Extending Power B and R

Second Edition

Perform advanced analysis using the power of analytical languages

Luca Zavarella

Extending Power BI with Python and R

Second Edition

Senior Publishing Product Manager: Gebin George
Acquisition Editor – Peer Reviews: Gaurav Gavas
Project Editor: Rianna Rodrigues
Senior Development Editor: Elliot Dallow
Copy Editor: Safis Editing
Technical Editor: Aneri Patel
Proofreader: Safis Editing
Indexer: Manju Arasan
Presentation Designer: Rajesh Shirsath
Developer Relations Marketing Executive: Vignesh Raju

First published: November 2021
Second edition: March 2024

Production reference: 1260324

Published by Packt Publishing Ltd.
Grosvenor House
11 St Paul's Square
Birmingham
B3 1RB, UK.

ISBN 978-1-83763-953-3

www.packt.com

Dedicated to my beloved wife, Nicoletta, whose unwavering patience endured the many hours this book demanded of our time together.

To my treasured circle, the "5-5-5 Tables," whose words were a beacon of motivation and support during the most challenging phases of this journey.

Gratitude to the SolidQ mentors, whose wisdom nurtured my curiosity and resilience, and equipped me with the skills necessary to navigate the most complex technical challenges.

To the technical community, a wellspring of knowledge from which I draw daily and which has been instrumental in connecting the myriad technical aspects presented in this book.

And to each and every person I have met along my professional journey who has contributed significantly to my deep understanding of the subjects I now master.

-Luca Zavarella

"Creativity is just connecting things. When you ask creative people how they did something, they feel a little guilty because they didn't really do it, they just saw something. It seemed obvious to them after a while. That's because they were able to connect experiences they've had and synthesize new things."

- Steve Jobs

Foreword

As an engineering leader at Power BI, I've been impressed by the transformative impact of integrating R and Python into our platform. These powerful languages have opened up new horizons for data professionals, enabling them to create sophisticated visualizations and perform advanced transformations and statistical analysis—all within the familiar Power BI environment.

It is with great pleasure that I introduce this book on R and Python support in Power BI, authored by the incredible Luca Zavarella, who is one of the most active data MVPs in this area. I've had the privilege of exchanging emails with him on and off for several years, and his passion for this field is contagious. He has also been the driving force behind a host of R/Python packages added to the service, numerous bug reports, documentation improvement requests, and ideas. He has also been actively answering questions from folks in the community and escalating to the product group when necessary.

As a speaker, blogger, and the author of this book, Luca has a wealth of experience in this area, and in this book he shares many use cases that he has witnessed over the years. These practical use cases will go a long way towards boosting your confidence when you start a new project.

As part of researching his book, I have seen him conduct various experiments, face errors, and even get into reverse engineering algorithms used in other parts of the Microsoft platform. There is no doubt that Luca has put a lot of effort into this book, and he was constantly on the lookout for more to share, improve, and add.

Congratulations to Luca and a big thank you for writing this book! This book will definitely help the Power BI community.

Rajat Talwar

Engineering Leader, Power BI

Contributors

About the author

Luca Zavarella has a rich background as an Azure Data Scientist Associate and Microsoft MVP, and holds a computer engineering degree from the University of L'Aquila. His decade-plus experience spans the Microsoft Data Platform, starting as a T-SQL developer on SQL Server 2000 and 2005, then mastering the full suite of Microsoft Business Intelligence tools (SSIS, SSAS, SSRS), and advancing into data warehousing. Recently, his focus has shifted to advanced analytics, data science, and AI, contributing to the community as a speaker and blogger, especially on Medium. Currently, he leads the Data & AI division at iCubed, and he also holds an honors degree in classical piano from the Alfredo Casella Conservatory in L'Aquila.

About the reviewer

Art Tennick is an author and freelance consultant with 30+ years of experience, specializing in Power BI, Python/R in Power BI, Analysis Services, SQL Server, and Fabric. His books on DAX, MDX, DMX, and SQL remain in print even after a decade. His extensive expertise includes editorial writing, with a tenure as a Windows columnist for leading computer magazines, as well as as a reviewer of tech literature. You can connect with him on LinkedIn, where he primarily talks about Power BI and Python.

Many thanks to Rita Mendoza (from the land of the coconuts), Lorna, and the two mischievous Emmas.

– Art Tennick

Learn more on Discord

To join the Discord community for this book – where you can share feedback, ask questions to the author, and learn about new releases – follow the QR code below:

https://discord.gg/MKww5g45EB

Table of Contents

Chapter 3: Configuring Python with Power BI   49

Chapter 4: Solving Common Issues When Using Python and R in Power BI   89

Chapter 11: Calling External APIs to Enrich Your Data   329

Chapter 12: Calculating Columns Using Complex Algorithms: Distances   349

Chapter 16: Adding Statistical Insights: Outliers and Missing Values   481

Chapter 18: Using SQL Server External Languages for Advanced Analytics and ML Integration in Power BI — 565

Chapter 19: Exploratory Data Analysis — 621

Preface

Welcome to the second edition of our book, where the journey into advanced analytics for Power BI deepens and expands your expertise in Python and R. This edition isn't just an update; it's an expansion into new territory, meticulously crafted to enhance your analytical prowess, whether you're using Power BI or diving directly into Python and R.

We've introduced new chapters that pave the way for optimizing your environment, harnessing the power of Intel's Math Kernel Library for speed, and tackling integration challenges with finesse. Imagine managing massive data sets effortlessly, using advanced techniques and the Swift parquet format for fast data processing. Imagine mastering the art of probabilistic fuzzy matching and navigating the potential of SQL Server External Languages to overcome traditional limitations in Power BI. You'll also be guided in creating stunning visualizations using not only R, but also Python, applying the Grammar of Graphics through a specialized package.

The remaining chapters have been carefully updated, expanded, and technically refined. They give you the skills to excel at validating data using regular expressions, leveraging data from a variety of uncommon external sources, and applying sophisticated data transformation algorithms. You'll explore advanced methods for protecting personal data in Power BI, including strategies for pseudonymization, anonymization, and data masking. This book also covers integrating external APIs to enrich your datasets, improve I/O efficiency, and leverage the powerful analytical capabilities of Python and R. Perform comprehensive analysis and uncover deep insights with statistical and machine learning methods, all without requiring the premium capacity. The text encourages you to visualize key statistical features of your data through a variety of graphical outputs as you develop machine learning models. In addition, each chapter has challenging questions and answers that reinforce your understanding and test your skills.

Join us on this challenging adventure where your analytical skills will soar to new heights.

Who this book is for

This book is intended for data analysts and developers who already have some experience with Power BI. In addition, ideally, readers should also be familiar with Python or R (or both), but the book is designed to still be accessible to beginners. For those more complex topics that require programming skills, the book provides in-depth learning resources. Newcomers are guided through each concept with clear explanations and annotated code examples, ensuring they will end up with a comprehensive understanding of how and why the code works.

What this book covers

Chapter 1, Where and How to Use R and Python Scripts in Power BI, provides a comprehensive overview of integrating R and Python scripts with Power BI. It delves into the capabilities of Power BI, emphasizing its utility beyond simple data visualization by incorporating advanced analytics through R and Python. The chapter covers key aspects such as injecting R or Python scripts into Power BI, the specific Power BI tools for script integration, and the limitations of these scripts on different Power BI products.

It also addresses the technical requirements for this integration and provides insights into data loading, transformation, and visualization using R and Python scripts. This chapter is critical to understanding the role of these scripts in extending the functionality of Power BI and how they interact with data at various stages of report development.

Chapter 2, Configuring R with Power BI, focuses on setting up and integrating R with Power BI. It walks you through installing and configuring the necessary R engines and development environments for use within Power BI. The chapter discusses various R distributions, including CRAN R and Microsoft R Open, and provides insight into improving R performance using Intel's **Math Kernel Library** (**MKL**). It also covers installing RTools and configuring Power BI Desktop and the Power BI service to work effectively with R. In addition, the chapter discusses the limitations of R script visualizations and the technical requirements for these configurations.

Chapter 3, Configuring Python with Power BI, delves into the integration of Python with Power BI. It walks through the installation and configuration of Python engines and IDEs, highlighting different Python distributions and how to choose the right engine. The chapter discusses setting up the Power BI desktop and service for Python, focusing on the limitations and technical requirements of the Python visualization. It focuses on using virtual environments for data transformations and Python script visualizations in Power BI. In addition, the chapter discusses improving Python performance in Power BI, including using Intel's MKL for optimized computational efficiency.

Chapter 4, Solving Common Issues When Using Python and R in Power BI, systematically addresses common problems encountered when developing solutions in Power BI using Python and R. It provides solutions to issues such as the `ADO.NET` error when running a Python script, the `Formula.Firewall` error, using multiple datasets in a Python/R script step, and handling dates/times in these scripts.

Chapter 5, Importing Unhandled Data Objects, focuses on using R and Python for data ingestion in Power BI. It covers importing RDS and PKL files into Power BI, which is useful for data that comes from external processing and is not managed directly by Power BI. The chapter is designed to guide through serialized files in Power BI, providing practical examples and detailed instructions.

Chapter 6, Using Regular Expressions in Power BI, explores the use of `regular expressions` (regex) to perform complex searches and replacements on strings in Power BI, improving data cleansing tasks. Key topics include a brief introduction to regex, validating data, loading complex log files, and extracting values from text using regex in Power BI. It also discusses the technical requirements for these processes and how to configure R and Python environments in Power BI to perform regex operations. The goal of this chapter is to provide you with the skills to use regex for high-quality data projects in Power BI.

Chapter 7, Anonymizing and Pseudonymizing Your Data in Power BI, focuses on techniques for de-identifying data in Power BI using Python and R scripts. The chapter emphasizes the importance of data privacy and compliance with regulations such as GDPR. It covers various de-identification methods, including information removal, data masking, swapping, generalization, perturbation, tokenization, hashing, and encryption. The chapter also distinguishes between anonymization and pseudonymization processes, and demonstrates their implementation in Power BI with real-world examples. It also discusses preserving the statistical properties of datasets during pseudonymization and anonymization.

Chapter 8, Logging Data from Power BI to External Sources, covers how to extract and log data from Power BI to external files or systems using Python and R. It covers various methods for logging data to CSV and Excel files, and demonstrates how to interact with SQL servers, including Azure SQL Server. The chapter provides detailed instructions and examples for each of these processes, demonstrating how to effectively manage and transfer data outside of Power BI for various purposes.

Chapter 9, Loading Large Datasets beyond the Available RAM in Power BI, focuses on working with large files, especially those that exceed the RAM capacity of your machine, in Power BI using Python and R. It covers practical techniques for importing, processing, and exporting large datasets. Key topics include typical analytical scenarios involving large datasets, importing and exporting large datasets in both Python and R, and the technical requirements for these operations. The chapter emphasizes the use of specific packages and distributed computing systems to provide a comprehensive guide to working with large datasets in Power BI.

Chapter 10, Boosting Data Loading Speed in Power BI with Parquet Format, discusses improving the performance of Power BI, especially for large data sources. The chapter focuses on converting data from the traditional CSV format to the more efficient Parquet file format. The goal of this conversion is to optimize query execution times and overall report performance in Power BI. The chapter provides technical requirements and detailed instructions on how to implement this conversion and illustrates the significant performance benefits of using the Parquet format. It also explains how to use Parquet files in Power BI for both Python and R users, highlighting practical applications and benefits.

Chapter 11, Calling External APIs to Enrich Your Data, teaches you how to extend existing data using external **application programming interfaces** (**APIs**), which are often exposed through web service endpoints. It covers understanding web services, using Bing Maps web services to geocode addresses in Python and R, and accessing these services through Power BI. The chapter includes detailed instructions for registering for Bing Maps web services, handling geocoding, and integrating these methods into Power BI, with an emphasis on technical requirements and practical examples.

Chapter 12, Calculating Columns Using Complex Algorithms: Distances, explores the use of distance measurements in data analysis. The chapter begins with an exploration of the concept of distance in various contexts, including geographic and string distances. Key topics include calculating the distance between two geographic locations and between strings. The chapter emphasizes the use of non-trivial algorithms for data analysis in Power BI, using R and Python for complex computations. It includes practical examples and the technical requirements necessary to implement these concepts.

Chapter 13, Calculating Columns Using Complex Algorithms: Fuzzy Matching, explores advanced data analysis techniques with a focus on fuzzy matching in Power BI. It covers the use of Microsoft Research's Jaccard distance-based fuzzy matching algorithm and delves into the specifics of probabilistic data association. The chapter includes practical examples and guidance on implementing these techniques in Power BI, highlighting key aspects such as standard fuzzy matching, probabilistic record association algorithms, and their application.

Chapter 14, Calculating Columns Using Complex Algorithms: Optimization Problems, explores how Power BI analysts can tackle mathematical optimization problems without extensive knowledge of advanced mathematics. It focuses on **linear programming** (**LP**) and its application to data analysis, particularly for real-world cases such as demand optimization in manufacturing. The chapter covers topics such as the basics of linear programming, how to solve optimization problems using Python and R, and the technical requirements for setting up Power BI with these programming languages. Practical examples are provided to demonstrate how to effectively apply LP techniques in Power BI.

Chapter 15, Adding Statistical Insights: Associations, focuses on statistical techniques used to extract insights from data, emphasizing the critical role of statistics in data analysis. This chapter covers exploring associations between variables, including correlations between numeric and categorical variables, and discusses the technical requirements for performing these analyses. Key concepts include understanding the behavior of variables, measuring the degree of association (correlation), and using mathematical concepts to define different types of correlations. The chapter also discusses the limitations of certain statistical methods and introduces alternatives such as Spearman's and Kendall's correlation coefficients. It also includes practical examples and instructions for implementing these techniques in Python, R, and Power BI.

Chapter 16, Adding Statistical Insights: Outliers and Missing Values, explores advanced statistical capabilities in Power BI, with a focus on detecting outliers and imputing missing values in datasets. It covers different methods for detecting and handling outliers, the impact of missing values on data analysis, and strategies for dealing with these issues. The chapter provides you with the skills to effectively use Power BI for these purposes, including a comprehensive explanation of outlier detection and missing value imputation algorithms. It also outlines the technical requirements for performing these operations in Power BI.

Chapter 17, Using Machine Learning without Premium or Embedded Capacity, focuses on integrating **machine learning** (**ML**) capabilities into Power BI workflows, particularly for users with Pro licenses. The chapter addresses the use of Python and R for machine learning within Power BI, despite the limitations of certain advanced AI tools. Key topics include interacting with ML in Power BI using data flows, AutoML solutions, embedding training code in Power Query, using trained models, and calling web services in Power Query. The chapter aims to provide practical insights into effectively applying ML techniques in Power BI environments.

Chapter 18, Using SQL Server External Languages for Advanced Analytics and ML Integration in Power BI, explores the integration of Python and R analytical engines within SQL Server (or Azure SQL Managed Instance) and their use in Power BI.

This approach is considered because of certain limitations in Power BI for handling Python and R directly. The chapter covers installing and configuring Python and R in SQL Server, using ML services, and importing preprocessed datasets into Power BI. It provides a detailed guide to managing and integrating these technologies to extend the capabilities of Power BI reports.

Chapter 19, *Exploratory Data Analysis*, focuses on the importance of thoroughly understanding the inherent characteristics of your data before applying ML models. It introduces **exploratory data analysis** (**EDA**) techniques that can help you make informed decisions about selecting appropriate ML models and feature engineering methods. The chapter covers topics such as the goals of EDA, techniques for performing EDA using Python and R, and EDA in Power BI. It emphasizes the critical steps of cleaning the dataset, understanding variable relationships, and deriving meaningful insights to build accurate models.

Chapter 20, *Using the Grammar of Graphics in Python with plotnine*, provides a comprehensive guide to the plotnine package in Python, drawing parallels to the popular ggplot2 tool in R. The chapter begins with an overview of plotnine, explaining its foundation in the grammar of graphics and its intuitive, powerful syntax. It then delves into practical applications, demonstrating how to analyze the Titanic dataset using various plotnine techniques, such as creating bar charts and histograms. In addition, the chapter covers the integration of plotnine with Power BI, providing detailed instructions on how to effectively use plotnine visualizations within Power BI environments. This includes methods for converting plotnine graphs for Power BI compatibility and ensuring their effective display in reports.

Chapter 21, *Advanced Visualizations*, focuses on creating advanced and visually appealing custom graphs, with an emphasis on circular bar plots. These bar plots are particularly useful for displaying periodic or cyclical data in a clear and space-efficient manner. The chapter covers topics such as selecting and implementing pie charts in R and Power BI. It also discusses the integration of R scripts into Power BI for rendering complex ggplot2 graphs and provides a detailed walkthrough for this process.

Chapter 22, *Interactive R Custom Visuals*, focuses on enhancing data visualizations with interactivity, building on the concepts introduced in previous chapters. It explores the transition from static charts to interactive visualizations using HTML widgets and Plotly in R, emphasizing their benefits for data interpretation. The chapter covers key topics such as adding interactivity with Plotly, using HTML widgets, and integrating these interactive visuals with Power BI. It also provides practical guidance on creating and importing custom visual packages into Power BI, giving readers the skills to create more dynamic and engaging data presentations.

Software used in this book

Power BI is currently undergoing frequent updates, many on which are making changes to the UI. Each chapter in this book includes a note which indicates the version of Power BI used for the screenshots and examples within. If you are using a different version, please be aware that some UI elements may have changed or moved.

To get the most out of this book

- You will need a working PC with a stable Internet connection. This setup will allow you to not only download the necessary software, but also access online resources that can enhance your learning experience. In addition, it is critical that you have Power BI Desktop installed on your computer. This software is the backbone of the concepts and labs that we will explore in this book.

- It is best to have a basic understanding of Power BI. Familiarity with the interface and basic concepts will help you navigate through the exercises and understand the more advanced topics more easily.

- If you are reading a digital version of this book, we recommend that you type the code examples yourself or access the code from the book's GitHub repository. A link to the repository is provided in the next section. This practice will help you avoid potential errors that can result from copying and pasting code directly.

Download the example code files

The code bundle for the book is hosted on GitHub at `https://github.com/PacktPublishing/Extending-Power-BI-with-Python-and-R-2nd-edition`. We also have other code bundles from our rich catalog of books and videos available at `https://github.com/PacktPublishing`. Check them out!

Download the color images

We also provide a PDF file that has color images of the screenshots/diagrams used in this book. You can download it here: `https://packt.link/gbp/9781837639533`.

Conventions used

There are a number of text conventions used throughout this book.

`CodeInText`: Indicates code words in text, database table names, folder names, filenames, file extensions, pathnames, dummy URLs, user input, and Twitter handles. For example: "Activate the environment that gives you the error you saw before using the `conda activate <your-environment-name>` command."

A block of code is set as follows:

```
re.search('test', 'TeSt', re.IGNORECASE)
re.match('test', 'TeSt', re.IGNORECASE)
re.sub('test', 'xxxx', 'TesTing', flags=re.IGNORECASE)
```

When we wish to draw your attention to a particular part of a code block, the relevant lines or items are set in bold:

```
import pandas as pd
import numpy
df = pd.DataFrame(dir(numpy))
```

Any command-line input or output is written as follows:

```
successfully initialized (spaCy Version: 3.5.0, language model: en_core_web_lg)
(python options: type = "condaenv", value = "C:\ProgramData\Miniconda3\envs\
presidio_env")
```

Bold: Indicates a new term, an important word, or words that you see on the screen. For instance, words in menus or dialog boxes appear in the text like this. For example: "**Personally Identifiable Information (PII)**, also known as **personal information** or **personal data**, is any information about an identifiable individual."

Warnings or important notes appear like this.

Tips and tricks appear like this.

Get in touch

Feedback from our readers is always welcome.

General feedback: Email feedback@packtpub.com and mention the book's title in the subject of your message. If you have questions about any aspect of this book, please email us at questions@packtpub.com.

Errata: Although we have taken every care to ensure the accuracy of our content, mistakes do happen. If you have found a mistake in this book, we would be grateful if you reported this to us. Please visit http://www.packtpub.com/submit-errata, click **Submit Errata**, and fill in the form.

Piracy: If you come across any illegal copies of our works in any form on the internet, we would be grateful if you would provide us with the location address or website name. Please contact us at copyright@packtpub.com with a link to the material.

If you are interested in becoming an author: If there is a topic that you have expertise in and you are interested in either writing or contributing to a book, please visit http://authors.packtpub.com.

Share your thoughts

Once you've read *Extending Power BI with Python and R, Second Edition*, we'd love to hear your thoughts! Scan the QR code below to go straight to the Amazon review page for this book and share your feedback.

https://packt.link/r/1837639531

Your review is important to us and the tech community and will help us make sure we're delivering excellent quality content.

Download a free PDF copy of this book

Thanks for purchasing this book!

Do you like to read on the go but are unable to carry your print books everywhere?

Is your eBook purchase not compatible with the device of your choice?

Don't worry, now with every Packt book you get a DRM-free PDF version of that book at no cost.

Read anywhere, any place, on any device. Search, copy, and paste code from your favorite technical books directly into your application.

The perks don't stop there, you can get exclusive access to discounts, newsletters, and great free content in your inbox daily

Follow these simple steps to get the benefits:

1. Scan the QR code or visit the link below

https://packt.link/free-ebook/9781837639533

2. Submit your proof of purchase
3. That's it! We'll send your free PDF and other benefits to your email directly

1

Where and How to Use R and Python Scripts in Power BI

Power BI is Microsoft's flagship **self-service business intelligence** product. It consists of a set of on-premises applications and cloud-based services that help organizations integrate, transform, and analyze data from a wide variety of source systems through a user-friendly interface.

The platform is not limited to data visualization. Power BI is much more than this when you consider that its analytics engine (**Vertipaq**) is the same as **SQL Server Analysis Services** (**SSAS**), **Azure Analysis Services**, and **Power Pivot in Excel** and it is also the engine used for reports and datasets published to the Power BI service. In addition, it uses **Power Query** as its data extraction and transformation engine, which we find in both Analysis Services and Excel. The engine comes with a very powerful and versatile formula language (**M**) and GUI, thanks to which you can "grind" and shape any type of data into any form.

Moreover, Power BI supports **DAX** as a data analytics formula language, which can be used for advanced calculations and queries on data that has already been loaded into tabular data models.

Such a versatile and powerful tool is a godsend for anyone who needs to do data ingestion and transformation in order to build dashboards and reports to summarize a company's business.

Recently, the availability of huge amounts of data, along with the ability to scale the computational power of machines, has made the area of **advanced analytics** more appealing. So, new mathematical and statistical tools have become necessary in order to provide rich insights. Hence the integration of analytical languages such as **Python** and **R** within Power BI.

R or Python scripts can only be used within Power BI with specific features. Knowing which Power BI tools can be used to inject R or Python scripts into Power BI is key to understanding whether the problem you want to address is achievable with these analytical languages.

This chapter will cover the following topics:

* Injecting R or Python scripts into Power BI

- Using R and Python to interact with your data
- Python and R compatibility across Power BI products

Technical requirements

This chapter requires you to have **Power BI Desktop** already installed on your machine (you can download it here: `https://aka.ms/pbiSingleInstaller`). The version used in this chapter is 2.110.1161.0 64-bit (October 2022).

Injecting R or Python scripts into Power BI

In this first section, Power BI Desktop tools that allow you to use Python or R scripts will be presented and described in detail. Specifically, you will see how to add your own code during the **data loading**, **data transforming**, and **data viewing** phases.

Data loading

One of the first steps required to work with data in Power BI Desktop is to **import** it from external sources:

There are many connectors that allow you to do this, depending on the respective data sources, but you can also do it via scripts in Python and R. In fact, if you click on the **Get data** icon in the ribbon, not only are the most commonly used connectors shown but you can also select other ones from a more complete list by clicking on **More...**:

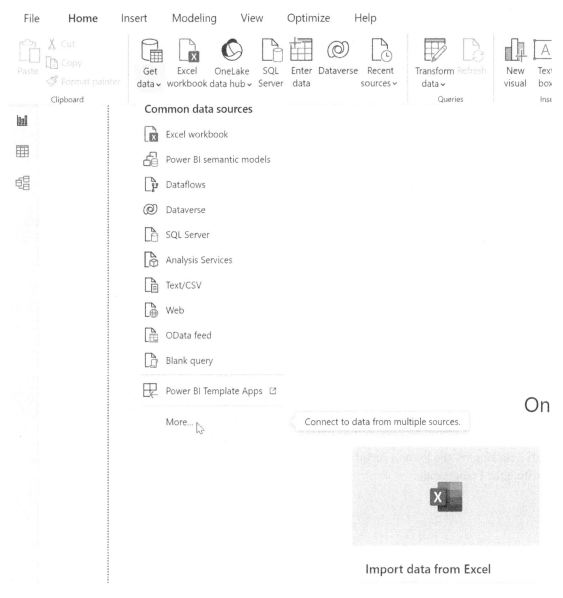

Figure 1.1: Browse more connectors to load your data

In the new **Get Data** window that pops up, simply start typing the word script into the search box, and immediately the two options for importing data via Python or R appear:

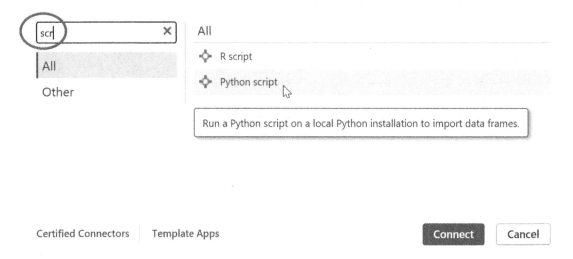

Figure 1.2: Showing R script and Python script in the Get Data window

Reading the contents of the tooltip, obtained by hovering the mouse over the **Python script** option, two things should immediately jump out at you:

    a.   A local installation of Python is required.

    b.   What can be imported through Python is a data frame.

The same two observations also apply when selecting **R script**. The only difference is that it is possible to import a **pandas DataFrame** when using Python (a DataFrame is a data structure provided by the pandas package), whereas R employs the two-dimensional array-like data structure called an **R data frame**, which is provided by default by the language.

After clicking on the **Python script** option, a new window will be shown containing a text box for writing the Python code:

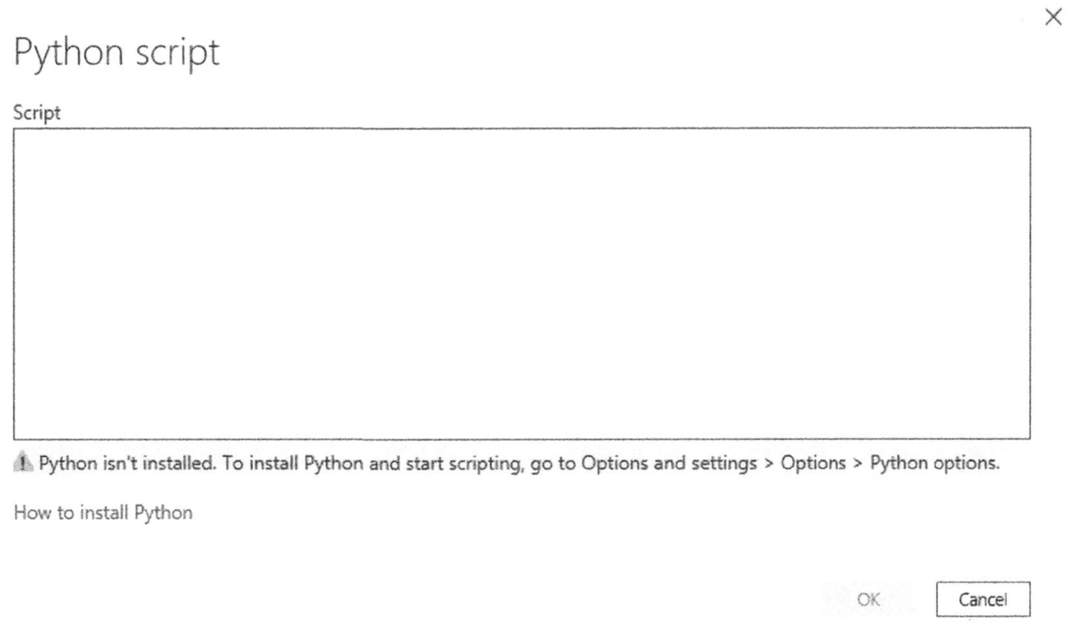

Python script

Script

✕

⚠ Python isn't installed. To install Python and start scripting, go to Options and settings > Options > Python options.

How to install Python

OK   Cancel

Figure 1.3: Window showing the Python script editor

As you can see, it's definitely a very skimpy editor, but in *Chapter 3*, *Configuring Python with Power BI*, you'll discover how you can utilize your preferred IDE to create your scripts within a more comprehensive and feature-rich editor.

Taking a look at the warning message, Power BI reminds you that no Python engine has been detected, so it must be installed. If you already have Python installed and configured, you will not see this message. Clicking on the **How to install Python** link will cause a Microsoft Docs web page to open, explaining the steps to install Python.

Microsoft suggests installing the base Python distribution, but in order to follow some best practices on **environments** (self-contained spaces that allow developers to manage dependencies, libraries, and configurations specific to individual projects), we will install the **Miniconda** distribution. The details of how to do this and why will be covered in *Chapter 3*.

If you had clicked on **R script** instead, a window for entering code in R, similar to the one shown in *Figure 1.4*, would have appeared:

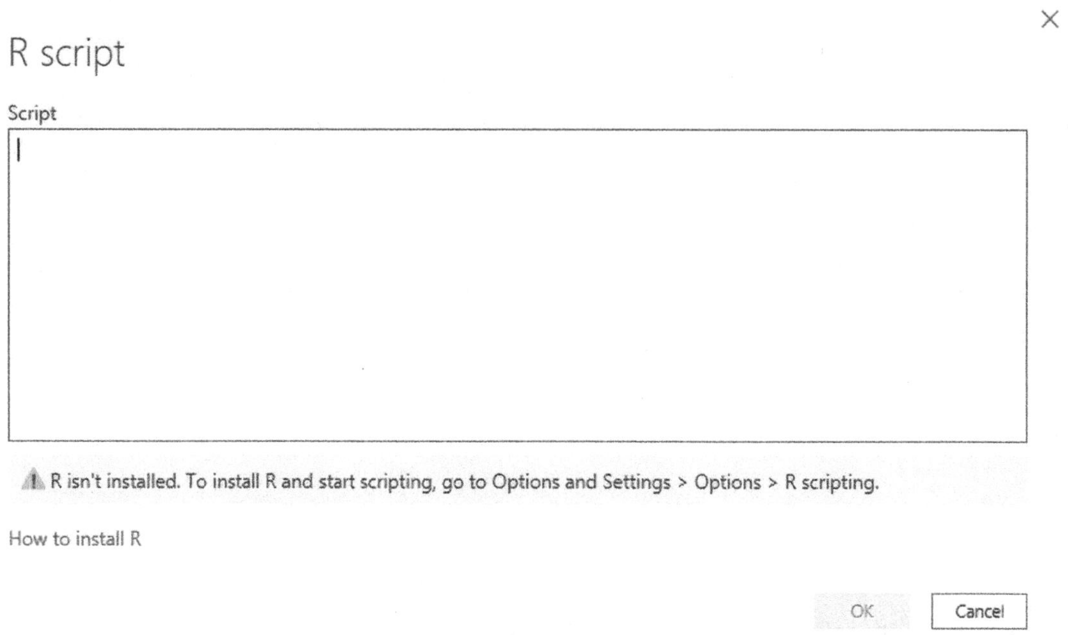

×

R script

Script

⚠ R isn't installed. To install R and start scripting, go to Options and Settings > Options > R scripting.

How to install R

OK   Cancel

Figure 1.4: Window showing the R script editor

As with Python, in order to run code in R, you need to install the R engine on your machine. Clicking on the **How to install R** link will open a Docs page where Microsoft suggests installing either **Microsoft R Open** or the classic **CRAN R**. *Chapter 2, Configuring R with Power BI,* will show you which engine to choose and how to configure your favorite IDE to write code in R.

In order to import data using Python or R, you need to write code in the editors shown in *Figure 1.3* and *Figure 1.4,* which assign a pandas DataFrame or an R data frame to a variable, respectively. You will see concrete examples throughout this book.

Next, let's look at transforming data.

Data transformation

It is possible to apply a transformation to data already imported or being imported, using scripts in R or Python. Should you want to test this on the fly, you can import the following CSV file directly from the web: `http://bit.ly/iriscsv`. Follow these steps:

1. Simply click on **Get data** and then **Web** to import data directly from a web page:

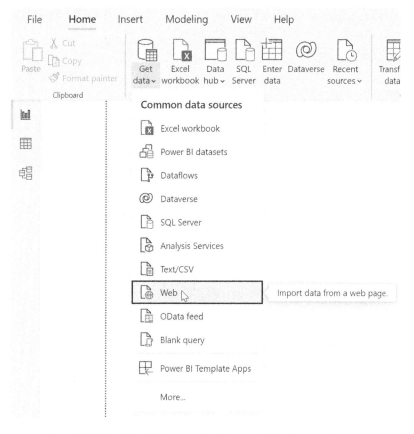

Figure 1.5: Select the Web connector to import data from a web page

2. You can now enter the previously mentioned URL in the window that pops up:

Figure 1.6: Import the Iris data from the web

3. Right after clicking **OK**, a window will pop up with a preview of the data to be imported.

   In this case, instead of importing the data as is, click on **Transform Data** in order to access the Power Query data transformation window:

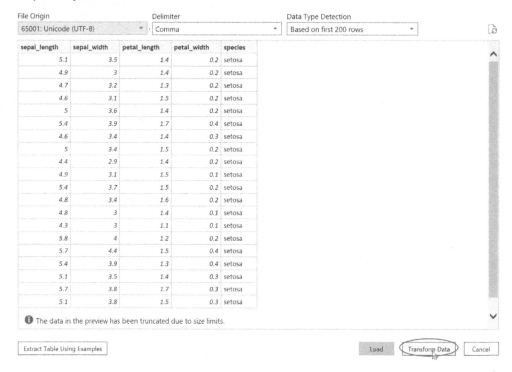

Figure 1.7: Imported data preview

It is at this point that you can add a transformation step using a Python or R script by selecting the **Transform** tab in **Power Query Editor**:

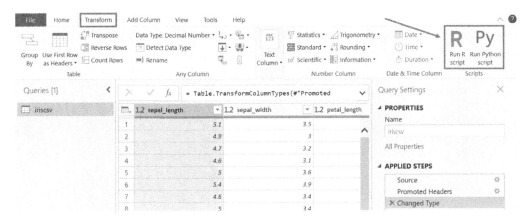

Figure 1.8: R and Python script tools in Power Query Editor

By clicking on **Run Python script**, you'll cause a window, similar to the one you've already seen in the data import phase, to pop up:

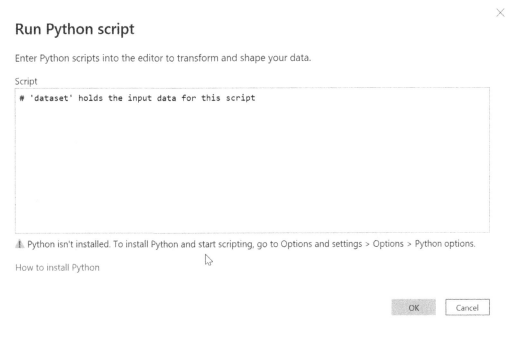

Figure 1.9: The Run Python script editor

If you carefully read the comment in the text box, you will see that the dataset variable is already initialized and contains the data present at that moment in Power Query Editor, including any transformations already applied. At this point, you can insert your Python code in the text box to transform the data into the desired form.

A similar window will open if you click on **Run R script**:

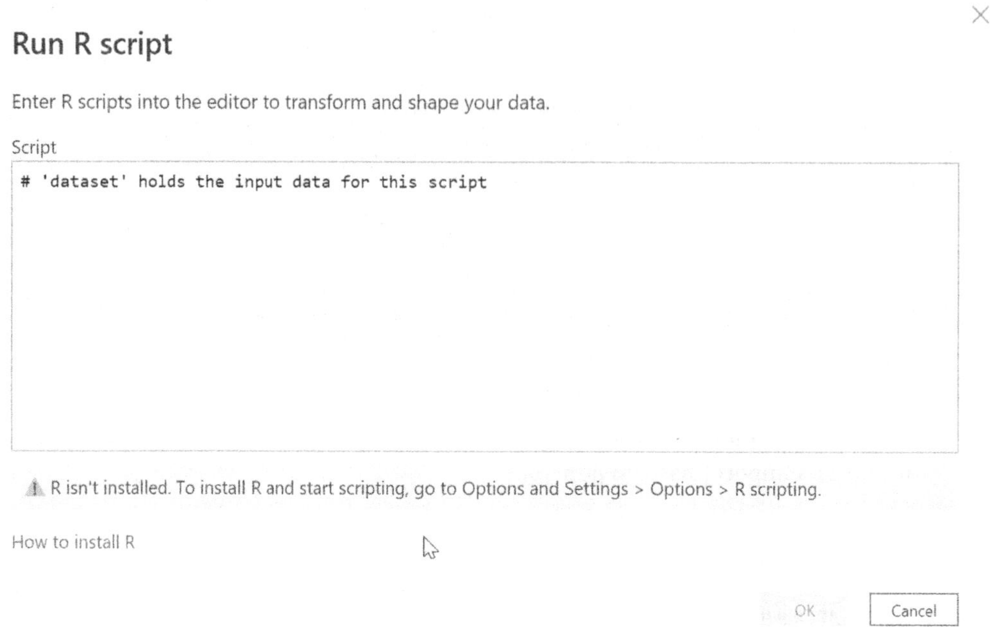

Run R script

×

Enter R scripts into the editor to transform and shape your data.

Script

```
# 'dataset' holds the input data for this script
```

⚠ R isn't installed. To install R and start scripting, go to Options and Settings > Options > R scripting.

How to install R   ⌕

OK   Cancel

Figure 1.10: The Run R script editor

Also, in this case, the dataset variable is already initialized and contains the data present at that moment in Power Query Editor. You can then add your own R code and reference the **dataset** variable to transform your data in the most appropriate way.

Next, let's look at visualizing data.

Data visualization

Finally, your own Python or R scripts can be added to Power BI to create new visualizations, in addition to those already present in the tool out of the box:

1. Assuming we resume the data import activity started in the previous section, once the **Iris** dataset is loaded, simply click **Cancel** in the **Run R script** window, and then click **Close & Apply** in the **Home** tab of Power Query Editor:

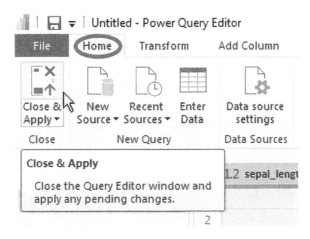

Figure 1.11: Click Close & Apply to import the Iris data

2. After the data import is complete, you can select either the **R visual** or **Python visual** option in the **Visualizations** pane of Power BI:

Figure 1.12: The R and Python script visuals

If you click on **Python visual,** a window pops up asking for permission to enable script code execution, as there may be security or privacy risks:

Figure 1.13: Enable the script code execution

3. After enabling code execution, in Power BI Desktop, you can see a placeholder for the Python visual image on the report canvas and a **Python script editor** pane at the bottom:

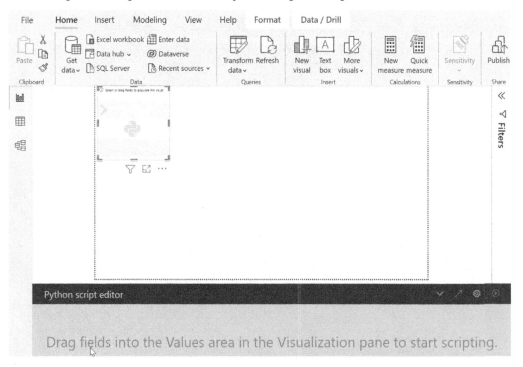

Figure 1.14: The Python visual layout

Once you drag the fields you want to use in your Python script into the **Values** area, you can write your own custom code into the Python script editor and run it to generate a Python visualization.

A pretty much identical layout occurs when you select **R visual.**

Using R and Python to interact with your data

In the previous section, you saw all the ways you can interact with your data in Power BI via R or Python scripts. Beyond knowing how and where to inject your code into Power BI, it is very important to know how your code will interact with that data. It's here that we see a big difference between the effect of scripts injected via Power Query Editor and scripts used in visuals:

- **Scripts via Power Query Editor:** This type of script will transform the data and persist transformations in the model. This means that it will always be possible to retrieve the transformed data from any object within Power BI. Also, once the scripts have been executed and have taken effect, *they will not be re-executed unless the data is refreshed*. Therefore, it is recommended to inject code in R or Python via Power Query Editor when you intend to use the resulting insights in other visuals, or in the data model.

- **Scripts in visuals:** The scripts used within the R and Python script visuals extract particular insights from the data and only make them evident to the user through **visualization**. Like all the other visuals on a report page, the R and Python script visuals are also interconnected with the other visuals. This means that the script visuals are subject to **cross-filtering** and therefore, *they are refreshed every time you interact with other visuals in the report*. That said, it is not possible to persist the results obtained from the script visuals in the data model.

TIP

Thanks to the interactive nature of R and Python script visuals due to cross-filtering, it is possible to inject code that is useful for extracting real-time insights from data. The important thing to keep in mind is that, as previously stated, it is then only possible to visualize such information, or at the most, to write it to external repositories (as you will see in *Chapter 8, Logging Data from Power BI to External Sources*). Also, although it is possible to access resources on the internet from a visual script when developing in Power BI Desktop, it is no longer possible to do so when the report is published to the Power BIs Service (you will see what this is about in the next section) due to security issues. This restriction doesn't exist for scripts used in Power Query.

In the final section of this chapter, let's look at the limitations of using R and Python when it comes to various Power BI products.

Python and R compatibility across Power BI products

The first question once you are clear on where to inject R and Python scripts in Power BI could be: "*Is the use of R and Python code allowed in all Power BI products?*" In order to cover that, let's briefly recap the various Power BI products and their usage in general. Here is a concise list:

- **Power BI service:** This is sometimes called **Power BI Online**, and it's the **Software as a Service (SaaS)** version of Power BI. It was created to facilitate the sharing of visual analysis between users through **dashboards and reports**.

- **Power BI Report Server:** This is the on-premises version of Power BI and it extends the capabilities of **SQL Server Reporting Services,** enabling the sharing of reports created in **Power BI Desktop** (for **Report Server**) and **Power BI Report Builder** for Power BI paginated reports.

- **Power BI embedded:** A Microsoft Azure service that allows dashboards and reports to be embedded in an application for users who do not have a Power BI account.

- **Power BI Desktop:** A free desktop application for Windows that allows you to use almost all of the features that Power BI offers. It is not the right tool for sharing results between users, but it allows you to share them on the Power BI service and Power BI Report Server. The desktop versions that allow publishing on the two mentioned services are distinct and support slightly different sets of features. They are named Power BI Desktop and Power BI Desktop for Power BI Report Server, respectively.

- **Power BI mobile:** A mobile application, available on Windows, Android, and iOS, that allows secure access to the Power BI service and Power BI Report Server, and that allows you to browse and share dashboards and reports, but not edit them.

- **Power BI Report Builder:** A free desktop application for Windows that allows you to create paginated reports. These can then be published and shared in the Power BI service and Power BI Report Server.

Apart from the licenses, which we will not go into here, a summary figure of the relationships between the previously mentioned products follows:

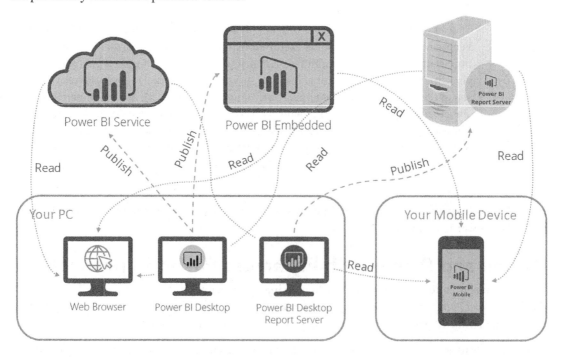

Figure 1.15: Interactions between Power BI products

Unfortunately, of all these products, only **the Power BI service, Power BI Embedded,** and **Power BI Desktop** allow you to enrich data via code in R and Python:

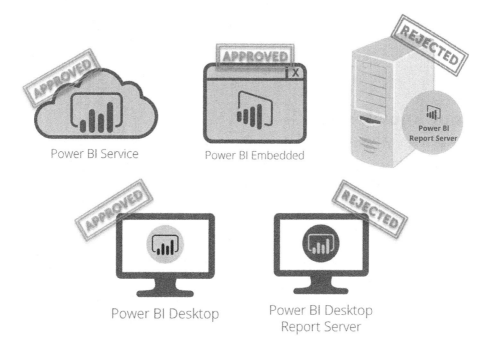

Figure 1.16: Power BI products, compatibility with R and Python

IMPORTANT NOTE

From here on out, when we talk about the Power BI service in terms of compatibility with analytical languages, what we say will also apply to Power BI embedded.

So, if you need to develop reports using advanced analytics through R and Python, make sure the target platform supports them.

Summary

This chapter has given a detailed overview of all the ways in which you can use R and Python scripts in Power BI Desktop. During the data ingestion and data transformation phases, Power Query Editor allows you to add steps containing R or Python code. You can also make use of these analytical languages during the data visualization phase thanks to the R and Python script visuals provided by Power BI Desktop.

It is also very important to know how the R and Python code will interact with the data already loaded or being loaded in Power BI. If you use Power Query Editor, both when loading and transforming data, the result of script processing will be persisted in the data model. Also, if you want to run the same scripts again, you have to refresh the data. On the other hand, if you use the R and Python script visuals, the code results can only be displayed and are not persisted in the data model. In this case, script execution occurs whenever cross-filtering is triggered via the other visuals in the report.

Unfortunately, at the time of writing, you cannot run R and Python scripts in every Power BI product. The only ones that provide for running analytics scripts are Power BI Desktop and the Power BI service.

In the next chapter, we will see how best to configure the R engine and RStudio to integrate with Power BI Desktop.

Test your knowledge

1. At what stages of Power BI report development can scripts in Python or R be used?
2. Is it possible to use a Python dictionary as a data source for a Power BI report?
3. Is it possible to use an R list as a data source for a Power BI report?
4. When you insert a Python or R script step immediately after other transformation steps that return a specific result set, what is the name of the variable you will need to use in your script to access the data obtained in the step just before?
5. After adding a Python or R visual script to your canvas, what do you need to do to enable the script editor to take a script that generates a plot?
6. What are the ways by which to force the re-execution of Python or R scripts added via Power Query?
7. What are the ways by which to force the re-execution of Python or R scripts added in a script visual?
8. In what case is it not possible to access the internet from a Python or R script in Power BI?
9. In which Power BI products can Python or R scripts be used?

Learn more on Discord

To join the Discord community for this book – where you can share feedback, ask questions to the author, and learn about new releases – follow the QR code below:

https://discord.gg/MKww5g45EB

2

Configuring R with Power BI

Power BI Desktop is not equipped with the analytical language engines presented in the previous chapter by default. Therefore, it is necessary to install these engines and properly configure Power BI Desktop to correctly interface with them. It is also recommended to install an **Integrated Development Environment (IDE)**, enabling you to work in the way you are most comfortable.

We'll look at how to get those engines up and running and give you some general guidelines on how to pick the most appropriate one for your needs. After that, we'll look at how to make these engines interface with both Power BI Desktop and the Power BI service.

Finally, we will give some important tips on how to overcome some stringent limitations of R script visuals within the Power BI service.

In particular, this chapter will deal in detail with the following topics:

- The available R engines
- Choosing an R engine to install
- Installing an IDE for R development
- Linking Intel's **Math Kernel Library (MKL)** to R
- Installing RTools
- Configuring Power BI Desktop to work with R
- Configuring the Power BI service to work with R
- R script visuals limitations

Technical requirements

This chapter requires you to have a working internet connection and **Power BI Desktop** already installed on your machine. It also requires you to have signed up for the Power BI service in the last part of the chapter (here's a how-to: `http://bit.ly/signup-powerbiservice`). A **Power BI free** license is enough to test all the code in this book, as you will share reports only in your personal **workspace**.

The available R engines

There is more than one R distribution available on the market that you can use for free for your advanced analytics projects. In this section, we'll explore the main details of each of them.

The CRAN R distribution

When it comes to installing the R engine, we almost always think of the open source software environment, *par excellence*, developed by a collective of contributors over the years known as **CRAN R**, also called **base R** (https://cran.r-project.org). To be exact, the **Comprehensive R Archive Network** (**CRAN**) is a network of web servers and FTP servers around the world whose goal is to preserve multiple identical and up-to-date versions of the R source code and the entire ecosystem of R packages developed by the community, along with all the R documentation.

One of the biggest advantages of CRAN R is its very active community of developers. Their contribution to the creation of new packages on CRAN is invaluable. That's why if you think you need a particular feature to process your data, it's almost certain that it has already been developed by the R community and released as a free usable R package.

However, not everyone knows that CRAN R is not the only R distribution available on the market.

The Microsoft R Open distribution and MRAN

Even Microsoft has contributed to the community by releasing its own open source R "distribution" for both Windows and Linux, under the terms of the *General Public License version 2*. Starting from 2016, Microsoft released its own distribution of R, called **Microsoft R Open** (**MRO**) and sometimes referred to simply as **Microsoft R**, which reflects the same versions released by CRAN R and is 100% compatible with it.

IMPORTANT NOTE

If you take any code written in CRAN R, using any CRAN package, and run it with the same version of the MRO engine, everything will work fine.

In addition, there are only a few Microsoft-owned functions (including `RevoUtils` and `RevoUtilsMath`) that return information about the engine installation (such as path and memory usage) and the maximum number of threads that the **MKL** can run.

The benefit of the MRO release was that it brought important improvements for the R community:

- The multi-threaded **Intel MKL** included out of the box.
- A high-performance mirror of the CRAN repository called **Microsoft R Application Network** (**MRAN**, https://mran.microsoft.com), which gives you a "time machine" tool to get a snapshot of CRAN packages at the selected time.

Unfortunately, Microsoft announced in late June 2021 (`https://bit.ly/r-future-in-azure-sql`) that **MRO** would be phased out in favor of the official CRAN R distribution.

> **IMPORTANT NOTE**
>
> The last release of MRO was 4.0.2. Any, applications that depended on it (like SQL Server ML Services and the Power BI service) switched to using CRAN R. The `RevoScaleR` and `revoscalepy` packages were open-sourced.
>
> After that, in early January 2023, Microsoft publicly announced the following:
>
> The MRAN website would be shut down within 6 months of the announcement (so it would run until the end of June 2023). Along with MRAN, CRAN Time Machine would also be shut down.

In light of these decisions, you should definitely use CRAN R for R scripts, configuring it appropriately to gain additional benefits according to the target of the scripts you will write. Microsoft suggests using the miniCRAN package instead of CRAN Time Machine. Unfortunately, however, miniCRAN relies on the packages available in the CRAN repository, which does not maintain all snapshots of the compiled packages when individual versions of R are released online. For example, if you look at the packages available for Windows at `https://cran.r-project.org/bin/windows/contrib`, the oldest version available at the time of this writing is 3.6. So if you need to use packages that are compatible with R version 3.4, you can't. Fortunately, however, Posit, the company that maintains RStudio and its entire ecosystem of services, has made available the public Package Manager, which is a true replacement for MRAN's CRAN Time Machine. Later we will show you how to use it.

However, we feel it is appropriate to describe MRO in detail as it is an engine that could still be used in "legacy" installations. Let's see in detail what they are.

Multi-threading in MRO

CRAN R is linked to the single-threaded **Basic Linear Algebra Subprograms** (**BLAS**) and **Linear Algebra Package** (**LAPACK**) libraries by default. This implies the ability to perform basic vector and matrix operations and to solve simultaneous systems of linear equations, least-squares solutions of systems of linear equations, eigenvalue problems, and singular-value problems by exploiting a single thread. CRAN R can also link to multi-threaded versions of BLAS and LAPACK, but you must install and configure these libraries manually. You will see how to do that later in the chapter.

Installing MRO would have offered the advantage of having the engine already preconfigured and optimized for Intel processors thanks to MKL, with the purpose of performing mathematical calculations in parallel.

To get an idea of the gain in computational time, look at the benchmark results obtained comparing R 3.4.1 and MRO 3.4.1 in *Figure 2.1* (source: `bit.ly/msropen-bnchmrk`):

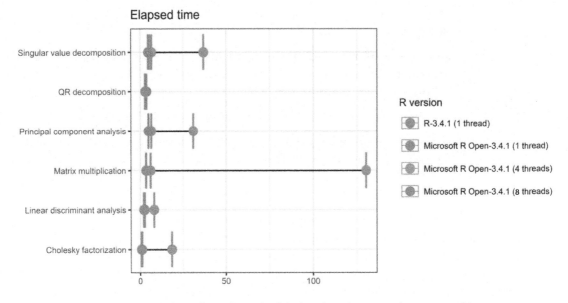

Figure 2.1: Total elapsed time for each of the benchmark tests on the same machine

As you can easily see in *Figure 2.1*, the time taken by CRAN R (installed as is without linking the MKL BLAS libraries) in the matrix calculation is significantly higher than that taken by MRO. Therefore, it is highly recommended to use CRAN R linked with MKL in future installations if you use a lot of math routines for data science, engineering, financial analysis, and so on.

Let's first see which version of the CRAN R engine is best to install.

Choosing an R engine to install

Once it is decided that CRAN R is the R distribution to adopt, the first question when installing an R engine is: *"Which version should I install? Do I choose the latest one, or do I opt for a previous one?"* The usual answer to these kinds of questions is: *"It depends!"* In our case, the goal is to use the R engine within Power BI, so we need to understand which versions are used by the various products that admit the use of R within them.

The R engines used by Power BI

We saw in *Chapter 1, Where and How to Use R and Python Scripts in Power BI,* that only two Power BI products are allowed to use scripts in R and Python: Power BI Desktop and the Power BI service (remember that Power BI embedded is implicitly included when talking about the Power BI service). So, the answer *"It depends!"* has a clearer connotation now: if you need to share your reports with people inside your organization, then you have to install the engines that work well with the Power BI service; if, instead, you need to create reports for your own use, without even publishing it on **My Workspace**, you can install the engines suitable for Power BI Desktop.

There is a substantial difference between the use of analytic engines by these two products. **Power BI Desktop** relies on the R engine installed by the user on the same machine on which Power BI Desktop is running. It is the user who chooses which version of the engines and which packages to install. Power BI Desktop simply ensures that any R code entered through its interface runs directly on that engine.

The **Power BI service** is the **Software as a Service** (**SaaS**) product among those covered by Power BI. The user does not have to take on the maintenance of its underlying IT infrastructure, and the user cannot decide to install components on it at will.

IMPORTANT NOTE

The R engine and the packages used by the Power BI service for **R script visuals** are prein-stalled on the cloud and therefore the user must adapt to the versions adopted by the service.

It is also important to know exactly which R distribution and version is used by the R script visuals in the Power BI service.

IMPORTANT NOTE

To date, the Power BI service still relies on the **MRO 3.4.4** runtime when implementing an R script visual. It is important to always keep an eye on the version of the R engine and the packages provided by the Power BI service with each release to ensure that the reports to be published work properly. See the following link for more information: `http://bit.ly/powerbi-r-limits`.

If, instead, you have to do data ingestion or data transformation using R scripts and you need to refresh your data, the Power BI service does not use the same engine for R script visuals in this case.

IMPORTANT NOTE

The R engine used by the Power BI service during the data refresh phase for R scripts in Power Query has to be installed on any machine of your choice outside the service, and on that same machine, you have to install the **Power BI on-premises data gateway** in **personal mode**. Note that you must use external engines even if the data to be refreshed does not flow through the gateway, but comes from data sources not referenced by the gateway itself (e.g., a CSV dataset from the web).

As long as the R engine to be referenced via the data gateway is the only one, it is sufficient that both are installed on the same machine. Otherwise, the following note applies.

IMPORTANT NOTE

If you need to use multiple R engines installed on the machine for your Power Query transformations, you must also install Power BI Desktop. It allows you to switch the routing of the
data gateway to the selected engine through its options by updating the `C:\Users\<your-
username>\AppData\Local\PowerBIScripting\RSettings.xml` configuration file. This
file allows the override of the R engine referenced by the data gateway by default.

If you need to learn more about the on-premises data gateway (in the *enterprise* and *personal* modes),
we suggest reading the Microsoft Docs page at this link: `http://bit.ly/onprem-data-gateway`.

In summary, with the preceding scenarios in mind, if you need to create reports for personal use on
your desktop, you have no limitations on which R engine to use, so you can install the R versions and
packages that suit you best. If, however, you know in advance that the reports you are going to create
contain R script visuals and are intended to be shared with colleagues on the Power BI service, there
are stringent limitations on both the version and the packages to be pre-installed in the service.

Let's now move on to the installation of the engines.

Installing the suggested R engines

Managing dependencies of R scripts injected within reports developed for the Power BI service can
be complex in the long run. Keeping in mind that it is possible to install more than one R engine on
the same machine, we suggest reading on to learn about a useful tip.

The R engine for data transformation

You have seen that the R scripts used in Power Query to make changes to the data model must use
an external R engine through the on-premises data gateway in personal mode, even if you use the
Power BI service.

TIP

We recommend installing the latest available version of CRAN R. Unfortunately, with the
default installation, CRAN R will not benefit from the performance advantages of the
MKL library, as it did with MRO, but in the next sections, you'll be shown how to link it
to a classic CRAN R installation.

Installing CRAN R is very simple:

1.   Go to `https://cran.r-project.org/` and click on the **Download R for Windows** link in the
     middle of the page.
2.   Then, click on the **base** link on the left, under the **Subdirectories** label.
3.   Finally, click on the **Download R x.x.x for Windows** link (where **x.x.x** corresponds to the actual,
     available version) on the top left of the next page.

4. Once the `R-x.x.x-win.exe` file is downloaded, double-click on it and select the language to be used during the installation.

5. The next screen, **Information**, shows you the license of the software. Click on "**Next**".

6. In the next window, you can select the destination location of the software. Keep the default one and click on "**Next**".

7. In the "**Select Components**" window, you can choose which components to install. By default, all are selected, and "**User installation**" is chosen. Click on "**Next**".

8. In the "**Startup options**" window, keep the default (**No**) and click on "**Next**".

9. In the "**Select Start Menu Folder**" window, keep the default and click on "**Next**".

10. In the "**Select Additional Tasks**" window, you can choose to add additional shortcuts for your convenience. Keep the default selected and click on "**Next**".

11. The installation will start. Click "**Finish**" at the end of it.

And that's it! You are now ready to be able to write and run your R code on CRAN R.

IMPORTANT NOTE

Usually, the Power BI Desktop installation on which you develop reports is located on a separate machine from the one selected as the Power BI service's R engine machine, where the data gateway in personal mode is also installed. In that case, you must also install the R engine on the machine on which your Power BI Desktop instance is installed to test your reports.

If you want, you can already write code on the very rudimentary GUI installed by default with CRAN R:

Figure 2.2: The R GUI installed by MRO

We'll see later in this chapter how to install the IDE preferred by most R developers: **RStudio**.

The R engine for R script visuals on the Power BI service

As previously mentioned, R visual scripts published on the Power BI service run on a pre-installed R engine on the cloud, the version of which may change based on new releases of the Power BI service itself. Should you need to share a report containing an R script visual with colleagues, you need to be sure that your R code works correctly on the pre-installed engine.

TIP

We strongly recommend that you also install on your machine an instance of CRAN R at the same version of MRO (or CRAN R in the near future) as that used for R script visuals by the Power BI service.

In order to install the CRAN R version compatible with the Power BI service, the process is very simple:

1. Go to http://bit.ly/powerbi-r-limits and check the actual version of MRO (in the near future, CRAN R) used by the Power BI service:

Requirements and Limitations of R packages

There are a handful of requirements and limitations for R packages:

- Current R runtime: Microsoft R 3.4.4 ◄

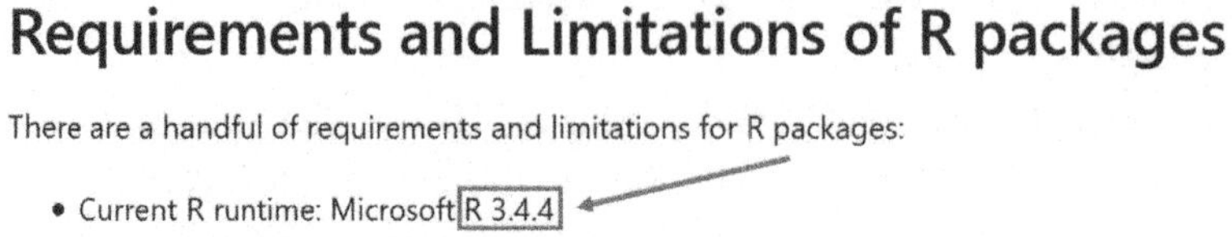

Figure 2.3: The actual MRO version used by the Power BI service

2. Then, go to https://cran.r-project.org/, click on **"Download R for Windows"**, click on **"base"**, and then click on the **"Previous releases"** link you can find at the bottom of the page:

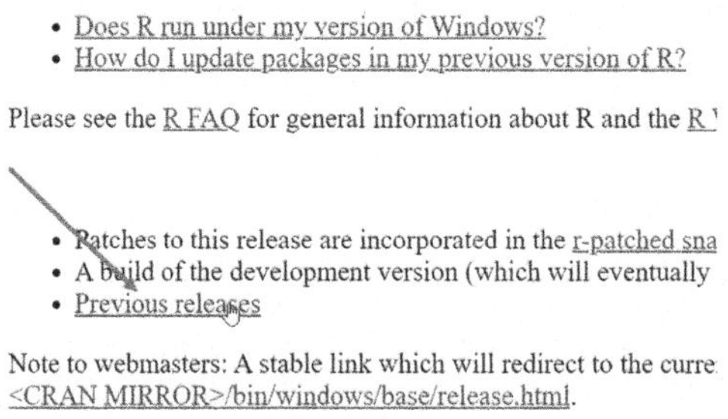

- Does R run under my version of Windows?
- How do I update packages in my previous version of R?

Please see the R FAQ for general information about R and the R '

- Patches to this release are incorporated in the r-patched sna
- A build of the development version (which will eventually
- Previous releases

Note to webmasters: A stable link which will redirect to the curre <CRAN MIRROR>/bin/windows/base/release.html.

Figure 2.4: Link to previous releases of CRAN R for Windows

3. Then, click on the CRAN R version of your interest and click on the **"Download R x.x.x for Windows"** link on the next page.

4. After downloading the executable, simply follow the steps outlined in the previous section to install this specific version of the CRAN R engine. Note that in contrast to newer versions, earlier versions of R also installed the 32-bit version of the engine, an option set by default by the installer.

At this point, you need to make sure that the versions of the packages you want to download in the future are compatible with those provided by the Power BI service. To do this you need to set the CRAN snapshot from which to download packages. This is precisely where Posit's public Package Manager comes in.

Posit's public Package Manager is a versatile and reliable tool for the data science community, designed to make the lives of R and Python users easier and more efficient. It was developed in collaboration with Microsoft as a successor to the retiring Microsoft R Application Network.

It goes beyond simply preserving MRAN's features, it enhances them. While MRAN was an invaluable resource that provided daily snapshots of the CRAN website, Posit's focus is on the packages themselves, with full compliance to CRAN standards. This makes it possible for users to install packages directly using conventional commands such as install.packages(). Every business day, Posit takes a snapshot of all the CRAN packages available at that time. These snapshots are then stored and made available to users via specific URLs, allowing them to download and install specific versions of packages corresponding to the date of the snapshot.

As you can imagine, the Posit Package Manager URL you need simply points to the release date snapshot of the R engine version used by the Power BI service to ensure you are using packages compatible with that version. The URL you can use is the following: `https://packagemanager.posit.co/cran/2018-04-10`.

This snapshot setting must be done each time the version 3.4.4 of the engine is used, so the engine must trigger it each time it runs. Therefore, we will update the `Rprofile.site` file in the R etc folder to control the behavior of R sessions.

What you are going to do now is simply install this installation package in R 3.4.4. Let's see how to do it:

1. Open the File Explorer in the R Home folder, which for 64-bit installations by default looks like the following: `C:\Program Files\R\R-x.x.x\`. In our case, the version we are working on is 3.4.4, so replace x.x.x with this version.

2. Inside the R Home there is the etc folder, in which there is already the Rprofile.site file. Open this file in your favorite editor using the Administrator mode.

3. This file contains commented lines of code:

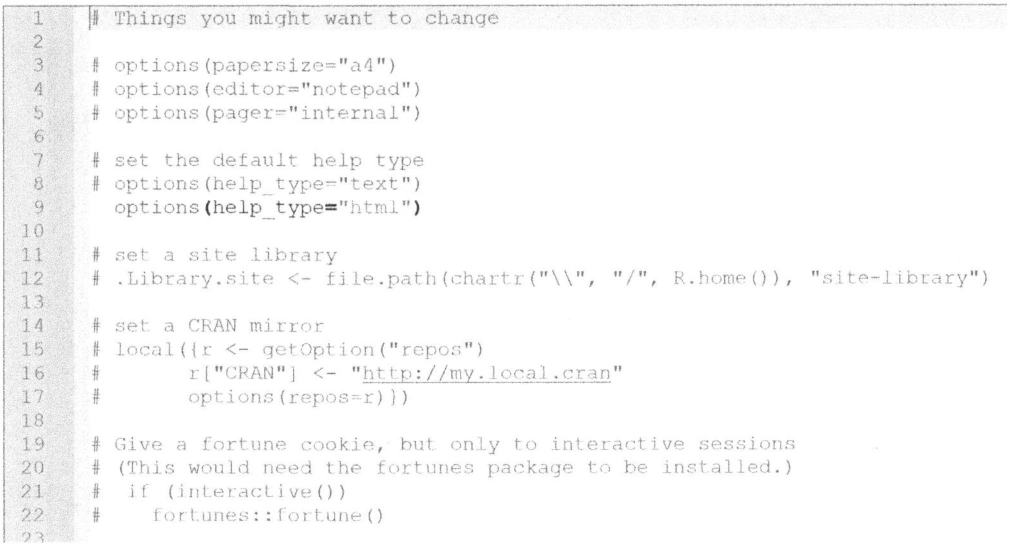

```
1   # Things you might want to change
2
3   # options(papersize="a4")
4   # options(editor="notepad")
5   # options(pager="internal")
6
7   # set the default help type
8   # options(help_type="text")
9     options(help_type="html")
10
11  # set a site library
12  # .Library.site <- file.path(chartr("\\", "/", R.home()), "site-library")
13
14  # set a CRAN mirror
15  # local({r <- getOption("repos")
16  #       r["CRAN"] <- "http://my.local.cran"
17  #       options(repos=r)})
18
19  # Give a fortune cookie, but only to interactive sessions
20  # (This would need the fortunes package to be installed.)
21  #  if (interactive())
22  #    fortunes::fortune()
23
```

Figure 2.5: Default content of the Rprofile.site file

4. Add the following code after what is already there. You can replace the correct date of the default snapshot repository with the R engine release date (in our case 2018-04-10). However, since we will need a slightly updated version of dplyr in Chapter 21, Advanced Visualizations, we will use the date of October 31, 2018:

```
Repos_date <- "2018-10-31"


local({
    # set a CRAN mirror
    r <- getOption("repos")
```

```
    r["CRAN"] <-
        paste0("https://packagemanager.posit.co/cran/",
               repos_date)
    options(repos=r)
    cat("\nDefault CRAN mirror snapshot taken on ",
        repos_date, ".", sep = "")
    cat("\n", "See: https://packagemanager.posit.co/.",
        sep="")
    cat("\n\n")
})
```

Then save the file.

5.   Open the `Rgui 3.4.4` clicking on the R x64 3.4.4 application in the **Start** menu. You'll see something like this:

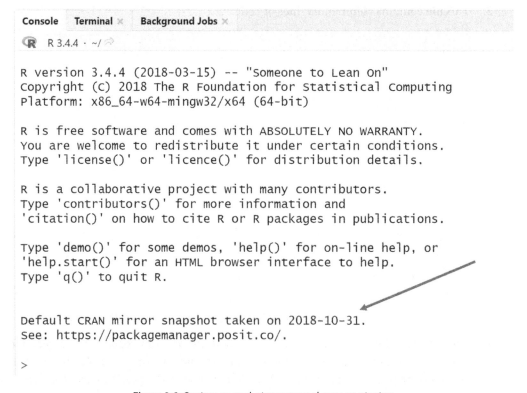

Figure 2.6: Custom snapshot message shown on startup

6.   To check that everything is working, try installing the `Ggplot` package using the `install.packages("ggplot2")` command. You should see a message like this:

```
> install.packages("ggplot2")
WARNING: Rtools is required to build R packages but is not currently installed. Please download and install
the appropriate version of Rtools before proceeding:

https://cran.rstudio.com/bin/windows/Rtools/
trying URL 'https://packagemanager.posit.co/cran/2018-10-31/bin/windows/contrib/3.4/ggplot2_3.1.0.zip'
Content type 'binary/octet-stream' length 3486989 bytes (3.3 MB)
downloaded 3.3 MB

package 'ggplot2' successfully unpacked and MD5 sums checked

The downloaded binary packages are in
        C:\Users\lucazav\AppData\Local\Temp\2\RtmpYfIUwY\downloaded_packages
```

Figure 2.7: Ggplot successfully installed from CRAN snapshot

The installation of the dedicated R script visuals engine, including the first R package chosen, is now complete.

What to do when the Power BI service upgrades the R engine

It may happen that you have already installed a version of CRAN R specifically to be aligned with the R script visual engine on the Power BI service at a certain date, and after a while, Microsoft updates the Power BI service, also upgrading the pre-installed R engine. This scenario causes two separate events:

- The R engine is more up to date than its predecessor and may contain breaking changes that could make previously developed reports unusable. This is a very rare eventuality since very often, such changes are mitigated by the introduction of "deprecated" functions or parameters, thus ensuring backward compatibility.

- Many of the packages installed on the release date of the previous R engine will be updated to a later version, corresponding to the release date of the new version of the R engine. Updating a package to a newer version is one of the most frequent causes of errors due to the incompatibility of a script written for the previous version of the package.

In this case, you should verify that all your reports that have R script visuals and are published to the Power BI service also work with the updates made to the service.

TIP

In light of the preceding observations, and considering the fact that the pre-installed R engine of the Power BI service is very rarely updated, it is better to directly install the new version of CRAN R on your machine (remember to edit the `Rprofile.site` file in order to set the CRAN snapshot correctly) and test your reports, making sure that Power BI Desktop references the new version of the engine. You need to fix any code issues in the failing R script visuals. After that, you can publish the reports back to the Power BI service.

Once you've made sure that all of the preceding reports are working properly, it's up to you to decide whether you want to uninstall the previous version of CRAN R to free up disk space and avoid confusion in handling these particular reports.

As you may have noticed, the R GUI that CRAN R provides is really minimal. You will see in the next section how to install an R IDE that has many more functions than the R GUI installed by default by CRAN R.

Installing an IDE for R development

The need to install a state-of-the-art R IDE for the development of code in Power BI comes from the need to have all the tools necessary to identify any bugs and quickly test the results of code chunks on the fly.

> **TIP**
>
> It is strongly suggested to test your R code in the IDE and verify the results before using it in Power BI.

There are many IDEs for R development on the market. Some examples are **R-Brain IDE (RIDE)**, **IntelliJ IDEA**, and **JupyterLab**, but it is estimated that over 90% of R programmers use **RStudio** as their primary IDE because of the countless features that simplify their daily work. For this reason, we suggest that you also use this IDE to test the code you will encounter in this book.

Installing RStudio

Installing RStudio (at the time of writing the chapter, the version is 2022.07.2+576) on your machine is very simple:

1. Go to `https://posit.co/download/rstudio-desktop/` and click the **DOWNLOAD RSTUDIO DESKTOP FOR WINDOWS** button at the bottom of the page:

Figure 2.8: Download RStudio for Windows

2. After the download is completed successfully, double-click on the executable, and click on the **Next** button on the RStudio setup welcome window.

3. In the next window, you are asked for the folder in which to install RStudio. Leave the default one and click on **Next**.

4. The following window asks you to select the **Start** menu folder in which to create the shortcuts. Leave the default one and click on **Install**.

5. When the installation is complete, click on **Finish**.

Just to make sure you installed everything smoothly, check that you have the option to select one of the two newly installed R engines from the RStudio options:

1. Open the newly installed RStudio from the start menu:

Figure 2.9: Run RStudio from the Start menu

2. Once opened, you may be asked whether you want to anonymously send any crash reports to RStudio to improve the product. Select **Yes** or **No**, whichever you want.

3. As you can see in the **Console** messages, RStudio has already selected an R engine by default. In your case, it will be the latest version installed on your machine:

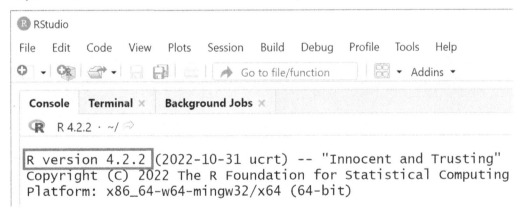

Figure 2.10: The default R engine selected in RStudio

4. Click on the **Tools** menu and then **Global Options...** to see the available engines:

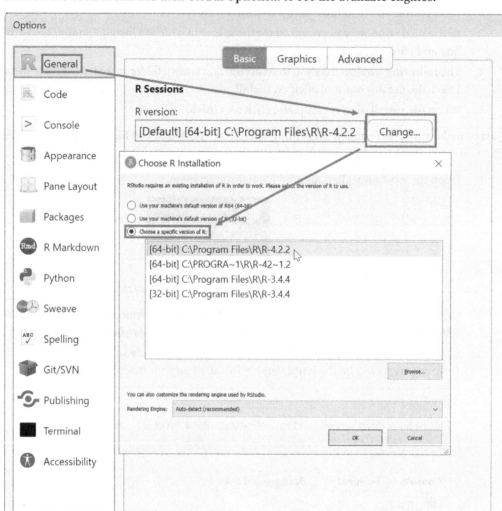

Figure 2.11: Choose your preferred R engine to use with RStudio

In the **General** menu of the **Options** window, you have the possibility to select the engine you want to use in RStudio by clicking on **Change...** and then selecting one of the available engines. Usually, we would not advise considering the engine containing C:\PROGRA~1\... as the root of the path because it is simply the engine that is currently selected in RStudio. Just select one of the other engines from the list.

5. For now, select the most recent version of R (in our case, R 4.2.2), make sure that the selected rendering engine is **Auto-detect (recommended)**, and then click **OK** in the **Choose R Installation** window. You will be notified that the rendering engine has been changed and will need to restart RStudio for the selected changes to take effect.

6. Click **OK** in the **Choose R Installation** window, and then **OK** in the **Options** window. Sometimes, you'll have the option to restart by selecting **Yes** in the dialog box that is shown immediately afterward. If not, just exit RStudio and open it again.

Well done! Now you're ready to manually link Intel's MKL to your R engines for better performance.

Installing RTools

When you install a package, it may not be specifically compiled for the R engine you are using. Sometimes, however, problems may arise with the compatibility of the package with the engine, so it may be necessary to compile the package appropriately.

In the Windows environment, it is necessary to have **RTools** installed to properly compile an R package from its source code or build R itself from the source. So, let's install it:

1. Go to the link `https://bit.ly/install-rtools`.
2. As we're using R 4.2.2, click on **RTools 4.2**.
3. Click on the **Rtools42 installer** link in the middle of the page to start downloading the installer.
4. Double-click on the installer and click **Next** to go to the first setup window.
5. Keep everything selected in the **Select Additional Tasks** window and click **Next**.
6. Click **Install** and then click **Finish**.

Since the RTools installer for earlier versions of R 4.2 is distinct from the one you just used, you may be wondering how to install a different version of RTools on your own machine to compile R 3.4.4 packages.

TIP

You do not need to install RTools for R 3.4.4 since the packages you install for this engine are selected specifically for that version of the engine using the Posit's public Package Manager.

In order to have all the tools needed to compile an R package, you need to install `devtools`. The main goal of `devtools` is to facilitate package development by providing R functions that simplify common tasks. It also provides the `install_github()` function to install the latest developments of a package from GitHub, before the new version of the package is released on CRAN. Let's follow the steps below to install it and check that RTools is installed correctly:

1. Open RStudio.
2. Enter the command `install.packages("devtools")` in the bottom-left Console.
3. A popup may appear asking if you want to install the required devtools dependency packages from the source. If it appears, it means that RTools is working behind the scenes, so click **Yes**.
4. Enter the command `devtools::find_rtools()` in the Console to verify that RTools is correctly installed. If the output is `TRUE`, all is OK.

If RTools is not found, you can try adding the RTools utilities path to the `PATH system variable`.

You can do this by following the instructions at this link: `https://bit.ly/rtools-install-win`. You have just installed RTools and devtools for R 4.2.2 the right way! Well done! Now you're ready to manually link Intel's MKL to your R engines for better performance.

Linking Intel's MKL to R

As anticipated earlier, the installation of CRAN R provides single-threaded versions of **BLAS** and **LAPACK** by default. You can check for the presence of the above libraries for both installed engines in the folder `C:\Program Files\R\R-x.y.z\bin\x64`, where `x.y.z` identifies the engine version. For example, for R 4.2.2, the above libraries are in the folder you can see in *Figure 2.14*:

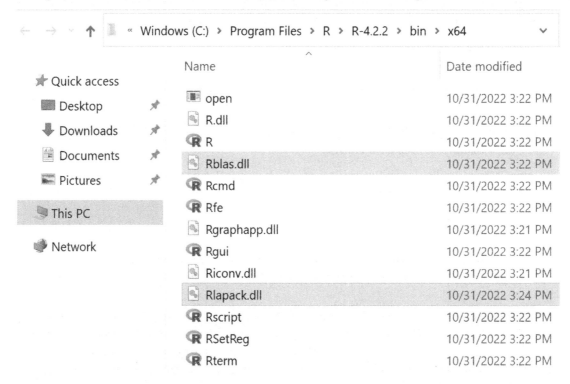

Figure 2.12: Single-threaded BLAS and LAPACK libraries in CRAN R

As already mentioned, these libraries provide the functions necessary for the R executable to perform specific mathematical operations. The addition of these functions to the executable is done by the **linking operation**, done by an operating system mechanism called a **dynamic loader**, which first reads the executable into memory, then reads all the dynamic libraries referenced by the executable into memory, and then modifies all calls to these libraries in the executable so that they point directly to the memory locations where the libraries were loaded. Thus, keeping these libraries separate makes the executable lighter, as well as allowing other applications to use the same libraries.

To get an idea of the benchmark performance using these libraries in single-threaded mode, let's do an experiment. You will use a benchmark designed by Philippe Grosjean, which you can find at this link: https://bit.ly/r-benchmark. A copy of the same script can be found in the GitHub repository associated with the book in the folder that references this chapter.

Once the file is downloaded to your machine, open it in RStudio using the **Open File...** option in the **File** menu. The contents of the loaded script can be displayed in a tab with the file name as the title:

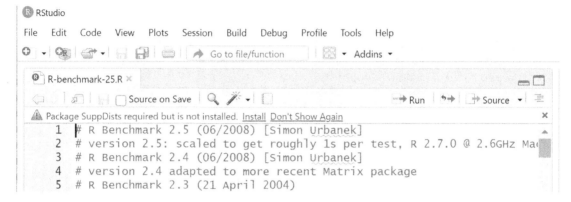

Figure 2.13: The R benchmark script loaded in RStudio

As you can see, RStudio notices if any package is used in the script that you have not yet installed in the engine. Should it find any, it suggests that you install them by clicking on the simple **Install** link on the yellow warning banner.

In the case of the benchmark, install the reported SuppDists package by clicking on the link. After the installation is finished, click on the **Source as Background Job...** option you can find in the **Source** menu on the top right of the tab with the script:

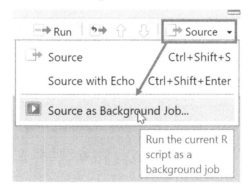

Figure 2.14: Running the script in a background job

Then, click **Start** in the next pop-up window. The script will run as a background job in a separate thread, and when it is finished executing, the results of the benchmark will be shown clearly in the **Background Jobs** tab at the bottom left of RStudio.

On a machine with an Intel(R) Xeon(R) Platinum 8272CL CPU at 2.60GHz (8 threads) and 32 GB RAM, the results are as follows:

```
Loading required package: Matrix


   R Benchmark 2.5
   ================
Number of times each test is run_____: 3


   I. Matrix calculation
   ---------------------
Loading required package: SuppDists
Creation, transp., deformation of a 2500x2500 matrix (sec): 0.863333333333333
2400x2400 normal distributed random matrix ^1000____ (sec): 0.923333333333333
Sorting of 7,000,000 random values_____ (sec): 0.816666666666667
2800x2800 cross-product matrix (b = a' * a)_____ (sec): 18.4433333333333
Linear regr. over a 3000x3000 matrix (c = a \ b')___ (sec): 8.09333333333333
                              ------------------------------------------------
               Trimmed geom. mean (2 extremes eliminated):  1.86160763076357

   II. Matrix functions
   --------------------
FFT over 2,400,000 random values_____ (sec): 0.393333333333336
Eigenvalues of a 640x640 random matrix_____ (sec): 0.793333333333327
Determinant of a 2500x2500 random matrix_____ (sec): 3.86
Cholesky decomposition of a 3000x3000 matrix_____ (sec): 5.99666666666667
Inverse of a 1600x1600 random matrix_____ (sec): 3.03333333333333
                              ------------------------------------------------
               Trimmed geom. mean (2 extremes eliminated):  2.10210488539771

   III. Programmation
   ------------------
3,500,000 Fibonacci numbers calculation (vector calc)(sec): 0.709999999999999
Creation of a 3000x3000 Hilbert matrix (matrix calc) (sec): 0.303333333333332
Grand common divisors of 400,000 pairs (recursion)__ (sec): 0.296666666666662
Creation of a 500x500 Toeplitz matrix (loops)_____ (sec): 0.406666666666666
Escoufier's method on a 45x45 matrix (mixed)_____ (sec): 0.400000000000006
                              ------------------------------------------------
               Trimmed geom. mean (2 extremes eliminated):  0.366780497256686


Total time for all 15 tests_____ (sec): 45.3333333333333
Overall mean (sum of I, II and III trimmed means/3)_ (sec): 1.12801858656321
                         --- End of test ---
```

Figure 2.15: Benchmark results using a single thread

Now, let's try to use the multi-threaded functions of the BLAS and LAPACK packages provided by the **Intel oneAPI MKL**. Here are the steps to follow:

1.   Go to this link: https://bit.ly/onemkl-download.

2. Select "**Windows**" as the operating system and "**Online**" as the distribution. Click the **Download** button, which you can find at the bottom of the page, and then click the **Continue as Guest** link in the following popup. The latest version will start downloading (in our case, the version is 2022.2.1).

3. Double-click on the downloaded installer and then click **Continue** to begin the installation.

4. Accept the terms of the license by checking the checkbox and click **Continue** to proceed with the recommended installation.

5. In the next window, just click on the right arrow, as you don't have Microsoft Visual Studio installed.

6. Select the radio button you want according to your preferences about the collection of your information, and then click **Install**.

7. Click **Finish** after the intel-optimized math library for numerical computing has been installed correctly.

8. Open the binary folder of R 4.2.2 (`C:\Program Files\R\R-4.2.2\bin\x64`) in File Explorer and keep it open.

9. Open another instance of File Explorer and go to the following path: `C:\Program Files (x86)\Intel\oneAPI\compiler\2022.2.1\windows\redist\intel64_win\compiler` (notice the folder named after the installed version in the middle of the path; you may need to change it).

10. Copy all the content of the `compiler` folder into the R 4.2.2 binary folder in the other instance of File Explorer.

11. Open another instance of File Explorer and go to the following path: `C:\Program Files (x86)\Intel\oneAPI\mkl\2022.2.1\redist\intel64` (notice the folder named after the installed version in the middle of the path; you may need to change it).

12. Copy all the content of the `intel64` folder into the R 4.2.2 binary folder in the other instance of File Explorer.

13. Find the files `Rlapack.dll` and `Rblast.dll` in the R 4.2.2 binaries folder (`bin/x64`) and rename them to `Rlapack.dll.old` and `Rblast.dll.old` respectively.

14. Find the file `mkl_rt.2.dll` in the R 4.2.2 binaries folder (`bin/x64`), duplicate it, and rename the copy `Rlapack.dll` (the original `mkl_rt.2.dll` file must be kept).

15. Find the file `mkl_rt.2.dll` in the R 4.2.2 binaries folder (`bin/x64`), duplicate it, and rename the copy `Rblast.dll` (the original `mkl_rt.2.dll` file must be kept).

Basically, what you did was replace the old `Rlapack.dll` and `Rblast.dll` files with a copy of the `mkl_rt.2.dll` library, which contains all the functions of the two old libraries, but enabled for multi-threading and specialized for Intel processors. When the R 4.2.2 engine is linked to the two old libraries by the OS, in their place will be the new performance functions of oneMKL. We have to thank the developer Guilherme Higashi (`https://www.linkedin.com/in/guilherme-higashi/`), who shared the idea with the community that the `mkl_rt.2.dll` library could replace both the old BLAS and LAPACK libraries.

Let's verify that the substitution was successful:

1. Close and restart RStudio. If it loads correctly without giving any error message, that is already a good indicator that the replacement was successful. Otherwise, it is likely that you made misspellings when you renamed the copies of the new library. Just fix them and try again.

2. If there are no errors, we check the maximum number of threads "seen" by BLAS by installing the `RhpcBLASctl` package. Enter the command `install.packages("RhpcBLASctl")` in the Console in the bottom left of RStudio and press *Enter*.

3. Still in the Console, enter the following command: `RhpcBLASctl::omp_get_max_threads()` and press **Enter.** In our case, the output is 8 (you might get a different value depending on the hardware you are using):

```
Console   Terminal ×   Background Jobs ×

R  R 4.2.2 · ~/

> install.packages("RhpcBLASctl")


package 'RhpcBLASctl' successfully unpacked and MD5 sums checked

The downloaded binary packages are in
        C:\Users\lucazav\AppData\Local\Temp\3\Rtmpmo82kZ\downloaded_packages
> RhpcBLASctl::omp_get_max_threads()
[1] 8
>
```

Figure 2.16: Checking the number of threads seen by BLAS

Wow, that's great! You just got your R engine to use the new multi-threading-enabled oneML libraries! For example, in our case, the BLAS library is now using 8 threads!

TIP

Repeat the same steps to install the oneMKL libraries for the R 4.2.2 engine as well.

Let us verify the performance improvement by running the benchmark script again with the R 4.2.2 engine. This time, it is not possible to run the script via the **Source as Background Job...** option because this execution is performed using multi-threading and would conflict with the mathematical operations performed in multi-threading in the script. Therefore, this time, simply click on **Source** to rerun the benchmark script. At the end of the execution, in the Console, you can see the following:

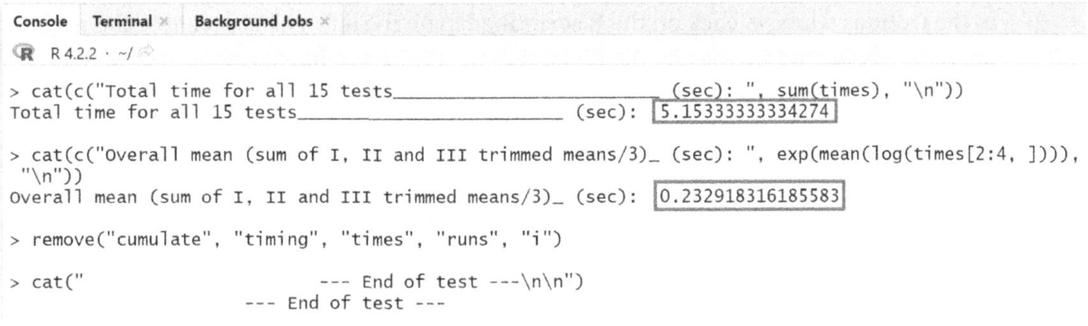

Console
Terminal
Background Jobs
R 4.2.2 · ~/
> cat(c("Total time for all 15 tests_____________________________ (sec): ", sum(times), "\n"))
Total time for all 15 tests_____________________________ (sec): 5.15333333334274
> cat(c("Overall mean (sum of I, II and III trimmed means/3)_ (sec): ", exp(mean(log(times[2:4,]))), "\n"))
Overall mean (sum of I, II and III trimmed means/3)_ (sec): 0.232918316185583
> remove("cumulate", "timing", "times", "runs", "i")
> cat("   --- End of test ---\n\n")
--- End of test ---

Figure 2.17: Benchmark results using multiple threads

The results are impressive! Comparing them with *Figure 2.17*, we observe that the total time required to run all the tests is 8.8 times faster (just like the number of threads seen), and the overall average trimmed time is 4.84 times faster! Congratulations, you managed to link the brand-new oneMKL libraries to your R engine!

Now that the R engines are configured and up to speed, let's also configure Power BI Desktop so that it interfaces properly with them.

Configuring Power BI Desktop to work with R

Once you have installed the R engines necessary for the development of your reports and the RStudio IDE, you must configure Power BI Desktop so that it properly references these tools. This is really a very simple task:

1. In Power BI Desktop, go to the **File** menu, click on the **Options and settings** tab, and then click on **Options**:

New
Open report
Save
Save as
Get data
Import
Export
Publish
Options and settings
Get started
Options and settings
Options
Data source settings

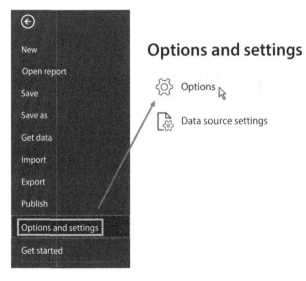

Figure 2.18: Opening the Power BI Desktop Options and settings window

2. In the **Options** window, click on the **R scripting** tab on the left. The contents of the panel on the right will update, giving you the option to select the R engine to reference and the R IDE to use for R script visuals:

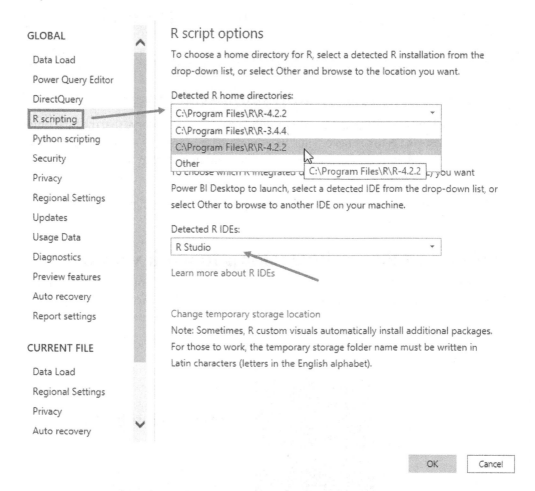

Figure 2.19: Choosing the engine and the IDE to work with in Power BI Desktop

3. As you can see, Power BI Desktop automatically identifies the installed R engines and IDEs. For the moment, select the latest version of the engine (in our case, it is 4.2.2), in order to be aligned with the one already selected in RStudio.

You can use the R IDE detected by Power BI Desktop when you need to debug the code you write within an R script visual. Let's explore how to do that next.

Debugging an R script visual

Once you drag some data fields into the R script visual values, the R script editor will be activated so that you can interact with its tools, provided in the upper-right corner:

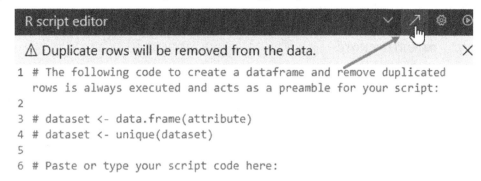

Figure 2.20: Opening the R code of an R script visual in RStudio

Clicking the arrow in the upper-right corner of the R script editor opens a block of code in RStudio that loads the dataset provided as input to an R script visual as a CSV file and then allows you to run the rest of the code to debug it:

Figure 2.21: Debugging the R code of an R script visual in RStudio

Now you know that the code you see in *Figure 2.23* will be executed on every refresh of the R script visual. Also, if you play around with this feature a bit, you will be able to guess the first of the most relevant possible problems that occur when debugging directly from the R script visual.

> **IMPORTANT NOTE**
>
> Whenever you debug the code of an R script visual on the referenced IDE, Power BI Desktop creates a folder in which it downloads the data present at the time as input to the R script visual in CSV format, and saves the script wrapper you saw in *Figure 2.23*. If you have meanwhile clicked the R script visual's external debug arrow several times while the same IDE instance was open, multiple temporary folders will have been created. Closing the IDE will delete only the last temporary folder created, leaving all other previous temporary folders in the `C:\Users\<user-name>` folder. The remaining folders will be deleted after closing Power BI Desktop.

Some users who have used earlier versions of Power BI Desktop have complained about some cases where such folders were not deleted. Should that happen, such a bug could cause the hard drive to fill up if you did a lot of debugging from the R script visual.

Therefore, our suggestion is as follows:

IMPORTANT NOTE

Before writing R code directly into the script visual, develop it separately in the IDE by referencing the data directly from the source. If this is not possible because the input data of the R script visual is the result of a series of transformation steps in Power BI, debug it once externally from the script visual only to retrieve the CSV of the source data. At that point, finish developing the rest of your code directly in the IDE. When development is complete, always make sure that any temporary folders generated by Power BI Desktop are properly deleted; otherwise, delete them yourself.

A question may arise about the size of the CSV file that Power BI Desktop can generate: Could the CSV file occupy many GB of data? The answer is as follows:

IMPORTANT NOTE

As you will see in a later section on the limitations of R script visuals, a script visual can handle a dataset of only 150,000 rows. Any rows in excess are simply truncated. Therefore, the size of the CSV generated by Power BI can be quite large, but not excessively large because of the previous limitation. By the way, this limitation should not be a problem because an R script visual is used exclusively to graphically represent data. Keep in mind that a graphical representation is mostly based on aggregations of data that make up a dataset of a few rows, not huge datasets. Plotting millions of points is in most cases not the right choice. Should it be necessary to do so, an R script visual is not the right tool.

We have seen how to best configure Power BI Desktop with R and RStudio. Now let's look at everything you need to configure in order to interact properly with the Power BI service.

Configuring the Power BI service to work with R

As you learned in the *The R engines used by Power BI* section of this chapter, the Power BI service uses different R engines depending on whether the scripts are used in R script visuals or in Power Query for data transformation. In the first case, the engine is pre-installed on the cloud.

IMPORTANT NOTE

If the data sources of your report come exclusively from online services (e.g., Azure SQL Database) or the web, and if the R scripts in your report are used only in the R script visuals, you don't need to install the data gateway in personal mode to refresh the datasets.

In the second case, or if at least one dataset in your report is fed from an on-premises data source or on an Azure VM, you need to install the on-premises data gateway in personal mode on any machine of your choice in order to make the Power BI service communicate with the R engine you installed on that machine.

Installing the on-premises data gateway in personal mode

We have emphasized the fact that you will need to install the data gateway in personal mode for an important reason: R scripts are not supported for the on-premises data gateway in enterprise mode.

In your case, you will install the data gateway on the same computer on which you have installed the R engines and Power BI Desktop. The steps to do this are as follows:

1. Make sure you can log in to the Power BI service (`https://app.powerbi.com`). You will see a home page like the following, customized with your company logo if you have already set one up:

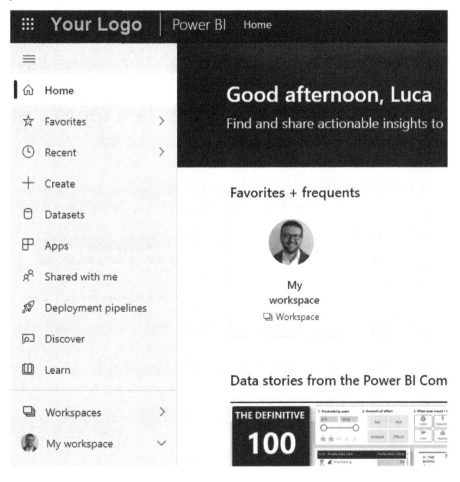

Figure 2.22: The Power BI service home page

2. On the top right-hand side of the home page, you'll notice a downward-pointing arrow that allows you to access the download menu. Click on this, and then select **Data Gateway**:

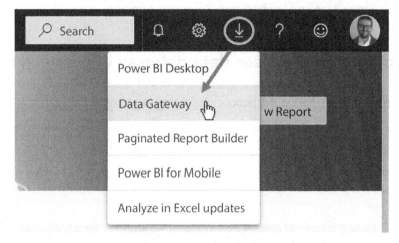

Figure 2.23: The Download menu on your the Power BI service home page

3. You will be redirected to a web page from which you can download the data gateway. Be sure to download the **personal mode** version:

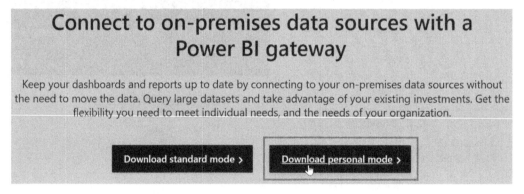

Figure 2.24: Download the personal mode version of the data gateway

4. Running the newly downloaded executable immediately opens an initial window that asks you to check the minimum installation requirements given in a link, set the installation folder of the software, and accept the terms of use for the software:

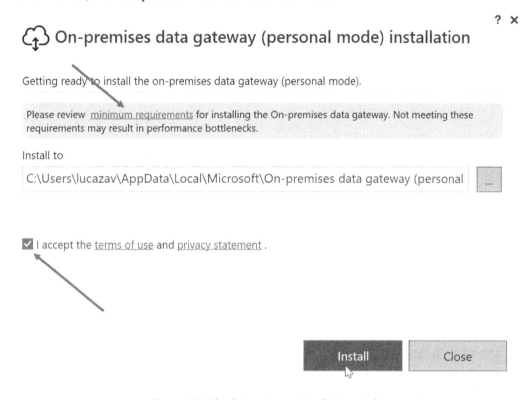

Figure 2.25: The data gateway installation window

You can leave the default folder selected, click on the terms of use acceptance checkbox, and click **Install** to move on.

5. Once the data gateway installation is complete, a sign-in window will open where you will need to enter the email address with which you registered with the Power BI service, and then your password:

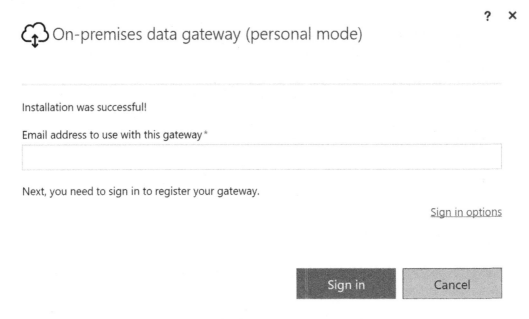

Figure 2.26: The data gateway sign-in window

6. When the sign-in operation is successful, a green tick will appear with the words **The gateway is online and ready to be used.**:

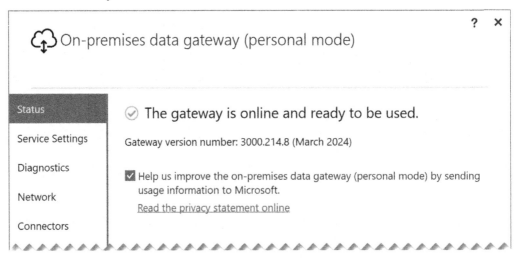

Figure 2.27: The data gateway up and running

7. You can close the on-premises data gateway window.

Now, the Power BI service is directly connected to your machine and can access it whenever there is a need to refresh a published dataset with which your newly installed data gateway is associated.

IMPORTANT NOTE

Keep in mind that a Power BI user can only have one personal data gateway associated. If you try to install multiple on-premises data gateways in personal mode on several different machines, logging in on one of them will force a disconnection for all other data gateways.

Sharing reports that use R scripts in the Power BI service

In the previous sections, you learned that thanks to the data gateway newly installed in personal mode, you can publish a report that uses R scripts in the Power BI service to your personal workspace for sure. But assuming you have a Pro license, can you also publish this report to shared workspaces? There is often a lot of confusion about this.

IMPORTANT NOTE

No one forbids you from publishing your report on shared workspaces as well! Although you have used a data gateway in personal mode, other users can view your report. But not only that! Other users can also refresh the dataset behind the report. They will do this "on your behalf," pointing to the machine referenced by your data gateway. The important thing is that your machine is turned on!

But then, if you can still share your reports with others using a data gateway in personal mode, what is the advantage of using a data gateway in Enterprise mode?

Using just one data gateway in Enterprise mode, multiple users in your organization can access on-premises data to which they already have access permission. It goes without saying that other users can view and refresh your report, but they cannot develop their own reports using R code by referencing your machine with R engines through your personal data gateway. This one is the true limitation.

In light of the preceding information, there is an unofficial architecture, frequently used in companies, that allows all reports that make use of R code in Power Query to reference a single machine on which the R engine has been installed using a personal data gateway.

TIP

This unofficial architecture makes use of a personal data gateway associated not with a physical person, but with a fictitious "service" user. The credentials of this user are shared between all the analysts who use R code to transform data into their reports. Also, since the machine with the R engine referenced by the data gateway is shared, it must remain on during periods of scheduled activity. For this reason, an Azure Windows virtual machine on which both the R engine and the data gateway run is often used in this architecture.

Since a picture is worth a thousand words, *Figure 2.22* summarizes this architecture:

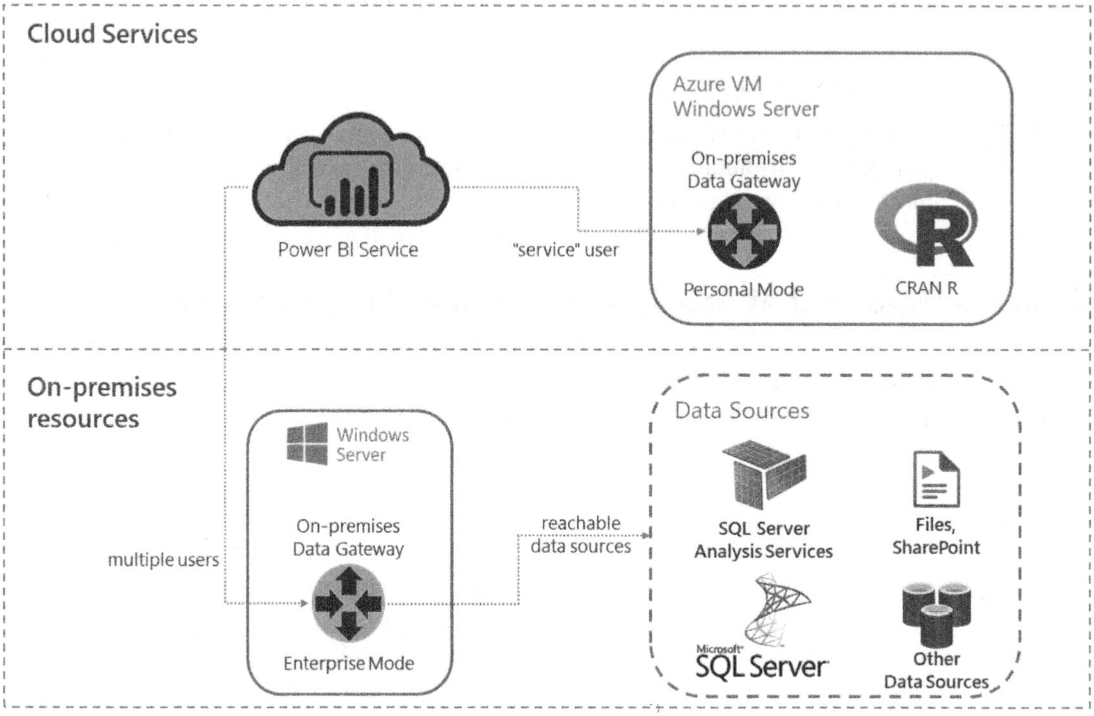

Figure 2.28: Enterprise architecture to use R for data transformations

Thanks to this architecture, it is possible to allow a group of analysts to use R scripts in their reports, despite the limitations imposed by the on-premises data gateway in personal mode.

That said, in addition to the limitations seen for R scripts in Power Query, there are some important ones to be aware of for R script visuals as well.

R script visuals limitations

R script visuals have some important limitations regarding the data they can handle, both as input and output:

- An R script visual can handle a data frame with only 150,000 rows. If there are more than 150,000 rows, only the first 150,000 rows are used and a relevant message is displayed on the image.
- R script visuals have an output size limit of 2 MB.

You must also be careful not to exceed the 5 minutes of runtime calculation for an R script visual in order to avoid a time-out error. Moreover, in order not to run into performance problems, note that the resolution of the R script visual plots is fixed at 72 DPI.

As you can imagine, some limitations of R script visuals are different depending on whether you run the visual on Power BI Desktop or the Power BI service.

If you think you need to develop reports intended only for Power BI Desktop, without the need to publish them on the service, you can do any of the following:

- Use any kind of package (CRAN, GitHub, or custom) in your R script visuals.
- Use only CRAN packages in your custom R script visuals (you will see an example in *Chapter 22, Interactive Custom Visuals in R*).
- Access the internet from both an R script visual and a custom R script visual.

When you create reports to share through the Power BI service, note the following:

- For both R script visuals and custom R script visuals, you can use only the CRAN packages listed at this link: `https://bit.ly/powerbi-r-limits`.
- You cannot access the internet from either R script visuals or custom R script visuals.

As you may have noticed, although the CRAN packages that can be used in an R script visual on the Power BI service are limited, you can still count more than 900 packages in that list! In addition to the fact that R was the first analytical language introduced into Power BI, this shows that R is de facto considered one of the most versatile and professional languages for creating engaging visualizations.

As you probably already know, once one of your reports is published on the Power BI service, you can decide to share it on your blog, on one of your websites, or on social media via the **Publish to web** option. R script visuals are not allowed to be published on the web.

 IMPORTANT NOTE

Custom R visuals overcome the limitation of publishing to the web.

So, if you have to publish a report to the web, and that report contains a visualization created using R code, you must develop a custom R visual.

Summary

In this chapter, you learned about the most popular free R engines in the community. In particular, you learned about the performance advantages introduced by Microsoft in its distribution of R, even if this distribution will be retired in the near future. You also learned how to enhance the standard CRAN R with the oneMKL libraries for multi-threaded calculations.

Taking note of the unique features of Power BI Desktop and the Power BI service, you have learned how to properly choose the engines and how to install them.

You have also learned about the most popular IDE in the R community and how to install it.

In addition, you were introduced to all of the best practices for properly configuring both Power BI Desktop and the Power BI service with R, whether in a development or enterprise environment.

Finally, you learned about some of the limitations of using R with Power BI, knowledge of which is critical to avoid making mistakes in developing and deploying reports.

In the next chapter, we'll see which Python engines and IDEs to install and configure in Power BI in order to develop and test Python scripts in comfort.

Test your knowledge

1. What are the most popular R engines to date and which of them will be phased out?

2. What is the most obvious advantage of Microsoft's R distributions?

3. Is it possible to introduce the advantage in *question 2* for CRAN R as well? If so, can this be done directly from the software installer?

4. You decide to install the latest available version of CRAN R, and through this, you develop some transformation steps in Power Query. What do you need to be able to publish your report to the Power BI service and allow it to be refreshed regularly?

5. Suppose you have installed only the R engine mentioned in *Question 4* and you also add a plot made with an R script visual to the same report mentioned in *Question 4*. What are the problems you'll encounter on Power BI Desktop? What are the problems you'll encounter when you publish the report to the Power BI service?

6. Is it possible to refresh datasets of a published report using R scripts without having to install a data gateway in personal mode? If yes, in which case?

7. Why within Power BI would you interact with the R IDE configured in Power BI options?

8. How does the passing of data to the external R IDE take place?

9. Suppose you made a report containing an R script visual that uses the `RgoogleMaps` package to query Google's internet services and make a beautiful map. The version of the R engine you are using is aligned with the version of the engine used in the Power BI service. Will you get an error when you publish the report and try to refresh the datasets?

10. You need to embed a Power BI report that contains an R script visual on your technical blog via the "**Publish to web**" feature. Is it possible to do this?

Learn more on Discord

To join the Discord community for this book – where you can share feedback, ask questions to the author, and learn about new releases – follow the QR code below:

`https://discord.gg/MKww5g45EB`

3

Configuring Python with Power BI

Just as in *Chapter 2*, *Configuring R with Power BI*, you had to install the R engines in order to interact with Power BI, you will now have to install the Python engines on your machine. You'll also see how to configure some IDEs so you can develop and test Python code comfortably before using it in Power BI. Therefore, similar to what we have already seen in *Chapter 2*, *Configuring R with Power BI*, the following topics will be discussed in this chapter:

- The available Python engines
- Installing an IDE for Python development
- Installing an IDE for Python development
- Configuring Power BI Desktop to work with Python
- Configuring the Power BI service to work with Python
- Limitations of Python visuals

Technical requirements

This chapter requires you to have a working internet connection and **Power BI Desktop** already installed on your machine (we used version 2.110.1161.0 64-bit, October 2022). The last part of the chapter also requires you to be signed up for the Power BI service (here's a how-to: `http://bit.ly/signup-powerbiservice`). A **Power BI Free** license is enough to test all the code in this book, as you will share reports only in your personal **workspace**.

The available Python engines

As with R, there are several distributions you can install for Python: **standard Python, ActivePython, Anaconda**, and so on. Typically, "pure" developers download the latest version of the Python engine from `https://www.python.org/`, and then install various community-developed packages useful for their projects from the **Python Package Index** (**PyPI**). Other vendors, such as ActiveState and Anaconda, pre-package a specific version of the Python engine with a set of packages for the purpose of accelerating a project's startup.

While the standard Python and ActiveState distributions are more aimed at general-purpose developers, Anaconda is the distribution preferred by data scientists and by those who work more closely with machine learning projects. In turn, Anaconda comes in two distinct distributions itself: Anaconda and **Miniconda**.

The Anaconda distribution, with its more than 150 included packages, can be considered the best do-it-yourself supermarket for data scientists, where commonly used utilities, libraries, and Python packages are ready and configured for use. The Miniconda distribution, on the other hand, is considered the minimum indispensable toolbox for the data scientist seeking to trim the resources to the right level.

There is one fundamental tool that Anaconda and Miniconda have in common: it is **conda**, one of the most popular package managers for Python. Conda provides the developer with an easy-to-use system for the management of so-called **virtual environments**. A virtual environment, or **environment** for short, aims to encapsulate the installation of a Python engine with a set of version-specific packages. The goal is to create an isolated environment, often associated with a project or task, that can guarantee the **reproducibility of results**. This is a very important concept, essential to ensure that Python projects run smoothly when dealing with a large community of developers who create and maintain their own packages independently of each other.

IMPORTANT NOTE

Contrary to what you saw in *Chapter 2, Configuring R with Power BI*, the Python community does not have a "time machine" like the Posit's public Package Manager that easily references a specific version of the Python engine at its release date and a snapshot of the entire ecosystem of Python packages at the versions they were at on that date. It is up to you to build your own "time capsules" using environments in order to ensure the reproducibility of your code.

Conda is a very versatile tool. Besides managing the environments, it can also install various packages (regardless of the programming language used, not only Python), carefully managing all their dependencies. Generally, the most widely used tool for installing Python packages is **pip**, which installs only packages written in Python and is generally installed along with the Python engine. This is because pip is based on PyPI, which contains the vast majority of packages developed in Python and shared with the community. Conda, on the other hand, provides multiple channels. The *default* channel is maintained by Anaconda Inc and provides a smaller number of packages, sometimes less up to date than their counterparts found on PyPI, thus trying to provide more stability. But there is also the *conda-forge* channel, which is less constrained and dedicated to the community. We will see how to use them later.

That said, beyond the extent of "bodywork" mounted around the Python engine, the various Python distributions do not add features that dramatically improve engine performance, unlike what we saw in *Chapter 2, Configuring R with Power BI*, with the Microsoft R engines. For this reason, we will not go into detail about the features installed by each distribution. What can really make a difference is installing some essential packages for numerical computation with pip or conda. You will see this in one of the next sections.

Choosing a Python engine to install

Back to our scenario, to develop Python code for use in Power Query or Python visuals, what you need for sure is the following:

- A Python engine
- A package manager, to install the minimum number of packages needed to transform the data or visualize it appropriately

To select the products that best suit your needs, you will need to understand your Power BI requirements in more detail.

The Python engines used by Power BI

Just as with R visuals in the Power BI service, the following note applies to Python visuals.

IMPORTANT NOTE

The Python engine and packages used by the Power BI service for **Python visuals** are preinstalled on the cloud and therefore the user must adapt to the versions adopted by the service.

As you can imagine, the version of the engine adopted by the Power BI service is a bit behind the latest release (now 3.11.0). See the following note for more details.

IMPORTANT NOTE

To date (December 2022), the Power BI service still relies on the **Python 3.7.7** runtime when implementing a Python visual. It is important to always keep an eye on the version of the Python engine and packages provided by the Power BI service with each release to ensure that the reports to be published work properly. See the following link for more information: `http://bit.ly/powerbi-python-limits`.

The behavior of the Power BI service is the same as that we've already seen for the R script in the case of doing data transformation in Power Query.

IMPORTANT NOTE

The Python engine used by the Power BI service during the data refresh phase for Python scripts in Power Query has to be installed on any machine of your choice outside the service, and on that same machine you have to install the **on-premises data gateway** in **personal mode**. Note that you must use external engines even if the data to be refreshed does not flow through the gateway, but comes from data sources not referenced by the gateway itself (e.g., a CSV dataset from the web).

As long as the Python environment to be referenced via the data gateway is the base one, it is sufficient that both are installed on the same machine. Otherwise, the following note applies.

IMPORTANT NOTE

If you need to use multiple environments installed on the machine for your Power Query transformations, you must also install Power BI Desktop. It allows you to switch the routing of the data gateway to the selected environment through its options by updating the configuration file at `C:\Users\<your-username>\AppData\Local\PowerBIScripting\PythonSettings.xml`. This file allows the overriding of the Python environment referenced by the data gateway by default. Keep in mind that you can refer to only one environment. The content of this file updates automatically when you change configurations in the Python scripting tab of the Power BI Desktop options.

In a nutshell, regardless of whether you want to run R or Python scripts, the infrastructure required by Power BI Desktop and the Power BI service is managed in the same way. Therefore, again, if you need to do reports *for personal use on your desktop*, you have no limitations on which Python engine to use, so you can install the Python versions and packages that suit you best. If, on the other hand, you know in advance that the reports you will create *contain Python visuals and are intended to be shared with colleagues* on the Power BI service, then there are strict limitations on both the version and the packages pre-installed in the service.

But let's get down to business and start installing the Python stuff!

Installing the suggested Python engines

Managing dependencies of Python scripts injected inside reports can be complex in the long run. Keeping in mind that it is possible to create multiple environments on the same machine, we suggest the following tip.

TIP

We recommend that you dedicate a machine to run the Python engines used by Power BI reports. Our suggestion is to create a Python environment for each possible need that may arise when developing Python scripts in Power Query or for Python visuals. If you have already prepared a machine dedicated to running R scripts, as seen in *Chapter 2, Configuring R with Power BI*, then you could use the same machine to install Python engines on as well. Keep in mind that in this case, you need to make sure that the resources of the machine are sufficient to run all the engines and to satisfy the various requests coming from the various reports.

Let's first install the latest version of the Python engine to use for our data transformation.

The Python engine for data transformation

Certainly, to enrich your reports using Python, you won't need a large number of pre-installed packages. Also, in order to easily manage your environments, conda is a tool to include in your arsenal. Bearing in mind that the engine we are about to install will be used as an external Python engine by the Power BI service to transform data via Power Query through the on-premises data gateway in personal mode, the following tip applies.

TIP

We suggest adopting the latest version of **Miniconda** as the default distribution. This is because, besides pre-installing very few packages giving you the possibility to choose which packages to install, it also includes conda in the distribution.

The installation of Miniconda is very simple:

1. Go to `https://docs.conda.io/en/latest/miniconda.html` and then click on Latest Miniconda installer links by Python version.
2. Click on the latest Python version available in Miniconda for your OS (3.9 as of the time of writing):

Windows installers

Python version	Name	Size
Python 3.9	Miniconda3 Windows 64-bit	71.2 MiB
Python 3.8	Miniconda3 Windows 64-bit	70.6 MiB
Python 3.7	Miniconda3 Windows 64-bit	69.0 MiB
Python 3.9	Miniconda3 Windows 32-bit	67.8 MiB
Python 3.8	Miniconda3 Windows 32-bit	66.8 MiB
Python 3.7	Miniconda3 Windows 32-bit	65.5 MiB

Figure 3.1: Download the latest version available of Miniconda

3. Once the file is downloaded, double-click on it, click **Next** on the welcome window that pops up, and then click on **I Agree** to accept the License Agreement.
4. In the next window, you'll be asked if you want to install Miniconda just for you or for other users as well. Leave the default setting (all users) if you have admin privileges, otherwise select **Just Me**. Then click **Next**.

5. Leave the default folder for the installation on the next screen and click **Next**. Keep in mind that the installation path if you selected **All Users** is the following: C:\ProgramData\Miniconda3. If it has been installed just for you, the installation path will be in this form: C:\Users\<your-username>\miniconda3.

6. In the next window, check **Register Miniconda3 as the system** (or **my default** if installing just for yourself) **Python 3.10.9** and click **Install**:

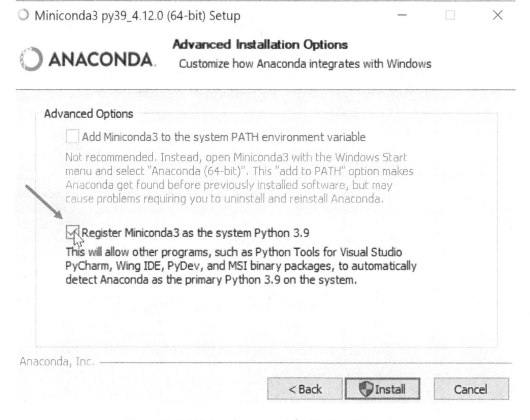

Figure 3.2: Set Miniconda as your default Python 3.9 engine

7. At the end of the installation, an **Installation Complete** window will inform you that the installation was completed successfully. Then, click **Next**.

8. The last screen gives you the possibility to open documents containing tips and resources to start working with Miniconda. You can unflag the two options and click **Finish**.

And that's it! Now you are ready to write and run your Python code with Miniconda.

IMPORTANT NOTE

As a best practice, the Power BI Desktop installation on which you develop reports should be located on a different machine than the machine selected as the Power BI service Python engine machine, which is often where the data gateway is installed. In this case, you will also need to install Miniconda on the machine where your Power BI Desktop instance is installed to test your reports.

At the end of the installation, under the **Anaconda3 (64-bit)** folder in the **Start** menu, you will find shortcuts to two command-line interfaces (the standard **Command Prompt** and **PowerShell**), which ensure that you can activate **conda** behind the scenes and interact with the tools provided by Miniconda:

Figure 3.3: Anaconda prompts that are useful for interacting with Miniconda

Our favorite command line is **Anaconda Prompt** and we'll show you how to use it very shortly.

As we said in the *The available Python engines* section, both **conda** and **pip** are very good package managers. As a package dependency solver, conda is better, although a bit slower than pip. But the reason pip is often used as a package manager is that it pulls packages directly from PyPI, which is a far more complete repository than Anaconda's one. For the same reason, *we will also use pip as our default package manager*.

Creating an environment for data transformations using pip

Contrary to what you have seen with R engines, for which two separate installations of two engines with different versions was done, in the case of Python there is one single installation and *only the environments vary*.

Here, we will create an environment dedicated to data transformations and containing one of the Python versions made available by Miniconda along with a small number of packages essential to make the initial transformations. In general, it is best to avoid installing the latest versions of Python (especially if they were only released a few months ago), because often all the major packages you will use will take some time to be updated to support the latest versions.

First of all, you have to find the most recent version of Python present in the distribution you just installed:

1. Open Anaconda Prompt from the **Start** menu as shown previously.

2. If the prompt has small fonts, just right-click on its title bar, select **Properties**, and then change the fonts as you like in the **Font** tab.

    The first thing to notice is the word **(base)** before the current path. The string before the path indicates *the name of the current environment*. The **base** environment is the default environment created during the installation of the Miniconda distribution.

3. Enter the `conda search python` command and press *Enter*.

4. You will see the list of available Python versions:

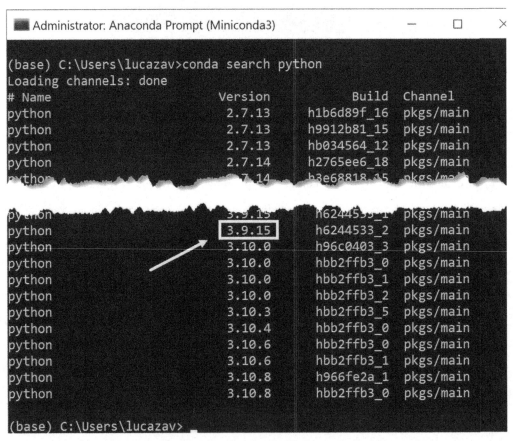

Figure 3.4: List of all the available Python versions

An appropriate version to install may be `3.9.15`, just before 3.10.0, because the Miniconda version you downloaded is also aligned with Python 3.9, as you can see in *Figure 3.1*.

Once we have found the latest version of Python available, we can create our environment dedicated to the data transformation in Power Query, which we will call pbi_powerquery_pip_env, as we will use pip to install the packages needed:

1. Enter the following command to create a new environment named pbi_powerquery_pip_env containing Python version 3.9.15:

```
conda create --name pbi_powerquery_pip_env python==3.9.15
```

You would achieve the same thing if, instead of ==3.9.15, you used the form =3.9 (with a single =), leaving it up to conda to find the latest micro-version.

2. Anaconda Prompt will ask you to install some packages needed to create the environment. At the **Proceed ([y]/n)?** prompt, type **y** and press **Enter**.

When the package installation is complete, you will still see (base) as the prompt prefix:

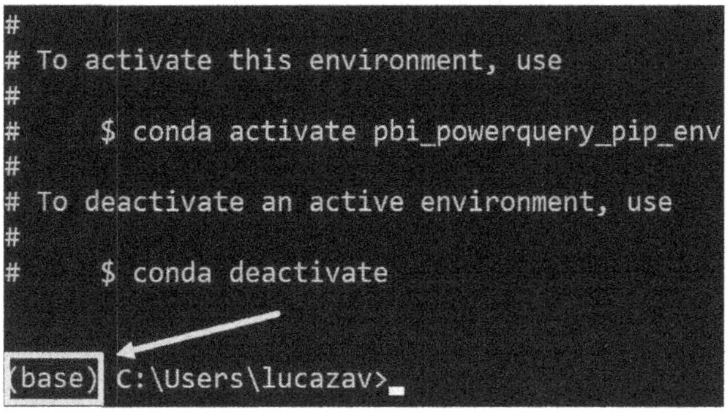

Figure 3.5: After creating the new environment, you are still in the old one called base

This means that you are still in the base environment. Are you sure you created the new environment correctly? Let's check it:

1. Try to list the environments present on the system by entering the conda env list command:

Figure 3.6: List of conda environments in the system

Fortunately, the new environment is listed, but it is not the active one. The active environment is identified by an asterisk.

2. In order to install our packages inside the newly created environment, you must first *activate* it using the conda `activate pbi_powerquery_pip_env` command:

```
(base) C:\Users\lucazav>conda activate pbi_powerquery_pip_env
(pbi_powerquery_pip_env) C:\Users\lucazav>
```

Figure 3.7 – Activating the new environment

Now your prompt prefix correctly indicates that you are in your new environment.

3. To be on the safe side, check that the version of Python within the new environment is the one you expect using the `python --version` command:

```
(pbi_powerquery_pip_env) C:\Users\lucazav>python --version
Python 3.9.15
(pbi_powerquery_pip_env) C:\Users\lucazav>
```

Figure 3.8: Checking the Python version installed in the new environment

You are inside your new environment and Python is correctly installed! You can now start installing some of the packages you'll need later. The packages to be installed are as follows:

- **NumPy**: The most widely used library in Python for working with arrays, and with functions on linear algebra, Fourier transforms, and matrices.
- **SciPy**: Used to solve scientific and mathematical problems; it is built on the NumPy extension and allows the user to manipulate and visualize data.
- **pandas**: A Python package that provides fast, flexible, and expressive tabular, multidimensional, and time-series data.
- **Requests**: Allows you to send HTTP requests extremely easily.
- **BeautifulSoup**: A library that makes it easy to scrape information from web pages.
- **PyYAML**: Allows you to easily read and write YAML files.

The last three packages in the previous list will be used in one of the next sections, where you will use some web scraping techniques thanks to a ready-made script!

But let's get back to it, and proceed with the installation of each package. One question you might have is whether, by installing a package via the simple `pip install` command, you can be sure that you download the correct version of the package and its dependencies so that they are compatible with the Python version you are using. First, check the pip version installed using the `pip --version` command:

```
(pbi_powerquery_pip_env) C:\Users\lucazav>pip --version
pip 22.2.2 from C:\ProgramData\Miniconda3\envs\pbi_powerquery_pip_env\lib\site-packages\pip (python 3.9)
```

Figure 3.9: Checking the pip version installed in the new environment

You have just verified that by directly running the `pip install` command, you are implicitly installing packages compatible with Python version 3.9.

IMPORTANT NOTE

If you have multiple installations of Python, you should run the `python -m pip install your-package` command to make sure that you are installing packages compatible with a specific version of Python, ensuring that you reference the correct version of the Python executable.

In this case, to install each of these packages, type the appropriate command as shown below and press **Enter**:

- **NumPy:** `pip install numpy==1.23.5`
- **SciPy:** `pip install scipy==1.9.3`
- **pandas:** `pip install pandas==1.5.2`
- **Requests:** `pip install requests==2.28.1`
- **BeautifulSoup:** `pip install beautifulsoup4==4.11.1`
- **PyYAML:** `pip install pyyaml==6.0`

Check that all packages have been installed correctly with the `conda list` command:

```
(pbi_powerquery_pip_env) C:\Users\lucazav>conda list
# packages in environment at C:\ProgramData\Miniconda3\envs\pbi_powerquery_pip_env:
#
# Name                    Version                   Build  Channel
beautifulsoup4 ◄──        4.11.1                    pypi_0    pypi
ca-certificates           2022.10.11              haa95532_0
certifi                   2022.9.24           py39haa95532_0
charset-normalizer        2.1.1                     pypi_0    pypi
idna                      3.4                       pypi_0    pypi
numpy ◄──                 1.23.5                    pypi_0    pypi
openssl                   1.1.1s                  h2bbff1b_0
pandas ◄──                1.5.2                     pypi_0    pypi
pip                       22.2.2              py39haa95532_0
python                    3.9.15                  h6244533_2
python-dateutil           2.8.2                     pypi_0    pypi
pytz                      2022.6                    pypi_0    pypi
pyyaml ◄──                6.0                       pypi_0    pypi
requests ◄──              2.28.1                    pypi_0    pypi
scipy ◄──                 1.9.3                     pypi_0    pypi
setuptools                65.5.0              py39haa95532_0
six                       1.16.0                    pypi_0    pypi
soupsieve                 2.3.2.post1               pypi_0    pypi
sqlite                    3.40.0                  h2bbff1b_0
tzdata                    2022f                   h04d1e81_0
urllib3                   1.26.13                   pypi_0    pypi
vc                        14.2                    h21ff451_1
vs2015_runtime            14.27.29016             h5e58377_2
wheel                     0.37.1                  pyhd3eb1b0_0
wincertstore              0.2                 py39haa95532_2

(pbi_powerquery_pip_env) C:\Users\lucazav>_
```

Figure 3.10: Checking all the selected Python packages are installed

Awesome! Your new environment is now properly configured.

You saw in *Chapter 2, Configuring R with Power BI*, how it is possible to use multithreading-aware libraries that optimize certain types of calculations in R. Is it possible to prepare an optimized Python environment for the same type of calculations? You will see in the next section.

Creating an optimized environment for data transformations using conda

As you have already seen in *Chapter 2, Configuring R with Power BI*, the specific operations of numerical linear algebra are handled through the specialized libraries BLAS and LAPACK. These libraries now define a standard interface for those types of operations. But depending on which implementation of them you choose, there can be significant differences in performance.

There are many implementations made under different licenses. For example, the **standard BLAS and LAPACK** libraries that you often find pre-installed on your system (such as those in CRAN R), do not support multi-threading. The **Automatically Tuned Linear Algebra Software** (**ATLAS**) implementation achieves good performance and uses the BSD license. Then there is **OpenBLAS**, another open-source implementation with very good performance due to multi-threading. Finally, we have the **Intel oneAPI Math Kernel Library** (**MKL**), optimized for Intel multi-core processors, which uses the **Intel Simplified Software License**. This license, beyond some copyright constraints, a prohibition on using the Intel name to promote the product, and a prohibition on reverse engineering, decompiling, and disassembly of the library, provides no licensing or ownership rights from Intel for those who use it in their products.

Linear algebra calculations in Python are possible thanks to the NumPy package, which links the BLAS and LAPACK libraries behind the scenes. Considering the fact that you installed NumPy in your pbi_powerquery_pip_env environment, let's see what implementations of the preceding libraries NumPy is using:

1. If you closed it, open Anaconda Prompt again.
2. Make sure you are in the newly created environment. If you are in the base environment instead, activate the new one via the conda activate pbi_powerquery_pip_env command.
3. Enter the python command and press **Enter**. A Python prompt consisting of three "greater than" symbols (>>>) is displayed, indicating that the Python shell is started and waiting for any Python script.
4. Enter the import numpy as np script and press **Enter**.
5. Enter the np.show_config() script and press **Enter**. This is what you get in the console:

```
(pbi_powerquery_pip_env) C:\Users\lucazav>python
Python 3.9.15 (main, Nov 24 2022, 14:39:17) [MSC v.1916 64 bit (AMD64)] on win32
Type "help", "copyright", "credits" or "license" for more information.
>>> import numpy as np
>>> np.show_config()
openblas64__info:
    library_dirs = ['D:\\a\\numpy\\numpy\\build\\openblas64__info']
    libraries = ['openblas64__info']
    language = f77
    define_macros = [('HAVE_CBLAS', None), ('BLAS_SYMBOL_SUFFIX', '64_'), ('HAVE_BLAS_ILP64', None)]
blas_ilp64_opt_info:
    library_dirs = ['D:\\a\\numpy\\numpy\\build\\openblas64__info']
    libraries = ['openblas64__info']
    language = f77
    define_macros = [('HAVE_CBLAS', None), ('BLAS_SYMBOL_SUFFIX', '64_'), ('HAVE_BLAS_ILP64', None)]
openblas64__lapack_info:
    library_dirs = ['D:\\a\\numpy\\numpy\\build\\openblas64__lapack_info']
    libraries = ['openblas64__lapack_info']
    language = f77
    define_macros = [('HAVE_CBLAS', None), ('BLAS_SYMBOL_SUFFIX', '64_'), ('HAVE_BLAS_ILP64', None), ('HAVE_LAPACKE', None)]
lapack_ilp64_opt_info:
    library_dirs = ['D:\\a\\numpy\\numpy\\build\\openblas64__lapack_info']
    libraries = ['openblas64__lapack_info']
    language = f77
    define_macros = [('HAVE_CBLAS', None), ('BLAS_SYMBOL_SUFFIX', '64_'), ('HAVE_BLAS_ILP64', None), ('HAVE_LAPACKE', None)]
Supported SIMD extensions in this NumPy install:
    baseline = SSE,SSE2,SSE3
    found = SSSE3,SSE41,POPCNT,SSE42,AVX,F16C,FMA3,AVX2,AVX512F,AVX512CD,AVX512_SKX
    not found = AVX512_CLX,AVX512_CNL,AVX512_ICL
>>>
```

Figure 3.11: Checking the BLAS and LAPACK implementation used in your environment

6. Type `quit()` to exit the Python command line.

Since the packages in the above environment were installed via `pip`, the following applies:

IMPORTANT NOTE

The implementation of the BLAS and LAPACK libraries used in the built distribution (**wheel**) of **NumPy** in PyPI is **OpenBLAS.** This means that if you install NumPy via `pip`, you implicitly use the OpenBLAS implementation.

You will surely be curious to check the performance of OpenBLAS. To do this, you will use a script that performs specific algebraic calculations shared by *Markus Beuckelmann* in this blog post: `https://bit.ly/boosting-numpy-blas-arch`. You can find the same script in the book's GitHub repository, in the *Chapter 3* folder, under the name *blas-lapack-benchmark.py*. The machine on which I am running the benchmark is an Azure VM Intel(R) Xeon(R) Platinum 8370C CPU @ 2.80 GHz (4 cores, 8 threads) with 32 GB, running Windows Server 2022 Datacenter Azure Edition. You can run the script directly from Anaconda Prompt as follows:

1. Make sure that the `pbi_powerquery_pip_env` environment is enabled in Anaconda Prompt.
2. Download the aforementioned benchmark script to your machine and locate its full path (which will be something like `C:\<your-path>\blas-lapack-benchmark.py`).

3. Enter the python `"C:\<your-path>\blas-lapack-benchmark.py"` command and press **Enter**.
    After a while, the output on the console will be as follows:

```
(pbi_powerquery_pip_env) C:\Users\lucazav>python "C:\Users\lucazav\OneDrive\MVP\Packt
Book\Code\Extending-Power-BI-with-Python-and-R-2nd-edition\Ch03 - Configuring Python
with Power BI\blas-lapack-benchmark.py"
Dotted two 8192x8192 matrices in 6.02 s.
Dotted two vectors of length 1048576 in 0.30 ms.
SVD of a 4096x2048 matrix in 9.36 s.
Cholesky decomposition of a 4096x4096 matrix in 1.03 s.
Eigendecomposition of a 4096x4096 matrix in 51.56 s.
```

Figure 3.12: NumPy benchmark results on the pbi_powerquery_pip_env environment

Basically, you have performed a scalar product operation between matrices, one between vectors, a **singular value decomposition (SVD)**, a *Cholesky decomposition*, and an *eigendecomposition* on fairly large matrices or vectors. As you can see, the most onerous operations are SVD and eigendecomposition, which take about 9 seconds and 52 seconds, respectively.

Now you will create a new Python environment, called pbi_powerquery_env, for which you will use conda to install packages. As mentioned before, using conda you can install packages persisted in different remote repositories called **conda channels**. If you don't specify anything, the conda install command will download packages from *Anaconda's default channel* (the repository at https://repo. anaconda.com/pkgs/), which is managed by Anaconda Inc with the goal of ensuring consistency across dependencies between packages. If, on the other hand, you want to download a package from a specific channel other than the default channel, you must declare it via the conda install --channel <your-channel> command. Along with specific channels, such as the *bioconda* channel specializing in Bioinformatics, there is the **conda-forge** channel, which is instead maintained by the community. conda-forge is very close in "philosophy" to PyPI. Indeed, you have the possibility of finding packages in PyPI with more recent versions than the same ones on conda-forge, and you can even find packages that are missing on conda-forge. Clearly, all this freedom with conda-forge implicitly shifts all the responsibility for verifying package compatibilities onto the user.

That said, let's proceed with installing NumPy and the other packages from the default channel:

1. If you are still in the pbi_powerquery_pip_env environment, you must first deactivate it and return to the base one with the conda deactivate command.

2. Enter the conda create --name pbi_powerquery_env python==3.9.15 command to create the above new environment and then enter y to proceed with installing the suggested packages.

3. Activate the new pbi_powerquery_env environment using the conda activate pbi_powerquery_ env command.

4. **NumPy:** conda install numpy==1.23.4. During installation, you will be asked to also accept the installation of some dependent packages:

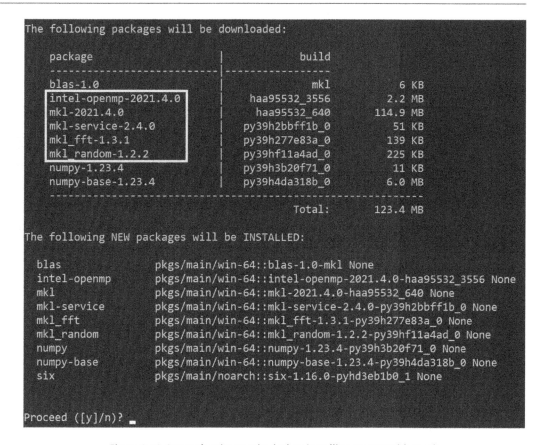

Figure 3.13: Dependencies required when installing NumPy with conda

As you can see, the dependent packages that are being installed contain the **Intel MKL** libraries.

- **SciPy:** `conda install scipy==1.9.3` .
- **pandas:** `conda install pandas==1.5.1` .
- **Requests:** `conda install requests==2.28.1` .
- **BeautifulSoup:** `conda install beautifulsoup4==4.11.1` .
- **PyYAML:** `conda install pyyaml==6.0`.

The following is evident at this point.

IMPORTANT NOTE

The implementation of the BLAS and LAPACK libraries used in the built distribution (conda package) of **NumPy** in conda using the **conda default channel** is **Intel MKL**. This means that if you install NumPy via conda without specifying any channels, you are implicitly using the Intel MKL implementation.

Let's try now the NumPy performance using the Intel MKL implementation of BLAS and LAPACK libraries on the same machine:

1. Enter the `python "C:\<your-path>\blas-lapack-benchmark.py"` command and press **Enter**. After a while, the output on the console will be as follows:

```
(base) C:\Users\lucazav>conda activate pbi_powerquery_env

(pbi_powerquery_env) C:\Users\lucazav>python "C:\Users\lucazav\OneDrive\MVP\PacktBook
\Code\Extending-Power-BI-with-Python-and-R-2nd-edition\Ch03 - Configuring Python with
 Power BI\blas-lapack-benchmark.py"
Dotted two 8192x8192 matrices in 4.69 s.
Dotted two vectors of length 1048576 in 0.11 ms.
SVD of a 4096x2048 matrix in 2.53 s.
Cholesky decomposition of a 4096x4096 matrix in 0.50 s.
Eigendecomposition of a 4096x4096 matrix in 33.91 s.
```

Figure 3.14: NumPy benchmark results on the pbi_powerquery_env environment

Wow! As you can verify by comparing these results with those obtained in *Figure 3.12*, although Open-BLAS is still multi-threading aware, Intel MKL can be as much as 3 times more performant in certain computations when the machine is based on Intel processors. Therefore, the following applies.

IMPORTANT NOTE

Since both Power BI Desktop and the Power BI data gateway are applications developed only for Windows operating systems, and most machines with such operating systems mount Intel processors, we suggest installing the packages that make use of algebraic calculations (NumPy and SciPy) via **conda**, so that the Intel MKL libraries can be used behind the scenes. Note that AMD processors can also benefit from the Intel MKL boost (`https://bit.ly/intel-mkl-amd`).

If you need to use the OpenBLAS libraries in specific projects, you can still install the above packages via conda, but this time using the conda-forge channel.

Now that you have optimized your environment dedicated to Power Query transformations, let's configure a new environment dedicated to Python script visuals.

Creating an environment for Python script visuals on the Power BI service

As already mentioned, Python script visuals published on the Power BI service run on a pre-installed Python engine on the cloud, the version of which may change with new releases of the Power BI service itself. Should you need to share a report containing a Python visual with colleagues, you need to be sure that your Python code works correctly on the pre-installed engine.

TIP

We strongly recommend that you also create on your machine an environment with the same version of Python that is used for Python visuals by the Power BI service.

Keep in mind that these limitations would not be there if your reports using Python visuals were not to be shared and you only used them through Power BI Desktop. In this case, it is the engine on your machine that is used for the visuals.

To create the new environment, you must check which versions of both Python and the allowed packages are supported by the Power BI service. You can check these requirements at this link: `http://bit.ly/powerbi-python-limits`. Currently, the supported version of Python is still 3.7.7.

Requirements and Limitations of Python packages

There are a handful of requirements and limitations for Python packages:

- Current Python runtime: Python 3.7.7.

Figure 3.15: Python version supported for visuals on the Power BI service

In addition, as of November 1, 2022, the number of packages provided increased from 8 to 21, with a version upgrade of some packages already there. The first thing that jumps out at you is the far smaller number of packages compared to the R packages that the Power BI service provides (21 Python packages versus more than 900 R packages!). This evident imbalance of available packages is primarily due to two reasons:

- **Python** was introduced more recently than R (February 2019), so the Python packages introduced are mostly those essential to transforming and visualizing data.
- **R** is a language primarily for data analysis, and this is immediately clear because it provides a variety of packages that are designed for scientific visualization. **Python**, on the other hand, is a general programming language that can also be used for data analysis.

The following applies to Python script visuals.

TIP

Because of the small number of Python packages supported by the Power BI service, we suggest creating a dedicated environment for Python scripts to run on the Power BI service, directly installing all the currently allowed packages.

Keep in mind that you can't properly run a Python visual without installing some default packages. See the following note.

IMPORTANT NOTE

In order to properly run a Python script visual, regardless of whether you do it on Power BI Desktop or the Power BI service, the **pandas** and **Matplotlib** packages are required. So you have to install them in the new environment.

That said, you could already proceed to create another environment that satisfies the aforementioned version specifications, following the steps already used to create the previous environment. Even though the Power BI service engines are updated infrequently, this manual task would still be tedious. Unfortunately, there are no ready-made "snapshots" that you can install on the fly to reproduce the environment, as you saw in the case of R engines. But there is a shortcut. To avoid unnecessary manual work, we created a Python script that scrapes the web page containing the Python engine requirements on the Power BI service and automatically generates a YAML file to be used in the creation of the new environment. **YAML** (AKA *"Yet Another Markup Language"*, also defined by some funny guy using the recursive acronym **YAML Ain't Markup Language**) is a language useful for serializing data (it's a bit of a rival to JSON) and is human-readable. It is often used to serialize the contents of a computer system's configuration files.

In our case, a YAML file helps us gather all the specifications we need to create our new environment. We thought about a YAML file because conda also permits the use of a YAML file as a parameter to create an environment. Our new environment, which we will call `pbi_visuals_env`, should have the following:

- The Python engine version 3.7.7
- The pip package manager
- All of the 21 packages seen previously, each at the required version, installed using `pip`

The above assumes that the Python packages displayed on the Microsoft Docs page actually match the packages installed on the Python engine of the Power BI service. As you will see in Chapter 20, Using the Grammar of Graphics in Python with plotnine, this is not always the case!

The preceding requirements can be summarized in a YAML file as follows:

```
name: pbi_visuals_env
dependencies:
- python==3.7.7
- pip
- cycler==0.11.0
- joblib==1.1.0
- kiwisolver==1.4.4
```

```
- matplotlib==3.2.2
- numpy==1.21.6
- packaging==21.3
- pandas==1.3.5
- patsy==0.5.2
- pip==22.1.2
- pyparsing==3.0.9
- python-dateutil==2.8.2
- pytz==2022.1
- scikit-learn==1.0.2
- scipy==1.7.3
- seaborn==0.11.2
- setuptools==63.2.0
- six==1.16.0
- statsmodels==0.13.2
- threadpoolctl==3.1.0
- typing-extensions==4.3.0
- xgboost==1.6.1
```

So, let's generate the YAML file using our Python script as follows:

1. Open your **Anaconda Prompt** (if you didn't close it before, it should still be open) and make sure that pbi_powerquery_env is the activated environment. If not, activate it using the conda activate pbi_powerquery_env command.

2. Your current path should be in the form of C:\Users\<your-username>. If not, go to your user folder using the command: cd C:\Users\<your-username>.

3. Let's create a new folder called py-environments (this will contain the Python script for web scraping, along with the YAML file) using the md py-environments command.

4. Now, go to the book's GitHub repository at https://github.com/PacktPublishing/Extending-Power-BI-with-Python-and-R-2nd-edition.

5. If you have already downloaded the .zip file of the whole repository and unzipped it on your hard drive, you will find the Python script file that we are interested in in the Chapter03 folder, with the name 01-create-pbi-service-py-packages-env-yaml-file.py.

6. If you haven't downloaded the entire repository, click **Code** on top right of the page at the preceding link, and then click **Download ZIP**:

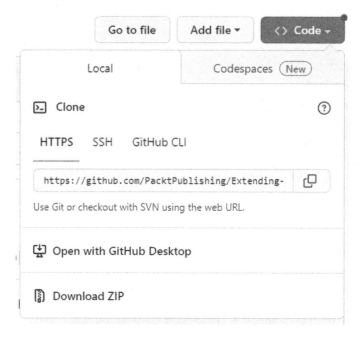

Figure 3.16: Download the entire zipped repository

After unzipping it, you'll find the file we need in the Chapter03 folder.

7. Now copy the file, `01-create-pbi-service-py-packages-env-yaml-file.py`, into the `C:/Users/<your-username>/py-environments` folder using File Explorer.

8. Go back to Anaconda Prompt and change your current folder to `py-environments` using this command: `cd py-environments`.

9. Now you can finally run the Python script that does the web scraping and generates the YAML file with this command: `python 01-create-pbi-service-py-packages-env-yaml-file.py`. You will see the contents of the YAML file printed at the prompt as follows:

```
(pbi_powerquery_env) C:\Users\lucazav\py-environments>python
 01-create-pbi-service-py-packages-env-yaml-file.py
channels:
- defaults
- conda-forge
dependencies:
- python==3.7.7
- pip
- cycler==0.11.0
- joblib==1.1.0
- kiwisolver==1.4.4
- matplotlib==3.2.2
- numpy==1.21.6
- packaging==21.3
- pandas==1.3.5
- patsy==0.5.2
- pip==22.1.2
- pyparsing==3.0.9
- python-dateutil==2.8.2
- pytz==2022.1
- scikit-learn==1.0.2
- scipy==1.7.3
- seaborn==0.11.2
- setuptools==63.2.0
- six==1.16.0
- statsmodels==0.13.2
- threadpoolctl==3.1.0
- typing-extensions==4.3.0
- xgboost==1.6.1
name: pbi_visuals_env
```

Figure 3.17: Execute the Python script to create the YAML file

You can also verify that the YAML file was generated correctly by looking again at the contents of the folder at C:/Users/<your-username>/py-environments:

Figure 3.18: The YAML file correctly created

10. At this point, we can directly create the new environment using the `conda env create -f visuals_environment.yaml` command and then press **Enter**.

11. When both Python and the packages' installations are complete, activate the newly created environment using the `conda activate pbi_visuals_env` command and then press **Enter**.

12. Then check if the Python version is the one defined for this environment in the YAML file by entering the `python --version` command. You should see Python 3.7.7 as output.

Excellent! You have finally created the new environment that will be used when developing your Python script visuals for publishing on the Power BI service. If you are interested in understanding in detail how the previous Python script managed to capture all the information needed to create the environment, you can open it in any code editor and read the very detailed comments on the code.

What to do when the Power BI service upgrades the Python engine

As we did in *Chapter 2, Configuring R with Power BI*, let's assume that you have already developed and published reports containing Python visuals using the new environment you created earlier. Suppose that Microsoft decides to upgrade the Python version supported by the Power BI service, and consequently to upgrade the versions of the currently supported packages as well. As you may have already guessed, it is likely that these updates can cause the code to fail (it is a rare event as very often, backward compatibility is guaranteed).

> **TIP**
>
> In such circumstances, it is often more convenient to create a new environment on the fly, aligned to the updated requirements from Microsoft, through the Python script you have already used previously. Next, you'll need to test reports containing Python visuals that were already published on the service on Power BI Desktop, making sure that they reference the newly created environment. You need to fix any code issues in those Python visuals, after which you can publish those reports back to the Power BI service.

Once you've made sure that all the reports are working properly, it's up to you to decide if you want to uninstall the "old" environment to free up disk space and avoid confusion in handling these reports.

At this point, we can move on to the configuration and installation of some IDEs that facilitate the development of Python scripts.

Installing an IDE for Python development

In *Chapter 2, Configuring R with Power BI*, you installed RStudio to conveniently develop your own R scripts. Did you know that, starting with version 1.4, you can write and run Python code directly in RStudio, making use of advanced tools for viewing instantiated Python objects?

Let's see how to configure your RStudio installation to also run Python code.

Configuring Python with RStudio

In order to allow RStudio to communicate with the Python world, you need to install a package called `reticulate`, which contains a comprehensive set of tools for interoperability between Python and R thanks to embedded Python sessions within R sessions. After that, it's a breeze to configure Python within RStudio. Let's see how to do it:

1. Open RStudio and make sure the referenced engine is the latest one, in our case **CRAN 4.2.2**. As seen in *Chapter 2, Configuring R with Power BI*, you can set up your R engine in RStudio by going to the **Tools** menu and then **Global Options....**

2. You can now install the reticulate package by clicking on the **Packages** tab on the bottom-right panel in RStudio, clicking on **Install**, entering the `reticulate` string in the textbox, and finally, clicking on the **Install** button:

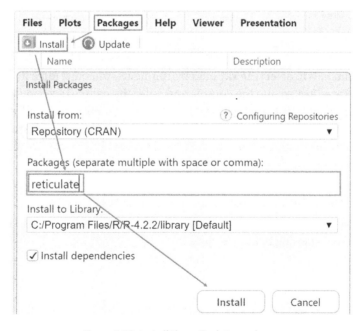

Figure 3.19: Install the reticulate package

3. After that, go to the **Tools** menu and then **Global Options....** In the **Options** windows that pops up, click on **Python,** then click on **Select...** to choose your Python interpreter executable. Note that you should have as many executables as the number of environments you have created in the **Conda Environments** tab:

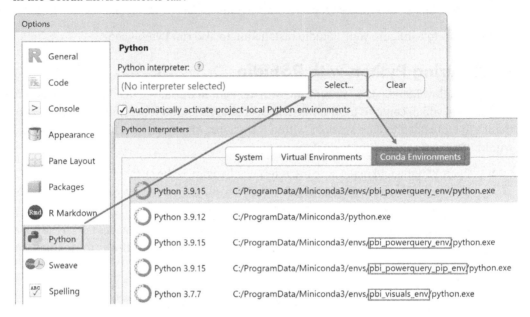

Figure 3.20: Set your preferred Python interpreter in RStudio

4. If RStudio fails to detect the various environments, you must force it to see them correctly via `reticulate`. Just go into the console and enter the `reticulate::py_config()` command. At first, a message is displayed stating that the system cannot detect any Python installations. Then you will be asked if you want to install Miniconda. Answer no by entering n at the prompt. Soon after, following some forced activity by `reticulate` in the background, the already configured environments are finally recognized.

5. Choose the Python interpreter with the latest version (in our case 3.9.15) and click **Ok**. You'll be asked to restart the current R session. Choose **Yes**.

6. Now you can open a new Python script file by clicking on the green "+" icon in the upper-left corner and choosing **Python Script:**

Figure 3.21: Create a new Python script in RStudio

7. Write the code a = [1, 2] in the new script file, highlight it, and then click the **Run** icon in the top right:

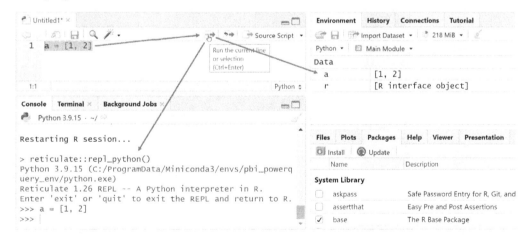

Figure 3.22: Run your first Python script in RStudio

You can see from the console that RStudio uses reticulate behind the scenes. Moreover, on the top-right panel, you can inspect the Python variables created after the execution of your code.

Great! You have successfully configured RStudio to run your Python code.

Configuring Python with Visual Studio Code

If you're an R language lover, chances are you'd prefer to run both R and Python code on RStudio. However, if you have the spirit of a true *Pythonista*, you'll definitely enjoy using one of the advanced editors that has been all the rage lately: **Visual Studio Code** (**VS Code**). Let's install and configure it!

1. Download VS Code from this link (`https://code.visualstudio.com/`) by clicking on the **Download for Windows** button.

2. Run the executable. The setup may warn you that you're trying to install the user installer, not the system installer. The user installer is sufficient for you, so click **OK** to continue with the user installer.

3. Accept the agreement and click **Next** on the next window.

4. Then keep the default destination folder and click **Next**.

5. Also, keep the default **Start** menu folder on the following window and click **Next**.

6. On the **Additional Tasks** window, choose the tasks you prefer and click **Next**.

7. Click **Install** on the recap window.

8. After the installation is completed, keep the **Launch Visual Studio Code** checkbox flagged and click **Finish**.

9. After VS Code has started, choose your preferred color theme, click on the **Extensions** icon on the left, then start entering the python string and click on the **Install** button next to the **Python extension**:

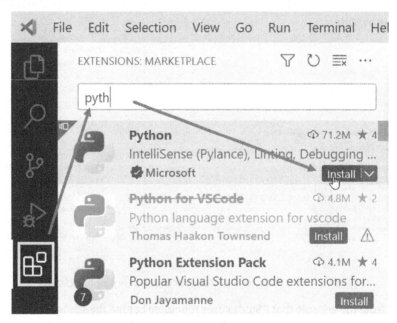

Figure 3.23: Install the Python extension in VS Code

10. Once installed, click on the Python extension label to open the extension main page, then click on its settings gear icon, and then on **Extension Settings:**

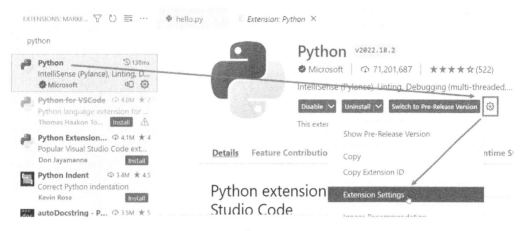

Figure 3.24: Entering the extension settings page

11. The option you need to set is the path to the conda executable. In our case, the path is `C:\ProgramData\Miniconda3\Scripts\conda.exe`:

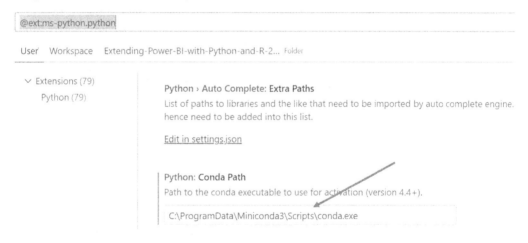

Figure 3.25: Entering conda.exe path setting

12. Now go to the **File** menu at the top and click **Open Folder...**.

13. Go to the `Documents` folder and create a new test folder named `Hello` from the **Open Folder** window and then select that folder:

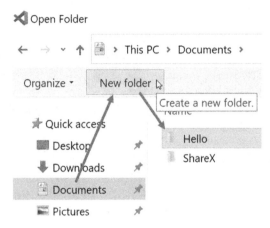

Figure 3.26: Create a new folder on the fly and select it in the Open Folder window

14. You may be asked to trust the authors of the files in this folder. If so, check the checkbox to apply your choice to all files in the folder and select **Yes, I trust the authors**.

15. Now you have to select the Python interpreter by accessing the **Command Palette** using *Ctrl + Shift + P*. Then start entering the `interpreter` string and click **Python: Select Interpreter**:

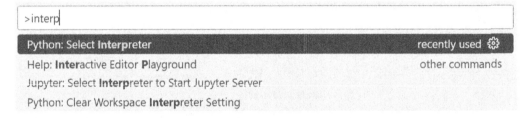

Figure 3.27: Choose the "Python: Select Interpreter" option in the Command Palette

16. You'll be prompted to select one of the actual environments you have on your machine. Choose the `pbi_powerquery_env` environment:

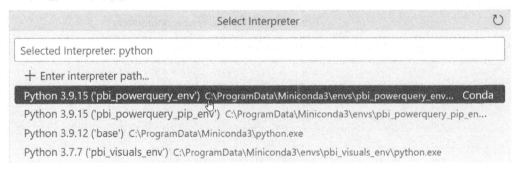

Figure 3.28: Select your preferred environment

17. Go back to your HELLO folder in the Explorer panel on the left. Click on the **New File** icon next to the **HELLO** label and name the new file hello.py:

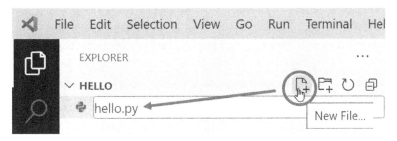

Figure 3.29: Create a new file named hello.py in the Hello folder

18. Once you have created a file in the Hello folder, for which a specific Python interpreter has been chosen, you can see what environment is selected on the status bar at the bottom right:

Figure 3.30: Check the selected environment

19. Enter the following code in the new file:

```
msg = "Hello World"
print(msg)
```

Then click the **run** icon (the arrow pointing to the right) on the top right of the main panel:

Figure 3.31: Enter the sample code and run it

20. Behind the scenes, VS Code activates the selected conda environment for the folder and then executes the `hello.py` file. You can see the result in the Terminal output:

```
PROBLEMS    OUTPUT    DEBUG CONSOLE    TERMINAL    JUPYTER                  [>] Python  + ∨  ⊟  🗑  ∧  ✕

pbi_powerquery_env/python.exe c:/Users/lucazav/Documents/Hello/hello.py
Hello World
PS C:\Users\lucazav\Documents\Hello> & C:/ProgramData/Miniconda3/envs/pbi_powerquery_env/
python.exe c:/Users/lucazav/Documents/Hello/hello.py
Hello World  ←————————————————————————————————————————————————
PS C:\Users\lucazav\Documents\Hello> []
```

Figure 3.32: Your first Python script run in VS Code

Very good! Your VS Code instance is now correctly configured to run Python scripts.

Working with the Python Interactive window in Visual Studio Code

You may have heard of **Jupyter notebooks**. They are a tool that allows you to easily combine **Markdown** text (a markup language in plain text that is intended to facilitate writing for the internet) and executable Python source code into a single canvas, called a notebook. A notebook is organized into *cells*, each of which can either contain some Markdown text, or Python code that you can run through an installed Python engine. Generally, Jupyter notebooks are the most commonly used tool by data analysts and data scientists precisely because they allow them to annotate and format the content of analyses very quickly, while at the same time allowing the results of the analyses to be achieved through code that can be executed inline. The good news is that VS Code fully supports Jupyter notebooks, and this comes in very handy when you need to debug your Python code.

In general, a Jupyter notebook is a structured file in a specific format that has the extension `.ipynb`. In VS Code you can benefit from the cell structure of Jupyter notebooks to run your Python code step-by-step without necessarily having to use a Jupyter notebook. You can do this via Jupyter-like code cells within the Python code using the comment `# %%`. Let's try it with the example code you just wrote in the `hello.py` file:

1. Insert a line before the code `msg = "Hello World"` and write the comment `# %%` there.
2. Like magic, the code below the comment you just entered will be encapsulated in a cell, which has execute/debug commands just above the comment:

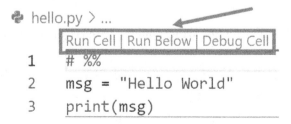

Figure 3.33: Commands of a Jupyter-like code cell

3. Click on the **Run Cell** command to run the code inside that cell.

4. In order to run a Jupyter notebook cell, Jupyter-specific packages are needed. Since they have not been installed in the pbi_powerquery_env environment, VS Code notices this and shows you a warning that you either have to install them or reference a Python interpreter that has such packages already installed:

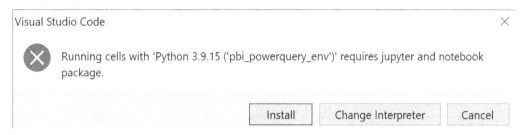

Figure 3.34: Warning to install missing packages or change the interpreter

5. Click **Install** to install the required packages.

6. After VS Code has finished installing all Jupyter Notebook package dependencies behind the scenes, the cell is executed as requested and the output is shown in an **Interactive window** opened next to the code window:

Figure 3.35: Code executed via a Jupyter cell in an Interactive window

Great! Now you can debug your code very easily and quickly with VS Code.

Configuring Power BI Desktop to work with Python

Since you have everything you need installed, you can now configure Power BI Desktop to interact with Python engines and IDEs. This is really a very simple task:

1. In Power BI Desktop, go to the **File** menu, click on the **Options and settings** tab, and then click on **Options**.

2. In the **Options** window, click on the **Python scripting** link on the left. The contents of the panel on the right will update, giving you the option to select the Python environment to reference and the Python IDE to use for Python visuals.

In order to select a specific environment, you need to choose **Other** and then click **Browse** and supply a reference to your environment folder:

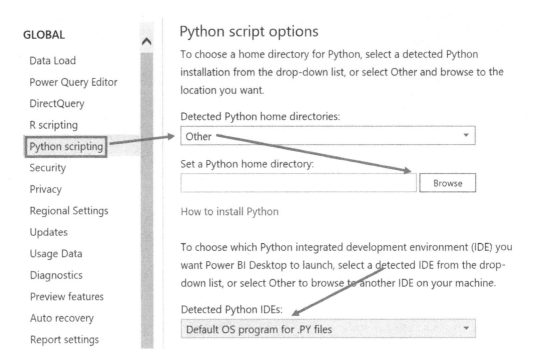

Figure 3.36: Configuring your Python environment and IDE in Power BI

Usually, you can find the default environments folder in `C:\ProgramData\Miniconda3\envs\` (for all-user installations) or `C:\Users\<username>\miniconda3\envs\` (for just your user installation). If you cannot see the hidden `ProgramData` folder, open File Explorer, click on the **View** tab in the top ribbon, and then under **Options**, select **Change folder and search options**:

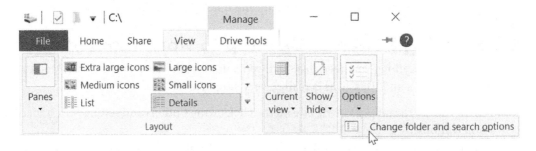

Figure 3.37: Change the folder and search options

In the next window click on the **View** tab and be sure to select the **Show hidden files, folders, and drives** option:

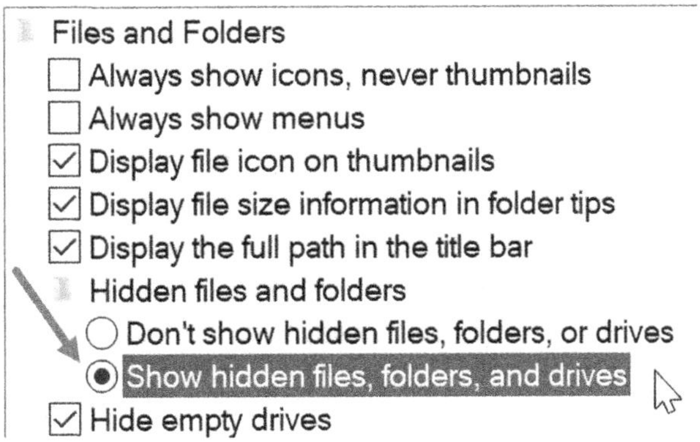

Files and Folders
☐ Always show icons, never thumbnails
☐ Always show menus
☑ Display file icon on thumbnails
☑ Display file size information in folder tips
☑ Display the full path in the title bar
   Hidden files and folders
    ○ Don't show hidden files, folders, or drives
    ◉ Show hidden files, folders, and drives
☑ Hide empty drives

Figure 3.38: Select the option to show hidden files and folders

At this point the **ProgramData** folder will be visible:

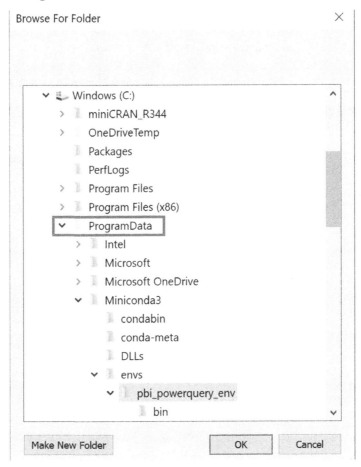

Figure 3.39: Now the ProgramData folder is visible

Then select your pbi_powerquery_env subfolder.

3. As you can see in *Figure 3.36*, Power BI Desktop will use the default Windows program associ-
    ated with files having the .py extension. If you want to indicate a specific executable, you can
    select **Other** from the drop-down menu and then indicate the path to the executable using the
    Browse button that appears. Usually, the VS Code executable is Code.exe and it's located in
    your C:\Users\<username>\AppData\Local\Programs\Microsoft VS Code\ path. Feel free
    to associate the .py extension with VS Code by selecting **Open with...** from the menu, and
    checking the **Always use this app to open .py files** option before opening the file. Otherwise,
    select the conda.exe executable from the above folder and press **OK**.

4. Then press **OK** in the main Options window.

You can debug Python code written in Python Visuals in your favorite Python IDE in the same way as
seen for R in *Chapter 2, Configuring R with Power BI*. By clicking on the arrow at the top right of the
Python script editor of a Python visual, a block of code is opened in VS Code that loads the dataset provided as input to the Python visual and then allows you to run the rest of the code in order to debug it:

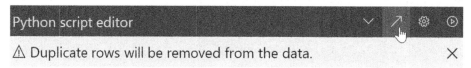

Figure 3.40: Opening the Python code of a Python visual in VS Code

The code opened in VS Code highlights the Python wrapper injected by Power BI in order to load the
dataset data as input to the Python visual:

```
 PythonEditorWrapper.PY 3  X                                                                          ▷

C: > Users > lucazav > PythonEditorWrapper_a09beeb2-22e6-44a5-a66f-cfe431b8701e >  PythonEditorWrapper.PY > ...
  1    # Prolog - Auto Generated #
  2    import os, uuid, matplotlib
  3    matplotlib.use('Agg')
  4    import matplotlib.pyplot
  5    import pandas
  6
  7    import sys
  8    sys.tracebacklimit = 0
  9
 10    os.chdir(u'C:/Users/lucazav/PythonEditorWrapper_a09beeb2-22e6-44a5-a66f-cfe431b8701e')
 11    dataset = pandas.read_csv('input_df_c37c4675-480d-40cb-941f-1cde571a613a.csv')
 12
 13    matplotlib.pyplot.figure(figsize=(5.55555555555556,4.16666666666667), dpi=72)
 14    matplotlib.pyplot.show = lambda args=None,kw=None: matplotlib.pyplot.savefig(str(uuid.uuid1()))
 15    # Original Script. Please update your script content here and once completed copy below section
       back to the original editing window #
 16    ###############################
 17
 18    # Epilog - Auto Generated #
 19    os.chdir(u'C:/Users/lucazav/PythonEditorWrapper_a09beeb2-22e6-44a5-a66f-cfe431b8701e')
```

Figure 3.41: Debugging the Python code of a Python script visual in VS Code

You can see from *Figure 3.41* that some libraries are imported by default into a Python script visual. Nevertheless, the code you'll find in the following chapters reloads some of those libraries deliberately, in order to make the code itself more readable and make it reproducible in contexts other than Power BI. Keep in mind that this wrapper code will be executed on every refresh of the Python script visual.

In addition, as also seen for R script visuals, the following applies:

IMPORTANT NOTE

Whenever you debug the code of a Python script visual on the referenced IDE, Power BI Desktop creates a folder in which it downloads the data present at that time as input to the Python script visual in CSV format, and saves the script wrapper you saw in *Figure 3.41*. If you click the Python script visual's external debug arrow several times while the same IDE instance was opened, multiple temporary folders will be created. Closing the IDE will delete only the last temporary folder created, leaving all other previous temporary folders in the `C:\Users\<username>` folder. The remaining folders will be deleted after closing Power BI Desktop.

Regarding the approach to the development of Python scripts, we suggest developing Python code separately in the IDE by referencing the data directly from the source before writing it directly into the script visual. If this is not possible and the input data of the Python script visual is the result of a series of transformation steps in Power BI, debug it once externally from the script visual only to retrieve the CSV of the source data. At that point, finish developing the rest of your code directly in the IDE. When the development is complete, always make sure that any temporary folders generated by Power BI Desktop are properly deleted; otherwise, delete them yourself.

If you are concerned about the size of CSV files created by Power BI Desktop to develop in the reference IDE, note that a script visual can handle a dataset of only 150,000 rows, as you will see in a later section on the limitations of Python script visuals. Any rows in excess are simply truncated. Therefore, the size of the CSV generated by Power BI can be quite large, but not excessively large because of the aforementioned limitation. By the way, this limitation should not be a problem because a Python script visual is used exclusively to graphically represent data. Keep in mind that a graphical representation is mostly based on aggregations of data that make up a dataset of a few rows, not huge datasets. Plotting millions of points is in most cases not the right choice. Should it be necessary to do so, a Python script visual is not the right tool.

Now let's see how to properly configure your environment to be able to use Python with the Power BI service.

Configuring the Power BI service to work with Python

As you have already learned from *Chapter 2*, *Configuring R with Power BI*, in order to allow the Power BI service to use R in the data transformation steps with Power Query, you must install the **on-premises data gateway** in **personal mode** on an external machine, on which an R engine is installed. The same thing applies to Python with Power Query in the Power BI service, with the following exception:

IMPORTANT NOTE

If the data sources of your report come exclusively from online services (e.g., an Azure SQL database) or the web, and if the Python scripts in your report are used only in the Python script visuals, you don't need to install the data gateway in personal mode to refresh the datasets.

If, on the other hand, your Python scripts are in Power Query, or if at least one dataset in your report is fed from an on-premises data source or on an Azure VM, you need to install the **on-premises data gateway** in **personal mode** on any machine of your choice in order to make the Power BI service communicate with the Python engine you installed on that machine.

So, if you have not installed the on-premises data gateway yet, do it by following the steps in *Chapter 2*.

IMPORTANT NOTE

Python engines and R engines can be installed on the same external machine and referenced by a single data gateway. You must make sure, however, that the machine's resources are sufficient to handle the load of requests coming from the Power BI service.

Sharing reports that use Python scripts in the Power BI service

What was said about how to share reports that use R scripts for data transformations in the Power BI service in *Chapter 2, Configuring R with Power BI*, also applies to reports that use Python scripts. Consider the following tip in summary.

TIP

You can use an unofficial architecture that makes use of a personal data gateway associated not with a physical person, but with a fictitious "service" user. The credentials of this user are shared between all those analysts who use Python (along with R) code to transform data in their reports using the same virtual environment. Also, since the machine with the Python engines referenced by the gateway is shared, it must remain on during periods of scheduled activity. The same machine often hosts the R engines too. An Azure Windows Virtual Machine, on which the R and Python engines and the data gateway run, is often used in this architecture.

As a reminder, *Figure 3.42* summarizes the aforementioned architecture:

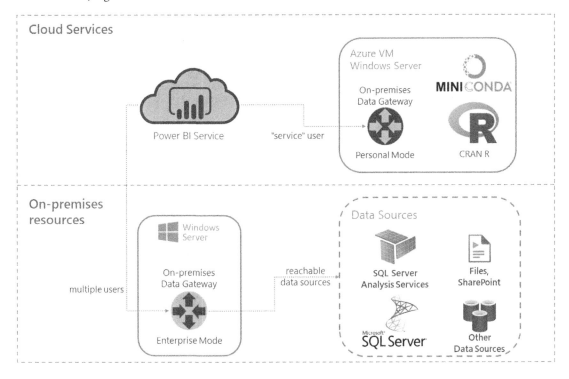

Figure 3.42: Enterprise architecture for the use of Python and R in data transformations

Thanks to this architecture, it is possible to allow a group of analysts to be able to use Python scripts in their reports, despite the limitations imposed by the on-premises data gateway in personal mode.

That said, in addition to the limitations seen for Python scripts in Power Query, there are some important ones to be aware of for Python visuals as well.

Limitations of Python visuals

Python visuals have some important limitations regarding the data they can handle, both input and output:

- A Python visual can handle a *dataframe of up to 150,000 rows only*. If there are more than 150,000 rows, only the first 150,000 rows are used.
- Python visuals have an *output size limit of 2 MB*.

You must also be careful not to exceed the 5-minute runtime calculation for a Python visual in order to avoid a time-out error. Moreover, in order not to run into performance problems, *the resolution of the Python visual plots is fixed at 72 DPI.*

As you can imagine, some limitations of Python script visuals are different depending on whether you run the visual on Power BI Desktop or the Power BI service.

If you think you need to develop reports intended *only for the Power BI Desktop*, without the need to publish them on the service, you can do any of the following:

- Install any kind of package (Conda, PyPI, or custom) in your engine for Python visuals.
- Access the internet from a Python script visual.

When you create reports to share through the *Power BI service*, you can do the following:

- You can *only use the Python packages listed at this link*: https://bit.ly/powerbi-python-limits.
- You *cannot access the internet* from a Python script visual.

You may have noticed that the custom Python script visuals were not mentioned. In fact, the following applies:

IMPORTANT NOTE

In contrast to the case of R script visuals, you do not have the option of developing a custom Python script visual.

Once one of your reports is published on the Power BI service, you can decide to share it on your blog, on one of your websites, or on social media via the **Publish to web** option. Unfortunately, Python script visuals (as well as R script visuals) are not usable on reports that will be published publicly on the web. This was done by Microsoft by design.

TIP

If you absolutely need to publish a particular visualization to the web, remember that custom R visuals overcome this restriction on publishing to the web. So, you need to switch from Python to R.

Summary

In this chapter, you learned about the most popular free Python distributions in the community and the best practices for their use.

Using the unique features of Power BI Desktop and the Power BI service, you have learned how to properly create specific Python environments.

You also learned that the most popular IDE in the R community (RStudio) can also run Python code. In addition, you have installed and configured VS Code, which is to date one of the most widely used advanced editors for Python.

You were also introduced to all of the best practices for properly configuring both Power BI Desktop and the Power BI service with Python, whether in a development or enterprise environment.

Finally, you've learned some of the limitations of using Python with Power BI, knowledge of which is critical to avoid making mistakes when developing and deploying reports.

In the next chapter, we will show you the most common problems you might run into when using Python and R script steps in Power Query.

Test your knowledge

Keep in mind that many of the questions asked in *Chapter 2* about R also apply to Python. It is therefore recommended that you answer those as well, if you have not already done so.

1. Which Python distributions are most widely used by data scientists?
2. What are the most commonly used tools for installing packages in Python? What are their most important differences?
3. How many instances of the engine should be installed to ensure reproducibility of results for Python scripts in Power Query and Python script visuals?
4. A colleague of yours has prepared a virtual environment dedicated to Python script visuals, containing the latest Python release allowed by Miniconda. Did he follow the best practices stated in this chapter?
5. Suppose you created a report with a Python script visual that highlights insights from a dataset created by uploading data from an HTML table available on the web. What do you need to allow a refresh of the data once the report is published to the Power BI service?
6. You need to port an algorithm written in R that performs many dot products of very large matrices to Python. Your goal is to write code that performs at its best. You have two options: either use a simple user function that adopts the `sum()` and `zip()` functions to avoid installing NumPy, or use NumPy's `dot()` function. What do you decide to do? Explain the reasons for your choice.
7. What is the purpose of the #%% code within a Python script used in VS Code?
8. Suppose you need to develop a plot via a Python script visual using a series of transformations of the source data as input, done via multiple steps in Power Query. If you want to develop the plot on your favorite editor separately, how do you retrieve the output data of the transformations so you can test your code?
9. You need to publish a Power BI report, which makes use of Python to draw a plot, on your public blog. Since you can't use a Python script visual to publish to the web, can you use a custom Python visual to circumvent the problem?
10. Suppose you and your colleague create two reports, each of which contains a Python script step in Power Query. During the development, your Power BI Desktop references the Python environment A, while your colleague's Power BI Desktop references the Python environment B. The two environments have different sets of packages installed, each needed by the Python script step that uses it.

Both you and your friend decide to publish your reports to Power BI service using the unofficial architecture suggested in this chapter (one personal data gateway associated with a fictitious service user). Both you and your friend make sure that your environments (A and B) with their installed packages are present on the data gateway machine. Once the two reports are published, the dataset of one of them gives an error when you try to update it. What happens?

Learn more on Discord

To join the Discord community for this book – where you can share feedback, ask questions to the author, and learn about new releases – follow the QR code below:

`https://discord.gg/MKww5g45EB`

4

Solving Common Issues When Using Python and R in Power BI

Sometimes you may run into some problems that are quite common for those developing solutions in Power BI using Python and R. This chapter systematically addresses those most common problem cases by providing the most appropriate solutions to each of them.

This chapter will cover the following topics:

- Avoiding the ADO.NET error when running a Python script in Power BI
- Avoiding the *Formula.Firewall* error
- Using multiple datasets in one Python and R script step
- Dealing with dates/times in Python and R script steps

Technical requirements

This chapter requires you to have a working internet connection and **Power BI Desktop** already installed on your machine (we used version 2.112.603.0 64-bit, December 2022).

Avoiding the ADO.NET error when running a Python script in Power BI

We assume you have followed the steps in *Chapter 3*, *Configuring Python with Power BI*, to properly install Python and to best configure it to interact with Power BI. That said, let's assume that you have already created two Python environments to use for reports, in both of which you have installed NumPy in addition to the other necessary packages.

Sometimes (but not always!), switching the Power BI Desktop **Options** from one environment to the other and then running your Python script, you might see an error like this:

 DataSource.Error: ADO.NET: Python script error.

<pi> C:\Users\LucaZavarella\miniconda3\envs\azureml_scoring_env\lib\site-packages\numpy_init_.py:140: UserWarning: mkl-service package failed to import therefore Intel(R) MKL initialization ensuring its correct out-of-the box operation under condition when Gnu OpenMP had already been loaded by Python process is not assured. Please install mkl-service package, see http://github.com/IntelPython/mkl-service

from . import _distributor_init

Traceback (most recent call last):

File "PythonScriptWrapper.PY", line 2, in <module>

import os, pandas, matplotlib

File "C:\Users\LucaZavarella\miniconda3\envs\azureml_scoring_env\lib\site-packages\pandas_init_.py", line 17, in <module>

"Unable to import required dependencies:\n" + "\n".join(missing_dependencies)

ImportError: Unable to import required dependencies:

numpy

Figure 4.1: A strange Python error referring to MKL and NumPy

Such an error can also occur by running the following simple Python code when loading data (**Get Data à More... à Python script**):

```
import pandas as pd
import numpy
df = pd.DataFrame(dir(numpy))
```

The message in *Figure 4.1* refers to an error loading the Intel MKL libraries and to the non-presence of the NumPy package in the selected environment. But NumPy was already installed in the environment in question, so the error is rather weird, and frankly, from the error message you can't tell more than that.

At this point, one question may arise: is it possible that you have correctly selected the Python environment to be referenced in the **Options**, but that Power BI Desktop cannot activate it correctly? Let's test this hypothesis.

The real cause of the problem

In order to validate the above hypothesis, you must find a way to force Power BI Desktop to run in a context that defaults to the Python executable contained in the selected environment folder. In other words, the Power BI Desktop instance must exist in a context in which the environment in question has been activated.

So, let's try running the Power BI Desktop executable in Anaconda Prompt after activating the environment:

1. Open **Anaconda Prompt**.
2. Activate the environment that gives you the error you saw before using the `conda activate <your-environment-name>` command.
3. Launch the Power BI Desktop executable (usually you can find it in `C:\Program Files\ Microsoft Power BI Desktop\bin\PBIDesktop.exe`) from **Anaconda Prompt**:

```
Administrator: Anaconda Prompt (Miniconda3)                                         —  □  ×

(base) C:\Users\lucazav>conda activate pbi_powerquery_env

(pbi_powerquery_env) C:\Users\lucazav>"C:\Program Files\Microsoft Power BI Desktop\bin\PBIDesktop.exe"
```

Figure 4.2: Executing Power BI Desktop from Anaconda Prompt

At this point, the Power BI Desktop instance opens. Make sure, of course, that the environment selected in **Options** is the same as the one activated before running Power BI Desktop. If you now try adding the same Python script to the Power Query transformation steps that previously failed, you will see that everything will work without errors. Therefore, the following applies.

TIP

Unlike the standard Python distribution, to avoid errors with an Anaconda environment, Power BI Desktop can only reference it correctly if it is enabled.

This problem is also highlighted in Microsoft's Power BI Docs (`https://bit.ly/power-bi-python-config`) but often goes unnoticed, because the script sometimes runs without returning an error, even though the conda environment wasn't activated. Just think that during the writing of the first edition of this book, we never got that error, although we always used conda environments!

In our opinion, this is for all intents and purposes a very important bug or missing feature in Power BI Desktop, especially considering that VS Code, for example, solves this very easily. Therefore, on the advice of the product team, we opened a Microsoft Idea (`https://bit.ly/power-bi-solve-python-env-activation`) to try to point the team to the implementation of the feature. If you are interested, you can vote on the idea.

Okay, now you've figured out a workaround! But opening Anaconda Prompt to activate the necessary environment and then running the Power BI Desktop executable from there every time you need to use Python in Power BI is quite frustrating. Is there a more convenient and simple solution that speeds up operations? Let's see it together.

A practical solution to the problem

It would be convenient to have an icon with which, by double-clicking on it, you could start a Power BI Desktop instance that refers to a specific active environment.

This can be done with a specific batch script (you can find it here: `https://bit.ly/batch-run-powerbi-conda`):

```
1    @echo OFF
2    rem How to run Power BI Desktop in a given conda environment from a batch
     file.
3
4    rem It doesn't require:
5    rem - conda to be in the PATH
6    rem - cmd.exe to be initialized with conda init
7
8    rem Define here the path to your conda installation
9    rem If you installed [Anaconda/Miniconda] just for your user, you'll find
     the installation folder in C:\Users\your-username\[AnacondaX/MinicondaX]
10   rem If you installed [Anaconda/Miniconda] for all the users, you'll find
     the installation folder in C:\ProgramData\[AnacondaX/MinicondaX]
11   set CONDAPATH=C:\Users\your-username\miniconda3
12   rem Define here the name of the environment. Use "base" for the base
     environment
13   set ENVNAME=your-environment-name
14
15   rem The following command activates the base environment.
16   rem call C:\ProgramData\Miniconda3\Scripts\activate.bat
     C:\ProgramData\Miniconda3
17   if %ENVNAME%==base (set ENVPATH=%CONDAPATH%) else (set
     ENVPATH=%CONDAPATH%\envs\%ENVNAME%)
18
19   rem Activate the conda environment
20   rem Using call is required here, see: https://stackoverflow.com/questions/
     24678144/conda-environments-and-bat-files
21   call %CONDAPATH%\Scripts\activate.bat %ENVPATH%
22
23   rem Run a python script in that environment
24   "C:\Program Files\Microsoft Power BI Desktop\bin\PBIDesktop.exe"
25
26   rem Deactivate the environment
27   call conda deactivate
28
29   rem If conda is directly available from the command line then the
     following code works.
30   rem call activate your-environment-name
31   rem "C:\Program Files\Microsoft Power BI Desktop\bin\PBIDesktop.exe"
32   rem conda deactivate
33
34   rem One could also use the conda run command
35   rem conda run -n your-environment-name "C:\Program Files\Microsoft Power
     BI Desktop\bin\PBIDesktop.exe"
```

Figure 4.3: Batch script to run Power BI Desktop "under" an activated conda environment

As stated in the script comments, be sure to appropriately change the path to the Miniconda installation folder (in our case, C:\ProgramData\Miniconda3\), and specify the name of the Conda environment (in your case, pbi_powerquery_env).

After saving the run_power_bi_in_conda_env.bat batch file to a favorite folder of yours (you can also find it in the book's GitHub repo), do the following:

1. Create a shortcut to it on your desktop by right-clicking on it, selecting **Send to,** and then selecting **Desktop (create shortcut).**
2. Rename the shortcut on your desktop as Power BI - pbi_powerquery_env.
3. Right-click on it and select **Properties.**
4. Go to the **Shortcut** tab and click on **Change Icon...:**

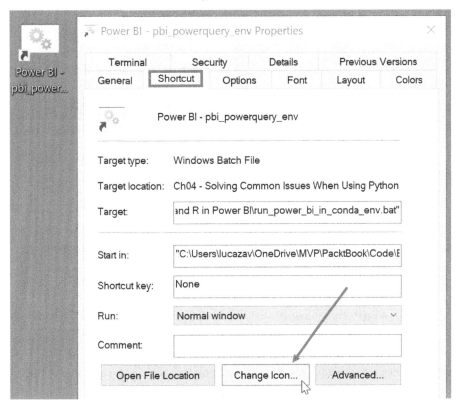

Figure 4.4: Changing the icon of your Power BI shortcut

5. A message will be displayed indicating that the `.bat` file contains no icon. Click **OK**, then **Browse**, select the Power BI Desktop executable (`PBIDesktop.exe`) located in the `C:\Program Files\Microsoft Power BI Desktop\bin` folder, and click **Open**:

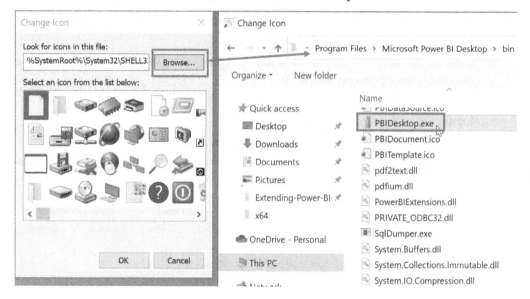

Figure 4.5: Selecting the icon from PBIDesktop.exe

6. Then select the Power BI icon and click **OK**.

7. Click **OK** on the shortcut Properties window.

You will finally have a convenient icon, useful for running an instance of Power BI Desktop that references the conda `pbi_powerquery_env` environment. The following applies:

TIP

We suggest creating as many shortcuts as there are different conda environments that will be used for report development by creating specific batch files.

In your case, you could already prepare a convenient desktop icon to run a Power BI Desktop instance referencing the `pbi_visuals_env` environment.

Avoiding the Formula.Firewall error

Another problem one runs into when dealing with R or Python scripts (but not only them) is that of data flow blocking by Power Query's **Data Privacy Firewall** (aka the **Firewall**).

The Firewall was created with the goal of preventing any sensitive data from one data source from being sent to another data source inadvertently through the mechanism called **query folding**.

This is not the place to go into detail about what the query folding mechanism is (there is a whole section of the Docs here: `https://bit.ly/powerbi-query-folding` and an in-depth topic here: `https://bit.ly/powerbi-firewall`). To understand how data can pass from one source to another, imagine that *data source A* from an Excel file contains the attributes of a healthcare company's customers, also including information about the diseases the customer has had; *data source B*, on the other hand, is generated by a query on a SQL Server database to get information about orders, for each of which there is only the customer code. If you try to perform a join (**Merge Queries**) between the two datasets via the user interface, Power BI Desktop tries, behind the scenes, to optimize the query to be sent to the SQL Server engine. During the optimization phase, the engine could inject all the client data obtained from Excel into SQL Server. Hence the possible leaking of data. To avoid this, the Firewall raises specific errors.

The two types of error that the Firewall raises are the following:

- *Formula.Firewall: Query 'Query1' (step 'Source') is accessing data sources that have privacy levels which cannot be used together. Please rebuild this data combination.*
- *Formula.Firewall: Query 'Query1' (step 'Source') references other queries or steps, so it may not directly access a data source. Please rebuild this data combination.*

The *first type* concerns the compatibility of the **privacy levels** of the datasets. Basically, if the levels are incompatible with each other, the Firewall raises the error to avoid possible data leakage.

These are the data source privacy levels available in Power BI Desktop:

- **Private:** Data sources set as Private contain sensitive or confidential information. Visibility may be restricted to authorized users. Data from a private data source is not folded into other data sources, including other private data sources.
- **Organizational:** Data sources set to Organizational can fold into private and other organizational data sources. They cannot fold into public data sources. Visibility is set to a trusted group.
- **Public:** Files, internet data sources, and workbook data can be set to Public. Data can fold into other data sources. Visibility is available to everyone.

Please, note the following:

These settings, including privacy options in both the **Global** and **Current File** sections, apply only to Power BI Desktop. After publishing a report, if you use the on-premises data gateway (enterprise and personal mode), you must also configure the data privacy settings on the sources used by the dataset in the Power BI portal.

The *second type* of Firewall error, on the other hand, is more obscure. Power Query transformations can be broken down into one or more **partitions**, each of which is a set of steps found in the **Applied Steps** panel. Sometimes, when writing queries in Power Query, there may be one partition that references another. In this case, the Firewall checks for compatibility between the privacy levels of the partitions involved. However, when there are data sources accessed within the referenced partition, the Firewall can no longer perform the gatekeeper function and therefore raises the second error seen above.

But let us see in practice in what cases it is possible to receive these errors using Python or R scripts, and how to resolve the related data flow blocks imposed by the Firewall.

Incompatible privacy levels

For simplicity, you will use only R scripts in these tests. But everything you learn will continue to apply when you use Python scripts.

To have the Firewall raise the privacy level incompatibility error, proceed as follows:

1. Open **Power BI Desktop**.
2. Import the Excel file with the name `dummy-data.xlsx` found in the `Chapter 4` folder of the GitHub repository associated with the book:

Figure 4.6: Importing the dummy Excel file

3. After selecting the **Dummy** sheet, click on **Transform Data** to directly open the Power Query Editor.
4. Click on the **Transform** tab on the ribbon and then click on **Run R script**:

Figure 4.7: Adding an R script step to transform data

5. Enter the df <- head(dataset, 2) script into the **Run R script** editor to select the first two rows of the dummy dataset and click **OK**:

Run R script

Enter R scripts into the editor to transform and shape your data.

Script
```
# 'dataset' holds the input data for this script
df <- head(dataset, 2)
```

Figure 4.8: Entering a simple R script

6. A warning about data privacy may appear in a yellow ribbon just below the Formula Bar. If you have never set a privacy level for R scripts, then the following pop-up window will appear:

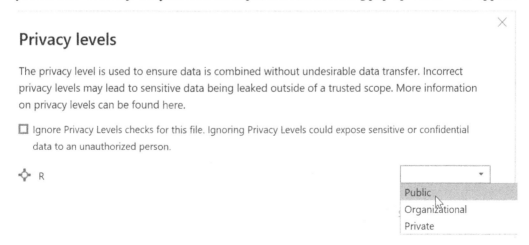

Figure 4.9: Show the Privacy levels pop-up window to set R privacy

7. You could simply choose to disable the Firewall controls on the privacy levels, but in this case, the solution to the blockage is simple to apply. Just select the **Public** privacy level for R scripts. You could also select another type of privacy level, but keep in mind that, as you learned from *Chapter 2* and *Chapter 3*, when publishing a Power BI report that contains R or Python scripts on the service, their privacy level must be set to Public.

8. If, on the other hand, you have already set the privacy level for R scripts, but not for the folder from which you import Excel data, you will see this popup:

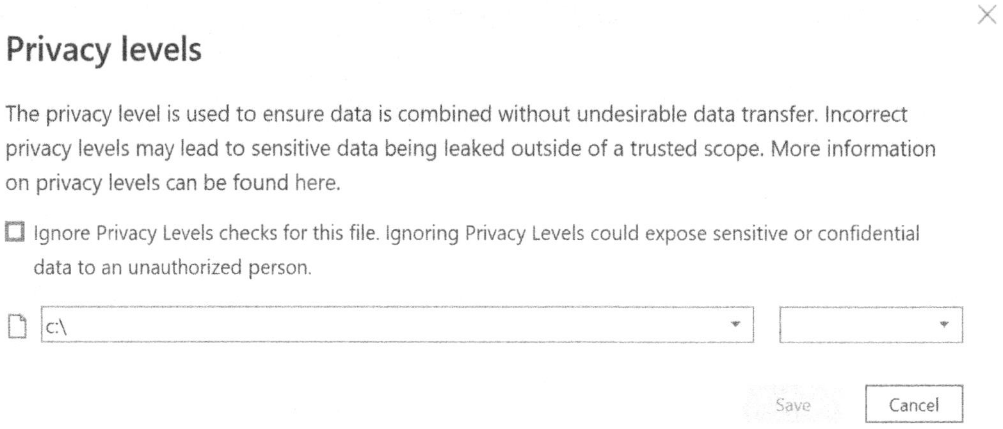

✕

Privacy levels

The privacy level is used to ensure data is combined without undesirable data transfer. Incorrect privacy levels may lead to sensitive data being leaked outside of a trusted scope. More information on privacy levels can be found here.

☐ Ignore Privacy Levels checks for this file. Ignoring Privacy Levels could expose sensitive or confidential data to an unauthorized person.

| 🗋 | c:\ | ▾ | | ▾ |

Save | Cancel |

Figure 4.10: Show the Privacy levels pop-up window to set folder privacy

9. Here you can select the folder in which the Excel file is located, or one of its parent folders. Then assign the Public privacy level to the main folder C and click **Save.**

10. In either of the above cases, or if you have already set privacy levels for the folder and R scripts previously, a warning may appear containing the same message as the first firewall error:

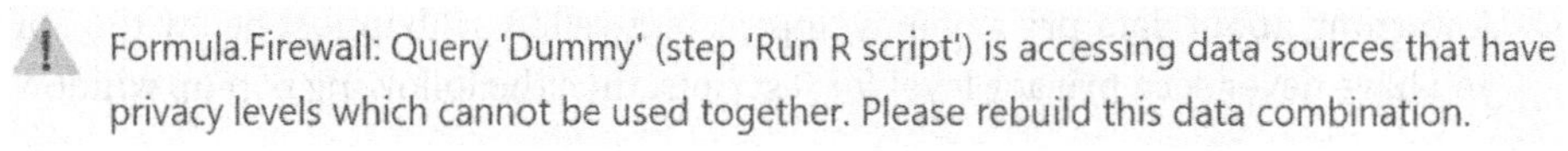

⚠ Formula.Firewall: Query 'Dummy' (step 'Run R script') is accessing data sources that have privacy levels which cannot be used together. Please rebuild this data combination.

Figure 4.11: The incompatible privacy levels warning

11. This means that you have to manually configure the privacy levels of the folder and the script so that they are compatible according to what we saw at the beginning of this section.

12. Click on the **File** tab of the ribbon, select **Options and settings**, and then click on **Data source settings:**

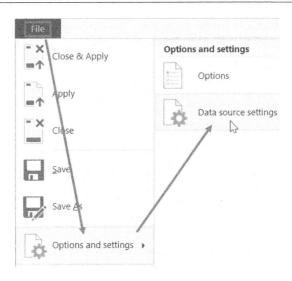

Figure 4.12: Open Data source settings

13. Make sure both data sources have the privacy level Public by selecting them one at a time and clicking on **Edit permissions...** and then click **Close**:

Data source settings

Manage settings for data sources that you have connected to using Power BI Desktop.

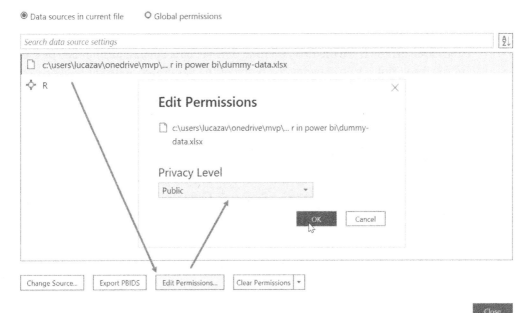

Figure 4.13: Set the privacy level for both the data sources

14. At this point, it may be necessary to force the execution of the R script step again. To do this, click the **Home** tab and then click **Refresh All** from the **Refresh Preview** menu:

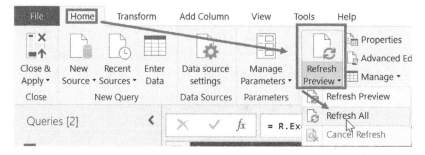

Figure 4.14: Refresh all the queries

15. This time the warning should disappear, and you may be able to expand any of the dataframes created by the R script:

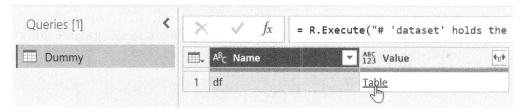

Figure 4.15: Choose the dataframe to expand

16. In your case, the only dataframe exposed by the R script is **df**, so click on the Table link next to the name **df**. You'll see the first two rows of Excel data appear (as intended by the R script) and you'll see a new step showing the name of the dataframe added at the end of the list of transformation steps:

Figure 4.16: The output of the R script is shown

17. To finish the transformations, click on the **Home** tab of the ribbon and click **Close & Apply**:

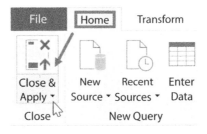

Figure 4.17: Close the Power Query Editor and apply all the transformations done

Wow! You just learned how to solve the block due to incompatible dataset privacy levels imposed by the Firewall.

Let's now see how to resolve the other type of error often raised by the Firewall.

Indirect access to a data source

In order to have the Firewall raise the indirect data source access error, you can create a new query in Power Query by referencing an existing one. After that, simply add an R script step to the new query.

Keep in mind that a **reference query** directly uses the output of the referenced query by calling its name in the M code as follows:

```
let
    Source = #"titanic-dataset-csv"
in
    Source
```

Referencing another dataset ensures that any changes to the referenced query will be reflected on the referrer query without having to manually work on the latter.

That said, proceed as follows:

1. Open **Power BI Desktop**.
2. Import the Titanic dataset directly from the internet by clicking on **Get Data**, selecting **Web**, and then entering the bit.ly/titanic-dataset-csv URL. Then click **OK**.

3. Immediately after a preview of the data appears, click **Transform Data** to directly access the Power Query Editor:

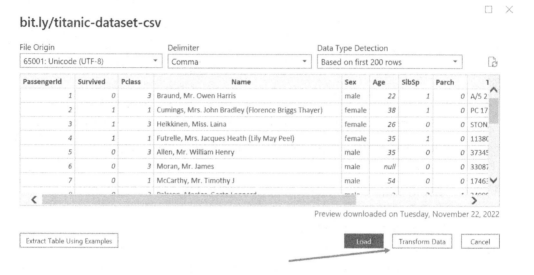

Figure 4.18: Titanic data imported from the Web

4. On the left side of the Power Query Editor, in the **Queries** panel, right-click on the **titanic-dataset-csv** query you just created and click on **Reference**:

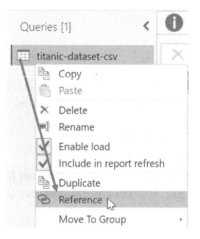

Figure 4.19: Create a reference to your first query

5. The new **titanic-dataset-csv (2)** query will be created, which you can rename to `titanic-dataset-csv-R-ref` for clarity by right-clicking on it and selecting **Rename**.

6. Now add an R script to the **titanic-dataset-csv-R-ref** query, making sure it is selected, then click on the **Transform** tab of the ribbon and then on **Run R script**.

7. Enter the script `df <- head(dataset, 20)` in the R script editor and then click **OK**.

8. Power Query Editor will immediately raise the error of indirect access to a data source:

Formula.Firewall: Query 'titanic-dataset-csv-R' (step 'Run R script') references other queries or steps, so it may not directly access a data source. Please rebuild this data combination.

Figure 4.20: Indirect access error for the reference query

9. Let's take a look at the query dependencies to see what they look like. Click on the **View** menu on the ribbon and then **Query Dependencies**:

Figure 4.21: Select the Query Dependencies view

10. Query dependencies look as follows:

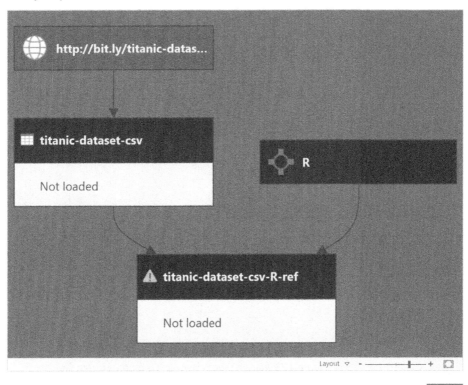

Figure 4.22: Query dependencies

In this case, it is evident how the **titanic-dataset-csv-R-ref** query on which the R script step is added references the **titanic-dataset-csv** query, which directly accesses the data source on the web. Therefore, the Firewall fails to perform its gatekeeper function and raises the error in *Figure 4.20*.

This time it is not enough to set the privacy levels correctly for each data source to overcome the block. There are several strategies to overcome the block though. Let's see what they are.

The easy way

As mentioned earlier, you can turn off the controls on privacy levels and everything else done by the Firewall through a setting in the Power BI Desktop **Options**. Here's how you do it:

1. Click on the **File** tab of the ribbon, then **Options and settings**, and then **Options**.
2. Click on the **Privacy** tab on the left side of the **Options** window under the **CURRENT FILE** section and select **Ignore the Privacy Levels and potentially improve performance**. Then click **OK**:

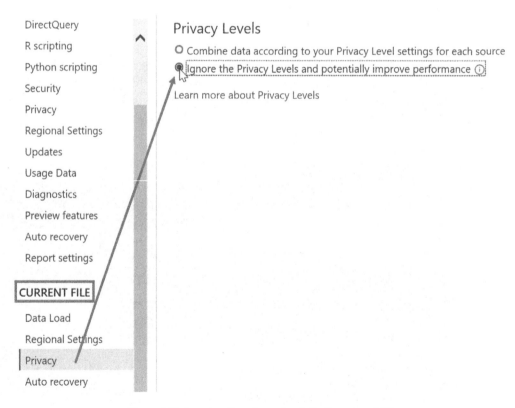

Figure 4.23: Ignoring the privacy levels for the current file

Note the following:

> After a report has been published, if you are using **on-premises data gateway** in **personal mode**, you can configure it on the Power BI service to ignore the data privacy settings. Unfortunately, if you are using the Enterprise on-premises data gateway in standard mode (formerly known as Enterprise Data Gateway) to load your data, there is currently no way to configure the gateway to ignore data privacy levels on the Power BI service.

3. Now click the **Home** tab and the **Refresh All** under the **Refresh Preview** menu.

4. You can see that the warning has disappeared and that the df dataframe calculated in the R script is correctly available:

Figure 4.24: Dataframe df available without warnings

5. If you see the screen shown in *Figure 4.24*, expand the df table by clicking on its link to have the first 20 rows of the Titanic dataset.

This is the most straightforward approach, but it is not always advisable to turn off controls on privacy levels. Here is a list of pros and cons of ignoring privacy levels:

Pros:

- *Easy Data Exploration*: Ignoring privacy levels allows you to quickly connect to and explore data from various sources without having to configure and manage privacy settings. This can be helpful during the initial stages of data exploration and prototyping.

- *Simplified Development*: By ignoring privacy levels, you can simplify the development process, especially when working on small-scale or personal projects. It reduces the need for configuring privacy settings and enables faster development iterations.

- *Quick Data Mashup*: Ignoring privacy levels can make it easier to combine and mash up data from different sources without encountering privacy-related errors. It allows for more flexibility in data blending and can be beneficial for certain ad hoc analysis or data preparation tasks.

Cons:

- *Security Risks*: Ignoring privacy levels can introduce security risks by bypassing data privacy safeguards. Power BI's privacy levels are designed to prevent unauthorized access to sensitive data, and ignoring them may expose confidential information to unintended users.

- *Compliance Issues*: Ignoring privacy levels can result in non-compliance with data governance and regulatory requirements, such as the **General Data Protection Regulation (GDPR)** or the **Health Insurance Portability and Accountability Act** (HIPAA). Failure to adhere to these privacy regulations can lead to legal consequences and reputational damage.

- *Reduced Collaboration*: Ignoring privacy levels can hinder collaboration within a team or organization. Each user may have different access privileges and privacy requirements, and ignoring privacy levels can undermine data sharing and collaboration efforts by exposing sensitive data to unauthorized individuals.

If you want to be sure to respect the privacy levels of the data sources you use, you can avoid selecting the option to ignore them and proceed in a different way.

First, however, remember to reset the privacy level for the current file set as in *Figure 4.23* to **Combine data according to your Privacy Level settings for each source.**

Combining queries and/or transformations

As you saw in the previous session, a reference query allows you to reuse the output of a set of transformation steps wrapped in a query as the basis for further transformations. In addition, any changes made to the referenced query are automatically inherited by the referrer query. The second method of solving the blockage caused by the Firewall requires you to go without these benefits.

Specifically, instead of using a reference query, a **duplicate query** must be used in this method. In this way, all the transformation steps of the referenced query are replicated in the new query. It goes without saying that, should you make a change to the source query, that change must also be carried over by hand into the new query. At the end of all replicated transformations, the transformations specific to the new query will be added.

Let's look at a practical example:

1. Right-click on the **titanic-dataset-csv** query you just created in the **Queries** panel and then click on **Duplicate**:

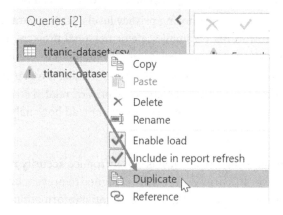

Figure 4.25: Duplicate the first query

2.   The new **titanic-dataset-csv (2)** query will be created, which you can rename to `titanic-dataset-csv-R-dup` for clarity by right-clicking on it and selecting **Rename**.

3.   Now add an R script to the **titanic-dataset-csv-R-dup** query making sure it is selected, then click on the **Transform** tab of the ribbon and then on **Run R script**.

4.   Enter the script `df <- head(dataset, 20)` in the R script editor and then click **OK**.

5.   Power BI will automatically create the additional **df** step and will show the first twenty rows of the full Titanic dataset. In this case, the Firewall did not throw up any kind of error. Let's check what the query dependencies look like now.

6.   Click on the **View** menu on the ribbon and then **Query Dependencies**:

Query Dependencies

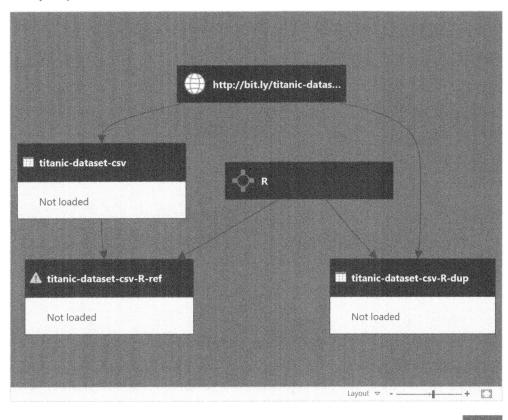

Figure 4.26: Checking both query dependencies

As you can see, the **titanic-dataset-csv-R-dup** query directly references the main data source, so the Firewall can do its job without any problems.

Encapsulating queries into functions

There is a way to not lose the benefits highlighted earlier for referenced queries. It is to use functions. Let's see how:

1. Right-click on the **titanic-dataset-csv** query you just created in the **Queries** panel and then click on **Create Function...**:

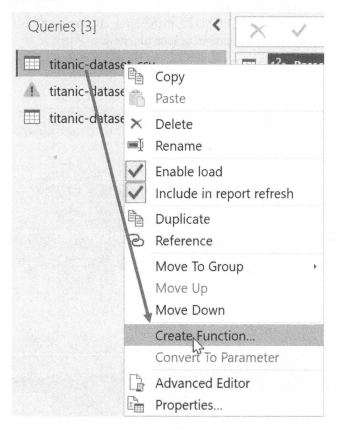

Figure 4.27: Creating a function starting from the first query

2. An alert will be shown stating that the query on which to create a function does not reference parameters that can be used as parameters of the function itself. Proceed anyway by clicking **Create**.

3. You will be prompted to enter the name of the function. Enter func-titanic as the name and click **OK**.

4. The newly created **func-titanic** function and the **titanic-dataset-csv** query are moved inside the folder named after the function. The remaining queries end up in the Other Queries folder:

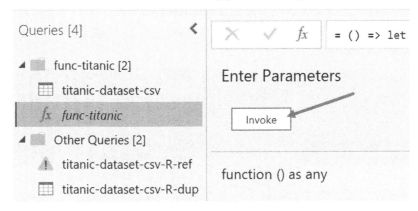

Figure 4.28: Invoking the just created func-titanic function

5. Now click **Invoke** to call the function you just created and generate its output.

6. The new query, Invoked Function, is created, which is the result of the function call. Right-click on it and click **Rename** to rename it to titanic-dataset-csv-R-inv:

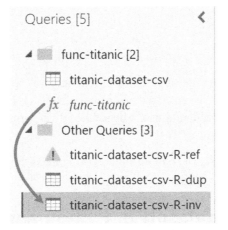

Figure 4.29: Query created by invoking the function

7. Now add an R script to the **titanic-dataset-csv-R-inv** query, making sure it is selected, then click on the **Transform** tab of the ribbon and then on **Run R script**.

8. Enter the script df <- head(dataset, 20) in the R script editor and then click **OK**.

9.   Also, in this case, Power BI will automatically create the additional **df** step and will show the first twenty rows of the full Titanic dataset. Again, the Firewall did not throw up any kind of error. Let's check how the query dependencies look now:

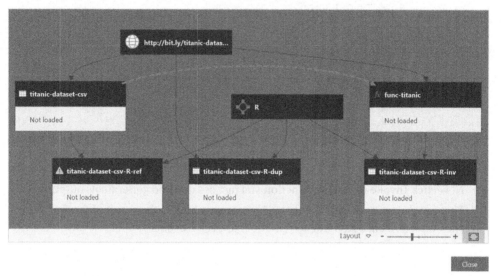

Figure 4.30: Query dependencies induced by the introduction of the function

From the query dependencies, it can be seen that the function created on the main query has the effect of creating a reference, but it is unrelated to the query itself and is tied directly to the data source that feeds it. Therefore, the function retains the benefits of the reference seen earlier without causing the Firewall to block the data flow.

At this point, you are able to easily handle any Firewall blocks that might arise by introducing Python or R steps into your transformations.

Using multiple datasets in Python and R script steps

You may have noticed how each query in Power Query has its own queue of transformation steps, leading from the initial data to the final dataset in the desired form. You may need to add a Python or R script step that uses a function to which you need to pass two dataframes as parameters to a query.

Assuming I have the two queries, query_A and query_B, which return the two datasets to be used as parameters for the above function, how do I reference the result of query_B in my script if I'm adding the script step to query_A?

There are several ways to do this. Let's see them.

Applying a full join with Merge

The first trick that comes to mind for any analyst who is used to dealing with data is to apply a full join between the two datasets and thus generate a third dataset on which to apply the script step. Within the script step, the reverse merge transformation is applied, that is, separating the columns of the two original datasets and applying a distinct operation.

Suppose, for simplicity's sake, that you need to write a Python script that returns rows not in common between two tables, even though this can be done directly using Power Query's basic transformations. Let's look at an example:

1. Run Power BI Desktop using the batch file that activates the pbi_visuals_env conda environment (you should have created it for practice) to avoid the ADO.NET error, as you learned at the beginning of this chapter.
2. Make sure your Power BI Desktop is referencing the pbi_visuals_env conda environment you created in *Chapter 3*:

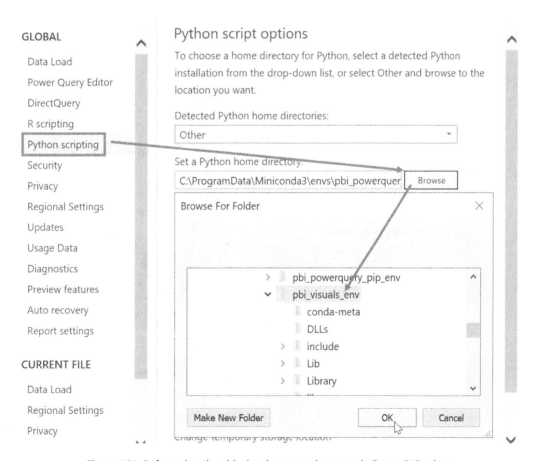

Figure 4.31: Referencing the pbi_visuals_env environment in Power BI Desktop

3. In the GitHub repository associated with the book, you will find the two Excel files `cars-data-01.xlsx` and `cars-data-02.xlsx` in the folder pertaining to *Chapter 4*. Load their respective `cars-01` and `cars-02` sheets into Power BI. When these tasks are completed, you will see the two tables present in the **Fields** panel on the right side of the workspace:

Figure 4.32: Cars tables correctly imported in Power BI

4. Now you need to do some transformations, so click on **Transform data** on the **Home** ribbon to open the Power Query editor window:

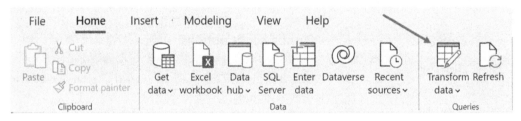

Figure 4.33: Open the Power Query editor by clicking on the "Transform data" icon

5. Then right-click on the **cars-01** query and click **Duplicate**. The new **cars-01 (2)** query will be created.

6. Right-click on the just created query and click **Rename**. Rename the new query to `cars-diff`.

7. Now, making sure the **cars-diff** query is selected, click on **Merge Queries** on the right of the **Home** menu on the ribbon:

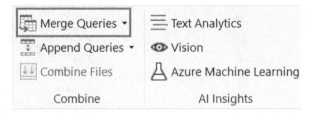

Figure 4.34: The Merge Queries transformation

8. Select the **cars-02** query in the second drop-down menu provided in the **Merge** window and select both **CarType** columns of both tables by clicking on them. Then select **Full Outer (all rows from both)** from the **Join Kind** drop-down menu:

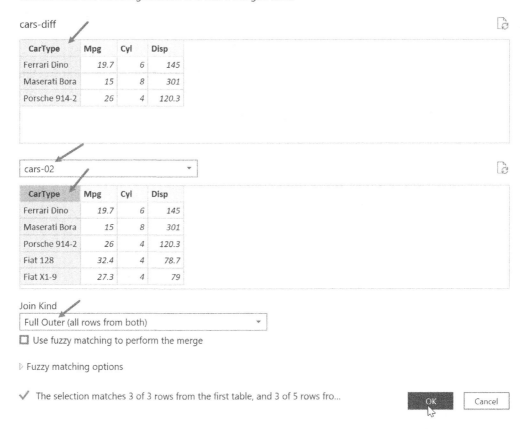

Figure 4.35: Merging the two tables using full join

Then click **OK**.

9. Now expand the content of all the tables calculated by the merge transformation by clicking on the double arrow icon on the right of the cars-02 header:

Figure 4.36: Expanding the merged table

10. Leave all selected in the next pop-up and click **OK**. Columns of table **cars-02** will be added to the current fields, using the table name as a prefix:

1.2 Disp	ABC cars-02.CarType	1.2 cars-02.Mpg	1²3 cars-02.Cyl	1.2 cars-02.Disp
145	Ferrari Dino	19.7	6	145
301	Maserati Bora	15	8	301
120.3	Porsche 914-2	26	4	120.3
null	Fiat 128	32.4	4	78.7
null	Fiat X1-9	27.3	4	79

Figure 4.37: Columns of table cars-02 added

11. As you can see, rows associated with values in the **CarType** column (the join key) that do not match in the other table (Fiat cars) are still added, leaving null values in the fields of that table.

12. At this point, the merge table is complete, so you need to add a Python script step by clicking on the **Transform** menu and then on **Run Python script**.

13. Enter the following script into the Python editor. We won't go into detail about the functions used (but they are commented on):

```
# 'dataset' holds the input data for this script
import pandas as pd


# Extract df1 from the merged dataset, selecting the
# first 4 columns, removing rows having all null values
# and removing duplicates
df1 = dataset[["CarType", "Mpg", "Cyl", "Disp"]].dropna(how='all').drop_
duplicates()


# Extract df2 from the merged dataset, selecting the
# second 4 columns, removing rows having all null values,
# removing duplicates and renaming the columns like the df1 ones
df2 = dataset[["cars-02.CarType", "cars-02.Mpg", "cars-02.Cyl", "cars-02.
Disp"]].dropna(how='all').drop_duplicates().\
    rename(columns={"cars-02.CarType": "CarType", "cars-02.Mpg": "Mpg",
"cars-02.Cyl": "Cyl", "cars-02.Disp": "Disp"})


# Get the rows not in common between the two dataframes
df_diff = pd.concat([df1,df2]).drop_duplicates(keep=False)
```

You can also find this script in the `multiple-tables-from-merge.py` file in the folder related to chapter 4 of the GitHub repository. Then click **OK**.

14. Again, if the Firewall controls have not been disabled, the usual error you are familiar with by now is raised:

Formula.Firewall: Query 'cars-diff' (step 'Run Python script') references other queries or steps, so it may not directly access a data source. Please rebuild this data combination.

Figure 4.38: The usual Formula.Firewall error

15. The Python script interacts with the merge query, which by definition contains the references to the two data sources, so the Firewall fails to enforce its privacy rules. Therefore, in this case, you must turn off the Firewall check.

16. If the Firewall error popped up for you, then go to the Power Query editor **Options,** click on **Privacy** in the **Current File** section, select the **Ignore the Privacy Levels and potentially improve the performance** option, and click **OK.**

17. Go to the **Home** menu and click **Refresh Preview.**

18. Now the dataframes defined in your Python script are shown as tables in Power BI:

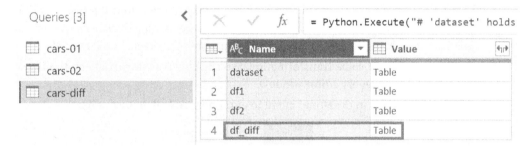

Figure 4.39: All the dataframes defined in the Python script are now available

19. Then click on the **Table** link corresponding to the **df_diff** dataframe.

20. Power BI now shows the rows not in common between the two original tables:

Figure 4.40: Rows not in common between the two original tables are shown

21. Click the **Close & Apply** icon in the **Home** menu.

Great! You managed to use two tables as input to a Python script step thanks to the merge transformation.

Keep the following in mind:

 In the merge transformation, you could have used two tables that had no fields in common. By selecting any column in the two tables as the join key, you would still have obtained a reasonable merge table containing a lot of null values for non-matches. From this merge table, you would still have been able to get back to the contents of the two original tables with the same Python script you used earlier.

However, there is a more immediate method that allows you to achieve the same result. Let's see what it is.

Using arguments of the Python.Execute function

In this section, you will learn how to use two tables as input for a step script without having to resort to the merge transformation, but simply passing them as parameters to the M function used to execute the script code. Let's take an example:

1. Run Power BI Desktop using the batch file that activates the pbi_visuals_env conda environment (you should have created it for practice) to avoid the ADO.NET error, as you learned at the beginning of this chapter.

2. Make sure your Power BI Desktop is referencing the pbi_visuals_env conda environment you created in *Chapter 3*.

3. In the GitHub repository associated with the book, you will find the two Excel files cars-data-01.xlsx and cars-data-02.xlsx in the folder pertaining to *Chapter 4*. As you did in the previous case, load their respective cars-01 and cars-02 sheets into Power BI.

4. Now you need to do some transformations, so click on **Transform data** on the Home ribbon to open the Power Query editor window.

5. Click on **Enter Data** in the **Home** menu to enter new table data manually:

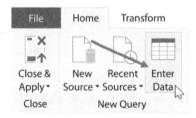

Figure 4.41: Enter a new table manually

6. Leave the table data empty and name the new table cars-diff, then click **OK**:

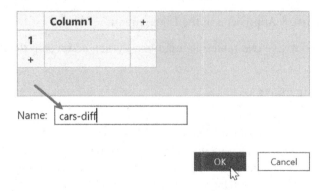

Figure 4.42: Create the empty cars-diff table

7. Click on **Run Python script** in the **Transform** menu, keeping the **cars-diff** query selected.

8. Leave just the default comment in the Python editor without entering any new code and click **OK**.

9. Go back to the **Home** menu and click **Advanced Editor**, keeping the **cars-diff** query selected:

Figure 4.43: Open Advanced Editor for the cars-diff query

10. As you can see, Power Query adds some M code corresponding to the empty table:

Figure 4.44: cars-diff M code shown in the Advanced Editor

11. Just remove the code from Source to text}}), (including the comma) and make sure the code you are left with is the following:

```
let
    #"Run Python script" = Python.Execute("# 'dataset' holds the input
data for this script#(lf)",[dataset=#"Changed Type"])
in
    #"Run Python script"
```

12. Basically, you have the execution of an empty Python script in the M script. For now, do not click **Done**.

13. If you look closely at the final code in the previous point, the `Python.Execute` function, in addition to accepting the string containing the Python script, also accepts the list of dataframes to be considered as input. By default, there is only the `dataset` dataframe referencing a table as input. And here's the catch:

 Replace the default `[dataset=#"Changed Type"]` parameters list with the following: `[df1=#"cars-01", df2=#"cars-02"]`.

14. Basically, you are passing the Python script the two tables, `cars-01` and `cars-02`, as parameters `df1` and `df2` respectively. Ultimately, your M code will look like this:

```
let
    #"Run Python script" = Python.Execute("# 'dataset' holds the input
data for this script#(lf)",[df1=#"cars-01", df2=#"cars-02"])
in
    #"Run Python script"
```

15. Then, click **Done**.

16. Now, if the Firewall controls have not been disabled, the usual error you are familiar with is raised:

 Formula.Firewall: Query 'cars-diff' (step 'Run Python script') references other queries or steps, so it may not directly access a data source. Please rebuild this data combination.

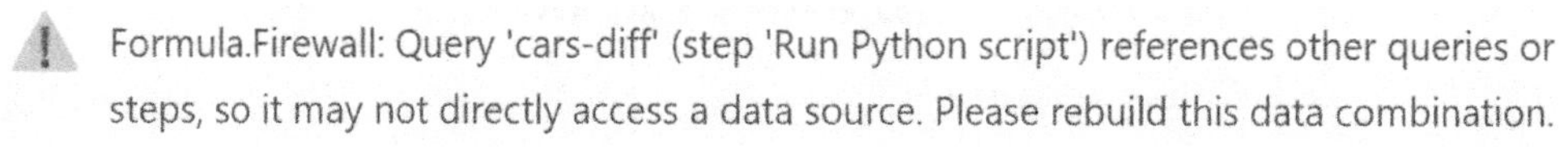

Figure 4.45: The usual Formula.Firewall error

17. The `Python.Execute` function references the two car queries, each of which contains loading calls to different data sources, so the Firewall fails to enforce its privacy rules. Therefore, in this case, you must turn off the Firewall check.

18. If the Firewall error popped up for you, then go to the Power Query editor **Options**, click on **Privacy** in the **Current File** section, select the **Ignore the Privacy Levels and potentially improve the performance** option, and click **OK**.

19. Go to the Home menu and click **Refresh Preview**.

20. Sometimes it is necessary to give Power BI permission to run Python code. If so, click **Permission required** in the yellow warning ribbon and click **OK** in the next window.

21. At this point, you can finally enter the Python code that provides the rows that are not common to the two tables provided as input. To do this, select the **cars-diff** query, and click on the gearwheel next to the **Run Python script** step in the **Applied Steps** panel:

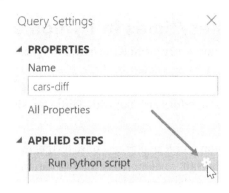

Figure 4.46: Edit the Python script of the cars-diff query

22. The Python script editor will pop up. Enter the following simple script:

```python
import pandas as pd


df_diff = pd.concat([df1,df2]).drop_duplicates(keep=False)
```

23. Then click **OK**.

24. Now the dataframes defined in your Python script are shown as tables in Power BI:

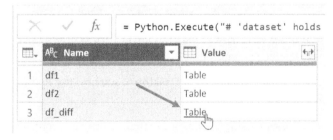

Figure 4.47: Expand the df_diff table

25. Then click on the **Table** link corresponding to the **df_diff** dataframe.

26. Power BI now shows the rows not in common between the two original tables:

Figure 4.48: Rows not in common between the two original tables are shown

27. Click the **Close & Apply** icon in the **Home** menu.

Amazing! You were able to use two tables in a single Python script step with a simple modification of the execution function generated by default by Power BI.

It goes without saying that the same technique is also valid for R scripts with the R.Execute function.

Dealing with dates/times in Python and R script steps

The handling of date, date/time, and time fields is native in Power BI. If you want to add a Python or R script step from a dataset containing a date/time field, you would expect to find that field in the default `dataset` dataframe with the corresponding data type depending on whether it is a Python or R script. Unfortunately, it is not so straightforward. But with a little forethought, it is possible to handle these data types in the right way.

The code used in both Python and R makes use of date-specific functions with which you may not be too familiar. It is not important to completely know them for the purposes of understanding the section; you can delve into them later when you need to.

In the folder pertaining to *Chapter 4* in the GitHub repository associated with the book, you will find the `date-time-fields.xlsx` Excel file containing the `dates` sheet with only date, date/time, and time fields:

	A	B	C
1	DateField	DateTimeField	TimeField
2	2023-01-02	2023-01-02 08:00:00	08:00:00
3	2023-01-03	2023-01-02 09:00:00	09:00:00
4	2023-01-04	2023-01-03 10:00:00	10:00:00
5	2023-01-05	2023-01-04 11:00:00	11:00:00

Figure 4.49: Content of the dates/times Excel file

By way of background, the data type in Excel of `DateField` is **Short Date**, that of `DateTimeField` is **Custom** (`yyyy-mm-dd hh:mm:ss`), and that of `TimeField` is **Time**.

Let's try loading this Excel file into Power BI Desktop to see how the Python and R script steps behave with the dates/times fields:

1. Run Power BI Desktop using the batch file that activates the `pbi_visuals_env` conda environment (you should have created it for practice) to avoid the ADO.NET error, as you learned at the beginning of this chapter.

2. Make sure your Power BI Desktop is referencing the `pbi_visuals_env` conda environment you created in *Chapter 3*.

3. In the GitHub repository associated with the book, you will find the `date-time-fields.xlsx` Excel file seen before in the folder pertaining to *Chapter 4*. As you did in the previous case, load the `dates` sheet into Power BI.

4. Now you need to do some transformations, so click on **Transform data** on the ribbon to open the Power Query editor window.

5. You can see that Power BI Desktop correctly mapped the **Date** and **Date/Time** data types to **DateField** and **DateTimeField**, respectively. There is only a problem with **TimeField**, displayed in Excel as time only, but handled in Power BI Desktop always as **Date/Time**, using the minimum expected date (`1899-12-31`):

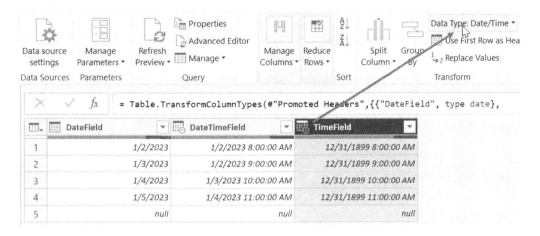

Figure 4.50: Excel Time data type mapped as Date/Time in Power BI

6. In order to have a data type representative of time as the source, select **Time** from the **Data Type** menu on the Transform ribbon for **TimeField**. You will be prompted to replace the existing conversion. Do so by clicking on **Replace current**. You will see **TimeField** in the right way now:

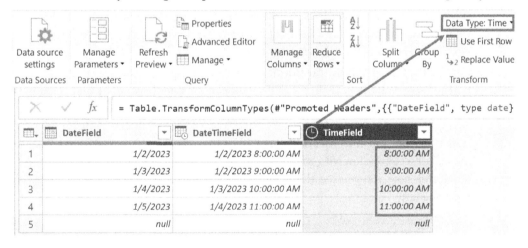

Figure 4.51: Time data correctly managed in Power BI Desktop

7. Now right-click on the **dates** query and click **Duplicate**. Then rename the new **dates query** (2) to dates-R.

8. Click on **Run R script** in the **Transform** menu, keeping the **dates-R** query selected.

9. Enter the following self-explanatory script into the R script editor to check the data types inherited by Power Query:

```
df <- dataset
```

Then click **OK**.

10. The Firewall error for incompatible privacy levels of the Excel file and R code may appear. If so, first set privacy levels of both the sources to **Public** via the **Data source settings**, as you have already seen in the previous sections. Then go to the **Home** menu and click **Refresh Preview**.

11. If prompted, expand the **df** table. You will see the following:

	A^BC DateField	A^BC DateTimeField	A^BC TimeField
1	Microsoft.OleDb.Date	2023-01-02T08:00:00.0000000	Microsoft.OleDb.Time
2	Microsoft.OleDb.Date	2023-01-02T09:00:00.0000000	Microsoft.OleDb.Time
3	Microsoft.OleDb.Date	2023-01-03T10:00:00.0000000	Microsoft.OleDb.Time
4	Microsoft.OleDb.Date	2023-01-04T11:00:00.0000000	Microsoft.OleDb.Time
5			

Figure 4.52: Direct output of date/time fields passing through an R script step

12. As you can see from the icons near the headers, all the fields are **Text.** In addition, fields with **Date** and **Time** data types are not handled properly, since the values are not even interpreted as strings, and only the name of the corresponding data type in .NET is displayed (*Microsoft. OleDb.Date* and *Microsoft.OleDb.Time*) instead of the values. In order to properly handle the values of the **Date** and **Time** fields, at least as strings, you must transform their data type to **Text** before running the R script step.

13. Click on the **Changed Type** transformation step in the **Applied Steps** related to the **dates-R** query. Then select all the fields in the table shown in the middle panel by first clicking **DateField** and then **TimeField** while holding down the **Shift** key. Change the **Data Type** of all of them to **Text** in the **Home** or Transform menu. First, you will be prompted to insert an intermediate step. Go ahead and click **Insert**. Immediately afterwards you are given the option to replace the existing conversion with the new one. Go ahead by clicking on **Add new step.** Selecting the **df** step now, you will see all the fields transformed correctly, each with an **ABC** icon next to its header:

	A^BC DateField	A^BC DateTimeField	A^BC TimeField
1	1/2/2023	1/2/2023 8:00:00 AM	8:00 AM
2	1/3/2023	1/2/2023 9:00:00 AM	9:00 AM
3	1/4/2023	1/3/2023 10:00:00 AM	10:00 AM
4	1/5/2023	1/4/2023 11:00:00 AM	11:00 AM
5	*null*	*null*	*null*

Figure 4.53: Field data types correctly transformed in Text

Now the output values look correctly interpreted by the R step, although only their string representation is shown, not the correct date/time formats. Let's see what data types these fields take on in the context of the R script.

14. Click on the **Run R script** step just before the df one, click on the gearwheel, and replace the existing code with the following:

```
df <- dataset


# Apply the class function to all columns of dataset
dataTypesVec <- sapply(df, function(c) class(c)[[1]])


# Create a dataframe having a column for field names
# and another one for their data type
data_type_df <- data.frame(Field = names(dataTypesVec), DataType =
dataTypesVec)
```

Then click **OK.**

15. This time, expand the **data_type_df** table. Click **Continue** and you will see the data type of each column in the **date-R** table when running the script:

	ᴬᴮC **Field**	ᴬᴮC **DataType**
1	DateField	character
2	DateTimeField	character
3	TimeField	character

Figure 4.54: Data types inherited by the R script step

This means that all fields are imported as if they were characters and, therefore, they are automatically transformed into the character data type (by default, the R script step does that with strings). Thus, it is necessary to transform them correctly into date/time data types using specific R functions if needed, for example, to apply functions for calculating dates by adding or subtracting days.

16. Again, go back to the **Run R script** step, click on the gearwheel, and replace the code with the following:

```
df <- dataset

Sys.setenv(TZ='GMT')
df$DateField <- as.Date(df$DateField, format = "%m/%d/%Y")
df$DateTimeField <- as.POSIXct(df$DateTimeField, format="%m/%d/%Y
%H:%M:%S")


# Apply the class function to all columns of dataset
dataTypesVec <- sapply(df, function(c) class(c)[[1]])
```

```
# Create a dataframe having a column for field names
# and another one for their data type
data_type_df <- data.frame(Field = names(dataTypesVec), DataType =
dataTypesVec)
```

Then click **OK.**

17. As you can see, there is no code for casting the Time field into a specific data type, as R doesn't have a native class for storing times. You need to use special libraries such as **hms** or **lubridate** for timing storage, but this is not the place to present them.

18. Again, expand the **data_type_df** table, click **Continue**, and you will see updated data types:

⊞	A^BC Field		A^BC DataType	
1	DateField		Date	
2	DateTimeField		POSIXct	
3	TimeField		character	

Figure 4.55: Updated data types

19. Go back to the **Run R script** step, expand the **df** table this time, and click **Continue** to see how Power BI Desktop handles the new data types returned by the R script step:

⊞	▦ DateField		🕓 DateTimeField		A^BC TimeField	
1	1/2/2023		1/2/2023 8:00:00 AM	8:00 AM	
2	1/3/2023		1/2/2023 9:00:00 AM	9:00 AM	
3	1/4/2023		1/3/2023 10:00:00 AM	10:00 AM	
4	1/5/2023		1/4/2023 11:00:00 AM	11:00 AM	
5	null		null		

Figure 4.56: Output of the R script step in Power BI

Great! Power BI correctly recognizes date/time data types returned by the R script step.

20. Let's try now with Python. First, right-click on the **dates** query and then click **Duplicate.** Rename the new **dates (2)** query **dates-Python.**

21. Click on **Run Python script** in the **Transform** menu, keeping the **dates-Python** query selected.

22. Enter the following self-explanatory script into the Python script editor to check the data types inherited by Power Query:

```
df = dataset
```

Then click **OK.**

23. The firewall error for incompatible privacy levels may appear. If so, first set the Python data source permission to **Public** via the **Data source settings**, in order to be consistent with other data sources. Then go to the **Home** menu and click **Refresh Preview**.

24. First, expand the **df** table. You will see the following:

	A^BC **DateField**		DateTimeField		A^BC **TimeField**	
1	Microsoft.OleDb.Date		1/2/2023 8:00:00 AM		Microsoft.OleDb.Time	
2	Microsoft.OleDb.Date		1/2/2023 9:00:00 AM		Microsoft.OleDb.Time	
3	Microsoft.OleDb.Date		1/3/2023 10:00:00 AM		Microsoft.OleDb.Time	
4	Microsoft.OleDb.Date		1/4/2023 11:00:00 AM		Microsoft.OleDb.Time	
5			*null*			

Figure 4.57: Direct output of date/time fields passing through a Python script step

As you can see from the icons near the headers, only the **DateTimeField** is recognized as a **DateTime** data type. Also, in this case, fields with the **Date** and **Time** data types are not handled properly, since the values are not even interpreted as strings, and only the name of the corresponding data type in .NET is displayed (*Microsoft.OleDb.Date* and *Microsoft.OleDb.Time*) instead of the values. In order to properly handle the values of the **Date** and **Time** fields at least as strings, you must transform their data type to **Text** before running the Python script step.

25. Click on the **Changed Type** transformation step in the **Applied Steps** related to the **dates-Python** query. Then select all the fields in the table shown in the middle panel by first clicking **DateField** and then **TimeField** while holding down the **Shift** key. Change the **Data Type** of all of them to **Text** in the **Home** or **Transform** menu. First, you will be prompted about inserting an intermediate step. Go ahead and click **Insert**. Immediately afterwards you are given the option to replace the existing conversion with the new one. Go ahead by clicking on **Add new step**. You will see all the fields transformed correctly, each with an **ABC** icon next to its header:

	A^BC **DateField**		A^BC **DateTimeField**		A^BC **TimeField**	
1	1/2/2023		1/2/2023 8:00:00 AM		8:00 AM	
2	1/3/2023		1/2/2023 9:00:00 AM		9:00 AM	
3	1/4/2023		1/3/2023 10:00:00 AM		10:00 AM	
4	1/5/2023		1/4/2023 11:00:00 AM		11:00 AM	
5		*null*		*null*		*null*

Figure 4.58: Field data types correctly transformed in Text

26. Now the output values look correct, although they are still strings and not date/time formats. Let's see internally, in the context of the Python script, what type of data these fields take on.

27. Click on the **Run Python script** step, click on the gearwheel, and replace the code with the following, then click **OK**:

```
df = dataset


data_type_df = df.dtypes.to_frame('dtypes').reset_index().rename(columns
= {'index':'Field', 'dtypes':'DataType'})
```

28. This time, expand the **data_type_df** table. Click **Continue** and you will see the data type of each column in the **date-Python** table when running the script:

⊞ ▾	^{AB}C **Field** ▾	^{AB}C **DataType** ▾
1	DateField	object
2	DateTimeField	object
3	TimeField	object

Figure 4.59: Data types inherited by the Python script step

29. This means that all fields are automatically transformed into the generic object (string) data type. So, you need to properly transform them into date/time data types using Python functions.

30. Again, go back to the **Run Python script** step, click on the gearwheel, and replace the code with the following, then click **OK**:

```
import pandas as pd


df = dataset


df['DateField'] = pd.to_datetime(df['DateField']).dt.date
df['DateTimeField'] = pd.to_datetime(df['DateTimeField'])
df['TimeField'] = pd.to_datetime(df['TimeField'],format='%I:%M %p').
dt.time


data_type_df = df.dtypes.to_frame('dtypes').reset_index().rename(columns
= {'index':'Field', 'dtypes':'DataType'})
```

In contrast to R, the time format is handled natively in Python via the pre-installed Datetime module, loaded indirectly in the previous script by pandas. We have set the region so that we have the 12-hour clock, so we have used the appropriate formatting as highlighted in the code. If you need different formatting for your region, you can refer to the handy table of format codes here: https://strftime.org/.

31. Again, expand the **data_type_df** table, click **Continue**, and you will see the updated data types:

	ᴬᴮс Field	ᴬᴮс DataType
1	DateField	object
2	DateTimeField	datetime64[ns]
3	TimeField	object

Figure 4.60: Updated data types

32. Go back to the **Run Python script** step, expand the **df** table, and this time click **Continue** to see how Power BI Desktop handles the new data types returned by the Python script step:

	DateField	DateTimeField	TimeField
1	1/2/2023	1/2/2023 8:00:00 AM	8:00:00 AM
2	1/3/2023	1/2/2023 9:00:00 AM	9:00:00 AM
3	1/4/2023	1/3/2023 10:00:00 AM	10:00:00 AM
4	1/5/2023	1/4/2023 11:00:00 AM	11:00:00 AM
5	null	null	null

Figure 4.61: Output of the R script step in Power BI

Amazing! Power BI correctly recognizes all the date/time data types returned by the Python script step.

33. Click **Close & Apply**.

Well done! Thanks to this section, you will also be able to handle any tables containing dates and times in a Python or R script step in the most appropriate way.

Summary

In this chapter, you covered some of the types of issues that are common when integrating Python or R scripts into Power BI.

In particular, you learned how to avoid the indecipherable ADO.NET error that can occur when you use Power BI with a conda environment that is not properly enabled. You learned about the different levels of privacy that are managed in Power BI and how to resolve incompatibility issues between them that are caused by the Formula Firewall. You also learned new techniques for referencing more than one dataset in a Python or R script, even though the step stack in which the script is inserted references only one dataset. Finally, you learned how to properly handle data types for date and time fields in step scripts in Python and R.

In the next chapter, you'll start working with Python and R scripts in Power BI to perform data ingestion and import data sources that Power BI doesn't handle by default.

Test your knowledge

1. Why does Power BI Desktop sometimes raise the ADO.NET error referring to the inability to import the NumPy library, even though the package is correctly installed in the conda environment referenced in the Options?

2. What's the goal of the Data Privacy Firewall, aka the Firewall?

3. List the two types of errors that the Firewall can raise and describe their characteristics.

4. Suppose you need an on-premises data gateway in enterprise mode to allow some datasets to be refreshed after publishing your report to the Power BI service. Will the published datasets have privacy levels aligned with those set on Power BI Desktop?

5. Suppose you have a query that directly accesses a data source and involves a Python script step. The query has a privacy level set to Organizational, whereas the Python script has the privacy level set to Public. Does the firewall raise errors? If yes, which ones?

6. What are the pros and cons of the two methods of resolving the indirect access error to a data source (combination of transformations vs. encapsulation in functions)?

7. Does the method of applying a full join between two queries in order to be passed into a Python or R script step necessarily require at least one field in common that can be joined between the two resulting tables?

8. Should the list of tables passed by parameter to `Python.Execute` or `R.Execute` functions include the renamed "dataset" table obtained from the transformations prior to the step that calls it?

9. Why is it necessary to transform any Date, Date/Time, or Time type fields into Text format before adding a Python or R script step?

10. If you don't have the ability to install new packages and you have to work with the Time data type within a script step, is it better to use a Python script step or an R script step?

Learn more on Discord

To join the Discord community for this book – where you can share feedback, ask questions to the author, and learn about new releases – follow the QR code below:

`https://discord.gg/MKww5g45EB`

5

Importing Unhandled Data Objects

In this chapter, you'll look at using R and Python in what is typically the first phase of report creation: **data ingestion**. Power BI is a very powerful tool from this point of view because it has many connectors to various data sources out of the box. In addition to being able to import data directly by connecting to data sources, you can easily solve more complex data-loading scenarios with Power BI. For example, you can merge multiple CSV files or multiple Excel workbook sheets dynamically directly from Power BI, even using the **M language** to apply special logic to the merge step. You can also scrape any web page by just clicking on the web page contents without using any code. All this is possible thanks to Power BI's standard features, without having to use R or Python.

There are, however, cases in which the data to be imported and used in Power BI comes from **processing done on external systems**, which persists data in formats that are not directly managed by Power BI. Imagine being a Power BI report developer and having to interface with a team of data scientists. Some complex processing done by them on fairly large datasets might require non-trivial runtimes. That's why data scientists often **serialize the result** of such processing in files of an acceptable size, so they can deserialize them very quickly if needed. Now, suppose the data scientist team provides you with one of these files serialized in R or Python and asks you to use it for some calculations needed to create a visual in your report. How would you do it?

In this chapter, you will see how to work with serialized files from R (.rds) and Python (.pkl) in Power BI. The following topics will be discussed in this chapter:

- Importing RDS files in R
- Importing PKL files in Python

Technical requirements

This chapter requires you to have a working internet connection and **Power BI Desktop** already installed on your machine (we used version 2.112.603.0 64-bit, December 2022). RStudio was updated to version 2022.12.0 build 353. You must have properly configured the R and Python engines and IDEs, as outlined in *Chapter 2, Configuring R with Power BI*, and *Chapter 3, Configuring Python with Power BI*.

Importing RDS files in R

In this section, you will develop mainly R code. We will provide you with various examples to demonstrate the concepts. First, we will give you an overview of what we are going to do, outlining the steps involved. Then, we will proceed to walk you through the process, explaining each step in detail. If you have little experience with R, you should familiarize yourself with the data structures that R provides by starting with this quickstart: `http://bit.ly/r-data-struct-quickstart`. Take a look at the *References* section for more in-depth information.

A brief introduction to Tidyverse

A data scientist using R as an analytical language for data analysis and data science must know the set of packages that goes by the name of **Tidyverse** (`https://www.tidyverse.org`). It provides everything needed for data wrangling and data visualization, giving the analyst a consistent approach to the entire ecosystem of packages it provides. This way, it tries to heal the initial "chaos" situation, where R functionalities are provided by packages developed by developers who had not agreed on a common framework.

> **IMPORTANT NOTE**
>
> If you are new to **Tidyverse**, you might want to start with this quickstart by Software Carpentry to get familiar with the main concepts: `http://bit.ly/tidy-quickstart`. The *References* section also contains links to in-depth information about Tidyverse.

The fundamental data type to know about in Tidyverse to be able to work with tabular data is the **tibble**. Tibbles (the New Zealand pronunciation of "tables") are a modern version of R **dataframes**. Starting from a tibble, you can perform all the data transformations you want with simple functions provided by the Tidyverse packages.

Today, you will often find the use of the `%>%` **pipe** (the R language allows symbols wrapped in % to be defined as functions, and the > implies a chaining) in data analyses performed in the Tidyverse world. Borrowed from the **magrittr** package included in Tidyverse, the pipe has the function of forwarding the object on its left inside the function on its right as the first parameter. In short, if you need to select the `my_col` column from a `my_tbl` tibble, instead of using `select( my_tbl, my_col )`, you can use the piped form, `my_tbl %>% select( my_col )`, making the code much more readable.

IMPORTANT NOTE

R Core introduced a native graphical form of the pipe, which is |>, starting from CRAN R 4.1. However, this pipe cannot be a dry substitute for the **magrittr** pipe; it works slightly differently. That is why you still find it very infrequently in the code. If you are curious to understand how different the native pipe is, please check out the following article: `https://bit.ly/native-r-pipe`.

For the purpose of understanding the code used in this section, we will describe it piece by piece, explaining the functionality of each R object used.

Creating a serialized R object

Now, imagine for a moment that you are part of the data scientist team that has to do the complex processing of a dataset and then serialize the result obtained in a file to be reused as needed. The first thing to do is to configure the environment to install the latest version of Tidyverse.

Configuring the environment and installing Tidyverse

In this section, we will show you how to work with an RStudio project and install all the packages provided by the Tidyverse ecosystem. Open RStudio and proceed as shown here:

1. Make sure the most recent R engine (4.2.2 in our case) is selected (**Tools** and **Global Options...**).
2. Create a new project by clicking on the **Project** icon in the upper-right corner and then **New Project...**:

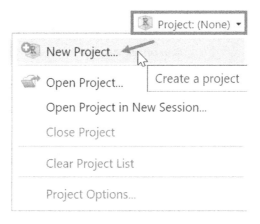

Figure 5.1: Creating a new RStudio project

An RStudio project makes it straightforward to divide your work into multiple contexts, each with its own working directory, workspace, history, and source documents.

3. Click on **New Directory** and then on **New Project:**

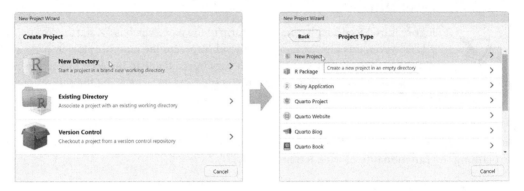

Figure 5.2: Selecting New Directory and New Project

4. Now, enter a name for the project folder, choose in which folder you want to place it, and click **Create Project:**

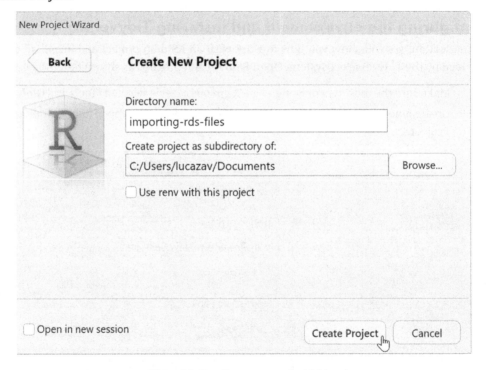

Figure 5.3: Creating a new project folder

You can also find this project ready for you in the GitHub repository in the `importing-rds-files` subfolder of the `Chapter 5` folder.

RStudio will restart the R session, and the project folder you have just created will become the working directory of your project.

5. Now, let's install all Tidyverse packages by simply running the following command on the console: `install.packages("tidyverse")` (it's equivalent to installing it through the GUI, by clicking on the **Packages** tab at the bottom right and then on **Install**).

Awesome! You have just installed the latest version of Tidyverse. Now, let's see how to serialize an R object into an RDS file that can be used in Power BI.

Creating the RDS files

We will now walk you through creating the serialization of an R object in an RDS file. Suppose that the computation time required to create this object is very high (tens of hours), and therefore, it is not convenient to perform the computation each time to obtain the object, but it *is* convenient to serialize the object on the file system. An object will also be created that is not a simple tibble and, therefore, cannot be easily exported to CSV for later import into Power BI. Let's start:

1. Open a new R script in your project by pressing *Ctrl + Shift + N* (or by clicking the + **New File** icon and then **R Script**).

2. Now, you will load in memory both the Tidyverse packages (using the `library` command) and the *growth population* tibble contained in the **tidyr** package (using the `data` command), consisting of a subset of data taken from the *World Health Organization Global Tuberculosis Report*:

```r
library(tidyverse)
data("population")
# Let's have a look at the tibble
population
```

The latest command (which matches the name of the tibble) allows you to observe the contents of the first few lines of the tibble and its columns' data types. Highlight all the commands and press *Ctrl + Enter* (or click on the **Run** icon at the top-right of the panel) to run them.

It is possible, in some cases, that the following warning will be displayed just after the execution of the command that loads all the Tidyverse packages:

```
Warning message:
In Sys.timezone() : unable to identify current timezone 'C':
please set environment variable 'TZ'
```

Figure 5.4: Timezone warning

The timezone is required for some loaded Tidyverse packages, and in this case, your machine does not have a default timezone set. To fix this issue, in RStudio, you can customize the settings for each R session by creating or editing the `.Rprofile` file at the user level. To do this, proceed as follows:

1. Enter the `usethis::`**edit_r_profile**`()` command in the console to open the `.Rprofile` file in RStudio. A new tab named `.Rprofile` will open.

2. Identify the timezone you want to set on your machine. In our case, we will use **Coordinated Universal Time** (UTC). Then, enter the `Sys.setenv(TZ='UTC')` command into the new tab to set the environment variable `TZ` to `UTC` for each new R session, and press *Ctrl + S* to save its content in the `.Rprofile` file. You will see the file saved in your `Documents` folder.

This way, the next time you start a new R session, you will no longer get the warning.

You will see the following result:

```
> data("population")
>
> # Let's have a look at the tibble
> population
# A tibble: 4,060 × 3
   country       year population
   <chr>        <dbl>      <dbl>
 1 Afghanistan   1995   17586073
 2 Afghanistan   1996   18415307
 3 Afghanistan   1997   19021226
 4 Afghanistan   1998   19496836
 5 Afghanistan   1999   19987071
 6 Afghanistan   2000   20595360
 7 Afghanistan   2001   21347782
 8 Afghanistan   2002   22202806
 9 Afghanistan   2003   23116142
10 Afghanistan   2004   24018682
# … with 4,050 more rows
# i Use `print(n = ...)` to see more rows
```

Figure 5.5: Loading the "population" tibble

Everything that follows # is a comment.

3. Now, let's check how many distinct countries there are in the tibble. You'll use the `distinct` function and then the `pull` one to extract the single column of distinct countries from the tibble in the vector format:

```
population %>%
  distinct(country) %>%
  pull()
```

You'll see a long list of all the distinct countries, like this one:

```
> population %>%
+    distinct(country) %>%
+    pull()
  [1] "Afghanistan"
  [2] "Albania"
  [3] "Algeria"
  [4] "American Samoa"
  [5] "Andorra"
```

```
[214]  Viet Nam
[215] "Wallis and Futuna Islands"
[216] "West Bank and Gaza Strip"
[217] "Yemen"
[218] "Zambia"
[219] "Zimbabwe"
>
```

Figure 5.6: List of distinct countries

4. Now, we want to group the year and population information into separate tibbles for each country. In short, we want to have a tibble that contains the countries and, for each of them, another tibble with the demographic information by year. You can do that using the nest function:

```
nested_population_tbl <- population %>%
  tidyr::nest( demographic_data = -country )
nested_population_tbl
```

You have just assigned the `nested_population_tbl` variable the new tibble containing the nested demographic data. Observe that we made the `nest` function call explicit by calling it from its `tidyr` source package, using `::`. Also, observe how easy it is to "nest" everything except the `country` column (note the minus sign) into a list of tibbles contained in the new `demographic_data` column.

By highlighting and running the previous chunk of code, you'll see the following result:

```
> nested_population_tbl <- population %>%
+   tidyr::nest( demographic_data = -country )
> nested_population_tbl
# A tibble: 219 × 2
   country                 demographic_data
   <chr>                   <list>
 1 Afghanistan             <tibble [19 × 2]>
 2 Albania                 <tibble [19 × 2]>
 3 Algeria                 <tibble [19 × 2]>
 4 American Samoa          <tibble [19 × 2]>
 5 Andorra                 <tibble [19 × 2]>
 6 Angola                  <tibble [19 × 2]>
 7 Anguilla                <tibble [19 × 2]>
 8 Antigua and Barbuda     <tibble [19 × 2]>
 9 Argentina               <tibble [19 × 2]>
10 Armenia                 <tibble [19 × 2]>
# ... with 209 more rows
```

Figure 5.7: Tibble of nested demographic data

Note that the new demographic_data column is a list of tibbles.

5. Now, you can finally serialize the nested_population_tbl object into an RDS file using the saveRDS function:

```
saveRDS(nested_population_tbl, "nested_population_tbl.rds")
```

You can find the R code shown here in the GitHub repository associated with the book in the Ch05 - Importing Unhandled Data Objects\importing-rds-files\01-create-object-to-serialize.R file.

To properly execute the code in the following section, you must open the R project found in the GitHub repository. To do that, follow these steps:

1. Close the current project created at the beginning of this section by clicking on the project name at the top-right of RStudio, and then clicking on **Close Project**:

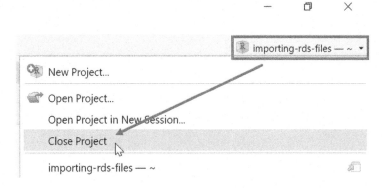

Figure 5.8: Closing the current R project

2. After that, open the project file with the same name as the closed one via the Ch05 - Importing Unhandled Data Objects\importing-rds-files\importing-rds-files.Rproj file. Then, you can open the previously mentioned R script using the **Files** tab in the bottom-right panel of RStudio and execute it.

Awesome! You can verify that a file has been serialized correctly by taking a look at the same panel:

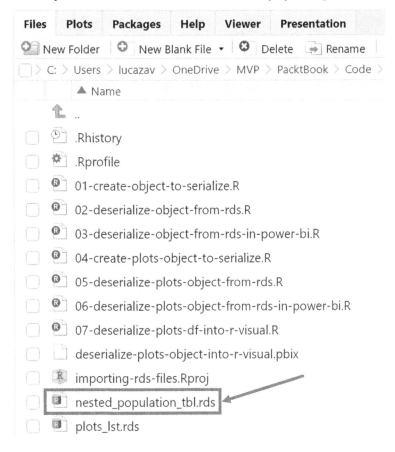

Figure 5.9: The RDS file correctly created

In the same way, you'll create an RDS object that contains time series views for four selected countries. The time series data is the same as the population growth data you saw earlier. Let's see how you can generate this file:

1. Install the fantastic timetk package by Matt Dancho by entering the install.packages("timetk") command into the RStudio console. It makes it easy to visualize, wrangle, and feature engineer time series data for forecasting and machine learning predictions. For more details, see the tutorials in the *Getting Started* links here: https://business-science.github.io/timetk/#getting-started. The installation may require compiling the package for your specific installed version of R. Click **Yes** on the popup if it appears.

2. Open the `Ch05 - Importing Unhandled Data Objects\importing-rds-files\04-create-plots-object-to-serialize.R` file by clicking on its filename in the RStudio **Files** panel. The first part of the file contains code already seen in the previous section and is used to generate the nested tibble `nested_population_tbl` for the population. Run it again.

3. Immediately after creating the nested tibble `nested_population_tbl`, you'll see how to plot the time series data related to Sweden. Every single R function used is explained in the code:

```r
selected_country <- "Sweden"
nested_population_tbl %>%
  # Get the row related to the selected country
  filter( country == selected_country ) %>%
  # Get the content of 'demografic_data' for
  # that row. Note that it is a list
  pull( demographic_data ) %>%
  # Extract the 'demografic_data' tibble from
  # the list (it has only 1 element)
  pluck(1) %>%
  # Now plot the time series declaring the date variable
  # and the value one.
  timetk::plot_time_series(
    .date_var = year,
    .value = population,
    .title = paste0("Global population of ", selected_country),
    .smooth = FALSE,      # --> remove the smooth line
    .interactive = FALSE # --> generate a static plot
  ) +
  # Thousand separators
  scale_y_continuous(
    labels=function(x) format(x, big.mark = ".",
                              scientific = FALSE))
```

Here is the result:

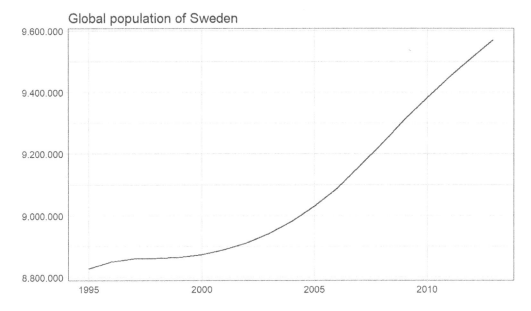

Figure 5.10: Population growth time series plot for Sweden

4. You will now create a time series graph for each country in the nested tibble following the previous example. The great thing is that thanks to the power of **functional programming** provided by the **map functions** of the purrr package, you can do this in one go using only one function. As always, you'll find detailed explanations in the code:

```
nested_population_plots_tbl <- nested_population_tbl %>%
  # Select a subset of countries
  filter( country %in% c("Italy", "Sweden", "France", "Germany") ) %>%
  # Add a new column called 'plot' applying the plot_time_series
  # function to the values of the demographic_data tibble (.x)
  # for each country (.y) in the 'country' field.
  # Do this thanks to the map2 function.
  mutate(
    plot = map2( demographic_data, country, ~ timetk::plot_time_series(
      .data = .x,
      .date_var = year,
```

```
      .value = population,
      .title = paste0("Global population of ", .y),
      .smooth = FALSE,
      .interactive = FALSE) +
        scale_y_continuous(
          labels=function(x) format(x, big.mark = ".",
                                    scientific = FALSE))
      )
  ) %>%
  # Return just the 'country' and 'plot' columns.
  select( country, plot )
```

5. After that, only the plots list extracted by the `nested_population_plots_tbl` tibble is serialized in an RDS file:

```
# Now extract the named list of plots for each country from the nested
tibble.
plots_lst <- nested_population_plots_tbl %>%
    # converts two-column data frames to a named list, using
    # the first column as name and the second column as value
    deframe()
# Serialize the list of plots
saveRDS(plots_lst, "plots_lst.rds")
```

Well done! You've serialized your R objects into RDS files.

You are now ready to use the nested tibble serialized in a file directly in Power BI.

Using an RDS file in Power BI

It's clear that an RDS file must be used via R scripts in Power BI. As you may have learned by now, there are two Power BI objects through which you can use R scripts: the **Power Query Editor** and **R visuals**. Let's start with the simplest case, which is to import the RDS file into the Power Query Editor.

Importing an RDS file into the Power Query Editor

You'll import a serialized R object into the Power Query Editor when you know *you can extract tabular information from the object* and want to persist it in the Power BI data model. Let's see how it's done:

1. If it is not already, open the R project you used in the previous section, and then open the `02-deserialize-object-from-rds.R` file.

2. Load the RDS file via the `readRDS` function and assign it to the new `deserialized_tbl` variable, like so:

```
library(tidyverse)
deserialized_tbl <- readRDS("nested_population_tbl.RDS")
```

Since we are in an R project and running the code in RStudio, it is sufficient to pass as a parameter to the readRDS function just the filename to read the file that is in the same folder as the project file.

3. Now, try extracting the demographics of Sweden from the nested tibble, as follows:

```
sweden_population_tbl <- deserialized_tbl %>%
  filter( country == "Sweden" ) %>%
  pull( demographic_data ) %>%
  pluck(1)
sweden_population_tbl
```

In this piece of code, we assign to the sweden_population_tbl variable the content of the deserialized_tbl variable, to which we apply the following transformations:

a. We filter it for the country Sweden through the filter function (thus obtaining the row associated with the country Sweden).

b. From this row, we detach the content of the demographic_data field from the original tibble using the pull function (you'll get a list).

c. Since the content of the demographic_data column is a list containing only one tibble, the content must be unlisted using the pluck function. The result is the Sweden demographic data organized in one tibble, as shown in *Figure 5.11*:

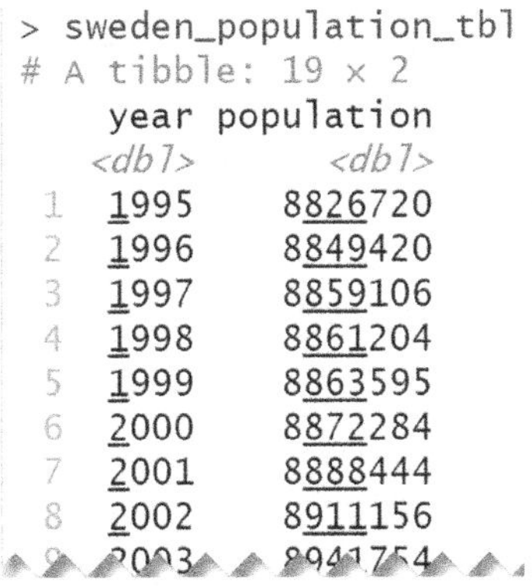

```
> sweden_population_tbl
# A tibble: 19 × 2
    year population
   <dbl>      <dbl>
 1  1995    8826720
 2  1996    8849420
 3  1997    8859106
 4  1998    8861204
 5  1999    8863595
 6  2000    8872284
 7  2001    8888444
 8  2002    8911156
 9  2003    8941754
```

Figure 5.11: The content of the Sweden demographic data organized in a tibble

4. Let's try to execute the same code in Power BI Desktop, so open it and make sure it references the most recent CRAN R engine (version 4.2.2 in our case). Click on **Get data** and then **More....** Start typing script into the search textbox, and double-click on R script. The R script editor will pop up.

5. Keep in mind that Power BI Desktop doesn't have the concept of "projects" that RStudio does and, therefore, needs an absolute path to locate the file correctly. So you need something like this:

```
project_folder <- "C:/<your>/<absolute>/<project_folder>/<path>"
deserialized_tbl <- readRDS( file.path(project_folder, "nested_
population_tbl.RDS") )
```

Note that, in R, you can use either the **escaped backslash** (\\) or the simple slash (/) as a separator in path strings. You will find the full code using the absolute path in the `03-deserialize-object-from-rds-in-power-bi.R` file. Copy and paste its content into the R script editor, changing the absolute path accordingly, and then click on **OK**.

6. The **Navigator** window will open, giving you the option to select which dataframe to import:

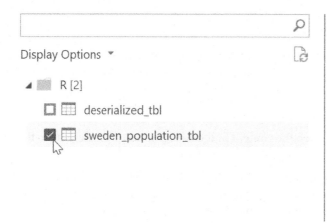

Figure 5.12: Import the deserialized dataframe into Power BI

You will see as many dataframes (remember that tibbles are specializations of dataframes) as you have defined within your script. Select the `sweden_population_tbl` dataframe and click **Load**.

7. When loading is finished, click on the table icon on the left menu of Power BI Desktop to verify that the data has been imported correctly in tabular form:

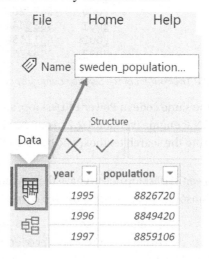

Figure 5.13: The dataframe is correctly imported

Great! You have correctly imported your RDS file into Power BI to use its contents with Power Query in the most appropriate way.

IMPORTANT NOTE

As you may have noticed, the only R data structure that Power BI can work with is a dataframe (or data table) with columns that have standard data types. It isn't possible to import any other type of R objects. If you had imported the `deserialized_tbl` dataframe directly, the values in the `demographic_data` column would have generated an error and would have been unavailable.

Sometimes, it may happen that you can't deserialize an RDS file in the Power Query Editor and extract its information in a tabular format to persist it in the Power BI data model. You may need to deserialize the content of an RDS file on the fly in an R visual to use its information in a visualization. You'll see how to solve this scenario in the next section.

Importing an RDS file in an R script visual

Now, let's assume that you have received the RDS file that contains the time series charts for each country from the team of data scientists. Your goal is to allow the report user to view the charts by selecting a country.

The problem you are facing is as follows. Reading from files is often time-consuming. Having to deserialize an object in Power BI Desktop from the file system every time you select from a slicer in Power BI will definitely make the report unresponsive.

IMPORTANT NOTE

Note that once the report is published to the Power BI service, the R engine is hosted and access to the file system of the hosted environment is restricted. Therefore, if a report loads a file into a script visual, that file will no longer be accessible through the Data Gateway once the report is published.

For the above reasons, it is convenient to deserialize the object once in Power Query and reuse it multiple times. But there is a problem. You know that to import any information from the Power Query Editor through the R script, it must be in a tabular format and use standard data types. The charts made available by data scientists are grouped in a list of objects in the *ggplot* format (**ggplot** offers a powerful graphics language for creating elegant and complex plots in R), which is not a standard data type. So how do you import them into Power BI? You'll need a little bit of *lateral thinking*.

IMPORTANT NOTE

As you probably already know, it is possible to serialize any programming object in its **byte representation** (the raw vector in R). The byte representation can in turn be transformed into its **string representation**. Once you have strings (a standard data type), you can organize them into a dataframe. After that's done, you can import that dataframe into Power BI.

When working with an R visual and needing to "feed" it with data, it is important to keep the following points in mind. If you choose multiple columns from different tables within the Power BI data model (with a relationship between them) as the values for an R visual, these values will be combined into a single deduplicated dataframe. This resulting dataframe will then be referenced in the R script of the visual.

In some cases, you may want to not delete duplicate rows. In that case, you can add an index field to your dataset (row number) that causes all rows to be considered unique and prevents grouping.

It wouldn't make sense to import a dataframe containing a string representation of something in the Power Query Editor if you couldn't transform it back to the original object. Fortunately, the previously mentioned direct transformation operations are all reversible, so you can use the inverse transformations within an R visual to extract and display plots appropriately. Also part of this process is a limitation of the data handled in R visuals that appear to be undocumented:

IMPORTANT NOTE

If a string is longer than 32,766 characters, once it is passed into the default dataframe to be referenced within an R visual, it is truncated. To avoid truncation, it is necessary to split the string into smaller chunks (we chose an arbitrary length of 10,000) and persist those chunks in a dataframe column before using the data in the R visual.

That said, in summary, what you will be doing in this section is as follows:

1. Import the RDS file containing the named list of plots into the **Power Query Editor**. From it, extract a dataframe of country names and a dataframe containing the plots information.
2. Use the countries dataframe in a slicer with a single choice.
3. Each time a country is selected from the slicer, the **R visual** will display the plot of the time series for the population growth of that country.

Let's summarize all the processes of wrangling the plots data in a figure that contains the functions you will find in the code:

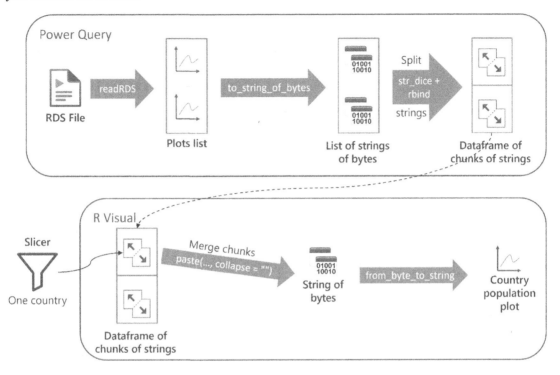

Figure 5.14: Deserialize the RDS file content into an R visual

In case you were wondering, it would not be possible to directly import the single dataframe containing the country names and corresponding graphs because the ggplot data type is not a native R data type, so the R engine would return the ENVSXP error.

In the following steps, we will not explain in detail all the functions used, simply because we will refer to the code shared in the GitHub repository associated with this book, in which every single detail is commented. So let's start:

1. Open Power BI Desktop and go to **Get data**, then **More…**, and then **R Script** to import the RDL files.

2. Open the 06-deserialize-plots-object-from-rds-in-power-bi.R file from the GitHub repository, copy the content, changing the absolute path to the RDL file accordingly, paste it into the R script editor, and click **OK**.

3. Power Query will detect three dataframes created in your script. Select only the `plots_df` dataframe (the one containing the string representation of bytes of plots) and the `selected_countries_df` one. Then, click **Load**:

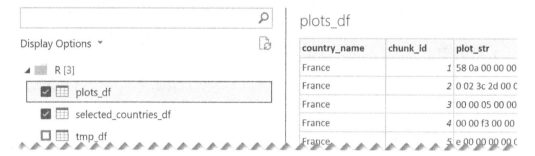

Figure 5.15: Select the two dataframes containing useful data

4. Click on the **Data** icon on the left ribbon, and then click on the **Manage relationships** button:

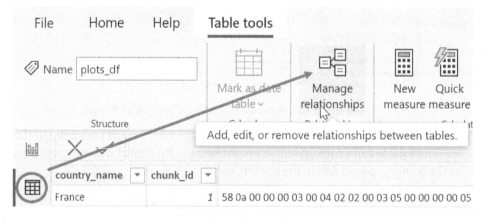

Figure 5.16: The Manage relationships button

5. The engine has automatically created the relationship between the two imported tables, using columns with the same name (`country_name`):

Manage relationships

Figure 5.17: Relationship between tables automatically detected

Click **Close**.

6. Go back to the report canvas by clicking on the **Report** icon on the left ribbon:

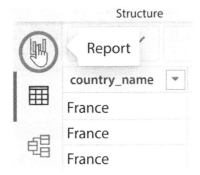

Figure 5.18: The Report icon

7. Now, click on the **Slicer** icon:

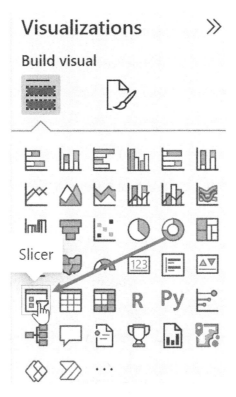

Figure 5.19: The Slicer icon

8. Keeping the **Slicer** visual region selected on the canvas, expand the `selected_countries_df` table in the **Fields** panel, and then select the `country_name` field:

Figure 5.20: Selecting the country_name column for the Slicer visual

9. Then, click the **Format** icon of the **Slicer** and enable the **Single select** option:

Figure 5.21: Allowing only the single selection

It is very important to set **Single select**, because the logic inside the R visual will manage the deserialization of a single plot.

10. Now, the **Slicer** visual will show all the countries contained in `selected_countries_tbl`:

Figure 5.22: This is what the Slicer visual looks like

11. Click on the report canvas in order to deselect the **Slicer** visual, and then click on the **R script visual** icon:

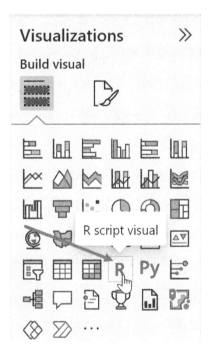

Figure 5.23: The R script visual icon

The usual **Enable script visuals** window pops up. Click on **Enable**.

12. Move and stretch the R visual borders in order to cover almost all the report canvas. Keeping it selected, expand the `plots_df` table in the **Fields** panel and select the `chunk_id`, `country_name`, and `plot_str` fields:

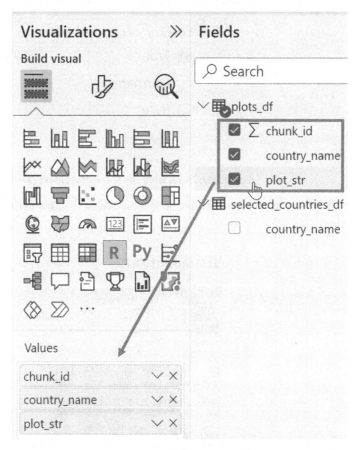

Figure 5.24: Selecting the fields to use in the R script visual

Feel free to turn the R script visual title off in the **Format** tab.

13. Open the `07-deserialize-plots-df-into-r-visual.R` file from the GitHub repository, copy the content, and paste it into the R visual's script editor. Then, click on the **Run** icon at the top-right of the R script editor.

14. Now, you can click on each country in the Slicer to see its population time series:

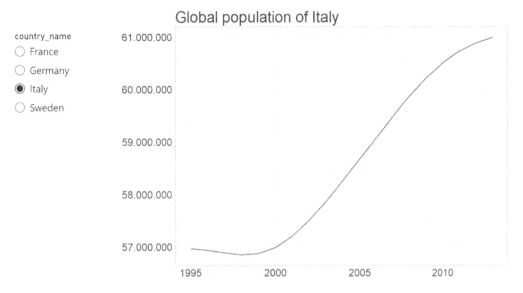

Figure 5.25: Showing the population growth for Italy

Outstanding! You have just created a report using an unusual technique that you may have only seen in this book!

IMPORTANT NOTE

This technique can be very useful when you need to build complex visualizations in R that require the use of packages not provided by the R visual in Power BI, and which need only the ggplot package to be simply displayed (not implemented). These visualizations can be made "offline," serialized to a file, and then used on a shared report on the service.

You've just seen how to import an RDS file despite not being able to do so out of the box in Power BI, and how you can then use it directly within an R script visual.

In the next section, you'll see how you can do the same thing for files serialized with Python.

Importing PKL files in Python

Let's give you an overview of what you're going to implement using the Python code on GitHub. If you are not familiar with Python, you should familiarize yourself with the basic structures through this tutorial: `http://bit.ly/py-data-struct-quickstart`. For a more detailed study of how to implement algorithms and data structures in Python, we suggest this free e-book: `https://runestone.academy/ ns/books/published/pythonds/index.html`.

A very short introduction to the PyData world

The **PyData** world is made up of users and developers who are passionate about data analytics and love to use open-source data tools. The PyData community also loves to share best practices, new approaches, and emerging technologies for managing, processing, analyzing, and visualizing data. The most important and popular packages used by the Python data management community are as follows:

- **NumPy**: This is the main library for scientific computing in Python. It provides a high-performance multidimensional array object and tools for working with data.

- **SciPy**: A library for scientific computing using NumPy. SciPy stands for *Scientific Python*. It provides multiple utility functions for optimization, statistics, and signal processing.

- **pandas**: The *Python Data Analysis Library* (pandas comes from *panel data*) is built upon NumPy and takes data in a tabular format (such as a CSV file, TSV file, or SQL database table), in order to create a Python object with rows and columns called a **DataFrame**. This object is very similar to a table in statistical software, and people familiar with R conceptually equate the pandas DataFrame with R's dataframe data type.

- **Matplotlib**: This is a Python package used to produce plots. It began as a project in the early 2000s to use Python to visualize electronic signals in the brains of patients with epilepsy. The creator of Matplotlib was a neurobiologist and was looking for a way to replicate MATLAB's graphing capabilities with Python.

- **Scikit-learn**: Also known as **sklearn**, this derives its name from a shortcut of *SciPy Toolkit*. It is a free and robust machine learning library for Python, designed to interact with NumPy, SciPy, pandas, and Matplotlib, among others.

Going into detail about what is possible using these libraries is not the purpose of this book.

IMPORTANT NOTE

If you want to start learning how to work with data in Python by taking advantage of these libraries, we recommend starting with this free book: `http://bit.ly/data-science-py-ebook`. After that, for further study, you can't miss the opportunity to study this fantastic book: *Python Machine Learning: Machine Learning and Deep Learning with Python, scikit-learn, and TensorFlow 2*, Third Edition, by Sebastian Raschka, also from Packt Publishing.

In order to summarily understand the code used in this section, we will try to describe its functionality piece by piece, referring you to the comments in the code on GitHub for more details.

Creating a serialized Python object

As we did in the previous section, imagine that you are part of another team of data scientists that needs to do some complex, time-consuming data analysis with Python. Needing to reuse the results obtained in other processes, the team decides to use a **Pickle file (PKL)**. It is obtained by serializing and then writing to a file any Python object, using the **pickle** library. As you have already seen in the previous section, serializing means converting an object in memory into a stream of bytes that can be either saved to disk or sent over a network. Obviously, this is an easily reversible operation. In fact, there is the possibility to deserialize a serialized object.

So let's start to install what we need in our environment and initialize the IDE appropriately.

Configuring the environment and installing the PyData packages

Open your **Anaconda Prompt** (from the **Start** menu) and proceed as follows:

1. Make sure to use the pbi_powerquery_env environment, entering this code:

   ```
   conda activate pbi_powerquery_env
   ```

   Now, you will install some missing packages that are necessary to be able to use the code in this section.

2. Enter the following command to install matplotlib: pip install matplotlib

Great! Your Python environment is now ready to run your scripts. Now, open Visual Studio Code and proceed as shown:

1. Go to **File** and then **Open Folder….** Make sure to choose the importing-pkl-files folder contained in the GitHub repository you previously unzipped, under the Chapter 05 folder. Click **Select Folder.**
2. Open the 01-create-object-to-serialize-in-pkl.py file, clicking on it in the Explorer on the left, under the selected folder.
3. Remember that you have to choose the environment in which to run your script. So, press *Ctrl + Shift + P* to open the Visual Studio Code palette, and start entering the text interpreter. Then, select **Python: Select Interpreter**, and then choose the pbi_powerquery_env environment.

Excellent! Now, you are ready to serialize your first Python object.

Creating the PKL files

Two of the most commonly used data structures in Python are **lists** and **dictionaries**. While by now you're familiar with lists, which you've seen before in R, if you've never developed in a programming language, perhaps dictionaries sound new to you. Dictionaries are data structures that consist of a collection of **key-value pairs**. You can define them using curly braces ({…}). Specifically, in this section, you will create a dictionary with key-value pairs, consisting of the country name and a dataframe containing data about the growth of the country's population.

The data you will use is the same data you used in the previous section. This time, instead of loading it from a package in memory, you'll do it directly from a CSV file. Let's go:

1. Since the `01-create-object-to-serialize-in-pkl.py` file is already open in Visual Studio Code, just run the code via the arrow icon in the upper-right corner (**Run Python File**). This way, the whole script will be executed (depending on how you open the file in Visual Studio Code, you may need to change the main path).

2. You won't see anything particular in the console, just the **Terminal** tab that runs `python.exe` with the current script path as a parameter. But if you look in the Explorer on the left, you will see that the `nested_population_dict.pkl` file has been created correctly:

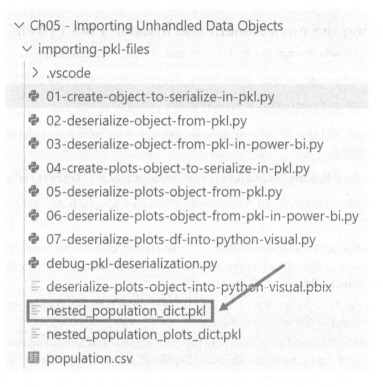

Figure 5.26: Your first PKL file has been created

3. Just like in RStudio, you can only run pieces of code by highlighting them and pressing *Ctrl + Enter* in R, or *Shift + Enter* in Python. You need to change a **settings** option to allow the use of the **interactive window** with Python. Go to **Settings**, pressing *Ctrl + ,* (comma), then start entering `Send Selection To Interactive Window` in the search bar, and check the selected option:

Jupyter: Send Selection To Interactive Window
☑ When pressing shift+enter, send selected code in a Python file to the Jupyter interactive window as opposed to the Python terminal.

Figure 5.27: Enabling the execution of Python code chunks in the Jupyter interactive window

4. Now, you have to install the IPython kernel (ipykernel) in your pbi_powerquery_env environment. Usually, this operation is done automatically by Visual Studio Code, but sometimes, you can run into errors. So, it's better to do it manually. Open your Anaconda Prompt (referencing the base environment) and enter the following command: conda init. And then, enter the conda install --name pbi_powerquery_env ipykernel -y command.

5. Now, select the code from the beginning (import pandas as pd) to the line where countries is defined (countries = population_df.country.unique()), and then press *Shift* + *Enter*. Your chunk of code will be sent to the interactive window:

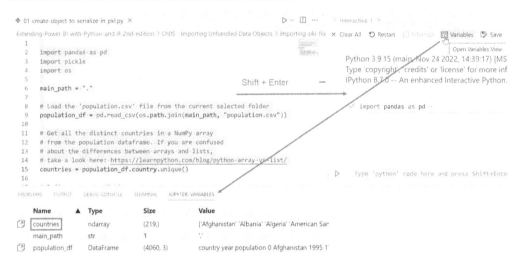

Figure 5.28: Running selected chunks of script in Visual Studio Code

By clicking on the **Variables** icon in the interactive window, as shown in *Figure 5.28*, you can also inspect the content of each variable created during the execution of the chunk code.

Hey, maybe you didn't notice, but with minimal effort, you have just created your first PKL file! You can train yourself to deserialize the newly created PKL file by running the code in the 02-deserialize-object-from-pkl.py file.

Now, we will guide you in creating a second PKL file that contains a serialized dictionary, with pairs composed of the country and the respective time series on population growth. This time, however, you will keep only four countries in the dictionary for simplicity. Let's proceed:

1. Open the 04-create-plots-object-to-serialize-in-pkl.py file from the explorer on the left.

2. You can run the code a piece at a time to better understand how it works. First, run the chunk from the first row to row 25 (nested_population_dict[c] = selected_population_df.loc[…])

3. About halfway through the script, you will find the following code:

```
# Let's try to plot the time series for Sweden
selected_country = "Sweden"
x = nested_population_dict[selected_country].year
y = nested_population_dict[selected_country].population
```

```
# Create a figure object
fig_handle = plt.figure()
# Plot a simple line for each (x,y) point
plt.plot(x, y)
# Add a title to the figure
plt.title("Global population of " + selected_country)
# Show the figure
fig_handle.show()
```

Select that chunk of code and run it.

4.   After running it, an interactive window will open, in which the time series graph of Sweden is shown:

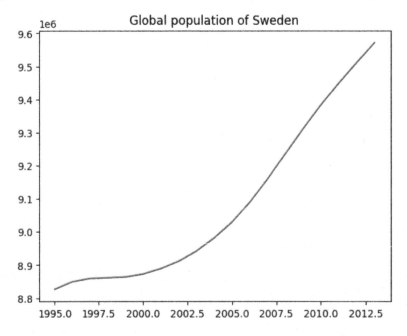

Figure 5.29: Interactive window showing the time series plot of Sweden

5.   The last piece of code (from line 43) creates a new dictionary, containing graphs for each country, and serializes it to a file. Once executed, you can see the nested_population_plots_dict. pkl file in the explorer on the left:

Figure 5.30: The new dictionary is correctly serialized in a PKL file

Amazing! You serialized your second dictionary as well. You can practice deserializing it using the code in the `05-deserialize-plots-object-from-pkl.py` script.

Now, you're ready to test your PKL files in Power BI, either in the Power Query Editor or in Python visuals.

Using a PKL file in Power BI

Just like we saw when working with R, it is evident that a PKL file must be exclusively utilized through Python scripts in Power BI. As a result, there are two Power BI components that enable the usage of Python scripts: the **Power Query Editor** and **Python visuals**. To begin, let's explore the simplest scenario, which involves importing the PKL file into the Power Query Editor.

Importing a PKL file into the Power Query Editor

You will import a serialized Python object into the Power Query Editor once you know how to extract tabular information from the object, and then persist it in the Power BI data model. Let's take a look at how to do this:

1. Open Power BI Desktop through the shortcut that activates the `pbi_powerquery_env` environment.

2. Make sure that Power BI Desktop references the `pbi_powerquery_env` environment in the **Options**.

3. Then, click on **Get data** and then **More....** Start typing `script` into the search textbox and double-click on the Python script. The Python script editor will pop up.

4. Open the `03-deserialize-object-from-pkl-in-power-bi.py` file in Visual Studio Code and copy its content. Then, paste it into the Python script editor in Power BI Desktop, changing the absolute path to the PKL file accordingly, and click **OK**.

5. The **Navigator** window will open, giving you the option to select which dataframe to import:

Figure 5.31: Import the deserialized dataframe into Power BI

Select the `sweden_population_tbl` DataFrame and click **Load**.

6. When loading is finished, click on the **table** icon on the left menu of Power BI Desktop to verify that the data has been imported correctly in a tabular form:

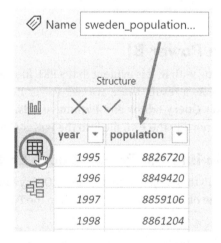

Figure 5.32: The dataframe is correctly imported

Nice job! You have correctly imported your PKL file into Power BI to use its contents with Power Query in the most appropriate way.

IMPORTANT NOTE

As with R scripts, the only Python data structure that Power BI can work with are pandas DataFrames with columns that have standard data types. It is not possible to import any other type of Python object. That's precisely why you couldn't import the dictionary directly.

As should be clear to you by now from the previous section, it can happen that a PKL file doesn't contain information in a tabular format that can be extracted in Power Query Editor. You may need to deserialize the contents of a PKL file directly within a Python visual to use that information to create a plot. You will see how to solve this scenario in the next section.

Importing a PKL file in a Python script visual

Now, let's assume that you received a PKL file containing the time series graphs for each country from the data scientists' team. Your goal is to allow the report user to view the graphs by selecting a country.

The problem you face is the following: you know that in order to import any information into the Power Query Editor via Python scripts, it must be in a tabular format and use standard data types. The plots provided by the data scientists are grouped in a dictionary in the **figure format** of **Matplotlib**, which itself is not a standard data type. So how do you import the dictionary into Power BI? The same "trick" used with R in the previous section applies.

In summary, what you will do in this section is this:

1. Import the PKL file containing the dictionary of plots into the Power Query Editor. Extract the file's keys (countries) and expose them in a dataframe. Use its byte stream representation in strings to fill another dataframe.
2. Use the `countries` dataframe as a slicer with a single choice.
3. Each time a country is selected from the slicer, the Python script visual will deserialize the byte stream into the input dataframe, and it will display the time series plot for the population growth of that country.

Also, in this case, when you select more than one column from more than one table in the Power BI data model (there must be a relationship between them) as values of a Python script visual, these values will form a single dataframe (deduplicated) to be referenced in the Python script of the visual.

In addition, the same suggestion that was made for the R dataframe input applies. You may want to not delete duplicate rows; if so, you can add an `index` field to your pandas dataset (row number) that causes all rows to be considered unique and prevents grouping.

Again, even the Python visuals add a size limitation to the data it imports, which appears to be un-documented.

IMPORTANT NOTE

If a string is longer than 32,766 characters, it is truncated once passed into the input dataframe of a Python visual. To avoid truncation, we need to split the string into chunks of 32,000 characters each (this is an arbitrary value chosen by us) and persist these chunks in a column of the dataframe, before using the data in the Python visual.

Here is the process summarized in a figure that contains the functions you will find in the code:

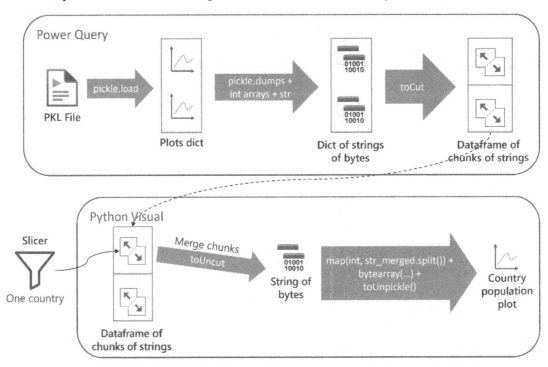

Figure 5.33: Deserializing the PKL file content into a Python visual

In the following steps, we will not explain in detail all the Python functions used, simply because we will refer to the code shared in the GitHub repository associated with this book, where every single detail is commented. So let's get started:

1. Open Power BI Desktop through the shortcut that activates the pbi_powerquery_env environment.

2. Make sure Power BI Desktop references the pbi_powerquery_env environment in the **Options**.

3. Then, click on **Get data** and then **More…**. Start typing script into the search textbox and double-click on the Python script. The Python script editor will pop up.

4. Open the 06-deserialize-plots-object-from-pkl-in-power-bi.py file from the GitHub repository, copy the content, paste it into the Python script editor, changing the absolute path to the PKL file accordingly, and click **OK**.

5. Power Query will detect three dataframes created in your script. Select only the plots_df (the one containing the chunks of byte strings for each plot) and selected_countries_df (the one containing the country names) dataframes:

Figure 5.34: Selecting the two dataframes containing useful data

Then, click **Load**.

6. Click on the **Data** icon in the left ribbon, and then click on the **Manage relationships** button:

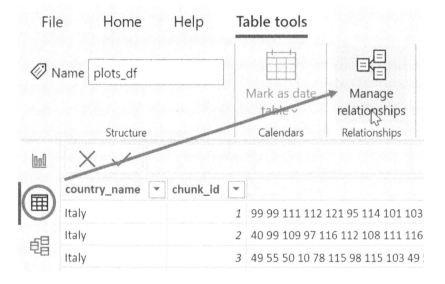

Figure 5.35: The Manage relationships button

7. The engine has automatically created the relationship between the two imported tables:

Active	From: Table (Column)	To: Table (Column)
☑	plots_df (country_name)	selected_countries_df (country_name)

Figure 5.36: Relationship between the tables automatically detected

Click **Close** and go back to the report canvas, using the **Report** icon in the left ribbon.

8. Now, click on the **Slicer** visual icon:

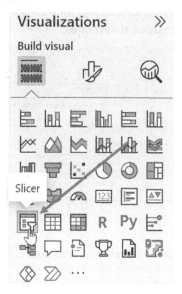

Figure 5.37: The Slicer visual icon

9. Keeping the Slicer visual region selected on the canvas, expand the selected_countries_df table on the **Fields** panel and select the country_name field:

Figure 5.38: Selecting the country_name column for the Slicer visual

10. Then, click the **Format** icon of the Slicer as you did in the previous section; expand first the **Slicer** settings, then **Selection**, and enable the **Single select** option. The Slicer visual will show all the country names contained in the selected_countries_df table. It is very important to set **Single select**, because the logic inside the Python visual will manage the deserialization of a single plot.

11. Click on the report canvas to deselect the Slicer visual region, and then click on the **Python visual** icon:

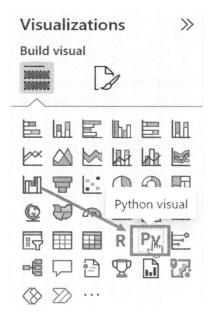

Figure 5.39: The Python visual icon

The usual **Enable script visuals** window pops up. Click on **Enable**.

12. Move and stretch the Python visual borders in order to cover almost all the report canvas. Keeping it selected, click on the plots_df table in the **Fields** panel and select all three chunk_id, country_name, and plot_str fields:

Figure 5.40: Selecting the fields to use in the Python visual

Feel free to turn the Python visual title off in the **Format** tab.

13. Open the `07-deserialize-plots-df-into-python-visual.py` file from the GitHub repository, copy the content, and paste it into the Python visual script editor. Then, click on the **Run** icon at the top-right of the Python script editor.

14. Now, you can click on each country in the Slider in order to see the population time series:

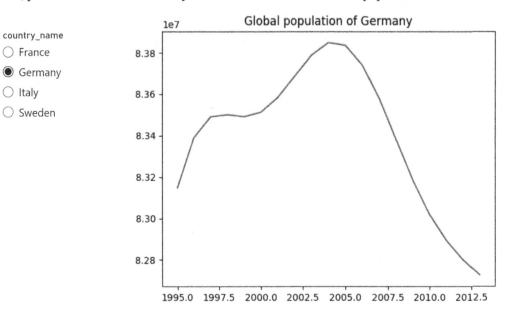

Figure 5.41: Showing the population growth for Germany

Brilliant! You have just completed a report using a unique technique that may have been introduced to you exclusively through this book!

IMPORTANT NOTE

This technique can be very useful when you need to build complex visualizations in Python that require the use of packages not provided by Python visuals in Power BI. These visualizations can be made offline, serialized to a file, and then used in a shared report on the service.

Summary

In this chapter, you got to learn about the Tidyverse approach to R development and how to serialize R objects to files. After that, you learned how to use these serialized files, both in the Power Query Editor and in R visuals.

You then approached the same issues using Python. Specifically, you learned which packages are most used by the PyData community, how to serialize Python objects to files, and how to use them in Power BI, both in the Power Query Editor and in Python visuals.

In the next chapter, you'll have a chance to learn how powerful regular expressions are and what benefits they can bring to your Power BI reports.

References

For additional reading, check out the following books and articles:

- *An Introduction to R* by R Core (`https://cran.r-project.org/doc/manuals/r-release/R-intro.html`)
- *R for Data Science* by Hadley Wickham (`https://r4ds.had.co.nz/index.html`)
- *Machine Learning with R, 4th Edition* by Brett Lantz, Packt Publishing ()
- *ggplot2: Elegant Graphics for Data Analysis* (`https://ggplot2-book.org/`)
- *Python for Data Analysis* (`https://wesmckinney.com/book/`)
- *Matplotlib User Guide* (`https://matplotlib.org/stable/users/index`)

Test your knowledge

1. What could be the reason why you may want to import serialized files into R (`.rds`) or Python (`.pkl`)?
2. Is there a specific format of an R object that needs to be serialized so that it can then be deserialized in Power BI?
3. Why use an alternative method to inject a serialized object from a Python or R script step in Power Query into a Python or R script visual, when it is possible to deserialize the object directly in the visual?
4. Can you briefly summarize the alternative method for injecting a serialized object from Power Query into a script visual?
5. Why is it important to provide a relationship between the object name table (used in the slicer) and the table containing the byte string representation of objects and their names?

Learn more on Discord

To join the Discord community for this book – where you can share feedback, ask questions to the author, and learn about new releases – follow the QR code below:

`https://discord.gg/MKww5g45EB`

6

Using Regular Expressions in Power BI

Often, many data cleansing tasks involve carrying out complex searches and substitutions between strings. The usual search and replace tools are sometimes not enough to get the desired results. For instance, let's suppose you need to match strings, not in an exact way (for instance, via equality conditions) but using similar criteria between them. Knowing how to use tools such as regular expressions (alias regex) can make all the difference in projects that require high-quality data. To illustrate the power of regular expressions in data cleansing, consider a scenario involving a dataset of user names with inconsistent formatting. Some usernames contain spaces, numbers, special characters, or a mix of uppercase and lowercase letters. By using a specific regex pattern, [^a-zA-Z0-9_], we can efficiently search for and remove all the unwanted characters, making each username the same. Thanks to R and Python, you can add these tools to your arsenal.

In this chapter, we will cover the following topics:

- A brief introduction to regexes
- Validating data using regex in Power BI
- Loading complex log files using regex in Power BI
- Extracting values from text using regex in Power BI

Technical requirements

This chapter requires you to have a working internet connection and **Power BI Desktop** already installed on your machine (we used version 2.112.603.0 64-bit, December 2022). You need to properly configure the R and Python engines and IDEs, as outlined in *Chapter 2, Configuring R with Power BI*, and *Chapter 3, Configuring Python with Power BI*.

A brief introduction to regexes

A **regular expression** (usually shortened to **regex**) is defined by a series of characters that *identify an abstract search pattern*. Essentially, it is a mathematical technique that was developed in 1951 by experts in formal language and theoretical computer science. It is used to **validate** input data or to *search for and extract* information from texts.

If you don't know the syntax of a regex, at first glance, it might look really tricky:

$$\text{\textasciicircum[A-Z0-9.\_\%+-]+@[A-Z0-9.-]+\textbackslash.[A-Z]\{2,\}\$}$$

Figure 6.1: An example of a regex pattern

Fortunately, there are online regex visualization tools that make it easier to understand patterns (you can find one of them at `https://regexper.com`). For example, the regex highlighted in *Figure 6.1* can be visualized as follows:

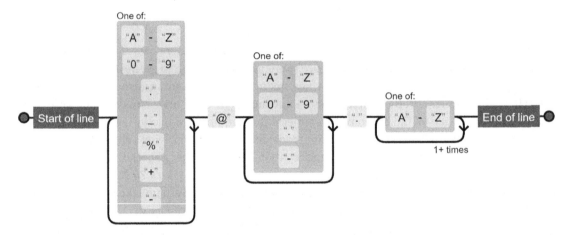

Figure 6.2: A visualization of a regex

From *Figure 6.2*, we can see that the regex in *Figure 6.1* will identify email addresses in a piece of text.

Mastering regex is certainly not easy, and going that far is not the purpose of this section. Here, we will explain the basic rules that will allow you to create simple, yet effective, search patterns. For more details, please refer to the *References* section at the end of this chapter.

The basics of regexes

We will try to explain the basic principles of regexes through the use of examples, which is perhaps the most immediate way to start using them. Each subsequent subsection will explain a function of regexes. To test our regex, we will use the tool made available at `https://www.regexpal.com/`. Let's get started!

Literal characters

To include one or more literal characters in a regex, it is necessary to make use of the "search" feature. Let's try searching for the *owe* string inside the *May the power of extending Power BI with Python and R be with you!* text:

Figure 6.3: Searching for "owe" using a regex

Note that the tool uses the **Global search flag** in the search by default. A specific flag is indicated with a letter (in our case, **g**) right after the regex delimiters, */.../*. The possible flags that can be used are as follows:

- **g (global)**: This will match all of the occurrences, keeping the index of the last match.
- **m (multiline)**: When enabled, the string anchors (you'll see them later) will match the start and end of a line instead of the whole string.
- **i (ignore case)**: This searches the pattern irrespective of the case (lower or upper) of the string.

Bear in mind that not all programming languages use flag syntax, as mentioned earlier. For example, Python's re package (the default one for regexes) provides parameters in the search, match, and sub functions:

```
re.search('test', 'TeSt', re.IGNORECASE)
re.match('test', 'TeSt', re.IGNORECASE)
re.sub('test', 'xxxx', 'TesTing', flags=re.IGNORECASE)
```

This is the same for R's regex() function of the stringr package:

```
str_detect('tEsT this', regex('test', ignore_case=TRUE))
```

You can also use **global modifiers** directly in line with your regex pattern. These are (?i) for case-insensitive and (?m) for multiline. For example, in R, you can also run the following script:

```
str_detect('tEsT this', regex("(?i)test"))
```

Note that Python doesn't allow inline global modifiers.

Special characters in regex

Regex uses 12 special characters (also called **metacharacters**), where each has a special meaning. They are the following:

Symbol	Name
|	Pipe
\	Backslash
$	Dollar Sign
?	Question Mark
^	Caret
*	Asterisk
+	Plus Sign
.	Dot
( )	Parentheses
[	Opening Square Bracket
{	Opening Curly Bracket

Table 6.1: A list of the Regex special characters

If you need to search for one of the previously mentioned characters, you have to escape it using the backslash. So, if you want to match exactly 123$, you need to use 123\$ as the regex pattern.

Next, you will learn about the meaning and use of metacharacters.

The ^ and $ anchors

Anchor characters serve the special purpose of placing the regex match at a specific position in the string. The caret, ^, is used to indicate *the beginning of the string* (or line), and the dollar sign, $, is used to indicate *the end of the string* (or line). An example visualization is worth a thousand words:

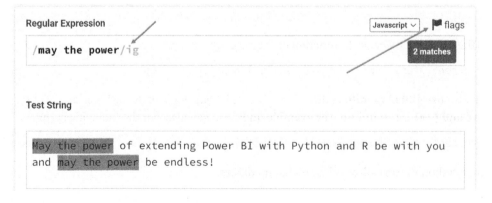

Figure 6.4: Case-insensitive and global search

In *Figure 6.4*, the "ignore case" flag is set by clicking on the **flags** icon and then checking "ignore case." In this way, both occurrences are matched. Now, add a caret, ^, before the m character:

Figure 6.5: Case-insensitive and global search using the caret, ^

In this case, only the first occurrence (that is, the one at the beginning of the string) is matched.

If you also add a dollar sign at the end of the regex, nothing will be matched, as you are asking for a match of the may the power string that is at the beginning and that also ends the text.

OR operators

You might need to match one of the individual sets of characters or strings. For example, if you want to find the letter **s** or **t** right after the letters **ye**, use the regex **ye[st]**. Here, [st] is a character class that matches either **s** or **t**, making **ye[st]** look for yes or yet. This is so that it will match both the yes and yet strings. Character classes can also be used to match an occurrence in a range of characters using the hyphen, -. For example, [0-9] matches a single digit between 0 and 9, while [A-Z] matches a single uppercase letter from A to Z. Additionally, you can combine multiple ranges into one character class. For instance, [A-Z0-9] matches only a digit or an uppercase letter.

To match one of two strings, you can use the pipe, |, to separate them within opening and closing parentheses, such as (string1|string2). Here is a complete example:

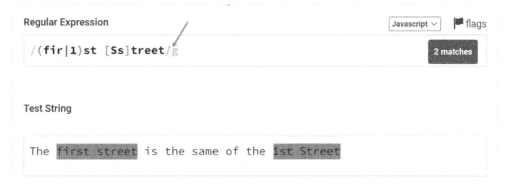

Figure 6.6: A complete example of OR operators

Note that in the case of *Figure 6.6*, the **ignore case** flag is turned off (the i is missing) and upper and lower cases are explicitly managed with a character class to handle case sensitivity only for the word Street.

The character class can also be used to match any character different from a specific character that is given. This is thanks to the **negated character class**.

Negated character classes

The caret symbol (^), when placed immediately after the opening square bracket in a regex pattern, serves to negate the character class. This means that the regex will match any character not listed inside the parentheses. For example, consider the regex pattern [^abc]. This pattern will match any single character except a, b, or c. For a practical example, imagine you're processing some text and you want to find any character that isn't a vowel. You could use the regex [^aeiou]. This pattern would match consonants, digits, spaces, punctuation, etc., but skip vowels.

Shorthand character classes

There are some character classes that are used very often. For this reason, we have defined some abbreviations to allow you to include them in regexes quickly. Here is a list of the most commonly used ones:

- \w: This matches an alphanumeric character, including the underscore. Example: in Item_01, Cost: $30, \w matches Item_01, Cost, and 30, ideal for extracting structured data like product codes.

- \W: This is the opposite of \w, so it matches a single non-alphanumeric character, excluding the underscore. Example: in Username: John_Doe!, \W matches the colon : and the exclamation mark !, useful for identifying and handling special characters or punctuation in text.

- \d: This matches a single digit. Example: in 1234 Elm St., Apt 56, \d matches 1234 and 56, essential for extracting numbers like street and apartment numbers.

- \D: This is the opposite of \d, so it matches a single non-digit character. Example: in Temperature: 23°C, \D matches Temperature: and °C, useful for isolating text in datasets with numbers and text.

- \s: This matches "whitespace characters" such as space, tab, newline, and carriage return. Example: in First Name\tLast Name\nAge, \s matches the tab and newline, crucial for parsing formatted documents or data files.

We'll use shorthand character classes relatively often throughout this chapter.

Quantifiers

Quantifiers indicate the number of times a *character* or *expression* must be matched. Here is a list of the most used ones:

- +: This matches what precedes it one or more times. For example, test\d+ will match the test string followed by one or more digits. The test(-\d\d)+ regex will match the test string followed by one or more times a dash that is then followed by two digits:

Figure 6.7: Repeating a group of characters using +

- {n}: This one matches what precedes it *n* times. For example, \d{4} will match any integer number made up of 4 digits.

- {n,m}: This one matches what precedes it between *n* and *m* times. For example, prod-\d{2,6} will match the prod- string followed by an integer number made up of between 2 and 6 digits.

- {n, }: This one matches *n* or more times what precedes it.

- ?: This one matches one or zero times what precedes it. For example, Mar(ch)? will match both March and Mar. Alternatively, the colou?red regex will match both colored and coloured.

- *: This one matches zero or more times what precedes it. For example, code\d* will match code, code1, or code173846.

The dot

The dot corresponds to a single character, regardless of what that character is, except for line-break characters. It's a very powerful regex metacharacter and gives you a chance to be lazy. This is precisely why you have to be careful not to abuse it because, sometimes, you might include unintended results in the matches.

Consider the regex a.b, which is intended to match any three-character string that starts with a and ends with b. This regex would match acb, a-b, a9b, but also a b. So, it may match parts of words or phrases that you didn't intend to include, which can interfere with data extraction or manipulation processes.

Greedy and lazy matches

The +, *, and repetition of {...} are **greedy quantifiers**. Greedy means that *they will consume the longest possible string*. This fact can have adverse effects when processing strings, especially if you're not careful about how you use them. Here are some key points to keep in mind:

- **Overmatching**: Greedy quantifiers match as much as they can, potentially capturing more of the string than intended. For example, using <.*> in a pattern to match HTML tags such as <a>link</a> may inadvertently match the entire string, including both tags and the text between them, rather than individual tags. An example is shown below.

- **Performance issues:** Greedy quantifiers can cause performance inefficiencies, especially with long strings or complex patterns. The regex engine may be forced to perform significant back-tracking if the first, longest possible match does not meet the overall pattern requirements. This can slow down the processing of large datasets.

- **Unintended matches in nested structures:** In nested structures, such as parentheses in mathematical expressions or nested HTML tags, greedy quantifiers can cause false matches. For example, if you want to match only the internal parentheses in the string (a(b)c), a greedy pattern like \(.+\) would match the whole string (a(b)c) instead of stopping at the first closing parenthesis.

Let's take a practical example. Suppose that you only want to match the tags used in the <em>Power BI rocks</em> string. The first attempt a beginner would make is to use the <.+> regex, which, expressed in words, becomes "get the <, then get any non-newline character one or more times, and finally, in the end, get the >". The expected result is made up of two matches, <em> and </em>. Let's take a look at the result:

Regular Expression		Javascript ∨	🚩 flags
/<.+>/g			1 match

Test String

"<em>Power BI rocks</em>"

Figure 6.8: The greediness of .+

It is evident that the combination of .+ captures everything contained between *the first* occurrence of < and the last occurrence of >, hence the definition of the **greediness** of the quantifiers.

So, is it possible to force a greedy quantifier to stop at the first detected occurrence of the next character, preventing it from "eating" anything until the last occurrence of it? In other words, is it possible to turn a greedy quantifier into a **lazy** one? The answer is "yes," it is possible to do so by adding the ? metacharacter just after the +. So, the <.+> regex becomes <.+?>. Here is the result:

Figure 6.9: Making a greedy quantifier lazy thanks to the ? metacharacter

Bear in mind, however, that *lazy quantifiers are underperforming*. Whenever possible, it is always preferable to *use negated character classes instead*. In our example, simply using the `<[^>]+>` regex (that is, a < character, any non-> character one or more times, and a > character) will achieve the same result without consuming computational resources:

Figure 6.10: Using a negated character class instead of a lazy quantifier

So far, with what you've learned about regexes, you have the minimum foundation required to understand the more complex regexes that we'll be using in the next few examples. We'll start by using what we've learned to check the validity of email addresses.

Checking the validity of email addresses

If you were asked to validate an email address using the concepts you just learned, one of your first attempts might look like the following: `^.+@.+\..+$`. Translating this regex into spoken language gives us the following:

1. `^`: This matches the beginning of the string or a line if the multiline flag is enabled.

2. `.+`: This matches any character one or more times, except the line break.

3. `@`: This matches an "@" character.

4. .+: This matches any character one or more times, except the line break.

5. \.: This matches a "." character.

6. .+: This matches any character one or more times, except the line break.

Of course, this regex will validate a correct email address. But are you sure it can also detect the obvious syntactic errors of bad emails? Let's perform a test in https://www.regexpal.com/ with the wrong email, example@example.c (the top-level domain, that is, the portion of the domain after the dot, must contain a minimum of two characters):

Figure 6.11: Using a simple regex to validate a wrong email address

Well, that's not much of an outcome: an obviously wrong email would pass as correct. For this reason, it is often necessary to use more complex regexes that can respect well-defined syntactic rules.

In this specific case, we'll use a specific regex for email validation that we often adopt in production. It also takes into account whether the domain IP is used. For the purpose of displaying it in full, the regex is as follows:

```
^(([^<>()[\]\\.,;:\s@\""]+(\.[^<>()[\]\\.,;:\s@\""]+)*)|(\"".+\""))@((\[?[0-
9]{1,3}\.[0-9]{1,3}\.[0-9]{1,3}\.[0-9]{1,3}\]?)|(([a-zA-Z\-0-9]+\.)+[a-zA-Z]
{2,}))$
```

At first glance, this regex is sure to cause confusion. However, if we attempt to break it down into its essential parts, it becomes much more readable. Let's do that now.

 If you think this regex is really complex, take a look at the one that takes into account all, and I mean all, the syntactic rules provided by the *Standard for the Format of Arpa Internet Text Messages*, which you can find at https://url.uk.m.mimecastprotect.com/s/wcZ gCLY21tRgWAzFPiJnT?domain=pdw.ex-parrot.com! Pretty impressive, huh?

The format of an email address is defined as `local-part@domain`. You can find the complete specifications on Wikipedia at `https://en.wikipedia.org/wiki/Email_address`. We are going to match the minimum number of rules (not all of them!) that will allow us to validate a significantly different number of email addresses. So, considering we're going to match the domain name or the domain IP, the general structure of the regex is as follows:

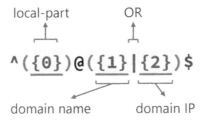

Figure 6.12: The structure of the complex regex for email validation

In *Figure 6.12*, the `{0}`, `{1}`, and `{2}` strings are just placeholders, not characters to match. That said, let's start by defining each token:

1. The `{0}` token matches the **local-part** regex of the email. In this case, it's much easier to explain what the *local-part* regex does with a diagram rather than with words. In *Figure 6.13*, the labels explain every single detail of the subparts:

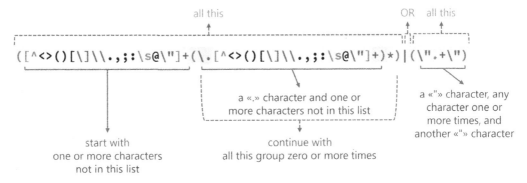

Figure 6.13: The local-part regex explained in detail

Bear in mind that *parentheses group regex patterns together*. Parentheses allow you to apply regex operators to the entire grouped expression and to get a part of the match as a separate item in the result array. The text that corresponds to the regex expression is captured within them as a **numbered group**, and it can be reused with a numbered backreference. For example, in `(abc)(def)`, abc is group 1, and def is group 2. You can refer back to these groups within the same pattern using `\1`, `\2`, etc., for repeated or mirrored patterns, or in replacements for reordering or restructuring text. You'll learn how to use this feature later.

Remember that, in order to have the match of a metacharacter be a real character, the escape backslash must be placed before it. So, for example, `\]` will be the] character.

2.   The {1} token matches the domain name of the email. Again, we will use a diagram to explain what the domain name regex does:

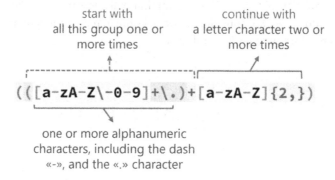

Figure 6.14: The domain name regex explained in detail

3.   The {2} token matches the **domain IP** of the email. It is the easier sub-regex, and you can find out what it matches by looking at *Figure 6.14*:

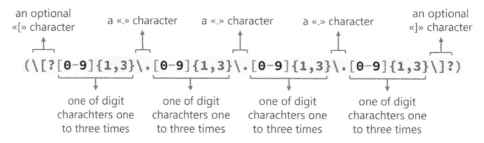

Figure 6.15: The domain IP regex explained in detail

If you want to view the *whole regex* in a visualization, please refer to the following one, which is taken from https://jex.im/regulex:

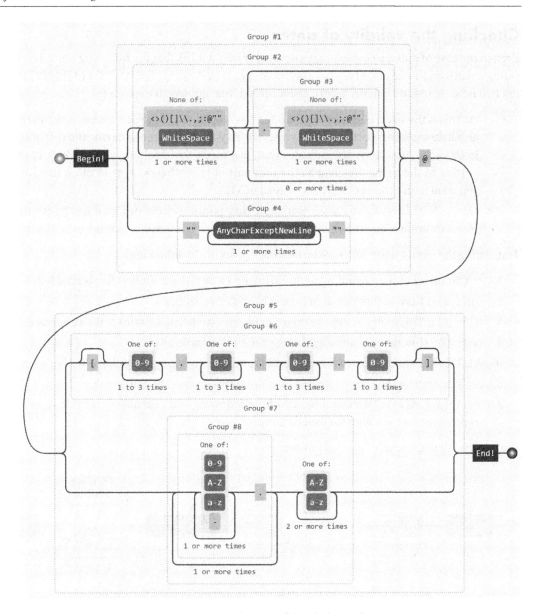

Figure 6.16: A visualization of the whole email regex

Now, let's proceed with the validation of another important type of information, which is very often subject to typing errors: dates.

Checking the validity of dates

Even in the case of dates, a clueless regex developer might think that the following regex is enough to validate dates (in the format of dd-mm-yyyy): ^\d{1,2}([\-\/])\d{1,2}\1(?:\d{4}|\d{2})$. There are two new expressions, never before encountered, that are worth exploring:

- \1: This is the **backreference** to group 1. As we explained in the previous section, parentheses also help capture a portion of the string, which you can reference during the rest of the regex. In this case, the \1 syntax indicates that, at exactly that position, you can expect the same portion of the string matched by the first pair of parentheses. Bear in mind that, in Python, you need to use the \g<1> syntax instead of \1.

- (?: …): This is the so-called **non-capturing group**. Sometimes, you need parentheses to correctly apply a quantifier, but you don't want their contents to be reported in the results.

Translating the whole regex into spoken language gives us the following:

1. ^: This matches the beginning of the string or a line if the multiline flag is enabled.
2. \d{1,2}: This matches any digit between 1 and 2 repetitions.
3. ([\-\/]): This matches any character between - and /, and captures the result as group 1.
4. \d{1,2}: This matches any digit between 1 and 2 repetitions.
5. \1: This backreferences to the captured group 1. So, it expects any character between - and /.
6. .+: This matches any character one or more times, except the line break.
7. (?:\d{4}|\d{2}): This matches one of the following two alternatives: any digit for exactly 4 repetitions and any digit for exactly 2 repetitions.

You can visualize the whole regex as follows:

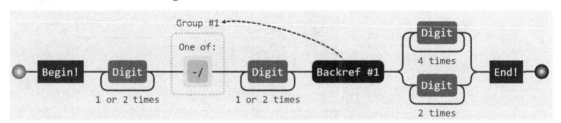

Figure 6.17: A visualization of the first attempt of a regex for validating dates

As you might have guessed, this regex validates dates in the following formats: dd-mm-yyyy, dd-mm-yy, d-m-yyyy, and d-m-yy, using / or - as separators. However, it does not account for errors due to invalid dates, such as February 30 or September 31.

If you want a regex that also accounts for these errors, then you must use the following:

```
^(?:(?:31[\-\/](?:(?:0?[13578])|(1[02]))[\-\/](19|20)?\d\d)|(?:(?:29|30)[\-\/]
(?:(?:0?[13-9])|(?:1[0-2]))[\-\/](?:19|20)?\d\d)|(?:29[\-\/]0?2[\-\/](?:19|20)
(?:(?:[02468][048])|(?:[13579][26])))|(?:(?:(?:0?[1-9])|(?:1\d)|(?:2[0-8]))[\-
\/](?:(?:0?[1-9])|(?:1[0-2]))[\-\/](?:19|20)?\d\d))$
```

Again, viewed in this way, this regex is difficult to interpret. However, looking at it "from above" a bit more, you realize that it consists of four alternatives:

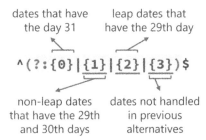

Figure 6.18: The structure of the complex regex for date validation

Also, in this case, the {0}, {1}, {2}, and {3} strings are just placeholders, not characters to match. That said, let's start by defining the {0} token.

The {0} token matches the dates that have the 31st day. As in previous cases, it's much easier to explain what this regex does with a visualization rather than with words. In *Figure 6.19*, the labels explain every single detail of each component:

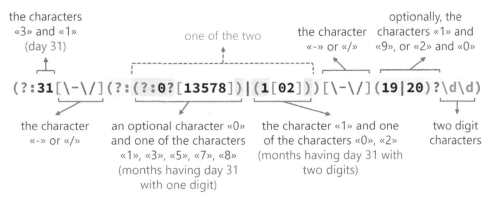

Figure 6.19: The regex part for dates that have the 31st day explained in detail

The regexes used for the other placeholders are very similar to the one we just explained. Therefore, we will leave the explanation of the others as an exercise for the reader.

If you want to see the whole regex in a visualization, please refer to the following diagram, which is taken from `https://jex.im/regulex`:

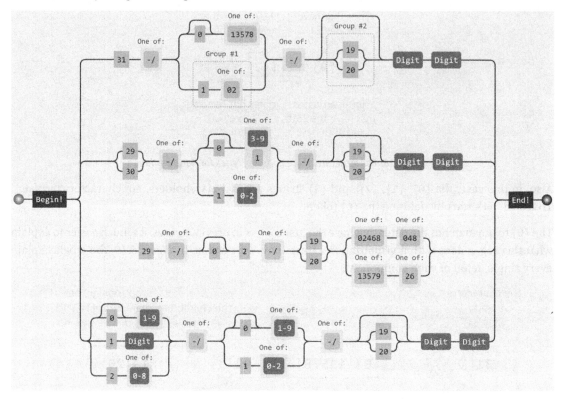

Figure 6.20: The visualization of the whole date regex

The regex that we just examined allows the validation of the `dd-mm-yyyy` format with all of its variants. In the code, we will demonstrate how you can implement date validation in Power BI. Additionally, you will find regexes that allow you to validate dates in the `mm-dd-yyyy` and `yyyy-mm-dd` formats with all of their variants (where the year is made of two digits, the month is made of one digit, and so on).

Now that you understand what's behind the complex regexes presented earlier, let's move on to implementing them in Power BI to validate your data.

Validating data using regex in Power BI

To date, Power BI has no native feature in Power Query to perform operations via regexes. There are cases when you can't avoid using regexes to extract useful information from data in text form. The only way to be able to use regexes is through R scripts or Python scripts. The only cons you have in this case is that, if you need to publish the report on the Power BI service, to allow Power Query to use external R or Python engines, you must also install the on-premises data gateway in personal mode.

However, let's get right into it with some real-world type examples.

Let's say you work for a retail company that has a team dedicated to identifying fraudulent customers. As soon as a team member identifies a fraudster, they fill out an Excel spreadsheet, in which the *Email* and *BannedDate* columns are included along with others. Your task is to load the data from this Excel file into Power BI and, from other data sources, select only the fraudster's information in order to carry out specific analysis on their purchases.

Having the correct fraudster emails within the Excel file is critically important to be able to properly join them with the other data. Having the correct ban dates is also important in order to know whether further orders from that fraudster have slipped through the cracks after that date. As you know, the filling in of an Excel file by several users is done without any kind of validation of the entered data; therefore, it is subject to human errors. So, identifying any errors when filling out certain fields and highlighting them allows the fraud team to be able to correct them. It is precisely in this case that regexes come to your aid.

Using regex in Power BI to validate emails with Python

In the repository that comes with this book, you can find the `Users.xlsx` Excel file inside the `Ch06 - Using Regular Expressions in Power BI` folder. Its content is shown in *Figure 6.21*:

	A	B	C	D	E
1	UserId	Email	BannedDate	IsEmailValidByDefinition	IsDateValidByDefinition
2	1	_____@example.com	05/29/2018	1	1
3	2	example1@example.com/example2@example.com	06/07/2019	0	1
4	3	example33@example.com.	02/05/2018	0	1
5	4	firstname-lastname@example.com	06/07/2019	1	1
6	5	example@example.com --> check	02/29/18	0	0
7	6	email@example-one.com	11/06/2017	1	1

Figure 6.21: The content of the Users.xlsx file

In this section, we will focus exclusively on the `Email` column. This contains the email addresses of fraudsters entered manually by the fraud team, which was described at the beginning of the section. These email addresses are not all syntactically correct. Moreover, in the Excel file, there is also the `IsEmailValidByDefinition` column, whose values (*1=yes*; *0=no*) indicates whether the email corresponding to that value is actually valid or not.

Python has a built-in package, called `re`, which contains all the functions you need to work with regexes. Additionally, in `pandas`, there are several methods for a series or dataframe object, which accept regexes to find a pattern in a string. These methods work in the same way as the ones you will find in Python's `re` module. We will be using the `match` method shortly.

You will learn about the use of the `r'...'` syntax to create strings. This is a **raw string** that allows you to treat the backslash (\) as a literal character and not as an escape character.

So, open Power BI Desktop, make sure the Python environment you use is `pbi_powerquery_env`, and let's get started:

1. Open Power BI Desktop through the shortcut that activates the `pbi_powerquery_env` environment.

2. Make sure Power BI Desktop is referencing the pbi_powerquery_env environment in **Options**.

3. From the ribbon, click on the **Excel workbook** icon to import data from Excel:

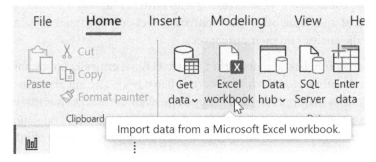

Figure 6.22: Importing data from Excel

4. From the **Open** dialog box, select the previously mentioned Users.xlsx file.

5. From the **Navigator** window, select the **Users** sheet and then click on **Transform Data**:

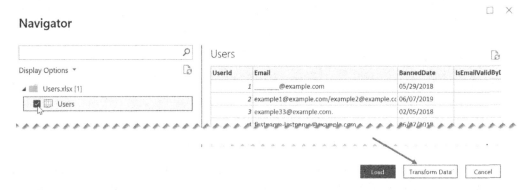

Figure 6.23: Selecting the Users sheet and clicking on Transform Data

6. Click on the **Transform** menu, and then click on **Run Python Script**.

7. Then, copy and paste the following code into the Python script editor and click on **OK**:

```python
import pandas as pd
import re
df = dataset
regex_local_part = r'([^<>()[\]\\.,;:\s@\""]+(\.[^<>()[\]\\.,;:\s@\""]+)*
)|(\"".+\"")'
regex_domain_name = r'(([a-zA-Z\-0-9]+\.)+[a-zA-Z]{2,})'
regex_domain_ip_address = r'(\[?[0-9]{1,3}\.[0-9]{1,3}\.[0-9]{1,3}\.[0-9]
{1,3}\]?)'
pattern = r'^({0})@({1}|{2})$'.format(regex_local_part, regex_domain_
name, regex_domain_ip_address)
df['isEmailValidFromRegex'] = df['Email'].str.match(pattern).astype(int)
```

You can also find this Python script in the 01-validate-emails-with-regex-with-python. py file, which is inside the repository that comes with the book, in the 01-validating-data-using-regex subfolder of the Ch06 - Using Regular Expressions in Power BI mail folder.

8. Power BI Desktop may trigger the Firewall privacy level mismatch error. If so, follow *Step 9*; otherwise, you can jump to *Step 10*.

9. Go to **File**, **Option and settings**, then click on **Data source settings**. Make sure to select the same privacy level for both the Python script and the Users Excel file by clicking **Edit Permissions...** for each of them. If you select the **Organizational** level for both, everything will work fine on Power BI Desktop. However, if you plan to publish your reports to the *Power BI service (or Embedded)*, you *must use the "Public" level*. For both options, select the **Public** level. Click Close and then click **Refresh Preview** on the **Home** tab.

10. We are only interested in the df dataset. So, click on its **Table** value:

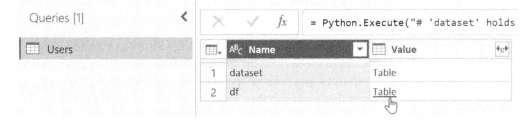

Figure 6.24: Selecting the df dataset as a result of the Python script transformation

11. As you can see, the **isEmailValidFromRegex** column is added and it contains the Boolean values resulting from the validation of the emails by your regex. If you check them, you will see that they match the values given by the definition in the **IsEmailValidByDefinition** column:

Email	BannedDate	IsEmailValidByDefinition	IsDateValidByDefinition	isEmailValidFromRegex
_____@example.com	05/29/2018	1	1	1
example1@example.com/example2@example.com	06/07/2019	0	1	0
example33@example.com.	02/05/2018	0	1	0
firstname-lastname@example.com	06/07/2019	1	1	1
example@example.com --> check	02/29/18	0	0	0
email@example-one.com	11/06/2017	1	1	1
email@example.co.jp	012/05/2018	1	0	1
email@example.name	06/7/2019	1	1	1
example	10/22/2018	0	1	0
email@example.com	9/04/2017	1	1	1
email@subdomain.example.com	11/22/2018	1	1	1
email@123.123.123.123	07/31/17	1	1	1
.@example.com	04/24/018	0	0	0
firstname.lastname@example.com	11/22/18	1	1	1
firstname+lastname@example.com	05/16/2018	1	1	1
example@example.c	6/7/2019	0	1	0
1234567890@example.com	05/16/2018	1	1	1
email@example.museum	03/26/2018	1	1	1
email@[123.123.123.123]	06/31/2017	1	0	1

Figure 6.25: The regex validation results for emails

Your regex did a great job! The result is a perfect match with the real email checks. Now you can go back to the **Home** menu and click on **Close & Apply**.

Thanks to the **isEmailValidFromRegex** column, you can now filter the correct email addresses from the incorrect email addresses, and perhaps even report the matter to the fraud team in a special report.

Using regex in Power BI to validate emails with R

If you want to use R for your email validation using regex, the process is pretty much the same except for a few things.

First of all, *R only allows the use of raw strings as of version 4.0.0*. Also, the syntax for raw strings is slightly different from Python's. Instead of r'...', you must use r'(...)', r'[...]', or r'{...}'. Additionally, instead of using numeric placeholders in curly brackets inside the string and then assigning them via the format() function, as you would in Python, in R you can simply use the variable names in curly brackets directly as placeholders when using the str_glue() function from the stringr package. Note that as of Python 3.6, you can also use F-strings, which allow you to use variable names directly in curly brackets in Python too. They have the form: f'This is the value of the variable myvar: {myvar}'.

That said, the second thing you need to pay attention to is the following: you have to be careful so that, in R, not only] is considered a metacharacter, but also [. Therefore, when you want to use both square brackets as literal characters, you must prepend the backslash escape character (\) for both. Therefore, the part of the regex that identifies the character class in the local-part regex of the email is slightly different:

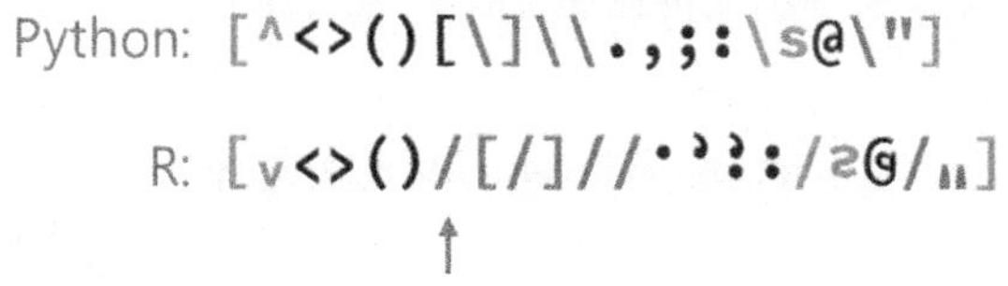

$$\text{Python: } [\char`\^<>()[\backslash]\backslash\backslash.,;:\backslash s@\backslash"]$$

$$\text{R: } [\char`\v<>()/[/]//\cdot\char`\'?:/\char`\2 G/\char`\"]$$

$$\uparrow$$

Figure 6.26: You must escape the opened square bracket when it is a literal character in R

R Base provides two functions that enable you to use regexes: grep() and grepl():

- grepl() returns a Boolean value based on whether a pattern exists in a character string.
- grep() returns the indexes of the occurrences in the vector of characters that contains a match or the specific strings that have the match.

Since we want to adopt the *Tidyverse paradigm*, we will use the wrapper functions provided by the stringr package, which are str_detect() and str_which(), respectively.

Having clarified these differences, the process to validate the emails present in the Users.xlsx Excel file in Power BI using the R script is practically the same as that discussed in the previous section where we used Python:

1. Repeat *Steps 1 to 3* of the previous section (*Using regex in Power BI to validate emails with Python*) to import the data contained in the Users.xlsx file.
2. Click on the **Transform** menu, and then click on **Run R Script**.

3. Then, copy and paste the following code into the R script editor and click on **OK**:

```
library(dplyr)
library(stringr)
regex_local_part <- r'(([^<>()\[\]\\.,;:\s@\"]+(\.[^<>()\
[\]\\.,;:\s@\"]+)*)|(\".+\"))'
regex_domain_name <- r'((([a-zA-Z\-0-9]+\.)+[a-zA-Z]{2,}))'
regex_domain_ip_address <- r'((\[?[0-9]{1,3}\.[0-9]{1,3}\.[0-9]{1,3}\.
[0-9]{1,3}\]?))'
pattern <- str_glue(
  '^({regex_local_part})@({regex_domain_name}|{regex_domain_ip_
address})$'
)
df <- dataset %>%
  mutate( isEmailValidFromRegex = as.integer(str_detect(Email, pattern))
)
```

You also can find this R script in the `02-validate-emails-with-regex-with-r.R` file, which is the repository that comes with the book, in the `01-validating-data-using-regex` folder.

4. Power BI Desktop may trigger the Firewall privacy level mismatch error. If so, follow *Step 5*; otherwise, you can jump to *Step 6*.

5. Also, select the *Organizational* level for R scripts. Go to **File**, **Option and settings**, then click on **Data source settings**. Make sure to select the same privacy level for both the R script and the Users Excel file by clicking **Edit Permissions...** for each of them. If you select the **Organizational** level for both, everything will work fine on Power BI Desktop. However, if you plan to publish your reports to the *Power BI service (or Embedded)*, you *must use the "Public" level*. For both options, select the **Public** level. Click Close and then click **Refresh Preview** on the **Home** tab.

6. We are only interested in the `df` dataset. So, click on its **Table** value:

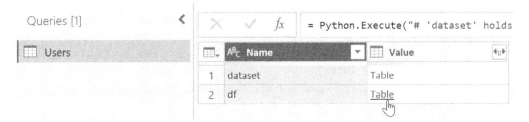

Figure 6.27: Selecting the df dataset as a result of the R script transformation

7. As you can see, the **isEmailValidFromRegex** column has been added, and it contains the Boolean values (converted to 1 and 0) resulting from the validation of the emails by your regex. When you check them, they match the values given by the definition in the **IsEmailValidByDefinition** column.

Also, in this case, your regex did a great job! Now you can go back to the **Home** menu and click on **Close & Apply**.

Thanks to the isEmailValidFromRegex column, you can now appropriately filter the correct and incorrect email addresses in your reports.

Now, let's take a look at how to validate dates in Power BI with Python.

Using regex in Power BI to validate dates with Python

As an example of the dates to validate, we will use the Users.xlsx Excel file that we used earlier. It contains the *BannedDate* column that has string values representing dates in the mm/dd/yyyy format with all its variants. The Excel file also contains the *IsDateValidByDefinition* column, whose values (1=yes; 0=no) indicate whether the date matching this value is valid or not.

By now, you already know the Python functions needed to use a regex. So, let's get started:

1. Repeat *Steps 1 to 3* of the *Using regex in Power BI to validate emails with Python* section to import the data contained in the Users.xlsx file.

2. Click on the **Transform** menu and then click on **Run Python Script**.

3. Then, copy and paste the following code into the Python script editor and click on **OK**:

```python
import pandas as pd
import re
df = dataset
regex_dates_having_day_31 = r'(?:(?:(?:0?[13578])|(?:1[02]))[\-\/]31[\-
\/](?:19|20)?\d\d)'
regex_non_leap_dates_having_days_29_30 = r'(?:(?:(?:0?[13-9])|(?:1[0-2]))
[\-\/](?:29|30)[\-\/](?:19|20)?\d\d)'
regex_leap_dates_having_day_29 = r'(?:0?2[\-\/]29[\-\/]
(?:19|20)?(?:(?:[02468][048])|(?:[13579][26])))'
regex_remaining_dates = r'(?:(?:(?:0?[1-9])|(?:1[0-2]))[\-\/](?:(?:1\
d)|(?:0?[1-9])|(?:2[0-8]))[\-\/](?:19|20)?\d\d)'
pattern = r'^(?:{0}|{1}|{2}|{3})$'.format(regex_dates_having_day_31,
regex_non_leap_dates_having_days_29_30, regex_leap_dates_having_day_29,
regex_remaining_dates)
df['isValidDateFromRegex'] = df['BannedDate'].str.match(pattern).
astype(int)
```

You can find a more exhaustive Python script in the 03-validate-dates-with-regex-with-python.py file, which can be found in the repository that comes with the book. That script handles dates in the formats mm-dd-yyyy, dd-mm-yyyy, and yyyy-mm-dd with all their variances, including both - and / as separators.

4. If Power BI requires you to provide it with data privacy information, you already know how to proceed based on what we've discussed in the previous sections.

5. As you can see after clicking on the df table, the isValidDateFromRegex column has been added, and it contains the Boolean values resulting from the validation of the emails through your regex. If you do a check, they coincide with the values given by definition in the IsDateValidByDefinition column:

ABC BannedDate	123 IsEmailValidByDefinition	123 IsDateValidByDefinition	123 isValidDateFromRegex
05/29/2018	1	1	1
06/07/2019	0	1	1
02/05/2018	0	1	1
06/07/2019	1	1	1
02/29/18	0	0	0
11/06/2017	1	1	1
012/05/2018	1	0	0
06/7/2019	1	1	1
10/22/2018	0	1	1
9/04/2017	1	1	1
11/22/2018	1	1	1
07/31/17	1	1	1
04/24/018	0	0	0
11/22/18	1	1	1
05/16/2018	1	1	1
6/7/2019	0	1	1
05/16/2018	1	1	1
03/26/2018	1	1	1
06/31/2017	1	0	0

Figure 6.28: The regex validation results for the dates

Your regex did a great job again! Now you can go back to the **Home** menu and click on **Close & Apply**.

Thanks to the isValidDateFromRegex column, you can now filter the correct and incorrect email addresses and work appropriately with them.

Using regex in Power BI to validate dates with R

If you want to use R for your date validation using regex, in this case, the process is pretty much the same except for what you have already learned in the *Using regex in Power BI to validate emails with R* section. Starting from the same Users.xlsx Excel file that we used in the previous section, here are the steps to follow:

1. Repeat *Steps 1 to 3* of the *Using regex in Power BI to validate emails with Python* section to import the data contained in the Users.xlsx file.
2. Click on the **Transform** menu, and then click on **Run R Script**.
3. Then, copy and paste the following code into the R script editor and click on **OK**:

```
library(dplyr)
library(stringr)
df <- dataset
```

```r
regex_dates_having_day_31 <- r'((?:(?:(?:0?[13578])|(?:1[02]))[\-\/]31[\-
\/](?:19|20)?\d\d))'
regex_non_leap_dates_having_days_29_30 <- r'((?:(?:(?:0?[13-9])|(?:1[0-
2]))[\-\/](?:29|30)[\-\/](?:19|20)?\d\d))'
regex_leap_dates_having_day_29 <- r'((?:0?2[\-\/]29[\-\/]
(?:19|20)?(?:(?:[02468][048])|(?:[13579][26]))))'
regex_remaining_dates <- r'((?:(?:(?:0?[1-9])|(?:1[0-2]))[\-\/](?:(?:1\
d)|(?:0?[1-9])|(?:2[0-8]))[\-\/](?:19|20)?\d\d))'
pattern <- str_glue(
  '^(?:{regex_dates_having_day_31}|{regex_non_leap_dates_having_
days_29_30}|{regex_leap_dates_having_day_29}|{regex_remaining_dates})$'
)
df <- dataset %>%
  mutate( isDateValidFromRegex = as.integer(str_detect(BannedDate,
pattern)) )
```

You can find a more exhaustive R script in the `04-validate-dates-with-regex-with-r.R` file, which can be found in the repository that comes with the book, in the `01-validating-data-using-regex` folder. That script handles dates in the formats mm-dd-yyyy, dd-mm-yyyy, and yyyy-mm-dd with all their variances, including both - and / as separators.

4. If Power BI requires you to provide it with data privacy information, you already know how to proceed based on what we've discussed in the previous sections.

5. As you can see, the **isValidDateFromRegex** column has been added, and it contains the Boolean values resulting from the validation of the emails through your regex. If you do a check, they coincide with the values given by definition in the **IsDateValidByDefinition** column.

Your regex also did a great job in this case! Now you can go back to the **Home** menu and click on **Close & Apply**.

Thanks to the **isDateValidFromRegex** column, you can now appropriately filter the correct and incorrect dates in your reports.

In the next section, you will learn how to import the contents of a semi-structured log file using Python and R.

Loading complex log files using regex in Power BI

Log files are a very useful tool for developers and administrators of computer systems. They record what happened to the system, when it happened, and which user actually caused the event. Thanks to these files, you can find information about any system failure, which allows you to diagnose the causes of these failures more quickly.

Logs are often **semi-structured data**, information that cannot be persisted in a relational database in the format in which it was generated. In order to be analyzed with standard tools, this data must first be transformed into a more suitable format.

Because it is not structured data, it is difficult to import it into Power BI as is, unless someone has developed a custom connector to do so. In these scenarios, using a regex in languages like Python or R can help us get the results we want.

Apache access logs

Let's suppose your company has a website published through an Apache web server. Your manager asks you to carry out an analysis regarding which web pages of the site are the most clicked on. The only way to get this information is to analyze the *access log file*. This file records data about all requests made to the web server. Here is an example of an Apache access log:

```
1  83.149.9.216 - - [17/May/2015:10:05:03 +0000] "GET
   /presentations/logstash-monitorama-2013/images/kibana-search.png HTTP/1.1" 200 203023
   "http://semicomplete.com/presentations/logstash-monitorama-2013/  " "Mozilla/5.0 (Macintosh;
   Intel Mac OS X 10_9_1) AppleWebKit/537.36 (KHTML, like Gecko) Chrome/32.0.1700.77 Safari/537.36"
2  83.149.9.216 - - [17/May/2015:10:05:43 +0000] "GET
   /presentations/logstash-monitorama-2013/images/kibana-dashboard3.png HTTP/1.1" 200 171717
   "http://semicomplete.com/presentations/logstash-monitorama-2013/  " "Mozilla/5.0 (Macintosh;
   Intel Mac OS X 10_9_1) AppleWebKit/537.36 (KHTML, like Gecko) Chrome/32.0.1700.77 Safari/537.36"
```

Figure 6.29: An example of an Apache access log

As you can see, at first glance, there is a fairly organized structure to the information in this log. If no one has customized the output of the Apache log files, it uses the **Common Log Format** (**CLF**) by default. You can find a real example of an Apache access log in the apache_logs.txt file, which is inside the repository that comes with this book, in the 02-loading-complex-log-files-using-regex folder. We can find it in the GitHub repository at http://bit.ly/apache-access-log (click on **Download** to view it).

If you go ahead and read the documentation of those log files, you will deduce that the information recorded in the access log follows the *NCSA extended/combined log format*. So, the data that is recorded is as follows:

1. The remote host name (the IP address).
2. The remote log name (if empty, you'll find a dash; it is not used in the sample file).
3. The remote user if the request was authenticated (if empty, you'll find a dash).
4. The datetime that the request was received, in the [18/Sep/2011:19:18:28 -0400] format.
5. The first line of the request made to the server between double quotes.
6. The HTTP status code for the request.
7. The size of the response in bytes, excluding the HTTP headers (could be a dash).
8. The Referer HTTP request header, which contains the absolute or partial address of the page making the request.
9. The User-Agent HTTP request header, which contains a string that identifies the application, operating system, vendor, and/or version of the requesting user agent.

Once you know both the nature of the information written in the log and the form in which it is written, you can take advantage of the powerful tools provided by regexes to better structure this information and import it into Power BI.

Importing Apache access logs in Power BI with Python

As mentioned earlier, you can find a real example of an Apache access log in the apache_logs.txt file, which is inside the repository that comes with this book, in the 02-loading-complex-log-files-using-regex folder. You will load the information in this file using a Python script, not a Power BI connector.

Compared to what you've learned before about regexes and Python, in the 01-apache-access-log-parser-python.py Python script (which you'll find in the preceding folder), you will encounter the new constructs that we will highlight below.

To be able to read a text file line by line in Python, you'll use the open(file, mode) functions and the readlines() method. Specifically, you're going to read the apache_logs.txt file as read-only ('r') and read each of its lines to store them in a list.

In regexes, it is possible to refer to groups identified by round brackets not only by a numerical index but also *by a name*. This is thanks to **named capturing groups**. Usually, the generic regex syntax that is used to assign a name to a group is (?<group-name>…). In Python, it is (?P<group-name>…):

- In Python, you can define a list of regex parts that can be merged (join) using a separator. In our case, the separator is defined by one or more space characters (\s+). Also note that in the various patterns below, the character class \S (uppercase) is used to denote a character that is not one of the spaces identified by \s (lowercase):

```
regex_parts = [
    r'(?P<hostName>\S+)',
    r'\S+',
    r'(?P<userName>\S+)',
    r'\[(?P<requestDateTime>[\w:/]+\s[+\-]\d{4})\]',
    r'"(?P<requestContent>\S+\s?\S+?\s?\S+?)"',
    r'(?P<requestStatus>\d{3}|-)',
    r'(?P<responseSizeBytes>\d+|-)',
    r'"(?P<requestReferrer>[^"]*)"',
    r'"(?P<requestAgent>[^"]*)?"',
]
pattern = re.compile(r'\s+'.join(regex_parts) + r'$')
```

Note that, in this case, the re.compile() function is used since the match must be done many times on all lines of the log; therefore, precompiling the regex could have computational advantages.

- Pattern matching is done for each line in the log:

```
for line in access_log_lines:
    log_data.append(pattern.match(line).groupdict())
```

The groupdict() method returns a dictionary with the group names as the key and the matched strings as the value for that key. All the dictionaries for each line are appended to the log_data list.

We leave it up to the reader to interpret how each regex part goes about capturing the desired string.

Now that we've clarified a few points in the code, let's import the log into Power BI:

1. Open Power BI Desktop through the shortcut that activates the pbi_powerquery_env environment.

2. Make sure Power BI Desktop is referencing the pbi_powerquery_env environment in **Options**.

3. Go to **Get Data, More … pyt** and select the Python script.

4. Copy and paste the script from the 01-apache-access-log-parser-python.py file into the Python script editor, making sure to change the path to the Apache log file. Then click on **OK**.

5. Then, select the **df** dataframe from the **Navigator** window and click on **Load**:

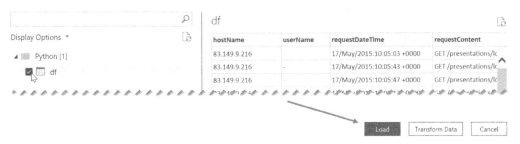

Figure 6.30: Selecting the df dataframe returned by the Python script

6. If you click on the **Data** icon, you can view the entire log loaded as a structured table:

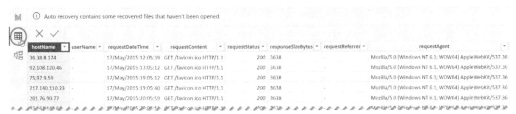

Figure 6.31: The Apache access log is loaded in Power BI with Python

Awesome! As you can see, Python has done all the magic of transforming semi-structured data into table-structured data thanks to regexes! So now you can easily import what looked like a complex log file to manage into Power BI.

Importing Apache access logs in Power BI with R

In this section, you will load the information of the apache_logs.txt file, but this time, using an R script.

Compared to what you've learned previously about regexes in R, in the `02-apache-access-log-parser-r.R` script (which you'll find in the same preceding folder), you'll encounter these new constructs:

- To be able to read a text file line by line in R, you'll use the `read_lines()` function from the readr package. Specifically, you're going to read each line of the `apache_logs.txt` file in order to persist them to a vector.

- In order to take full advantage of named capturing groups in R, you need to install and use the features of a package called `namedCapture`. Thanks to this package, both regex syntaxes for named groups are allowed: the standard (`?<group-name>…`) regex syntax and the (`?P<group-name>…`) regex syntax.

- Just as we did in the Python script, in R, you'll also define a vector of regex parts, which you'll merge with the `paste(..., collapse = '...')` function. Essentially, the regex components within the vector are combined using the text specified in the `collapse` argument. Specifically, this function will join regex parts together through the `\s+` separator. After merging all of the parts, the `$` character is added to the end of the resulting string using the `paste0(…)` function. Remember that raw strings have a different syntax in R than in Python. In this case, we will use the `r'{...}'` syntax:

```r
regex_parts <- c(
    r'{(?P<hostName>\S+)}'
  , r'{\S+}'
  , r'{(?P<userName>\S+)}'
  , r'{\[(?P<requestDateTime>[\w:/]+\s[+\-]\d{4})\]}'
  , r'{"(?P<requestContent>\S+\s?\S+?\s?\S+?)"}'
  , r'{(?P<requestStatus>\d{3}|-)}'
  , r'{(?P<responseSizeBytes>\d+|-)}'
  , r'{"(?P<requestReferrer>[^"]*)"}'
  , r'{"(?P<requestAgent>[^"]*)?"}'
)
pattern <- paste0( paste(regex_parts, collapse = r'{\s+}'), '$' )
```

- Pattern matching is done using the `str_match_named()` function of the namedCapture package over the whole log vector, using a single-line command:

```r
df <- as.data.frame( str_match_named( access_log_lines, pattern = pattern
) )
```

Again, we leave it to the reader to interpret how each individual regex part goes about capturing the desired string.

IMPORTANT NOTE

Toby Dylan Hocking, author of the namedCapture package, has developed a newer package called nc, which uses user-friendly functions for extracting a data table from non-tabular text data using regular expressions. For the sake of training on this very topic, we use the old namedCapture package in this case, because it avoids hiding the construction of the entire pattern used for matching.

Now that we've clarified a few points in the code, let's import the log into Power BI:

1. First, you need to install the namedCapture package. So, open RStudio and make sure that the engine being referenced is the latest one (CRAN R 4.2.2 in our case) in **Global Options**.

2. Now, go to the console and enter and run the following code:

```
install.packages("namedCapture")
```

3. Open Power BI Desktop, go to **Get Data**, More … and select the R script.

4. Copy and paste the script from the 02-apache-access-log-parser-r.R file into the R script editor and then click on **OK**.

5. Then, select the **df** dataframe from the **Navigator** window and click on **Load**:

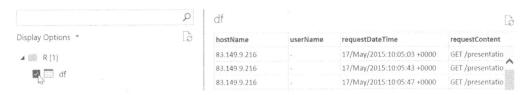

Figure 6.32: Selecting the df dataframe returned by the R script

6. If you click on the **Data** icon, you can view the entire log loaded as a structured table:

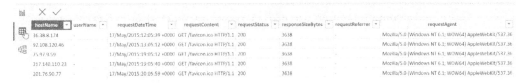

Figure 6.33: The Apache access log loaded in Power BI with R

Great job! You were able to import a semi-structured log file into Power BI even with R.

Extracting values from text using regex in Power BI

The last use case we want to present happens very often when it comes to shipping goods to customers. Sometimes a fraudster manages to steal the goods addressed to a customer and the company has to refund the customer.

The defrauded customer then contacts Customer Care to request a refund. If the management system provided to the Customer Care operator who has to manage the case does not allow you to enter the refund information in a structured way, the operator must resort to the only possible method: the entry of a *free text note* associated with the order, which specifies the *amount*, the *reason*, and the *date* of the refund.

You already know that information entered in free text is every analyst's nightmare, especially when your boss asks you to analyze the very information entered in those infamous notes.

In the repository that comes with this book, you can find the OrderNotes.xlsx Excel file inside the Ch06 - Using Regular Expressions in Power BI folder. Its content is shown in *Figure 6.34*:

	A	B
1	OrderNumber	Notes
2	ORD000001	EUR 5.00 Theft in delivery inserted in wire transfer 11/02/2021
3	ORD000002	EUR 29.00 Refund for theft in delivery 04/06/2020
4	ORD000003	53.00€ Refund for theft in delivery 24/09/2020
5	ORD000004	29/10/2020 EUR45.00 Refund for theft in delivery
6	ORD000005	EUR 522.00 PA for theft in delivery 20/08/2020
7	ORD000006	€ 266.00 - Theft in delivery inserted in wire transfer 10/12/2020
8	ORD000007	EUR68.50 - Refund for theft in delivery 02/07/2020
9	ORD000008	EUR 50.00 - Refund for theft in delivery - 30/07/2020
10	ORD000009	30/07/2020 209.00 € - Refund for theft in delivery

Figure 6.34: Free text notes entered by the operator for some orders

As you can see, by looking at the contents of the Excel file, the relevant information to extract from the notes is as follows:

- The refund amount
- The refund reason
- The refund date

The problem is that the Customer Care agents used a lot of imagination to enter this information, without the slightest predetermined rule about how to structure it. From this, we can see the following:

- The refund amount was entered as *EUR xx.yy*, *EURxx.yy*, *xx.yy EUR*, *€ xx.yy*, *xx.yy€*, and *xx.yy €*.
- The "separator" between all of the pieces of information can be made by one or more whitespaces or by a dash surrounded by one or more spaces.
- The refund date is always in the dd/mm/yyyy format (you are lucky here!).
- The refund reason could contain any text.

Given all the generality of the notes entered, is it possible to correctly extract the information needed for the analysis your boss wants? The answer is certainly "yes" if you know how to use regexes in the best possible way.

One regex to rule them all

With the experience you gained in the previous sections, you will immediately understand the solution we are going to propose. Look at the following regex parts:

- **Currency:** `(?:EUR|€)`
- **Separator:** `(?:\s+)?-?(?:\s+)?`
- **Refund amount:** `\d{1,}\.?\d{0,2}`
- **Refund reason:** `.*?`
- **Refund date:** `\d{2}[\-\/]\d{2}[\-\/]\d{4}`

Remember the syntax of a **non-capturing group**, `(?:…)`? Well, with this syntax, you're explicitly saying to the regex engine that you don't want to capture the content inside those brackets, as this isn't important information to extract. That said, the final regex is nothing more than multiple alternative combinations of these parts, such as the one you can see in *Figure 6.35*:

```
^(?
({currency}{separator}{amount}{separator}{reason}{separator}{date})
OR
({amount}{separator}{currency}{separator}{reason}{separator}{date})
OR
({date}{separator}{currency}{separator}{amount}{separator}{reason})
OR
({date}{separator}{amount}{separator}{currency}{separator}{reason})
)$
```

Figure 6.35: The full regex structure for extracting information from notes

If you're curious to see it in full, the final complete regex is as follows:

```
^(?:(?:(?:EUR|€)(?:\s+)?-?(?:\s+)?(?P<RefundAmount>\d{1,}\.?\d{0,2})(?:\
s+)?-?(?:\s+)?(?P<RefundReason>.*?)(?:\s+)?-?(?:\s+)?(?P<RefundDate>\d{2}[\-
\/]\d{2}[\-\/]\d{4})(?:\s+)?-?(?:\s+)?)|(?:(?P<RefundAmount>\d{1,}\.?\d{0,2})
(?:\s+)?-?(?:\s+)?(?:EUR|€)(?:\s+)?-?(?:\s+)?(?P<RefundReason>.*?)(?:\
s+)?-?(?:\s+)?(?P<RefundDate>\d{2}[\-\/]\d{2}[\-\/]\d{4})(?:\s+)?-?(?:\
s+)?)|(?:(?P<RefundDate>\d{2}[\-\/]\d{2}[\-\/]\d{4})(?:\s+)?-?(?:\s+)?(?:EUR|€)
(?:\s+)?-?(?:\s+)?(?P<RefundAmount>\d{1,}\.?\d{0,2})(?:\s+)?-?(?:\
s+)?(?P<RefundReason>.*?)(?:\s+)?-?(?:\s+)?)|(?:(?P<RefundDate>\d{2}[\-\/]\d{2}
[\-\/]\d{4})(?:\s+)?-?(?:\s+)?(?P<RefundAmount>\d{1,}\.?\d{0,2})(?:\s+)?-?(?:\
s+)?(?:EUR|€)(?:\s+)?-?(?:\s+)?(?P<RefundReason>.*?)(?:\s+)?-?(?:\s+)?))$
```

Let's implement it in Power BI using Python.

Using regex in Power BI to extract values with Python

As you saw from *Figure 6.35*, our regex contains named groups that are *reused multiple times* within it. Unfortunately, the reuse of the same named group within a regex is not supported by the Python re module, which is also the module used behind the scenes in pandas. To use more advanced features of regex, such as the previously mentioned *identically named groups* or the *lookbehind* and *lookahead* syntaxes (which are not covered in this chapter), you must use the regex module. So, first, you need to install it in your pbi_powerquery_env environment. Then, you have to load the OrderNotes.xlsx Excel file, located in the Ch06 - Using Regular Expressions in Power BI folder, into Power BI Desktop. After that, you can transform that dataset using a Python script. So, let's get started:

1. Open your Anaconda Prompt, switch to your pbi_powerquery_env environment using the conda activate pbi_powerquery_env command, and then install the regex package using this code: pip install regex.

2. Open Power BI Desktop through the shortcut that activates the pbi_powerquery_env environment.

3. Make sure Power BI Desktop is referencing the pbi_powerquery_env environment in the **Options**.

4. From the ribbon, click on the **Excel workbook** icon to import data from Excel and open the OrderNotes.xlsx file.

5. Select the **Sheet1** dataset from the **Navigator** window and click on **Transform Data**:

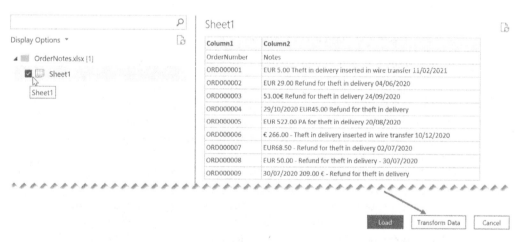

Figure 6.36: Loading the order notes from Excel and transforming the data

6. Declare the first row of loaded data as column headers by clicking on **Use First Row as Headers**:

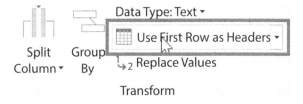

Figure 6.37: Clicking on the Use First Row as Headers button

7. Then, go to the **Transform** tab menu and click on **Run Python script**.

8. Open the Python script that you can find inside the `01-order-notes-parser-python.py` file, which is in the `03-extracting-values-from-text-using-regex` subfolder of the `Ch06 - Using Regular Expressions in Power BI` main folder. Copy and paste the script into the **Run Python script** editor and then click on **OK**.

9. If there are any issues with the compatibility levels of the datasets, simply open the **Data source settings** window from **Options** and set the permissions of each dataset to `Public` using **Edit Permissions....** Then, click on **Refresh Preview**.

10. We are only interested in the `df` dataset. So, click on its **Table** value.

11. You can see that the resulting table has three more columns, each of which refers to a named group matched by regexes:

Figure 6.38: Values extracted from free text notes using regexes with Python

Finally, go to the **Home** menu and click on **Close & Apply**.

Awesome! You've just managed to reorganize the data contained in the free text order notes using regexes in Python. Your boss will be more than happy!

Using regex in Power BI to extract values with R

In R, we can still use the `namedCapture` package to manage named groups that are reused multiple times in the same regex. We can do this by prepending the `(?J)` modifier in front of it (this allows multiple named capture groups to share the same name). Unlike Python, in R, the `str_match_named()` function of the `namedCapture` package does not return a one-time result captured by the named group.

It returns as many columns as it has used:

	RefundAmount	RefundReason	RefundDate	RefundAmount.1	RefundReason.1	RefundDate.1	RefundDate.2	RefundAmount.2	RefundReason.2
1	5.00	Theft in delivery inserted in wire transfer	11/02/2021						
2	29.00	Refund for theft in delivery	04/06/2020						
3				53.00	Refund for theft in delivery	24/09/2020			
4							29/10/2020	45.00	Refund for theft in delivery
5	522.00	PA for theft in delivery	20/08/2020						
6	266.00	Theft in delivery inserted in wire transfer	10/12/2020						
7	68.50	Refund for theft in delivery	02/07/2020						
8	50.00	Refund for theft in delivery	30/07/2020						

Figure 6.39: The intermediate data frame of the R script using namedCapture

Therefore, we had to further manipulate the result; first, by replacing the blank characters with the null value of `NA`, and second, by applying the `dplyr`'s `coalesce()` function, which merges multiple column values into one by keeping the first non-null value.

>
>
> **IMPORTANT NOTE**
>
> We pointed out this limitation to Toby Dylan Hocking, the author of the `namedCapture` package, who recently implemented the feature inside the new version of the package, named nc. Details of the implementation can be found at `https://github.com/tdhock/namedCapture/issues/15`. The new version of the nc package has not yet been released on CRAN at the time of this writing. Therefore, we thought it appropriate to keep the use of the `namedCapture` package in our code. However, there is an additional script (`03-order-notes-parser-nc-r.R`) in the repository that uses the new features introduced in the nc package after my suggestion to the author. You just need to install the nc and `data.table` packages directly from GitHub using the command `remotes::install_github(c("Rdatatable/data.table", "tdhock/nc@suggest-re2"))` in the RStudio console.

That said, let's start to extract values from the order notes using R in Power BI:

1. Open Power BI Desktop and make sure the referenced R engine is the latest one (in our case, this is *CRAN R 4.4.2*).
2. From the ribbon, click on the **Excel workbook** icon to import data from Excel, and open the `OrderNotes.xlsx` file you can find in the `Ch06 - Using Regular Expressions in Power BI` folder.
3. Select the **Sheet1** dataset from the **Navigator** window, and click on **Transform Data** as you did in the previous section.
4. Declare the first row of loaded data as column headers by clicking on **Use First Row as Headers**.
5. Then, go to the **Transform** menu and click on **Run R script**.
6. Open the R script that you can find inside the `02-order-notes-parser-namedcapture-r.R` file, which is in the `extracting-values-from-text-using-regex` subfolder. Copy and paste the script into the **Run R script** editor and then click on **OK**.
7. We are only interested in the df dataset. So, click on its **Table** value.

8. You can see that the resulting table has three more columns, each one related to a named group:

	OrderNumber	Notes	RefundAmount	RefundDate	RefundReason
1	ORD000001	EUR 5.00 Theft in delivery inserted in wire transfer 11/02/2021	5.00	11/02/2021	Theft in delivery inserted in wire transfer
2	ORD000002	EUR 29.00 Refund for theft in delivery 04/06/2020	29.00	04/06/2020	Refund for theft in delivery
3	ORD000003	53.00€ Refund for theft in delivery 24/09/2020	53.00	24/09/2020	Refund for theft in delivery
4	ORD000004	29/10/2020 EUR45.00 Refund for theft in delivery	45.00	29/10/2020	Refund for theft in delivery
5	ORD000005	EUR 522.00 PA for theft in delivery 20/08/2020	522.00	20/08/2020	PA for theft in delivery
6	ORD000006	€ 266.00 - Theft in delivery inserted in wire transfer 10/12/2020	266.00	10/12/2020	Theft in delivery inserted in wire transfer
7	ORD000007	EUR68.50 - Refund for theft in delivery 02/07/2020	68.50	02/07/2020	Refund for theft in delivery
8	ORD000008	EUR 50.00 - Refund for theft in delivery - 30/07/2020	50.00	30/07/2020	Refund for theft in delivery
9	ORD000009	30/07/2020 209.00 € - Refund for theft in delivery	209.00	30/07/2020	Refund for theft in delivery

Figure 6.40: Values extracted from the free text order notes using regex with R

Finally, go to the **Home** menu and click on **Close & Apply**.

Amazing! You've just demonstrated that you know how to use regexes to rearrange the data contained in the order notes, even with R.

Summary

In this chapter, you were introduced to the basics of how to use regexes. Using the bare minimum, you were able to effectively validate strings representing email addresses and dates in Power BI, using both Python and R.

You also learned how to extract information from semi-structured log files using regexes and how to import the extracted information into Power BI in a structured way.

Finally, you learned how to use regex in Python and R to extract information from seemingly unprocessable free text thanks to the real-world case of notes associated with sales orders.

In the next chapter, you'll learn how to use some de-identification techniques in Power BI to anonymize or pseudonymize datasets that show sensitive data about individuals in plain text before they are imported into Power BI.

References

For additional reading, please refer to the following books and articles:

- **Regular Expressions**: *The Complete Tutorial, Jan Goyvaerts* (`https://www.regular-expressions.info/tutorial.html`)
- `nc`, an R package that simplifies the process of extracting and organizing information in a tabular format with regular expressions (`https://github.com/tdhock/nc`))

Test your knowledge

1. What are the main purposes of using regexes?
2. What are the main Python packages that implement regex functionality?
3. What are the main R packages that implement regex functionality?
4. Can you briefly summarize the method used to extract useful information from a free-text note?

Learn more on Discord

To join the Discord community for this book – where you can share feedback, ask questions to the author, and learn about new releases – follow the QR code below:

```
https://discord.gg/MKww5g45EB
```

7

Anonymizing and Pseudonymizing Your Data in Power BI

It is often the case that those who develop a specific software product for one customer want to re-package it and sell it to another customer who is interested in similar features. However, if you want to show some screenshots of the software in a demo to the new customer, you should avoid showing any data that might be sensitive. Getting in there and trying to manually mask the data from a copy of the original software database was definitely one of the tasks the poor hapless developer had to do in the past, maybe even a few days before the demo.

The scenario described does not require data to be shared with a third-party recipient but is intended to successfully demonstrate a product to a customer by presenting simulated data for illustrative purposes. Therefore, there is no concern about a potential brute-force attack by professional analysts to derive the original data prior to the de-identification operation.

Things definitely change when you need to share an entire dataset with a third-party recipient. The issue has become more sensitive since 2018, especially in Europe, where the need to pay more attention to data privacy and **personally identifiable information (PII)** has become imperative for organizations to comply with the requirements of the **General Data Protection Regulation (GDPR)**.

The goal of this chapter is to introduce de-identification techniques using **Python** and **R** scripts that can help the **Power BI** developer prevent a person's identity from being associated with the information displayed in the report.

In this chapter, you will learn about the following:

- De-identifying data
- Anonymizing data in Power BI
- Pseudonymizing data in Power BI

Technical requirements

This chapter requires you to have a working internet connection and **Power BI Desktop** already installed on your machine (we used version 2.114.664.0 64-bit, February 2022). You must have properly configured the R and Python engines and IDEs as outlined in *Chapter 2, Configuring R with Power BI*, and *Chapter 3, Configuring Python with Power BI*.

De-identifying data

PII, also known as **personal information** or **personal data,** is any information about an identifiable individual. There are two types of PII – *direct* and *indirect*. Examples of **direct identifiers** include your name, your address, a photograph of you, or a **Radio Frequency Identification** (**RFID**) tag associated with you. **Indirect identifiers**, on the other hand, are any elements of information that don't explicitly refer to you as an individual, but somehow make it easier to identify you. Examples of indirect identifiers include your license plate number, your bank account number, the link to your profile on a social networking site, or your place of employment.

The practice of **de-identifying** data is to manipulate PII so that it is no longer possible to identify the person referenced by them.

There are two ways to deal with direct and indirect personal identifiers – either you decide to destroy them completely, or you decide to keep them separate from the rest of the data and implement security measures to prevent anyone from re-identifying the data subject. But first, let's explore what some of the most common de-identification techniques are.

De-identification techniques

De-identification is a process that is invisible to end users. After doing a careful study with a team of analysts, it is usually the data manager (or the person acting on their behalf) who decides what information should be de-identified. The following sections discuss the most commonly used de-identification techniques, such as:

- Information removal
- Data masking
- Data swapping
- Generalization
- Data perturbation
- Tokenization
- Hashing
- Encryption

Let's take a closer look at these techniques.

Information removal

The simplest form of de-identification is the removal of sensitive information from the dataset to reduce the risk of data breaches and ensure compliance with privacy regulations. Determining sensitive information for removal requires an assessment of the nature and context of the data. Information such as names, addresses, or banking information that can directly or indirectly identify an individual is often considered sensitive. The decision also depends on the potential for harm if the data is mishandled and the risk of re-identification, where data elements, alone or in combination with other information, could reveal an individual's identity. This process requires a deep understanding of the data and its broader context.

An example of information removal is shown in *Figure 7.1*:

Name	Email	Gender	Country	NumOfOrders
Johann Lucas Idler	j.lucas.idler@bluewin.ch	male	SWITZERLAND	15
Ruth Connelly	clevecon@outlook.com	female	UNITED STATES	1
Francisco Javier Diez Gonzalez	francis1971diez@gmail.com	male	MEXICO	1
Alexei Fabius Malenkiy-Fransk	fabius-fransk@hotmail.com	male	UKRAINA	1
Hilma Kitzmann	hilmakit234@gmx.de	female	GERMANY	6
Luke Romba	rombaluke77@gmail.com	male	UNITED STATES	1
John Romkanid	romkaj69@gmail.com	male	UNITED STATES	2

Gender	Country	NumOfOrders
male	SWITZERLAND	15
female	UNITED STATES	1
male	MEXICO	1
male	UKRAINA	1
female	GERMANY	6
male	UNITED STATES	1
male	UNITED STATES	2

Figure 7.1: Anonymization, information removal

Obviously, there could be more than one drawback to this simplistic approach:

- Over-de-identification can lead to the loss of valuable information, potentially reducing the utility and accuracy of the dataset for research and analysis.
- The final dataset no longer conforms to the schema expected by the application that needs to consume it.

Data masking

Data masking hides information that users with certain roles shouldn't see. It can consist of modifying data by replacing words or characters. For example, you can replace a value character with a symbol, such as * or x.

The following is a typical example of data masking:

Name	Email	Gender	Country	NumOfOrders
Johann Lucas Idler	j.lucas.idler@bluewin.ch	male	SWITZERLAND	15
Ruth Connelly	clevecon@outlook.com	female	UNITED STATES	1
Francisco Javier Diez Gonzalez	francis1971diez@gmail.com	male	MEXICO	1
Alexei Fabius Malenkiy-Fransk	fabius-fransk@hotmail.com	male	UKRAINA	1
Hilma Kitzmann	hilmakit234@gmx.de	female	GERMANY	6
Luke Romba	rombaluke77@gmail.com	male	UNITED STATES	1
John Romkanid	romkaj69@gmail.com	male	UNITED STATES	2

Name	Email	Gender	Country	NumOfOrders
Roberto Hall	*@bluewin.ch	male	SWITZERLAND	15
Amber Cole	*@outlook.com	female	UNITED STATES	1
Christopher Patel	*@gmail.com	male	MEXICO	1
Douglas Singleton	*@hotmail.com	male	UKRAINA	1
Brittany Harrison	*@gmx.de	female	GERMANY	6
John Trujillo	*@gmail.com	male	UNITED STATES	1
Stephen Thomas	*@gmail.com	male	UNITED STATES	2

Figure 7.2: Anonymization, data masking

Note that if the readable domain name in the email address is not public and belongs to a recognizable legal entity, applying data masking may not comply with GDPR rules if it allows the workplace to be identified. When determining which users should have access to the unmasked data, factors such as their role, need for information, and data security clearance are critical. Some products offer out-of-the-box **dynamic data masking** solutions that selectively mask or block sensitive information based on user roles, locations, and privileges. This masking can be applied to various types of sensitive data, including phone numbers, user IDs, personally identifiable information, and other potentially identifiable information, ensuring that only authorized personnel have access to the full, unmasked record.

IMPORTANT NOTE

For example, **Microsoft SQL Server** and **Azure SQL Database** provide dynamic data masking as a solution to prevent sensitive data from being exposed to unauthorized users. The data in the database is not altered, because the masking rules are applied to the query results.

Data swapping

Data swapping involves shuffling the values of a column containing sensitive data across the entire dataset. For example, if you have a column that contains a person's date of birth, the shuffling technique can be used to effectively anonymize that information.

An advantage of this technique is that it preserves the statistical properties of the original dataset, making it suitable for analysis while protecting individual privacy. It's also a relatively simple method to implement.

However, there are drawbacks. A major challenge is maintaining data integrity, especially in datasets where relationships between different columns are important. Incorrect implementation of data swapping can lead to misleading or inaccurate analysis. In addition, if the process isn't managed carefully, it can result in partial or complete loss of the original data ordering, making it difficult to restore the original state.

In cases where problems arise during data exchange, it's critical to have a rollback plan in place. This typically involves maintaining a secure, encrypted copy of the original dataset that can be used to restore the data to its original state if necessary. However, this approach must be carefully managed to prevent unauthorized access to the original sensitive data, to ensure compliance with data privacy regulations, and to maintain data security.

Generalization

Generalization is a data de-identification technique that replaces specific values in a dataset with broader, less specific categories. For example:

- An *age* of 25 can be transformed in the values >=18, or *between 18 and 30*.
- A *birth date*, like 04/11/1989, can be replaced by the *year of birth* 1989. It involves replacing specific values with broader categories to which the original values belong.
- A *postal zip code* can be replaced by a broader *regional zip code*.

This method is particularly useful in preserving the utility of the data while reducing the risk of identifying individual data subjects.

The primary benefit of generalization is that it allows for a balance between data utility and privacy. By categorizing data into broader groups, it becomes more difficult to pinpoint individual identities, thereby protecting personal information. This approach is beneficial in fields such as medical research, where preserving the overall structure and patterns in data is critical, but identifying individual patients is unnecessary and potentially harmful.

However, the technique has its challenges. Overgeneralization can result in a significant loss of detail, making the data less useful for specific analyses. Determining the right level of generalization requires a careful assessment of the intended use of the data and the associated privacy risks.

Data perturbation

Data perturbation is a method of data anonymization that involves modifying original data values to protect privacy. This is typically done in one of two ways: by adding random noise or by creating synthetic data.

Adding random noise introduces small, random variations into the original data values. For example, in a dataset of numerical values such as salaries, a random amount might be added to or subtracted from each salary number.

The goal is to change the data just enough so that the individual values are no longer accurate representations of the original data, but the overall statistical properties of the dataset (such as means and variances) remain largely unchanged. This technique is particularly useful in scenarios where the overall statistical analysis of the dataset is more important than the precision of individual data points.

Creating synthetic data, on the other hand, involves generating entirely new data points that are statistically similar to the original dataset but do not correspond to actual individuals. This method uses algorithms to understand patterns and correlations in the original data and then uses this understanding to generate new, artificial data points. The resulting synthetic dataset maintains the statistical properties of the original data, making it useful for analysis without risking the exposure of individual identities.

It's important to note that while data perturbation can enhance privacy, it also introduces a trade-off between data accuracy and utility. The added noise or synthetic elements can sometimes result in the loss of important information, potentially making the data less useful for certain types of precise analysis. The key challenge is in determining the right amount of perturbation: enough to protect privacy, but not so much that the data becomes meaningless.

Tokenization

Tokenization is a data security technique that involves replacing sensitive data elements with non-sensitive equivalents called **tokens** that have no exploitable meaning or value. The tokens are randomly generated alphanumeric strings, and each token is uniquely mapped to the original sensitive data. This mapping is critical to the tokenization process, and it's securely maintained in a dedicated database, often referred to as a token vault.

The token vault securely stores the association between each token and its corresponding original value. This database is heavily protected by various security measures. These include encryption, access controls, and often additional layers of security protocols to prevent unauthorized access. Encryption ensures that even if someone gains access to the token vault, they cannot decipher the relationship between the tokens and the original data without the proper decryption key.

The role of the dedicated token server is critical in this process. The token server is responsible for generating tokens, maintaining the token vault, and managing the mapping between tokens and original data. When a system or application needs to process sensitive data, it sends a request to the token server. The server then either retrieves the corresponding original data for an existing token or generates a new token for a new piece of sensitive data.

The token server ensures that the actual sensitive data does not travel throughout the system, significantly reducing the risk of data breaches. It acts as a central, secure point for all tokenization processes, handling both the creation of tokens and the translation back to the original data when required. This centralized approach enables better management and control of access to sensitive data.

Furthermore, since there is no mathematical algorithm that relates the token to the original data, the ability to reverse engineer the original information from the token is virtually non-existent. This lack of direct correlation between the token and the sensitive data it represents provides a high level of security to the tokenization process.

Hashing

Hashing is a technique similar to tokenization, except that the resulting *token*, called a **hash value**, is generated by a mathematical algorithm, has a fixed length, and is nearly impossible to transform back to the original value. If you use the same hash function with the same input value, you'll always get the same hash value as the original output. In the hashing process, the use of *salt* plays a critical role in increasing security, especially against brute-force attacks. A salt is a random string that is added to the input value before the hash function is applied. The primary purpose of salt is to ensure that the same input does not always result in the same hash value, significantly increasing the complexity and security of the hash.

When a hash function is used without salt, it produces the same output for the same input every time. This consistency can be exploited by attackers using methods such as rainbow tables, which are precomputed tables for inverting cryptographic hash functions. Essentially, if an attacker knows the hash function being used, they can precompute the hash values for a wide range of possible inputs and then simply look up the hash value to find the corresponding input.

Encryption

Encryption is a method of securing sensitive data by transforming it into a format that cannot be easily understood without a specific key, known as a decryption key. Unlike hashing, which is a one-way process, encryption is reversible, allowing the original data to be recovered. This two-way transformation is critical in many applications where data must be securely transmitted or stored, but also retrieved and used in its original form.

The process of encryption involves using a mathematical algorithm, called a cipher, to convert the original data (plaintext) into an encrypted form (ciphertext). This conversion is done using an encryption key, a string of bits that the cipher uses to transform the data. To convert the ciphertext back to plaintext, a decryption key is required. Depending on the encryption method used, this decryption key can be the same as the encryption key (symmetric encryption) or a different key (asymmetric encryption).

The use of an encrypted mapping table can greatly improve the efficiency of data decryption. An encrypted mapping table stores a relationship between the encrypted data and some form of reference data. This allows you to more quickly look up and decrypt specific pieces of data without having to decrypt an entire dataset. This approach is particularly useful in database systems where certain fields need to be accessed frequently and quickly.

The incorporation of end-to-end encryption in productivity tools and database systems represents a significant advancement in data security. End-to-end encryption ensures that data is encrypted at its origin and decrypted only at its intended destination.

IMPORTANT NOTE

Two examples are Microsoft SQL Server or Azure SQL databases, which have the Always Encrypted feature out of the box. It works by encrypting the data on the client side and hiding the encryption keys from the server. Even database administrators cannot read information stored in an encrypted column without having explicit permission.

Now that you have an idea of the most common transformations used to de-identify sensitive information, you will see how they are used in anonymization and pseudonymization.

Understanding pseudonymization

Pseudonymization is a de-identifying process that separates direct or indirect identifiers from the remaining data while ensuring the following:

- Replacement of one or more pieces of PII with **pseudonyms** (a random real name, or more often a random numeric or alphanumeric identifier), which ensures the non-identification of the subject. Analytical correlations are guaranteed by the fact that the pseudonym is always the same for the same input. Thus, the analysis of pseudonymized data doesn't lose any value.

- Do not destroy the original PII, but ensure that the entire dataset can be reconstructed (re-identify the data), for example, using lookup tables between PII and pseudonyms, or digital secret keys to pseudonymize inputs to the same output.

- Take appropriate technical and organizational measures to make it difficult to trace the identity of an individual from the remaining data.

During this process, you can perform some de-identification transformations on some PII that you want to keep in the accessible data. For example, you can replace PII values with similar-looking pseudonyms, making sure to keep track of the replacement to ensure re-identification.

An example of a pseudonymization process is shown in *Figure 7.3*, where a lookup table is used to guarantee the mapping for the inverse transformation:

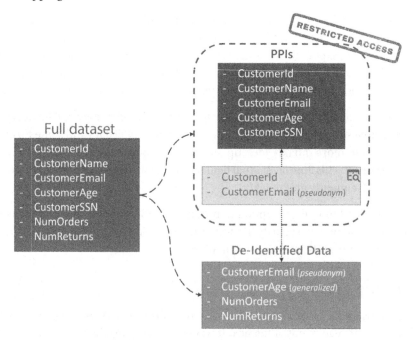

Figure 7.3: The process of pseudonymization

The figure shows a complete dataset on the left, containing various customer-related PII, such as CustomerId, CustomerName, CustomerEmail, CustomerAge, CustomerSSN, NumOrders, and NumReturns. The upper-right portion of the image represents the PII elements, highlighted in red, that have restricted access due to their sensitive nature. These PII elements include CustomerId, CustomerName, CustomerEmail, CustomerAge, and CustomerSSN.

In the bottom-right corner of *Figure 7.3*, we see a subset of this data, labeled "De-Identified Data," that has undergone pseudonymization. In this de-identified section, CustomerEmail has been replaced with a pseudonym to mask the original identity while still allowing for individual tracking or analysis. Additionally, CustomerAge appears to have been generalized, meaning it has been replaced with a less specific value to prevent direct identification. The NumOrders and NumReturns fields are included in the de-identified data as non-PII elements and remain unchanged.

Figure 7.3 highlights the presence of a lookup table, indicated by a lens icon, that serves as a key for re-identifying the pseudonymized data when necessary. This lookup table securely stores the association between the original PII values and their corresponding pseudonyms, allowing the original data to be restored in a controlled manner when appropriate permissions and conditions are met.

The key elements that should be noted from *Figure 7.3* are the following:

- The complete record contains both PII and non-PII elements.
- PII elements are highly sensitive and are placed under restricted access.
- Pseudonymization replaces sensitive PII with non-identifiable proxies, such as pseudonyms, for CustomerEmail.
- Generalization is applied to CustomerAge to obfuscate specific values.
- A secure lookup table maintains the association between the original and pseudonymized data.
- The de-identified dataset still contains certain elements, such as NumOrders and NumReturns, that do not require pseudonymization.

Such an architecture also ensures the ability to satisfy any requests for deletion of personal data by individuals (as required by GDPR) by meeting the following conditions:

- It will be impossible to identify the subject from that moment on, by simply removing the corresponding association from the lookup table. When a subject requests that their personal data be deleted, the system responds by removing the entry that links the pseudonymized identifier in the de-identified record to the subject's actual identity in the lookup table. Once this link is removed, the record no longer contains any direct or indirect means of identifying the subject, rendering them anonymous within the record.
- De-identification transformations ensure that the usefulness of the dataset for research or business analysis is retained even after specific personal data is removed, because the statistical relationships and patterns are largely unaffected. This approach allows organizations to comply with GDPR's data protection requirements without sacrificing their ability to gain insights from their data assets.

IMPORTANT NOTE

The moment you permanently lose the link between a set of accessible data and their respective PII, that set becomes completely anonymized and thus falls outside of GDPR's control.

So, we have introduced the concept of anonymization. Let's take a look at what this means.

What is anonymization?

Anonymization is a rigorous process that ensures the complete destruction of both direct and indirect identifiers, or any links to their de-identified counterparts, making it extremely unlikely that an attacker can reconstruct the identity of individuals from the data. The essence of this process is to make inversion impossible. When data is anonymized, any lookup tables or cross-referencing tools that map de-identified data back to real people are securely eliminated. This step is critical because it removes the ability to match anonymized data with identifiable information to reveal individual identities. For this reason, the following becomes true: **anonymized data is outside the scope and control of GDPR because anonymized data is no longer personal data**.

The most obvious disadvantage of anonymization is that it removes significant value from the data involved. This is because once the process is complete, it is impossible to trace the identities that generated the data. It is therefore advisable to assess all relevant risks before anonymizing a dataset.

The second disadvantage of anonymization is that it usually uses randomly generated de-identified strings, so *some statistical information about the dataset is permanently lost*, making any work a data scientist would have to do futile.

Anonymized data may be vulnerable to **de-anonymization attacks**. They consist of enriching the anonymized dataset with available external information, thus imputing the anonymized elements. These attacks are more likely to succeed because the anonymized data is rich, granular, and relatively stable over time and context.

To address and mitigate this vulnerability, it is essential to employ additional protection measures. These include the use of **differential privacy**, which adds a layer of randomness to the data, making it more difficult for attackers to use external information to determine individual identities. Regular audits and updates to anonymization protocols are also critical, as they help identify and respond to new threats. In addition, limiting access to anonymized data based on roles and minimizing the level of detail in shared records can reduce risk. Finally, continuous monitoring for potential breaches and a robust response strategy can significantly improve the security of anonymized data against de-anonymization attempts.

The most commonly used de-identification techniques for secure anonymization are as follows:

- Tokenization
- Encryption

Now let's see how you can apply these concepts to a real-world case using Power BI.

Anonymizing data in Power BI

One of the possible scenarios that could happen to you during your career as a report developer in Power BI is the following. Imagine that you are given an Excel dataset to import into Power BI to create a report for another department in your company. The Excel dataset contains sensitive personal information, such as the names and email addresses of people who have made multiple attempts to pay for an order with a credit card. The following is an example of the contents of the Excel file:

	A	B	C	D	E	F	G
1	Name	Email	Country	NumOfOrders	OrderAmount	NumCreditCardAttempts	Notes
2	Rachel Rodriguez-Bailey	rrodriguezb@yahoo.com	UNITED STATES	15	2228.57	21	It seems the customer has another account with the name Ashley Stevenson and email kevin123b@hotmail.com
3	Vada Kling	kingv@gmail.com	UNITED STATES	1	2868.57	3	
4	Stacy Connely	stacycon@outlook.com	UNITED STATES	1	612.22	2	

Figure 7.4: Excel data to be anonymized

You are asked to create the report while anonymizing the sensitive data.

The first thing you will notice is that not only do you need to anonymize the **Name** and **Email** columns, but also, some names or email addresses can be contained in the text of **Notes**. While it is quite easy to find email addresses using regular expressions, it is not so easy to find names in free text. For this purpose, it is necessary to use a **natural language processing** (**NLP**) technique called **named entity recognition** (**NER**). Thanks to NER, it's possible to identify and classify named entities (such as people, places, etc.) in free text.

The basic idea is to replace both full names and email addresses with random *tokens*. Depending on the analytical language used, there are different solutions driven by the different packages available that lead to the same result.

Anonymizing data using Python

Python is one of the most widely used languages for performing de-identification transformations in anonymization processes. There are a number of packages that implement such solutions. In particular, Microsoft has released the open-source package **Presidio** (https://microsoft.github.io/presidio/), which is recognized as a comprehensive privacy and anonymization solution. It provides rapid forms of identification and anonymization for entities found in free text and images, such as credit card numbers, names, locations, social security numbers, email addresses, financial information, and more. **PII recognizers** use NER, regular expressions, rule-based logic, and checksums to identify the relevant context in multiple languages. Behind the scenes, Presidio uses NLP engines to recognize the entities – it supports both **spaCy** (the default one) and **Stanza**. One of the most interesting features of Presidio is its *extensibility*. In fact, it is very easy to extend the Presidio analyzer by adding *custom PII entities*. This means that if an organization has unique forms of PII or operates in a multilingual environment, it can train Presidio to recognize and protect that data accordingly.

Once the sensitive entities are identified, you need to replace them with tokens. These are generated in Python using the `secrets` module.

That said, you can find an implementation of this in the Python file 01-anonymize-data-in-power-bi-python.py, in the Ch07 - Anonymizing and Pseudonymizing Your Data in Power BI folder of the GitHub repository that comes with this book. It performs the following operations:

1. Loads the libraries needed to run the code. You will be using the pandas module, some functions from the presidio_analyzer and presidio_anonymizer modules, and the secrets module.

2. Defines two custom functions, one to anonymize emails and the other to anonymize person names. Use both the analyzer.analyze() Presidio function to identify the entities to be anonymized and the secrets module to generate the tokens for the anonymizer.anonymize() function.

3. Initializes the main objects of the Presidio analyzer and Presidio anonymizer.

4. For each row of the dataset previously loaded into Power BI Desktop (or via the pandas read_excel() function if you want to test the code in **VSCode**), it applies the anonymizeEmail function to the **Email** and **Notes** columns and applies the anonymizeName function to the Name and Notes columns. To apply a function to each individual value of a column, we use the apply() function followed by a construct called a lambda function (introduced by the keyword lambda). It is a small function defined without a name (anonymous) to be used inline. Here is an example:

```
df.Name = df.Name.apply(lambda x: anonymizeName(x))
```

However, to continue, it is best to configure *a new Python environment* dedicated to Presidio to avoid package conflicts.

These are the steps needed to configure the new environment:

1. Open Anaconda Prompt.

2. Enter and run the following code to create the new presidio_env environment with Python 3.8:

```
conda create --name presidio_env python=3.8
```

3. Enter and run the following code to switch to the newly created environment:

```
conda activate presidio_env
```

4. Enter and run the following code to install the Presidio analyzer:

```
pip install presidio_analyzer
```

5. Enter and run the following code to install the Presidio anonymizer:

```
pip install presidio_anonymizer
```

6. The analyzer also installs spaCy behind the scenes. So, you must also install spaCy's *trained pipeline for written English text* (we chose the one ideal for blogs, news, and comments) using this code:

```
python -m spacy download en_core_web_lg
```

This is the largest pipeline used by spaCy and takes up about 588 MB.

7. Enter and run the following code to install pandas:

```
pip install pandas
```

8. If you want to use pandas to directly load Excel with Python and then test the code before entering it in Power BI, you'll also need the openpyxl module:

```
pip install openpyxl
```

9. Enter and run the following code to install matplotlib, needed by the Power BI wrapper used with Python scripts:

```
pip install matplotlib
```

You are now ready to apply anonymization in Power BI to the content of the CustomersCreditCardAttempts. xlsx Excel file, which you can find in the Ch07 - Anonymizing and Pseudonymizing Your Data in Power BI folder.

So, let's get started:

1. As mentioned in the first section of *Chapter 4, Solving Common Issues When Using Python and R in Power BI*, create a batch script and an associated shortcut to run Power BI Desktop in the context of the newly created presidio_env environment.

2. Open Power BI Desktop from the newly created shortcut that activates the presidio_env environment.

3. Make sure the referenced Python environment is presidio_env in **Options** (its home directory should be C:\ProgramData\Miniconda3\envs\presidio_env). If you can't find the path to your Python environment, activate it at the Anaconda command prompt (conda activate <your-env>) and then type the where python command.

4. Import the aforementioned CustomersCreditCardAttempts.xlsx file content.

5. From the **Navigator** window, select the Customers sheet and then click on **Transform Data**:

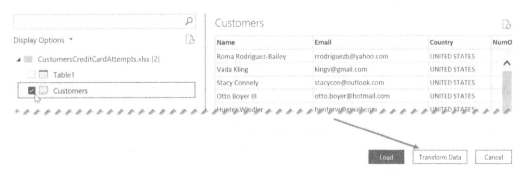

Figure 7.5: Selecting the Customers sheet and clicking on Transform Data

6. Click on the **Transform** menu and then click on **Run Python Script**.

7. Copy the script from the `01-anonymize-data-in-power-bi-python.py` file into the Python script editor and click **OK**.

8. If Power BI needs you to provide it with data privacy information, you already know how to proceed based on what you've seen in *Chapter 4, Solving Common Issues When Using Python and R in Power BI*. Set the privacy levels to **Public**.

9. We are only interested in the `df` dataset. So, click on its **Table** value.

10. You can now click **Close & Apply** in the **Home** tab.

11. Click on the **Table view** on the left of the canvas and select the **Customers** table. As you can see, person names in the `Name` and `Notes` columns and emails in the `Email` and `Notes` columns have been correctly anonymized:

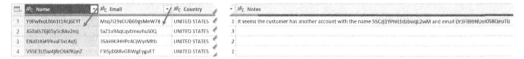

Figure 7.6: The transformed dataset as the result of the Python script

Note the data anonymized in the **Notes** column is the result of applying the NER algorithms used by the **spaCy** engine, which works under the hood of Presidio.

In addition, the de-identification technique used (tokenization) does not preserve the statistical properties of the dataset, because applying the procedure to the same personal data does not return the same de-identified string.

IMPORTANT NOTE

When you publish the report for which you have anonymized the data, the corresponding dataset is also published. Users who can access only the dataset (and not the source Excel file) will see only the anonymized data, without having the ability to learn about the associations with the original data that was replaced.

Thanks to anonymization, you can now develop your reports without worrying about the risk of exposing sensitive data.

Let's see how you can do the same thing in R.

Anonymizing data using R

You can also implement a data anonymization process in R. As long as you use regular expressions to identify strings in R, the processing is quite fast. However, when natural language processing techniques like NER need to be implemented, the most common R packages available are often wrappers around open-source modules developed in other languages. For example, the openNLP R package is an interface to the `Apache OpenNLP` toolkit, which is based on machine learning algorithms written in Java. In order for the openNLP package to interface with the `OpenNLP` software, its installation also requires the `rJava` package as a dependency, which enables the dialog between the R and Java worlds.

To implement the same anonymization features in R that were developed in Python in the previous section, you will make use of another widely used R package for NLP operations called spacyr. This library provides a convenient R wrapper around the Python spacy module. In the previous section, you saw that the Python module called presidio, behind the scenes, installs the same spacy module that spacyr uses. If you're wondering how to run Python code from an R module, remember that, in *Chapter 3, Configuring Python with Power BI*, you ran Python code through **RStudio** using the R package called reticulate. Just as rJava provides the interface between R and the Java VM, reticulate allows R to interface with a Python environment and execute Python code. In short, the R code you are going to develop does nothing more than execute the functionality of the spacy Python module you used in the previous section.

IMPORTANT NOTE

Remember that you could have used regular expressions to replace email addresses with dummy data. Instead, replacing person names in free text is only possible with an NLP function that recognizes named entities. Hence the need to use a package like spacyr.

As in the previous section, here you will use tokenization to anonymize the contents of the Excel file CustomersCreditCardAttempts.xlsx. Tokens in R are created using the stringi package.

The R code in the 02-anonymize-data-in-power-bi-r.R file, which you can find in the Ch07 - Anonymizing and Pseudonymizing Your Data in Power BI folder, performs the following operations:

1. Loads the libraries needed to run the code. In particular, you will use stringr, dplyr, and purrr from Tidyverse for data wrangling; spacyr and stringi are used for data anonymization.

2. Defines the anonymizeEmails function, which is used to anonymize emails into free text. It uses the spacyr function spacy_parse() with the additional like_email attribute. Since it can identify multiple email addresses in a single text, the str_replace_all() function is used to replace all the found occurrences with a token generated by the stri_rand_strings function of the stringi package.

3. Defines the anonymizeNames function, which is used to anonymize the names of people in free text. It contains more complex logic than the previous function because a person's name can consist of multiple tokens that are not always separated by a space (for example, the name Roma Rodriguez-Bailey). Therefore, to identify the set of all tokens that refer to a single person, we need to construct a regex that references the first and last tokens (from the previous example, Rachel.*?Bailey) and is able to match the entire name. As you can see, there was no need to implement all of this logic in the previous section, because the Python presidio module takes care of all of these cases.

4. You need to initialize spacyr to point to a Python environment with the spacy module installed. In general, if you haven't already installed spacy in an environment, you can use spacyr's spacy_install() function, which will set up a new Python environment with everything you need to make it work properly.

In our case, we've already created the Python environment, presidio_env, in the previous section, which contains both the spacy module and the trained en_core_web_lg model for extracting language attributes using written English samples taken from the web. It is then sufficient to reference the path of the environment presidio_env in the spacy_initialize() function to correctly configure spacyr. Here is the code:

```
spacy_initialize(
  model = "en_core_web_lg",
  condaenv = r"{C:\ProgramData\Miniconda3\envs\presidio_env}",
  entity = TRUE
)
```

5. Once the path to the conda environment presidio_env is set correctly, if you run it in RStudio, you'll get something similar to the following message if all is working correctly:

```
successfully initialized (spaCy Version: 3.5.0, language model: en_core_
web_lg)
(python options: type = "condaenv", value = "C:\ProgramData\Miniconda3\
envs\presidio_env")
```

6. For each row of the dataset that you previously loaded into Power BI (or you may have used the readxl package to test the code in RStudio), apply the anonymizeEmail function to the Email and Notes columns, and apply the anonymizeName function to the Name and Notes columns. To apply the two previously defined functions to each element of a column, we used the map() function from the purrr package. More specifically, map_chr() returns the output as a vector of strings, so that it can replace the column contents with them.

Having briefly explained what the R script does, let's get down to business. To use the spacyr R package, it must be installed in the latest R engine (in our case, CRAN R 4.4.2). These are the necessary steps:

1. Open **RStudio** and make sure the latest CRAN R engine is selected in the **Global Options** that you have already installed by following the steps in *Chapter 2, Configuring R with Power BI*.

2. Then, install the spacyr package by running the following code in the R console:

```
install.packages("spacyr")
```

You are now ready to apply anonymization in Power BI to the contents of the CustomersCreditCardAttempts. xlsx Excel file using R.

So, let's get started:

1. Open your Power BI Desktop, and make sure the referenced R engine is your latest CRAN R version in **Global Options**.

2. Click the **Excel workbook** icon on the ribbon to import data from Excel.

3. From the **Open** dialog box, select the CustomersCreditCardAttempts.xlsx file mentioned above.

4. In the **Navigator** pane, select the **Customers** sheet and then click on **Transform Data**.

5. Click on the **Transform** menu on the ribbon and then click on **Run R Script**.

6. Copy the script from the 02-anonymize-data-in-power-bi-r.R file into the R script editor and click **OK**. Remember to change your machine's conda environment path.

7. If Power BI requires you to provide it with data privacy information, set all privacy levels to **Public**.

8. We are only interested in the df dataset. So, click on its **Table** value.

9. As you can see, people's names in the Name and Notes column and emails in the Email and Notes columns have been correctly anonymized:

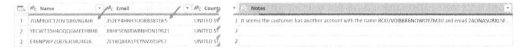

	A⁸ C Name	▾	A⁸ C Email	A⁸ C Coun	▾	Notes	▾
1	7GM9OiC12UV10HV8GAHI		3S2EY4H8H3ODR838TDF5	UNITED S	1	It seems the customer has another account with the name BOO7VOI8BR6NOWOYZM3U and email 2AONASU8XL5F...	
2	YECWT35H4OQQGMEEH8H8		XBHF5ENJRW8NHDN19R21	UNITED S	3		
3	E46NPWP2LB76308U46JR		2EY8QX4A1PEYNVXR5PE7	UNITED S	2		

Figure 7.7: The transformed dataset as the result of the R script

You can then click **Close & Apply** in the **Home** tab.

As you can see, the R script took longer to execute than the Python script. Clearly, the overhead of passing information through reticulate makes a difference.

IMPORTANT NOTE

If you need to anonymize a not-so-small dataset, it is advisable to do it directly using a Python script for much better performance.

Again, the dataset resulting from publishing this report will contain only the anonymized data, without providing Power BI users with the ability to retrieve the original data.

Now let's see how to pseudonymize the data in Power BI.

Pseudonymizing data in Power BI

Unlike anonymization, pseudonymization preserves the statistical properties of the dataset by transforming the same input string into the same output string, and keeps track of the replacements that have occurred, allowing those with access to this mapping information to recover the original dataset.

Imagine a healthcare research firm that has collected detailed patient data for analysis. The dataset contains sensitive information such as patient names, medical record numbers, and dates of birth. To analyze the data while protecting patient confidentiality, the company decides to use pseudonymization. Each patient name can be replaced with a unique identifier, such as "Patient001," "Patient002," and so on. Medical record numbers can also be converted to another set of alphanumeric strings that follow a specific format but do not reveal the original numbers. Birth dates can be modified to show only the year or month and year, reducing accuracy but retaining useful demographic information for analysis. The pseudonymized dataset retains the structure and statistical properties of the original data, so analyses such as disease prevalence across age groups or drug effectiveness can still be performed accurately.

However, the direct identifiers have been replaced with pseudonyms, significantly reducing the risk of patient re-identification. The research organization can maintain a secure, encrypted mapping of the original identifiers to the pseudonyms. This mapping is necessary when a situation arises where re-identification is legally required, such as for patient follow-up.

To make the de-identified data more realistic, pseudonymization can also replace sensitive data with **fake strings** (**pseudonyms**) that have the *same form* as the original.

Depending on the analytical language used, there are different solutions driven by the different packages available that lead to the same result. Let's see how to apply pseudonymization in Power BI to the contents of the same Excel file used in the previous sections with Python.

Pseudonymizing data using Python

The modules and code structure you will use are quite similar to those already used for anonymization. One difference is that once the sensitive entities are identified, they are replaced by fake entities of the same type. There are two main fake data generators in Python: **Faker** (`https://faker.readthedocs.io/`) and **Mimesis** (`https://mimesis.readthedocs.io/`). In our example, we'll use Faker, which is inspired by the library of the same name previously developed for **PHP**, **Perl**, and **Ruby**.

What also changes from the code used for anonymization is the logic of the two custom functions used to de-identify entities and the addition of the management of two dictionaries (`emails_dict` and `names_dict`) to maintain the mapping between personal data and fake data. The two dictionaries serve a critical function in the de-identification of personal data. Each dictionary acts as a reference system that maintains the relationship between the original data and the fake or pseudonymized data. First, they ensure that the pseudonymization process is consistent. If a name or email occurs multiple times in the dataset, it is always replaced with the same pseudonym, which is essential for maintaining the integrity of data relationships and enabling accurate analysis. Second, they provide a way to revert the pseudonymized data back to its original form if necessary.

We've also added a little more *salt* to the handling of the fake data handling – person names and email addresses are generated taking into account the country of each individual in the dataset, which is passed as a parameter in custom functions. For example, if the person is German, the generated person name will be a typical German name.

Let's take a closer look at what this is all about. The referenced Python file is `03-pseudonymize-data-in-power-bi-python.py`, which can be found in the `Ch07 - Anonymizing and Pseudonymizing Your Data in Power BI` folder:

1. While in the case of anonymization, the `anonymizer.anonymize()` function was used to replace all entities identified with the `analyzer.analyze()` function in one go, now, after the same entity identification, we must *first check if each identified entity is already mapped to a fake string*. If the entity is in its own specific dictionary, retrieve the associated fake string and use it to pseudonymize the text. Otherwise, you generate a new fake string using the `fake.safe_email()` or `fake.name()` function, depending on the type of string, and add it to the dictionary, associating it with the entity in question.

2. When the pseudonymization of all expected columns is complete, the mapping dictionaries (for both names and emails) are persisted in pkl files. These are unpickled and used as mapping dictionaries whenever new Excel data needs to be pseudonymized, and then whenever the dataset is refreshed. This ensures that the same pseudonyms are always used for the same personal data and also for new Excel rows containing the same personal data.

In order to use the faker module, as mentioned before, you need to install it in the presidio_env environment in the following way:

1. Open Anaconda Prompt.

2. Enter and run the following code to switch to the newly created environment:

```
conda activate presidio_env
```

3. Enter and run the following code to install Faker:

```
pip install Faker
```

Once this is done, you can start to implement pseudonymization in Power BI:

1. Open Power BI Desktop from the newly created shortcut that activates the presidio_env environment.

2. Make sure the referenced Python environment is presidio_env in **Options** (its home directory should be C:\ProgramData\Miniconda3\envs\presidio_env).

3. From the Power BI ribbon, click on the **Excel workbook** icon to import data from Excel.

4. From the **Open** dialog box, select the CustomersCreditCardAttempts.xlsx file mentioned above.

5. From the **Navigator** window, select the **Customers** sheet and then click on **Transform Data**.

6. Click on the **Transform** menu and then click on **Run Python Script**.

7. Copy the script from the file 03-pseudonymize-data-in-power-bi-python.py into the Python script editor and click **OK**. Remember to change the path of the pickle files to the main folder of the chapter.

8. If Power BI needs you to provide it with data privacy information, set all privacy levels to **Public**.

9. We are only interested in the df dataset. So, click on its **Table** value.

10. As you can see, people's names in the Name and Notes column and emails in the Email and Notes columns have been correctly pseudonymized:

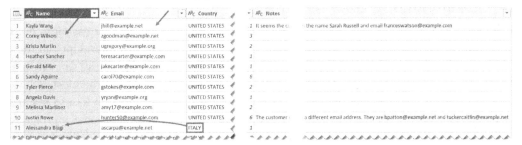

Figure 7.8: The transformed dataset as the result of the Python script

11. You can then click **Close & Apply** in the **Home** tab.

As in the case of anonymization, the Name, Email, and Notes columns have been correctly de-identified. What we have in addition is the following:

- The consistency of the people's names and emails with each person's country, although Faker does not currently allow you to maintain consistency between generated names and their corresponding emails. For example, in *Figure 7.8*, *line 11* shows an Italian name and an email that uses a different Italian name (the email doesn't use any form of the name *Alessandra Biagi*).

- Use of the emails_dict and names_dict mapping dictionaries to ensure that statistical analysis can be performed on the pseudonymized dataset.

- The fact that we can trace the original data thanks to these mapping dictionaries that are persisted to disk.

In this case, when you publish the report to share it with Power BI users, you should be aware of the following:

IMPORTANT NOTE

Power BI users who only have access to the dataset will only see the de-identified data. By also providing mapping dictionaries to those with the right permissions, you ensure that they can also trace the original data for any legal needs.

Did you notice that the Python script allowed you to write the information resulting from the data processing performed in Power BI to a file?

IMPORTANT NOTE

For example, instead of using serialized dictionaries in PKL files, you could have written the information to CSV or Excel files.

Simply put, you have the ability to log information outside of Power BI. You'll learn more about this option in *Chapter 8, Logging Data from Power BI to External Sources*.

Now let's see how pseudonymization can be implemented in R.

Pseudonymizing data using R

The libraries we will use for data pseudonymization in R are much the same as those used for anonymization in R. To fully simulate the functionality of the Python script developed in the previous section, we also need an R package that generates *fake data* to replace *sensitive data*, such as person names and email addresses. In Python, we used the Faker module, one of the most widely used for this purpose. A package with the same functionality has been developed in R, also inspired by the same code used for Faker, and is called charlatan (https://github.com/ropensci/charlatan). In addition, the R code for pseudonymization will follow the same logic already implemented in the Python script in the previous section, with the following minor differences:

- Use named lists instead of dictionaries to map pseudonyms to original entities.
- Named lists are serialized and persisted in RDS files, instead of PKL files.

In order to use the `charlatan` R package, it must be installed in the latest R engine (in our case, CRAN R 4.4.2). These are the necessary steps to follow:

- Open RStudio, and be sure to select in **Global Options** the most recent CRAN R engine you already installed following the steps in *Chapter 2, Configuring R with Power BI*.
- Then, install the `charlatan` package by running the following code in the console:

```
install.packages("charlatan")
```

You are now ready to apply pseudonymization in Power BI to the contents of the `CustomersCreditCardAttempts.xlsx` Excel file using R. So, let's get started:

1. Open your Power BI Desktop, and make sure the referenced R engine is your latest CRAN R version in **Global Options**.
2. From the ribbon, click on the **Excel workbook** icon to import data from Excel.
3. From the **Open** dialog box, select the `CustomersCreditCardAttempts.xlsx` file mentioned above.
4. From the **Navigator** window, select the **Customers** sheet and then click on **Transform Data**.
5. Click on the **Transform** menu and then click on **Run R Script**.
6. Copy the script from the `04-pseudonymize-data-in-power-bi-r.R` file into the R script editor and click **OK**. Remember to change the needed paths for the RDS file and for the Python environment used by spaCy in the code.
7. If Power BI needs you to provide it with data privacy information, you already know how to proceed based on what you've seen in *Chapter 6, Using Regular Expressions in Power BI*.
8. We are only interested in the `df` dataset. So, click on its **Table** value.
9. As you can see, person names in the `Name` and `Notes` column and emails in the `Email` and `Notes` columns have been correctly pseudonymized:

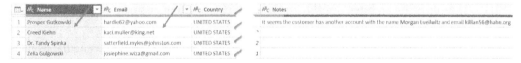

Figure 7.9: The transformed dataset as the result of the R script

You can then click **Close & Apply** in the **Home** tab.

Unfortunately, charlatan does not yet support the `it_IT` locale. But since it is an open-source project, it is possible that it will be implemented by the community soon. However, this does not prevent us from obtaining a very good pseudonymization of the dataset and of the report that will be published on the Power BI service, since, in the absence of a specific locale, the default one (`en_US`) is always used.

It has been said that the implementation of de-identification procedures in R is certainly less performant than in Python. However, the gap can be partially bridged by introducing the parallelization of operations using multitasking. We'll look at this technique in detail in *Chapter 11, Calling External APIs to Enrich Your Data*.

Summary

In this chapter, you learned about the main differences between anonymization and pseudonymization. You also learned which techniques are most commonly used to apply each de-identification process.

You also applied the anonymization process through tokenization and the pseudonymization process by creating similar pseudonyms in Power BI using both Python and R.

In the next chapter, you will learn how to log data derived from operations performed with Power Query in Power BI to external repositories.

References

For additional reading, check out the following books and articles:

- *Anonymization and Pseudonymization Policy* (`https://www.termsfeed.com/blog/gdpr-pseudonymization-anonymization/`)
- *Symmetric and Asymmetric Encryption* (`https://medium.com/hackernoon/symmetric-and-asymmetric-encryption-5122f9ec65b1`)
- *Cryptography with Python Tutorial* (`https://www.tutorialspoint.com/cryptography_with_python/`)
- *Encryption in R with cyphr* (`https://docs.ropensci.org/cyphr/articles/cyphr.html`)

Test your knowledge

1. What is the most obvious disadvantage of anonymization?
2. How does pseudonymization differ from anonymization?
3. How does the architecture shown for pseudonymization ensure compliance with GDPR deletion requirements?
4. Why is it necessary to use NLP techniques to identify PII instead of using the usual regexes?
5. What is one of the best Python packages for de-identifying PII? What NLP engines can be used behind the scenes?
6. Which R package was used to de-identify PII? What is special about this package as an engine for NLP?
7. What are pseudonyms?
8. Which Python and R packages were used to generate pseudonyms?

Learn more on Discord

To join the Discord community for this book – where you can share feedback, ask questions to the author, and learn about new releases – follow the QR code below:

https://discord.gg/MKww5g45EB

8

Logging Data from Power BI to External Sources

As you've learned in previous chapters, **Power BI** uses **Power Query** as a tool for **extracting, transforming,** and **loading** (ETL) operations. This tool is really very powerful – it allows you to extract data from a wide variety of data sources and then easily transform it with very user-friendly options. This includes a graphical query editor for point-and-click transformations, the ability to extract data from multiple sources, comprehensive column and row transformations, data cleaning functions, and the ability to perform simple calculations. The output of these transformations is persisted in the Power BI data model. Power Query is a read-only tool. In fact, its biggest limitation is its inability to write information outside of Power BI. However, by integrating analytical languages such as **Python** and **R**, you can persist information about Power Query loading and transformation processes to external files or systems. In this chapter, you will learn about the following topics:

- Logging to **CSV** files
- Logging to **Excel** files
- Logging to **(Azure) SQL Server**

Technical requirements

This chapter requires you to have a working internet connection and **Power BI Desktop** already installed on your machine (we used version 2.114.664.0 64-bit, February 2022). You must have properly configured the R and Python engines and IDEs as outlined in *Chapter 2, Configuring R with Power BI*, and *Chapter 3, Configuring Python with Power BI*.

Logging to CSV files

One of the most widely used formats for logging tabular structured information to files is **comma-separated values (CSV)**. Because a CSV file is still a flat text file, CSV is the most popular format for exchanging information between heterogeneous applications.

A CSV file is a representation of a rectangular dataset (**matrix**) containing numeric or string columns. Each row of the matrix is represented by a list of values (one for each column), separated by commas, and should have the same number of values. Sometimes, other value delimiters may be used, such as tab (\t), colon (:), and semicolon (;) characters. The first row might contain the column heads. Usually, a **line break** is used as a **row delimiter**, which is a **CRLF (Carriage Return Line Feed)** character (usually entered as \r\n), or simply by **LF** (\n) on Unix systems. Thus, an example of the contents of a CSV file might be as follows:

```
1  Col1,Col2,Col3CRLF
2  A,23,3.5CRLF
3  B,27,4.8CRLF
```

Figure 8.1: Example of CSV file content

Note that spaces become part of a string value! For example, if for the second line you had A,23, 3.5, the second numeric value would no longer be such, but a string: [space]3.5.

It may happen that a string value contains line breaks (CRLF), double quotes, or commas (as is common in free text fields such as Notes). In this case, the value should be enclosed in double quotes and any literal double quote must be escaped with another double quote. For example, the values "C,D", "E""F", and "G[CRLF]H" for the Col1 column are formatted as follows in a CSV file:

```
1  Col1,Col2,Col3CRLF
2  A,23,3.5CRLF
3  B,27,4.8CRLF
4  "C,D",18,2.1CRLF
5  "E""F",19,2.5CRLF
6  "GCRLF
7  H",21,3.1CRLF
```

Figure 8.2: Example of CSV values containing commas, double quotes, or CRLF

IMPORTANT NOTE

It's important to note that a CSV file does not have any size limitations per se.

Because it is a flat text file, the maximum size is determined by the limits imposed by the file system. For example, the default file system for Windows is the **New Technology File System (NTFS)**, and its current implementation allows a maximum file size of *16 TB*. However, its designed theoretical limit is *16 EB* (16 × 264 bytes) minus *1 KB*.

Instead the old **File Allocation Table** file system, in its 32-bit variant (**FAT32**), can only handle a maximum size of *4 GB*.

IMPORTANT NOTE

Keep in mind that handling large CSV files will lead to memory and/or CPU bottlenecks. You are very likely to get an OutOfMemory error if the CSV file you are trying to load is larger than the RAM you have available and if your libraries don't use parallelism/distribution/lazy loading mechanisms. You'll learn how to handle such large CSV files in *Chapter 9, Loading Large Datasets Beyond the Available RAM in Power BI*.

Let's see how to read and write CSV files using Python.

Logging to CSV files with Python

Python has a built-in CSV module that provides some functions for reading and writing CSV files. Very often, however, you need to import a CSV file whose contents are then transformed by pandas functions, or you need to export a DataFrame into CSV format that was previously processed by pandas. In these cases, it's much more convenient to use the built-in pandas functions directly with DataFrame objects. The files 01-read-csv-file-in-python.py and 02-write-csv-file-in-python.py in the Python subfolder of the Ch08 - Logging Data from Power BI to External Sources main folder show you how to use the CSV module. In the following section, we will focus only on the functionality provided by pandas.

Let's take a closer look at the pandas functions available for working with CSV files.

Using the pandas module

The functions provided by the pandas module to read and write a CSV file are very simple and straightforward. You can use the read_csv() function to read data from a CSV file. Below is the code that allows you to load the contents of the example.csv file into a DataFrame:

Ch08 - Logging Data from Power BI to External Sources\Python\03-read-csv-file-with-pandas.py

```
import pandas as pd
data = pd.read_csv(r'D:\<your-path>\ Ch08 - Logging Data from Power BI to
External Sources\example.csv')
data.head(10)
```

Here is the output using the **VS Code Interactive window**, running the code with *Shift + Enter*:

	Col1	Col2	Col3
0	A	23	3.5
1	B	27	4.8
2	C,D	18	2.1
3	E"F	19	2.5
4	G\r\nH	21	3.1

Figure 8.3: Output of the pandas DataFrame loaded with the contents of the sample CSV file

The read_csv function also allows you to pass the sep parameter to specify the value separator to use when reading the file.

On the other hand, if you need to write a CSV file from the contents of a DataFrame, you can use the to_csv() function. The following is an example of the code you might use:

Ch08 - Logging Data from Power BI to External Sources\Python\04-write-csv-file-with-pandas.py

```
import pandas as pd
data = {
    'Col1' : ['A', 'B', 'C,D', 'E"F', 'G\r\nH'],
    'Col2' : [23, 27, 18, 19, 21],
    'Col3' : [3.5, 4.8, 2.1, 2.5, 3.1]
}
data_df = pd.DataFrame(data)
data_df.to_csv(r'D:\<your-path>\Ch08 - Logging Data from Power BI to External
Sources\example-write.csv', index=False)
```

The to_csv() function also allows you to pass the sep parameter in order to define the value separator you want to use in the file. When you open the CSV file in Excel, select the cell that contains the 'G' to see that it also contains the 'H'.

As you can see, working with CSV files in Python is very simple. In the next section, you'll put this into practice in Power BI.

Logging emails to CSV files in Power BI with Python

As an example of how to generate a CSV file, we will use the same scenario from *Chapter 6, Using Regular Expressions in Power BI*, where you needed to validate email addresses and ban dates. The goal is to export the rows of the dataset that contain an incorrect email to a CSV file and to filter them out of the dataset so that only valid emails remain in Power BI. We will use the to_csv() function provided by pandas. The required steps are as follows:

1. Complete all of the steps in the *Using regex in Power BI to validate emails with Python* section of *Chapter 6, Using Regular Expressions in Power BI*, to the end, but do not click on **Close & Apply**.

2. Then, click on **Run Python Script** again and enter the following script, and click **OK**:

    ```
    import pandas as pd
    filter = (dataset['isEmailValidFromRegex'] == 0)
    dataset[filter].to_csv(r'D:\<your-path>\Ch08 - Logging Data from Power BI
    to External Sources\Python\wrong-emails.csv', index=False)
    df = dataset[~filter]
    ```

    You can find this Python script also in the Python\05-log-wrong-emails-csv-in-power-bi.py file. Note the ~ character that in this case is a negation of the Boolean condition defined by the filter variable.

3. Click on the df dataset's **Table** value.

4. Only rows containing valid emails will be kept:

1^2_3 UserId		A^B_C Email	A^B_C BannedDate		1^2_3 isEmailValidFromRegex	
1	1	_____@example.com	05/29/2018			1
2	4	firstname-lastname@example.com	06/07/2019			1
3	6	email@example-one.com	11/06/2017			1
4	7	email@example.co.jp	012/05/2018			1
5	8	email@example.name	06/7/2019			1
6	10	email@example.com	9/04/2017			1
7	11	email@subdomain.example.com	11/22/2018			1
8	12	email@123.123.123.123	07/31/17			1
9	14	firstname.lastname@example.com	11/22/18			1
10	15	firstname+lastname@example.com	05/16/2018			1
11	17	1234567890@example.com	05/16/2018			1
12	18	email@example.museum	03/26/2018			1
13	19	email@[123.123.123.123]	06/31/2017			1

Figure 8.4: A table containing only valid emails

In addition, the wrong-emails.csv file has been created in your Ch08 - Logging Data from Power BI to External Sources\Python folder.

5. Go back to the **Home** menu, and then click **Close & Apply**.

If you go and check the contents of the created CSV file, it matches the following:

```
wrong-emails.csv
1   UserId,Email,BannedDate,IsEmailValidByDefinition,IsDateValidByDefinition,isEmailValidFromRegex
2   2,example1@example.com/example2@example.com,06/07/2019,0,1,0
3   3,example33@example.com.,02/05/2018,0,1,0
4   5,example@example.com --> check,02/29/18,0,0,0
5   9,example,10/22/2018,0,1,0
6   13,.@example.com,04/24/018,0,0,0
7   16,example@example.c,6/7/2019,0,1,0
```

Figure 8.5: Contents of the wrong-emails-csv file

As you can see, the emails in the CSV file are all invalid ones. At this point, you can share the previous file with your colleagues so that they can correct the invalid emails.

Well done! You just learned how to log information from Power BI to a CSV file using Python. Now, let's see how you can do the same thing using R.

Logging to CSV files with R

The base R language provides some out-of-the-box functionality for working with CSV files. However, there is also the readr package, included in the **Tidyverse** ecosystem, which provides similar functionality but is faster at loading larger CSV files.

Let's see how to use them in detail.

Using Tidyverse functions

The readr package provides some functions that mirror those seen for reading and writing CSV files with R base. The advantage of these functions is that, in addition to respecting the common interface provided by the Tidyverse world functions, they are up to five times faster than the standard functions and also provide a progress meter. Make sure you have at least version 1.4.0 of the package installed (check it on the **Packages** tab, usually in the bottom-right panel in RStudio), otherwise update it (in our case, it is the 2.1.3 version).

Always using the usual example.csv file, similar to what we did in the previous section, you can load the data this way using the read_csv() function of the readr package:

```
library(readr)
data_df <- read_csv(r'{D:\<your-path>\Ch08 - Logging Data from Power BI to
External Sources\example.csv}')
```

As output, you can see the following specifications:

```
Rows: 5 Columns: 3
── Column specification ──────────────────────────────────────────────
Delimiter: ","
chr (1): Col1
dbl (2): Col2, Col3

i Use `spec()` to retrieve the full column specification for this data.
i Specify the column types or set `show_col_types = FALSE` to quiet this message.
```

Figure 8.6: Column specifications returned by read_csv()

Besides the fact that the read_csv() function returns a **tibble** instead of a DataFrame, there is one more thing to note:

IMPORTANT NOTE

The interesting thing is that the read_csv() function imports the carriage return character correctly by default.

If you check the newly imported tibble, you have the following:

```
> data_df
# A tibble: 5 × 3
  Col1      Col2  Col3
  <chr>    <dbl> <dbl>
1 "A"         23   3.5
2 "B"         27   4.8
3 "C,D"       18   2.1
4 "E\"F"      19   2.5
5 "G\r\nH"    21   3.1
```

Figure 8.7: Characters \r\n correctly imported by read_csv

As with R base, the readr package also provides the same functions, read_csv2(), read_tsv(), and read_delim(), to ensure a similar interface and thus is easy to use.

To persist data to a CSV file, the readr package provides the write_csv() function with its full family of functions, similar to R base (write_csv2, write_tsv, and write_delim). Unlike write.csv(), these functions do not include row names as columns in the written file. Also, the default end-of-line delimiter is just a new line (\n). So, if you want to export your data using the \r\n characters as a line separator, you have to pass them through the eol parameter:

```
library(readr)
data_df <- data.frame(
  Col1 = c('A', 'B', 'C,D', 'E"F', 'G\r\nH'),
  Col2 = c(23, 27, 18, 19, 21),
  Col3 = c(3.5, 4.8, 2.1, 2.5, 3.1)
)
write_csv(data_df, file = r'{D:\<your-path>\Ch08 - Logging Data from Power BI
to External Sources\R\example-write.csv}', eol = '\r\n')
```

Note that in this case, you must use both characters (\r\n) in your data if you want to extract it in exactly the same way. When you open a CSV file in Excel, select the cell that displays 'G' to reveal that it also includes 'H'.

As you can see, working with CSV files is just as easy in R as it is in Python. In the next section, you will log emails and dates using R in Power BI.

Logging dates to CSV files in Power BI with R

We will always use the scenario presented in *Chapter 6, Using Regular Expressions in Power BI*, where we need to validate both email addresses and ban dates. This time, we will use R to export invalid ban dates to a CSV file. The required steps are as follows:

1. Follow all the steps in the *Using regex in Power BI to validate dates with R* section of *Chapter 6, Using Regular Expressions in Power BI*, to the end, but do not click on **Close & Apply**.

2. Then click again on **Run R Script**, enter the following script, and click **OK**:

```
library(readr)
library(dplyr)
dataset %>%
  filter( isDateValidFromRegex == 0 ) %>%
  write_csv( r'{D:\<your-path>\Ch08 - Logging Data from Power BI to
External Sources\R\wrong-dates.csv}', eol = '\r\n' )
df <- dataset %>%
  filter( isDateValidFromRegex == 1 )
```

You can also find this R script in the R\01-log-wrong-emails-in-r.R file.

3. Click on the df dataset's **Table** value.

4. Only rows containing valid emails will be kept:

	1²₃ UserId		Aᴮ_C Email		Aᴮ_C BannedDate		1²₃ isDateValidFromRegex	
1		1	_____@example.com		05/29/2018	1		1
2		4	firstname-lastname@example.com		06/07/2019	1		1
3		6	email@example-one.com		11/06/2017	1		1
4		8	email@example.name		06/7/2019	1		1
5		10	email@example.com		9/04/2017	1		1
6		11	email@subdomain.example.com		11/22/2018	1		1
7		12	email@123.123.123.123		07/31/17	1		1
8		14	firstname.lastname@example.com		11/22/18	1		1
9		15	firstname+lastname@example.com		05/16/2018	1		1
10		17	1234567890@example.com		05/16/2018	1		1
11		18	email@example.museum		03/26/2018	1		1

Figure 8.8: A table containing only valid emails

In addition, the wrong-dates.csv file has been created in your Ch08 - Logging Data from Power BI to External Sources\R folder.

5. Go back to the **Home** menu, and then click **Close & Apply**.

At this point, you can share the wrong-emails.csv file you just created with your colleagues so that they can correct the invalid emails.

Awesome! You just learned how to log information from Power BI to a CSV file using R. Now let's see how you can use Excel files to log your information.

Logging to Excel files

As you probably already know, Microsoft Excel is a **spreadsheet** program available in the **Microsoft Office** suite. It's one of the most widely used tools in the world for storing and organizing data in a spreadsheet format. It is very popular in organizations because it allows business data to be shared between departments and allows individual users to perform their own data analysis directly and quickly without the help of the IT department.

Early versions of Excel stored information in **Excel Sheet** (XLS) format files. This is a proprietary Microsoft format, based on the **Binary Interchange File Format** (BIFF). It was the default format for versions from v7.0 (Excel 95) through v11.0 (Excel 2003). From version 8.0 to 11.0, the XLS format can handle *64K (2^{16} = 65,536) rows* and *256 columns (2^8)*. Starting with version v12.0 (Excel 2007), the default format has changed to **Excel Open XML Spreadsheet** (XLSX). This is based on the **Office Open XML** format, and it is based on text files that use XML to define all their parameters. The XLSX format can handle *1,024K (2^{20} = 1,048,576) rows and 16,384 (2^{14}) columns*, addressing the growing need to handle large volumes of data.

IMPORTANT NOTE

Did you know that an XLSX file contains data from multiple XML files compressed in the **ZIP** format? If you want to verify this, simply rename one of your XLSX files, for example, `example.xlsx`, and add the `.zip` extension to it (for example, `example.xlsx.zip`). Then, extract its contents using **File Explorer** or any other ZIP client (such as **7-Zip**).

This structure (a collection of XML files in a ZIP package) not only results in smaller file sizes but also enhances file recovery capabilities, making it possible to recover parts of a document even if it is corrupted.

Since the introduction of **Power Pivot** (starting with Excel 2013) and **Power Query** (starting with Excel 2016), most of the data ingestion and data analysis activities to create a prototype data model are often performed by power users thanks to Microsoft Excel. Power Query gives you a rich set of data transformation tools all in one place. Power Pivot gives you the ability to work with large amounts of data by overcoming Excel's 1,048,576-row limit. Once imported, you can use pivot tables and the **DAX** formula language on them because the behind-the-scenes engine is the same as **Analysis Service Tabular** and Power BI. That's why Excel and Power BI are the best tools for self-service BI on the **Microsoft data platform**.

Now, let's see how to interact with Excel files in Python. We will use the latest XLSX format from now on.

Logging to Excel files with Python

The fastest way to interact with Excel files in Python is to use the functions provided by pandas. However, you need to install the openpyxl package in your `pbi_powerquery_env` environment. If you remember correctly, you already installed this package in the **Presidio** environment (`presidio_env`) in *Chapter 7, Anonymizing and Pseudonymizing Your Data in Power BI*. To install this package in the `pbi_powerquery_env` environment as well, simply follow these steps:

1. Open **Anaconda Prompt**.
2. Set your current environment to `pbi_powerquery_env`, entering the following command and pressing **Enter**:

   ```
   conda activate pbi_powerquery_env
   ```

3. Enter the following command and press **Enter**:

   ```
   pip install openpyxl
   ```

As an example, you will find the `example.xlsx` file in the `Ch08 - Logging Data from Power BI to External Sources` folder. Let's see how to import its content with Python.

Using the pandas module

You can easily import your data into a pandas DataFrame using this code:

`Ch08 - Logging Data from Power BI to External Sources\Python\06-read-excel-file-with-pandas.py`

```
import pandas as pd
data = pd.read_excel(r'D:\<your-path>\Ch08 - Logging Data from Power BI to External Sources\example.xlsx', engine='openpyxl')
```

If you visualize the DataFrame in VS Code, you'll see something like the following:

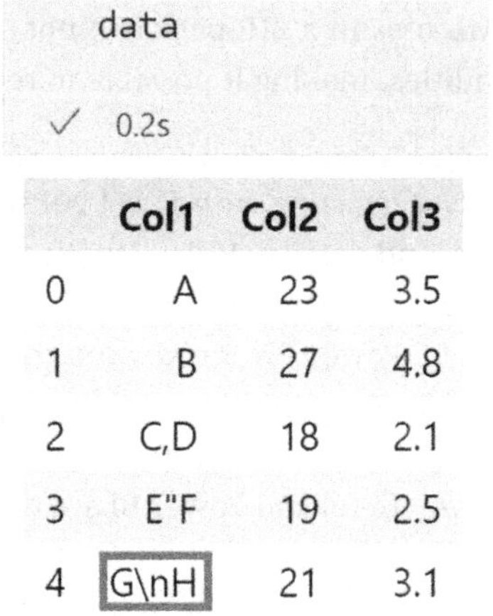
data
✓ 0.2s

	Col1	Col2	Col3
0	A	23	3.5
1	B	27	4.8
2	C,D	18	2.1
3	E"F	19	2.5
4	G\nH	21	3.1

Figure 8.9: Output of the pandas DataFrame loaded with the contents of the example.xlsx file

In this case, if an Excel cell contains a string with the characters `\r\n`, the carriage return (`\r`) is lost after import, as you can see in *Figure 8.9*.

As you probably already know, an Excel file (**workbook**) can contain one or more sheets (**worksheets**) that contain data. If you want to import data from a specific worksheet, you can use this code:

```
data = pd.read_excel(r'D:\<your-path>\Ch08 - Logging Data from Power BI
to External Sources\example.xlsx', sheet_name='<your-worksheet-name>',
engine='openpyxl')
```

Similarly, you can use this code to write the contents of a DataFrame to Excel files:

`Ch08 - Logging Data from Power BI to External Sources\Python\07-write-excel-file-with-pandas.py`

```
import pandas as pd
data = {
    'Col1' : ['A', 'B', 'C,D', 'E"F', 'G\r\nH'],
    'Col2' : [23, 27, 18, 19, 21],
    'Col3' : [3.5, 4.8, 2.1, 2.5, 3.1]
}
data_df = pd.DataFrame(data)
```

```
data_df.to_excel(r'D:\<your-path>\Ch08 - Logging Data from Power BI to External
Sources\Python\example-write.xlsx', index = False, engine='openpyxl')
```

The resulting Excel file will have a default Sheet1 worksheet, and its content will look like the following:

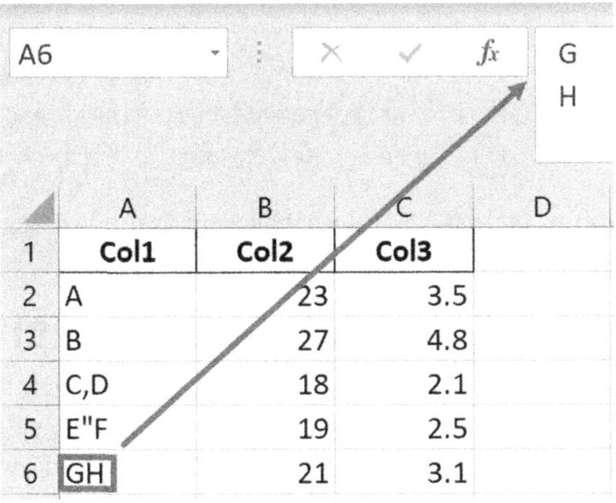

Figure 8.10: The content of the Excel file created using pandas functions

If you copy the contents of cell A6 into an advanced editor (such as Notepad++), you can verify that the \r\n characters are preserved.

If you want to write the contents of your dataset to a specific named worksheet in *a new Excel file*, then you can use the following code:

```
data_df.to_excel(r'D:\<your-path>\Ch08 - Logging Data from Power BI to External
Sources\Python\example-write-named-sheet.xlsx', sheet_name='My data', index =
False, engine='openpyxl')
```

The result will be as follows:

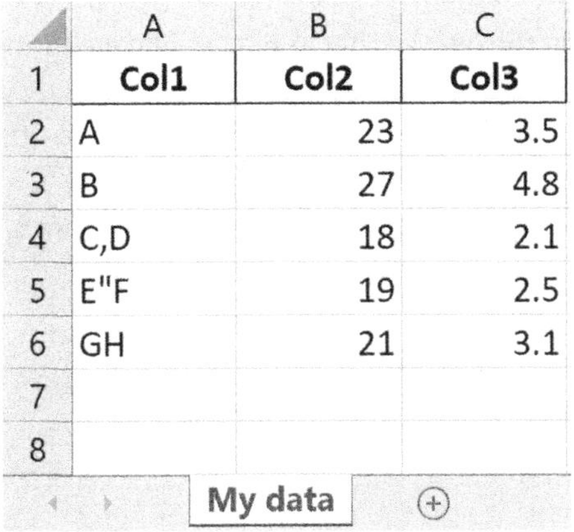

Figure 8.11: The content is now written into a named worksheet

If, instead, you want to write the contents of your dataset to a specific named worksheet in *an existing Excel file*, then you need to use the pandas `ExcelWriter` class in the following way:

Ch08 - Logging Data from Power BI to External Sources\Python\08-write-excel-file-named-sheet-with-pandas.py

```
with pd.ExcelWriter(r'D:\<your-path>\Ch08 - Logging Data from Power BI to
External Sources\Python\example-write-named-sheet.xlsx', mode='a') as writer:
    data_df.to_excel(writer, sheet_name='My data', index = False)
```

Note that `mode='a'` stands for *"append."* Now let's look at an example of logging in Power BI using the previous pandas functions.

Logging emails and dates to Excel files in Power BI with Python

Let's go back to the same scenario we used in the previous sections, namely, the one we analyzed in *Chapter 6, Using Regular Expressions in Power BI*, where you needed to validate email addresses and ban dates. This time, however, the goal is to export invalid emails and invalid dates to two separate worksheets in an Excel file and then share them with the team. Therefore, for convenience, we have reported the Python code that validates both emails and dates in one script.

Now let's get started:

1.   Open Power BI Desktop through the shortcut that activates the `pbi_powerquery_env` environment.

2.   Make sure Power BI Desktop is referencing the `pbi_powerquery_env` environment in **Options**.

3.   Click on the **Excel workbook** icon on the ribbon to import data from Excel.

4.   From the **Open** dialog box, select the `Users.xlsx` file located in the `Ch06 - Using Regular Expressions in Power BI` folder.

5.   In the **Navigator** window, select the **Users** sheet and then click on **Transform Data**.

6.   Click on the **Transform** menu, and then click on **Run Python Script**.

7.   Copy the code found in the `09-validate-emails-dates-with-regex-in-power-bi.py` file in the `Ch08 - Logging Data from Power BI to External Sources/Python` folder, and paste it into the Python script editor. This code is just a merge of the scripts you already used to validate emails and dates separately. Then, click **OK**.

8.   Select only the **Table** value related to the `df` table name and you will see something like this:

Figure 8.12: The transformed data contains both valid email and date flags

Now, you have both the `isEmailValidFromRegex` and `isValidDateFromRegex` flags, which allow you to select emails and correct dates.

9. Click **Run Python Script** again, copy and paste the script you found in the `10-log-wrong-emails-dates-excel-in-power-bi.py` file, making sure to change the path to the destination file there where it appears, then click **OK**.

10. Select only the **Table** value related to the `df` table name and you will see a table where only rows with valid emails and dates are kept:

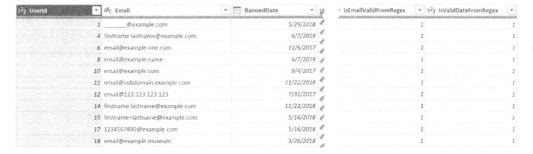

Figure 8.13: Output data containing rows with valid emails and dates

In addition, the `wrong-data.xlsx` file has been created in your `Ch08 - Logging Data from Power BI to External Sources/Python` folder and it contains two worksheets: `Wrong emails` and `Wrong dates`.

11. Go back to the **Home** menu, and then click **Close & Apply**.

Amazing! You just learned how to log information from Power BI to an Excel file in multiple sheets using Python. Now, let's see how you can do the same thing using R.

Logging to Excel files with R

To be able to read and write Excel files in R, we recommend using two separate packages:

- **readxl**: This is a package that is part of the Tidyverse world and allows you to read the information contained in an Excel file in the simplest and most flexible way.
- **openxlsx**: This is a package that provides a high-level interface for creating and editing Excel files. Unlike other packages that do the same, openxlsx removes the **Java** dependency behind the scenes.

We recommend using both the readxl and openxlsx packages for handling Excel files due to their complementary strengths and functionalities. The readxl package, a member of the Tidyverse ecosystem, is designed for simplicity and flexibility in reading Excel files. On the other hand, openxlsx excels at creating and editing Excel files without relying on Java, providing a high-level interface that simplifies the manipulation of Excel documents.

To go on, you must first install the openxlsx package:

1. Open **RStudio**, and make sure that the latest **CRAN R** engine is selected in the **Global Options** (in our case, CRAN R 4.2.2).
2. Type install.packages("openxlsx") in the console.

Now you are ready to learn how to read and write data in Excel files.

Using the readxl and openxlsx packages

The readxl package provides two separate functions – read_xls(), to read Excel files in XLS format, and read_xlsx(), to read files in XLSX format. If you want to read the contents of the example.xlsx file located in the Ch08 - Logging Data from Power BI to External Sources folder, you can use the following code:

```
library(readxl)
data_tbl <- read_xlsx(r'{D:\<your-path>\Ch08 - Logging Data from Power BI to
External Sources\example.xlsx}')
data_tbl
```

The result will be a tibble:

```
> data_tbl
# A tibble: 5 × 3
  Col1          Col2  Col3
  <chr>        <dbl> <dbl>
1 "A"             23   3.5
2 "B"             27   4.8
3 "C,D"           18   2.1
4 "E\"F"          19   2.5
5 "G\r\nH"        21   3.1
```

Figure 8.14: Reading Excel data with the read_xlsx function

As you can see, the line breaks and newline characters (\r\n) are preserved. If you want to read data from a specific worksheet instead, you can use this code:

```
data_tbl <- read_xlsx(r'{D:\<your-path>\Ch08 - Logging Data from Power BI to
External Sources\example.xlsx}', sheet = 'My sheet')
```

To write your data to Excel files, you can use the `write.xlsx()` function of the openxlsx package, as follows:

```
library(dplyr)
library(openxlsx)
data_df <- data.frame(
    Col1 = c('A', 'B', 'C,D', 'E"F', 'G\nH'),
    Col2 = c(23, 27, 18, 19, 21),
    Col3 = c(3.5, 4.8, 2.1, 2.5, 3.1)
)
data_df %>%
    write.xlsx(file = r'{D:\<your-path>\Ch08 - Logging Data from Power BI to
External Sources\R\example-write.xlsx}', colNames = TRUE)
```

Note that in this case, you must use the *Unix convention* regarding the new lines, and that is to use only the \n character in the strings of your data to have the standard Windows \r\n characters in Excel.

If you want to write the contents of your dataset to a specific named worksheet in a new Excel file, you can use the following code:

```
data_df %>%
    write.xlsx(file = r'{D:\<your-path>\Ch08 - Logging Data from Power BI to
External Sources\R\example-write.xlsx}', colNames = TRUE, sheetName = 'My
data', append = FALSE)
```

On the other hand, if you need to add a worksheet to *an existing Excel file*, you must use a named list of DataFrames/tibbles as the input to the write.xlsx function. This is the code to use if you can manually assign a string name to each sheet:

```
df_named_lst <- list("My data 1" = data_df, "My data 2" = data_df)
write.xlsx(df_named_lst, file = r'{D:\<your-path>\Ch08 - Logging Data from
Power BI to External Sources\R\example-write.xlsx}')
```

Note that if you need to use a list of DataFrames/tibbles (df_lst) and a list of worksheet names (names_lst) separately, you can use the following code to write all your data into an Excel workbook:

```
df_named_lst <- setNames(df_lst, names_lst)
write.xlsx(df_named_lst, file = r'{D:\<your-path>\<your-file>.xlsx}')
```

Now let's look at an example of logging in Power BI using the previous R functions.

Logging emails and dates to Excel in Power BI with R

The example we will use is still the one from *Chapter 6, Using Regular Expressions in Power BI*, where you needed to validate email addresses and ban dates. The end goal will always be to export invalid emails and invalid dates to two separate worksheets in an Excel file and then share them with the team.

Now, open Power BI Desktop, make sure your latest CRAN R is referenced in the options, and let's get started:

1. Make sure Power BI Desktop is referencing the latest R engine version you've installed (in our case, version 4.2.2) in **Options**.
2. Click the **Excel workbook** icon on the ribbon to import data from Excel.
3. From the **Open** dialog box, select the Users.xlsx file located in the Ch06 - Using Regular Expressions in Power BI folder.
4. In the **Navigator** window, select the **Users** sheet and then click on **Transform Data**.
5. Click on the **Transform** menu, and then click on **Run R Script**.
6. Copy the code found in the 02-validate-emails-dates-with-regex-in-power-bi.R file in the Ch08 - Logging Data from Power BI to External Sources/R folder, and paste it into the R script editor. This code is just a merging of the scripts you already used to validate emails and dates separately. Then click **OK**.
7. If it doesn't automatically expand, select just the **Table** value related to the df table name and you will see something like this:

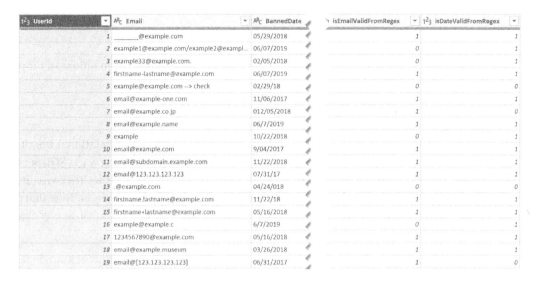

1²₃ UserId	Aᴮ꜀ Email	Aᴮ꜀ BannedDate	isEmailValidFromRegex	1²₃ isDateValidFromRegex
1	_____@example.com	05/29/2018	1	1
2	example1@example.com/example2@exampl...	06/07/2019	0	1
3	example33@example.com.	02/05/2018	0	1
4	firstname-lastname@example.com	06/07/2019	1	1
5	example@example.com --> check	02/29/18	0	0
6	email@example-one.com	11/06/2017	1	1
7	email@example.co.jp	012/05/2018	1	0
8	email@example.name	06/7/2019	1	1
9	example	10/22/2018	0	1
10	email@example.com	9/04/2017	1	1
11	email@subdomain.example.com	11/22/2018	1	1
12	email@123.123.123.123	07/31/17	1	1
13	.@example.com	04/24/018	0	0
14	firstname.lastname@example.com	11/22/18	1	1
15	firstname+lastname@example.com	05/16/2018	1	1
16	example@example.c	6/7/2019	0	1
17	1234567890@example.com	05/16/2018	1	1
18	email@example.museum	03/26/2018	1	1
19	email@[123.123.123.123]	06/31/2017	1	0

Figure 8.15: The transformed data containing both the valid email and date flags

Now you have both the `isEmailValidFromRegex` and `isDateValidFromRegex` flags, which allow you to select the correct emails and dates.

8. Click **Run R Script** again, copy and paste the script you can find in the `03-log-wrong-emails-dates-excel-in-power-bi.R` file, and click **OK**. Remember to change the paths in the code.

9. Select only the **Table** value associated with the `df` table name and you will see a table where only rows with valid emails and dates are kept:

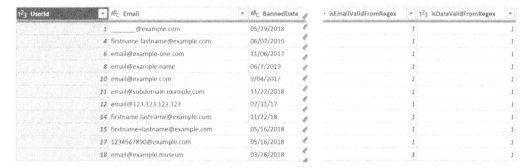

1²₃ UserId	Aᴮ꜀ Email	Aᴮ꜀ BannedDate	isEmailValidFromRegex	1²₃ isDateValidFromRegex
1	_____@example.com	05/29/2018	1	1
4	firstname-lastname@example.com	06/07/2019	1	1
6	email@example-one.com	11/06/2017	1	1
8	email@example.name	06/7/2019	1	1
10	email@example.com	9/04/2017	1	1
11	email@subdomain.example.com	11/22/2018	1	1
12	email@123.123.123.123	07/31/17	1	1
14	firstname.lastname@example.com	11/22/18	1	1
15	firstname+lastname@example.com	05/16/2018	1	1
17	1234567890@example.com	05/16/2018	1	1
18	email@example.museum	03/26/2018	1	1

Figure 8.16: The output data contains rows containing valid emails and dates

In addition, the `wrong-data.xlsx` file has been created in your `Ch08 - Logging Data from Power BI to External Sources/R` folder and it contains two worksheets: `Wrong emails` and `Wrong dates`.

10. Go back to the **Home** menu, and then click **Close & Apply**.

Awesome! You have just learned how to log information from Power BI to an Excel file in multiple sheets using R.

In the next section, you will learn how to log information from Power BI to either an **on-premises SQL Server** or **Azure SQL Server**.

Logging to (Azure) SQL Server

In the vast majority of organizations, business information is stored in a **Relational Database Management System (RDBMS)**. Microsoft's quintessential relational database server is **SQL Server** in its on-premises version if the company has adopted the Microsoft data platform. Otherwise, it is **Azure SQL Server**, which is a **Platform as a Service (PaaS)**, cloud-hosted database server. Note that an Azure SQL Server can contain multiple Azure SQL Databases, just as an on-premises SQL Server can contain multiple databases.

In general, it is a good idea to centralize all of a company's critical information in a single repository. That's why it can be useful to know how to log information from within a Power BI process to a SQL Server database or an Azure SQL database.

If you already have access to an on-premises instance of SQL Server or Azure SQL Server, you just need to make sure that the **ODBC Driver for SQL Server** is installed on your machine. In fact, both Python and R will connect to (Azure) SQL Server via an ODBC connection. You can install the driver directly on your machine (using the link `http://bit.ly/ODBC-SQLServer`), but more often this driver is installed indirectly when you install the ultimate client for managing any SQL infrastructure, which is **SQL Server Management Studio (SSMS)**.

On the other hand, if you don't have access to either an on-premises SQL Server instance or an Azure SQL Server, then you have two options for testing the examples in this section:

- Install a free instance of **SQL Server Express Edition** (or **Developer**).
- Create an Azure SQL Database (and thus an Azure SQL Server indirectly) from the Azure portal using your account.

Let's see how to proceed for each of these options in detail.

Installing SQL Server Express

In this section, we will show you how to install the Express edition of SQL Server. This is the free version of Microsoft's database engine that can also be used in production for desktop and small server data-driven applications. Of course, the Express edition has limitations that distinguish it from the top-of-the-line **Enterprise edition**. Here are a few examples:

- A maximum of 1,410 MB of memory is used by an instance of the database engine.
- A maximum size of 10 GB for a single database.
- The compute capacity used by a single instance is limited to the lesser of one socket or four cores.

Despite these limitations, SQL Server Express is still an excellent production solution for small applications. On the other hand, if you need to be able to test the more advanced features of the engine, knowing that your application will use a more complete edition (Standard or Enterprise) in production, you can install the **Developer edition** on your machine. This edition allows you to test all the features of the Enterprise edition without paying for an Enterprise license. The main limitation is, of course, that the Developer edition cannot be used in production. For example, if a project is expected to scale significantly or requires the use of advanced data analytics, high availability, or robust security features exclusive to the Standard or Enterprise editions, the Developer edition becomes a strategic choice. It allows developers to build, test, and refine applications with these complex features to ensure compatibility and performance optimization before deploying to a production environment using a paid edition.

Having said that, there are many tutorials on how to install the latest version of SQL Server Express available today. One of the many we recommend for installation is the following, which has you install the 2019 version (just before the very latest 2022 version, which has just been released):

https://www.sqlshack.com/how-to-install-sql-server-express-edition

If you follow the instructions and click the links on the Microsoft site, you will automatically be redirected to download the latest 2022 version. Instead, use the following link to download the 2019 version:

https://www.microsoft.com/en-US/download/details.aspx?id=101064

Just keep these observations in mind:

1. The **Feature Selection** screen suggests that you also install **SQL Server Replication** and **Machine Learning Services**. Deselect them and it's up to you whether you want to keep the full-text option selected. It is also recommended that you deselect the Java option:

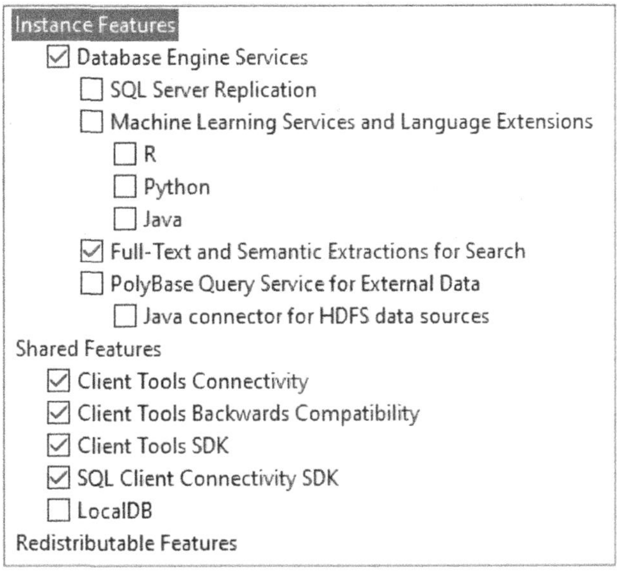

Figure 8.17: Suggested instance features

It is important to leave **Shared Features** selected by default so that the ODBC drivers needed to connect to the instance are also installed.

2. On the **Instance Configuration** screen, the tutorial suggests that you create a **named instance** (SQLEXPRESS). Instead, you must select the **Default Instance** option, which automatically changes the instance name to MSSQLSERVER.

3. Remember to save the password for the sa (system administrator) user in a safe place, as it will provide access to the instance you are installing as an administrator.

4. The tutorial will ask you to install SSMS in *Step 5*. If you haven't already installed it, do so now.

5. To connect to your SQL Server Express instance with SSMS, you can use . (a simple dot) or your computer name alone as the **server name** instead of the computer name and then the instance name. However, the tutorial suggests that you test your connection using **SQL Server Authentication** with the sa account credentials. Remember that you can also connect to your instance directly using **Windows authentication**, because your user is automatically added to the **SQL Server Administrators** group. As the tutorial says, if the login window closes without problems after you click **Connect**, it means that the connection is working properly.

Just stop at the *For the Windows authentication* section. The following applies:

IMPORTANT NOTE

It is important that the connection to the new instance works properly from SSMS. This confirms that the instance was installed correctly.

After the installation is complete, you can verify that the ODBC drivers are installed by following these steps:

1. Click the Windows **Start** button, and start entering the string ODBC. You will see something like this:

Figure 8.18: The Windows ODBC Data Sources configuration tools

2. Click on the 32-bit app or the 64-bit app, and then click on the **Drivers** tab. You'll see **ODBC Driver 17 for SQL Server** installed:

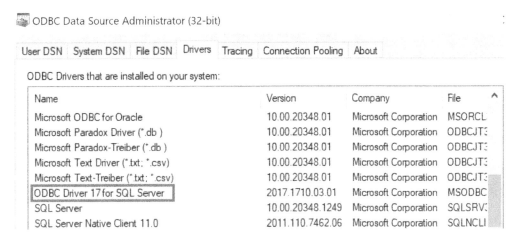

Figure 8.19: ODBC Driver 17 for SQL Server correctly installed

Fantastic! Now your default instance is working properly.

Let's also see how to configure an Azure SQL Database instance using the Azure portal.

Creating an Azure SQL Database

To create an Azure SQL Database, you must subscribe to Azure services. This allows you to access the **Azure portal** (https://portal.azure.com/) to manage all of your tenant's Azure resources. Once you have access to the portal, follow these steps:

1. Search for SQL databases in the main search box and click on it:

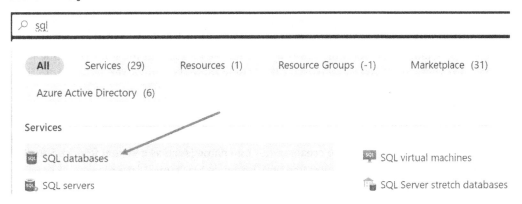

Figure 8.20: Selecting SQL databases in the Azure portal

2. Click on **Create** at the top left of the page:

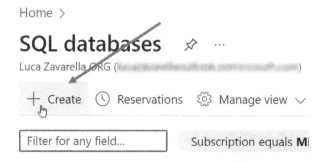

Figure 8.21: Clicking to create a SQL database

3. Beginning in late 2023, you can activate and use an Azure SQL Database for free within certain limits, as shown on the **Create SQL Database** page in *Figure 8.22*:

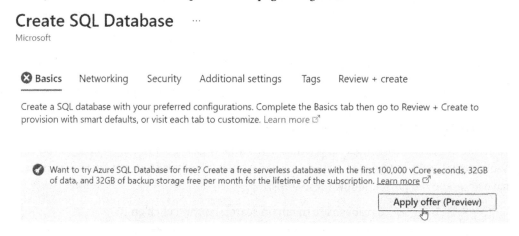

Figure 8.22: Select the Azure SQL Database free option

For details on the monthly limits of this option, please visit the following link: `https://bit.ly/azure-sql-db-free-limits`. Click **Apply offer (Preview)**. You will see the free monthly options in **Cost summary** on the right side of the page.

4. You need to select a **subscription** associated with your account (usually, the selected default one is OK if you have only one subscription associated) and then a **resource group** to collect all the resources you want to create under one name (such as a virtual folder). Select a resource group if you have already created one, or create a new one if necessary.

5. You must also specify the **database name** and **server**. As the database name, use `SystemsLogging`. If this is your first time creating an Azure SQL Database, you will also need to create a new server. To do this, click on **Create new** and specify a server name, a login, the related password, and the location you prefer (in our case, we already had a server available). After clicking **OK**, you'll see something like this:

Database details

Figure 8.23: Entering the database name and the new server

6. Under **Compute + storage**, click **Configure database**:

Figure 8.24: Configuring the database compute

By default, the **Auto-pause the database until next month** option is selected when the **Free database offer** is applied. In this way, the database will automatically become inaccessible if you exceed the limits imposed by the free option, thus preventing you from spending money. Keep it selected, leave all the other options as they are, and click on the **Apply** button.

7. You will be returned to the summary window of the options selected so far. Select the **Additional settings** tab at the top of the page and choose to install the sample data (i.e. the **AdventureWorkLT** demo database) by clicking on **Sample**. You will be asked if you want to change a backup compatibility option. Just click **OK**:

Figure 8.25: Choosing to install a sample database

8. Click on **Review + create**, and then on **Create** to deploy your brand-new Azure SQL Database.

9. Once the deployment is complete, click **Go to resource** and click on the **Overview** tab on the left to access the general dashboard of the newly created resource. In the upper-right corner, you will notice that the server name looks like this:

    ```
    <your-server-name>.database.windows.net
    ```

10. To access your Azure SQL Database from any client, you need to specify the client's IP address in the server firewall rules. To do this, click **Set server firewall** at the top of the dashboard:

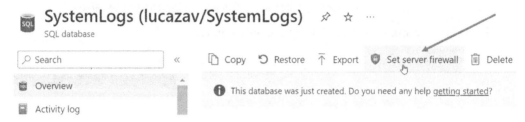

Figure 8.26: Setting rules on the Azure SQL server firewall

Among other options, you'll see some text boxes for entering the **rule name, start IP**, and **end IP**. By default, the all-in entry allows access to all IP addresses. If you want to restrict access for security reasons, you can remove it and add the IP address from which you are currently connected:

Figure 8.27: Adding your current IP address and using it in your rule

Note that if the public IP address of the computer is not static, the next time the computer reboots it will have a new IP address that is different from the previous one. This will force you to change the IP provided to the firewall each time you reboot. Therefore, if you frequently need to connect to the Azure SQL Database from your computer, it is advisable to have a **static public IP address** for the network you work from (internet providers often offer the option of having one for a small additional fee).

11. Click **Save** to save any changes to the firewall settings.

12. At this point, you can test the connection to your new Azure SQL Database using SSMS. If you haven't installed it yet, do so now by downloading the installer from the link `http://aka.ms/ssms`. Once installed, open the **Microsoft SQL Server Management Studio** app from the **Start** menu (you can find it in the `Microsoft SQL Server Tools XX` folder).

Use the server name in the `<your-server-name>.database.windows.net` format, choose **SQL Server Authentication** as the authentication method, and then enter the login and password you used during the creation of your Azure SQL Server. Then click **Connect**:

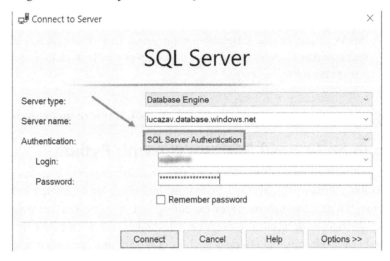

Figure 8.28: Connecting to your Azure SQL Database with SSMS

13. When the **Connect to Server** window disappears, you are connected to your server. In fact, if you open the **Databases** node in **Object Explorer** on the left, you can see your `SystemsLogging` database, which contains the `AdventureWorkLT` tables:

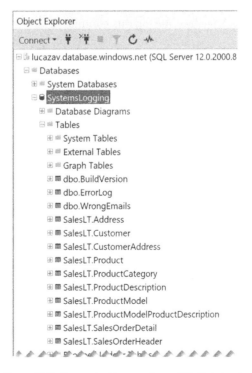

Figure 8.29: Connected to your Azure SQL Database

Awesome! Your Azure SQL database is up and running.

IMPORTANT NOTE

Note that Azure Entra authentication, including support for **multi-factor authentication (MFA)**, can also be used. However, configuring Azure Entra authentication is beyond the scope of this discussion and must be set up correctly to ensure secure access. See the references for more details.

Now let's try using Python to read from and write to a SQL server or an Azure SQL database.

Logging to an (Azure) SQL server with Python

The most common Python module for connecting to databases that you can connect to via ODBC drivers is **pyodbc**. It offers significant advantages, including broad compatibility with different database systems. It's easy to implement for executing SQL queries and retrieving data. It supports a standardized approach to database interactions. This makes it easier for developers to switch between different databases with minimal changes to their code. So, first, you need to install this package in the pbi_powerquery_env environment:

1. Open Anaconda Prompt.

2. Switch to the pbi_powerquery_env environment by entering this command:

    ```
    conda activate pbi_powerquery_env
    ```

3. Install the new package by entering this command:

    ```
    pip install pyodbc
    ```

At this point, you can start interacting with your database instances using Python.

Using the pyodbc module

To read from or write to a database, you must first connect to your database instance. You can do this with the connect() function, which takes a *connection string* as an argument. Depending on whether you need to connect to an on-premises or an Azure SQL Server instance, for the same type of authentication (SQL or Windows authentication), the connection string varies only in its server parameter.

You can use this code to connect to your local instance using Windows authentication:

```
import pyodbc
conn = pyodbc.connect(
    'Driver={ODBC Driver 17 for SQL Server};'
    r'Server=.;'
    'Database=master;'
    'Trusted_Connection=yes;')
```

You can also find the code snippets used here in the `11-read-write-on-azure-sql-server-with-python.py` file in the `Ch08 - Logging Data from Power BI to External Sources\Python` folder. Unlike the other Python script you found in the repository, this one has comments like `# %%`. As you learned in *Chapter 3, Configuring Python with Power BI*, these are placeholders that VS Code recognizes as **Jupyter-like code cells**. When VS Code identifies a cell, it automatically adds commands to execute its contents in the Interactive window, making it easier for the user to interact with the code:

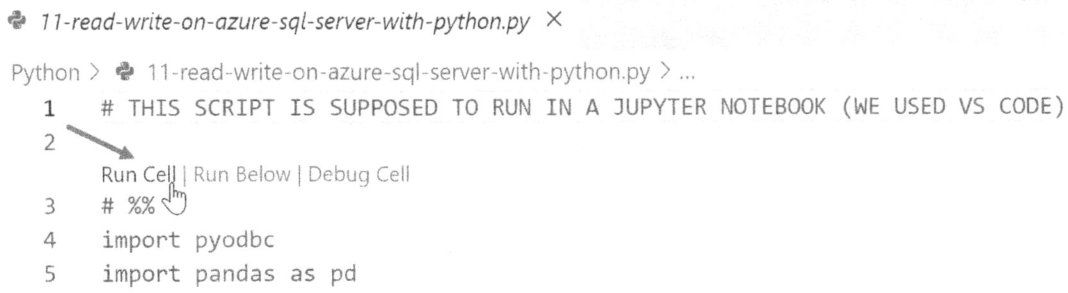

```
11-read-write-on-azure-sql-server-with-python.py ✕

Python >    11-read-write-on-azure-sql-server-with-python.py > ...
    1    # THIS SCRIPT IS SUPPOSED TO RUN IN A JUPYTER NOTEBOOK (WE USED VS CODE)
    2
         Run Cell | Run Below | Debug Cell
    3    # %%
    4    import pyodbc
    5    import pandas as pd
```

Figure 8.30: Using Jupyter notebook cells in VS Code

If you want to connect to the same instance using SQL authentication instead, you can use this code:

```
import pyodbc
conn = pyodbc.connect(
    'Driver={ODBC Driver 17 for SQL Server};'
    r'Server=.;'
    'Database=master;'
    'Uid=<your-username>;'
    'Pwd=<your-password>)
```

The format of the previous connection strings remains the same even when you want to connect to an Azure SQL Server. You must use the `<your-server-name>.database.windows.net` format for the server name. The authentication mode must necessarily be the SQL authentication mode. Therefore, the code to connect to your Azure SQL Database using the SQL authentication is as follows:

```
import pyodbc
conn = pyodbc.connect(
    'Driver={ODBC Driver 17 for SQL Server};'
    'Server=<your-server-name>.database.windows.net;'
    'Database=SystemsLogging;'
    'Uid=<your-username>;'
    'Pwd=<your-password>')
```

Once you have connected to an instance of your choice, you can read data from tables or views using the pandas `read_sql()` function, which takes a query in SQL (in our case, **T-SQL** for SQL Server) as a parameter.

For example, regardless of whether you are connected to your on-premises instance or to Azure, you can run the following code to read the database information available in the instance:

```
import pandas as pd
data = pd.read_sql("SELECT database_id, name FROM sys.databases", conn)
data.head()
```

In the case of Azure SQL Server, you will see this result:

	database_id	name
0	1	master
1	8	SystemsLogging

Figure 8.31: Result of a query to Azure SQL Server

Let's try writing something to a database instead. First, in the case of your *on-premises instance,* you need to create a new database to write your data to. You can do this in SSMS by following these steps:

1. Click on **Connect**, and then on **Database Engine...**:

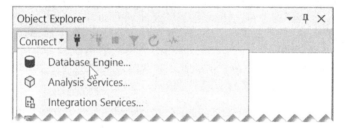

Figure 8.32: Connecting to a database engine in SSMS

2. Remember that you configured your on-premises SQL Server to be accessed using both the SQL and the Windows authentication. In this case, let's connect to your default instance using Windows authentication with the . (dot) string as the server name. Then, click on **Connect**:

Figure 8.33: Connecting to your default instance

3. Click on **New Query** on the toolbar at the top:

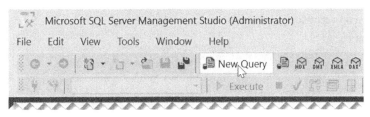

Figure 8.34: Opening a new query editor

4. Enter the `CREATE DATABASE SystemsLogging` script and then click on the **Execute** button with the green arrow (or just press *F5*).

5. Open the **Databases** node in **Object Explorer** and you can now see the brand-new SystemsLogging database:

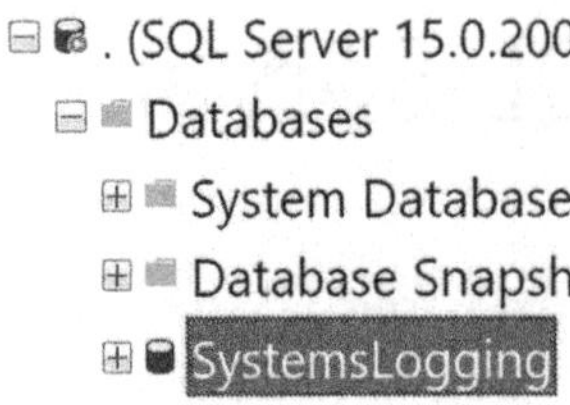

Figure 8.35: The new SystemsLogging database in your default instance

Now it's time to create the new WrongEmails table in the SystemsLogging database. It is usually prefer-able to execute **Data Definition Language (DDL)** commands (such as CREATE) directly in SSMS. In this case, we'll do it through Python to show you some special commands. You will first create a cursor object from the conn connection and then call its execute() method, passing it a CREATE TABLE query (the following scripts can always be found in the 11-read-write-on-azure-sql-server-with-python.py file):

```
conn = pyodbc.connect(
    'Driver={ODBC Driver 17 for SQL Server};'
    r'Server=.;'
    'Database=SystemsLogging;'
    'Trusted_Connection=yes;')
cursor = conn.cursor()
cursor.execute('''
            CREATE TABLE WrongEmails
            (
            UserId int,
            Email nvarchar(200)
            )
            ''')
conn.commit()
```

Remember that an Azure SQL or a SQL Server database collects its objects (tables, views, and so on) in **SQL schemas**. Typically, when you create a database object, you also specify the schema in the CREATE statement. For a table, you typically use the CREATE TABLE <your-schema>.<table-name> script. The WrongEmails table was created without specifying a schema. Therefore, it assumes the default schema, which is dbo.

Make sure to create the same table in your Azure SQL Database too:

```
conn = pyodbc.connect(
    'Driver={ODBC Driver 17 for SQL Server};'
```

```
        'Server=<your-server-name>.database.windows.net;'
        'Database=SystemsLogging;'
        'Uid=<your-username>;'
        'Pwd=<your-password>')
cursor = conn.cursor()
cursor.execute('''
                CREATE TABLE WrongEmails
                (
                UserId int,
                Email nvarchar(200)
                )
                ''')
conn.commit()
```

At this point, you can write pandas DataFrame content in the WrongEmails table row by row, using the cursor.execute() method, passing to it an INSERT INTO query. We will use the Azure SQL Database in the example since there is also the SalesLT.Customer table there (note the SalesLT schema) from which to read some customer data to write to the WrongEmails table:

```
# Get data from sample Customers
data = pd.read_sql('SELECT TOP 10 CustomerID, EmailAddress FROM SalesLT.
Customer', conn)
# Write Customers data into the WrongEmails table
cursor = conn.cursor()
# Write a dataframe into a SQL Server table row by row:
for index, row in data.iterrows():
    cursor.execute("INSERT INTO WrongEmails (UserId, Email) values(?,?)", row.
CustomerID, row.EmailAddress)
conn.commit()
cursor.close()
```

The iterrows() function iterates over the DataFrame columns and returns a tuple with the column name and content in the form of a series. Note that if you want to write to an on-premises SQL server, all you have to do is change the connection string, and the syntax you just saw remains valid. You can't run the code exactly as it is written in your default instance, simply because there is no AdventureWorksLT sample data there, so you will get an error.

To display the first few rows of the WrongEmails table, you can use this code:

```
df = pd.read_sql('SELECT TOP 10 UserId, Email FROM WrongEmails', conn)
df.head()
```

You will see something like this in VS Code:

	UserId	Email
0	202	a0@adventure-works.com
1	29943	a0@adventure-works.com
2	345	abigail0@adventure-works.com
3	29792	abigail0@adventure-works.com
4	511	abraham0@adventure-works.com

Figure 8.36: First few rows of the WrongEmails table

Now, be sure to empty the WrongEmails table with the following command so that it can be ready to be used later:

```
cursor = conn.cursor()
cursor.execute('TRUNCATE TABLE WrongEmails')
conn.commit()
```

When you have finished reading and writing to the database instance, remember to close the connection as follows:

```
conn.close()
```

Hey! You just learned how to read and write data from SQL Server or Azure SQL Database using Python. Easy, right? Let's apply what you've learned to Power BI.

Logging emails and dates to an Azure SQL Database in Power BI with Python

In this section, we will use the same scenario provided in *Chapter 6, Using Regular Expressions in Power BI*, where you validated email addresses and ban dates. The goal is to log the rows of the dataset that contain invalid emails to an Azure SQL Database and to filter them out of the dataset so that only valid emails remain in Power BI. This helps identify and analyze data quality issues, facilitates data cleansing and validation processes, and supports compliance and auditing efforts by providing a transparent record of data integrity efforts.

To run the following Python code correctly, you must ensure that you have created both the Azure SQL SystemsLogging database and its WrongEmails table as discussed in the previous section. If you prefer, you can also use your on-premises SQL Server instance by changing the server name in the connection string accordingly. In this case, make sure that the SystemsLogging database and its WrongEmails table exist.

The necessary steps are as follows:

1. Complete all of the steps in the *Using regex in Power BI to validate emails with Python* section of *Chapter 6, Using Regular Expressions in Power BI*, to the end, but do not click on **Close & Apply**.

2. Next, click on **Run Python Script** again, type the script you found in the `Python\12-log-wrong-emails-azure-sql-in-power-bi.py` file, and click **OK**.

3. Click on the `df` dataset's **Table** value.

4. Only rows with valid emails are retained:

1²₃ UserId	AᴮC Email	AᴮC BannedDate	isEmailValidFromRegex
1	_____@example.com	05/29/2018	1
4	firstname-lastname@example.com	06/07/2019	1
6	email@example-one.com	11/06/2017	1
7	email@example.co.jp	012/05/2018	1
8	email@example.name	06/7/2019	1
10	email@example.com	9/04/2017	1
11	email@subdomain.example.com	11/22/2018	1
12	email@123.123.123.123	07/31/17	1
14	firstname.lastname@example.com	11/22/18	1
15	firstname+lastname@example.com	05/16/2018	1
17	1234567890@example.com	05/16/2018	1
18	email@example.museum	03/26/2018	1
19	email@[123.123.123.123]	06/31/2017	1

Figure 8.37: A table containing only valid emails

Moreover, invalid emails have been written into the `WrongEmails` table of your `SystemsLogging` Azure SQL Database.

5. Go back to the **Home** menu, and then click **Close & Apply**.

To verify that invalid emails were actually written to the previous table, you can use SSMS as follows:

1. Use SSMS to connect to your Azure SQL Server using the string `<your-server-name>.database.windows.net` as the server name and SQL authentication.

2. Open the **Databases** node, open the **SystemsLogging** database node, then open the **Tables** node, right-click on the **dbo.WrongEmails** table, and click on **Select Top 1000 Rows**:

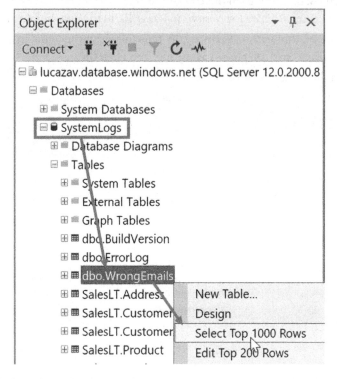

Figure 8.38: Querying the WrongEmails table in SSMS

You'll see the following output:

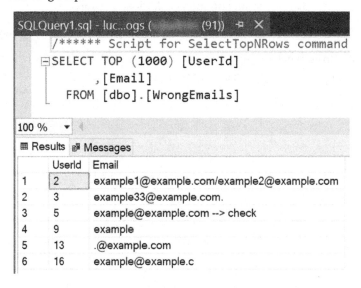

Figure 8.39: The content of the WrongEmails table in SSMS

Now, third-party systems can easily access your Azure SQL Database (even simply with Excel – see the *References* section) to read invalid emails and mobilize the appropriate team to fix them.

Well done! You just learned how to log information to an Azure SQL Database from Power BI using Python (you can do the same writing to an on-premises SQL Server database by simply changing the connection string). Now, let's see how you can do the same thing using R.

Logging to an (Azure) SQL Server with R

To connect to a database using ODBC drivers in R, we will use two packages: DBI and odbc. The job of the DBI package is to separate the database connection into a *front-end* and a *back-end*. The R code you'll write will only use the exposed front-end API. The back - end will take care of communicating with the specific DBMS through special drivers provided by the installation of other packages. On the other hand, the odbc package acts as a bridge between R and the database using ODBC drivers. It is specifically designed to communicate with various DBMSs, including SQL Server, whether hosted on-premises or on cloud platforms such as Azure.

IMPORTANT NOTE

You could have used odbc() directly to connect to both databases, on-premises and on Azure. Using DBI::dbConnect(odbc::odbc(), ...) instead of just odbc() offers important advantages: it adheres to a standardized interface for database operations, improves code readability and maintenance by making the connection method explicit, and ensures consistency across different database management systems. This approach leverages the DBI package's robust features for connection management and error handling, making your database interactions more reliable and efficient.

So, first you need to install these packages in your latest CRAN R engine:

1. Open RStudio, and make sure it is referencing your latest CRAN R in **Global Options**.
2. Enter this command into the console:

```
install.packages(c('odbc', 'DBI'))
```

At this point, you can start interacting with your database instances using R.

Using the DBI and odbc packages

In this case, you also need to *create a connection* to your database instance. You can do this with the DBI package's dbConnect() function, which takes a *driver object* (in our case, the odbc() one from the odbc package) and a *connection string* as arguments.

You can connect to your on-premises default instance using the Windows authentication with the code you can find in the file R\04-read-write-on-azure-sql-server-with-r.R:

```
library(odbc)
library(DBI)
conn <- dbConnect(
```

```
    odbc::odbc(), server = r'{.}',
    database = 'SystemsLogging', trusted_connection = 'yes',
    driver = '{ODBC Driver 17 for SQL Server}'
)
```

If you want to connect to the same instance using the SQL authentication instead, you can use this code:

```
conn <- dbConnect(
    odbc::odbc(), server = r'{.}',
    database = 'SystemsLogging', uid = '<your-username>',
    pwd = '<your-password>',
    driver = '{ODBC Driver 17 for SQL Server}'
)
```

The format of the previous connection strings remains the same even when you want to connect to an Azure SQL Database. You just need to use the `<your-server-name>.database.windows.net` format for the server name. In our case, the authentication mode used is the SQL authentication one. Therefore, the code to connect to your Azure SQL Database is as follows:

```
conn <- dbConnect(
    odbc::odbc(), server = '<your-server>.database.windows.net',
    database = 'SystemsLogging', uid = '<your-username>',
    pwd = '<your-password>',
    driver = '{ODBC Driver 17 for SQL Server}'
)
```

It is interesting to note that, once connected, RStudio allows you to browse the databases on your server using the **Connections** tab in the top-right corner. For example, *Figure 8.40* displays the contents of the SystemsLogging database of the default instance, going down to the detail of individual columns in a table:

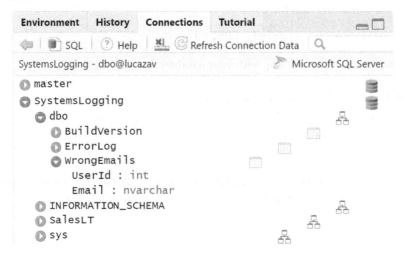

Figure 8.40: RStudio's Object Explorer of the established connection

Recall that the WrongEmails table was created in the previous section.

Once you have connected to an instance of your choice, you can easily read data from tables or views using DBI's dbGetQuery() function, which takes a SQL query (in our case, T-SQL for SQL Server) as a parameter. For example, just like in Python, you can run the following code to read the database information available on both on-premises instances and Azure SQL Servers:

```
data <- DBI::dbGetQuery(conn, "SELECT database_id, name FROM sys.databases")
head(data)
```

In the case of Azure SQL Server, you will see this result:

```
> head(data)
  database_id        name
1           1      master
2           6 SystemLogs
>
```

Figure 8.41: Result of a query to Azure SQL Server

Let's try writing something to a database instead. For example, you can *write the content of an R Data-Frame* to the WrongEmails table using the dbAppendTable() method. It simply takes the connection object, the name of the target table, and the DataFrame containing the source data. You just need to take care to properly rename the source data columns using aliases in the SQL query (using the AS keyword) when reading from the database, so that the names match those of the columns in the target table. In this example, we will use an Azure SQL Database because it also has the SalesLT.Customer table from which to retrieve the source data:

```
customers_df <- dbGetQuery(conn, "SELECT TOP 10 CustomerID AS UserId,
EmailAddress AS Email FROM SalesLT.Customer")
dbAppendTable(conn, name = 'WrongEmails', value = customers_df)
```

Note that if you need to create and populate the target table, you can use the one-time dbCreateTable() method, which takes the same parameters as the dbAppendTable() method. To display the first few rows of the WrongEmails table, you can use the following code:

```
df <- dbGetQuery(conn, "SELECT TOP 10 UserId, Email FROM WrongEmails")
head(df)
```

You will see something like this in VS Code:

```
> head(df)
  UserId                        Email
1    202         a0@adventure-works.com
2  29943         a0@adventure-works.com
3    345 abigail0@adventure-works.com
4  29792 abigail0@adventure-works.com
5    511 abraham0@adventure-works.com
6  30052 abraham0@adventure-works.com
>
```

Figure 8.42: The contents of the WrongEmails table

Now make sure you empty the WrongEmails table with the TRUNCATE TABLE SQL command inside the dbSendQuery() method (which just executes a query without retrieving any data) so that it is ready to use:

```
dbSendQuery(conn, "TRUNCATE TABLE WrongEmails")
```

When you have finished reading and writing to the database instance, remember to close the connection as follows:

```
dbDisconnect(conn)
```

Wow! You just learned how to use R to read and write data from SQL Server or Azure SQL Database! Let's apply what you've learned to Power BI.

Logging emails and dates to an Azure SQL Database in Power BI with R

In this section, we will use the same scenario that we used earlier to show how to log data to an Azure SQL Database from Power BI. To properly execute the following R code, you must ensure that you have created the Azure SQL SystemsLogging database and the WrongEmails table, as discussed in the *Logging to an Azure SQL Server with Python* section. If you prefer, you can also use your on-premises SQL Server instance by changing the server name in the connection string accordingly. In this case, make sure that the SystemsLogging database and the WrongEmails table are present. The required steps are as follows:

1. Complete all of the steps in the *Using regex in Power BI to validate emails with R* section of *Chapter 6*, *Using Regular Expressions in Power BI*, to the end, but do not click on **Close & Apply**.

2. Then, click on **Run R Script** again, type the script you found in the R\05-log-wrong-emails-azure-sql-in-power-bi.R file, and click **OK**. Remember to edit the server name and your credentials in the code.

3. Click the **Table** value of the df dataset.

4. Only rows with valid emails are kept:

Figure 8.43: A table that contains only valid emails

In addition, the invalid emails were written to the WrongEmails table in your Azure SQL database.

5. Go back to the **Home** menu, and then click **Close & Apply**.

As done before, you can use SSMS to verify that invalid emails were written to the previous table. You should see the following output:

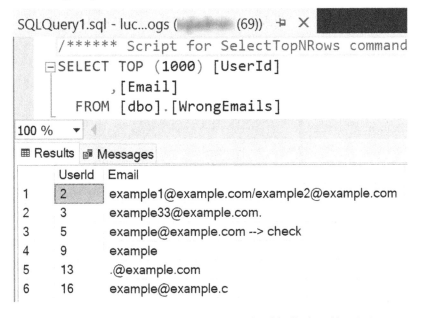

Figure 8.44: The contents of the WrongEmails table displayed by SSMS

Awesome! You've just logged your wrong emails to your (Azure) SQL Server database using R from Power BI.

Managing credentials in the code

As you have just seen, to connect to an instance of (Azure) SQL Server using SQL authentication, you need to specify the user and password in plain text in the connection string. As you can imagine, leaving such sensitive information exposed in Python or R code in Power BI is not a security best practice. We left the code this way for educational purposes, but there are some simple strategies you can adopt to prevent this dangerous exposure of sensitive data.

If you need to secure credentials in code in a Power Query step script, you can use **environment variables.** Let's take a closer look at how to implement this strategy.

Creating environment variables

The most common method is to create two **system environment variables** that contain your user ID and password as values. Then, you simply call the contents of these environment variables in your code.

Let's see how to do this:

1.   Click on the **Windows Start menu** and type the word environment. The **Edit the system envi-ronment variables** option will appear on the menu as you type. Click on it:

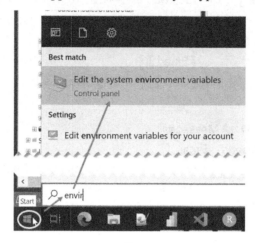

Figure 8.45: Editing the system environment variables

2.   The **System Properties** window will appear with the **Advanced** tab selected. Simply click on the **Environment Variables...** button:

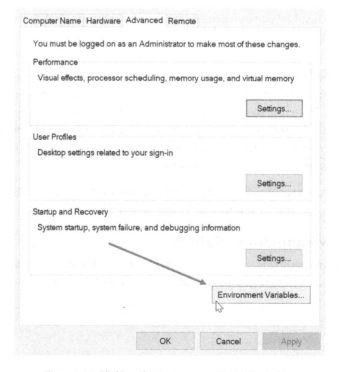

Figure 8.46: Clicking the Environment Variables button

3. The **Environment Variables** window appears. It has two panels in it: one for managing user environment variables, and one for managing system environment variables. Since you need to add system variables (valid for all the users logging on that computer), click the **New** button in the **System variables** panel:

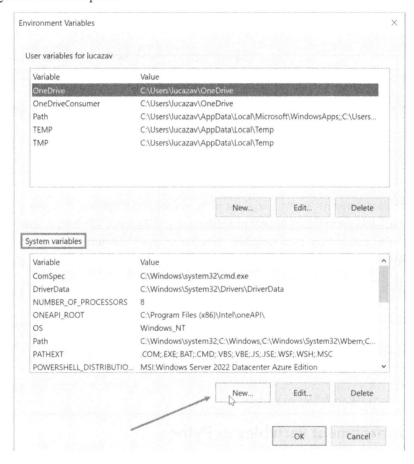

Figure 8.47: Creating a new system environment variable

4. Enter the SQLDB_USERNAME system variable and use your username to connect to your (Azure) SQL database. Then click **OK**:

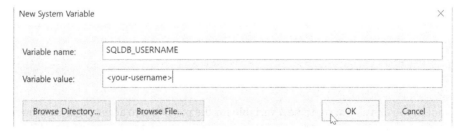

Figure 8.48: Entering the SQLDB_USERNAME system variable

5. Enter the `SQLDB_PASSWORD` system variable in the same way. If everything is okay, you will see both the new system variables in the **System variables** panel:

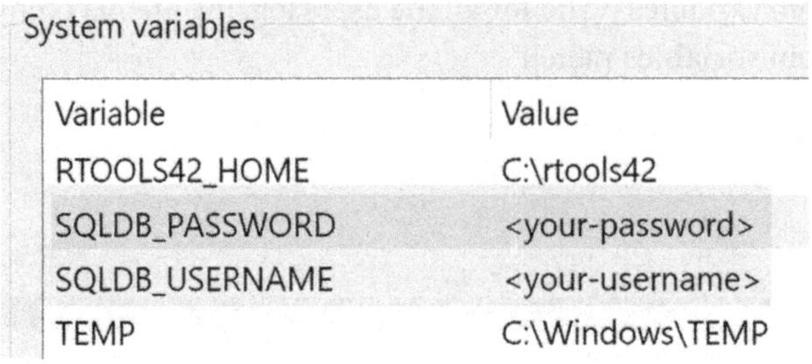

System variables

Variable	Value
RTOOLS42_HOME	C:\rtools42
SQLDB_PASSWORD	<your-password>
SQLDB_USERNAME	<your-username>
TEMP	C:\Windows\TEMP

Figure 8.49: Your system variables correctly entered

6. Click **OK** in the **Environment Variables** window and **OK** in the **System Properties** window.

Great! The first step required to use environment system variables is done!

For the new environment system variables to be visible from Python or R, you must restart the processes that will use them if they are running. Basically, if RStudio, VS Code, or Power BI Desktop were open when you entered the new variables, you must restart them if you want to "see" the variables in that software.

> **IMPORTANT NOTE**
>
> If a report published to the Power BI service requires access to environment system variables in Power Query Python or R step scripts, you must create those variables directly on the computer hosting the data gateway in personal mode.

So, let's use the new variables in Python.

Using environment variables in Python

If you want to get the environment variables in Python, you can utilize the os module that comes with the standard Python library. Once you import it, you can access the dictionary of environment variables by using the environ attribute. Here is the simple code to assign the value of the system environment variable SQLDB_USERNAME to a variable in the code and then use it:

```
import os

# Get the SQLDB_USERNAME environment variable
SQLDB_USERNAME = os.environ["SQLDB_USERNAME"]
print(SQLDB_USERNAME)
```

At this point, you can also assign a new variable for the password to access your instance of (Azure) SQL Server, and then use both variables in the connection string without directly exposing sensitive data.

It is possible to do the same thing in R. Let's see how.

Using environment variables in R

To get the contents of system environment variables in R, you can use the Sys.getenv function, as shown in the following code:

```
# Get the SQLDB_USERNAME environment variable
SQLDB_USERNAME <- Sys.getenv("SQLDB_USERNAME")
print(SQLDB_USERNAME)
```

Now you can create a new variable to hold your (Azure) SQL Server password and then include both variables in the connection string, thereby preventing direct exposure of confidential information.

Summary

In this chapter, you learned how to log some information processed in Power Query to CSV files, Excel, on-premises SQL Server database, and Azure SQL Database, in both Python and R, using very simple and straightforward commands.

In the next chapter, you will see how to handle very large CSV files that cannot be loaded from Power BI Desktop due to the RAM size of your machine not being sufficient.

References

For additional reading, check out the following books and articles:

* *Common Format and MIME Type for Comma-Separated Values (CSV) Files* (https://tools.ietf.org/html/rfc4180)

* *Excel (.xlsx) Extensions to the Office Open XML SpreadsheetML File Format* (https://bit.ly/ms-xlsx-specs)

* *Connect Excel to a database in Azure SQL Database* (https://bit.ly/excel-to-azuresqldb)

* *Configure and manage Microsoft Entra authentication with Azure SQL* (https://bit.ly/azuresql-entra-auth)

Test your knowledge

1. Which Python and R functions are used in this chapter to create CSV files? How do they differ in how they handle carriage returns and newline characters?

2. Which Python and R functions are used in this chapter to create Excel files?

3. Whether you want to connect to an on-premises SQL Server or an Azure SQL Database through a client, what technology was used in the chapter to enable communication?

4. Which packages used in this chapter allowed you to connect to an Azure SQL Database using Python and R?

5. How can you prevent exposing sensitive data in Python or R code that is required to connect to an Azure SQL Database that requires SQL authentication from a Power Query script step?

Learn more on Discord

To join the Discord community for this book – where you can share feedback, ask questions to the author, and learn about new releases – follow the QR code below:

https://discord.gg/MKww5g45EB

9

Loading Large Datasets Beyond the Available RAM in Power BI

In the previous chapter, you learned how to read from and write to a CSV file using both Python and R. When it comes to reading a file, whether you use Power BI's standard data import feature or the techniques shown in the previous chapter, the main limitation on the file size is the amount of RAM available on the machine where Power BI Desktop is installed.

In a data enrichment phase, it may be necessary to extract information needed for ongoing analysis from very large files (terabytes in size). In these cases, it is almost always necessary to implement big data solutions to be able to handle such large amounts of data. Very often, however, it is necessary to import files that are slightly larger than the available memory in order to extract aggregate information and then persist it in a small table for reuse during processing. In such cases, you don't need to worry about sophisticated big data platforms, but as we will discuss in this chapter, you can take advantage of the flexibility provided by specific packages that implement distributed computing systems in both Python and R, without having to resort to Apache Spark-based backends.

In this chapter, you will learn about the following topics:

- A typical analytic scenario using large datasets
- Importing large datasets using Python
- Importing large datasets using R
- Exporting large datasets in Parquet using Python and R

Technical requirements

This chapter requires you to have a working internet connection and **Power BI Desktop** already installed on your machine (we used version 2.114.664.0 64-bit, February 2022). You must have properly configured the R and Python engines and IDEs as outlined in *Chapter 2, Configuring R with Power BI*, and *Chapter 3, Configuring Python with Power BI*.

A typical analytic scenario using large datasets

One of the most common activities of a data scientist is to analyze a dataset of information relevant to a business scenario. The goal of the analysis is to be able to identify associations and relationships between variables that will somehow help to discover new measurable aspects of the business (insights) that can then be used to make it grow better. It may be the case that the available data is not sufficient to identify strong associations between variables, because any additional variables may not be considered. In this case, attempting to obtain new data that is not generated by your organization but that enriches the context of your dataset (a type of **data augmentation**) can improve the strength of the statistical associations between your variables. For example, being able to link weather forecast data to a dataset that reports the measurements of a dam's water level will certainly introduce significant variables to better interpret the phenomenon.

In this context, you often need to extract information from CSV files downloaded from external data sources. For example, imagine that you have been asked to analyze what factors influenced the profitability of a chain of shoe stores located in major airports in the U.S. from 1987 to 2012. The first thing that comes to your mind is that maybe flight delays are somehow related to the amount of time people spend at the airport. If you have to spend time at the airport, you definitely have more time to visit the various stores there, and therefore the likelihood of you making a purchase increases. So, how do you find data on the average airline delay at each U.S. airport for each day of the year? Fortunately, the *Research and Innovative Technology Administration (RITA)*, *Bureau of Transportation Statistics*, provides aggregated statistics (`http://bit.ly/airline-stats`) and raw data containing flight arrival and departure details for all commercial flights within the U.S. (`http://bit.ly/airline-stats-data`). A set of CSV files derived from the data collected by RITA, containing only monthly airline data from 1987 to 2012, has already been packaged and zipped by Microsoft and can be downloaded directly from this link: `https://bit.ly/airontime87to12`. For more information about the fields in the files, see: `https://bit.ly/airontime87to12-desc`.

The compressed file in question is about 4 GB in size and, once unzipped, contains many CSV files with detailed data of flights made in the U.S. across months ranging from 1987 to 2012, with a total size of 30 GB! Your goal is to calculate the average daily flight delay for each origin airport and to save the resulting dataset in a CSV file. How do you import all this data into Power BI? Let's first see how to do this in Python.

Importing large datasets with Python

In *Chapter 3*, *Configuring Python with Power BI*, we suggested that you install some of the most commonly used data management packages in your environment, including NumPy, pandas, and scikit-learn. The biggest limitation of these packages is that *they cannot handle datasets larger than the RAM of the machine on which they are used*, so they cannot scale to more than one machine. These packages are designed to work in memory, which means that the data they work with must be loaded into the computer's RAM. If the size of the dataset exceeds the available RAM, the packages cannot load or process the data efficiently, resulting in potential crashes or significantly slower performance due to the need to swap data in and out of memory.

To overcome this limitation, distributed systems based on **Spark**, which has become a dominant tool in the big data analytics landscape, are often used. However, moving to these systems forces developers to rethink code they have already written using an API called **PySpark**, which was created to use Spark objects with Python. This process is generally seen as causing delays in project delivery and causing frustration for developers who are much more comfortable with the libraries available for standard Python.

In response to the preceding issues, the community has developed a new library for parallel computing in Python called **Dask** (`https://dask.org/`). This library provides transparent ways for the developer to scale pandas, scikit-learn, and NumPy workflows more natively, with minimal rewriting. In fact, the Dask APIs are pretty much a copy of most of these modules' APIs, making the developer's job easier. Scaling is achieved through a combination of lazy evaluation and parallel execution, taking advantage of the machine's multiple cores or processors. Another advantage of Dask is that *you don't need to set up a cluster of machines to be able to manipulate 100+ GB datasets*. All you need is one of today's laptops with a multi-core CPU and 32 GB of RAM to handle them with ease. So, with Dask, you can analyze moderately large datasets (they exceed the memory capacity of standard laptops or desktops, which typically range from 8 to 32 GB of RAM) on your own laptop, without incurring the overhead typical of clusters, such as using Docker images on multiple nodes and complex debugging.

> **IMPORTANT NOTE**
>
> Apparently, even the Spark team recognized the inconvenience of using PySpark by developers accustomed to using pandas as a data wrangling module. For this reason, they have introduced **Koalas** (`https://koalas.readthedocs.io`), which provides a pandas API on top of Apache Spark.

The fact remains that Dask has many advantages over Spark when it comes to using a distributed system on your laptop only. For example, Spark is based on a **Java Virtual Machine** (**JVM**) infrastructure, and therefore requires Java and other components to be installed, while Dask is written in pure Python. Additionally, using Dask enables a faster transition from your laptop to a cluster in the cloud, which can be easily provisioned thanks to Azure, for example. This is made possible thanks to the **Dask Cloud Provider** package (`https://cloudprovider.dask.org/`), which provides classes for creating and managing temporary Dask clusters on different cloud platforms. See the references if you need to create a Dask cluster on Azure via Azure Spot Virtual Machines, or by using Azure Machine Learning compute clusters (for example, using NVIDIA RAPIDS for GPU-accelerated data science).

Coming back to the topic at hand, let's then see how to install Dask on your laptop.

Installing Dask on your laptop

You will install Dask in the `pbi_powerquery_env` environment, where the pandas and NumPy libraries are already installed. This time, it's not enough to simply run the `pip install dask` command, because that will only install the core parts of Dask. The correct way for Dask users is to install all components.

To display the graph of the execution plan of a Dask operation, a **Graphviz** module must also be installed. To do all of this, follow these steps:

1. Open your Anaconda prompt.
2. Switch to your pbi_powerquery_env environment and type this command:

    ```
    conda activate pbi_powerquery_env
    ```

3. Type the following command to install all components of Dask:

    ```
    pip install "dask[complete]"
    ```

4. Type the following command to install all components of Graphviz:

    ```
    pip install graphviz
    ```

You will also need to install the **Graphviz** executables on Windows:

1. Go to http://www.graphviz.org/download/, and then download and install the 64-bit stable Windows installation package (in our case, version 9.0.0).
2. During the installation, choose to add Graphviz to the system path for the current user.

At this point, let's explore the structures provided by Dask that allow you to extend common interfaces, such as those of NumPy, pandas, and Python iterators, to handle objects larger than the available memory.

Creating a Dask DataFrame

A **Dask DataFrame** is part of the Dask *big data* collections that allow pandas, NumPy, and Python iterators to scale easily. In addition to Dask DataFrames, which are the counterpart to pandas DataFrames, **Dask Array** (which mimics NumPy), **Dask Bag** (which mimics iterators), and **Dask Delayed** (which mimics loops) are also part of the collections. However, we will focus on Dask DataFrames, which will allow us to achieve the analysis goal we set at the beginning of this chapter.

A Dask DataFrame is nothing more than a set of pandas DataFrames that can reside on disk on a single machine or multiple nodes in a cluster, allowing you to manage datasets larger than the RAM on your laptop. We assume that you have already unzipped the CSV files containing data on U.S. flights from 1987 to 2012, as mentioned at the beginning of this chapter, into the C:\<your-path>\AirOnTimeCSV folder.

> **IMPORTANT NOTE**
>
> If you don't have a laptop with enough hardware resources (at least 16 GB of RAM), you should import a subset of CSV files first (such as 40-50 files) to test the scripts without having to wait for excessively long execution times or incurring memory errors.

Then, you can easily create your Dask DataFrame as follows:

```
import os
import dask.dataframe as dd
```

```
main_path = os.path.join('C:\\', 'your-path', 'AirOnTimeCSV')
ddf = dd.read_csv(
    os.path.join(main_path, 'airOT*.csv'),
    encoding='latin-1',
    usecols =['YEAR', 'MONTH', 'DAY_OF_MONTH', 'ORIGIN', 'DEP_DELAY']
)
```

Note that the * wildcard allows you to capture all the CSV files contained in the folder that have the form airOTyyyymm.csv, where yyyy is the year and mm is the month number of the flight departure date. In addition, the encoding of the CSV files is declared as latin-1.

IMPORTANT NOTE

There is no indication anywhere that the downloaded CSV files have such encoding. By simply trying to import them without declaring it (and therefore assuming utf-8 by default), loading returns the following strange error: UnicodeDecodeError: 'utf-8' codec can't decode byte 0xe4 in position 4: invalid continuation byte. By searching the web, it is easy to find out that this kind of error is encoding related and that latin-1 is the correct one.

It is also a good idea to *specify only the columns of interest* using the usecols parameter in order to limit the columns to be read. This practice also guarantees that only those columns are read that you are sure are not completely empty, thus avoiding reading errors due to the difference between the inferred data type and the real one.

IMPORTANT NOTE

Some columns may have a number of null values at the beginning and therefore Dask cannot infer the correct data type because it uses a sample to do so. In this case, you should explicitly declare the data type of these columns using the dtype parameter.

Now that the Dask DataFrame has been created, let's see how you can use it to extract the information we need.

Extracting information from a Dask DataFrame

If you ran the code to read all the CSV files, you will have noticed that the operation took very little time. Come to think of it, that's really not enough time to read 30 GB of data. Could it be that the read was not successful? The secret of most parallel computing frameworks lies in this very feature: the read operation was not physically performed but was added to a possible queue of operations to be performed when you explicitly request to use the data. This concept is known as **lazy evaluation** or **delayed computation**. Accordingly, your Dask DataFrame can be used in subsequent operations as if it already contained the data.

In our case, since we need the average airline delay at each U.S. airport for each day of the year, consider using the following code:

```
mean_dep_delay_ddf = ddf.groupby(['YEAR', 'MONTH', 'DAY_OF_MONTH', 'ORIGIN'])
[['DEP_DELAY']].mean().reset_index()
```

If you are a little bit familiar with the pandas DataFrame transformations, you will notice that the same methods are used for the Dask DataFrame. As with pandas, you must use *double square brackets* to output a DataFrame; otherwise, you would get a series with a single pair of brackets (see here: http://bit.ly/pandas-subset-df). Also, in order to use the indexes created by the groupby() method as columns in a DataFrame, you need to reset them with reset_index() (for more details, see: http://bit.ly/pandas-groupby).

This piece of code also takes very little time to execute. As you can imagine, the averaging operation was queued after the data read operation in the transformation queue, which in this case is associated with the mean_dep_delay_ddf DataFrame. If you want to get a better idea of what the execution plan of the transformations queued so far is, you can create a graph to represent it. For simplicity, we will implement the graph using only one CSV file as input. These are the necessary steps:

1. Create a folder called AirOnTimeCSVplot.

2. Copy only **the first two CSV files** you unzipped earlier to the previous folder.

3. Open a new Python script and run the following code in Visual Studio Code:

    ```
    import os
    import dask.dataframe as dd
    main_path = r'C:\<your-path>\AirOnTimeCSVplot'
    ddf_1_month = dd.read_csv(
        os.path.join(main_path, 'airOT*.csv'),
        encoding='latin-1',
        usecols =['YEAR', 'MONTH', 'DAY_OF_MONTH', 'ORIGIN', 'DEP_DELAY']
    )
    mean_dep_delay_1_month_ddf = ddf_1_month.groupby(['YEAR', 'MONTH', 'DAY_
    OF_MONTH', 'ORIGIN'])[['DEP_DELAY']].mean().reset_index()
    mean_dep_delay_1_month_ddf.visualize(filename='mean_dep_delay_1_month_
    dask.pdf')
    ```

The visualize() method allows you to visualize the graph of the tasks estimated by the engine to realize the queued transformations, even before they are executed. Specifically, the code will generate a PDF file in the same folder as the script you executed.

Starting at the bottom of *Figure 9.1*, which represents the contents of the newly generated PDF file, you can see that the single source CSV file is read by the read-csv function from two chunks split by the engine. The dataframe-groupby-count-chunk and dataframe-groupby-sum-chunk functions are applied to each chunk because, for each tuple defined by the keys of the grouping operation (YEAR, MONTH, DAY_OF_MONTH, and ORIGIN), we need to know the sum of the delay (DEP_DELAY) and the number of occurrences to compute the average.

The results of the two `dataframe-groupby-sum-chunk` operations on the two chunks are then aggregated by the `dataframe-groupby-sum-agg` function. Similarly, the `dataframe-groupby-count-agg` function aggregates the results of the two `dataframe-groupby-count-chunk` operations. Once the two DataFrames of sums and counts have been determined, the ratio between the two (i.e., the mean) is calculated for each grouping using the `truediv` function. Finally, the `reset_index` function returns the desired DataFrame, the result of the distributed averaging operation.

If you think about it, the famous problem-solving strategy called **Divide and Conquer** (also known as **Divide and Rule** or **Divide et Impera** in Latin) has been adopted. It consists of dividing the original problem into smaller and generally simpler subproblems, each solved recursively. The solutions of the subproblems are then properly combined to obtain the solution of the original problem. If you've had any experience with the Hadoop world, the **MapReduce** paradigm follows the same philosophy, which was maintained and optimized later by Spark.

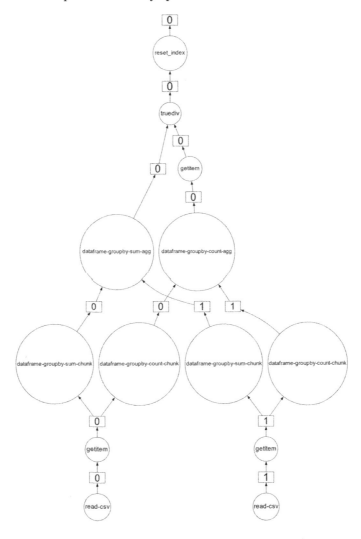

Figure 9.1: Computation of the underlying task graph

But let's go back to the original script. We defined the `mean_dep_delay_ddf` Dask DataFrame. All the transformations needed to get the desired result are queued. How do you tell Dask to actually do all the computations? You must explicitly ask for the result using the `compute()` method.

IMPORTANT NOTE

Note that `compute()` returns in-memory results. It converts Dask DataFrames to pandas DataFrames, Dask arrays to NumPy arrays, and Dask bags to lists. It is a method that should only be called if you are sure that the result will fit comfortably in your machine's RAM. Otherwise, you can write your data to disk using specific methods, such as `to_textfiles()` or `to_parquet()`.

When you instantiated a cluster, you could have chosen to persist the computed data not on disk but in memory using the `persist()` method. The result would still have been a distributed Dask object, but one that references precomputed results distributed over the cluster's memory.

To add some magic to your script, you can use the `ProgressBar()` object, which allows you to monitor the progress of your calculations. Unfortunately, it happens that even when the bar reaches 100%, it still takes some time for the workers to finish processing:

```
✓ with ProgressBar(): ⋯
```

```
[########################################] | 100% Completed | 198.31 s
```

Figure 9.2: The progress bar on Visual Studio Code

So, don't give up! Before you run the following line of code, keep in mind that on a Xeon Platinum 8171M machine with a 2.60 GHz CPU, 32 GB of RAM, and 8 virtual processors, it will take about 3 minutes to run. The script is as follows:

```
with ProgressBar():
    mean_dep_delay_df = mean_dep_delay_ddf.compute()
```

Your laptop will use all available logical processors to parallelize calculations, which you can see in the **Logical Processors** view of **Task Manager**:

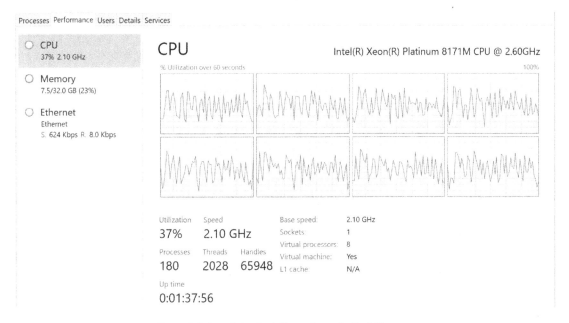

Figure 9.3: Parallel calculations shown in Task Manager

When processing is complete, your pandas DataFrame is available in memory, and you can view some of its rows as follows:

```
mean_dep_delay_df.head(10)
```

The output will be as follows:

✓ `mean_dep_delay_df.head(10)` ⋯

	YEAR	MONTH	DAY_OF_MONTH	ORIGIN	DEP_DELAY
0	1987	10	1	ABE	1.600000
1	1987	10	1	ABQ	2.494253
2	1987	10	1	ACV	14.000000
3	1987	10	1	AGS	2.000000
4	1987	10	1	ALB	5.843750
5	1987	10	1	ALO	0.000000
6	1987	10	1	AMA	0.086957
7	1987	10	1	ANC	1.142857
8	1987	10	1	APF	0.000000
9	1987	10	1	ATL	4.051604

Figure 9.4: First 10 rows of the pandas DataFrame output

You can also check the size of this DataFrame with this code:

```
print(mean_dep_delay_df.shape)
```

Here is the result:

```
print(mean_dep_delay_df.shape)
✓  0.4s

(2188888, 5)
```

Figure 9.5: Size of the resulting pandas DataFrame

The complete script for creating a Dask DataFrame and extracting information from it can be found in the `01-load-large-dataset-in-python.py` file in the `Ch09 - Loading Large Datasets` beyond the `Available RAM in Power BI\Python` folder.

Finally, you were able to get the dataset of a few thousand rows on average flight delays for each origin airport and for each day of the year by processing a 30 GB CSV set!

If you want to write the contents of a Dask DataFrame to a CSV file, without going through the generation of a Pandas DataFrame, you can call the `to_csv()` method directly, passing the path to the file to generate as a parameter, as the following example shows:

```
ddf.to_csv(r'D\<your-path>\mean_dep_delay_df.csv')
```

As you can well imagine, calling the `to_csv()` method triggers the actual execution of all queued transformations, just like the `compute()` method, since you're forcing Dask to read the DataFrame contents in order to write them to disk. For this reason, if you need to generate the CSV file and also create the pandas DataFrame to be used later in your code, you should not first call `to_csv()` from the Dask DataFrame and then call `compute()` to get the pandas DataFrame, because you would force the actual execution of the transformation pipeline twice. In this case, it is convenient to first generate the pandas DataFrame with `compute()` and then generate a CSV or an Excel file from it, as you learned in *Chapter 8*, *Logging Data from Power BI to External Sources*.

Now, let's try applying what you've learned so far to Power BI.

Importing a large dataset in Power BI with Python

You learned that Power BI can import data directly using a Python script and that the data must be organized in a pandas DataFrame in order to be used in the data model. Therefore, you will develop a script that uses the objects illustrated in the previous section in order to instantiate a pandas DataFrame that contains the data on average flight delays in the U.S. You will then generate a CSV file from this DataFrame. Here are the steps required to implement this in Power BI:

1. Open Power BI Desktop through the shortcut that activates the `pbi_powerquery_env` environment.

2. Make sure Power BI Desktop is referencing the pbi_powerquery_env environment in the **Options**.

3. Click on **Get data**, type Python, and then double-click on **Python script**.

4. Copy the contents of the 02-load-large-dataset-in-power-bi.py file into the Ch09 - Loading Large Datasets beyond the Available RAM in Power BI/Python folder and paste it into the Python script editor. Remember to edit the path to the CSV files (main_path) and the destination path of the CSV file to be generated, and then click **OK**.

5. After about 12 minutes (time required from data validation and data loading on the same machine as before), you will see the **Navigator** window showing the aggregated data in the mean_dep_delay_df DataFrame:

Navigator

Figure 9.6: The mean_dep_delay_df DataFrame loaded in Power BI

Select the DataFrame and click on **Load**. A **Load** popup will appear and remain active for about seven more minutes. When it disappears, your data is loaded into the data model.

Moreover, the script also generated the CSV file containing your aggregated data. You'll find the mean_dep_delay_df.csv file, sized about 60 MB, in your folder:

```
Python > 📊 mean_dep_delay_df.csv
1    YEAR,MONTH,DAY_OF_MONTH,ORIGIN,DEP_DELAY
2    1987,10,1,ABE,1.6
3    1987,10,1,ABQ,2.4942528735632186
4    1987,10,1,ACV,14.0
5    1987,10,1,AGS,2.0
```

Figure 9.7: Content of the CSV file created from the Python script in Power BI

Impressive! You just imported 30 GB of data to get aggregated results in your Power BI Desktop, with just a few lines of Python. Congratulations!

Did you know you could do the same thing in R? We're going to show you a technology that's very hot these days and can be used with both Python and R. Curious? Let's see what it's all about.

Importing large datasets with R

The same scalability limitations illustrated for Python packages used to manipulate data also exist for R packages in the **Tidyverse** ecosystem. Similarly, in R, users face scalability limitations with datasets exceeding the available RAM on the machine. The first solution that is adopted in these cases is also to switch to Spark-based distributed systems that provide the **SparkR** language. It provides a distributed implementation of the DataFrame you are used to in R, supporting filtering, aggregation, and selection operations as you do with the dplyr package. For those of us who are fans of the Tidyverse world, RStudio is actively developing the sparklyr package, which allows you to use all the functionality of dplyr, even for distributed DataFrames. However, using Spark-based systems to process CSVs that together take up little more than the RAM you have available on your machine may be overkill due to the overhead of all the Java infrastructure needed to run them.

In the previous edition of this book, we introduced the R disk.frame package as a fast, disk-based, parallelized data manipulation framework for larger-than-RAM data. Recently, this package has been soft deprecated in favor of a new technology that is gaining significant traction: the arrow package, which is the R implementation of **Apache Arrow**, a cross-language development platform for in-memory and larger-than-memory data, which implements a new columnar format.

Introducing Apache Arrow

Apache Arrow is a new language-independent framework designed specifically for managing flat and hierarchical data. It addresses the challenge of efficiently exchanging data between various software applications. In fact, it was created to solve a problem that many software developers face when working with data: how to move data between different applications and systems without losing speed or efficiency.

Traditionally, when data needs to be shared between applications, it must be converted into a format specific to each application's needs. This process can be slow and resource intensive, especially when dealing with large amounts of data. Apache Arrow solves this problem by using an in-memory columnar format that reduces the overhead associated with traditional row-based data formats. In a row-based format, data is stored in rows, where each row represents a record or observation, and each column represents a variable or feature. When performing operations on a row-based format, the entire row must be loaded into memory, even if only a few columns are needed. This can result in a lot of unnecessary data being loaded into memory and can slow down processing times. With a columnar format, only the relevant columns need to be loaded into memory, making data processing more efficient. Additionally, columnar formats are easier to compress because each column can be compressed independently. This can further reduce memory usage and improve processing times. The new file format introduced by Apache Arrow was originally known as **Feather** but has since been renamed **Arrow format**.

Apache Arrow has the unique advantage of supporting a wide range of programming languages, including C#, MATLAB, Python, and R. This means that if one data scientist applies transformations to a complex dataset using R, the result of the transformations can also be used by another data scientist who knows how to use Python, for example, as input to a pipeline.

IMPORTANT NOTE

You may be wondering why we did not also use Arrow for Python via the PyArrow package while choosing Dask. The reason is that Dask, in addition to being able to solve the problem of loading and transforming a dataset larger than the available memory, is a very popular and useful framework, especially for parallelizing operations in Python. Therefore, we thought it appropriate to include it because it will be very useful to you in other situations as well.

Note, however, that pandas 2.0 has been released, and the big new feature it will have is the Apache Arrow backend for pandas data.

As of version 6.0.0, the arrow package supports the aggregation functions of the dplyr package, such as n(), n_distinct(), sum(), and mean(). This makes it really easy to perform aggregation operations on large amounts of data.

Let's see how to use arrow in detail.

Installing arrow on your laptop

First, you need to install the arrow package in your R engine:

1. Open RStudio and make sure it is referencing your latest CRAN R engine (in our case, version 4.2.2).
2. Click on the console prompt and type this command: install.packages("arrow"). Make sure you install the latest version of the package (in our case, version 11.0.0.3).

At this point, you are ready to test it on RStudio.

Creating and extracting information from an Arrow Dataset object

Apache Arrow provides an efficient way of working with both single and multi-file datasets, even if the data is too large to fit into memory. You can upload individual files of different formats, such as csv, tsv, json, parquet, and arrow through the Arrow Table object. On the other hand, if you need to work with very large datasets based on multiple files, the Arrow Dataset object allows you to manage them using familiar dplyr syntax. The file formats allowed by an Arrow Dataset are parquet, arrow, csv, tsv, or text to handle non-standard field delimiters.

Instantiating an Arrow Dataset object is really quite simple. Once the arrow library is loaded, you simply call the open_dataset function, passing as parameters the folder containing the files to read and the format of those files:

```
library(arrow)
main_path <- r"{C:\<your-path>\AirOnTimeCSV}"
ds <- open_dataset(main_path, format = "csv")
```

Just as you saw for a Dask DataFrame, an Arrow Dataset is also a pointer to source files. In fact, the creation process is very fast. Again, any transformations you do on it will be queued and applied at the end (**lazy evaluation**). Let us then see what transformations to apply to the Arrow Dataset.

As we are interested in getting the average airline delay at each U.S. airport for each day of the year, a grouping operation is required on the entire dataset. There is nothing easier than this because, as expected, it is possible to use the dplyr syntax that all analysts using R are accustomed to.

The following code should be used to extract aggregated data:

```
library(arrow)
library(dplyr)
main_path <- r"{C:\Datasets\AirOnTimeCSV}"
ds <- open_dataset(main_path, format = "csv")
start_time <- Sys.time()
mean_dep_delay_df <- ds %>%
   select( YEAR, MONTH, DAY_OF_MONTH, ORIGIN, DEP_DELAY ) %>%
   group_by( YEAR, MONTH, DAY_OF_MONTH, ORIGIN ) %>%
   summarise( DEP_DELAY = mean(DEP_DELAY, na.rm = T) ) %>%
   collect() %>%
   ungroup()
end_time <- Sys.time()
dim(mean_dep_delay_df)
(create_dkf_exec_time <- end_time - start_time)
```

Again, as already seen for Dask in Python, there are functions that collect all the queued transformations and trigger the execution of calculations. In the case of arrow, the function is collect(). The duration of this operation is about 3 and a half minutes with the same machine used with Dask.

The end result is a tibble containing the desired air delay averages (these results may differ slightly depending on how the rows are sorted):

```
> head(mean_dep_delay_df, 10)
# A tibble: 10 × 5
     YEAR MONTH DAY_OF_MONTH ORIGIN DEP_DELAY
    <int> <int>        <int> <chr>      <dbl>
 1  1987    11            1 JFK         6.91
 2  1987    11            2 JFK         3.91
 3  1987    11            3 JFK         3.36
 4  1987    11            4 JFK         7.10
 5  1987    11            5 JFK        23.3
 6  1987    11            6 JFK        21.6
 7  1987    11            7 JFK         8.96
 8  1987    11            8 JFK        14.6
 9  1987    11            9 JFK         7.67
10  1987    11           10 JFK        13.5
>
```

Figure 9.8: First rows of the tibble containing the delay averages

Even in this case, you were able to get the dataset of a few thousand rows on average flight delays by processing a CSV set as large as 30 GB!

The following common-sense observation applies here as well:

IMPORTANT NOTE

If the results of previous time-consuming processing are to be reused often, it is best to persist them on disk in a reusable format. In this way, you can avoid all the onerous processing of the queued transformations.

Because the result of the collect function is a tibble, you can write it to disk as you learned in *Chapter 8, Logging Data from Power BI to External Sources*.

You can find the complete script for creating the mean departure delay DataFrame using an Arrow Dataset in the 01-create-diskframe-in-r.R file in the Ch09 - Loading Large Datasets beyond the Available RAM in Power BI\R folder.

So, let's see how you can apply what you've learned so far in Power BI.

Importing a large dataset in Power BI with R

The optimal solution for loading a dataset larger than the available RAM with R through Power BI is the same as you saw in the previous section. You can then use it in Power BI as follows:

1. Make sure Power BI Desktop is pointing to the latest R engine you've installed (in our case, version 4.2.2) in the **Options**.

2. Click on **Get data**, type `script`, and then double-click on **R script**.

3. Copy the contents of the `02-create-and-extract-info-from-arrow-in-power-bi.R` file in the `Ch09 - Loading Large Datasets beyond the Available RAM in Power BI\R` folder and paste it into the R script editor. Remember to edit the source folder path and the destination path of the CSV file to be generated, and then click **OK**.

4. After about seven minutes (using the same machine used before), you will see the **Navigator** window showing the aggregated data in the `mean_dep_delay_df` DataFrame.

Navigator

Figure 9.9: The mean_dep_delay_df DataFrame loaded in Power BI

Select the DataFrame and click on **Load**. A **Load** popup will appear, and it will remain active for about four more minutes. When it disappears, your data will be loaded into the data model.

The script also created the CSV file containing your aggregated data. You'll find the `mean_dep_delay_df.csv` file, which is about 60 MB in size, in the destination folder you selected:

```
C: > Temp >  ⊞ mean_dep_delay_df.csv
1    YEAR,MONTH,DAY_OF_MONTH,ORIGIN,DEP_DELAY
2    1987,11,1,JFK,6.909774436090226
3    1987,11,2,JFK,3.9140625
4    1987,11,3,JFK,3.3577235772357725
5    1987,11,4,JFK,7.096774193548387
```

Figure 9.10: Contents of the CSV file generated by the R script in Power BI

Awesome! Have you ever thought about importing 30 GB of data into your Power BI desktop to extract information from it in R? Well, you just did with just a few lines of code.

Summary

In this chapter, you've learned how to import datasets that are larger than the RAM available on your laptop into Python and R. You've also used this knowledge to import a set of CSV files that together take up more than the RAM available on your machine into Power BI Desktop.

In the next chapter, you will learn how to optimize the execution time of Power BI processing that requires the use of referenced queries.

References

For additional reading, check out the following books and articles:

- *Create Dask clusters on Azure using Azure (Spot) VMs* (`https://cloudprovider.dask.org/en/latest/azure.html`)
- *Library to turn Azure ML Compute into Ray and Dask cluster* (`https://bit.ly/azureml-ray-dask`)
- *The arrow package in R* (`https://arrow.apache.org/docs/r/`)
- *pandas 2.0 and the Arrow revolution (part I)* (`https://datapythonista.me/blog/pandas-20-and-the-arrow-revolution-part-i`)

Test your knowledge

1. What is the primary limitation when reading files in Power BI Desktop, and how does it impact file size?
2. How can you handle datasets larger than the available RAM in Power BI Desktop?
3. What method does Dask use to manage the reading of large datasets without immediately consuming memory?
4. How can Apache Arrow improve the handling of large datasets in R?

Learn more on Discord

To join the Discord community for this book – where you can share feedback, ask questions to the author, and learn about new releases – follow the QR code below:

`https://discord.gg/MKww5g45EB`

10

Boosting Data Loading Speed in Power BI with Parquet Format

Often, the analyses you are asked to perform in Power BI need to be based on fairly large data sources. In the previous chapter, you learned how to work with data that is larger than the RAM available on your machine, and you saw that query execution times are in the order of minutes.

Now consider a report that needs to perform several calculations on the same corpus database. Obviously, the performance of the overall execution time of the report is strongly related to the expected number of operations to be performed on the database. Therefore, being able to reduce the execution time of individual queries will allow you to have a report whose dataset is updated as quickly as possible with each refresh.

Queries implemented in a Power BI report most often need to retrieve aggregated measures that provide users with the information they need to take specific business actions. If the data is available in relational databases, such as Azure SQL Database, specific indexes can be created for the queries that the report will execute. Such indexes are intended to speed up the execution time of the aforementioned queries, making the report update time quite fast. On the other hand, if the source data is persisted in CSV files, it is not possible to interact with it to speed up the queries. However, it is possible to modify the format of such files to make the final format more performant for aggregation operations.

This chapter will cover the following topics:

- From CSV to the Parquet file format
- Using the Parquet format to speed up a Power BI report

Technical requirements

This chapter requires you to have a working internet connection and **Power BI Desktop** already installed on your machine (we used version 2.114.664.0 64-bit, February 2022). You must have properly configured the R and Python engines and IDEs as outlined in *Chapter 2, Configuring R with Power BI*, and *Chapter 3, Configuring Python with Power BI*.

From CSV to the Parquet file format

The traditional approach of storing structured data in CSV files has long been the method of choice for many organizations. As an illustration, consider the dataset used in *Chapter 9, Loading Large Datasets beyond the Available RAM in Power BI*. This dataset encompasses monthly U.S. flight data from 1987 to 2012, distributed across numerous CSV files. However, this approach has several significant limitations that can negatively impact data processing and analysis:

- The CSV file format, characterized by its simplicity and row-based storage, is inherently not optimized for columnar storage, resulting in slower read and write times, especially when dealing with large datasets. This inherent characteristic of CSV files means that data is stored in a sequence of rows, with each row representing a single record. This row-oriented approach requires reading the entire file, or large portions of it, to access or query specific columns of data, resulting in slower query execution times and reduced overall performance.

- Although CSV files can handle basic data types such as integers and strings, they can struggle when it comes to dealing with more complex data structures such as arrays and nested data types. This means that storing and analyzing data that requires more complex data structures may be challenging when working with CSV files.

To overcome these limitations, a new technology called **Parquet** was born. This storage format was originally developed as a joint project between Cloudera and Twitter. It then became part of the Apache Software Foundation in 2013 and is now one of the most popular file formats used in the big data ecosystem.

It consists of an open-source columnar storage format specifically designed to optimize file efficiency, as opposed to the more common row-based CSV files. By leveraging columnar storage, users can quickly filter out extraneous data when querying, making aggregation queries much less time-consuming compared to traditional row-based databases. The tremendous efficiency of this storage method translates into reduced hardware costs and dramatic reductions in data access latency.

In addition, Parquet uses a binary encoding format, which increases the complexity of identifying sensitive information for AI detectors, making it more difficult for them to accurately classify data points and extract insights from large-scale datasets. The complexity introduced by Parquet's binary encoding format in identifying sensitive information has a dual effect. On the one hand, it enhances data privacy and security by making unauthorized access more difficult and helping to comply with data protection regulations. On the other hand, it presents challenges, including added complexity in data management and potential barriers to fully leveraging data for insights. While this complexity can protect sensitive data from misuse, it also requires more sophisticated tools and processes for effective data analysis and management.

In light of its impressive capabilities, Apache Parquet is optimally suited to function alongside cutting-edge interactive and serverless technologies like Azure Synapse Analytics, Microsoft Fabric, and Azure Databricks. But as you might have guessed, it's also possible to use this format in Power BI, either natively or with Python and R. Before we take an in-depth look at this, let's first see why it is not recommended to use the native Parquet connector in Power BI.

Limitations of using Parquet files natively in Power BI

The Parquet connector in Power BI was made publicly available on 15 December 2020. The new support for reading Parquet has obviously generated a lot of excitement, especially when you consider the benefits it brings compared to reading CSV files.

One of the first advantages, as mentioned in the previous paragraphs, is the ability to select only the columns needed for analysis from a Parquet file, given its columnar compressed data format. The Power Query engine can often take advantage of this when, for example, it needs to perform GROUP BY transformations. In this case, it can easily use the Parquet connector to extract only the columns needed for the operation.

In other cases, the engine is not so efficient. For example, if you want to count the rows of the dataset derived from a Parquet file, the connector first loads all the columns and then counts the rows. In cases like this, simple manual intervention is all that is needed to optimize the query. For example, by first selecting only one column of the dataset (an ID or a particular transaction date) and then applying the count operation, a significant performance improvement is achieved.

Unfortunately, this is the only optimization strictly related to the Parquet format that the Power BI connector can perform. There are others that would significantly improve query execution times but are not applied by the connector. These are as follows:

- **Parallel processing:** To achieve parallel processing, a framework may use multiple threads or processes, each working on a separate Parquet file simultaneously. In this way, while one thread reads and processes one file, another thread can simultaneously work on another file. By distributing the workload across multiple threads or processes, the framework can take advantage of the processing power available in the system, resulting in faster data loading and improved performance. When you try to load multiple Parquet files from a folder, it appears that the combination of the folder and Parquet connectors in Power BI prevents the parallel loading of individual files. This fact affects the speed at which large datasets can be processed.

- **Predicate pushdown:** When queries are executed using a straightforward approach, filtering data is typically done at the end of the query execution process. By applying filters earlier in the query execution, you can significantly improve performance by getting rid of non-matching records earlier, saving unnecessary processing time and resources later. The Power BI Parquet connector doesn't do predicate pushdown or anything like it.

- **Partition pruning:** This involves dividing a dataset into smaller, more manageable partitions based on specific criteria or attributes, such as date or region. By doing this, the framework can efficiently process only the relevant partitions, instead of scanning the entire dataset. However, this is only possible if the Parquet files representing the dataset have been partitioned for the selected key fields used as filters. This approach can lead to significant improvements in query execution times, especially for very large datasets. However, the Power BI Parquet connector doesn't support partition pruning, meaning that it is unable to take advantage of this performance-enhancing feature.

In addition, another limitation of the connector is the inability to connect in DirectQuery to Parquet files.

Since the Power BI Parquet connector can't take advantage of these benefits, the only way to do it is to bypass the connector and use Python or R. Let's see how to do that.

Using Parquet files with Python

In *Chapter 9, Loading Large Datasets beyond the Available RAM in Power BI*, you loaded a dataset consisting of several CSV files with detailed data on flights in the United States for months from 1987 to 2012, with a total size of 30 GB, using Dask. You could then calculate the average flight delay by origin for each day of the year in the dataset.

Taking the same use case and using the same dataset, let's see the significant benefits of using the Parquet format with Dask.

Analyzing Parquet data with Dask

Now suppose you want to calculate the maximum delay per flight origin, for each day in the years 1999 and 2000 only. Using the example of the Python code already provided in the previous chapter, we have the following:

```python
import os
import dask.dataframe as dd
from dask.diagnostics import ProgressBar


main_path = 'C:\\Datasets\\AirOnTimeCSV'


ddf = dd.read_csv(
    os.path.join(main_path, 'airOT*.csv'),
    encoding='latin-1',
    usecols =['YEAR', 'MONTH', 'DAY_OF_MONTH', 'ORIGIN', 'DEP_DELAY']
)


flights_1999_2000_ddf = ddf.loc[(ddf['YEAR'].isin([1999, 2000]))]


max_dep_delay_by_day_1999_2000_ddf = flights_1999_2000_ddf.groupby(['YEAR',
'MONTH', 'DAY_OF_MONTH', 'ORIGIN'])[['DEP_DELAY']].max().reset_index()


with ProgressBar():
    max_dep_delay_by_day_df = max_dep_delay_by_day_1999_2000_ddf.compute()


max_dep_delay_by_day_df.head(10)
```

As you may have noticed, to filter a Dask dataset, we use the condition of interest in the loc[] function, following the same API syntax provided by pandas. You can find the above code in the Python\01-load-csv-and-analyze-dask.py file in the *Chapter 10* code folder.

Running it in VS Code on a Xeon Platinum 8171M machine with a 2.60 GHz CPU, 32 GB RAM, and 8 virtual processors, the progress bar shows a time of about *2 minutes and 40 seconds*:

```
✓ with ProgressBar(): ⋯

[########################################] | 100% Completed | 161.10 s
```

Figure 10.1: The progress bar on Visual Studio Code

And the first 10 rows of the result are the following:

```
✓ max_dep_delay_by_day_df.head(10) ⋯
```

	YEAR	MONTH	DAY_OF_MONTH	ORIGIN	DEP_DELAY
0	1999	1	1	ABE	51.0
1	1999	1	1	ABQ	208.0
2	1999	1	1	ADQ	35.0
3	1999	1	1	AGS	3.0
4	1999	1	1	ALB	67.0
5	1999	1	1	AMA	65.0
6	1999	1	1	ANC	130.0
7	1999	1	1	ATL	175.0
8	1999	1	1	AUS	159.0
9	1999	1	1	AVL	29.0

Figure 10.2: The result of the analysis of the max flight delays

If you recall, the code in the above example from the previous chapter also took the same three minutes to average over all years. This means that even though we filtered for specific years, Dask is still forced to read all the CSV files before it can properly filter them.

You can find all the code needed to analyze CSV files using Dask in the Python\01-load-csv-and-analyze-dask.py file in the *Chapter 10* code folder.

Now let's try to generate the Parquet files associated with the entire dataset, again using the Dask API.

Writing Parquet datasets

First, create the AirOnTimeCSVtoAppend folder in the same root as the AirOnTimeCSV folder. Then move the airOT201212.csv file from the AirOnTimeCSV folder to the AirOnTimeCSVtoAppend folder. These instructions are a preliminary step designed to facilitate a clear demonstration of two distinct operations: creating a new Parquet dataset and appending data to an existing Parquet dataset.

Once a Dask DataFrame has been created by referencing the CSV files in the `AirOnTimeCSV` folder, it is actually possible to simply use the **to_parquet()** function to generate the Parquet format of the dataset composed of the various CSV files. Let's see how to do this:

```
import os
import dask.dataframe as dd
from dask.diagnostics import ProgressBar

# Get the path to the folder containing all the CSV files
# (update it according to your folders structure)
main_path = 'C:\\Datasets\\AirOnTimeCSV'

ddf = dd.read_csv(
    os.path.join(main_path, 'airOT*.csv'),
    encoding='latin-1',
    usecols =['YEAR', 'MONTH', 'DAY_OF_MONTH', 'ORIGIN', 'DEP_DELAY']
)

with ProgressBar():
    ddf.to_parquet(path=r'C:\Datasets\AirOnTimeParquetDask',
                   overwrite=True)
```

In only about 2 and a half minutes, you were able to get the dataset in Parquet format corresponding to all the CSV files except the one related to flights in December 2012. The files of the Parquet dataset are in the `AirOnTimeParquetDask` folder:

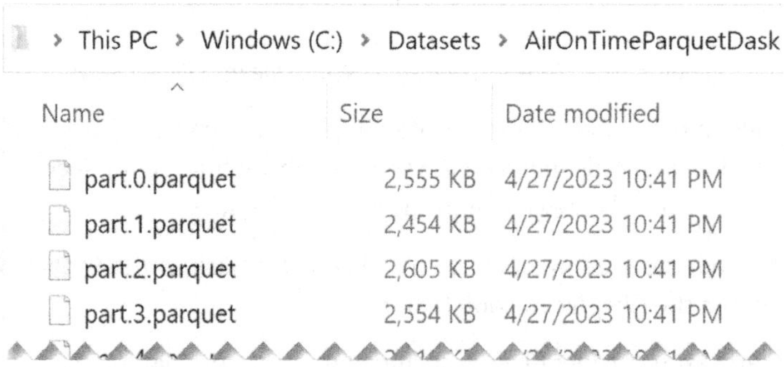

> This PC > Windows (C:) > Datasets > AirOnTimeParquetDask

Name	Size	Date modified
part.0.parquet	2,555 KB	4/27/2023 10:41 PM
part.1.parquet	2,454 KB	4/27/2023 10:41 PM
part.2.parquet	2,605 KB	4/27/2023 10:41 PM
part.3.parquet	2,554 KB	4/27/2023 10:41 PM

Figure 10.3: The Parquet files that represent the AirOnTime dataset

Have you noticed that a single dataset is transformed into multiple .parquet files? You may already know why, thanks to the concepts you learned in *Chapter 9*, but the following information box provides the reasons.

IMPORTANT NOTE

Dask creates multiple file parts when writing a Parquet dataset primarily to leverage its parallel and distributed computing capabilities. As Dask is designed for parallel and out-of-core computation, it divides the data into smaller chunks called partitions, which can be processed independently and in parallel across multiple cores or even distributed across multiple machines in a cluster.

To complete the Parquet dataset by including the December 2012 flights, let's see how to append the data contained in one or more CSV files to an existing Parquet dataset. After reading the CSV files to be added into a Dask DataFrame from the `AirOnTimeCSVtoAppend` folder, simply use the same to_parquet() function as before, this time using the **append=True** parameter instead of overwrite=True:

```
to_append_main_path = 'C:\\Datasets\\AirOnTimeCSVtoAppend'

to_append_ddf = dd.read_csv(
    os.path.join(to_append_main_path, 'airOT*.csv'),
    encoding='latin-1',
    usecols =['YEAR', 'MONTH', 'DAY_OF_MONTH', 'ORIGIN', 'DEP_DELAY']
)

with ProgressBar():
    to_append_ddf.to_parquet(
        path=r'C:\Datasets\AirOnTimeParquetDask',
        append=True)
```

After this operation, you will have a Parquet dataset containing data from all the CSV files of the flights you want to analyze.

As we mentioned at the beginning of this chapter, it is also possible to generate the partitioned Parquet files for specific columns contained in the dataset. **Partitioning** generally refers to the process of organizing and dividing a dataset into smaller, more manageable chunks based on specific attributes or criteria. This technique is particularly useful for improving the efficiency and performance of query operations on large datasets. By partitioning the data, the system can read and process only the relevant chunks (partitions), instead of scanning the entire dataset, resulting in faster query execution times and reduced I/O. In the context of the Parquet format, partitioning is often implemented on a columnar basis. This means that the dataset is divided into separate partitions based on the distinct values of a particular column. Each partition is then stored in a separate subdirectory, with the relevant Parquet files containing the data for that specific partition.

You can create partitioned Parquet files simply by passing the list of fields you want to partition to the partition_on parameter of the to_parquet() function. Let's see how to partition the files for the YEAR column:

```
with ProgressBar():
    ddf.to_parquet(
```

```
        path=r'C:\Datasets\AirOnTimeParquetPartitionedDask',
        partition_on=['YEAR'],
        overwrite=True)
```

Since we used the Dask DataFrame ddf in the code we just ran, we created a partitioned Parquet dataset that excludes the December 2012 flights.

Partitioning Parquet files based on the YEAR column is a strategic approach that significantly improves data management and query performance, especially for time-series data or datasets where temporal analysis is critical. By organizing data into separate directories or files for each year, this method allows for more efficient data access and processing. When queries are executed, only the relevant partitions corresponding to specific years are accessed, reducing the amount of data that needs to be read and processed.

As you can see, this time the AirOnTimeParquetPartitioned folder doesn't directly contain the Parquet files that represent the dataset, but there are as many folders as there are different values that the YEAR field takes, and the Parquet files are within these subfolders:

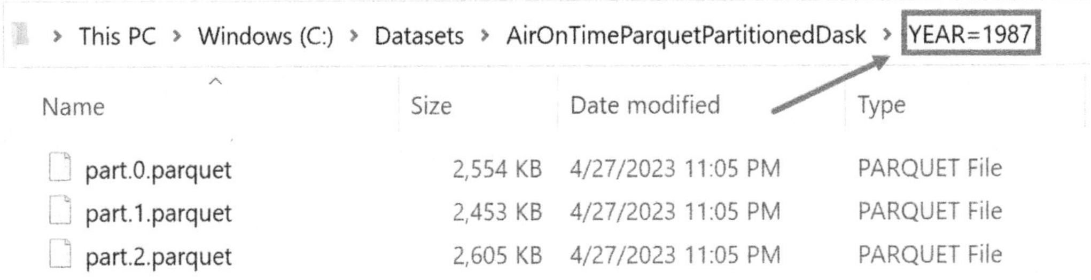

Name	Size	Date modified	Type
part.0.parquet	2,554 KB	4/27/2023 11:05 PM	PARQUET File
part.1.parquet	2,453 KB	4/27/2023 11:05 PM	PARQUET File
part.2.parquet	2,605 KB	4/27/2023 11:05 PM	PARQUET File

Figure 10.4: The partitioned Parquet files

Again, in order to be able to add the December 2012 flights to the Parquet dataset as well, simply perform an append operation on the CSV files (in our case only one) referenced by the Dask DataFrame to_append_ddf:

```
with ProgressBar():
    to_append_ddf.to_parquet(
        path=r'C:\Datasets\AirOnTimeParquetPartitionedDask',
        partition_on=['YEAR'],
        append=True)
```

The only difference from the append code used before is the presence of the partition_on=['YEAR'] parameter. You can find all the code needed to export Dask DataFrames to Parquet in the Python\02-create-parquet-dask.py file in the *Chapter 10* code folder.

At this point, the unpartitioned and partitioned Parquet datasets are ready to be used for data analysis.

Reading and transforming Parquet datasets

Now that you have successfully converted the data source of various CSV files to the Parquet format with Dask, let's try to perform the same analysis on the Parquet files that was performed directly on the CSV files.

We again compute the maximum delay by flight origin, only for each day of all the available years, from 1987 to 2012, this time loading the Dask DataFrame from the unpartitioned Parquet files, using the read_parquet() function:

```
import os
import dask.dataframe as dd
from dask.diagnostics import ProgressBar


main_path = 'C:\\Datasets\\AirOnTimeParquetDask'


ddf = dd.read_parquet(path=os.path.join(main_path, '*'))


max_dep_delay_ddf = ddf.groupby(['YEAR', 'MONTH', 'DAY_OF_MONTH', 'ORIGIN'])
[['DEP_DELAY']].max().reset_index()


with ProgressBar():
    max_dep_delay_df = max_dep_delay_ddf.compute()
```

Remember that the Parquet files are stored directly inside the AirOnTimeParquetDask folder, so the path passed as a parameter to the read_parquet() function contains a single asterisk (*wildcard*) at the end to indicate that all the files must be loaded.

Now look at the progress bar after the end of the calculation:

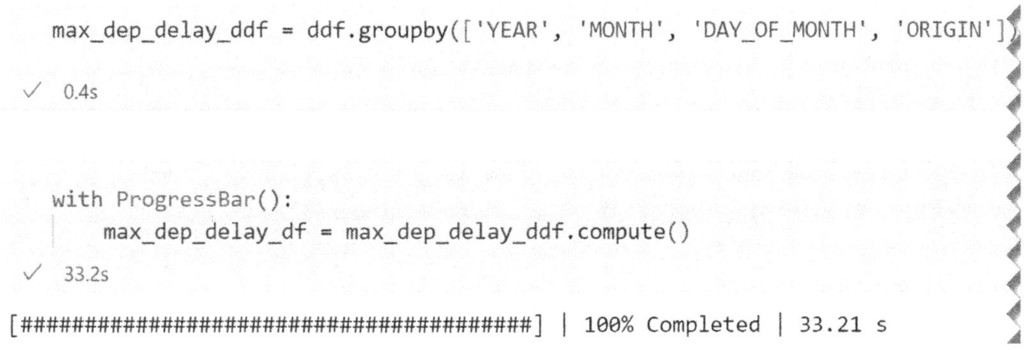

```
    max_dep_delay_ddf = ddf.groupby(['YEAR', 'MONTH', 'DAY_OF_MONTH', 'ORIGIN']
  ✓  0.4s



  with ProgressBar():
      max_dep_delay_df = max_dep_delay_ddf.compute()
  ✓  33.2s

[#######################################] | 100% Completed | 33.21 s
```

Figure 10.5: Calculation made on Parquet files

Impressive! The calculation on Parquet files took *only 33 seconds*! Compared to the similar calculation performed on CSV files in *Chapter 9, Loading Large Datasets beyond the Available RAM in Power BI*, which took about 3 minutes, you get a 6X improvement! Here are the first rows of the result:

 ✓ `max_dep_delay_df.head(10)` ⋯

	YEAR	MONTH	DAY_OF_MONTH	ORIGIN	DEP_DELAY
0	1987	10	1	ABE	21.0
1	1987	10	1	ABQ	28.0
2	1987	10	1	ACV	43.0
3	1987	10	1	AGS	15.0
4	1987	10	1	ALB	64.0
5	1987	10	1	ALO	0.0
6	1987	10	1	AMA	3.0
7	1987	10	1	ANC	15.0
8	1987	10	1	APF	0.0
9	1987	10	1	ATL	110.0

Figure 10.6: First rows of the result

Now let's see if the Parquet format allows us to take advantage of the performance improvements given by the *predicate pushdown* when applying a filter by year:

```
filters = [
    ("YEAR", "in", [1999, 2000])
]

flights_1999_2000 = dd.read_parquet(path=os.path.join(main_path, '*'),
filters=filters)

max_dep_delay_1999_2000_ddf = flights_1999_2000.groupby(['YEAR', 'MONTH', 'DAY_
OF_MONTH', 'ORIGIN'])[['DEP_DELAY']].max().reset_index()

with ProgressBar():
    max_dep_delay_1999_2000_df = max_dep_delay_1999_2000_ddf.compute()
```

This time, the progress bar marked the following time:

```
max_dep_delay_1999_2000_ddf = flights_1999_2000.groupby(['YEAR', 'MONTH', 'DA
✓ 0.7s


with ProgressBar():
    max_dep_delay_1999_2000_df = max_dep_delay_1999_2000_ddf.compute()
✓ 2.7s

[########################################] | 100% Completed | 2.71 sms
```

Figure 10.7: Effect of the predicate pushdown on the performance

This is huge! Compared to the same calculation performed on CSV files, which took 161 seconds (as you can see in *Figure 10.1*), this one took only 2.7 seconds, which is 60X faster!

Here are the first rows of the result:

```
✓ max_dep_delay_1999_2000_df.head(10) ···
```

	YEAR	MONTH	DAY_OF_MONTH	ORIGIN	DEP_DELAY
0	1999	1	1	ABE	51.0
1	1999	1	1	ABQ	208.0
2	1999	1	1	ADQ	35.0
3	1999	1	1	AGS	3.0
4	1999	1	1	ALB	67.0
5	1999	1	1	AMA	65.0
6	1999	1	1	ANC	130.0
7	1999	1	1	ATL	175.0
8	1999	1	1	AUS	159.0
9	1999	1	1	AVL	29.0

Figure 10.8: Result of the calculation on selected years

Let's see if partitioning the Parquet files instead helps improve the performance of the same calculation we just did. This time, you'll load your Dask DataFrame from the Parquet file in the AirOnTimeParquetPartitioned folder:

```
main_path_partitioned = os.path.join('C:\\', 'Datasets',
'AirOnTimeParquetPartitionedDask')
```

```
filters = [
    ("YEAR", "in", [1999, 2000])
]

flights_1999_2000_partitioned_ddf = dd.read_parquet(path=os.path.join(main_
path_partitioned, '**'), index='YEAR', filters=filters)

max_dep_delay_1999_2000_partitioned_ddf = flights_1999_2000_partitioned_ddf.
groupby(['YEAR', 'MONTH', 'DAY_OF_MONTH', 'ORIGIN'])[['DEP_DELAY']].max().
reset_index()

with ProgressBar():
    max_dep_delay_by_day_df = max_dep_delay_1999_2000_partitioned_ddf.compute()
```

Since the AirOnTimeParquetPartitionedDask folder no longer contains the files directly but the sub-folders in which the files are located, the path passed as a parameter to the read_parquet() function this time ends with a double asterisk (**), which is a **recursive wildcard**. It indicates that it will start from the specified folder and recursively fetch all possible files found not only in that folder but also in all subfolders. Let's take a look at the progress bar in this case:

```
    max_dep_delay_1999_2000_partitioned_ddf = flights_1999_2000_partitioned_ddf.groupby([

✓   0.7s


    with ProgressBar():
        max_dep_delay_by_day_df = max_dep_delay_1999_2000_partitioned_ddf.compute()
✓   2.9s

[#####################################] | 100% Completed | 2.91 sms
```

Figure 10.9: Time taken by calculation using partitioned Parquet files

This partition by year does not seem to improve computation time any more than predicate pushdown did. However, if you think about it, the reason is that the files you are doing the computations on are objectively few. Imagine that you have a sensor that measures some physical quantity, mounted on a production line, and it takes one measurement per second. In this case, the amount of data to be processed over several years would be much larger than in the example. Certainly, in this case, being able to filter the years by partitioning would improve performance, since it would prevent the predicate pushdown task from having to read the metadata associated with each individual file to know whether or not to discard it from being read.

You can find all the code needed to load data from the Parquet format and then analyze it with Dask in the Python\03-load-parquet-and-analyze-dask.py file in the *Chapter 10* code folder.

In this section, you have been reading and writing Parquet files simply by using Dask functions. But behind the scenes, Dask uses specific engines. By default, when you install the full version of Dask, **PyArrow**, which we discussed in the section *Importing large datasets with R* in *Chapter 9*, is also installed. Dask's Parquet format read and write functions will therefore use this engine, since they have the default engine parameter set to auto in the read_parquet() and to_parquet() functions. In addition to this value, the parameter can also take the following specific values: pyarrow and fastparquet. **FastParquet** is the historical engine used in Python to handle the Parquet format. Recently, however, it has become preferred to use PyArrow as the engine, since it is now widely used everywhere. Interestingly, if both engines were installed and the parameter was set to auto, the FastParquet engine would be selected and a deprecation warning would be displayed stating that the default selected engine would soon be PyArrow.

IMPORTANT NOTE

At the time of this writing, pandas 2.0 has also integrated the use of PyArrow as its backend to extend the functionality and improve the performance of various APIs.

Since Dask relies on PyArrow to handle the Parquet format, let's try to do the same analysis we did with Dask using PyArrow directly.

Analyzing Parquet data with PyArrow

As we did with Dask in the previous section, we'll try to calculate the maximum delay by flight origin for each day in the years 1999 and 2000 only with PyArrow by reading the CSV files directly. To do that, we must first introduce two specific entities used by this package:

- The first entity is the PyArrow **Dataset.** It excels in its ability to seamlessly handle large, partitioned datasets. When dealing with partitioned data, such as data split by time (e.g., years or months) or by certain categorical variables (e.g., flight origin), Dataset provides a highly efficient way to access and manipulate this data. It intelligently reads only relevant partitions based on the query filters applied, dramatically reducing I/O overhead for large datasets. This means that if you're trying to calculate the maximum delay by flight origin for each day, PyArrow can directly access only the partitions corresponding to the years 1999 and 2000 without having to load the entire dataset into memory.

- The second entity we refer to is the Table data type. It extends Dataset by providing a robust in-memory structure for managing filtered and selected data. After loading and filtering relevant data partitions with Dataset, they can be transformed into a table, which is optimized for columnar operations that are essential for analytics, such as calculating summaries and extremes. The columnar format allows for fast, memory-efficient operations through vectorization, which is critical for handling large datasets in high-performance tasks such as determining maximum daily flight delays by origin.

That said, here is the code we can use to achieve this:

```
import os
```

```python
import pyarrow as pa
import pyarrow.dataset as ds
import pyarrow.compute as pc


main_path = 'C:\\Datasets\\AirOnTimeCSV'


dataset = ds.dataset(source=main_path, format='csv')


flights_1999_2000_tbl = dataset.to_table(columns=['YEAR', 'MONTH', 'DAY_OF_
MONTH', 'ORIGIN', 'DEP_DELAY'],
                        filter=ds.field('YEAR').isin([1999, 2000]))


max_dep_delay_1999_2000_tbl = flights_1999_2000_tbl.group_by( ['YEAR', 'MONTH',
'DAY_OF_MONTH', 'ORIGIN'] ).aggregate([('DEP_DELAY', "max")])
```

In this case, the filtering of only the columns needed for the analysis is done not in the definition of the initial dataset (as in Dask) but in the dataset-to-table transformation, passing a list of column names to keep as the `columns` parameter and a filtering predicate in the filter parameter. It is precisely this transformation operation to table format that has to read all the CSV files and keep only the desired columns, and therefore it takes longer. The rest of the transformations (grouping and calculating the max) take a fraction of a millisecond, precisely because they are already done on a table, which is an in-memory optimized data structure for these transformations.

To see how much time it takes to obtain data useful for analysis, it is enough to perform all these transformations in a single cell of the Jupyter notebook in VS Code:

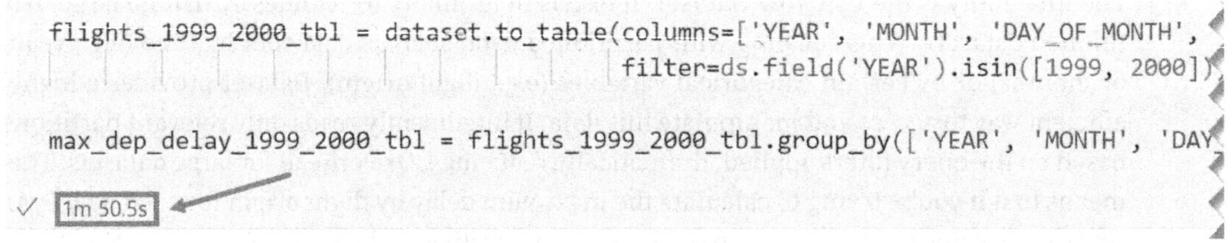

```python
flights_1999_2000_tbl = dataset.to_table(columns=['YEAR', 'MONTH', 'DAY_OF_MONTH',
                            filter=ds.field('YEAR').isin([1999, 2000])


max_dep_delay_1999_2000_tbl = flights_1999_2000_tbl.group_by(['YEAR', 'MONTH', 'DAY
```

✓ `1m 50.5s` ⬅

Figure 10.10: Time needed to perform analysis directly on CSV files with PyArrow

PyArrow also takes 2 minutes to perform the analysis directly on CSV files, which is a little better than Dask. To see the rows of the result, you must first transform the table into a pandas DataFrame:

```python
max_dep_delay_1999_2000_df = max_dep_delay_1999_2000_tbl.to_pandas()


max_dep_delay_1999_2000_df.head(10)
```

This is the output:

```
max_dep_delay_1999_2000_df = max_dep_delay_1999_2000_tbl.to_pandas() ···
```

	DEP_DELAY_max	YEAR	MONTH	DAY_OF_MONTH	ORIGIN
0	175.0	1999	1	1	ATL
1	798.0	1999	1	2	ATL
2	277.0	1999	1	3	ATL
3	217.0	1999	1	4	ATL
4	331.0	1999	1	5	ATL
5	436.0	1999	1	6	ATL
6	225.0	1999	1	7	ATL
7	690.0	1999	1	8	ATL
8	254.0	1999	1	9	ATL
9	829.0	1999	1	10	ATL

Figure 10.11: First rows of the analysis output

You can find all the code needed to analyze CSV files using PyArrow in the `Python\04-load-csv-and-analyze-pyarrow.py` file in the *Chapter 10* code folder.

Writing Parquet datasets

Now let's try to write the entire dataset in Parquet format with PyArrow. Unfortunately, at the time of writing, there is no direct and simple way, as already seen, for Dask to append a new CSV dataset to a Parquet dataset without first going through tables. This is because of how the Dask API was designed by its developers. Therefore, you will create the Parquet dataset by taking all the CSV files, both those in the `AirOnTimeCSV` folder and those in the `AirOnTimeCSVtoAppend` folder.

To select only certain columns from the dataset, use the `schema()` function, passing it both the name and the data type of each column that will be part of the Parquet dataset. At this point, writing to Parquet is done with the `write_dataset()` function. Let's see how to do this:

```
import os
import pyarrow as pa
import pyarrow.dataset as ds

def getFilePathsFromFolder(directory_path):
    # Get a list of file paths in the directory with the .csv extension
    file_paths = [os.path.join(directory_path, file_name) for file_name in
os.listdir(directory_path) if os.path.isfile(os.path.join(directory_path, file_
name)) and file_name.endswith('.csv')]

    return file_paths
```

```
main_path = 'C:\\Datasets\\AirOnTimeCSV'
to_append_path = 'C:\\Datasets\\AirOnTimeCSVtoAppend' Make sure you have
defined the file path correctly.

file_paths = getFilePathsFromFolder(main_path)
to_append_file_paths = getFilePathsFromFolder(to_append_path)

file_paths.extend(to_append_file_paths)

myschema = pa.schema([
    ('YEAR', pa.int64()),
    ('MONTH', pa.int64()),
    ('DAY_OF_MONTH', pa.int64()),
    ('ORIGIN', pa.string()),
    ('DEP_DELAY', pa.int64())])

dataset = ds.dataset(file_paths, format='csv', schema=myschema)

output_path = r'C:\Datasets\AirOnTimeParquetPyArrow'

ds.write_dataset(dataset, format='parquet',
                 base_dir=output_path,
                 existing_data_behavior='overwrite_or_ignore')
```

In general, the dataset() function takes as its source parameter the path to a folder containing the files to be read. In our case, since we need to read CSV files from multiple folders, it is possible to pass the function a list of individual paths to each CSV file to be read. When writing with the write_dataset() function, the overwrite_or_ignore value of the existing_data_behavior parameter will cause any existing data to be ignored and files with the same name as an output file to be overwritten. Other existing files are ignored.

The time it takes to write to the Parquet format is more or less 3 minutes. Here is the output:

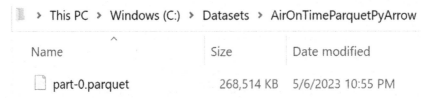

Figure 10.12: Single Parquet file created by PyArrow

As you can see, unlike with Dask, there is only one file here. This difference in the write behavior of the two libraries highlights the fundamental difference in their approach to data management.

IMPORTANT NOTE

While PyArrow is multi-threaded and can utilize multiple cores for certain operations (e.g., compression or decompression), it does not inherently support the parallel or distributed processing of data like Dask does. When writing a Parquet file using PyArrow, the library writes the data as a single file because it processes the data sequentially rather than dividing it into partitions or chunks for parallel processing.

The same thing happens if you want to partition Parquet files. The code is very simple. Just pass a list of columns to partition into a list for the `partition_cols` parameter:

```
output_partitioned_path = r'C:\Datasets\AirOnTimeParquetPartitionedPyArrow'

ds.write_dataset(dataset, format='parquet',
                base_dir=output_partitioned_path,
                partitioning=['YEAR'],
                partitioning_flavor='hive',
                existing_data_behavior='overwrite_or_ignore')
```

Setting the `partitioning_flavor` parameter to 'hive' ensures that the partitioning scheme used by PyArrow is compatible with that used by **Apache Hive**, a popular data warehousing tool that uses a specific directory structure. The result is the creation of as many subfolders as each value combination of the partitioning columns (in our case, only the YEAR column), just like the default in Dask. This allows for faster and more efficient querying of the data, particularly when filtering on the partitioning columns. Again, the difference with Dask is that within each subfolder you will find a single file, not more than one:

Figure 10.13: Subfolder for YEAR=1987 containing a single file

You can find all the code needed to export Dask DataFrames to Parquet in the `Python\05-create-parquet-pyarrow.py` file in the *Chapter 10* code folder.

Reading and transforming Parquet datasets

In order to replicate the same analysis done in the previous section, this time using PyArrow, you simply need to instantiate a dataset, this time of type Parquet. That said, here is the code to compute the maximum delay by flight origin for each day of all the available years:

```
import os
import pyarrow.dataset as ds

main_path = os.path.join('C:\\', 'Datasets', 'AirOnTimeParquet')
```

```
dataset = ds.dataset(source=main_path, format='parquet')

tbl = dataset.to_table()
max_dep_delay_tbl = tbl.group_by(['YEAR', 'MONTH', 'DAY_OF_MONTH', 'ORIGIN']).
aggregate([('DEP_DELAY', 'max')])
```

Once you have created the `Dataset` referencing the folder containing the Parquet files, you can instantiate the `Table` object using the `to_table()` function of `Dataset`. At this point, you can use the aggregation functions provided by the `Table` class.

PyArrow does not provide a function to generate a progress bar, but you can still measure the time taken by the calculation thanks to the Jupyter Notebook cells built into VS Code:

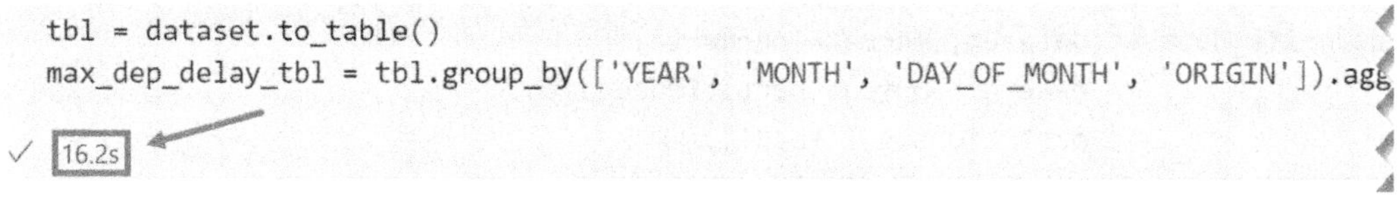

```
tbl = dataset.to_table()
max_dep_delay_tbl = tbl.group_by(['YEAR', 'MONTH', 'DAY_OF_MONTH', 'ORIGIN']).agg
```
✓ `16.2s`

Figure 10.14: Time taken by the calculation on all the years using PyArrow

But wait! The same calculation took 33 seconds with Dask (see *Figure 10.5*), while we got 16 seconds with PyArrow. That's an additional 2X improvement! Great!

If you want to visualize the first rows of the result, you need to convert the resulting table into a pandas DataFrame and then you can visualize it:

```
max_dep_delay_df = max_dep_delay_tbl.to_pandas()
max_dep_delay_df.head(10)
```

Here is the result:

✓ `max_dep_delay_df = max_dep_delay_tbl.to_pandas()` ···

	DEP_DELAY_max	YEAR	MONTH	DAY_OF_MONTH	ORIGIN
0	98.0	1987	10	1	JFK
1	70.0	1987	10	2	JFK
2	165.0	1987	10	3	JFK
3	144.0	1987	10	4	JFK
4	235.0	1987	10	5	JFK
5	41.0	1987	10	6	JFK
6	56.0	1987	10	7	JFK
7	58.0	1987	10	8	JFK
8	130.0	1987	10	9	JFK
9	80.0	1987	10	10	JFK

Figure 10.15: First rows of the calculation result

Let's now try filtering for specific years:

```
flights_1999_2000 = ds.dataset(source=main_path)

filters = ds.field('YEAR').isin([1999, 2000])
tbl_filtered = flights_1999_2000.to_table(filter=filters)

max_dep_delay_1999_2000_tbl = tbl_filtered.group_by(['YEAR', 'MONTH', 'DAY_OF_
MONTH', 'ORIGIN']).aggregate([('DEP_DELAY', "max")])

max_dep_delay_1999_2000_df = max_dep_delay_1999_2000_tbl.to_pandas()
max_dep_delay_1999_2000_df.head(10)
```

Here are the timing and the first rows of the result:

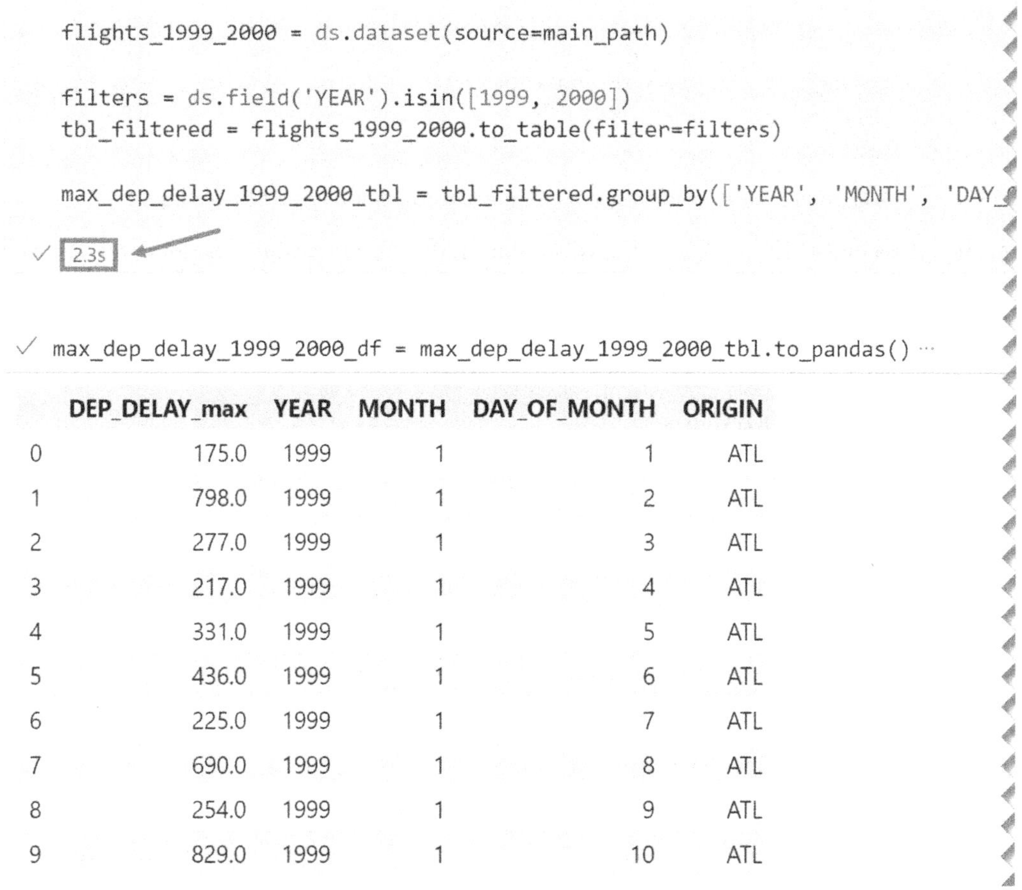

```
flights_1999_2000 = ds.dataset(source=main_path)

filters = ds.field('YEAR').isin([1999, 2000])
tbl_filtered = flights_1999_2000.to_table(filter=filters)

max_dep_delay_1999_2000_tbl = tbl_filtered.group_by(['YEAR', 'MONTH', 'DAY_

✓ [2.3s]  ◄——

✓ max_dep_delay_1999_2000_df = max_dep_delay_1999_2000_tbl.to_pandas() ⋯
```

	DEP_DELAY_max	YEAR	MONTH	DAY_OF_MONTH	ORIGIN
0	175.0	1999	1	1	ATL
1	798.0	1999	1	2	ATL
2	277.0	1999	1	3	ATL
3	217.0	1999	1	4	ATL
4	331.0	1999	1	5	ATL
5	436.0	1999	1	6	ATL
6	225.0	1999	1	7	ATL
7	690.0	1999	1	8	ATL
8	254.0	1999	1	9	ATL
9	829.0	1999	1	10	ATL

Figure 10.16: Timing and result of the filtered calculation

Wow! We got the same time of 2.3 seconds as with Dask (see *Figure 10.7*).

Let's see if there will be any improvement with PyArrow using partitioned Parquet files:

```python
main_path_partitioned = os.path.join('C:\\', 'Datasets',
'AirOnTimeParquetPartitionedPyArrow')
flights_1999_2000_partitioned = ds.dataset(source=main_path_partitioned,
format='parquet', partitioning='hive')
filters = ds.field('YEAR').isin([1999, 2000])
tbl_filtered_partitioned = flights_1999_2000_partitioned.to_
table(filter=filters)

max_dep_delay_1999_2000_tbl = tbl_filtered_partitioned.group_by(['YEAR',
'MONTH', 'DAY_OF_MONTH', 'ORIGIN']).aggregate([('DEP_DELAY', "max")])
```

Here's the timing:

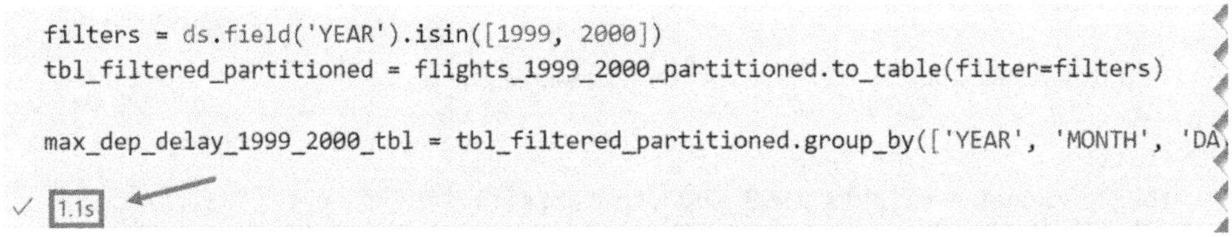

```python
filters = ds.field('YEAR').isin([1999, 2000])
tbl_filtered_partitioned = flights_1999_2000_partitioned.to_table(filter=filters)

max_dep_delay_1999_2000_tbl = tbl_filtered_partitioned.group_by(['YEAR', 'MONTH', 'DA)
```

✓ 1.1s ◄

Figure 10.17: Timing and result of the filtered calculation on partitioned Parquet

Amazing, 1.1 seconds! This time, a 2X improvement over predicate pushdown alone was achieved by also using partitioning pruning with PyArrow!

Note that in order to properly read the folders and files in the partitioned Parquet dataset, it was necessary to use the `partitioning = 'hive'` parameter.

Here is the output of the first rows:

```python
✓ max_dep_delay_1999_2000_df = max_dep_delay_1999_2000_tbl.to_pandas() ⋯
```

	DEP_DELAY_max	YEAR	MONTH	DAY_OF_MONTH	ORIGIN
0	175.0	1999	1	1	ATL
1	798.0	1999	1	2	ATL
2	277.0	1999	1	3	ATL
3	217.0	1999	1	4	ATL
4	331.0	1999	1	5	ATL
5	225.0	1999	1	7	ATL
6	690.0	1999	1	8	ATL
7	254.0	1999	1	9	ATL
8	436.0	1999	1	6	ATL
9	829.0	1999	1	10	ATL

Figure 10.18: Output of the first rows

You can find all the code needed to load data from the Parquet format and then analyze it with PyArrow in the `Python\06-load-parquet-and-analyze-pyarrow.py` file in the *Chapter 10* code folder.

You may be wondering why there are such differences in performance between Dask and PyArrow. Let's take a look at what's driving these differences.

Performance differences between Dask and PyArrow

The performance differences you observed between Dask and PyArrow are due to several factors:

1. *Overhead*: Dask has additional overhead due to its parallel and distributed computing capabilities. Dask breaks the data into smaller chunks and schedules tasks to process these chunks. This overhead might not be significant for larger datasets but could be noticeable for smaller datasets or when compared against more optimized libraries like PyArrow.

2. *Optimization*: PyArrow is a lower-level library and is optimized for working with Arrow-based data structures (like Parquet files), which can result in faster performance for specific operations like reading Parquet files and performing group by and aggregation operations.

3. *Data size*: Dask is designed for parallel and out-of-core computation, which provides significant benefits when dealing with larger-than-memory datasets. However, if the dataset can be contained in memory, or is not excessively larger than it, it may be more efficient to use PyArrow or pandas, since they can take advantage of memory-based optimizations and avoid the overhead of parallel and distributed processing.

At this point, we can try to implement the same analyses in R as we did in this section. Let's see how to do that.

Using Parquet files with R

There is no counterpart to the Python Dask package in R. Therefore, in R it is only possible to work with datasets larger than the available memory and with the Parquet format because of the Arrow library, as you learned in *Chapter 9*, *Loading Large Datasets beyond the Available RAM in Power BI*.

In this section, we will implement what you saw in the previous section, but using R. Therefore, you will see how to create, read, and analyze Parquet datasets in R, providing the same benefits that you saw using Python.

Analyzing Parquet data with Arrow for R

In the same way as we did in the previous section, we try to calculate the maximum delay by flight origin for each day in the years 1999 and 2000 alone, this time with Arrow for R, reading the CSV files directly. As we saw in *Chapter 9*, using Arrow in R is really quite simple. Once you have instantiated an Arrow dataset (in this case, using the CSV format), you can apply whatever transformations you want to it using the syntax provided by `dplyr`. So, for the end user, working with a standard R data frame, a tibble, or an Arrow Dataset is practically the same. The only thing that changes is that to go from an Arrow Dataset to a tibble after applying the transformations to the dataset in a lazy way, you have to call the Arrow `collect()` function (similar to what used to happen with Dask in Python).

Here is the code to perform the above analysis:

```
library(arrow)
library(dplyr)

main_path <- r"{C:\Datasets\AirOnTimeCSV}"

ds <- open_dataset(main_path, format = "csv")

start_time <- Sys.time()

mean_dep_delay_df <- ds %>%
  select( YEAR, MONTH, DAY_OF_MONTH, ORIGIN, DEP_DELAY ) %>%
  filter( YEAR %in% c(1999, 2000) ) %>%
  group_by( YEAR, MONTH, DAY_OF_MONTH, ORIGIN ) %>%
  summarise( DEP_DELAY = max(DEP_DELAY, na.rm = T) ) %>%
  collect() %>%
  ungroup()

end_time <- Sys.time()

(create_ds_exec_time <- end_time - start_time)
```

To conform to the PyArrow API seen in the previous section, the filtering of only the columns needed for the analysis is again done not in the definition of the initial dataset (as in Dask), but in the dataset-to-tibble transformation, using the default select() function provided by dplyr.

To see how much time it takes to obtain data useful for analysis, simply run the code:

```
> (create_ds_exec_time <- end_time - start_time)
Time difference of 3.057925 mins
```

Figure 10.19: Time needed to perform analysis directly on CSV files with Arrow for R

Arrow takes 3 minutes to perform the analysis directly on CSV files, the same as Dask. To see the rows of the result, just run the following:

```
head(mean_dep_delay_df, 10)
```

This is the output:

```
> head(mean_dep_delay_df, 10)
# A tibble: 10 × 5
    YEAR MONTH DAY_OF_MONTH ORIGIN DEP_DELAY
   <int> <int>        <int> <chr>      <dbl>
 1  1999     1            1 ATL          175
 2  1999     1            2 ATL          798
 3  1999     1            3 ATL          277
 4  1999     1            4 ATL          217
 5  1999     1            5 ATL          331
 6  1999     1            6 ATL          436
 7  1999     1            7 ATL          225
 8  1999     1            8 ATL          690
 9  1999     1            9 ATL          254
10  1999     1           10 ATL          829
```

Figure 10.20: First rows of the analysis output

You can find all the code needed to analyze CSV files using Dask in the `R/01-load-csv-and-analyze.R` file in the *Chapter 10* code folder.

Writing Parquet datasets

Now let's try to write the entire dataset in Parquet format with Arrow. Even in the case of the API for R, Arrow does not allow us to append data to an existing Parquet dataset in a straightforward manner as Dask does. Therefore, we will load the entire dataset consisting of the different CSV files spread over the two separate folders, `AirOnTimeCSV` and `AirOnTimeCSVtoAppend`. If the CSV files were in a single folder, it would have been possible to just specify the path to the folder containing them as the source. In our case, as with the Python API, we will create a vector of URLs for each file to be uploaded.

Once an Arrow Dataset has been created by referencing the CSV files above, you just have to select the columns you want to keep using the `dplyr` syntax, and then you can use the **write_dataset()** function to generate the Parquet format of the dataset. Let's see how to do this:

```
library(arrow)
library(dplyr)

getFilePathsFromFolder <- function(directory_path) {
  # Get a list of file paths in the directory with the .csv extension
  files <- list.files(directory_path, full.names = TRUE)
  file_paths <- files[grep("\\.csv$", files, ignore.case = TRUE)]

  return(file_paths)
}
```

```
main_path <- r"{C:\Datasets\AirOnTimeCSV}"
to_append_path <- r"{C:\Datasets\AirOnTimeCSVtoAppend}"

file_paths = getFilePathsFromFolder(main_path)
to_append_file_paths = getFilePathsFromFolder(to_append_path)

ds <- open_dataset(c(file_paths, to_append_file_paths), format = "csv")

output_path <- r'{C:\Datasets\AirOnTimeParquetArrowR\}'

start_time <- Sys.time()

ds %>%
  select( YEAR, MONTH, DAY_OF_MONTH, ORIGIN, DEP_DELAY ) %>%
  write_dataset( path = output_path, format = 'parquet' )

end_time <- Sys.time()

(create_ds_exec_time <- end_time - start_time)
```

The total time it takes to read from CSV and write to the Parquet format is more or less 3 minutes. Just like PyArrow, we get a single .parquet file:

Figure 10.21: Single Parquet file created by Arrow

The same thing happens if you want to partition a Parquet dataset. The code is very simple. Just pass a column or a vector of columns to partition into the partitioning parameter of the write_dataset() function:

```
output_partitioned_path <- r'{C:\Datasets\AirOnTimeParquetPartitionedArrowR\}'

start_time <- Sys.time()

ds %>%
  select( YEAR, MONTH, DAY_OF_MONTH, ORIGIN, DEP_DELAY ) %>%
  write_dataset( path = output_partitioned_path, format = 'parquet',
```

```
                        partitioning = 'YEAR')

end_time <- Sys.time()

(create_ds_exec_time <- end_time - start_time)
```

The result is the creation of as many subfolders as the YEAR variable expects from the dataset, just as was the case with PyArrow:

Figure 10.22: Subfolder for YEAR=1987 containing a single file

You can find all the code needed to export Dask DataFrames to Parquet in the R/02-create-parquet.R file in the *Chapter 10* code folder.

Reading and transforming Parquet datasets

Let's try to replicate the same analysis we did before reading data from Parquet files. All you need to do is instantiate a dataset, this time of type Parquet. That said, here is the code to compute the maximum delay by flight origin for each day of all available years:

```
library(arrow)
library(dplyr)

main_path <- r'{C:\Datasets\AirOnTimeParquetArrowR\}'

ds <- open_dataset(main_path, format = "parquet")

start_time <- Sys.time()

mean_dep_delay_df <- ds %>%
  select( YEAR, MONTH, DAY_OF_MONTH, ORIGIN, DEP_DELAY ) %>%
  group_by( YEAR, MONTH, DAY_OF_MONTH, ORIGIN ) %>%
  summarise( DEP_DELAY = max(DEP_DELAY, na.rm = T) ) %>%
  collect() %>%
  ungroup()

end_time <- Sys.time()

(create_ds_exec_time <- end_time - start_time)
```

Here is the time it took:

```
> (create_ds_exec_time <- end_time - start_time)
Time difference of 13.40664 secs
```

Figure 10.23: Time taken by the calculation on all the years using PyArrow

If you want to visualize the first rows of the result, run the following code:

```
head(mean_dep_delay_df, 10)
```

Here is the result:

```
> head(mean_dep_delay_1999_2000_df, 10)
# A tibble: 10 × 5
     YEAR MONTH DAY_OF_MONTH ORIGIN DEP_DELAY
    <int> <int>        <int> <chr>      <dbl>
 1   1987    10            1 JFK           98
 2   1987    10            2 JFK           70
 3   1987    10            3 JFK          165
 4   1987    10            4 JFK          144
 5   1987    10            5 JFK          235
 6   1987    10            6 JFK           41
 7   1987    10            7 JFK           56
 8   1987    10            8 JFK           58
 9   1987    10            9 JFK          130
10   1987    10           10 JFK           80
```

Figure 10.24: First rows of the calculation result

Now let's try filtering for certain years to see the effect of predicate pushdown:

```
start_time <- Sys.time()

mean_dep_delay_1999_2000_df <- ds %>%
  select( YEAR, MONTH, DAY_OF_MONTH, ORIGIN, DEP_DELAY ) %>%
  filter( YEAR %in% c(1999, 2000) ) %>%
  group_by( YEAR, MONTH, DAY_OF_MONTH, ORIGIN ) %>%
  summarise( DEP_DELAY = max(DEP_DELAY, na.rm = T) ) %>%
  collect() %>%
  ungroup()

end_time <- Sys.time()

(create_ds_exec_time <- end_time - start_time)

head(mean_dep_delay_1999_2000_df, 10)
```

Here are the time and the first lines of the result:

```
> (create_ds_exec_time <- end_time - start_time)
Time difference of 1.951251 secs
>
> head(mean_dep_delay_1999_2000_df, 10)
# A tibble: 10 × 5
      YEAR MONTH DAY_OF_MONTH ORIGIN DEP_DELAY
     <int> <int>        <int> <chr>      <dbl>
  1   1999     1            1 ATL          175
  2   1999     1            2 ATL          798
  3   1999     1            3 ATL          277
  4   1999     1            4 ATL          217
  5   1999     1            5 ATL          331
  6   1999     1            6 ATL          436
  7   1999     1            7 ATL          225
  8   1999     1            8 ATL          690
  9   1999     1            9 ATL          254
 10   1999     1           10 ATL          829
```

Figure 10.25: Time and result of the filtered calculation

Not bad at all! It took about 2 seconds!

Let's see if you will see any improvement using partitioned Parquet files:

```
main_partitioned_path <- r'{C:\Datasets\AirOnTimeParquetPartitionedArrowR\}'

partitioned_ds <- open_dataset(main_partitioned_path, format = "parquet",
partitioning = hive_partition())

start_time <- Sys.time()

mean_dep_delay_1999_2000_partitioned_df <- partitioned_ds %>%
  select( YEAR, MONTH, DAY_OF_MONTH, ORIGIN, DEP_DELAY ) %>%
  filter( YEAR %in% c(1999, 2000) ) %>%
  group_by( YEAR, MONTH, DAY_OF_MONTH, ORIGIN ) %>%
  summarise( DEP_DELAY = max(DEP_DELAY, na.rm = T) ) %>%
  collect() %>%
  ungroup()

end_time <- Sys.time()

(create_ds_exec_time <- end_time - start_time)
```

Here is the timing:

```
> (create_ds_exec_time <- end_time - start_time)
Time difference of 0.900707 secs
```

Figure 10.26: Time and result of the filtered calculation on partitioned Parquet

Amazing, 0.9 seconds! This time, a 2X improvement over predicate pushdown alone was achieved by also using partitioning pruning!

Here is the output of the first rows:

```
> head(mean_dep_delay_1999_2000_partitioned_df, 10)
# A tibble: 10 × 5
     YEAR MONTH DAY_OF_MONTH ORIGIN DEP_DELAY
    <int> <int>        <int> <chr>      <dbl>
 1   1999     1            1 ATL          175
 2   1999     1            2 ATL          798
 3   1999     1            3 ATL          277
 4   1999     1            4 ATL          217
 5   1999     1            5 ATL          331
 6   1999     1            7 ATL          225
 7   1999     1            8 ATL          690
 8   1999     1            9 ATL          254
 9   1999     1            6 ATL          436
10   1999     1           10 ATL          829
```

Figure 10.27: Output of the first rows

You can find all the code needed to load data from the Parquet format and then analyze it with PyArrow in the R/03-load-parquet-and-analyze-pyarrow.R file in the *Chapter 10* code folder.

Wow, great! Now you will be able to use datasets in the Parquet format with R as well.

Let's try to apply what you've learned about the Parquet format in Power BI.

Using the Parquet format to speed up a Power BI report

Now that you have learned how to take advantage of the Parquet format in both Python and R, you can apply this knowledge to real-world cases in Power BI. An example might be as follows.

Suppose you need to integrate a report commissioned by your boss with data on the longest flight delays in the U.S. on each day of the past two months for each departure airport. At the beginning of each month, a CSV can be retrieved with information on the above-mentioned flights for the previous month. To be consistent with the data we have available, assume that this integration was commissioned for you in December 2012 and that you were able to find all data for flights from October 1987 through November 2012.

In order to implement a data flow that optimizes both the time it takes to load new flight data and the time it takes to perform analysis on all the data in the history, the workflow to be followed will be as follows:

1. First, the Parquet dataset of historical data from October 1987 to November 2012 is created separately, which will serve as the basis for future data to be appended.

2. The Power BI report will have a Python script that first checks for new CSV files to add to the history. If these files are found, they are appended to the historical Parquet dataset (Dask will be used to append data).

3. The Power BI report will include an additional script, this time in either Python or R, that performs the necessary analysis of the data history in Parquet format and returns a table with the aggregated data resulting from the analysis.

Since we are forced to use Dask for append operations in Python because, as seen above, PyArrow and Arrow for R do not allow us to do so easily, it is convenient at this point to use Dask to generate the data history as well. Let's see how to do that.

Transforming historical data in Parquet

You have already learned how to create a dataset in Parquet format from a set of CSV files using Python and Dask. For clarity, you'll want to create a new folder (which we'll call `AirOnTimePowerBI`) in the root that already contains the datasets you created in this chapter:

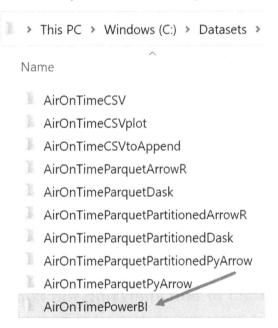

Figure 10.28: New folder to store data for the Power BI report

The Parquet dataset you are going to create will be partitioned by the YEAR column, so that you can also take advantage of the performance improvements from *partition pruning* if the dataset grows significantly over time. Here is the code:

```
import os
import dask.dataframe as dd
```

```python
from dask.diagnostics import ProgressBar

# %%
# Get the path to the folder containing all the CSV files
# (update it according to your folders structure)
main_path = 'C:\\Datasets\\AirOnTimeCSV'

# %%
ddf = dd.read_csv(
    os.path.join(main_path, 'airOT*.csv'),
    encoding='latin-1',
    usecols =['YEAR', 'MONTH', 'DAY_OF_MONTH', 'ORIGIN', 'DEP_DELAY']
)

# %%
with ProgressBar():
    ddf.to_parquet(path=r'C:\Datasets\AirOnTimePowerBI',
                   partition_on=['YEAR'],
                   overwrite=True)
```

You can find all of the above code in the `Python\07-create-parquet-historical-data.py` file in the `Chapter 10` code folder.

So, do the following:

1. Make sure that among the CSV files in the `AirOnTimeCSV` folder, you do not have the `airOT201212.csv` file, which should be in the `AirOnTimeCSVtoAppend` folder if you followed the instructions at the beginning of this chapter.

2. Run the entire script in the `Python\07-create-parquet-historical-data.py` file to create the Parquet dataset with historical data up to and including November 2012.

Now let's see how to develop Python code that will append new CSV files to the newly created Parquet dataset and analyze it.

Appending new data to and analyzing the Parquet dataset

To add one or more CSV files of new data that will arrive at the beginning of each month to the Parquet dataset, we will use Dask in the same way as you have seen in the previous sections. We will add some more code to be able to move the new CSV files arriving from the input folder to the folder of all CSV files representing the history once the new ones have been added to the Parquet dataset. For this purpose, we assume that new CSV files to be added to the Parquet dataset arrive in the `AirOnTimeCSVtoAppend` folder at the beginning of each month. Remember that the Parquet dataset of historical data is partitioned by year, so you will need to take this into account in the append operation as well. Here is the code:

```python
import os
```

```python
import pandas as pd
import dask.dataframe as dd

# %%
to_append_main_path = os.path.join('C:\\', 'Datasets', 'AirOnTimeCSVtoAppend')
csv_destination_path = os.path.join('C:\\', 'Datasets', 'AirOnTimeCSV')
partitioned_data_path = os.path.join('C:\\', 'Datasets', 'AirOnTimePowerBI')

# Check if there are any csv files in the folder
files = os.listdir(to_append_main_path)
csv_files = [file for file in files if file.lower().endswith(".csv")]

if len(csv_files) > 0:

    # Append new CSV files to the Parquet
    to_append_ddf = dd.read_csv(
        os.path.join(to_append_main_path, 'airOT*.csv'),
        encoding='latin-1',
        usecols =['YEAR', 'MONTH', 'DAY_OF_MONTH', 'ORIGIN', 'DEP_DELAY']
    )

    to_append_ddf.to_parquet(path=partitioned_data_path,
                             partition_on=['YEAR'],
                             append=True)

    # Move appended CSV file to the historical data folder
    for file in csv_files:

        # Construct the full path to the file
        file_path = os.path.join(to_append_main_path, file)

        # Construct the full path to the destination file
        destination_path = os.path.join(csv_destination_path, file)

        # Rename the file to include the full path to the destination
        os.rename(file_path, destination_path)

dummy_df = pd.DataFrame()
```

As you can see, an empty pandas DataFrame is created at the end of this script. The goal is to be able to use this script as the first data import step in Power BI (as you know, Power BI expects a DataFrame in the output), which must be done in Python because of the append issue.

After that, it will be possible to add a next step where the required analysis is done in Python or R as desired.

You can find all of the above code in the `Python\08-append-parquet-powerbi.py` file in the Chapter 10 code folder.

Let's see how to proceed with analysis using Python in a Power BI report.

Analyzing Parquet data in Power BI with Python

Once the new CSV files, if any, have been appended to the historical Parquet dataset, we will compute the dataset containing the maximum U.S. flight delays for each destination for the two months before the date of the report analysis.

The logic in Python to take only the last two months of data from today's date is present in the script, but it is commented out because the data we have goes back to December 2012 at most. For demonstration purposes, we will only consider data from November 2012 in this report, but if you need to apply this code to your own similar use case fed by data updated to the present, you can uncomment the relevant code to calculate the year and month from which to start the analyses. Here is the code:

```python
import os
import datetime
import pyarrow.dataset as ds


partitioned_data_path = os.path.join('C:\\', 'Datasets',
  'AirOnTimePowerBI')


dataset_partitioned = ds.dataset(source=partitioned_data_path,
  format='parquet',
                                 partitioning='hive')


# today = datetime.date.today()
# first_day_of_this_month = datetime.date(today.year, today.month, 1)
# last_day_of_previous_month = first_day_of_this_month - datetime.
timedelta(days=1)
```

```
# last_day_of_2_months_ago = (last_day_of_previous_month - datetime.
timedelta(days=last_day_of_previous_month.day)) - datetime.timedelta(days=1)
# year = last_day_of_2_months_ago.year
# month = last_day_of_2_months_ago.month

year = 2012
month = 11

filters = (ds.field('YEAR') >= year) & (ds.field('MONTH') >= month)
partitioned_latest_2_months_tbl =
dataset_partitioned.to_table(filter=filters)

max_dep_delay_latest_2_months_tbl = partitioned_latest_2_months_tbl.group_
by(['YEAR', 'MONTH', 'DAY_OF_MONTH', 'ORIGIN']).aggregate([('DEP_DELAY',
"max")])

max_dep_delay_latest_2_months_df = max_dep_delay_latest_2_months_tbl.to_
pandas()
```

You can find all of the above code in the Python\09-analyze-parquet-powerbi.py file in the Chapter 10 code folder.

Before proceeding with report development, you need to move the airOT201212.csv file from the AirOnTimeCSVtoAppend folder to the Datasets root folder, leaving the AirOnTimeCSVtoAppend folder empty. This will simulate the fact that the December 2012 CSV file has not yet arrived.

Let's now proceed to implement the report. Here are the steps required to implement this in Power BI:

1. Open Power BI Desktop through the shortcut that activates the pbi_powerquery_env environment.

2. Make sure Power BI Desktop is referencing the pbi_powerquery_env environment in **Options**.

3. Click on **Get data, More...**, type Python, and then double-click on **Python script**.

4. Copy the contents of the Python\08-append-parquet-powerbi.py file in the Chapter 10 folder and paste it into the Python script editor. Remember to edit the paths (to_append_main_path, csv_destination_path, and partitioned_data_path) accordingly, and then click **OK**.

5. Select the **dummy_df** table in **Navigator** and click **Transform Data**:

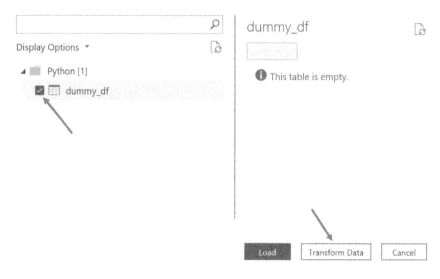

Figure 10.29: Select the dummy empty table and click Transform Data

6. Click on the **Transform** ribbon menu and click on **Run Python Script** to add the analysis script step.

7. Copy the contents of the Python\09-analyze-parquet-powerbi.py file into the Chapter 10 folder and paste it into the Python script editor. Remember to edit the paths (to_append_main_ path, csv_destination_path, and partitioned_data_path) accordingly, and then click **OK**.

8. Click on the **max_dep_delay_latest_2_months_df** dataset's **Table** value and you will see the imported aggregated values.

9. Click on the **Home** ribbon menu and then **Close & Apply**.

10. Click on the **Card** visualization on the right:

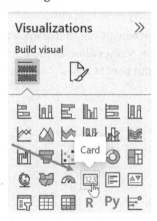

Figure 10.30: Add a Card visualization

11. Keeping the **Card** on the canvas selected, expand the **dummy_df** table under the **Data** panel, select the **YEAR** field, and choose **Maximum** as the aggregation type:

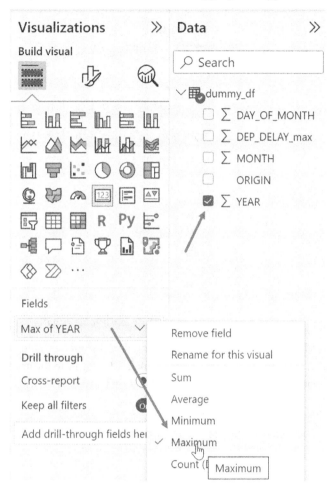

Figure 10.31: Selecting Max of YEAR as the Card value

12. Click in the center of the canvas to unselect the **Card** and repeat step 10 to add a new **Card**.

13. Keeping this new **Card** on the canvas selected, expand the **dummy_df** table under the **Data** panel, select the **MONTH** field, and choose **Maximum** as the aggregation type.

14. Click in the center of the canvas to unselect the **Card** and click on the **Table** visual:

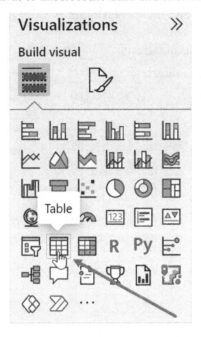

Figure 10.32: Adding a Table visual

15. Stretch the visual a bit and, keeping it selected in the canvas, select the **YEAR, MONTH, DAY_OF_MONTH, ORIGIN,** and **DEP_DELAY_max** fields from the **dummy_df** table in this specified order. For each selected column, choose the **Don't summarize** aggregation type:

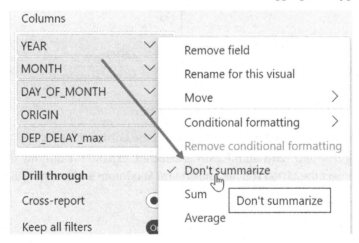

Figure 10.33: Choosing the aggregation type of columns

16. Click on the **MONTH** field within the table in order to display the detail rows sorted by descending month number:

Figure 10.34: Ordering details by descending month number

17. It is therefore clear that the data in the Parquet dataset stops at November 2012.

18. Now let us try to simulate the arrival of a new CSV file. Take the `airOT201212.csv` file in the `Datasets` folder and move it back to the `AirOnTimeCSVtoAppend` folder. Now click **Refresh** on the **Home** menu.

19. After a few seconds, you will see the report update to show December 2012 as the latest date in the Parquet dataset:

2012
Max of YEAR

12
Max of MONTH

YEAR	MONTH	DAY_OF_MONTH	ORIGIN	DEP_DELAY_max
2012	12	1	ABE	-3
2012	12	1	ABI	-5
2012	12	1	ABQ	344
2012	12	1	ABR	-1
2012	12	1	ABY	-5
2012	12	1	ACT	-4
2012	12	1	ACV	218
2012	12	1	ADQ	-17
2012	12	1	AEX	-1
2012	12	1	AGS	0

Figure 10.35: Updated report with data from December 2012

You will also see that the new CSV file in the `AirOnTimeCSVtoAppend` folder has been correctly moved to the `AirOnTimeCSV` folder, indicating that it has been processed correctly.

Maybe you didn't even realize it, but not only did you manage to perform a summary analysis on a detailed dataset much larger than the RAM you have available in a matter of seconds, but you also managed to do an incremental load of that dataset at the same time. This is a big one!

If you are more comfortable with R for data analysis, you can replicate this report using R for the analysis part only. Let's see how to do that.

Analyzing Parquet data in Power BI with R

As we mentioned earlier, the logic that implements the appending of new data must be developed in Python, because it is implemented in Dask and not in Arrow – although the analysis part can be safely created in R.

If you have already completed all of the steps in the previous section to create the report in Power BI with Python, you now need to perform steps that return the data you are processing to its initial state. They are listed below:

1. Move the `airOT201212.csv` file from the `AirOnTimeCSV` folder to the `Datasets` root folder.
2. Go to the `AirOnTimePowerBI` folder, select all of its subfolders (press *CTRL + A*), and delete them all (press **CANC**).
3. Run all the code in the `Python\07-create-parquet-historical-data.py` script to regenerate historical data in Parquet format back to November 2012.

At this point, you are ready to develop the Power BI report by following these steps:

1. Repeat steps 1 through 5 from the previous section, *Analyzing Parquet data in Power BI with Python*.
2. Click on the **Transform** ribbon menu and click on **Run R Script** to add the analysis script step.
3. Copy the contents of the `R/04-analyze-parquet-powerbi.R` file into the `Chapter 10` folder and paste it into the Python script editor. Remember to edit the paths (`partitioned_data_path`) accordingly, and then click **OK**.
4. Click on the **max_dep_delay_latest_2_months_df** dataset's **Table** value and you will see the imported aggregated values.
5. Click on the **Home** ribbon menu and then **Close & Apply**.
6. Repeat steps 10 through 16 from the previous section, *Analyzing Parquet data in Power BI with Python*. You will see the report showing data from November 2012:

2012   11

Max of YEAR   Max of MONTH

YEAR	MONTH	DAY_OF_MONTH	ORIGIN	DEP_DELAY_MAX
2012	11	1	ABE	3.00
2012	11	1	ABI	-1.00
2012	11	1	ABQ	109.00
2012	11	1	ABR	-5.00
2012	11	1	ABY	-1.00
2012	11	1	ACT	-9.00
2012	11	1	ACV	125.00
2012	11	1	ADK	7.00
2012	11	1	ADQ	-1.00
2012	11	1	AEX	33.00

Figure 10.36: Ordering details by descending month number

7. Let us try to again simulate the arrival of a new CSV file. Take the air0T201212.csv file in the Datasets folder and move it back to the AirOnTimeCSVtoAppend folder. Now click **Refresh** on the **Home** menu.

8. After a few seconds, you will see the report update, showing December 2012 as the latest date in the Parquet dataset:

2012   12

Max of YEAR   Max of MONTH

YEAR	MONTH	DAY_OF_MONTH	ORIGIN	DEP_DELAY_MAX
2012	12	1	ABE	-3.00
2012	12	1	ABI	-5.00
2012	12	1	ABQ	344.00
2012	12	1	ABR	-1.00
2012	12	1	ABY	-5.00
2012	12	1	ACT	-4.00
2012	12	1	ACV	218.00
2012	12	1	ADQ	-17.00
2012	12	1	AEX	-1.00
2012	12	1	AGS	0.00

Figure 10.37: Updated report with data from December 2012

Amazing! You were able to perform a summary analysis on a detailed dataset that was much larger than the available RAM, and an incremental load of the same dataset in seconds, even in R.

Summary

In this chapter, we discussed the limitations of the native Parquet connector in Power BI. You learned that these limitations can be overcome by using specific packages in both Python and R. We are talking about Dask and Arrow, the latter being available in both APIs for Python and R. In the last part of the chapter, you saw how to use these techniques in a Power BI report to append new data to very large datasets and query them in a very short amount of time.

In the next chapter, we'll finally start working with R and Python scripts in Power BI, doing data ingestion and data transformation.

References

- *Parquet File Performance In Power BI/Power Query* (`https://blog.crossjoin.co.uk/2021/03/21/parquet-file-performance-in-power-bi-power-query/`)
- *Optimising The Performance Of Combining Data From Multiple Parquet Files In Power Query/Power BI* (`https://blog.crossjoin.co.uk/2021/03/29/optimising-the-performance-of-combining-data-from-multiple-parquet-files-in-power-query-power-bi/`)
- *Parquet and CSV: Querying & Processing in Power BI* (`https://www.datalineo.com/post/parquet-and-csv-querying-processing-in-power-bi`)

Test your knowledge

1. What are the main features of the Parquet format?
2. What are the benefits and limitations of the native Parquet connector in Power BI?
3. What's the difference between predicate pushdown and partition pruning?
4. How do you explain the differences in performance between Dask and PyArrow?
5. Is there a specific API to transform referenced data from an Arrow dataset into R?

Learn more on Discord

To join the Discord community for this book – where you can share feedback, ask questions to the author, and learn about new releases – follow the QR code below:

`https://discord.gg/MKww5g45EB`

11

Calling External APIs to Enrich Your Data

In the previous chapter, you saw an example of how to enrich existing data with external information. In that case, the data was exposed via CSV files, but this is not always the case. Very often, the data that is useful for enrichment is exposed through external **application programming interfaces** (**APIs**), most often in the form of web service endpoints. Power BI allows you to read data from a web service through a dedicated UI, but most of the time it is unusable. So, you have to resort to writing **M code** to get it done. Writing M code isn't too difficult, but it's not easy. You also have to be careful not to write code that causes refresh problems when you publish the report to the Power BI service. In addition, Power BI does not allow you to parallelize more than one call to the same web service to reduce latency when retrieving data. Using Python or R to retrieve data from a web service solves all of these issues very easily.

In this chapter, you will learn the following topics:

- What is a web service?
- Registering for Bing Maps web services
- Geocoding addresses using Python
- Geocoding addresses using R
- Accessing web services using Power BI

Technical requirements

This chapter requires you to have a working internet connection and **Power BI Desktop** already installed on your machine (we used version 2.116.966.0 64-bit, April 2023). You must have properly configured the R and Python engines and IDEs as outlined in *Chapter 2, Configuring R with Power BI*, and *Chapter 3, Configuring Python with Power BI*.

What is a web service?

In the course of your work as an analyst, you might sometimes need to use specialized interfaces for data retrieval, such as direct database queries or proprietary protocols. However, this is a rare case because today almost all external data sources are exposed as web services, even within an enterprise. Web services are the most common and popular way to communicate information between heterogeneous information systems, and they offer several advantages. They enable seamless integration by using standard internet protocols, ensuring broad compatibility across platforms and languages. Web services facilitate scalability and flexibility, allowing systems to adapt to changing needs without extensive reconfiguration. They also support secure data transmission through encryption and authentication mechanisms, improving data privacy and integrity. In addition, web services can significantly reduce development time and costs by leveraging reusable components and facilitating easier maintenance and updates. A web service is basically a software module hosted on a server that is available over the internet to provide data in response to specific requests from a client.

There are two main types of design models for web services:

- **Simple Object Access Protocol (SOAP)**: SOAP relies heavily on **XML** and defines a highly typed messaging structure through schemas. All messages exchanged between the service and the client are encoded using the **Web Service Definition Language** (**WSDL**), which, in turn, is based on the XML format. One of the most important aspects of WSDL is that it defines a binding contract between the service provider and each service consumer. Therefore, any change to the API requires a change to the client. These days, almost everything that matters runs on HTTP. But remember that SOAP can take advantage of any other transport protocol (such as **Simple Mail Transfer Protocol (SMTP)** and **Transmission Control Protocol (TCP)**) in addition to HTTP.

- **Representational state transfer (REST)**: REST is becoming the standard design model for all public APIs. It is an architecture that relies exclusively on the HTTP protocol (as opposed to SOAP). It doesn't use WSDL contracts, making it more flexible and faster to implement. REST can handle data in any format, such as XML or YAML, but the most commonly used format is **JSON**. Unlike SOAP, which is function driven, REST is very **data driven**. For this reason, the REST architecture is dominant in the development of web services for data enrichment (see the references at the end of the chapter for more details) and can generate output in any format – not only JSON but also CSV or **Really Simple Syndication** (**RSS**), for example! Basically, REST provides a simpler way to interact with the service, using URLs in most cases to receive or send information. In a RESTful architecture, each resource, such as a user or a product, has a unique URL for identification purposes. For example, a client could send a GET request to a URL such as `http://example.com/api/users/123`, where 123 is the user ID, to retrieve information about a user. Similarly, a PUT request with the updated data in the request body could be sent to the same URL to update a user's information. This use of HTTP methods (`GET`, `POST`, `PUT`, and `DELETE`), in combination with resource-specific URLs, allows intuitive mapping of standard web operations to CRUD operations. This makes interacting with web services simple and efficient.

You may have heard about web service **endpoints**. In general, a web service works by accepting GET requests from the client and returning responses. In the context of a REST API, an endpoint is a URL where a client application can access the web service. A web service may provide more than one endpoint. For example, if you look at the **Bing Maps REST Services**, the endpoint used for geocoding is as follows: dev.virtualearth.net/REST/v1/Locations. The one used instead to provide a route between two waypoints is this one: dev.virtualearth.net/REST/v1/Routes.

Now that it's clear what a web service is and what the meanings of the technical terms often associated with it are, we can move on to showing you how to use a RESTful service.

Registering for Bing Maps web services

In this chapter, we will use Bing Maps web services as an example. Therefore, you must create a free Bing Maps basic key through your Microsoft account. The necessary steps to do this are as follows:

1. Go to the *Bing Dev Center* (https://www.bingmapsportal.com/) and click **Sign in** at the top right of the page to sign in with your Microsoft Account.

2. Once logged in, hover over the **My account** menu and select **My keys**. If it's the first time you have logged in to this portal, you will see a welcome page in which you are informed about *Azure Maps*. We don't need Azure Maps in this chapter, so go ahead and click on the **Yes, let's create a new account** link.

3. On the next page, enter your account information, select the option to agree to the Bing terms of use, and click **Create**.

4. You'll be logged into the Dev Center, and you'll see **Announcement** and **Important reminder** on the page. On this page, hover over the **My account** menu again and select **My keys**.

5. You will be presented with a form asking for a new key. Simply fill in the required fields, typing geocoding-test in the **Application name** field, leaving Basic as the **Key type** and Dev/Test as the **Application type**. Then, click on **Create**.

6.　You will see a page confirming that the key has been created, similar to the following:

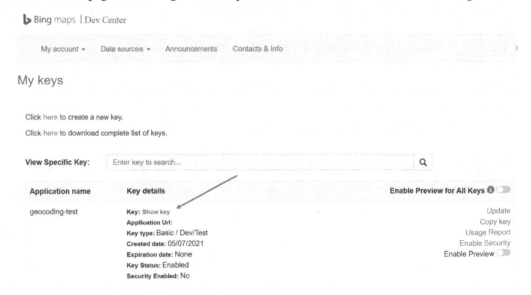

Figure 11.1: Bing Maps key confirmation

7.　Click on **Show key** to see and copy the key you'll use in the next examples.

8.　In your browser URL bar, type the following URL, replacing the `<your-bing-maps-api-key>` string with your key: `http://dev.virtualearth.net/REST/v1/Locations/1%20Microsoft%20 Way%20Redmond%20WA%2098052?key=<your-bing-maps-api-key>`. Then, press **Enter**.

9.　Some browsers, such as Firefox, beautify the JSON responses returned by web services. In your case, if all goes well, you should see a result like the following:

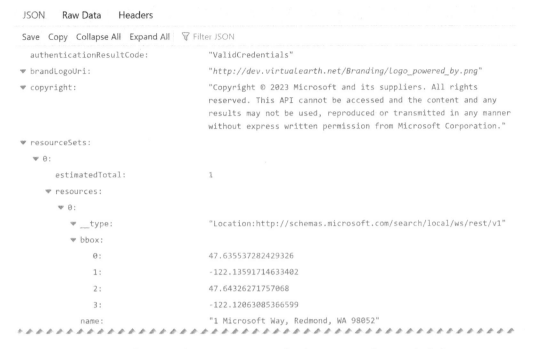

JSON   Raw Data   Headers

Save   Copy   Collapse All   Expand All   ▽ Filter JSON

    authenticationResultCode: "ValidCredentials"

▼ brandLogoUri: "*http://dev.virtualearth.net/Branding/logo_powered_by.png*"

▼ copyright: "Copyright © 2023 Microsoft and its suppliers. All rights
reserved. This API cannot be accessed and the content and any
results may not be used, reproduced or transmitted in any manner
without express written permission from Microsoft Corporation."

▼ resourceSets:

  ▼ 0:

     estimatedTotal: 1

    ▼ resources:

      ▼ 0:

        ▼ __type: "Location:http://schemas.microsoft.com/search/local/ws/rest/v1"

        ▼ bbox:

          0:            47.635537282429326

          1:            -122.13591714633402

          2:            47.64326271757068

          3:            -122.12063085366599

         name: "1 Microsoft Way, Redmond, WA 98052"

Figure 11.2: Your first geocoding experience using the Bing Maps Locations API via the browser

Congratulations! You just geocoded an address that was passed as a query parameter to the Bing Maps Locations API! Now, let's see how you can use Python to automate this process.

Geocoding addresses using Python

In this section, we'll show you how to make calls to the Bing Maps Locations API using both a direct call to the URL via the GET method (which is ultimately equivalent to the example call you made earlier via the browser) and a special Python **software development kit** (**SDK**), which makes the query easier.

Using an explicit GET request

If we want to get geocoded data for an address from the Bing API, we need to make a request to the web service by passing the address of interest as a parameter. The parameters are passed by appropriately concatenating the parameters with the endpoint URL. In our case, the full format of the endpoint URL that is useful for geocoding an address is as follows:

$$[\texttt{base\_url}]\texttt{query=}[\texttt{address}]\texttt{?key=}[\texttt{AUTH\_KEY}]$$

Figure 11.3: The URL format of a GET request to the Bing Maps Locations API

The following is the definition of each string token shown in *Figure 11.3*:

- base_url: The endpoint URL string, i.e., `https://url.uk.m.mimecastprotect.com/s/GdIYC NE2KC0QWAgSrfaL9?domain=dev.virtualearth.net/`.

- address: The string of the address that you want to geocode, transformed using the *percent encoding* technique to avoid using special characters in the final URL (you can use the *URL Decode and Encode* service at this link to encode your strings: `https://www.urlencoder.org/`).

- AUTH_KEY: Your Bing key.

Once the URL is constructed in this way, it can be used to make a GET request using the get() method of the requests module. After receiving the data as a result of the request, you'll capture the content of the web service response, which contains JSON, and from that, you can extract the values of interest. For example, in order to extract the formattedAddress value, you need to navigate into the data structure, as shown in *Figure 11.4*:

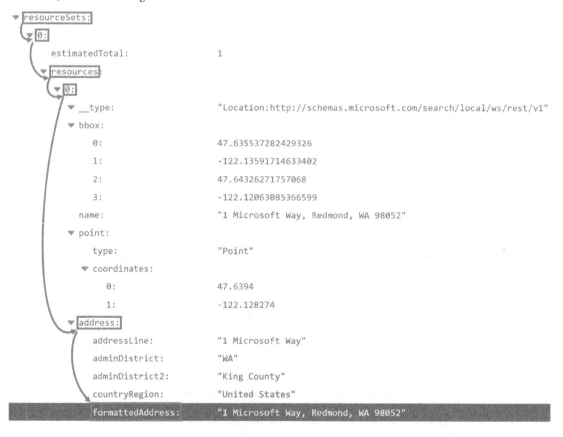

Figure 11.4: The visual structure of the Bing Maps Locations API response

So, you can navigate your data JSON variable in the same way to get this value, like this:

```
data['resourceSets'][0]['resources'][0]['address']['formattedAddress']
```

From *Figure 11.4*, you can see that the *resources* node can have more than one child node, identified by an integer. This is because, sometimes, the geocoding engine cannot accurately identify the geographic point from the given address and therefore returns more than one result. The estimatedTotal attribute indicates the number of possible geocodes identified. For simplicity, we extracted the last identified resource from the JSON, which is the one with the highest identifier.

In addition to the response in JSON format, you can also extract other values from the request, such as the reason for the response state (useful for understanding whether the GET operation was successful or not), the full content of the response in text format, and the URL used for the GET request. You will need the requests, urllib, json, pandas, and time modules. The latter is used to measure the geocoding execution time of all addresses in the dataset. Everything can be encapsulated in a handy function called bing_geocode_via_address():

```python
def bing_geocode_via_address(address):
    # trim the string from leading and trailing spaces using strip
    full_url = f"{base_url}query={urllib.parse.quote(address.strip(),
safe='')}?key={AUTH_KEY}"
    r = requests.get(full_url)
    try:
        data = r.json()
        # number of resources found, used as index to get
        # the latest resource
        num_resources = data['resourceSets'][0]['estimatedTotal']
        formattedAddress = data['resourceSets'][0]['resources'][num_
resources-1]['address']['formattedAddress']
        lat = data['resourceSets'][0]['resources'][num_resources-1]['point']
['coordinates'][0]
        lng = data['resourceSets'][0]['resources'][num_resources-1]['point']
['coordinates'][1]
    except:
        num_resources = 0
        formattedAddress = None
        lat = None
        lng = None

    text = r.text
    status = r.reason
    url = r.url

    return num_resources, formattedAddress, lat, lng, text, status, url
```

The code chunks contained in this section are available in the Python\01-geocoding-with-python. py file inside the Chapter 11 folder.

Assuming we have a list of addresses to geocode in a pandas DataFrame, it makes sense to write a handy function that takes as input a DataFrame row and the column name in which the address is stored. It will invoke the previous function to get geocoding values to add to the current row and will return it:

```python
def enrich_with_geocoding(passed_row, col_name):
    address_value = str(passed_row[col_name])

    num_resources, address_formatted, address_lat, address_lng, text, status,
url = bing_geocode_via_address(address_value)

    passed_row_copy = passed_row.copy()

    passed_row_copy['numResources'] = num_resources
    passed_row_copy['formattedAddress'] = address_formatted
    passed_row_copy['latitude'] = address_lat
    passed_row_copy['longitude'] = address_lng
    passed_row_copy['text'] = text
    passed_row_copy['status'] = status
    passed_row_copy['url'] = url

    return passed_row_copy
```

You can test these functions using the test dataset at this link: http://bit.ly/geocoding-test-addresses. It's also available in the Chapter 11 folder.

You simply need to pass the previous function as a parameter to the addresses' DataFrame apply() method to apply it to each of its rows, as shown in the following:

```python
base_url= "http://dev.virtualearth.net/REST/v1/Locations/"
AUTH_KEY = os.environ.get('BINGMAPS_API_KEY')
df_orig = pd.read_csv(r'D:\<your-path>\Ch11 - Calling External APIs To Enrich
Your Data\geocoding_test_data.csv', encoding='latin-1')
df = df_orig[['full_address','lat_true','lon_true']]
tic = time.perf_counter()
enriched_df = df.apply(enrich_with_geocoding, col_name='full_address', axis=1)
toc = time.perf_counter()
print(f"{df.shape[0]} addresses geocoded in {toc - tic:0.4f} seconds")
```

Note that the Bing Maps service key is set using the os.environ.get('BINGMAPS_API_KEY') function call. This way of accessing sensitive data avoids having to write it in plain text in the code. So, it has to be written to the BINGMAPS_API_KEY environment variable first. You can also do this in Python with the following script:

```python
os.environ['BINGMAPS_API_KEY'] = '<your-bing-api-key>'
```

This way, however, the variable is lost each time you restart Visual Studio Code. Setting an environment variable with os.environ in Python only affects the current process in which the Python script is running and its child processes. It does not affect system-level environment variables or the environment variables of other applications, including future instances of Visual Studio Code. To have it permanently available, you must set up a user variable environment directly through your operating system. On Windows, you can follow this guide: https://phoenixnap.com/kb/windows-set-environment-variable. Once the user variable environment has been added, you must restart Visual Studio Code to make it visible to your code.

> **IMPORTANT NOTE**
>
> We preferred loading the CSV file directly into the Python script. This is equivalent to first loading the CSV file using the Power BI **Text/CSV** connector and then adding a transformation step that would execute the Python code we just analyzed.

The geocoding process takes about *25 seconds* for 120 addresses on our machine. Part of the content of the final DataFrame is as follows:

Figure 11.5: The content of the geocoded DataFrame

You may notice that not all addresses are geocoded correctly. Incorrect geocoding can occur for a variety of reasons. These include incomplete or ambiguous addresses, poor data quality in the geocoding database, complex or unconventional address formats, typos and misspellings in the address, addresses that are very similar to others in different locations, lack of contextual information such as city or country, and technical limitations of the geocoding service itself. Nevertheless, the result is impressive! You geocoded up to 120 addresses in about 25 seconds with just a few lines of Python code.

But did you know that you could also parallelize GET requests by geocoding all your addresses in less time? Let's see how you do it.

Using an explicit GET request in parallel

As you learned in *Chapter 9, Loading Large Datasets Beyond the Available RAM in Power BI*, the Swiss Army knife that allows you to parallelize your computations in Python is Dask. The great thing is that a Dask DataFrame exposes the apply() method, which has the same functionality as the apply() function of a pandas DataFrame, except that it is parallelized. Therefore, the code used in the previous section is practically reusable with a few minor modifications to achieve significantly reduced execution times. You can find the full script in the Python\02-geocoding-parallel-with-python.py file in the Chapter 11 folder.

IMPORTANT NOTE

If the API requires it, it is preferable to provide multiple inputs using **batch mode** rather than making multiple calls in parallel. However, if batch mode is not covered by the API, multiple parallel calls are the only way to improve performance. The Bing Maps Locations API supports batch mode, but for demonstration purposes, we preferred using the multiple-call technique.

The `enrich_with_geocoding()` and `bing_geocode_via_address()` functions remain as they are. Instead, the Dask DataFrame is introduced already at the data read stage, as follows:

```
import dask.dataframe as dd
ddf_orig = dd.read_csv(r'D:\<your-path>\Ch11 - Calling External APIs To Enrich
Your Data\geocoding_test_data.csv', encoding='latin-1')
ddf = ddf_orig[['full_address','lat_true','lon_true']]
```

Internally, a Dask DataFrame is divided into many partitions, where each partition is a pandas DataFrame. Now, it happens that if the data is not a large amount, it can be loaded into a single partition by `read_csv()`. In fact, if you run `ddf.npartitions`, you will see that it returns 1. For this reason, in such cases, it is necessary to repartition the Dask DataFrame into an appropriate number of partitions to take advantage of parallelism, as follows:

```
ddf = ddf.repartition(npartitions=os.cpu_count()*2)
```

For the number of partitions in a DataFrame, the following applies:

IMPORTANT NOTE

There is no exact rule for determining the ideal number of partitions in a DataFrame. The formula used earlier is valid for the dataset we are considering here and was determined empirically.

At this point, you simply need to call the `apply()` method of the Dask DataFrame by passing it the `enrich_with_geocoding()` function, as you did with the `apply()` method of the pandas DataFrame in the previous section:

```
enriched_ddf = ddf.apply(enrich_with_geocoding, axis=1, col_name='full_
address', meta={'full_address': 'string', 'lat_true': 'float64', 'lon_true':
'float64', 'numResources': 'int32', 'formattedAddress': 'string', 'latitude':
'float64', 'longitude': 'float64', 'text': 'string', 'status': 'string', 'url':
'string'})
```

In this case, we needed to specify the expected metadata of the output. This is because many operations on DataFrames rely on knowing the name and type of the column. Internally, the Dask DataFrame propagates this information through all operations.

Usually, this is done by evaluating the operation on a small sample of dummy data. However, sometimes this operation may fail in user-defined functions (such as in the case of apply). In these cases, many functions support an optional meta keyword, which allows you to specify the metadata directly, bypassing the inference step.

IMPORTANT NOTE

Dask DataFrame's apply() method now supports only the axis=1 mode (row-wise).

You've just defined a lazy transformation. To actually execute it, you need to use the compute() function, so in this case, you can measure the time it takes to geocode all the addresses:

```
tic = time.perf_counter()
enriched_df = enriched_ddf.compute()
toc = time.perf_counter()
print(f'{enriched_df.shape[0]} addresses geocoded in {toc - tic:0.4f} seconds')
```

The end result is stunning: 120 addresses were geocoded in *just 3.5 seconds* versus 25 seconds for sequential code on our machine! You may achieve a 7X improvement in execution time thanks to Dask!

As you've seen in this section and the previous one, perhaps the most inconvenient part of the code is retrieving each value from the JSON returned by the web service (the logic in the bing_geocode_via_address() function) because you need to know the structure of the returned result in advance. However, there are Python modules that contain functions that make it easier to interact with specific web services. Let's see how to use the Geocoder library, which simplifies the use of the most popular geocoding providers, such as Google and Bing.

Using the Geocoder library in parallel

The **Geocoder** module (https://geocoder.readthedocs.io/) is a simple and consistent geocoding library written in Python. It provides consistent responses from expected geocoding providers using a unique JSON schema. Some of the available providers are Google, Bing, Mapbox, and TomTom.

First, you need to install the Geocoder library in the pbi_powerquery_env environment. You can do that by following these steps:

1. Open the **Anaconda prompt**.
2. Switch to the pbi_powerquery_env environment by typing this command: conda activate pbi_powerquery_env.
3. Install the Geocoder library by typing: pip install geocoder==1.38.1.

Thanks to Geocoder, the GET request for an address is simply transformed into the r = geocoder.bing(address, key = AUTH_KEY) command. The great thing is that the returned object, r, already contains the attributes useful for geocoding, such as r.address, r.lat, or r.lng.

As a result, the `bing_geocode_via_address()` function you encountered in the previous sections is embarrassingly simplified, as follows:

```
def bing_geocode_via_address(address):
    r = geocoder.bing(address, key = AUTH_KEY)
    return r.address, r.lat, r.lng, r.json, r.status, r.url
```

In this case, if the geocoding operation returns more than one match, Geocoder will select the most appropriate match, saving you further headaches. The option to return multiple results is currently under development. In newer versions of the package, it is possible to pass the `MaxRows` parameter to the geocoding functions with a value greater than one to get as many possible results as the passed value. In this way, the analyst can choose the result that meets his needs.

You can find the complete script that uses the Geocoder library to geocode addresses in parallel in the `Python\03-geocoding-parallel-using-sdk-with-python.py` file in the `Chapter  11` folder.

Now, you can understand that having an SDK available, which is designed to make your life easier when using a specific API, is a huge boon.

IMPORTANT NOTE

One of the overarching principles we always suggest is to avoid reinventing the wheel. If you need to accomplish a goal (in our case, geocoding an address), chances are that someone before you has already thought of it, and perhaps shared a library with the community that will make your life easier. Always spend half an hour searching the web for possible pre-existing solutions that can intelligently solve your problem. Not only will you save valuable time, but you will avoid the risk of going crazy over complexities that others have already solved for you.

Although we knew of the existence of the Geocoder library, we still wanted to show you how to make `GET` requests to the web service from scratch in the previous sections. This is because it is not certain that SDKs exist for all the web services you might need in the future.

Now, let's see how to get the same results using R.

Geocoding addresses using R

You have just learned how to use Python to query a web service via raw `GET` requests to the endpoint and via a handy SDK. As you might have guessed, you can do both with R. Let's see how it's done.

Using an explicit GET request

The package that allows URL calls in R is `httr` (installed by default with the engine). Thanks to this, making a `GET` request is simply translated to `GET(your_url)`. As you saw in the previous sections, you need to apply **percent encoding** to the address you want to pass as a web parameter to the Bing Maps Locations API endpoint.

The function that allows you to apply this type of encoding to a string is found in the RCurl package and is called `curlPercentEncode()`. In addition, the handy `tictoc` package is used to measure runtimes. Both the `RCurl` and `tictoc` packages need to be installed, as shown in the following steps:

1. Open **RStudio** and make sure it is pointing to your latest CRAN R engine in **Global Options**.
2. Click on the **Console** window and type the following command: `install.packages("RCurl")`. Then, press the **Enter** key. In our case, version 1.98-1.12 was installed.
3. Enter this command: `install.packages("tictoc")`. Then, press **Enter**. In our case, version 1.2 was installed.

At this point, once you have defined the `base_url` and `AUTH_KEY` variables that are specific to the web service you are querying, it is sufficient to run the following code to obtain the result of a `GET` request:

```
encoded_address <- RCurl::curlPercentEncode(address)
full_url <- stringr::str_glue('{base_url}query={encoded_address}?key={AUTH_
KEY}')
r <- httr::GET(full_url)
```

The `str_glue()` function from the `stringr` package was used to concatenate the strings. The `AUTH_KEY` variable can be set from an environment variable using `AUTH_KEY = Sys.getenv('BINGMAPS_API_KEY')`. This means that the environment variable must be set beforehand. You can set it directly in your R session with the following R script:

```
Sys.setenv(BINGMAPS_API_KEY = '<your-bing-api-key>')
```

However, each time you restart RStudio, this variable will be lost. To have it permanently available, you need to set up a user variable environment directly through your operating system. In Windows, you can follow this guide: `https://phoenixnap.com/kb/windows-set-environment-variable`. Once added, you must restart RStudio to make it visible to your code.

Once you have the result of the request, you can proceed to parse the JSON content to get the geocoding values you want. Everything that was discussed in the previous sections about parsing the result still applies. So, again, you will need to deal with the multiple results that some geocoding operations may return. As with the Python scripts used previously, all of this logic can be encapsulated in the `bing_geocode_via_address()` function in R, which returns a list of values obtained as a result of geocoding a given address. You can find the code in the `R\01-geocoding-with-r.R` file in the `Chapter 11` folder.

Once you have loaded the contents of the `geocoding_test_data.csv` file into the `tbl_orig` tibble and selected the columns of interest in `tbl`, you will use the convenience of the `purrr` package's `map()` function to call the previously defined `bing_geocode_via_address()` function for each address extracted from the tibble:

```
tic()
tbl_enriched <- tbl %>%
    pull( full_address ) %>%
    map_dfr( ~ bing_geocode_via_address(.x) ) %>%
    bind_cols( tbl, . )
toc()
```

Notice how we used the `pull()` function to convert the `full_address` tibble column to a vector and then passed it as a parameter to the `map_dfr()` function, which only accepts lists or vectors as input. You may wonder what the `map_dfr()` function is for. It is part of the `purrr` family of `map()` functions. While `map()` returns a list of results (each obtained by applying the input function to each element of the input vector) as output, `map_dfr()` binds rows directly if each element of the `map()` output is a named DataFrame, list, or vector. Thus, the final result of `map_dfr()` is a DataFrame/tibble composed of the elements returned by the input function, arranged row by row. The whole logic is wrapped by the pair of functions, `tic()` and `toc()`. By running the entire block of code (from `tic()` to `toc()`), you can very conveniently get the execution time of the code inside.

You may have noticed in this case that there is no need for an intermediate function like `enrich_with_geocoding()`, which takes the individual lines of the tibble as parameters. Since the `bing_geocode_via_address()` function returns a named list, the `map_dfr()` function manages to interpret it correctly and bind it into a single tibble.

IMPORTANT NOTE

We preferred loading the CSV file directly into the R script. It would have been equivalent to first loading the CSV file through the Power BI **Text/CSV** connector and then adding a transformation step that would execute the R code we just analyzed.

Since `map_dfr()` returns only one tibble of geocoding values, you need to bind this tibble to the initial `tbl` one in order to have a single enriched tibble. For this reason, we used the `bind_cols(tbl, .)` function, where the `.` parameter is the tibble of geocoding values passed as a parameter by the piping operation. However, the whole geocoding operation takes about 23 seconds (which is comparable to the result obtained with Python), and the final tibble will look like this:

```
> tbl_enriched
# A tibble: 120 × 11
   full_address                                 lat_true lon_true numOfResources formattedAddress        lat      lng statu…¹ statu…² text  url
   <chr>                                           <dbl>    <dbl>          <int> <chr>                 <dbl>    <dbl> <chr>     <int> <chr> <chr>
 1 200 K St NE, Washington DC, 20002                38.9    -77.0              1 200 K St NE, Was… 38.9    -77.0 OK          200 "{\"… http…
 2 200 K St North East, Washington DC, 20002        38.9    -77.0              1 200 K St NE, Was… 38.9    -77.0 OK          200 "{\"… http…
 3 200 K St Northeast,  DC                          38.9    -77.0              1 200 K St NE, Was… 38.9    -77.0 OK          200 "{\"… http…
 4 500 L'enfant Plaza SW, Washington DC, 200024     38.9    -77.0              1 500 L'Enfant Pla… 38.9    -77.0 OK          200 "{\"… http…
 5 500 Lenfant Plaza SW, Washington DC, 200024      38.9    -77.0              4 Quéry, Calvados,… 49.1   -0.708 OK          200 "{\"… http…
 6 500 Lenfant Plaza SW, DC                         38.9    -77.0              5 Southwest          5.06     9.23 OK          200 "{\"… http…
 7 2197 Plumleigh Dr, Fremont, CA, 94539            37.5   -122.               1 2197 Plumleigh D… 37.5   -122.  OK          200 "{\"… http…
 8 2197 Plumleegh Dr, Fremont, CA, 94539            37.5   -122.               1 2197 Plumleigh D… 37.5   -122.  OK          200 "{\"… http…
 9 2197 Plumleegh Dr, Fremon                        37.5   -122.               5 Fremont, NE        41.4    -96.5 OK          200 "{\"… http…
10 5034 Curtis St, Fremont, CA 94538                37.5   -122.               1 5034 Curtis St, … 37.5   -122.  OK          200 "{\"… http…
# … with 110 more rows, and abbreviated variable names ¹statusDesc, ²statusCode
```

Figure 11.6: The content of the DataFrame geocoded with R

Well done! You were able to geocode addresses via the web service even with R. Easy, right? Now, are you curious to learn how to do this using the parallelism of your machine? Let's see how you can do it.

Using an explicit GET request in parallel

Just as in Python, we have to use the Dask module to parallelize computations; in R, we need to introduce a new package to accomplish the same thing. The new package is called `furrr` (https:// furrr.futureverse.org/), and it is intended to combine the expressive power of the `purrr` family of mapping functions with the parallel processing capabilities of the **future** package (https://future. futureverse.org/).

Both the furrr and future packages are part of an interesting framework called **Futureverse** (https://www.futureverse.org/), which aims to parallelize existing R code without needing to significantly alter the original code. In practical terms, furrr allows you to replace purrr's map() and map_*() functions with furrr's future_map() and future_map_*() functions with minimal effort, and your code will magically run in parallel.

First of all, you need to install the furrr package. Just run the install.packages("furrr") command in RStudio's **Console** window and you're done. In our case, version 0.3.1 was installed. To apply what has just been said to the code analyzed in the previous section, it is sufficient to modify the last part of it as follows to obtain the same result (and, of course, to load the furrr library instead of purrr), but with the computations parallelized:

```
n_cores <- availableCores() - 1
plan(cluster, workers = n_cores)
tic()
tbl_enriched <- tbl %>%
    pull( full_address ) %>%
    future_map_dfr( ~ bing_geocode_via_address(.x) ) %>%
    bind_cols( tbl, . )
toc()
```

Thanks to the availableCores() function, it is possible to determine the number of virtual processors available on the machine. It is good practice not to use all of them, as this can make the machine unresponsive. The plan() function of a future instance allows you to define the strategy with which the future engine will perform the calculations (synchronously or asynchronously). It also allows you to define the number of workers that will work in parallel.

IMPORTANT NOTE

In general, the default strategy used on Windows computers is **multisession**, which works well when running code in RStudio. We found that with this strategy, Power BI cannot handle the multiple sessions created to parallelize calculations. In contrast, with the versions of Power BI Desktop used in the previous edition of the book, we found that by selecting the **cluster** strategy, even if the computer is unique, Power BI was able to complete the calculations. Unfortunately, with the latest versions of Power BI Desktop, you are no longer able to use futures correctly, and the load gets stuck without making any progress.

While it is not yet possible to use parallelism with R futures in Power BI, for the sake of completeness, we will provide the code to do so in RStudio.

Another minimal change was to declare the base_url and AUTH variables associated with the web service directly in the function called by future_map_dfr() instead of in the main code for simplicity. Passing variables to functions called via furrr is done slightly differently than in standard practice (see https://furrr.futureverse.org/articles/articles/gotchas.html), and we wanted to avoid adding additional complexity so as not to distract from the main concept.

The complete script can be found in the `R\02-geocoding-parallel-with-r.R` file in the `Chapter 11` folder.

When you run the code, the results are impressive: 120 addresses were geocoded in *just 3 seconds* after the cluster was allocated, versus 23 seconds for sequential code! Also, in this case, you achieved a 10X improvement in runtime thanks to `furrr`! Simple as that, right?

You can further simplify the code you just ran by using a geocoding package that does most of the work or calling the web service for you. Let's see what that's all about.

Using the tidygeocoder package in parallel

Although it is not yet possible to use parallelism with R in Power BI, for completeness we will provide the code to do so in RStudio using the tidycoder package. The `tidygeocoder` package (`https://jessecambon.github.io/tidygeocoder/`) provides a unified high-level interface for a selection of supported Geocoder services and returns results in tibble format. Some of the available providers are Google, Mapbox, TomTom, and Bing (starting with version 1.0.3).

First of all, you need to install it. You can simply run the `install.packages ("tidygeocoder")` command in the **Console** window. In our case, version 1.0.5 was installed.

Thanks to Tidygeocoder, the `GET` request for an address is simply transformed into the `details_tbl <- geo(address, method = 'bing', full_results = TRUE)` command, and the great thing is that the returned object already contains the attributes useful for geocoding, such as `details_tbl$bing_address.formattedAddress`. Therefore, the `bing_geocode_via_address()` function you encountered in the previous sections is embarrassingly simplified, as shown in the following code block:

```
bing_geocode_via_address <- function(address) {
    details_tbl <- geo(address, method = 'bing', full_results = TRUE)
    details_lst <- list(
        formattedAddress = details_tbl$bing_address.formattedAddress,
        lat = details_tbl$point.coordinates[[1]][1],
        lng = details_tbl$point.coordinates[[1]][2],
        details_tbl = details_tbl
    )
    return( details_lst )
}
```

Also in this case, if the geocoding operation returns more than one result, the `tidygeocoder` package will select the most appropriate match, saving you further headaches.

IMPORTANT NOTE

Note that Tidygeocoder assumes that the `BINGMAPS_API_KEY` environment variable is set and uses it to log in to the web service.

The complete script that uses the Geocoder library to geocode addresses in parallel can be found in the R\03-geocoding-parallel-using-sdk-with-r.R file in the Chapter 11 folder.

As you've probably figured out by now, using SDKs available to the community makes your life easier and is a winning choice. If an SDK is not available for a particular web service, you have still learned how to make a raw GET request with R.

Now, let's look at the benefits of what we've learned so far by implementing web service data enrichment solutions with R and Python in Power BI.

Accessing web services using Power BI

Power BI comes with out-of-the-box features that allow you to access the data exposed by a web service in Power Query. There are two main modes:

- Through the GUI (click on **Get data**, then **Web**, and then you can set advanced options if needed).
- Through the M language, using the Web.Contents() function.

Using the GUI is very cumbersome and almost always fails to produce the desired results. The only way to effectively connect to a web service using native Power BI features is to write M code. Writing code in M is not too difficult. However, there are some disadvantages to using it, which are as follows:

- There are some complications with using the Web.Contents() function that arise when publishing a report that uses the Power BI service. In short, you must be careful if you need to dynamically construct the URL to be used in the GET request using the **relative path** and the **query options**. If you do not use this particular construct, the service will not be able to refresh the data.
- The Power BI service does not allow you to securely store sensitive data, such as the API key, forcing you to embed this information in your code.
- M doesn't allow you to make multiple calls to an endpoint in parallel.

For these reasons, we recommend using R or Python to access web services, especially when SDKs are available to facilitate their use.

IMPORTANT NOTE

If the report that uses web service data needs to be published to the Power BI service, you can only query web services through Power Query, not within R Visuals, because the environment they use on the service is not exposed to the internet.

However, to be able to geolocate addresses using the Bing Maps Locations API in Power BI using the scripts we provide, you must define the BINGMAPS_API_KEY environment variable as a user environment variable on your operating system. If the report that uses the data extracted from the web service will be published to the Power BI service, be sure to create the same environment variable on the data gateway machine as well.

Now, let's see how you can use Python to extract data from a web service in Power BI.

Geocoding addresses in Power BI with Python

In Power BI, we will use the Python code that calls the web service through the Geocoder SDK and exploits the parallelism thanks to Dask. The code to be used is practically identical to that already analyzed previously. Remember to first set the `BINGMAPS_API_KEY` environment variable directly from the operating system, as shown in the following link: `https://phoenixnap.com/kb/windows-set-environment-variable`. Therefore, it is sufficient to follow these steps:

1. Open Power BI Desktop through the shortcut that activates the `pbi_powerquery_env` environment.

2. Make sure Power BI Desktop is referencing the `pbi_powerquery_env` environment in `Options`.

3. Click on **Get data, More…**, type **Python**, and then double-click on **Python script**.

4. Copy the contents of the `Python\04-geocoding-parallel-using-sdk-in-power-bi-with-python.py` file into the `Chapter 11` folder. Remember to edit the paths (`geocoding_test_data.csv`) accordingly, and then click **OK**.

5. After a few seconds, you will see the **Navigator** window appear, where you can select the `enriched_df` table:

Figure 11.7: The enriched_df DataFrame loaded in Power BI

Then, click on **Load**.

You just queried the Bing Maps Locations API from within Power BI in parallel using Python! Easy, right?

It's possible to do the same thing with R. Let's see how you do it.

Geocoding addresses in Power BI with R

In the versions of Power BI Desktop used in the previous edition of this book, it was possible to use R code that called the web service using the `Tidygeocoder` SDK and exploited parallelism using the `furrr` package. Unfortunately, the latest versions of Power BI Desktop do not resolve R futures correctly, even when using different strategies (cluster and multisession). Therefore, you are forced to use the non-parallelized code in R using direct web service calls. If you have not already done so, remember to first set the `BINGMAPS_API_KEY` environment variable directly from the operating system, as shown in the following link: `https://phoenixnap.com/kb/windows-set-environment-variable`. Therefore, it is sufficient to follow these steps:

1. Open Power BI Desktop and make sure it references your latest CRAN R engine.

2. Click on **Get data, More...**, type R script, and then double-click on **R script**.

3. Copy the contents of the R\04-geocoding-in-power-bi-with-r.R file into the Chapter 11 folder. Remember to edit the paths (geocoding_test_data.csv) accordingly, and then click **OK**.

4. After a few seconds, you will see the **Navigator** window appear, where you can select the enriched_df table:

Figure 11.8: The tbl_enriched DataFrame loaded in Power BI

Then, click on **Load**.

You just queried the Bing Maps Locations API from within Power BI using R, too!

Summary

In this chapter, you've learned how to query RESTful web services using Python and R. In addition to learning how to execute raw GET requests with both languages, you've also learned how to parallelize multiple calls to the same endpoint by taking advantage of your machine's multithreading capabilities. You've also seen some of the Bing Maps Locations API SDKs, both for Python and R, that make accessing the data much easier. Finally, you've seen how all of this is easily implemented in Power BI.

In the next chapter, you'll see how to enrich your data by applying complex algorithms to the data you already have. In doing so, you will create new variables that will shed new light on your data and make it more useful for achieving your goal.

References

For additional reading, check out the following books and articles:

- *What RESTful actually means* (https://codewords.recurse.com/issues/five/what-restful-actually-means)

- *Bing Maps REST Services* (https://docs.microsoft.com/en-us/bingmaps/rest-services)

- *A Future for R: A Comprehensive Overview* (https://cran.r-project.org/web/packages/future/vignettes/future-1-overview.html)

- *[VIDEO] Accessing API and web service data using Power Query* (https://www.youtube.com/watch?v=SoJ52o7ni2A)

- *Invoking M Functions In Parallel Using List.ParallelInvoke()* (https://blog.crossjoin.co.uk/2018/09/20/invoking-m-functions-in-parallel-using-list-parallelinvoke/)

Test your knowledge

1. What is the design model that is becoming the standard for all public web services, and how does it handle data?

2. Through which method can you perform a web service call for each row of the DataFrame in Python?

3. How do you parallelize web service calls for each row of the DataFrame in Python?

4. What functionality do you use in R to perform a function for each value in a column?

5. How do you introduce parallelism for web service calls in R?

6. What is the advantage of using an SDK to make web service calls?

7. What technology can you use in Power BI to parallelize calls to a web service?

Learn more on Discord

To join the Discord community for this book – where you can share feedback, ask questions to the author, and learn about new releases – follow the QR code below:

```
https://discord.gg/MKww5g45EB
```

12

Calculating Columns Using Complex Algorithms: Distances

The data ingestion phase allows you to gather all the information you need for your analysis from any data source. Once the various datasets have been imported, some of this information may not be useful in describing a phenomenon from an analytical point of view. After the data ingestion phase, it's not uncommon to find that some of the raw information doesn't directly contribute to analytical insights as is. Recognizing this, it is essential to refine and enhance the dataset with additional computations that can provide new perspectives and answers to our questions. This often involves the creation of calculated columns that provide measures that are more aligned with our analytical goals. For example, in the context of our exploration, the calculation of the distance between two geographic points or the dissimilarity between two strings can transform seemingly abstract or unrelated data into powerful tools for analysis. These computed measures allow us to delve deeper into our investigation and provide a more nuanced understanding of the phenomena under study.

In this chapter, we embark on a fascinating exploration of the concept of distance and its remarkable versatility in a variety of scenarios. Our journey begins with an examination of its role in the measurement of geographic points, where we delve into the intricacies of spatial measurement and its significance in various domains. We also embark on a fascinating exploration of how distance manifests itself in the realm of strings, uncovering the methods and techniques used to measure the dissimilarity between two distinct sequences.

It's often necessary to apply non-trivial algorithms to the data you have to get measures or indicators that do the trick, and Power BI often doesn't have the tools to calculate them. Fortunately, thanks to R and Python, we have access to everything we need to calculate our measures.

This chapter will cover the following topics:

- What is a distance?
- The distance between two geographic locations
- The distance between two strings

Technical requirements

This chapter requires you to have a working internet connection and **Power BI Desktop** already installed on your machine (we used version 2.114.664.0 64-bit, February 2023). You must have properly configured the R and Python engines and IDEs as outlined in *Chapter 2, Configuring R with Power BI*, and *Chapter 3, Configuring Python with Power BI*.

What is a distance?

A **distance**, in the context of data analysis and pattern recognition, is a quantitative measure that captures the dissimilarity or similarity between objects or points in a given space. It provides a numerical representation of the extent to which two entities are separate or close to each other and allows us to objectively quantify the relationships and differences between data points so that we can systematically compare and analyze them.

The concept of distance is particularly valuable because it provides a common metric for *comparing and evaluating different types of data*. Whether dealing with numerical attributes, categorical variables, or even complex structures such as images or text, distances can be defined and calculated to quantify the dissimilarity between instances. By using the concept of distance, analysts and data scientists gain insight into the relationships, patterns, and structures inherent in their data.

The concept of distance finds application and meaning in several scientific disciplines that actively study and use it to understand phenomena, relationships, and interactions at various scales. Mathematics, as a fundamental science, makes extensive use of distance in various branches such as geometry, topology, and mathematical analysis. These fields use distances to define and study the properties of spaces, shapes, and mathematical structures. For example, in geometry, distances between points determine the lengths of lines, the areas of shapes, and the angles between vectors, as seen in the following diagram:

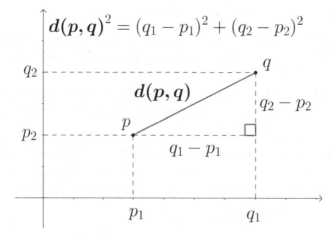

$$d(p, q)^2 = (q_1 - p_1)^2 + (q_2 - p_2)^2$$

Figure 12.1: The two-dimensional Euclidean distance

Physics, the fundamental science of matter and energy, uses distance to study the relationships and interactions between particles, objects, and fields. Biology also uses the concept of distance in many ways. In genetics, for example, distances between DNA sequences or genetic markers help to analyze evolutionary relationships and genetic diversity. In particular, social science uses distance to quantify and analyze relationships between individuals, groups, or entities. Social network analysis uses distance measures to assess centrality, connectivity, and influence within social networks.

Computer science and data analytics rely heavily on the concept of distance in many areas. In machine learning, distances are critical to clustering algorithms, which group objects or data points together based on their similarity or proximity. Similarly, in data mining and pattern recognition, distances serve as the basis for identifying patterns, detecting anomalies, and making predictions.

There is even a science that specifically studies the distances between strings. It is known as **stringology**. Stringology is a subfield of computer science and mathematics that focuses on the study of strings, which are sequences of characters. The field is concerned with developing algorithms, techniques, and theories for efficiently analyzing, manipulating, and comparing strings. In this chapter, you will see some examples of applications of this science.

As you can see, the concept of distance is of immense importance in various domains, providing a quantitative measure of the separation or dissimilarity between objects or points. By systematically analyzing distances, you gain valuable insight into the relationships, patterns, and structures inherent in data, enabling informed decision making and problem solving.

In the next section, we explore another critical aspect: the distance between two geographic locations. Understanding geographic distance is critical in many applications, including navigation, logistics, urban planning, and spatial analysis.

Let's see what it's all about.

The distance between two geographic locations

It is often the case that you have coordinates in your dataset, expressed in latitude and longitude, that identify points on the globe. Depending on the purpose of the analysis you want to perform, you can use these coordinates to calculate measures that best describe the scenario you want to address. For example, assuming you have the geographic coordinates of some hotels in a dataset, it might be useful to calculate the distance of each hotel to the nearest airport if you want to provide an additional value of interest to a visitor.

Some theory first

To fully understand a phenomenon well, to know what it consists of and what technologies have been developed to deal with it, it is necessary to go deeper into the theory behind it. Since we are talking about measuring the distance between two points on the globe, the first thing that comes to mind is to simplify the phenomenon by using a model that approximates reality. So let's take a closer look at the distance between two points on a **sphere** or **spheroid**, which is very similar to a globe.

Spherical trigonometry

The study of measuring triangles (**trigonometry**) has been of great interest in the past. The ancient Egyptians and Babylonians had already studied the relationships between sides, although they did not yet have the concept of an angle. It is thanks to Hellenistic mathematics that the concepts of trigonometric functions as we know them today began to spread around the world, even reaching India and China.

It was the ancient Greeks who, after exploring all the properties associated with a triangle drawn on a plane, came up with the idea of imagining a triangle drawn on a sphere. The importance of measuring distances between points on a sphere was immediately recognized as being of interest to navigation, and astronomy in later centuries. Therefore, several minds were eagerly devoted to the discovery of important properties that today can be summarized under the name of **spherical trigonometry**.

If you draw a spherical triangle, you will immediately notice how different it is from a flat triangle:

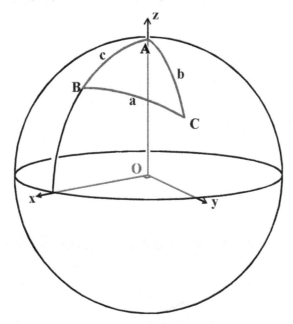

Figure 12.2: A spherical triangle

The main difference from plane triangles is that the sides of spherical triangles are arcs of **great circles** or **geodesics** (circumferences that always divide the sphere in half), and since the central angles (near the center, *O*) are proportional to the lengths of their respective arcs (*length = π x angle*), the sides *a*, *b*, and *c* are measured in *angle units* rather than linear units. If you want to visualize the fact that the sides of the spherical triangle belong to three great circles, *Figure 12.3* can help:

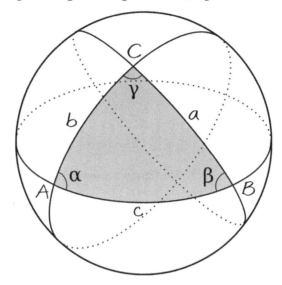

Figure 12.3: The great circles that generate a spherical triangle

The mathematics that describes spherical trigonometry makes it possible to define all the distances between two points on the sphere that have been highlighted by the great mathematicians of the past.

As for the distances between two geographic points, the reference coordinate system will be the one that uses **latitude** and **longitude**. Obviously, we will not go into the mathematical details of the distance proofs that we will propose shortly (because some of them would be very complex indeed). However, we wanted to provide an introduction that would lay the groundwork for the most commonly used concepts of geographic distance.

Now let's explore the simplest distance between two points, the law of Cosines distance.

The law of Cosines distance

The **law of Cosines distance** (also called the **great circle distance**) is the shortest distance between two points on the surface of a sphere, measured along the surface of the sphere. Given two points, *P* and *Q*, a unique great circle passes through them. The two points divide the great circle into two distinct arcs.

The length of the shorter arc is the distance of the great circle between the points:

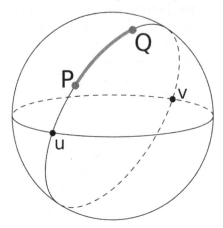

Figure 12.4: The great circle distance between the points P and Q

Note that if the two points from which the distance is to be calculated are at the antipodes of the sphere (the **antipodal points** u and v), then the great circles that pass through them are infinite, and the distance between these two points is very easy to calculate, since it measures exactly half the circumference of the sphere.

If, on the other hand, the points are not antipodal, it is possible to derive the preceding distance thanks to the **spherical law of Cosines** (see references at the end of this chapter), which governs spherical trigonometry (that is why we call it the law of Cosines distances). Without going through the tedious mathematical steps, the formula that calculates the law of Cosines (or great circle) distance between two points on a sphere is as follows

$$d = 2r \arcsin\left(\sqrt{\sin^2\left(\frac{\varphi_2 - \varphi_1}{2}\right) + \cos\varphi_1 \cdot \cos\varphi_2 \cdot \sin^2\left(\frac{\lambda_2 - \lambda_1}{2}\right)}\right)$$

Figure 12.5: The formula of the law of Cosines distance between two points

When you look at it, it's not the simplest, cleanest formula you've ever seen, right? Nevertheless, with the handy calculators available today, the preceding calculation remains feasible. Now imagine the ancient navigators who used the great circle distance between various points on the globe. How could they have used the preceding formula, even though they had sine and cosine tables that would only facilitate some of the calculations needed? It would have been a very complex activity and subject to errors that could have cost the sailors their lives.

IMPORTANT NOTE

If the two points are close together (for example, a few kilometers apart on the sphere) and you don't have a calculator with accurate precision, you may get more inaccurate results than if the two points are far apart.

For these reasons, mathematicians of the time introduced the new trigonometric **Haversine** function (or hav), which allows you to transform and smooth the great circle distance formula, avoiding the aforementioned error even for small distances. Let's see how it does this.

The law of Haversines distance

The function called haversine (from *half-versed sine*) is defined as follows:

$$\mathrm{hav}(\theta) = \sin^2\left(\frac{\theta}{2}\right) = \frac{1 - \cos(\theta)}{2}$$

Figure 12.6: Definition of the Haversine function

Thanks to this new function, it is possible to rewrite the Cosines distance law as follows:

$$\mathrm{hav}(\theta) = \mathrm{hav}(\varphi_2 - \varphi_1) + \cos(\varphi_1)\cos(\varphi_2)\,\mathrm{hav}(\lambda_2 - \lambda_1)$$

Figure 12.7: Definition of the law of Haversines distance

Once you have computed *hav(θ)* for the selected pair of points, you can then compute the angle distance using the inverse Haversine function *θ = archav(hav(θ))*. This new distance formulation is known as the **law of Haversines distance**. Its undoubted usefulness to navigators of the time becomes clear when you consider that, along with the tables of Sines and Cosines, tables of Haversines were also published. Therefore, the calculation of the distance between two points became immediate.

IMPORTANT NOTE

Even this formula suffers from rounding errors due to the special (and somewhat unusual) case of antipodal points.

To get a distance formula that is more accurate than the Haversine formula, you need to use *Vincenty's formula*. Let's see what it is.

Vincenty's distance

The winning assumption that led the geodesist Vincenty to a more precise formula for the distance between two points was to consider the Earth not as a sphere, but as an ellipsoid slightly flattened at the poles (the difference is only about 21 km):

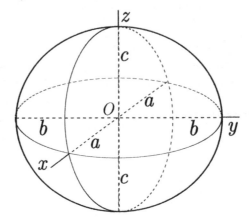

Figure 12.8: An ellipsoid representing the Earth

Unlike the Haversine method for calculating a distance on a sphere, **Vincenty's formulas** describe a method that must converge to a solution through several iterations. Specifically, a sequence of equations is computed, the output of which is fed back into the same sequence of equations with the goal of minimizing the computed value after a certain number of iterations. For this reason, Vincenty's formulas are more computationally demanding.

Vincenty's formulas are related to two problems:

- **Direct problem**: Find the endpoint, *(Φ2, L2)*, and azimuth, *α2*, given an initial point, *(Φ1, L1)*, and initial azimuth, *α1*, and a distance, *s*.
- **Inverse problem**: Find the azimuths *α1*, *α2* and the ellipsoidal distance, *s*, given the coordinates of the two points, *(Φ1, L1)* and *(Φ2, L2)*.

The inverse problem is what we are interested in, since we need to calculate the distance. To get an idea of the complexity of the formulas, take a look at the references section at the end of the chapter.

Vincenty's formulas are widely used in projects where there is a need for high precision in measurements because they are accurate to within 0.5 mm (0.020 in) of the Earth's ellipsoid.

IMPORTANT NOTE

If the points are nearly antipodal, the algorithm fails to converge and the error is much larger or converges slowly.

In 2013, Karney used Newton's method to give rapid convergence for all pairs of input points without any errors.

At this point, the question that arises is what kind of distance is it best to use and when. Let's try to understand that in the following section.

What kind of distance to use and when

Considering the strong limitation that the law of Cosines distance has for short distances between two points, the most used methods today in common applications are the law of Haversines (for short, Haversine) and Vincenty's formulas (for short, Vincenty). Here are our suggestions on which distance to use in certain scenarios:

- For *points located close to each other* (think short-range flights), the approximation of the Earth to a sphere is very accurate. Therefore, methods based on the spherical Earth model, such as Haversine, which are computationally simpler (hence faster), will be quite adequate.

- For *points located far away* (such as long-range flights, especially connecting opposite hemispheres), the spherical Earth model starts to be less tight and inaccurate. In these cases, Vincenty's inverse formula for ellipsoids, which is substantially more computationally complex (hence generally slower), will give a better result. If you have computational limitations, you need to consider whether the faster models give sufficiently accurate results for your purposes.

Now that you've become well versed in the theory, let's move on to implementing these algorithms in Python and R.

Implementing distances using Python

The scenario in which we will implement the distance algorithms described above is a dataset of U.S. hotels containing the latitude and longitude of each hotel. The goal is to enrich the dataset by adding the distances to the nearest airports.

The hotel data is publicly available on *Back4App* (`https://bit.ly/data-hotels-usa`). For convenience, we have extracted only 100 hotels from New York City, and for each of them we will compute the distances from LaGuardia and John F. Kennedy airports (you can find the airport data here: `https://datahub.io/core/airport-codes`) using the Haversine (spherical model) and Karney (ellipsoidal model) methods. You can find the already extracted datasets for your convenience in the `Chapter 12` folder of the GitHub repository. Specifically, the hotel data can be found in the `hotels-ny.xlsx` file, and the airport data in the `airport-codes.csv` file.

Calculating distances with Python

As we mentioned earlier, we are not the kind of people who like to reinvent the wheel, especially when there is a risk of running into complexities related to the domain of the problem to be solved. Fortunately, Python has a very active community of programmers with expertise in specific scientific domains who share their artifacts publicly. This is the case for the **PyGeodesy** package (`https://github.com/mrJean1/PyGeodesy`), created by Jean M. Brouwers, which implements in pure Python various computational tools for spherical and ellipsoidal models of the Earth that Chris Veness has made available for Java and Charles Karney himself has made available in C++.

To be able to use this module, you must of course install it in your environment, and since we want to use the distance formulas optimized by Karney, we must also install the **GeographicLib** library, which is maintained directly by him. Proceed as follows:

1. Open **Anaconda Prompt**.

2. Switch to the `pbi_powerquery_env` environment, enter the `conda activate pbi_powerquery_` `env` command, and then press **Enter**.

3. Install the `PyGeodesy` package, by typing `pip install PyGeodesy==23.5.23`, and then press **Enter**.

4. Install the `geographiclib` package, by typing `pip install geographiclib==2.0`, and then press **Enter**.

5. If you have not already done so, also install the `openpyxl` package by typing `pip install openpyxl`, and then press **Enter**.

At this point, you can proceed with the Python code. First, note that the **PyGeodesy** package includes a form of basic geodesic functions called **formy**. In this module, there are functions that directly calculate distances according to the Haversine and Vincenty formulas, but it doesn't contain the variant of the Karney formulas. Therefore, in addition to the standard pandas and NumPy modules, the following need to be imported:

```
from pygeodesy import formy as frm
from pygeodesy.ellipsoidalKarney import LatLon as kLatLon
```

To calculate the distance according to Karney, you need to use the objects provided by the `ellipsoidalKarney` module. Basically, you need to create the two points on the ellipsoid using the `LatLon` method of this model, and then calculate the distance. This is summarized in the following custom `karney` function:

```
def karney(lat1, lng1, lat2, lng2):
    return kLatLon(lat1, lng1).distanceTo(kLatLon(lat2, lng2))
```

Then, for convenience, a second user-defined function is created as a wrapper for the calls to calculate the various distances:

```
def geodistance(lat1, lng1, lat2, lng2, func):
    return func(lat1, lng1, lat2, lng2)
```

Then the hotel data is imported into the `hotel_df` dataframe and the airport data is imported into the `airports_df` dataframe. Since the airport dataframe has the `Coordinates` column, which contains a string of latitude and longitude separated by a comma, these two values are split into two separate columns using the `split()` function, and then appended to the same source dataframe without the now useless `Coordinates` column:

```
airports_df = pd.concat([
    airports_df.drop(['coordinates'], axis=1),
    airports_df['coordinates'].str.split(', ', expand=True).
rename(columns={0:'longitude', 1:'latitude'}).astype(float)], axis=1)
```

To conveniently access the latitude and longitude values of a specific airport, the custom airportLatLongList() function has been created, which takes as parameters both a dataframe containing the airport data with the iata_code, latitude, and longitude columns and the specific **IATA code** of the airport of interest. Remember that the IATA airport code is a three-letter code that identifies many airports and metropolitan areas around the world, as defined by the **International Air Transport Association (IATA)**. For example, John F. Kennedy International Airport is identified by the IATA code JFK and LaGuardia Airport is identified by the code LGA. Note that the airports_df dataframe contains about 58K rows, and only about 9K of those lines have an iata_code that is not null. This is because there are so many small airports that are not classified by the IATA. To find the coordinates of airports identified by an IATA code, you can use the following code:

```
jfk_lat, jfk_long  = airportLatLongList(airports_df, 'JFK')
lga_lat, lga_long = airportLatLongList(airports_df, 'LGA')
```

However, thanks to the geodistance() function, you only need to know the geographic coordinates of two points to calculate the distance between them. For example, if you want to calculate the Haversine distance between point A(lat1,lng1) and point B(lat2,lng2), all you have to do is use this code:

```
geodistance(lat1, lng1, lat2, lng2, func=frm.harvesine)
```

To calculate the Karney distance between them instead, you can take advantage of the karney() function and use this code:

```
geodistance(lat1, lng1, lat2, lng2, func=karney)
```

But what if you want to apply the geodistance() function not to two single points, but to a series of points contained in a dataframe column and a second fixed point? Since the previous function takes five input parameters, we could have used the apply() method of the pandas dataframe (as shown here: http://bit.ly/pandas-apply-lambda). Instead, we introduced a convenient way to evaluate a function over successive tuples of the input series. There is a concept in Python called **vectorization**, which refers to the process of transforming a function that operates on single elements into a function that can efficiently process entire arrays or matrices as input. This transformation allows the function to take advantage of optimized, vectorized operations provided by libraries such as NumPy. In our case, we are using functions (frm.haversine and kLatLon) that are provided as is by external packages. Therefore, we do not know if these functions use operations inside them that act on whole arrays or matrices to speed up execution time, rather than using simple loops. However, there is NumPy's **vectorize function**, which takes a scalar function as input and returns a new function that can efficiently operate on arrays or matrices element by element. While this function simplifies the syntax, it may not offer the same level of performance as fully optimized vectorized operations using built-in NumPy functions. Anyway, in this case, to vectorize a function, you have to call the np.vectorize() function and pass as a parameter the function to be applied to the series of geocoordinates. Then you must also pass the parameters of the input function as follows:

```
hotels_df['haversineDistanceFromJFK'] = np.vectorize(geodistance)(
    hotels_df['latitude'],
    hotels_df['longitude'],
```

```
    jfk_lat,
    jfk_long,
    func=frm.haversine)
```

The distances (in meters) resulting from the previous calculation are stored in the new column `haversineDistanceFromJFK` of the `hotels_df` dataframe. Similarly, the Karney distance can be calculated by simply referencing the `karney` function in the code chunk.

IMPORTANT NOTE

A truly vectorized function is not the same as a function used with `np.vectorize()`. A vectorized function is one that is built into NumPy and executed in the underlying compiled code (C or Fortran) so that special processor registers are used to operate on multiple elements at once. As you can imagine, vectorization is much more performant than, and preferable to, for loops. For more details, see the *References* section.

If you run the code for the `01-distances-from-airports-in-python.py` file in the `Python` folder, you'll get something like this:

name	haversineDistanceFromJFK	karneyDistanceFromJFK	haversineDistanceFromLGA	karneyDistanceFromLGA
Element New York Times Square West	22103.493557	22130.681538	10314.345715	10338.546883
Sanctuary Hotel New York Times Square	21696.697737	21720.930350	9541.202663	9563.793968
The Jane	22309.739387	22345.798923	12316.656741	12342.187319
Hotel Olcott	22651.190545	22669.169997	8832.336480	8854.870363
Fairfield Inn & Suites New York Manhattan/Time...	22156.605785	22184.919308	10568.505016	10593.031275
...	...	...	...	...

Figure 12.9: Haversine and Karney distances from hotels to JFK and LGA airports added

Amazing! You were able to calculate both the Haversine and Karney distances in meters between all the hotels and both airports using Python. At this point, it is easy to use similar code to calculate distances in Power BI. Let's see how to do it.

Calculating distances in Power BI with Python

It's time to put what you've learned into practice with Power BI. So launch Power BI Desktop and let's get started:

1. Open Power BI Desktop through the shortcut that activates the `pbi_powerquery_env` environment.

2. Make sure Power BI Desktop is referencing the `pbi_powerquery_env` environment in **Options**.

3. Click on **Excel workbook** to import the `hotels-ny.xlsx` file, which you can find in the `Chapter 12` folder. Select it and click **Open**.

4. Select the **Sheet 1** table from the **Navigator** window:

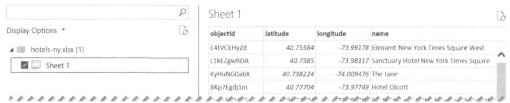

Figure 12.10: Selecting the Sheet 1 table

5. Then, click on **Transform Data**.

6. Click on the **Transform** menu, and then click on **Run Python script**.

7. Copy the script from the 02-distances-from-airports-in-power-bi-with-python.py file from the Python folder to the Python script editor. Remember to edit the airport-codes.csv path and then click **OK**.

8. You may be prompted to match the permissions in the Excel file to the permissions you initially selected for the scripts (in our case, **Public**). In this case, you already know how to proceed based on what you've seen in *Chapter 4, Solving Common Issues When Using Python and R in Power BI*. Then click on **Refresh Preview**.

9. We are only interested in the data in the dataset table. So, click on its **Table** value.

10. Power Query will transform your data by adding the distances from each hotel to the two airports, JFK and LGA, for the two methods, Haversines and Karney:

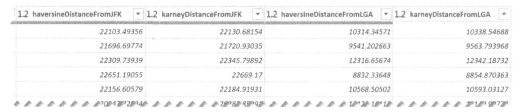

Figure 12.11: The result of the Python script transformation

11. You can then click **Close & Apply** on the **Home** tab.

Great! You just enriched your data by adding the distances between two geographic points in Power BI using Python. Let's see how you do the same thing in R.

Implementing distances using R

The scenario will be the same as the one described in the previous section. We will enrich the data of some hotels in New York City with the distances between them and the two main airports of New York, namely John F. Kennedy and LaGuardia.

The files containing the data to be processed can be found in the Chapter 12 folder of the GitHub repository. Specifically, the hotel data is in the hotels-ny.xlsx file and the airport data is in the airport-codes.csv file.

Calculating distances with R

The R community is also fortunate to have a freely available package that implements spherical trigonometry functions for geographic applications. The package is called **geosphere** (`https://cran.r-project.org/web/packages/geosphere/`) and, like the Python PyGeodesy package, it is inspired by the code released by Chris Veness and Charles Karney.

First, you need to install this new package:

1. Open RStudio and make sure it is referencing your latest CRAN R (version 4.2.2 in our case).
2. Click on the Console window and type this command: `install.packages('geosphere')`. Then, press **Enter**.

You are now ready to develop your code in R. In addition to the usual packages that allow you to read CSV and Excel files (`readr` and `readxl`) and facilitate data transformation operations (`dplyr` and `purrr`), you will, of course, need to load the package you just installed.

You can easily import hotel data into the `hotels_tbl` tibble using the `read_xlsx()` function and airport data into the `airport_tbl` tibble using the `read_csv()` function. At this point, the first operation to do is to split the contents of the coordinates column of `airports_tbl` into two new columns, `longitude` and `latitude`:

```
airports_tbl <- airports_tbl %>%
    tidyr::separate(
        col = coordinates,
        into = c('longitude', 'latitude'),
        sep = ', ',
        remove = TRUE,
        convert = TRUE )
```

Note the simplicity of using the `separate` function from the `tidyr` package:

1. The pipe passes the `airports_tbl` tibble as the first parameter for the function.
2. Declare the column to be split (`col = coordinates`).
3. Declare the two new target columns (`into = c('longitude', 'latitude')`).
4. Declare the separator found in the values of the column to be split (`sep = ', '`).
5. Remove the column to be split when the transformation is complete (`remove = TRUE`).
6. Let the data type of the target columns convert automatically if they are numeric columns (`convert = TRUE`).

Do it all in one step with maximum clarity. It's one of the reasons data analysts love R!

Again, we use a function to conveniently access the longitude and latitude values of a given airport. It is the `airportLongLatVec()` function, and it takes as parameters both a dataframe containing the airport data with the `iata_code`, `latitude`, and `longitude` columns and the specific IATA code of the airport of interest:

```
airportLongLatVec <- function(df, iata) {
    ret_vec <- df %>%
        filter( iata_code == iata ) %>%
        select( longitude, latitude ) %>%
        unlist()
    return(ret_vec)
}
```

The output is a named vector. So, the coordinates of the two airports can be easily found in this way:

```
jfk_coordinates <- airportLongLatVec(airports_tbl, 'JFK')
lga_coordinates <- airportLongLatVec(airports_tbl, 'LGA')
```

You are pretty much ready to transform the data. From the geosphere package, you will use the distHaversine() and distGeo() functions. The first one is self-explanatory. The distGeo() function calculates the shortest distance between two points on an ellipsoid according to Karney's formulas. Both functions take two pairs of coordinates (in the order of longitude and latitude) in vector form. To get the same results as in Python, the distHaversine() function must accept as a parameter the same mean radius of the Earth sphere model used by default by PyGeodesy. The radius in question is R1 (mean radius) as defined by the **International Union of Geodesy and Geophysics (IUGG)**, which is 6,371,008.771415 meters.

At this point, the enrichment operation on the hotels_tbl tibble can be performed using the map() family of functions from the purrr package that we have already seen. In the first step, we create a new column, p1, containing the latitude and longitude pairs in a vector using the map2() function. In the second step, we apply the distHaversine() and distGeo() functions to the newly created point, p1, and to the fixed points identifying the airports (jfk_coordinates and lga_coordinates) to create the new columns containing the distances. This is the required code:

```
hotels_tbl <- hotels_tbl %>%
mutate(
p1 = map2(longitude, latitude, ~ c(.x, .y))
    ) %>%
mutate(
haversineDistanceFromJFK = map_dbl(p1, ~ distHaversine(p1 = .x, p2 = jfk_
coordinates, r = 6371008.771415)),
karneyDistanceFromJFK = map_dbl(p1, ~ distGeo(p1 = .x, p2 = jfk_coordinates)),
haversineDistanceFromLGA = map_dbl(p1, ~ distHaversine(p1 = .x, p2 = lga_
coordinates, r = 6371008.771415)),
karneyDistanceFromLGA = map_dbl(p1, ~ distGeo(p1 = .x, p2 = lga_coordinates))
    ) %>%
select( -p1 )
```

Recall that the map2() function takes two vectors as input and executes them in parallel to pass their values to the function used after the ~ symbol (in our case, the c() function, which declares a vector). The map_dbl() function instead takes as input the column p1 (which contains the geographic coordinates of the hotels in vector format) and passes its elements to the function after the ~ (in our case, distGeo() and distHaversine() with other fixed parameters), which transforms the output into a vector of double numeric data types.

If you run the code for the 01-distances-from-airports-in-r.R file in the R folder, you'll get something like this:

```
# A tibble: 100 x 15
   objectId   latitude longitude name              type  address stars phone website state city  haver..'  karne..² haver..³ karne..⁴
   <chr>         <dbl>     <dbl> <chr>             <chr> <chr>   <dbl> <chr> <chr>   <chr> <chr>    <dbl>    <dbl>    <dbl>    <dbl>
 1 E4tVCEHyZd     40.8     -74.0 Element    es Square ... HOTEL 311 We...    3 1844... http:/... New ... New ... 22103.   22131.   10314.   10339.
 2 L1kEZgwRDA     40.8     -74.0 Sanctua    York Times... HOTEL 132 We...    4 1646... http:/... New ... New ... 21697.   21721.    9541.    9564.
 3 KyHuNG0abX     40.7     -74.0 The Jai           HOTEL 113 Ja...    2 +1 2... http:/... New ... New ... 22310.   22346.   12317.   12342.
 4 BKp7Egdj1m     40.8     -74.0 Hotel             HOTEL  27 W 7...    0 NA    NA      New ... New ... 22651.   22669.    8832.    8855.
 5 BvCu5xD7VF     40.8     -74.0 Fairfii    es New Yor... HOTEL 338 We...    2 1844... https:... New ... New ... 22157.   22185.   10569.   10593.
 6 22toTizkAB     40.7     -74.0 Sohote            HOTEL 341 Br...    3 1646... http:/... New ... New ... 20247.   20284.   12123.   12141.
 7 NCh0nzaBLj     40.8     -74.0 Amerit     square   HOTEL 230 we...    3 1646... http:/... New ... New ... 22065.   22088.    9398.    9421.
 8 Z2oxs3wPwR     40.7     -74.0 Lafaye            HOTEL  38 E 4...    3 +1 2... http:/... New ... New ... 20440.   20474.   11498.   11517.
 9 NhhvKalduo     40.7     -74.0 The Hoi           HOTEL  91 E B...    3 NA    http:/... New ... New ... 19875.   19913.   12422.   12438.
10 16c4HxxlCD     40.8     -74.0 Nation     ers      HOTEL 315 W ...    0 NA    NA      New ... New ... 22342.   22364.    9426.    9449.
# ... with 90 more rows, and abbreviated    ¹haversineDistanceFromJFK, ²karneyDistanceFromJFK, ³haversineDistanceFromLGA,
#   ⁴karneyDistanceFromLGA
```

Figure 12.12: The enriched hotels tibble with distances

Wow! You were able to calculate both the Haversine and Karney distances between all hotels and both airports also using R. At this point, it is straightforward to use similar code to calculate distances in Power BI. Let's see how to do it.

Calculating distances in Power BI with R

It's time to implement what you've just learned in Power BI. So, launch Power BI Desktop and let's get going:

1. Make sure Power BI Desktop is referencing your latest engine in **Options**. After that, click on the **Excel** workbook to import the hotels-ny.xlsx file, which you can find in the Chapter 12 folder. Select it and click **Open**.

2. Select the **Sheet 1** table from the **Navigator** window:

Navigator

Figure 12.13: Selecting the Sheet 1 table

3. Then, click on **Transform Data**.

4. Click on the **Transform** menu and then click on **Run R script**.

5. Copy the script from the 02-distances-from-airports-in-power-bi-with-r.R file from the R folder into the R script editor. Edit the path as needed and click **OK**.

6. We are only interested in the data in the **hotels_df** table. So, click on its **Table** value.

7. Power Query transforms your data by adding the distances from each hotel to the two airports, JFK and LGA, for the two methods, Haversines and Karney:

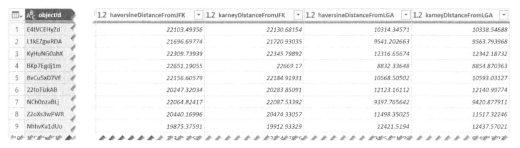

	A^B_C objectId	1.2 haversineDistanceFromJFK	1.2 karneyDistanceFromJFK	1.2 haversineDistanceFromLGA	1.2 karneyDistanceFromLGA
1	E4tVCEHyZd	22103.49356	22130.68154	10314.34571	10338.54688
2	L1kEZgwRDA	21696.69774	21720.93035	9541.202663	9563.793968
3	KyHuNG0abX	22309.73939	22345.79892	12316.65674	12342.18732
4	BKp7Egdj1m	22651.19055	22669.17	8832.33648	8854.870363
5	BvCu5xD7VF	22156.60579	22184.91931	10568.50502	10593.03127
6	22toTizkAB	20247.32034	20283.85091	12123.16112	12140.99774
7	NCh0nzaBLj	22064.82417	22087.53392	9397.765642	9420.877911
8	Z2oXs3wPWR	20440.16996	20474.33057	11498.35025	11517.32246
9	NhhvKa1dUo	19875.37591	19912.93329	12421.5194	12437.57021

Figure 12.14: The result of the R script transformation

8. You can then click **Close & Apply** in the **Home** tab.

Great! You just enriched your data by adding distances between two geographical points in Power BI using R.

The distance between two strings

When considering the concept of distance, our first thoughts often focus on measuring the physical space between two points in a well-defined environment. Whether it's solving problems in plane geometry or navigating the three-dimensional world we inhabit, distance plays a crucial role. However, it is important to recognize that the concept of distance extends beyond physical dimensions.

Some theory first

As you may recall from the introductory part of this chapter, there are numerous domains where distance is of immense importance in describing events and relationships. One such domain that may surprise you is *the space defined by strings of text*. Surprisingly, this includes the mathematical domain represented by strings of text. This domain encompasses a set or a range of all conceivable values or arrangements that can be embodied by an entity such as a string of text. That's right – it is perfectly possible to construct a meaningful metric for measuring the distance between two different strings of text. Here is a look at some of the most common distances in use today. Of course, this is not an exhaustive list.

The Hamming distance

In 1950, Hamming introduced the revolutionary **Hamming distance**, a simple yet powerful metric for measuring the dissimilarity between two strings of equal length. By counting the positions where the characters differ, this intuitive measure quickly became the go-to solution for error detection and correction codes in information theory.

However, while Hamming distance offers simplicity and clarity with a linear computational complexity of $O(n)$, its applicability is limited to strings of equal length and only considers single-character substitutions. As technology advanced and the need for more robust string distance measures arose, researchers and scientists pushed the boundaries of the field and unveiled more sophisticated techniques that take into account various operations involving multiple characters. One of them is the Levenshtein distance. Let's see what it is.

The Levenshtein distance

After the Hamming distance, the next string distance that gained significant popularity and importance was the **Levenshtein distance**. The Levenshtein distance, also known as the **edit distance**, is a metric used to measure the difference between two strings. It is applicable to strings of different lengths and calculates the minimum number of single-character edits (*insertions*, *deletions*, or *substitutions*) required to transform one string into another:

"Michael Jackson" to *"Mendelssohn"*

Figure 12.15: An example of a Levenshtein distance calculation

In *Figure 12.15*, each character transformation is associated with its respective operation type (no operation shown by a dash, insertion, deletion, or substitution).

Although the Levenshtein distance is relatively easy to understand and is used in a wide range of applications, it has some problems:

- Computing the Levenshtein distance between long strings is computationally expensive due to its quadratic time complexity $O(n2)$.
- It treats all edit operations as equally costly, which might not reflect the real-world significance of different types of edits.

- It does not explicitly account for *transpositions*, where two adjacent characters are swapped.
- It does not consider the context or meaning of the strings being compared, focusing solely on the number of edits required.

The transpositions problem is solved by an extension of the algorithm, which is named the **Damerau-Levenshtein distance**. Particularly useful in applications where transpositions are common, such as spell checking and **optical character recognition (OCR)**, it provides a more accurate measure of similarity between strings by accounting for the possibility that adjacent characters may be swapped. The computational complexity of calculating the Damerau-Levenshtein distance is slightly higher than that of the Levenshtein distance due to the additional transposition operation. There is also an extended version of the Damerau-Levenshtein distance that incorporates weighting or assigning different costs to individual edit operations. This variant is commonly known as the **Weighted Damerau-Levenshtein** distance.

While the Levenshtein distance provides a versatile measure of string similarity, another distance has gained prominence in applications such as name matching and record linkage, where handling transpositions and incorporating the prefix scale factor prove advantageous. Let's see what the distance is.

The Jaro-Winkler distance

The **Jaro-Winkler distance** was created by William E. Winkler in 1990 as an extension of the earlier Jaro distance introduced by Matthew Jaro in 1989. The Jaro-Winkler distance emerged as a specialized measure of similarity, specifically designed for comparing strings of short to medium length. It finds application in tasks such as name matching and record linkage, where dealing with transpositions and incorporating the *prefix scale factor* offers advantages. The **prefix scale factor** provides a higher similarity score for strings that share a common prefix, which is valuable in tasks such as name matching, where common prefixes such as surnames can help identify related records. Jaro-Winkler only considers matching characters and any necessary transpositions but gives them less weight. Since transpositions are less common in real-world data, the distance metric reflects this by reducing their impact on the overall similarity score.

The Jaro-Winkler distance also has some issues:

- Similar to other string distance metrics, the Jaro-Winkler distance does not take into account the context or meaning of the strings being compared. It treats all characters and operations equally, focusing only on the number of matching characters, transpositions, and prefix scale factor.
- The Jaro-Winkler distance is sensitive to string length, as longer strings can result in a higher number of transpositions and potentially affect the similarity score.
- While the Jaro-Winkler distance incorporates weighting for transpositions and the prefix scale factor, it does not provide the flexibility to assign different weights to other types of edits based on specific domain considerations.
- It can be computationally expensive due to its quadratic time complexity $O(n2)$.

From a mathematical point of view, Wikipedia reports the Jaro similarity definition as follows:

Jaro similarity   [edit]

The Jaro similarity sim_j of two given strings s_1 and s_2 is

$$sim_j = \begin{cases} 0 & \text{if } m = 0 \\ \frac{1}{3}\left(\frac{m}{|s_1|} + \frac{m}{|s_2|} + \frac{m-t}{m}\right) & \text{otherwise} \end{cases}$$

Where:

- $|s_i|$ is the length of the string s_i;
- m is the number of *matching characters* (see below);
- t is the number of *transpositions* (see below).

Figure 12.16: Mathematical definition of Jaro similarity

It also reports the Winkler modification as follows:

Jaro–Winkler similarity   [edit]

Jaro–Winkler similarity uses a prefix scale p which gives more favorable ratings to strings that match from the beginning for a set prefix length ℓ. Given two strings s_1 and s_2, their Jaro–Winkler similarity sim_w is:

$$sim_w = sim_j + \ell p(1 - sim_j),$$

where:

- sim_j is the Jaro similarity for strings s_1 and s_2
- ℓ is the length of common prefix at the start of the string up to a maximum of 4 characters
- p is a constant scaling factor for how much the score is adjusted upwards for having common prefixes. p should not exceed 0.25 (i.e. 1/4, with 4 being the maximum length of the prefix being considered), otherwise the similarity could become larger than 1. The standard value for this constant in Winkler's work is $p = 0.1$

The Jaro–Winkler distance d_w is defined as $d_w = 1 - sim_w$.

Figure 12.17: Mathematical definition of the Jaro-Winkler similarity

In addition to what we have seen so far, there are distance values that treat string characters from the point of view of a specific set of characters. One of them is the *Jaccard distance*.

The Jaccard distance

Jaccard distance is a widely used measure that quantifies the dissimilarity between two sets or binary vectors. It is based on Jaccard similarity (*Jaccard distance = 1 – Jaccard similarity*), which indicates the proportion of common elements or features between sets. Jaccard similarity is calculated by dividing the size of the intersection of two sets by the size of their union. The formula for Jaccard similarity is as follows: $J(A, B) = |A \cap B| / |A \cup B|$.

Basically, it focuses on the presence or absence of elements, disregarding their order or frequency. This makes it particularly useful in scenarios where set membership or binary feature comparison is important. It is effective when dealing with categorical data or binary features, such as document analysis (bag-of-words representation), set comparison, and clustering.

You may wonder how it is possible to use the Jaccard distance for strings when it is based on the ensemble concept. Quite simply, it is possible to make two types of assumptions for Jaccard similarity:

- *Character-based Jaccard similarity*: Each character in the string is treated as an element of a set. The sets are constructed by considering the unique characters present in each string.
- *Token-based Jaccard similarity*: The strings are split into **tokens**, which can be words, **q-grams** (contiguous sequences of q characters), or any other meaningful unit of text. Then the tokens in each string are treated as elements of a set, and Jaccard similarity is computed by comparing the sets of tokens.

IMPORTANT NOTE

Sometimes you can find n-gram instead of q-gram. The terms are interchangeable.

The weaknesses of Jaccard's distance are as follows:

- It is sensitive to the size of the sets being compared. Larger sets tend to have lower Jaccard similarity values, leading to higher Jaccard distances. This sensitivity can introduce bias or misinterpretation, especially when comparing sets of significantly different sizes.
- It does not provide detailed information about the specific elements that differ between sets. It only indicates the overall dissimilarity without distinguishing between different types or categories of differences.
- It can be computationally expensive due to its quadratic time complexity $O(n2)$.

That being said, let's take a look at some guidelines for figuring out what distance to use in a particular use case.

What kind of distance to use and when

The list of distances presented in this section is not exhaustive but simply reports the distances most commonly used to calculate the similarity of two strings. For example, there are algorithms that consider phonetic matching between strings (such as the *Match Rating Approach* algorithm) that were not included in the list. However, there are general principles for selecting specific distances for data analysis, regardless of the algorithms being considered.

To determine the best distance for a particular use case, first consider the following:

1. Determine the type of data you are working with. Is it binary, categorical, or continuous? This will help narrow down the choice of distance metrics.
2. Analyze the specific characteristics of the strings you are comparing. Consider factors such as length, the presence of typographical errors, or the need for order-independent comparison.

3. Clearly define the requirements of your task. Identify the specific aspects of string similarity or dissimilarity that are important for your application.

After that, you can start looking at specific distances as follows:

- For binary or categorical data of equal length, Hamming distance is a suitable choice.
- For strings with insertions, deletions, substitutions, and transpositions, Damerau-Levenshtein distance is appropriate.
- For strings with slight typographical errors, Jaro-Winkler distance can be effective.
- For comparing strings seen as a set of characters, Jaccard distance is a good option.
- And so on, considering any other algorithm.

When faced with the task of choosing a distance metric for your data, it's often helpful to consider several candidates and compare their performance. The process involves applying each metric to a representative subset of your data and evaluating the results based on certain factors. Two important factors to consider are *accuracy* and *computational efficiency*:

- The accuracy of a distance metric refers to how effectively it captures the desired similarity or dissimilarity between data points. Different distance metrics have different properties and assumptions, and they may be more suitable for specific types of data or applications. By evaluating the accuracy of each metric, you can determine which one best represents the relationships or patterns in your data.
- Another crucial consideration is the computational complexity of each distance metric, especially if you are working with large datasets. Some distance metrics require more computational resources and time to calculate than others. As a result, the efficiency of the metric becomes important when dealing with significant amounts of data.

After evaluating the results of applying multiple distance metrics to your data, it's important to refine your selection by considering trade-offs and the specific characteristics of your data and task. This refinement process often involves iterating and trying different distance metrics or adjusting parameters to find the best fit.

Note that if a single distance measure between strings does not meet your needs, you can combine multiple ones to create a new final normalized measure. Here's a general approach you can follow:

1. Familiarize yourself with the string distance metrics you want to combine.
2. Normalize each string distance metric to ensure that they have a consistent range or scale. Normalize them to a common range, such as [0, 1], where 0 represents no similarity and 1 represents exact similarity.
3. Determine the importance or relevance of each string distance metric to the final combined measure. Assign weights to each metric based on their significance or the specific requirements of your application.
4. Combine the normalized metrics ($m1, ..., mn$). A common approach is, for example, the weighted average (weights $w1, ..., wn$):

$$\text{combined measure} = \frac{w_1 m_1 \cdots w_n m_n}{w_1 + \cdots + w_n}$$

5. After combining the individual metrics, it's important to normalize the final combined metric to ensure it falls within the desired range, typically [0, 1]. If necessary, you can apply additional scaling or transformation techniques to achieve the desired normalization.

Now, let's look at a simple use case for the use of text distances in Python.

Deduplicating strings using Python and R

Imagine that you have been tasked with **deduplicating** a dataset that contains a column with some information in the form of strings. While these strings are not identical, they bear a striking resemblance to each other, indicating potential duplicates. The challenge is to identify and eliminate these duplicates to streamline data processing and analysis. In the field of data processing and analysis, the task of deduplicating information is a common challenge faced by many professionals. As datasets grow larger and more complex, the presence of duplicate records can hinder effective data management and analysis.

So let's see how to solve this duplicate problem with Python.

Deduplicating emails with Python

As an example, consider a small dataset that contains an email field associated with a person. There are several similar emails having the same domain associated with the same person in the dataset. Your goal is to eliminate the many similar email rows and leave only one. The data is provided in JSON format and can be found in the `email-addresses-to-dedup.json` file in the `Chapter 12` folder. A snippet of it, transformed into tabular form, is shown below:

	Name	Email	Phone Number
0	Amanda Scott	amanda.scott2@example.com	555-8888
1	Johnathan Garcia	johnathan.garcia2@example.com	555-9999
2	John Smith	jsmith@example.com	555-4321
3	Jane Doe	janed@example.com	555-8765
4	David Johnson	davidjo@example.com	555-9012
5	Sarah Miller	smiller@example.com	555-3456
6	Michael Brown	mbrown@example.com	555-7890
7	Emily Davis	edavis@example.com	555-2345

Figure 12.18: Extract of data to be deduplicated

Duplicates will appear after the first 15 lines (there are 15 unique names):

	Name	Email	Phone Number
0	Amanda Scott	amanda.scott2@example.com	555-8888
1	Johnathan Garcia	johnathan.garcia2@example.com	555-9999
2	John Smith	jsmith@example.com	555-4321
...	...	...	...
15	Amanda Scott	amanda.scott3@example.com	555-8888
16	Johnathan Garcia	johnathan.garcia3@example.com	555-9999
17	John Smith	j.smith@example.com	555-4321

Figure 12.19: Duplicated strings in evidence

In *Figure 12.19*, you can better see the duplicate emails we are talking about. It is very easy to identify them by eye, but how can you do it from an analytical point of view? This is where the distances between strings come in handy.

The basic idea behind implementing email deduplication is as follows:

1. An initially empty set is created to contain the unique emails.
2. For each row in the source dataset, the email associated with that row is extracted and then compared to each email in the set of unique emails by calculating the similarity (or distance, your choice) between them.
3. If the calculated similarity is greater (or the distance is less) than the given threshold, then the email extracted from the row is considered a duplicate. Otherwise, the extracted email is considered unique with respect to the set of unique emails and is added to this set.
4. The process identified in *steps 2* and *3* is repeated for each row of the source dataset.

The algorithm is fairly simple and straightforward, but before you implement it in Python, you need to understand how you want to calculate the distance between two strings. As you can well imagine, for the usual principle that it is not worth reinventing the wheel every time, you will use an existing package that is widely used by the analyst community. We are talking about the **TextDistance** package (https://github.com/life4/textdistance), a Python library for comparing distance and similarity between sequences by many algorithms.

The library is written in Python and is therefore not very performant compared to algorithms written in C++. That's why it is recommended to install the package with extras that provide additional libraries for maximum speed. The main algorithms in TextDistance try to call known external libraries (fastest first) if available (installed on your system) and possible (this implementation can compare this type of sequences).

Let's see how to install TextDistance including extras:

1. Open **Anaconda Prompt**.

2. Switch to the `pbi_powerquery_env` environment, enter the `conda activate pbi_powerquery_env` command, and then press **Enter**.

3. Install the `textdistance` package, by typing `pip install textdistance[extras]==4.5.0`, and then press **Enter**.

You may encounter an error when installing additional packages. When you install packages using `pip`, it first checks if a *wheel* is available for your specific platform and Python version. **Wheels** are precompiled package formats for Python. They contain pre-built binaries that can be installed directly without the need for compiling the source code. Unfortunately, not all packages have wheels available for all platforms or Python versions. In such cases, you will need to install additional tools to compile and build the packages from source. The process of building packages from source involves compiling the source code into binary code that your computer can run. This compilation process ensures that the package is compatible with the specific version of Python you're using and any other dependencies it requires. To facilitate this compilation and packaging process, `pip` often relies on tools such as compilers, linkers, and other development libraries that are specific to your operating system and version of Python. On Windows machines, you may need to install the *Microsoft Visual C++ Build Tools*, which includes the necessary compilers and libraries.

Let's see how to do it in case you need it:

1. Go to the web page `https://visualstudio.microsoft.com/visual-cpp-build-tools/` and click the **Download Build Tools** button on the left.

2. Run the executable and click **Continue** on the next window.

3. Select the **Desktop development with C++** option at the top left of the next window. Then leave only the first two optional installation details selected on the right (**MSVC – VS 2022 C++ x64/x86 build tools** and **Windows 11 SDK,** regardless of versions):

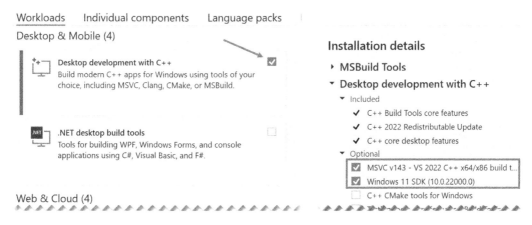

Figure 12.20: Installing Visual Studio Build Tools

Then click **Install while downloading.**

Once the Visual Studio build tools are installed, you can try to install TextDistance again using the `pip` command shown above. This time the installation will be successful.

TextDistance exposes different metrics for each distance algorithm it performs. For example, if we consider the Jaccard distance exposed by the `textdistance.jaccard` object, it takes as input a sequence of two or more strings to compare and exposes some defined metrics as follows:

- `distance()`: Calculate the distance between sequences.
- `similarity()`: Calculate similarity for sequences.
- `normalized_distance()`: Normalized distance between sequences. The return value is a float between 0 and 1, where 0 means equal, and 1 means totally different.
- `normalized_similarity()`: Normalized similarity for sequences. The return value is a float between 0 and 1, where 0 means totally different, and 1 means equal.

You can also invoke classes associated with the algorithms that allow you to change the comparison behavior by appropriately setting some input parameters. Most of them apply to all algorithms. For example, the `textdistance.Jaccard()` class takes the following parameters as tuning options:

- `qval`: Split sequences into q-grams. If 1 (default), then compare sequences of chars. If 2 or more, compare sequences of q-grams.
- `as_set`: Used in token-based algorithms. If `False` (default), then t is different from ttt. If `True`, then t is equal to ttt.
- `external`: If `True` (default), then use external libraries if available. If `False`, then use only internal algorithms.

There may also be parameters that are specific to the algorithm being used, which unfortunately are not well documented (only the source code can help you in this case). For example, the `textdistance.JaroWinkler()` class also takes the following specific parameters as input:

- `long_tolerance`: If `False` (default), don't adjust for long strings. If `True`, after matching leading characters, at least two or more must match, and matched characters must be greater than half of the remaining characters.
- `winklerize`: If `True` (default), apply the modification made by Winkler. If `False`, don't apply it.

When working with the Jaccard algorithm in TextDistance, you must be careful about the parameters to be used:

> To **adhere** to the standard definition of Jaccard similarity, items must be considered from a set perspective. In TextDistance, you then need to instantiate the `textdistance.Jaccard` class by setting the `as_set` parameter to `True`. If you use the `textdistance.jaccard` method directly, the intersection and union of the items would be calculated by not considering the elements uniquely, and the Jaccard similarity will have a different value than the usual one by definition.

That said, the algorithm described in meta language at the beginning of this section is as follows in Python:

```
import pandas as pd
import textdistance
```

```python
def deduplicate_data(data, similarity_metric,similarity_threshold):

    new_columns = data.columns.to_list()
    new_columns.append('Best Comparison')
    new_columns.append('Similarity')

    # Create a new DataFrame to store the deduplicated records
    deduplicated_data = pd.DataFrame(columns=new_columns)
    duplicated_data = pd.DataFrame(columns=new_columns)

    # Create a set to keep track of unique emails
    unique_emails = set()

    # Iterate through each row in the original dataset
    for index, row in data.iterrows():
        email = row['Email']
        is_duplicate = False
        best_comparison = ''
        best_similarity_score = 0.0

        # Compare the current email with unique emails using the
        # chosen similarity metric for unique_email in unique_emails:
            similarity_score = similarity_metric.normalized_similarity(email,
unique_email)

        # If the similarity score exceeds the threshold,
        # consider it a duplicate
            if similarity_score > similarity_threshold:
                is_duplicate = True

                df_to_append = pd.DataFrame([row])
                df_to_append['Best Comparison'] = unique_email
                df_to_append['Similarity'] = similarity_score

                duplicated_data = pd.concat(
                    [duplicated_data, df_to_append],
                    axis=0, ignore_index=True)
                break

            if similarity_score > best_similarity_score:
```

```
                    best_similarity_score = similarity_score
                    best_comparison = unique_email


        # If it's not a duplicate, add it to the deduplicated
        # dataset if not is_duplicate:
            unique_emails.add(email)

            df_to_append = pd.DataFrame([row])
            df_to_append['Best Comparison'] = best_comparison
            df_to_append['Similarity'] = best_similarity_score

            deduplicated_data = pd.concat(
                [deduplicated_data, df_to_append],
                axis=0, ignore_index=True)

    deduplicated_data.sort_values(by=['Name'], inplace=True)
    duplicated_data.sort_values(by=['Name'], inplace=True)

    # Return datasets
    return deduplicated_data, duplicated_data
```

All of the code used in this section can be found in the Python\03-deduplicate-emails.py file in *Chapter 12*.

The previous function returns two dataframes, one with the deduplicated data and one with the data that is considered duplicate. The function adds the email information and similarity value for the most similar comparison in the case of the deduplication dataset; it adds the email information and similarity value that contributed to the instance being considered a duplicate in the case of the duplications dataset. Notice how the algorithm uses the normalized similarity measure to calculate the closeness between strings. If you wanted, you could modify it to use the normalized distance or another measure of your choice.

By testing the standard Jaccard algorithm and considering a similarity threshold of 0.875 (chosen after a few tries), the following occurs:

```
deduplicated_data_jaccard, duplicated_data_jaccard = deduplicate_data(data,
    similarity_metric=textdistance.Jaccard(as_set=True),
    similarity_threshold=0.875)

deduplicated_data_jaccard
```

✓ 0.8s

	Name	Email	Phone Number	Best Comparison	Similarity
0	Amanda Scott	amanda.scott2@example.com	555-8888		0.000000
15	Amanda Scott	amanda.scott3@example.com	555-8888	amanda.scott2@example.com	0.875000
17	Amanda Scott	amanda.scott4@example.com	555-8888	amanda.scott3@example.com	0.875000
12	Brian Martinez	bmartinez@example.com	555-5555	mbrown@example.com	0.764706
4	David Johnson	davidjo@example.com	555-9012	janed@example.com	0.800000
16	David Johnson	d.johnson@example.com	555-9012	janed@example.com	0.866667
7	Emily Davis	edavis@example.com	555-2345	davidjo@example.com	0.866667
10	Eric Thompson	ethompson@example.com	555-3333	amanda.scott2@example.com	0.812500
3	Jane Doe	janed@example.com	555-8765	amanda.scott2@example.com	0.750000
8	Jason Lee	jlee@example.com	555-1111	janed@example.com	0.846154
13	Jessica Harris	jharris@example.com	555-6666	jsmith@example.com	0.875000
2	John Smith	jsmith@example.com	555-4321	johnathan.garcia2@example.com	0.736842
1	Johnathan Garcia	johnathan.garcia2@example.com	555-9999	amanda.scott2@example.com	0.650000
14	Kevin Turner	kturner@example.com	555-7777	bmartinez@example.com	0.722222
11	Lisa Anderson	landerson@example.com	555-4444	rwilson@example.com	0.812500

Figure 12.21: Using the standard Jaccard algorithm to deduplicate emails

As you can see in *Figure 12.21*, Jaccard's default algorithm does quite a good job. We found 0.875 to be the best choice, since it returns the most deduplicated emails. There is only a problem with Amanda Scott's emails *amanda.scott3* and *amanda.scott4*, which are only 0.875 away from *amanda.scott2*. The same similarity score is calculated between Jessica Harris' email and John Smith's email (highlighted in yellow). This means that if we lowered the threshold to 0.874 to prevent Amanda Scott's duplicates from entering, we would exclude Jessica Harris's email from the deduplication dataframe, which at this point is considered to be a duplicate of John Smith. In addition, David Johnson's two email addresses (*davidjo* and *d.johnson*) are considered to be completely different and not duplicates. In fact, each of them is considered to be more similar to the e-mail address of Jane Doe (*janed*) than to each other.

If you are curious about the similarity values identified in the matches that resulted in duplicates, you can inspect the `duplicated_data_jaccard` dataset returned by the previous function call:

```
duplicated_data_jaccard
```
✓ 0.3s

	Name	Email	Phone Number	Best Comparison	Similarity
10	Brian Martinez	b.martinez@example.com	555-5555	bmartinez@example.com	1.000000
5	Emily Davis	e.davis@example.com	555-2345	edavis@example.com	1.000000
8	Eric Thompson	e.thompson@example.com	555-3333	ethompson@example.com	1.000000
2	Jane Doe	jdoe@example.com	555-8765	jlee@example.com	0.916667
6	Jason Lee	j.lee@example.com	555-1111	jlee@example.com	1.000000
11	Jessica Harris	j.harris@example.com	555-6666	jharris@example.com	1.000000
1	John Smith	j.smith@example.com	555-4321	jsmith@example.com	1.000000

Figure 12.22: Checking the similarity values of duplicated data returned by the standard Jaccard algorithm

Let us try using the more complex Jaro-Winkler algorithm and a similarity threshold of 0.89 (which we found after trying different values):

```
deduplicated_data_jaro_winkler, duplicated_data_jaro_winkler = deduplicate_data(data,
    similarity_metric=textdistance.jaro_winkler,
    similarity_threshold=0.89)

deduplicated_data_jaro_winkler
```
✓ 0.9s

	Name	Email	Phone Number	Best Comparison	Similarity
0	Amanda Scott	amanda.scott2@example.com	555-8888		0.000000
12	Brian Martinez	bmartinez@example.com	555-5555	landerson@example.com	0.820437
4	David Johnson	davidjo@example.com	555-9012	jsmith@example.com	0.790588
15	David Johnson	d.johnson@example.com	555-9012	davidjo@example.com	0.851128
7	Emily Davis	edavis@example.com	555-2345	janed@example.com	0.883007
10	Eric Thompson	ethompson@example.com	555-3333	smiller@example.com	0.745698
3	Jane Doe	janed@example.com	555-8765	jsmith@example.com	0.753771
8	Jason Lee	jlee@example.com	555-1111	janed@example.com	0.866702
13	Jessica Harris	jharris@example.com	555-6666	jsmith@example.com	0.863048
2	John Smith	jsmith@example.com	555-4321	johnathan.garcia2@example.com	0.688538
1	Johnathan Garcia	johnathan.garcia2@example.com	555-9999	amanda.scott2@example.com	0.759475
14	Kevin Turner	kturner@example.com	555-7777	janed@example.com	0.853457
11	Lisa Anderson	landerson@example.com	555-4444	smiller@example.com	0.805503
6	Michael Brown	mbrown@example.com	555-7890	jsmith@example.com	0.814815
9	Rachel Wilson	rwilson@example.com	555-2222	mbrown@example.com	0.889498
5	Sarah Miller	smiller@example.com	555-3456	jsmith@example.com	0.807602

Figure 12.23: Using the standard Jaro-Winkler algorithm to deduplicate emails

In general, the Jaro-Winkler algorithm also does a very good job. Unfortunately, it also fails to solve the case of David Johnson's emails. In fact, if we look at the second case of the two matches highlighted in the box in *Figure 12.23*, we see that the similarity between David Johnson's two emails is also quite high according to Jaro-Winkler (0.85). However, if we try to lower the threshold from 0.89 to 0.85, David Johnson's emails will be correctly deduplicated, but we lose all the unique emails with similarity values between 0.85 and 0.89 that are now considered duplicates (e.g., Jessica Harris will be considered a duplicate of John Smith with a similarity of 0.86, as highlighted in red).

So should we throw in the towel and give up on the idea of properly deduplicating emails? If you recall, we said that the algorithms we have seen use sequences of characters taken individually by default. But what if, instead of using sequences of individual characters, we used sequences of *q-grams* obtained by splitting the strings to be compared? Let's see what happens when we apply the Jaccard algorithm to *3-grams* and consider a similarity threshold of 0.55:

```
deduplicated_data_jaccard_3grams, duplicated_data_jaccard_3grams = deduplicate_data(data,
    similarity_metric=textdistance.Jaccard(qval=3),
    similarity_threshold=0.55)

deduplicated_data_jaccard_3grams
```

✓ 0.1s

	Name	Email	Phone Number	Best Comparison	Similarity
0	Amanda Scott	amanda.scott2@example.com	555-8888		0.000000
9	Brian Martinez	bmartinez@example.com	555-5555	jlee@example.com	0.434783
4	David Johnson	davidjo@example.com	555-9012	janed@example.com	0.454545
12	Emily Davis	e.davis@example.com	555-2345	jharris@example.com	0.545455
13	Eric Thompson	e.thompson@example.com	555-3333	rwilson@example.com	0.541667
3	Jane Doe	janed@example.com	555-8765	jsmith@example.com	0.476190
7	Jason Lee	jlee@example.com	555-1111	janed@example.com	0.526316
10	Jessica Harris	jharris@example.com	555-6666	jlee@example.com	0.476190
2	John Smith	jsmith@example.com	555-4321	amanda.scott2@example.com	0.344828
1	Johnathan Garcia	johnathan.garcia2@example.com	555-9999	amanda.scott2@example.com	0.282051
11	Kevin Turner	kturner@example.com	555-7777	smiller@example.com	0.545455
14	Lisa Anderson	l.anderson@example.com	555-4444	rwilson@example.com	0.541667
6	Michael Brown	mbrown@example.com	555-7890	janed@example.com	0.476190
8	Rachel Wilson	rwilson@example.com	555-2222	mbrown@example.com	0.500000
5	Sarah Miller	smiller@example.com	555-3456	jsmith@example.com	0.500000

Figure 12.24: Using the Jaccard algorithm applied to 3-grams to deduplicate emails

Wow! Using the 3-grams and a threshold of 0.55, Jaccard's algorithm correctly deduplicates all email addresses! Obviously, the 3-grams make Jessica Harris's and John Smith's emails in *Figure 12.21* have much less overlapping between them, so we can correctly deduplicate Amanda Scott's ones with an appropriate threshold.

What if we also used the 3-grams with the Jaro-Winkler algorithm: would we be able to correctly deduplicate all emails? Let's see:

```
deduplicated_data_jaro_winkler_3grams, duplicated_data_jaro_winkler_3grams = deduplicate_data(data,
    similarity_metric=textdistance.JaroWinkler(qval=3),
    similarity_threshold=0.81)

deduplicated_data_jaro_winkler_3grams
```
✓ 0.9s

	Name	Email	Phone Number	Best Comparison	Similarity
0	Amanda Scott	amanda.scott2@example.com	555-8888		0.000000
9	Brian Martinez	bmartinez@example.com	555-5555	jlee@example.com	0.746867
4	David Johnson	davidjo@example.com	555-9012	janed@example.com	0.751634
12	Emily Davis	e.davis@example.com	555-2345	jharris@example.com	0.803922
13	Eric Thompson	e.thompson@example.com	555-3333	rwilson@example.com	0.804902
3	Jane Doe	janed@example.com	555-8765	jsmith@example.com	0.763889
7	Jason Lee	jlee@example.com	555-1111	janed@example.com	0.793651
10	Jessica Harris	jharris@example.com	555-6666	jlee@example.com	0.767507
2	John Smith	jsmith@example.com	555-4321	amanda.scott2@example.com	0.686594
1	Johnathan Garcia	johnathan.garcia2@example.com	555-9999	amanda.scott2@example.com	0.628556
11	Kevin Turner	kturner@example.com	555-7777	smiller@example.com	0.803922
14	Lisa Anderson	l.anderson@example.com	555-4444	rwilson@example.com	0.804902
6	Michael Brown	mbrown@example.com	555-7890	janed@example.com	0.763889
8	Rachel Wilson	rwilson@example.com	555-2222	mbrown@example.com	0.778186
5	Sarah Miller	smiller@example.com	555-3456	jsmith@example.com	0.778186

Figure 12.25: Using the Jaro-Winkler algorithm applied to 3-grams to deduplicate emails

Amazing! We managed to correctly deduplicate emails using the Jaro-Winkler algorithm with 3-grams and a similarity threshold of 0.81.

Let's see if it is possible to deduplicate the same email addresses using R.

Deduplicating emails with R

When it comes to approximate string matching in R, one of the most popular and widely used packages is *stringdist*. The **stringdist** package in R provides a low-level interface to several string distance algorithms commonly used to compare text strings in statistical text processing applications. It addresses the problem of scattered functionality in existing R packages, resulting in inconsistent interfaces and encoding handling. The package includes distance measures based on q-gram counting, edit-based distances, and other heuristic distance functions. In addition, the package provides inexact matching alternatives to R's exact matching functions, such as match and %in%. Let's try to use it to deduplicate the emails we encountered in the previous section.

Following the same approach as the algorithm described in the previous section for Python, we rewrote it in R using the stringdist package (you have to install it to use this code):

```r
library(dplyr)
library(stringdist)

deduplicate_data <- function(data, similarity_method, p=0.1, q=1, similarity_
threshold=0.8) {

  new_columns <- c(colnames(data), "Best Comparison", "Similarity")

  # Create new data frames to store deduplicated and duplicated records
  deduplicated_data <- tibble::tibble(!!!setNames(rep(list(NULL),
    length(new_columns)), new_columns))
  duplicated_data <- tibble::tibble(!!!setNames(rep(list(NULL),
    length(new_columns)), new_columns))

  colnames(deduplicated_data) <- new_columns
  colnames(duplicated_data) <- new_columns

  # Create a vector to keep track of unique emails
  unique_emails <- c()

  # Iterate through each row in the original dataset
  for (i in 1:nrow(data)) {
    email <- data$Email[i]
    is_duplicate <- FALSE
    best_comparison <- ''
    best_similarity_score <- 0.0

    # Compare the current email with unique emails
    # using the chosen similarity metric
    for (unique_email in unique_emails) {
      if (similarity_method == 'jw') {
        similarity_score <- stringsim(email,
          unique_email, method = similarity_method, q = q, p = p)

      } else {
        similarity_score <- stringsim(email,
          unique_email, method = similarity_method, q = q)

      }

      # If the similarity score exceeds the threshold,
```

```r
      # consider it a duplicate
      if (similarity_score > similarity_threshold) {
        is_duplicate <- TRUE

        row_to_append <- data[i, ]
        row_to_append['Best Comparison'] <- unique_email
        row_to_append['Similarity'] <- similarity_score

        duplicated_data <- bind_rows(duplicated_data,
          row_to_append)
        break
      }

      if (similarity_score > best_similarity_score) {
        best_similarity_score <- similarity_score
        best_comparison <- unique_email
      }
    }

    # If it's not a duplicate, add it to the deduplicated dataset
    if (!is_duplicate) {
      unique_emails <- c(unique_emails, email)

      row_to_append <- data[i, ]
      row_to_append['Best Comparison'] <- best_comparison
      row_to_append['Similarity'] <- best_similarity_score

      deduplicated_data <- bind_rows(deduplicated_data,
        row_to_append)
    }

  }

if (length(deduplicated_data) > 0)
  deduplicated_data <- deduplicated_data %>% arrange(Name)

if (length(duplicated_data) > 0)
  duplicated_data <- duplicated_data %>% arrange(Name)

# Return datasets
return(
```

```
        list(deduplicated_data=deduplicated_data,
        duplicated_data=duplicated_data) )

}
```

All of the code used in this section can be found in the R\03-deduplicate-emails.R file in *Chapter 12*.

As you can see, we used the stringsim() function exposed by the stringdist package, which calculates the similarity between two strings by taking as parameters, in addition to the two strings to compare, the method to use (Jaccard, Jaro-Winkler, etc.) and the number of q-grams to use (1 by default).

Once we have loaded the data in JSON format from the email-addresses-to-dedup.json file using the fromJSON() function of the jsonlite package, let's try to deduplicate the data with the above function using the Jaccard algorithm and a similarity threshold of 0.875:

```
> deduplicated_data_jaccard <- deduplicate_data(data, similarity_method = "jaccard", similarity_threshold = 0.875)
> deduplicated_data_jaccard[[1]]
# A tibble: 18 × 5
   Name             Email                        `Phone Number` `Best Comparison`                  Similarity
   <chr>            <chr>                        <chr>          <chr>                              <dbl>
 1 Amanda Scott     amanda.scott2@example.com    555-8888       ""                                 0
 2 Amanda Scott     amanda.scott3@example.com    555-8888       "amanda.scott2@example.com"        0.875
 3 Amanda Scott     amanda.scott4@example.com    555-8888       "amanda.scott2@example.com"        0.875
 4 Brian Martinez   bmartinez@example.com        555-5555       "mbrown@example.com"               0.765
 5 David Johnson    davidjo@example.com          555-9012       "janed@example.com"                0.8
 6 David Johnson    d.johnson@example.com        555-9012       "janed@example.com"                0.867
 7 Emily Davis      edavis@example.com           555-2345       "davidjo@example.com"              0.867
 8 Eric Thompson    ethompson@example.com        555-3333       "amanda.scott2@example.com"        0.812
 9 Jane Doe         janed@example.com            555-8765       "amanda.scott2@example.com"        0.75
10 Jason Lee        jlee@example.com             555-1111       "janed@example.com"                0.846
11 Jessica Harris   jharris@example.com          555-6666       "jsmith@example.com"               0.875
12 John Smith       jsmith@example.com           555-4321       "johnathan.garcia2@example.com"    0.737
13 Johnathan Garcia johnathan.garcia2@example.com 555-9999      "amanda.scott2@example.com"        0.65
14 Kevin Turner     kturner@example.com          555-7777       "bmartinez@example.com"            0.722
15 Lisa Anderson    landerson@example.com        555-4444       "amanda.scott2@example.com"        0.812
16 Michael Brown    mbrown@example.com           555-7890       "janed@example.com"                0.688
17 Rachel Wilson    rwilson@example.com          555-2222       "smiller@example.com"              0.867
18 Sarah Miller     smiller@example.com          555-3456       "jsmith@example.com"               0.75
```

Figure 12.26: Using the standard Jaccard algorithm to deduplicate emails

As you can see, the similarity values obtained from stringdist using Jaccard's algorithm are the same as those obtained in Python from TextDistance. Therefore, the issues highlighted in *Figure 12.26* are the same ones we discussed in the previous section.

Let's try to deduplicate the dataset using the Jaro-Winkler algorithm implemented in stringdist:

```
> deduplicated_data_jaro_winkler <- deduplicate_data(data, similarity_method = "jw", p = 0.1, similarity_threshold = 0.872)
> deduplicated_data_jaro_winkler[[1]] # deduplicated_data
# A tibble: 16 × 5
   Name             Email                        `Phone Number` `Best Comparison`                  Similarity
   <chr>            <chr>                        <chr>          <chr>                              <dbl>
 1 Amanda Scott     amanda.scott2@example.com    555-8888       ""                                 0
 2 Brian Martinez   bmartinez@example.com        555-5555       "landerson@example.com"            0.810
 3 David Johnson    davidjo@example.com          555-9012       "janed@example.com"                0.779
 4 David Johnson    d.johnson@example.com        555-9012       "davidjo@example.com"              0.851
 5 Emily Davis      edavis@example.com           555-2345       "janed@example.com"                0.872
 6 Eric Thompson    ethompson@example.com        555-3333       "smiller@example.com"              0.746
 7 Jane Doe         janed@example.com            555-8765       "jsmith@example.com"               0.742
 8 Jason Lee        jlee@example.com             555-1111       "janed@example.com"                0.856
 9 Jessica Harris   jharris@example.com          555-6666       "jsmith@example.com"               0.854
10 John Smith       jsmith@example.com           555-4321       "johnathan.garcia2@example.com"    0.710
11 Johnathan Garcia johnathan.garcia2@example.com 555-9999      "amanda.scott2@example.com"        0.752
12 Kevin Turner     kturner@example.com          555-7777       "janed@example.com"                0.853
13 Lisa Anderson    landerson@example.com        555-4444       "smiller@example.com"              0.806
14 Michael Brown    mbrown@example.com           555-7890       "jsmith@example.com"               0.815
15 Rachel Wilson    r.wilson@example.com         555-2222       "d.johnson@example.com"            0.823
16 Sarah Miller     smiller@example.com          555-3456       "jsmith@example.com"               0.796
```

Figure 12.27: Using the Jaro-Winkler algorithm to deduplicate emails

From the point of view of the functions exposed by `stringdist`, a peculiarity for the Jaro-Winkler case must be noted:

> Whether using the `stringdist()` function to calculate distance or `stringsim()` for the similarity, in the case where the method is "jw" (Jaro-Winkler), the `parameter` related to the prefix scale is also considered, but it takes the default value of 0, effectively applying Jaro's algorithm! Instead, to use the Jaro-Winkler algorithm, a `parameter` other than 0 must be passed (generally 0.1 is considered, at most 0.25).

However, you may notice a slight difference between the values calculated with stringdist and those you get with TextDifference. The original Jaro distance algorithm was originally described step by step by Matthew A. Jaro in the book "UNIMATCH: A Record Linkage System, User Manual" dated 1978. He then also described his algorithm in a technical report entitled "Advances in Record Linkage Methodology as Applied to Matching the 1985 Census of Tampa, Florida," which is more readily available than the book. However, this report does not provide a comprehensive and formal specification of the algorithm. The lack of a precise definition and detailed explanation led to different interpretations and implementations of the algorithm. The authors of stringdist use Jaro's algorithm as described in the original book. Obviously, the authors of TextDistance probably use a different definition of Jaro's distance.

As we have already done in Python, let us try to consider q-grams in the newly introduced algorithms with R. Let us see what happens when we apply Jaccard's algorithm to the 3-grams and consider a similarity threshold of 0.55:

```
> deduplicated_data_jaccard_3grams <- deduplicate_data(data, similarity_method = "jaccard", q = 3, similarity
_threshold = 0.55)
> deduplicated_data_jaccard_3grams[[1]] # deduplicated_data
# A tibble: 15 × 5
   Name             Email                          `Phone Number` `Best Comparison`        Similarity
   <chr>            <chr>                          <chr>          <chr>                         <dbl>
 1 Amanda Scott     amanda.scott2@example.com      555-8888       ""                                0
 2 Brian Martinez   bmartinez@example.com          555-5555       "jlee@example.com"            0.435
 3 David Johnson    davidjo@example.com            555-9012       "janed@example.com"           0.455
 4 Emily Davis      e.davis@example.com            555-2345       "davidjo@example.com"         0.545
 5 Eric Thompson    e.thompson@example.com         555-3333       "rwilson@example.com"         0.542
 6 Jane Doe         janed@example.com              555-8765       "jsmith@example.com"          0.476
 7 Jason Lee        jlee@example.com               555-1111       "janed@example.com"           0.526
 8 Jessica Harris   jharris@example.com            555-6666       "jlee@example.com"            0.476
 9 John Smith       jsmith@example.com             555-4321       "amanda.scott2@example.com"   0.345
10 Johnathan Garcia johnathan.garcia2@example.com  555-9999       "amanda.scott2@example.com"   0.282
11 Kevin Turner     kturner@example.com            555-7777       "smiller@example.com"         0.545
12 Lisa Anderson    l.anderson@example.com         555-4444       "rwilson@example.com"         0.542
13 Michael Brown    mbrown@example.com             555-7890       "janed@example.com"           0.476
14 Rachel Wilson    rwilson@example.com            555-2222       "mbrown@example.com"            0.5
15 Sarah Miller     smiller@example.com            555-3456       "jsmith@example.com"            0.5
```

Figure 12.28: Using the Jaccard algorithm applied to 3-grams to deduplicate emails

Great! The calculated distance values are the same as those calculated in Python, so thanks to the 0.55 threshold, you can perfectly deduplicate the example dataset.

Unlike TextDistance in Python, the stringdist library does not provide a Jaro-Winkler distance calculation via q-grams.

At this point, implementing the deduplication of a dataset in Power BI using Python or R is fairly straightforward. Let's see how to do it.

Deduplicating emails in Power BI

As an example, we will create two queries in Power BI, one with a Python step and the other with an R step, which aim to deduplicate the emails of a dataset with Jaccard's algorithm using 3-grams. Let's proceed:

1. Open Power BI Desktop through the shortcut that activates the pbi_powerquery_env environment.

2. Make sure Power BI Desktop is referencing the pbi_powerquery_env environment in the **Python scripting** tab, and the latest available engine (in our case 4.2.2) in the **R scripting** tab in **Options**.

3. Open the **Get Data, More...** menu on the **Home** ribbon, then select the **JSON** connector and click **Connect**:

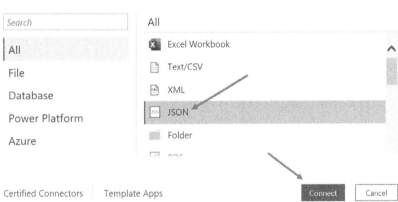

Figure 12.29: Selecting the JSON connector to load data

4. Select the email-addresses-to-dedup.json file in the Chapter 12 folder, and then click **Open**. Your dataset will be loaded as a new query called email-address-to-dedup:

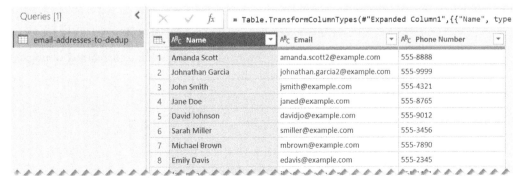

Figure 12.30: Data loaded in a new query

5. Rename the query by right-clicking on it, selecting **Rename**, and entering the new name, `email-addresses-to-dedup-Python`.

6. Duplicate the query by right-clicking on it and selecting **Duplicate**. The new query, `email-addresses-to-dedup-Python (2)`, will be created.

7. Rename the just-created query in `email-addresses-to-dedup-R` as you did in step 5. You'll end up with the following situation:

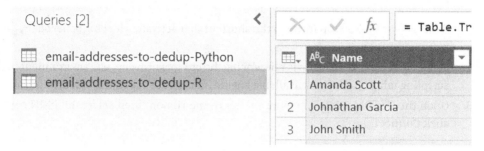

Figure 12.31: Two identical queries to start with

8. Click the **email-addresses-to-dedup-Python** query, click the **Transform** menu on the ribbon, and then click on **Run Python script**.

9. Copy the code in the `Python\04-deduplicate-email-in-powerbi.py` file, paste it into the Python script editor, and click **OK**.

10. If you get the Firewall privacy level mismatch error, select a **Public** privacy level for both the **email-addresses-to-dedup.json** and the **Python** data sources. Then click the **Home** menu on the ribbon, and click **Refresh Preview**.

11. Click the **Table** value at the right of the **deduplicated_data_jaccard_3grams** dataframe:

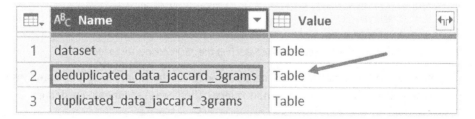

Figure 12.32: Expanding the right output dataframe

12. Now your `email-addresses-to-dedup-Python` query returns the correctly deduplicated emails with all the information they carry with them:

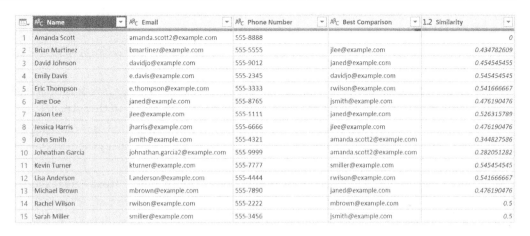

	Name	Email	Phone Number	Best Comparison	1.2 Similarity
1	Amanda Scott	amanda.scott2@example.com	555-8888		0
2	Brian Martinez	bmartinez@example.com	555-5555	jlee@example.com	0.434782609
3	David Johnson	davidjo@example.com	555-9012	janed@example.com	0.454545455
4	Emily Davis	e.davis@example.com	555-2345	davidjo@example.com	0.545454545
5	Eric Thompson	e.thompson@example.com	555-3333	rwilson@example.com	0.541666667
6	Jane Doe	janed@example.com	555-8765	jsmith@example.com	0.476190476
7	Jason Lee	jlee@example.com	555-1111	janed@example.com	0.526315789
8	Jessica Harris	jharris@example.com	555-6666	jlee@example.com	0.476190476
9	John Smith	jsmith@example.com	555-4321	amanda.scott2@example.com	0.344827586
10	Johnathan Garcia	johnathan.garcia2@example.com	555-9999	amanda.scott2@example.com	0.282051282
11	Kevin Turner	kturner@example.com	555-7777	smiller@example.com	0.545454545
12	Lisa Anderson	l.anderson@example.com	555-4444	rwilson@example.com	0.541666667
13	Michael Brown	mbrown@example.com	555-7890	janed@example.com	0.476190476
14	Rachel Wilson	rwilson@example.com	555-2222	mbrown@example.com	0.5
15	Sarah Miller	smiller@example.com	555-3456	jsmith@example.com	0.5

Figure 12.33: Deduplicated dataset using Python

13. Click the **email-addresses-to-dedup-R** query on the left, click the **Transform** menu on the ribbon, and click the **Run R script**.

14. Copy the code in the R\04-deduplicate-email-in-powerbi.R file, paste it into the R script editor, and click **OK**.

15. This time, the resulting dataframe will be automatically expanded and the email-addresses-to-dedup-R query correctly deduplicates the dataset using R, producing an identical table to the one shown in *Figure 12.33*.

16. Click the **Home** menu and click **Close & Apply**.

Amazing! You've just deduplicated a dataset using string distance algorithms in Power BI with Python and R like a pro!

Summary

In this chapter, we ventured into the fascinating realm of distances and their many applications. We began by exploring the calculation of geographic distances, introducing the remarkable formulas of the law of Cosines, the law of Haversines, and Vincenty's distance. Using the PyGeodesy package in Python and the geosphere library in R, we harnessed the power of computation to accurately measure distances between geographic locations.

Expanding our horizons, we delved into the realm of string distances. We encountered the metrics of Hamming, Levenshtein, Jaro-Winkler, and Jaccard distances, each offering unique insights into the dissimilarity or similarity between strings. Python's TextDistance package and R's stringdist library provided us with the essential tools to effortlessly compute these string distances.

In your study, you encountered a significant computational hurdle: the quadratic nature of the distance algorithms implemented. With the need to compute distances between a large number of strings, you face the daunting task of tackling this complexity head-on. The next chapter holds the key to some solutions that address this problem, and it also dives into the realm of linear optimization using Python and R in Power BI.

References

- *On Spherical Trigonometry* (https://web.archive.org/web/20220407174559/http://www.robingilbert.com/blog/2017-10-01-on-spherical-trigonometry/)
- *Calculate the Distance Between Two GPS Points with Python (Vincenty's Inverse Formula)* (https://nathanrooy.github.io/posts/2016-12-18/vincenty-formula-with-python/)
- *Vectorization and parallelization in Python with NumPy and pandas* (https://datascience.blog.wzb.eu/2018/02/02/vectorization-and-parallelization-in-python-with-numpy-and-pandas/)
- *How to Speed up Data Processing with Numpy Vectorization* (https://towardsdatascience.com/how-to-speedup-data-processing-with-numpy-vectorization-12acac71cfca)
- *Basic Stringology, from "Grammatical Inference" by Colin de la Higuera* (http://pagesperso.lina.univ-nantes.fr/~cdlh//book/Basic_Stringology.pdf)

Test your knowledge

1. Why is the concept of distance particularly valuable?
2. What was one of the most practical benefits introduced by the definition of the Haversine function?
3. What is the assumption that makes Vincenty's formula for calculating the distance between two geographic locations so much more accurate than others?
4. What libraries are used in Python and R to compute distances between geographic points?
5. If Hamming distance is very powerful, why is it not often used in common string comparison problems?
6. When is it recommended to use the Damerau-Levenshtein distance?
7. When is it recommended to use the Jaro-Winkler distance?
8. When is it recommended to use the Jaccard distance?
9. What libraries are used in Python and R to compute distances between strings?

Learn more on Discord

To join the Discord community for this book – where you can share feedback, ask questions to the author, and learn about new releases – follow the QR code below:

https://discord.gg/MKww5g45EB

13

Calculating Columns Using Complex Algorithms: Fuzzy Matching

In the previous chapter, we discussed the importance of distance measures in estimating the dissimilarity between two distinct strings. Continuing our exploration of data analysis techniques, this chapter delves into the world of fuzzy matching, a technique used to determine logical similarities and identity mismatches in duplicates. Unfortunately, finding a dissimilarity metric in string values can be challenging. However, Power BI comes with a complex, reliable, and scalable fuzzy matching algorithm implemented by the Microsoft Research team based on the Jaccard distance. Although this algorithm performs well enough for typical fuzzy matching problems, it's worth noting that there are other methods available if you require more precision and control. In this document, we will explore the topic of probabilistic data association, which is another powerful tool for your analytics arsenal. We will use a probabilistic approach to solve a deduplication problem commonly found in **Master Data Management (MDM)** systems.

This chapter will cover the following topics:

- Exploring default fuzzy matching in Power BI
- Introducing probabilistic record linkage algorithms
- Applying probabilistic record linkage algorithms

Technical requirements

This chapter requires you to have a working internet connection and **Power BI Desktop** already installed on your machine (we used version 2.114.664.0, 64-bit, February 2023). You must have properly configured the R and Python engines and IDEs as outlined in *Chapter 2, Configuring R with Power BI*, and *Chapter 3, Configuring Python with Power BI*.

Exploring default fuzzy matching in Power BI

Power BI provides advanced data matching and clustering capabilities through its fuzzy matching and fuzzy clustering tools. These tools are particularly useful for data analysts who need to compare and merge items from separate lists based on their similarity.

Fuzzy matching enables you to merge two tables in Power Query by identifying and matching similar items. On the other hand, **fuzzy clustering** leverages a fuzzy matching algorithm to group data points with similar values together. This is achieved by mapping the value of each column to the best-matched group.

Power Query provides users with the flexibility to apply both fuzzy matching and fuzzy clustering options during data transformations. Fuzzy matching options are available when merging two tables, while fuzzy clustering options can be accessed when adding a new column.

While Microsoft provides a simplified description of the algorithms used by Power BI saying that "Power Query uses the Jaccard similarity algorithm to measure the similarity between pairs of instances," it's worth noting that these features employ sophisticated algorithms developed by Microsoft Research. Jaccard similarity is just one part of the overall algorithmic implementation.

The fuzzy matching algorithm implemented in Power BI overcomes the most difficult problem when comparing two relatively large datasets: the computational complexity of the basic algorithms presented in the previous chapter, and thus the time required to perform the comparison. The naïve approach of evaluating the similarity function on each pair of records is not feasible for large datasets, so most techniques use a *filtering-verification architecture*. This architecture involves generating *signatures* for each string in the input tables, using a signature-based algorithm, and then verifying the similarity of candidate pairs. A signature is nothing more than a compact representation of a string that captures its essential characteristics, and its main purpose is to filter out pairs of records that are unlikely to have a similarity above the specified threshold. This implementation uses **Locality Sensitive Hashing** (**LSH**) to generate signatures, which allows high-frequency signatures to be *pruned* (i.e., removed) because they do not significantly affect the matching results due to their redundancy within each record. This results in improved performance and scalability. Essentially, to catch up with what was stated by Microsoft, a weighted version of Jaccard similarity is used in the LSH algorithm.

In addition, the algorithm we are discussing has the ability to scale efficiently across multiple nodes when deployed on a distributed compute cluster. This means that the same algorithm used in Power BI Desktop is also used in *Power BI dataflows* (`https://bit.ly/pbi-dataflow`) and the *Azure Data Factory data flow activity* (`https://bit.ly/adf-fuzzy-join`), although the single-node version is still used today. In the near future, this algorithm will allow for seamless scalability based on the compute resources that are available. See the *References* section for more details on the entire implementation.

Fuzzy clustering uses the fuzzy matching algorithm just described and then an unsupervised clustering algorithm. In detail:

1. The first step of the fuzzy clustering algorithm is to apply the fuzzy merge technique. This involves performing a self-fuzzy join on the input table to identify pairs of records that have a high degree of similarity above a predefined threshold. The fuzzy merge technique compares records and identifies those that share similar characteristics. By setting a threshold, only pairs of records with a similarity above the threshold are considered similar pairs. This step effectively groups records that have significant similarity, providing a basis for further clustering.

2. The second step of the fuzzy clustering algorithm uses **Agglomerative Hierarchical Clustering** (**AHC**) with *unweighted average linkage*, a method used in hierarchical clustering to measure the similarity between clusters. This clustering technique takes the output generated in Step 1 and further organizes the records into clusters based on their similarities. AHC is a bottom-up hierarchical clustering approach that first treats each record as an individual cluster. It then iteratively merges clusters based on a similarity metric, using unweighted average linkage to calculate the distance between clusters. This process continues until all records are grouped into a set of clusters, forming a dendrogram that represents the hierarchical structure of the clusters. This approach provides an effective way to organize records into clusters based on their similarities, creating a comprehensive clustering solution.

The use of fuzzy clustering is beyond the scope of this chapter. But let's look at an example of fuzzy matching using the algorithm that comes with Power BI out of the box.

Using Power Query's fuzzy merge

As a real-world use case, imagine that you have crawled products on some product price comparison sites and you need to group those products by some product categories that you have already normalized. Basically, you should compare each individual product description with the categories you have and identify the category that is closest to the product description in question.

This is a problem that can be solved using fuzzy matching techniques. The datasets we will use in this section are taken from Kaggle's *Product Clustering, Matching & Classification* datasets, which you can find here: https://bit.ly/product-matching-datasets. We simply took the data for mobile devices (pricerunner_mobile.csv) extracted from *PriceRunner*, a price comparison service, and reorganized it into the Excel file pricerunner-mobile-data.xlsx, which can be found in the *Chapter 13* code folder.

In this Excel file, there is a sheet (pricerunner_products) containing data on product descriptions (product_desc), each of which has the correct category (product_category_true) that the matching operation should identify:

product_id	product_desc	product_category_true
1	apple iphone 8 plus 64gb silver	Apple iPhone 8 Plus 64GB
2	apple iphone 8 plus 64 gb spacegrau	Apple iPhone 8 Plus 64GB
3	apple mq8n2b/a iphone 8 plus 64gb 5.5 12mp sim free smartphone in gold	Apple iPhone 8 Plus 64GB
4	apple iphone 8 plus 64gb space grey	Apple iPhone 8 Plus 64GB
5	apple iphone 8 plus gold 5.5 64gb 4g unlocked sim free	Apple iPhone 8 Plus 64GB
6	apple iphone 8 plus gold 5.5 64gb 4g unlocked sim free	Apple iPhone 8 Plus 64GB
7	apple iphone 8 plus 64 gb space grey	Apple iPhone 8 Plus 64GB
8	apple iphone 8 plus 64gb space grey	Apple iPhone 8 Plus 64GB
9	apple iphone 8 plus 64gb space grey	Apple iPhone 8 Plus 64GB

Figure 13.1: Contents of the pricerunner_products Excel sheet

There is another Excel sheet (product_categories) that instead provides the unique category descriptions that you need to match with the product descriptions:

product_category_id	product_category_desc
1	Apple iPhone 8 Plus 64GB
2	Apple iPhone 7 Plus 32GB
3	Apple iPhone 7 32GB
4	Apple iPhone 8 64GB
5	Apple iPhone X 64GB
6	Samsung Galaxy S8 64GB
7	Apple iPhone X 256GB
8	Apple iPhone 7 128GB
9	Apple iPhone 8 Plus 256GB
10	Apple iPhone 8 256GB

Figure 13.2: Contents of the product_categories Excel sheet

Before applying fuzzy matching techniques to strings, it is often beneficial to apply certain cleaning and transformation steps. This process standardizes and preprocesses the text, improving matching accuracy by removing inconsistencies and irrelevant variations that could hinder effective comparison. Here are some common cleaning transformations that can be applied:

- Convert both strings to lowercase to ensure case insensitivity. This step helps in matching strings regardless of their capitalization.

- Trim any leading or trailing spaces in the strings. Whitespace can affect the matching results and lead to false mismatches.

- Standardize date/time formats as strings in the yyyy-mm-dd hh:mm:ss format.

- Replace abbreviations with full words (e.g., standardize "St." to "Street").

- Remove commonly used words, known as **stopwords**, from the strings. Stopwords include words like "a," "the," and "and," which do not carry significant meaning and can negatively impact the matching accuracy.

- Reduce words to their base or root form using **stemming** or **lemmatization** techniques, used in natural language processing to reduce words to their base or root form. This step helps in matching words with similar meanings but different forms. For example, "running" and "runs" can be reduced to the base form "run."

- Decide whether to remove or preserve numerical values in the strings based on the specific use case. If numerical values are essential for matching, they should be preserved.

- Depending on the context, you may need to handle special characters or symbols in the strings. This can involve removing or replacing them as necessary to ensure consistent matching.

Since we are dealing with product and category descriptions, there is no need to apply complex techniques such as stopword removal or stemming/lemming. We will simply use lowercase, eliminate all trailing spaces, and eliminate all punctuation.

With that said, let's get started implementing fuzzy matching in Power BI:

1. Open Power BI Desktop, close the startup screen, and click on the **Excel workbook** button on the **Home** ribbon to load Excel data.

2. Select the **pricerunner-mobile-data.xlsx** file in the Chapter 13 folder and click **OK**.

3. Select both the **pricerunner_products** and **product_categories** sheets and click **Transform data**:

Figure 13.3: Importing data from both Excel sheets

4. Select the **pricerunner_products** query at the top left, click on the **Add Column** menu, and click on **Custom Column**:

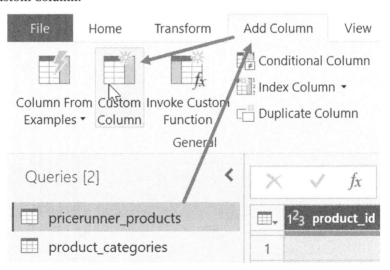

Figure 13.4: Adding a new custom column to the pricerunner_products query

5. Name the new column product_desc_cleaned and use the following formula for the **Custom column formula:** Text.Trim(Text.Lower(Text.Remove([product_desc], {".", "/", "&", "-", "(", ")"}))))

This will remove special characters, transform to lowercase, and trim trailing spaces in one shot. Then click **OK**:

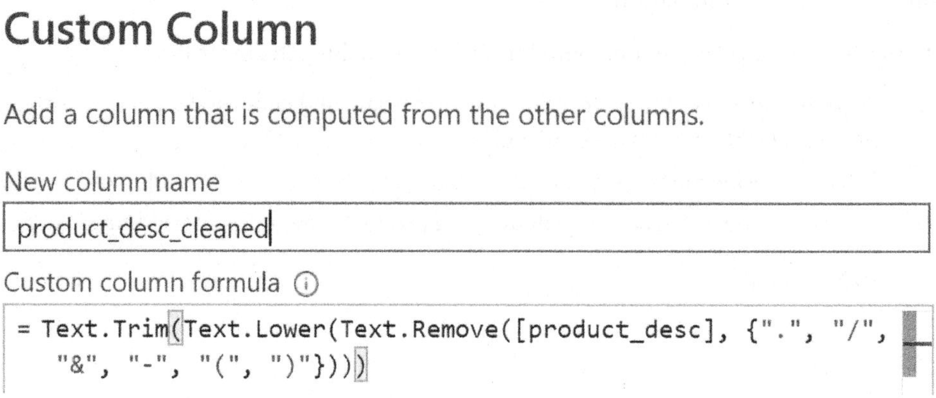

Custom Column

Add a column that is computed from the other columns.

New column name

product_desc_cleaned|

Custom column formula ⓘ

```
= Text.Trim(Text.Lower(Text.Remove([product_desc], {".", "/",
    "&", "-", "(", ")"})))
```

Figure 13.5: Adding the new custom column name and formula

6. Select the new **product_desc_cleaned** column, click on the **Transform** menu, and change its data type to **Text**:

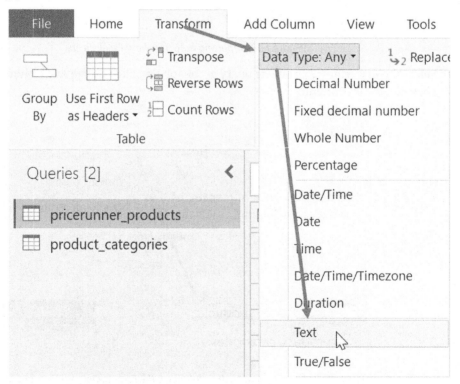

Figure 13.6: Changing the product_desc_cleaned data type to Text

This step is important because fuzzy merge works only on Text columns.

7. Select the product_categories query at the top left, click on the **Add Column** menu, and click on **Custom Column:**

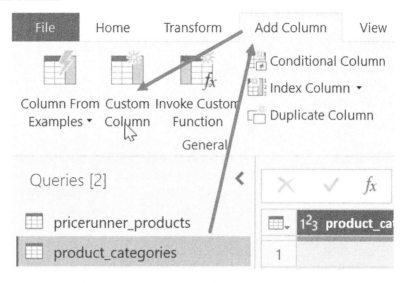

Figure 13.7: Adding a new custom column to the product_categories query

8. Name the new column product_category_desc_cleaned and use the following formula for the **Custom column formula:** Text.Trim(Text.Lower(Text.Remove([product_category_desc], {".", "/", "&", "-", "(", ")"})))

    This will remove special characters, transform to lowercase, and trim trailing spaces in one shot. Then click **OK**.

9. Select the new **product_category_desc_cleaned** column, click on the **Transform** menu, and change its data type to **Text**, as you did before.

10. Now click on the **pricerunner_products** query at the top left, click on the **Home** menu, open the **Merge Queries** submenu, and select **Merge Queries as New:**

Figure 13.8: Adding a new merge query

11. Select the **product_categories** table as the second table to use for the matching operation. Then select both the **product_desc_cleaned** and **product_category_desc_cleaned** columns as the merge keys by clicking on their headers:

Merge

Select tables and matching columns to create a merged table.

Figure 13.9: Selecting columns to use in the merge operation

12. In the lower part of the **Merge** window, keep **Left Outer** as the selected option for the **Join Kind** in order to keep all rows from the left table, select the **Use fuzzy matching to perform the merge** checkbox, and you will be notified that the selection matches 624 of 4081 rows from the first table using the default parameters:

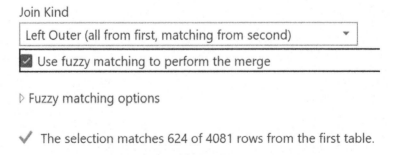

Figure 13.10: Performing fuzzy matching with default parameters

The low number of matches is a result of the default threshold value, which will be changed soon. Did you notice how fast the calculation of matches was, even though the theoretical number of matches to be made is *4081 x 4081 = 16,654,561*? That's the magic of Microsoft Research's implementation of fuzzy matching!

13. Expand the **Fuzzy matching options** menu, enter a **Similarity threshold** of 0.3 (the default value was 0.8, even if the text box is empty), and enter 1 as the **Maximum number of matches**. You will see that the actual selection matches 4008 of 4081 rows. Then click **OK**:

▲Fuzzy matching options

Similarity threshold (optional)

| 0.3 | ⓘ |

☑ Ignore case

☑ Match by combining text parts ⓘ

Maximum number of matches (optional)

| 1 | ⓘ |

Transformation table (optional)

| ▼ | ⓘ |

✓ The selection matches 4008 of 4081 rows from the first table.

Figure 13.11: Refining some fuzzy matching parameters

This means that by modifying the threshold from 0.8 to 0.3 and associating a single result with the matching operation of one description (the category with the minimum distance), 73 of all descriptions will not match. However, this does not mean that all other matches are correct! There will also be false positives.

14. You need to expand all matching results by clicking the **Expand** button on the **product_categories** column header of the new **Merge** query. Then select only the **product_category_desc** column of the merged product categories table, uncheck the **Use original column name as prefix** checkbox, and click **OK**:

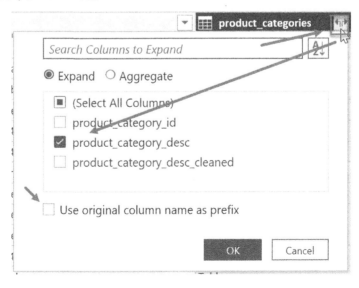

Figure 13.12: Expanding only the product_category_desc column from the joined table

You will see the matched categories thanks to the fuzzy matching operation.

15. Now, in order to understand if the matched category is the right one, we need to compare it to the true category of each row reported in the **product_category_true** column. To easily select correct matches, simply add a conditional column that compares the current match with the true match and returns 1 if the match is correct, and 0 otherwise. So, click on the **Add Column** menu and click the **Conditional Column** button:

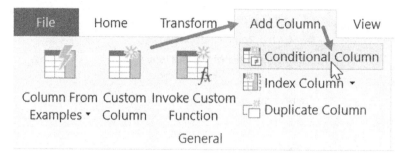

Figure 13.13: Adding a new conditional column

16. Enter is_wrong_category as the **New column name**, select **product_category_desc** in **Column Name**, and leave **Operator** as **equals**. Open the **Value** menu, click **Select a column**, and choose **product_category_true** as the column. Enter 0 as **Output** and enter 1 as **Else**. Then click **OK**:

Add Conditional Column

Add a conditional column that is computed from the other columns or values.

New column name

is_wrong_category

	Column Name	Operator	Value ⓘ		Output ⓘ
If	product_category... ▾	equals ▾	▦ ▾	product_category_true ▾ Then	ABC/123 ▾ 0

ABC/123 Enter a value

▦ Select a column

▦ Parameter

Add Clause

Else ⓘ

ABC/123 ▾   1

Figure 13.14: Setting the is_wrong_category conditional column

17. Select the new **is_wrong_category** column, click the **Home** menu, expand the **Data Type** menu, and select **Whole Number**.

18. Now, right-click on the **Merge1** query at the top left and select **Rename**:

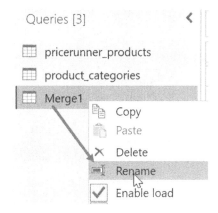

Figure 13.15: Renaming the new merge query FuzzyMerge

Rename the query by entering FuzzyMerge, then press **Enter**.

19. Click the **Home** menu and click **Close & Apply**.

20. Select the **Table** visual from the **Visualizations** panel:

Figure 13.16: Adding a Table visual

21. Keeping the table visual selected in the canvas, expand the **FuzzyMerge** table under the **Data** panel and select the **product_id**, **product_desc**, **product_category_true**, **produc_category_desc**, and **is_wrong_category** fields in the given order:

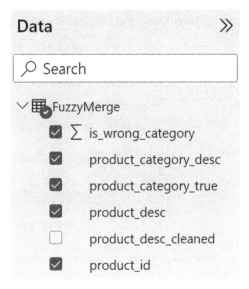

Figure 13.17: Selecting table fields to add to the Table visual

The table will show the selected columns.

22. You have to keep only the rows having a wrong categorization, so drag and drop the **is_wrong_category** field into the **Add data fields here** filter of the visual:

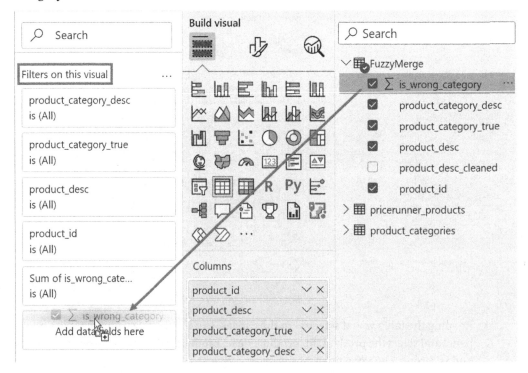

Figure 13.18: Adding the is_wrong_category field as a visual filter

Then select **Basic filtering** as **Filter type** and keep only the wrong matches by clicking on **1**:

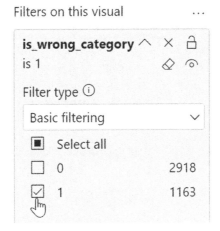

Figure 13.19: Keeping only wrong matches in the visual

23. Now you can see only the wrong matches in the table that add up to 1163:

product_id	product_desc	product_category_true	product_category_desc	Sum of is_wrong_category
471	10.16 cm 4 ips 640 x 1136 a9 m9 128gb lte 802.11ac blueto	Apple iPhone SE 128GB	Cyrus CM 16	1
412	10.16 cm 4 ips 640 x 1136 a9 m9 32gb lte 802.11ac bluetoo	Apple iPhone SE 32GB	Cyrus CM 16	1
1944	11.43 cm 4.5 854x480 55x98 mm 3.5 mm 142g li ion 2000 mah	Doro 8030	Nokia 2600	1
1906	11.43 cm 4.5 tft 480 x 854 gsm/wcdma/4g qualcomm msm8909 quad c	CAT S30 Dual SIM		1
275	11.938 cm 4.7 1334 x 750 3d touch a9 m9 128gb touch id 8	Apple iPhone 6S 128GB	HTC Touch 2	1
317	11.938 cm 4.7 1334 x 750 3d touch a9 m9 32gb touch id 80	Apple iPhone 6S 32GB	Nokia 150	1
Total				**1163**

Figure 13.20: Table showing only wrong matches

24. Select the table visual in the canvas, click on its **Format visual** icon, click on **General**, set the **Title** to **On**, expand it, and enter Fuzzy Merge as the title text:

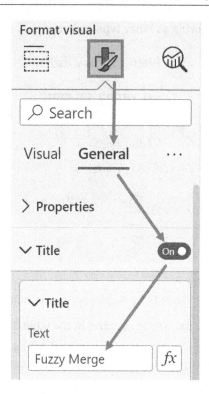

Figure 13.21: Entering a title for the table visual

25. Save your Power BI Desktop report as you will use it later on.

Awesome! You were able to apply fuzzy matching using the default fuzzy merge feature in Power BI. Note that Power BI's complex fuzzy matching implementation using the Jaccard algorithm cannot correctly match 1163 instances. There are inevitably inconsistencies that even the most complex algorithms cannot resolve.

However, there are problems that require fuzzy matching algorithms that cannot be easily solved with the standard Power BI features. In these cases, you need to use the analytical programming languages built into Power BI, such as Python or R. Let's look at a real-world case of such applications.

Introducing probabilistic record linkage algorithms

In addition to deterministic algorithms like the LSH seen above, there are **probabilistic record linkage** algorithms that use probabilistic techniques to determine the probability that two records refer to the same entity. In fact, they are specifically designed for fuzzy matching or linking records from different datasets. They typically involve calculating similarities between pairs of records based on various attributes (e.g., names, addresses, etc.) and assigning weights or probabilities to these similarities. Such algorithms then use these probabilities to make a decision about whether two records match or not.

One of the best-known algorithms of this type is the **Fellegi-Sunter model** proposed by Peter J. Fellegi and Alan B. Sunter in 1969. It has become a fundamental approach to probabilistic record linkage. The algorithm typically involves several steps:

1. *Comparison of attributes*: The algorithm compares the values of different attributes (e.g., name, address, date of birth) between pairs of records. It can use various similarity measures, such as string distance metrics like Jaccard's or Jaro-Winkler's.

2. *Estimation of parameters*: The model estimates the parameters needed for the probability calculation. This includes estimating the probabilities of attribute agreement and disagreement for matches and non-matches, along with the probabilities of agreeing on missing or unknown values. This estimation is done using an algorithm based on Bayes' theorem.

3. *Calculation of match probabilities*: Using the estimated parameters and the attribute comparisons, the algorithm calculates match probabilities for each pair of records. This is done by combining the attribute similarities using predefined rules. The weights or probabilities assigned to each attribute similarity play a critical role in determining the overall match probability.

4. *Decision-making*: The algorithm sets a threshold or cut-off point to decide whether two records are a match or not. If the calculated match probability exceeds the threshold, the records are considered a match – otherwise, they are considered a mismatch.

As you can see, the approach of this algorithm is completely different from the LSH-based approach seen in the previous section. Whereas LSH maps high-dimensional data into low-dimensional hash codes so that similar data points are likely to have similar hash codes, probabilistic record linkage algorithms use probabilistic techniques to calculate similarity probabilities and make linkage decisions.

The choice between using the LSH-based approach and the Fellegi-Sunter probabilistic record linkage method depends on the specific demands of the data analysis scenario:

*   LSH-based approaches are particularly effective when dealing with large-scale datasets and high-dimensional data. LSH is ideal for rapid processing needs, such as approximate nearest neighbor searches, big data analytics, multimedia retrieval, and real-time applications. Its efficiency, scalability, and simplicity make it preferable for tasks requiring quick, approximate matches without the computational overhead of probabilistic calculations.

*   The Fellegi-Sunter model is particularly effective for datasets with varying levels of data quality, such as inconsistencies and missing information. Its probabilistic approach provides a nuanced way to control matching criteria, enabling more sophisticated handling of complex matching requirements across datasets with diverse attributes. The Fellegi-Sunter model is particularly useful in fields where precise record linkage is crucial, such as healthcare and financial databases. Incorrect matches can have significant consequences, making the flexibility and accuracy of this model the preferred method in situations where match quality is more important than processing speed.

Both of these approaches are commonly used in **MDM** systems. MDM is a comprehensive approach to ensure the consistency, accuracy, and uniformity of an organization's critical data across multiple systems and applications. However, it comes with certain challenges, one of which is deduplication, which we will discuss next.

Applying probabilistic record linkage algorithms

Deduplication is one of the key challenges in MDM and refers to the accurate identification and linkage of duplicate records. Unlike the case of email deduplication applied to a single field, as you saw in the previous chapter, it is often necessary to deduplicate records based on multiple fields that may be similar. In this section, we'll see how to approach a case of deduplication using probabilistic record linkage in Python, R, and Power BI.

Applying probabilistic record linkage in Python

One of the most popular open-source Python libraries designed for probabilistic record linkage is **Splink** (`https://github.com/moj-analytical-services/splink`). It simplifies the process of implementing probabilistic record linkage by providing an easy-to-use and intuitive interface. It can efficiently handle large datasets, making it suitable for both small and large data applications.

Splink performs all data-linking operations by generating SQL statements and sending them to a user-selected backend for execution. For smaller input datasets, say 1-2 million records, users can perform data joins directly in Python on their laptop using the *DuckDB backend*, an in-memory analytical database specifically designed for analytical workloads. This is the recommended method because the DuckDB backend is automatically installed when Splink is installed via pip. No additional configuration is required.

However, for larger datasets that require compute-intensive calculations and produce datasets that are too large to handle on a regular laptop, it is recommended that you use one of Splink's big data backends, such as Spark or AWS Athena. In such cases, Splink generates SQL statements that are then sent to the selected backend for execution.

Before proceeding with some examples, we must first install the package:

1. Open Anaconda Prompt.
2. Switch to the `pbi_powerquery_env` environment by entering the `conda activate pbi_ powerquery_env` command, and then press **Enter**.
3. Install the `splink` package by typing `pip install splink==3.9.3`, and then press **Enter**.

The use case we will use as an example is the need to deduplicate a dataset containing names, addresses, cities, and types of restaurants from Fodor's and Zagat's guides (source: `https://www.cs.utexas.edu/users/ml/riddle/data.html`). Specifically, we converted the dataset to CSV format, selected a subset of its rows, and fixed some city names to avoid the need for geonormalization. We ended up with a dataset of 451 rows containing 224 duplicates (112 different restaurants). Here is an example of the dataset contents, where the `class` field identifies duplicate rows as those with the same numeric value:

id	name	addr	city	type	class
0	arnie morton's of chicago	435 s. la cienega blv.	los angeles	american	0
1	arnie morton's of chicago	435 s. la cienega blvd.	los angeles	steakhouses	0
2	art's delicatessen	12224 ventura blvd.	los angeles	american	1
3	art's deli	12224 ventura blvd.	los angeles	delis	1
4	hotel bel-air	701 stone canyon rd.	los angeles	californian	2
5	bel-air hotel	701 stone canyon rd.	los angeles	californian	2
6	cafe bizou	14016 ventura blvd.	los angeles	french	3
7	cafe bizou	14016 ventura blvd.	los angeles	french bistro	3
8	campanile	624 s. la brea ave.	los angeles	american	4
9	campanile	624 s. la brea ave.	los angeles	californian	4

Figure 13.22: Extract from the Restaurants dataset

First, as you learned at the beginning of this chapter, you should clean up the fields you are matching to get more accurate results. To do this, we will transform the name, addr, and city fields using the clean_string function, which applies some basic tricks:

```python
import os
import re
import numpy as np
import pandas as pd


def clean_string(input_string):
    # Convert to lower case
    cleaned_string = input_string.lower()

    # Remove trailing spaces
    cleaned_string = cleaned_string.strip()

    # Remove special characters
    cleaned_string = re.sub(r'[^a-zA-Z0-9\s]', '', cleaned_string)

    return cleaned_string

main_path = r'C:\<your-path>\Ch13 - Calculating Columns Using Complex
Algorithms, Fuzzy Matching & Optimization Problems'

restaurants_df = pd.read_csv(
    os.path.join(main_path, 'restaurants.csv'),
    skipinitialspace=True)
```

```
restaurants_df["name"] = restaurants_df["name"].apply(lambda x: clean_
string(x))
restaurants_df["addr"] = restaurants_df["addr"].apply(lambda x: clean_
string(x))
restaurants_df["city"] = restaurants_df["city"].apply(lambda x: clean_
string(x))
```

At this point, to use the splink package, you need to configure the behavior of the matching algorithm through some parameters in JSON format, defining its settings. The main configurations are:

- *Link type*: Splink offers the capability to perform data linking, deduplication, or a combination of both. Data linking involves establishing connections or links between different datasets, while deduplication focuses on identifying and establishing links within a single dataset.

- *Blocking rules*: Blocking rules play a crucial role in reducing computational complexity by specifying constraints on pairwise record comparisons. These rules limit the comparison process to only relevant pairs, significantly reducing the total number of comparisons generated. An example of a lock rule might be l.name = r.name and l.addr = r.addr, where l and r identify the left and right table aliases, respectively, in a comparison. Remember that the default repository used by Splink is DuckDB, which is a SQL-based engine. That's why the lock rules are like WHERE conditions in a SQL statement.

- *Comparisons*: One of the key features of Splink is the ability to customize how records are compared, allowing you to define similarity based on different types of data. During the blocking phase, pairwise record comparisons are performed according to the defined blocking rules. For example, you can define how names are compared (e.g., using the Jaro-Winkler algorithm) if your blocking rule contains l.name = r.name. You can use predefined comparison recipes baked for specific entities to compare, or you can define each step of the comparison using atomic functions. More details can be found here: https://moj-analytical-services.github.io/splink/topic_guides/customising_comparisons.html.

An example of settings configuration is the following:

```
from splink.duckdb.comparison_template_library import name_comparison
import splink.duckdb.duckdb_comparison_library as cl

settings = {
    "link_type": "dedupe_only",
    "blocking_rules_to_generate_predictions": [
        "l.name = r.name and l.addr = r.addr",
        "l.name = r.name and l.city = r.city",
        "l.name LIKE CONCAT('%',r.name,'%') or r.name LIKE CONCAT('%',l.
name,'%')",
    ],
    "comparisons": [
```

```
            name_comparison("name", jaro_winkler_thresholds=[0.9, 0.8]),
            name_comparison("addr", jaro_winkler_thresholds=[0.9, 0.8]),
            cl.exact_match("city"),
        ],
        "unique_id_column_name": "id",
        "retain_matching_columns": True,
        "retain_intermediate_calculation_columns": True,
        "max_iterations": 10,
        "em_convergence": 0.01
    }
```

From the settings we just defined, you can see that we are setting the algorithm to perform dedupli-cation only (`"link_type": "dedupe_only"`). In addition, the blocking rules (`"blocking_rules_to_generate_predictions"`) are quite intuitive: the first two are straightforward (the name and address of matches must be comparable; the name and city of matches must be comparable). The third rule seems a bit more complicated, but for those who have done a little SQL, it should be fairly obvious: basically, the name on the left of the match must be contained in the name on the right, or vice versa. You can find out more about the features that you can use in block rules here: https://duckdb.org/docs/sql/functions/overview.

Next, the comparison methods for each field in the block rules are defined. Specifically, the default template `name_comparison` from the *Comparison Template Library* is used for the name and addr fields. This template, applied to the name field, for example, is structured in a hierarchy as follows:

```
Comparison: name
├--- ComparisonLevel: Exact match
├--- ComparisonLevel: Up to one character difference
├--- ComparisonLevel: Names with Jaro-Winkler similarity of 0.9 or greater
├--- ComparisonLevel: Names with Jaro-Winkler similarity of 0.8 or greater
├--- ComparisonLevel: All other
```

Each `ComparisonLevel` is executed in the given order for the selected column, and the next one is executed if the previous one fails. You can also add more comparison levels using other string simi-larity functions, such as Levenshtein's. A direct similarity function taken from the `ComparisonLibrary`, specifically exact_match, was used for the city.

There are then specific options in the settings that define which column contains a unique row code (`"unique_id_column_name": "id"`), how many maximum iterations are performed during training (`"max_iterations": 10`), and the convergence tolerance for the *Expectation-Maximization* algorithm (`"em_convergence": 0.01`). In addition, any columns used by the comparison SQL expressions and intermediate calculation columns are retained in the output dataset (`"retain_matching_columns": True, "retain_intermediate_calculation_columns": True`).

From this simple example, you can see how powerful and granular this data linkage tool can be!

In the code you can find in the `Python\01-dedup-resturants-with-splink.py` file in the `Chapter 13` folder, after defining the linker object initialized with the settings just seen, we proceed to estimate the parameters of the m and u probabilities, specific to the Fellegi-Sunter model.

Without going into too much mathematical detail underlying this model, the m and u probabilities represent the match and non-match probabilities, respectively, for different attributes or characteristics of the individuals or entities being compared. The m probability (also known as the *matching probability* or *match weight*) represents the probability that two records with the same attribute value actually refer to the same entity. It quantifies the likelihood that the observed attribute values match by chance. On the other hand, the u probability (also known as the *non-matching probability* or *non-match weight*) represents the probability that two records with different attribute values refer to the same entity. It quantifies the likelihood that the observed attribute values differ even though they correspond to the same underlying entity.

Both the m and u probabilities are estimated using statistical methods. Specifically, u probabilities are estimated using the `estimate_u_using_random_sampling` function. It randomly samples subsets of the given dataset, and from this sample, pairwise record comparisons are generated, resulting in a Cartesian product. The u values, which represent the mismatch probabilities, are based on the assumption that these pairwise comparisons are predominantly mismatches, or at least have an extremely low probability of being matches. This assumption is usually true for large datasets.

To estimate the m probabilities, the `estimate_parameters_using_expectation_maximisation` function is used. It utilizes a blocking rule to generate pairwise record comparisons. By default, the m parameters are estimated for all comparisons except those included in the blocking rule. For instance, if the blocking rule is `l.name = r.name`, the parameter estimates will be made for all comparisons except those involving the name attribute in their SQL condition. The above function is called using different blocking rules to accurately estimate the m parameters for each attribute used in the matching. Here is the code:

```python
from splink.duckdb.linker import DuckDBLinker


linker = DuckDBLinker(restaurants_df, settings)


linker.estimate_u_using_random_sampling(max_pairs=1e6)


training_blocking_rule = "l.name = r.name and l.addr = r.addr"
training_session_names = linker.estimate_parameters_using_expectation_maximisation(training_blocking_rule)


training_blocking_rule = "l.name = r.name and l.city = r.city"
training_session_names = linker.estimate_parameters_using_expectation_maximisation(training_blocking_rule)


training_blocking_rule = "l.city = r.city and l.addr = r.addr"
```

```
training_session_names = linker.estimate_parameters_using_expectation_
maximisation(training_blocking_rule)
```

Sometimes, not all values of m and u can be estimated with the expected blocking rule. In this case, others must be added to complete the estimation.

Once the model training is complete (that is, all m and u values have been estimated), it can be applied to the dataset to obtain the match probabilities:

```
df_predict = linker.predict()
```

```
matches_df = df_predict.as_pandas_dataframe()
```

Examining the contents of the matches_df DataFrame, we can see that several matches identified by the pairs (id_l, id_r) were detected with high probability:

index	match_weight	match_probability	id_l	id_r	
0 0	6.9683704536	0.9920775937	6	7	
1 1	6.9683704536	0.9920775937	8	9	
2 2	6.9683704536	0.9920775937	10	11	
3 3	6.9683704536	0.9920775937	12	13	
4 4	6.9683704536	0.9920775937	22	23	
5 5	6.9683704536	0.9920775937	32	33	
6 6	6.9683704536	0.9920775937	36	37	

Figure 13.23: Output DataFrame with matching results

Notice that the matches_df DataFrame contains 197 rows, obtained by applying blocking rules. Some of these rows are associated with the same match pairs that have a different value of the match_key field. The latter represents the index associated with the blocking rules. Thus, there are matches that satisfy more than one blocking rule. This is a bug we have reported on the GitHub repository (https://github.com/moj-analytical-services/splink/discussions/1417). It will be fixed soon; in the meantime, we solved it by removing the match_key column and getting distinct rows. We know that the total number of duplicates is 224, so it is likely that we are missing some rows due to incorrect blocking rules or due to a too-high threshold applied to the working blocking rules.

In addition to the match probability, the DataFrame also contains the match_weight column. There are partial match weights in the Fellegi-Sunter model that capture the relative importance of different attributes present in the data. These partial match weights can be summed up to calculate the overall match score (the final match_weight you can see in the DataFrame) for each match.

Match scores greater than 1 correspond to match probabilities greater than 0.7, which are very likely matches. If you want to analyze the identified but uncertain matches instead, you can, for example, filter all matches with match_weight between 0 and 1 and display the *Match weights waterfall chart* for each of them with the following code:

```
low_prob_matches_dict = df[(df["match_weight"] >= 0) & (df["match_weight"] <
1)].to_dict(orient="records")


linker.waterfall_chart(low_prob_matches_dict)
```

This is the output plot for the first selected match:

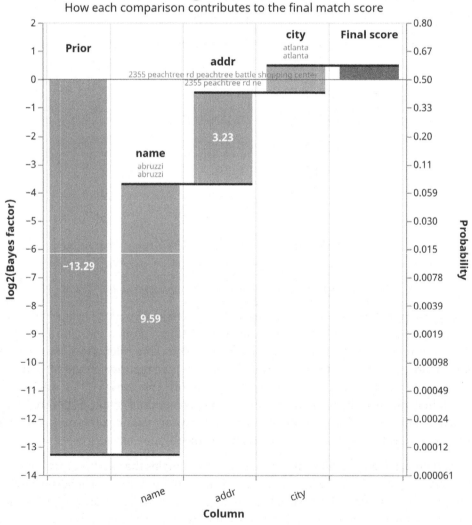

Figure 13.24: Match weights waterfall chart for the first selected match

The **Prior** you can see in *Figure 13.24* refers to the probability that two records drawn at random are a match. Then the two records are compared, increasing the match weight where columns agree, and decreasing it when columns disagree.

The waterfall chart provides valuable insights into the relative importance of different attributes in determining the probability of a match, and analysts can use it to aid in the record linkage decision process by fine-tuning the blocking rules used.

To get a rough idea of how the matching algorithm works, it is possible to use the class field information in the original Restaurants DataFrame. Two restaurants (two rows) are identified as the same business if they have the same integer value in the class field. With some transformation applied to this DataFrame, it is possible to obtain a final DataFrame containing the ID pairs associated with the same restaurant (the "truth" DataFrame, truth_df). Then, assuming that we want to consider as good matches all those that, for example, have a weighted_match greater than or equal to zero, we only need to compare whether the matches obtained in this way (whose check is in the match column) match those in the truth DataFrame. Here is the code to get the match and truth columns in the matches_df DataFrame:

```
matches_df = matches_df.drop(columns=['match_key']).drop_duplicates().
merge(truth_df, how='left', on=['id_l', 'id_r'])
matches_df['truth'] = matches_df['truth'].apply(lambda x: True if x == True
else False) matches_df.drop(columns=['id_x', 'id_y'])
weight_threshold = 0
matches_df['match'] = np.where(matches_df['match_weight'] >= weight_threshold,
True, False)
```

To understand how well the applied deduplication algorithm and the selected threshold work, a **confusion matrix** is often used. It provides a comprehensive summary of the model's predictions (fuzzy matches) and their corresponding actual values (the truth). The matrix is usually square and organized into four quadrants: **true positive** (TP), **false positive** (FP), **true negative** (TN), and **false negative** (FN). Here's a breakdown of the quadrants:

- *TP*: This represents the cases where the model predicted a positive class (match) correctly (true) as the actual value is indeed a match.
- *FP*: This indicates the cases where the model predicted a positive class (match) incorrectly (false) as the actual value is a mismatch.
- *TN*: This represents the cases where the model predicted a negative class (mismatch) correctly (true) as the actual value is indeed negative.
- *FN*: This indicates the cases where the model predicted a negative class (mismatch) incorrectly (false) as the actual value is positive.

Here is the code to get the confusion matrix:

```
# pass predicted and original labels to this function
def confusion_matrix(pred,original):
    matrix=np.zeros((2,2), dtype=np.int32)
```

```
    # adds up the frequencies of the tps,tns,fps,fns
    for i in range(len(pred)):
        if int(pred[i])==1 and int(original[i])==1:
            matrix[1,1]+=1 #True Positives
        elif int(pred[i])==0 and int(original[i])==1:
            matrix[0,1]+=1 #False Positives
        elif int(pred[i])==1 and int(original[i])==0:
            matrix[1,0]+=1 #False Negatives
        elif int(pred[i])==0 and int(original[i])==0:
            matrix[0,0]+=1 #True Negatives


    return matrix

print( confusion_matrix(matches_df['match'], matches_df['truth']) )
```

The output is the following:

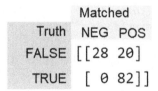

Figure 13.25: Confusion matrix of matches

Not bad! The algorithm with the previous settings correctly matches 82 pairs and it is only wrong for a total of 20 false matches. It is certainly possible to tweak the blocking rules to get a better result.

Let's see how the same principles of the Fellegi-Sunter model can be applied in R.

Applying probabilistic record linkage in R

A popular tool in the R programming language used for probabilistic record linkage and data deduplication tasks is the **Record Linkage Toolkit (reclin)**. Like Splink for Python, reclin for R implements the Fellegi-Sunter model introduced in the previous section. Although reclin was developed with performance and scalability in mind, implementing the main algorithms in C++, the package has recently been replaced by a much more performant version, registered on CRAN under the name **reclin2**. The main focus of reclin2 is to optimize performance, memory usage, CPU usage, and flexibility. To achieve superior performance, reclin2 uses the **data.table** library for the majority of its computations.

We have not discussed the data.table package for managing large datasets because we preferred to use Arrow R, an R interface to the Apache Arrow project, in *Chapter 9, Loading Large Datasets beyond the Available RAM in Power BI*. We chose it because it is a multilingual in-memory data development platform and because it also provides the Python interface you know as PyArrow. On the other hand, data.table is a widely adopted package specifically designed for data manipulation in R. It provides an optimized in-memory data structure and offers fast and memory-efficient operations for common data manipulation tasks.

This is why the author of reclin2 decided to base the new version of his product on the specialized "data table" data structure.

Back to reclin2, it also has the ability to distribute computations across multiple CPU cores or machines. Parallelization provides a straightforward approach to speed up the record linkage process, while the snow package allows data to be distributed across multiple machines, effectively utilizing the memory resources available on those machines.

For all these reasons, and also the fact that the reclin package was removed from CRAN in 2023, we will use reclin2 for our use case.

The theory on probabilistic data linkage expounded in the previous paragraph also applies here. The use case we will use is the same one we used in the previous section with Python – namely, the case of deduplicating a dataset containing names, addresses, cities, and types of restaurants from Fodor's and Zagat's guides.

First, let's install the `reclin2` package:

1. Open RStudio and make sure it is referencing your latest CRAN R (version 4.2.2 in our case).
2. Click on the **Console** window and type this command: `install.packages('reclin2')`. Then, press **Enter**.

You are now ready to deduplicate your data. You can find all the following code in the `R\01-dedup-resturants-with-reclin2.R` file in the `Chapter 13` folder.

After loading the dataset using the same `restaurant.csv` file used also with Python, you can define the blocking conditions using the `pair_minsim()` function:

```r
library(readr)
library(reclin2)
library(dplyr)



main_path <- r"{C:\<your-path>\Ch13 - Calculating Columns Using Complex
Algorithms, Fuzzy Matching & Optimization Problems}"

restaurants_df <- read_csv(file.path(main_path, "restaurants.csv"))

pairs <-
  pair_minsim(restaurants_df, deduplication = TRUE, on = "city",
             comparators = list(lcs(threshold = 0.7),
                                 jaro_winkler(threshold = 0.7)),
             minsim = 0.7, keep_simsum = TRUE)
```

The above function can take two DataFrame as input in the case of data joins. In our case, however, in addition to passing the one source DataFrame, you must declare that this is a deduplication (`deduplication = TRUE`) so that the record pairs are all generated from the one DataFrame passed as input.

In addition, after declaring which fields to match for the blocking conditions (on = "city"), you can select a list of comparators (list(lcs(threshold = 0.7), jaro_winkler(threshold = 0.7))), which are string functions used to compare the fields declared in the above conditions. The threshold passed to these functions indicates that all matches with a metric value equal to or greater than the specified normalized threshold are considered good. The only comparison functions implemented in reclin2 are identical(), jaro_winkler(), jaccard(), and lcs(). Besides identical(), which ensures that the values compared are identical, the only other string distance function ever encountered is lcs(), which stands for **Longest Common Subsequence**. It is a string distance metric used to measure the similarity or dissimilarity between two strings by calculating the minimum number of operations (insertions and deletions) required to transform one string into the other. For any need, you can still implement a custom comparison function. The minimum similarity score below which matches are excluded should also be specified (minsim = 0.7). At your option, you can choose to display the similarity scores in the resulting DataFrame (keep_simsum = TRUE).

Next, pairs must be compared on a set of common fields of your choice. This task is performed by the compare_pairs() function, which takes the output of one of the functions that specify the pairs to be considered in the comparison (one of these is pair_minsim, as you have seen), the fields to be used in the comparison, and the usual list of comparator functions to be used. You also have the option of specifying a default comparator, and whether the variable of the pairs passed as input should be changed in place by adding the result of the comparison. Here is an example:

```
compare_pairs(pairs, on = c("name", "addr", "city"),
              comparators = list(jaro_winkler(threshold = 0.9),
                                 jaro_winkler(threshold = 0.8),
                                 jaccard(threshold = 0.7)),
              default_comparator = jaro_winkler(threshold = 0.9),
              inplace = TRUE)
```

The contents of the pairs variable after this operation are as follows:

```
> print(pairs)
First data set:  451 records
Second data set: 451 records
Total number of pairs: 38 361 pairs

        .x    .y  simsum      name      addr  city
      <int> <int>  <num>     <num>     <num> <num>
   1:    1     2       1 1.0000000 0.9855072     1
   2:    1     3       1 0.5473401 0.5769537     1
   3:    1     4       1 0.5816667 0.5769537     1
   4:    1     5       1 0.4394872 0.5456229     1
   5:    1     6       1 0.5201282 0.5456229     1
  ---
38357:  448   450      1 0.6025641 0.6023745     1
38358:  448   451      1 0.5277778 0.4919897     1
38359:  449   450      1 0.5139194 0.6332669     1
38360:  449   451      1 0.4880952 0.5819121     1
38361:  450   451      1 0.5337607 0.6350000     1
```

Figure 13.26: Contents of pairs variable after the field comparison

The .x and .y fields represent the positions of the rows to be compared by indicators starting with the value 1. At this point, the information in the pair variable is used to estimate the m and u probabilities using the Expectation-Maximization algorithm, as expected by the Fellegi-Sunter model. The function used for this is problink_em(), to which you pass the pairs variable enriched with the comparison data, and the formula that relates the fields used in the comparison in the form ~ var1 + var2:

```
m <- problink_em(~ name + addr, data = pairs)
```

Here are the contents of the m variable:

```
> print(m)
M- and u-probabilities estimated by the EM-algorithm:
 Variable M-probability U-probability
     name     0.2072564  0.0005930717
     addr     0.9764372  0.0521685774

Matching probability: 0.008482069.
```

Figure 13.27: Estimated m and u probabilities for each field

The probability estimates shown in *Figure 13.27* are quite intuitive:

- The probability that two equal values of the name field represent the same restaurant (m probability) is 0.207, which is not very high. In fact, the names of two restaurants in the same chain may be the same, but the restaurants may be located at two different addresses. Instead, the probability that two records with different name values still refer to the same restaurant (u probability) is close to zero (0.0006), which makes a lot of sense.

- The probability that two equal values of the address field represent the same restaurant (m probability) is very high (0.976). In fact, in general, two businesses located at the same address are most likely the same business. On the other hand, the probability that two restaurants are the same business if they have different addresses (u probability) is very low (0.052).

- The estimated probability that two randomly selected records from the pairs are a match (matching probability) is also very low (0.008)

Once you have the probability estimates, you can predict weights and probabilities for pairs, adding them to the pairs variable:

```
pairs <- predict(m, pairs = pairs, add = TRUE)
```

Here is the new contents of the pairs variable:

```
> print(pairs)
   First data set:   451 records
   Second data set: 451 records
   Total number of pairs: 38 361 pairs

            .x    .y simsum        name        addr  city        weights
         <int> <int>  <num>       <num>       <num> <num>          <num>
     1:      1     2      1 1.0000000 0.9855072     1  8.549382888
     2:      1     3      1 0.5473401 0.5769537     1  0.327486875
     3:      1     4      1 0.5816667 0.5769537     1  0.362755443
     4:      1     5      1 0.4394872 0.5456229     1  0.122975748
     5:      1     6      1 0.5201282 0.5456229     1  0.185818149
   ---
 38357:    448   450      1 0.6025641 0.6023745     1  0.482140354
 38358:    448   451      1 0.5277778 0.4919897     1 -0.005609745
 38359:    449   450      1 0.5139194 0.6332669     1  0.510843040
 38360:    449   451      1 0.4880952 0.5819121     1  0.294077502
 38361:    450   451      1 0.5337607 0.6350000     1  0.535281428
```

Figure 13.28: Calculated weights and probabilities for pairs

The new variable, weights, represents a measure of the similarity of a match between two records. The higher the value of the variable, the more similar the two records are. After a few trials, it is possible to identify an optimal threshold of the weights variable, above which a match can be considered valid with a good probability. To apply this threshold, the select_threshold() function is used, specifying the pairs variable enriched with the match predictions, the name of the new logical variable that will signal whether a value is above the threshold or not, the name of the variable containing the weights, and the threshold to be applied:

```
pairs <- select_threshold(pairs, variable = "match",
                          score = "weights", threshold = 3)
```

Here is the code to get a sample of the records that have the new match variable set to true:

```
pairs %>% filter(match == TRUE)
```

The output is the following:

```
> pairs %>% filter(match == TRUE)
  First data set:  451 records
  Second data set: 451 records
  Total number of pairs: 108 pairs

        .x     .y simsum      name      addr  city  weights  match
      <int> <int>  <num>     <num>     <num> <num>    <num> <lgcl>
  1:     1     2      1 1.0000000 0.9855072     1 8.549383   TRUE
  2:     3     4      1 0.8518519 1.0000000     1 3.611968   TRUE
  3:     5     6      1 0.5897436 1.0000000     1 3.015967   TRUE
  4:     7     8      1 1.0000000 1.0000000     1 8.785827   TRUE
  5:     9    10      1 1.0000000 1.0000000     1 8.785827   TRUE
 ---
104:   215   216      1 0.7192982 1.0000000     1 3.209039   TRUE
105:   217   218      1 1.0000000 0.9399510     1 8.016931   TRUE
106:   219   220      1 1.0000000 1.0000000     1 8.785827   TRUE
107:   221   222      1 0.7849626 1.0000000     1 3.365664   TRUE
108:   223   224      1 1.0000000 1.0000000     1 8.785827   TRUE
```

Figure 13.29: Sample of records with a high probability of match

If you recall the contents of the original restaurant record, there is also the class variable, which contains integer values. It identifies two records that are duplicates with the same variable value, and it is provided to help you understand how good the implemented matching algorithm was. By performing a few transformations on the DataFrame, it is possible to obtain a DataFrame containing true matches (the truth DataFrame) in the following form:

```
> truth
# A tibble: 112 × 3
    id_x  id_y truth
   <dbl> <dbl> <lgl>
 1     1     2 TRUE
 2     3     4 TRUE
 3     5     6 TRUE
 4     7     8 TRUE
 5     9    10 TRUE
 6    11    12 TRUE
 7    13    14 TRUE
 8    15    16 TRUE
 9    17    18 TRUE
10    19    20 TRUE
# ... with 102 more rows
```

Figure 13.30: True matches DataFrame

At this point, you can merge the truth DataFrame with the probable match DataFrame to find out which matches were missed or false matches:

```
pairs <- pairs %>%
  left_join( truth, by = join_by(.x == id_x, .y == id_y) ) %>%
  mutate( truth = ifelse( is.na(truth), FALSE, truth) )
```

The goodness of the computed matches is most evident when using the so-called **confusion matrix**, which shows validated matches (the truth) in the columns and computed matches in the rows:

```
table(pairs$truth, pairs$match, dnn = c("Truth", "Matched"))
```

Here is the output:

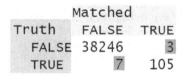

Figure 13.31: Confusion matrix of calculated matches

The matrix in *Figure 13.31* tells us that of all the pairs of items that do not actually match (the column `Matched=FALSE`), 38,246 were correctly identified as non-matches (negative class) by the algorithm, so they are true negatives; 7 were misclassified as non-matches (negative class), so they are false negatives. Of all the pairs that actually match (the column `Matched=TRUE`), 105 were correctly identified as matches (positive class) by the algorithm, so they are true positives; 3 were incorrectly identified as non-matches (negative class), so they are false positives.

Wow, not a bad deduplication result using fuzzy matching algorithms with R! Even if reclin2 is less flexible than Splink in Python, we get a better result than in the previous section (105 right matches vs. 82) using the less restrictive blocking conditions and tuned thresholds.

Let's see how you can apply what you learned in this section in Power BI.

Applying probabilistic record linkage in Power BI

We will apply the two approaches to deduplication through probabilistic data linkage in Python and in R in the same Power BI report. What we will do is identify duplicate pairs and then remove the right element of the pair from the original list of restaurants so that the deduplicated list is displayed. Let's proceed:

1. Open Power BI Desktop through the shortcut that activates the pbi_powerquery_env environment.

2. Make sure Power BI Desktop is referencing the pbi_powerquery_env environment in the **Python scripting** tab, and the latest available engine (in our case, 4.2.2) in the **R scripting** tab in the **Options**.

3. Open the **Get data** menu on the **Home** ribbon then select the **Text/CSV** connector and click **Connect**.

4. Select the file restaurants.csv in the Chapter 13 folder, and then click **Open**. Then click **Transform Data**. Your dataset will be loaded as a new query called **restaurants**:

Figure 13.32: Restaurants data loaded in Power BI

5. Duplicate the query by right-clicking on it and selecting **Duplicate**. The new query **restaurants (2)** will be created.

6. Rename the duplicated query by right-clicking on it, selecting **Rename**, and entering the new name restaurants-deduped-Python.

7. Duplicate the **restaurants** query again by right-clicking on it and selecting **Duplicate**. The new query **restaurants (2)** will be created.

8. Rename the duplicated query by right-clicking on it, selecting **Rename**, and entering the new name restaurants-deduped-R. You'll end up with the following situation:

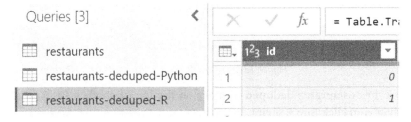

Figure 13.33: Situation after duplicating the query

9. Click the **restaurants-deduped-Python** query, click the **Transform** menu on the ribbon, and then click on **Run Python script**.

10. Copy the code in the file Python\02-dedup-resturants-in-powerbi.py, paste it into the Python script editor, and click **OK**.

11. If you get the Firewall privacy level mismatch error, select a **Public** privacy level for both the **restaurants.csv** and the **Python** data sources. Then click the **Home** menu on the ribbon, and click **Refresh Preview**.

12. Click the **Table** value to the right of the **restaurants_dedup_df** DataFrame:

	ABC Name	▼	Value	↤↦
1	dataset		Table	
2	matches_df		Table	
3	restaurants_dedup_df		Table ←	
4	restaurants_df		Table	

Figure 13.34: Expanding the right deduplicated DataFrame

13. Now your **restaurants-deduped-Python** query returns the deduplicated restaurant records, removing the rows with the IDs on the right part of the matching pairs:

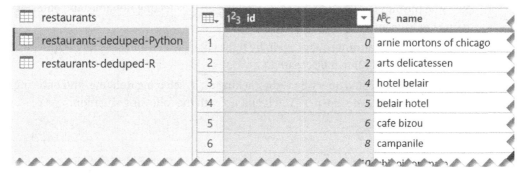

Figure 13.35: Deduplicated restaurants using Python

14. Click the **restaurants-deduped**-R query on the left, then click the **Transform** menu on the ribbon, and click **Run R script**.

15. Copy the code in the `R\02-dedup-resturants-in-powerbi.R` file, paste it into the R script editor, and click **OK**.

16. Click the **Table** value at the right of the **restaurants_dedup_df** DataFrame to get the deduplicated restaurants table:

	123 id	▼	ABC name	▼	ABC addr	
1		0	arnie morton's of chicago		435 s. la cienega blv.	
2		2	art's delicatessen		12224 ventura blvd.	
3		4	hotel bel-air		701 stone canyon rd.	
4		6	cafe bizou		14016 ventura blvd.	
5		8	campanile		624 s. la brea ave.	
6		10	chinois on main		2709 main st.	
7		12	citrus		6703 melrose ave.	
8		14	fenix		8358 sunset blvd. west	

Figure 13.36: Deduplicated restaurants using R

17. Click the **Home** menu and click **Close & Apply**.

Great! You have a deduplicated table using one of the most efficient fuzzy matching algorithms for large datasets based on probabilistic matching algorithms using both Python and R. If Power BI's standard fuzzy matching functionality does not meet your needs, you can turn to the more flexible probabilistic record linkage algorithms for both deduplication and two-table approximate matching solutions.

Summary

In this chapter, you learned how the default fuzzy matching feature in Power BI works and what it is. You also learned how to use another fuzzy matching algorithm based on probabilistic data linkage by implementing it in both Python and R. You then applied this knowledge to a real-world deduplication case in Power BI.

In the upcoming chapter, you will delve into the world of optimization and learn how to tackle simple optimization problems by solving their associated **Linear Programming** (**LP**) models.

References

- *Power Query Fuzzy Merge* (`https://learn.microsoft.com/en-us/power-query/merge-queries-fuzzy-match`)
- *Cluster values* (`https://learn.microsoft.com/en-us/power-query/cluster-values`)
- *Customizable and Scalable Fuzzy Join for Big Data* (`http://www.vldb.org/pvldb/vol12/p2106-chen.pdf`)
- *Locality Sensitive Hashing: How to Find Similar Items in a Large Set, with Precision* (`https://towardsdatascience.com/locality-sensitive-hashing-how-to-find-similar-items-in-a-large-set-with-precision-d907c52b05fc`)
- *Probabilistic record linkage* (`https://www.robinlinacre.com/probabilistic_linkage/`)
- *The mathematics of the Fellegi Sunter model* (`https://www.robinlinacre.com/maths_of_fellegi_sunter/`)
- *The Intuition Behind the Use of Expectation Maximisation to Train Record Linkage Models* (`https://www.robinlinacre.com/em_intuition/`)

Test your knowledge

1. What is fuzzy matching?
2. What are the benefits and use cases of fuzzy matching in data analysis?
3. What are the limitations of the default fuzzy matching algorithm in Power BI?
4. What are the common data cleaning steps performed before applying fuzzy matching algorithms?
5. How does the algorithm implemented in Power BI overcome the computational complexity of comparing large datasets?
6. How does probabilistic record linkage work?
7. Which libraries are used in this chapter to apply probabilistic record linkage algorithms?
8. How can the accuracy and performance of probabilistic record linkage algorithms be evaluated?

Learn more on Discord

To join the Discord community for this book – where you can share feedback, ask questions to the author, and learn about new releases – follow the QR code below:

```
https://discord.gg/MKww5g45EB
```

14

Calculating Columns Using Complex Algorithms: Optimization Problems

As a Power BI analyst, you may be faced with interesting mathematical optimization problems. There may be times when you need to solve basic, yet critical, optimization questions without having expertise in advanced mathematical concepts. **Linear programming** (**LP**) has made its way into data analysis with its simple requirements and immediate applicability. To show you how effective and easy it is to apply LP techniques to real-world cases, you will see how to solve a simple demand optimization problem for a manufacturing company using both Python and R in Power BI.

This chapter will cover the following topics:

- The basics of linear programming
- Handling optimization problems with Python and R

Technical requirements

This chapter requires you to have a working internet connection and **Power BI Desktop** already installed on your machine (we used version 2.114.664.0 64-bit, February 2023). You must have properly configured the R and Python engines and IDEs as outlined in *Chapter 2, Configuring R with Power BI*, and *Chapter 3, Configuring Python with Power BI*.

The basics of linear programming

LP algorithms are used in all areas where optimization, and therefore the economy of resources, is critical to the continuation of activities. To understand what this is all about, you need some basic math concepts. Let's brush up on some of the geometric concepts we learned in college.

Linear equations and inequalities

We have all encountered the term linear equation at least once in our lives. A **linear equation**, in its simplest sense, is a mathematical relationship between two variables, x and y, of the form $ax + by + c = 0$, which identifies a **straight line** on the Cartesian plane:

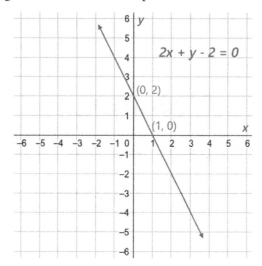

Figure 14.1: Representation of the linear equation $2x + y = 2$

Here, a and b are the coefficients that control the slope and direction of the line on the graph, determining how steep it is and whether it slopes up or down. c is the coefficient that adjusts the position of the line, determining where it crosses the vertical axis. Together, these components determine the appearance of the line on the Cartesian plane.

Obviously, the variables involved in a linear equation can be more than two. The representation of a linear equation is possible as long as we have three variables (the famous three dimensions we can see). In this case, a three-variable (x, y, and z) linear equation of the form $ax + by + cz + d = 0$ represents a **plane** in the space:

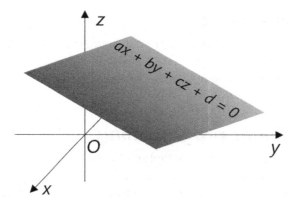

Figure 14.2: Representation of a generic linear equation $ax + by + cz + d = 0$

When you have more than three variables in a linear equation, we commonly refer to its representation as a **hyperplane** instead of a plane.

There are also **linear inequalities**, which are linear functions that contain inequalities (identified by the symbols $<$, $>$, $\leq$, and $\geq$). Just as with linear equations, you can plot linear inequalities with either two or three variables. They represent all points on either side of the line in the case of two variables (i.e., a region of the plane), or the points on either side of the straight plane in the case of three variables (i.e., a volume):

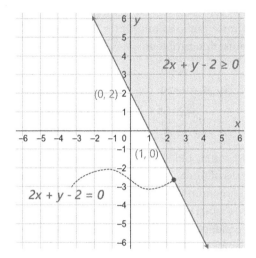
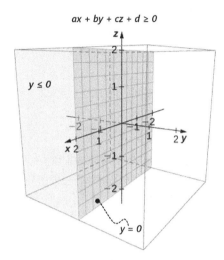

Figure 14.3: Representation of generic linear inequalities with two or three variables

Note that the regions identified by the inequalities are infinite but have an edge formed by the linear equation derived from the same inequality using the = sign instead of the inequality sign.

Very often, when we think about these concepts, we associate them only with the theoretical mathematical stuff, but that's not the case. Simple concepts related to transportation, manufacturing, shipping, and so on can be traced back to linear equations or inequalities. Let's look at an example.

Formulating a linear optimization problem

Imagine you work in a manufacturing company and you need to produce two products, P1 and P2. To produce them, you need a machine. Specifically, producing one unit of product P1 requires 30 minutes of processing time on the machine, while producing one unit of product P2 requires 25 minutes on the same machine. In addition, the number of hours that the machine, M, can remain on is 40 hours (= 40*60 minutes). This means that 30 minutes multiplied by the number of P1 products plus 25 minutes multiplied by the number of P2 products cannot exceed 40 hours of processing time. So, given x number of P1 products and y number of P2 products produced at the end of processing, the machine hours **constraint** (a rule or limit that you must work within) can be summarized as follows:

$$30x + 25y \leq 40 \cdot 60$$

Wow! You just used a simple linear inequality to describe a constraint on a manufacturing process.

Now imagine that you have received requests from customers for both P1 and P2 products. Specifically, if you add up all the requests, you must produce at least 45 units of P1 and 25 units of P2 to satisfy your customers. These demand constraints can be summarized as follows:

$$x \geq 45$$
$$y \geq 25$$

Awesome! You've added two more linear constraints to your problem. If you add a goal to these business constraints, for example, that you want to maximize the total number, z, of units of P1 and P2, the set of constraints and the goal form a linear optimization problem:

$$
\begin{aligned}
\textit{maximize:} \quad & z = x + y \\
\textit{subject to:} \quad & 30x + 25y \leq 40 \cdot 60 \\
& x \geq 45 \\
& y \geq 25
\end{aligned}
$$

Simple as that, right? If we want to be a little more formal, LP, also known as linear optimization, consists of a set of techniques useful for solving systems of linear equations and inequalities with the goal of maximizing or minimizing a linear objective function. Specifically, the variables x and y are called **decision variables** and the objective that is set is called the **objective function** or **cost function**. In this example, the business case only required inequality constraints, but there may be equality constraints as well. For example, imagine that the company must fill an order that requires exactly twice as many units of P1 as P2 to satisfy customer demand. This would create an equality constraint on the relationship between the number of products P1 and P2 produced. The equality constraint could be expressed as $x=2y$.

Cool! But now that we have the problem set up from a mathematical standpoint, how do we solve it? First, we need to take all the inequalities and plot them on the axes (in this case, you can, because they only contain two variables). As we saw at the beginning, a linear inequality represents a portion of a plane bounded by the line, given the sign of equality in the inequality itself. By intersecting all these planes, we come to identify an area common to all the inequalities, called the **feasible region**. In principle, all points in this region satisfy all the constraints imposed by the inequalities.

If you want to plot the feasible region associated with the constraints of the example just presented, there is no need to go through all the geometry you learned in high school, but just use **WolframAlpha** (https://www.wolframalpha.com/). Enter the following string in the search engine: `plot 30x+25y<=2400 and x>=45 and y>=25`. All constraints must be satisfied simultaneously, hence the use of the and operator. Press **Enter** and you will see this result:

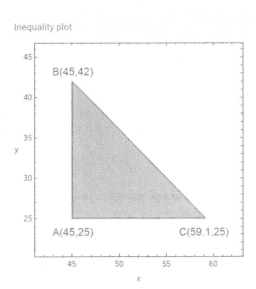

Figure 14.4: The feasible region drawn by WolframAlpha

To the WolframAlpha result, we have added the x and y coordinates of the vertices of the feasible region, which is a triangle. For instance, vertex A is located at x-axis 45 and y-axis 25.

 It is shown that if the optimization problem is solvable, the solution that maximizes or minimizes the objective function lies precisely at one of the vertices of the feasible region.

For those who are curious about how to calculate the coordinates of the vertices, we need to solve linear equations considering the values of the constraints given by the equations. For example, the x value of vertex x is calculated by substituting the value $y=25$ in the equation $30x+25y=2400$. So, $x=(2400-(25*25))/30=59.1666$. For simplicity, we assume the x value of vertex C is `59.1`. Obviously, it is not possible to have a fractional part of the product P1 since it is not possible to produce only a fraction of one unit. The closest integer value should then be considered, which is 59. Therefore, if the business problem requires having **integer values** for the decision variables, then the problem becomes one of **Mixed-Integer Linear Programming (MILP)**.

In our case, then, we consider the vertices A, B, and $C^*=(59,25)$ as possible solutions to our problem and substitute their coordinates into the objective function, $z = x + y$:

-    $A: z = 45 + 25 = 70$
-    $B: z = 45 + 42 = 87$
-    $C^*: z = 59 + 25 = 84$

We conclude that the solution of our problem is given by the vertex B with a maximum value of 87 units, namely $P1 = 45$ and $P2 = 42$.

 In summary, producing 45 units of product P1 and 42 units of product P2 satisfies the machine's hourly production constraint and the customer demand constraints, while maximizing total production.

Did you ever think you could solve a linear optimization problem before today? Well, you just did! Of course, it is possible to solve these problems by hand when they are that simple. But as the number of decision variables grows, it becomes impossible to draw the feasible region and, therefore, impossible to locate the vertices in a multi-dimensional space by eye. In these cases, it is mathematics, and in particular, the packages provided by the community for Python and R that allow us to solve the problem. Let's first consider a more complex real-world case of an LP problem.

Definition of the LP problem to solve

This time, imagine that you work for a company that needs to ship a product from different warehouses around the world to different countries. You have to handle the following:

-    The quantities of product available in warehouses:

warehouse_name	product_qty
Warehouse ITA	50000
Warehouse DEU	30000
Warehouse JPN	40000
Warehouse USA	55000

Figure 14.5: Quantities of product available in warehouses

-    The amount of product needed by the different countries:

country_name	product_qty
Italy	40000
France	15000
Germany	25000
Japan	45000
China	25000
USA	25000

Figure 14.6: Quantities of product required by different countries

- Shipping costs from each warehouse to all requesting countries:

warehouse_name	country_name	shipping_cost
Warehouse ITA	Italy	8
Warehouse ITA	France	18
Warehouse ITA	Germany	14
Warehouse ITA	Japan	40
Warehouse ITA	China	40
Warehouse ITA	USA	25
Warehouse DEU	Italy	12
Warehouse DEU	France	10
Warehouse DEU	Germany	8
Warehouse DEU	Japan	18
Warehouse DEU	China	40
Warehouse DEU	USA	18

Warehouse JPN	Italy	34
Warehouse JPN	France	32
Warehouse JPN	Germany	30
Warehouse JPN	Japan	10
Warehouse JPN	China	33
Warehouse JPN	USA	35
Warehouse USA	Italy	25
Warehouse USA	France	20
Warehouse USA	Germany	18
Warehouse USA	Japan	35
Warehouse USA	China	30
Warehouse USA	USA	10

Figure 14.7: Costs of shipping from warehouses to countries

Your goal is to minimize your company's costs by meeting all of the requirements of customers from the different countries.

Formulating the LP problem

As seen in the previous section, you must first formulate the problem mathematically. Let's use some numerical indices, i and j, to identify the quantities shipped and the costs. Specifically, consider the quantity xij of product that will be shipped from *Warehouse i* to *Country j* according to this matrix that defines the decision variables and costs:

Definitions	Italy (j=1)	France (j=2)	Germany (j=3)	Japan (j=4)	China (j=5)	USA (j=6)
Warehouse ITA (i=1)	x_{11}, C_{11}	x_{12}, C_{12}	x_{13}, C_{13}	x_{14}, C_{14}	x_{15}, C_{15}	x_{16}, C_{16}
Warehouse DEU (i=2)	x_{21}, C_{21}	x_{22}, C_{22}	x_{23}, C_{23}	x_{24}, C_{24}	x_{25}, C_{25}	x_{26}, C_{26}
Warehouse JPN (i=3)	x_{31}, C_{31}	x_{32}, C_{32}	x_{33}, C_{33}	x_{34}, C_{34}	x_{35}, C_{35}	x_{36}, C_{36}
Warehouse USA (i=4)	x_{41}, C_{41}	x_{42}, C_{42}	x_{43}, C_{43}	x_{44}, C_{44}	x_{45}, C_{45}	x_{46}, C_{46}

Figure 14.8: Definition matrix of the quantity of products sent and costs

The quantity xij is an integer and non-negative ($xij \geq 0$).

Given the preceding definitions, the target of the problem is to minimize the objective function, which can be written as the sum of the product between the cost of shipping from *Warehouse i* to *Country j* (Cij) and the quantity of product shipped from *Warehouse i* to *Country j* (xij):

$$\min_{i,j} \left(\sum_{i=1}^{4} \sum_{j=1}^{6} C_{ij} x_{ij} \right)$$

Written out in full, organized by warehouse for ease of reading, and using the shipping cost amounts from *Figure 14.7*, the previous objective function can be rewritten as follows:

$$\min \begin{bmatrix} (8x_{11} + 18x_{12} + 14x_{13} + 40x_{14} + 40x_{15} + 25x_{16}) \\ + \\ (12x_{21} + 10x_{22} + 8x_{23} + 18x_{24} + 40x_{25} + 18x_{26}) \\ + \\ (34x_{31} + 32x_{32} + 30x_{33} + 10x_{34} + 33x_{35} + 35x_{36}) \\ + \\ (25x_{41} + 20x_{42} + 18x_{43} + 35x_{44} + 30x_{45} + 10x_{46}) \end{bmatrix} \begin{matrix} (W_{ITA}) \\ \\ (W_{DEU}) \\ \\ (W_{JPN}) \\ \\ (W_{USA}) \end{matrix}$$

To complete the formulation of the problem, you must formalize the constraints, which are of two types – the *warehouse supply constraints* and the *customer demand constraints*:

- **Warehouse supply constraints:** Once a warehouse is fixed (for example, *Warehouse ITA*, for which $i = 1$), the sum of the products shipped from that warehouse to all countries (the sum of $x1j$) cannot exceed the maximum quantity of products contained in that warehouse (for *Warehouse ITA*, 50,000 products; see *Figure 14.5*). That is, for all six countries, we have:

$$x_{11} + x_{12} + x_{13} + x_{14} + x_{15} + x_{16} \le 50.000$$

Therefore, you will have a similar constraint for each warehouse (four constraints in total).

- **Customer demand constraints:** Regardless of which warehouse the goods come from, you must satisfy the demand for products in each country. Therefore, the sum of the products sent from all the warehouses to a given country (for example, *France*, where $j = 2$) must be at least equal to the demand of that country (*France* demands at least 15,000 products; see *Figure 14.6*). Therefore, considering all four warehouses, we have:

$$x_{12} + x_{22} + x_{32} + x_{42} \ge 15000$$

You will have a similar constraint for each country (six constraints in total).

Therefore, the final linear optimization problem can be formulated as follows:

$$z = \sum_{i=1}^{4} \sum_{j=1}^{6} C_{ij} x_{ij}$$

minimize:

subject to: (warehouse supply constraints)

$$x_{11} + x_{12} + x_{13} + x_{14} + x_{15} + x_{16} \le 50000 \quad (W_{ITA})$$
$$x_{21} + x_{22} + x_{23} + x_{24} + x_{25} + x_{26} \le 30000 \quad (W_{DEU})$$
$$x_{31} + x_{32} + x_{33} + x_{34} + x_{35} + x_{36} \le 40000 \quad (W_{JPN})$$
$$x_{41} + x_{42} + x_{43} + x_{44} + x_{45} + x_{46} \le 55000 \quad (W_{USA})$$

(country demand constraints)

$$x_{11} + x_{21} + x_{31} + x_{41} \ge 40000 \quad \text{(Italy)}$$
$$x_{12} + x_{22} + x_{32} + x_{42} \ge 15000 \quad \text{(France)}$$
$$x_{13} + x_{23} + x_{33} + x_{43} \ge 25000 \quad \text{(Germany)}$$
$$x_{14} + x_{24} + x_{34} + x_{44} \ge 45000 \quad \text{(Japan)}$$
$$x_{15} + x_{25} + x_{35} + x_{45} \ge 25000 \quad \text{(China)}$$
$$x_{16} + x_{26} + x_{36} + x_{46} \ge 25000 \quad \text{(USA)}$$

(non-negative constraints)
$$x_{ij} \ge 0, i = 1..4, j = 1..6$$

Awesome! You have managed to formulate a non-trivial business problem in mathematical terms. Now let's see how you can solve it with Python and R.

Handling optimization problems with Python and R

As you've probably noticed, the large community that develops Python packages never stands still. Even in this case, it has provided a module that helps us solve linear optimization problems. Its name is **PuLP** (https://github.com/coin-or/pulp) and it is an LP modeler written in Python. It interfaces with the most common free and non-free engines that solve LP, **Mixed-Integer Programming (MIP)**, and other related problems, such as the **GNU Linear Programming Kit (GLPK)**, **COIN-OR Branch and Cut (CBC)**, which is the default one, and **IBM ILOG CPLEX**. Using PuLP is fairly straightforward. Let's put it into practice right away with the problem from the previous section.

Solving the LP problem in Python

The code that will be explained to you in this section can be found in the `Python\01-linear-optimization-in-python.py` file in the `Chapter 14` folder of the repository.

First, you have to install the PuLP module in your environment:

1. Open Anaconda Prompt.
2. Enter the `conda activate pbi_powerquery_env` command.
3. Enter the `pip install pulp==2.7.0` command.

You can then define the values that will make up the constraints and costs using NumPy vectors and matrices:

```python
import pandas as pd
import numpy as np
import pulp as plp
warehouse_supply_df = pd.read_excel(r'C:\<your-path>\Ch14 - Calculating Columns
Using Complex Algorithms, Optimization Problems\RetailData.xlsx', sheet_
name='Warehouse Supply', engine='openpyxl')
warehouse_supply = warehouse_supply_df['product_qty'].to_numpy()
country_demands_df = pd.read_excel(r'C:\<your-path>\Ch14 - Calculating Columns
Using Complex Algorithms, Optimization Problems\RetailData.xlsx', sheet_
name='Country Demand', engine='openpyxl')
country_demands = country_demands_df['product_qty'].to_numpy()
cost_matrix_df = pd.read_excel(r'C:\<your-path>\Ch14 - Calculating Columns
Using Complex Algorithms, Optimization Problems\RetailData.xlsx', sheet_
name='Shipping Cost', engine='openpyxl')
n_warehouses = cost_matrix_df.nunique()['warehouse_name']
n_countries = cost_matrix_df.nunique()['country_name']
cost_matrix = cost_matrix_df['shipping_cost'].to_numpy().reshape(n_
warehouses,n_countries)
```

The script file also contains the code to import the values directly from the `RetailData.xlsx` file in the `Chapter 14` folder.

It is then possible to define an `LpProblem` object by giving it a name and the type of optimization you want to apply to the objective function (`minimize` or `maximize`):

```python
model = plp.LpProblem("supply-demand-minimize-costs-problem", plp.LpMinimize)
```

You can later add an objective function and constraints to this empty object.

To construct the objective function, we must first define the decision variables (xij) using the `LpVariable` function, which takes the variable name, the full list of strings representing the variable indices, the category of the variable (continuous, integer, or binary), and any upper or lower bound values. The index list is simply constructed using a nested **list comprehension** (http://bit.ly/nested-list-comprehensions):

```
var_indexes = [str(i)+str(j) for i in range(1, n_warehouses+1) for j in
range(1, n_countries+1)]
print("Variable indexes:", var_indexes)
```

This is the output as an example:

```
Variable Indices: ['11', '12', '13', '14', '15', '16', '21', '22', '23', '24',
'25', '26', '31', '32', '33', '34', '35', '36', '41', '42', '43', '44', '45',
'46']
```

You can now easily define the decision variables as follows:

```
decision_vars = plp.LpVariable.matrix(
name="x",
indexs=var_indexes,
cat="Integer",
lowBound=0 )
```

Since the decision variables are to be multiplied by the Cij costs defined earlier in cost_matrix, it is appropriate to format the decision_vars list in the same form as the cost matrix in order to be able to perform element-wise multiplication, also known as the *Hadamard product*:

```
shipping_mtx = np.array(decision_vars).reshape(n_warehouses,n_countries)
print("Shipping quantities matrix:")
print(shipping_mtx)
```

It returns the following output:

```
Shipping quantities matrix:
[[x_11 x_12 x_13 x_14 x_15 x_16]
 [x_21 x_22 x_23 x_24 x_25 x_26]
 [x_31 x_32 x_33 x_34 x_35 x_36]
 [x_41 x_42 x_43 x_44 x_45 x_46]]
```

The objective function is then defined as the sum of the element-wise product of the cost and shipping matrices:

```
objective_func = plp.lpSum(cost_matrix * shipping_mtx)
print(objective_func)
```

The output is as follows:

```
8*x_11 + 18*x_12 + 14*x_13 + 40*x_14 + 40*x_15 + 25*x_16 + 12*x_21 + 10*x_22 +
8*x_23 + 18*x_24 + 40*x_25 + 18*x_26 + 34*x_31 + 32*x_32 + 30*x_33 + 10*x_34 +
33*x_35 + 35*x_36 + 25*x_41 + 20*x_42 + 18*x_43 + 35*x_44 + 30*x_45 + 10*x_46
```

If you recall, this expression is the same as the fully written objective function that you saw in the previous section.

You can then add the objective function to the model, as follows:

```
model += objective_func
```

Constraint inequalities are also added in the same way:

```
for i in range(n_warehouses):
    model += plp.lpSum(shipping_mtx[i][j] for j in range(n_   countries)) <=
warehouse_supply[i], "Warehouse supply    constraints " + str(i)
for j in range(n_countries):
    model += plp.lpSum(shipping_mtx[i][j] for i in range(n_   warehouses)) >=
country_demands[j] , "Country demand    constraints " + str(j)
```

Finally, we can move on to solving the problem by running this simple script:

```
model.solve()
```

The first thing to do is to check the state of the solution, which can take the values Optimal, Not Solved, Infeasible, Unbounded, or Undefined:

```
status = plp.LpStatus[model.status]
print(status)
```

In our case, the state is Optimal, so an optimal solution to the problem has been found. So let's see what the value of the objective function is for the solution you found:

```
print("Total Cost:", model.objective.value())
```

The value is equal to €2,270,000, which is the lowest possible cost while satisfying all imposed constraints. If you want to see the solution values of the variables that make up the shipping matrix in a very readable way, you'd better transform them into a pandas DataFrame:

```
decision_var_results = np.empty(shape=(n_warehouses * n_countries))
z = 0
for v in model.variables():
try:
  decision_var_results[z] = v.value()
  z += 1
except:
  print("error couldn't find value")
decision_var_results = decision_var_results.reshape(n_warehouses,n_countries)
col_idxs = ['Italy','France','Germany','Japan','China','USA']
row_idxs = ['Warehouse ITA','Warehouse DEU','Warehouse JPN','Warehouse USA']
dv_res_df = pd.DataFrame(decision_var_results, columns=col_idxs, index=row_
idxs)
dv_res_df
```

The result is as follows:

	Italy	France	Germany	Japan	China	USA
Warehouse ITA	40000.0	0.0	10000.0	0.0	0.0	0.0
Warehouse DEU	0.0	10000.0	15000.0	5000.0	0.0	0.0
Warehouse JPN	0.0	0.0	0.0	40000.0	0.0	0.0
Warehouse USA	0.0	5000.0	0.0	0.0	25000.0	25000.0

Figure 14.9: Quantities shipped according to the solution found

For example, it is easy to see that French customers need to receive 10,000 units from the German (**DEU**) warehouse and 5,000 units from the **USA** warehouse to meet their demand.

Instead, if you want to check the total quantities shipped from each warehouse, you can run this code:

```
warehouse_shipped_qty = np.zeros(shape=(n_warehouses))
z = 0
for i in range(n_warehouses):
warehouse_shipped_qty[z] = plp.lpSum(shipping_mtx[i][j].value() for j in
range(n_countries)).value()
  z += 1
  w_shipped_df = pd.DataFrame(warehouse_shipped_qty,    columns=['qty'],
index=row_idxs)
  w_shipped_df
```

You will get this result:

	qty
Warehouse ITA	50000.0
Warehouse DEU	30000.0
Warehouse JPN	40000.0
Warehouse USA	55000.0

Figure 14.10: Total quantities shipped from each warehouse

Impressive! You've managed to solve a non-simple linear optimization problem with just a few lines of Python code. Would you have guessed that was possible? Now let's see how you can apply what you've learned in Power BI.

Solving the LP problem in Power BI with Python

Applying what we just saw in Power BI is not as straightforward as in the other cases we saw in the previous chapters. To start, we need to input data on the demand for the country, supply from the warehouse, and shipping costs into the model.

This information can come from different sources. In our case, we have them ready in Excel, so we will proceed to load them in Power BI Desktop:

1. Open Power BI Desktop through the shortcut that activates the pbi_powerquery_env environment.

2. Make sure Power BI Desktop is referencing the pbi_powerquery_env environment in the **Python scripting** tab.

3. Click **Excel workbook** on the ribbon (or **Import data from Excel** in the main canvas), select the RetailData.xlsx file in the Chapter 14 folder, and click **Open**.

4. Select the **CountryDemand, ShippingCost,** and **WarehouseSupply** tables (the ones with the blue header) and then click **Transform data:**

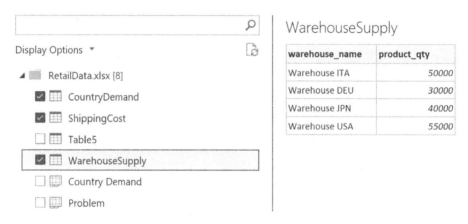

Figure 14.11: Selecting the three tables from Excel

You are now in the situation described earlier. At this point, each of the three queries in Power Query has its own stack of applied steps that generated it:

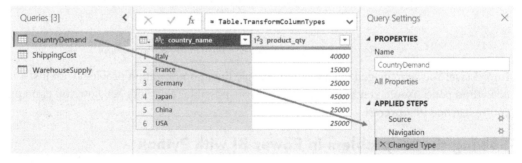

Figure 14.12: The CountryDemand query with its stack of applied steps

In the previous section, you saw that *you must be able to use all three datasets in a Python script* in order to calculate the optimal allocations. If you add a Python script as a step in one of the three queries listed previously, you can only interact with the data from that single query in the script. So how do you create a script that can use all of the available data? If you recall, we addressed this question in *Chapter 4, Solving Common Issues When Using Python and R in Power BI*. Specifically, we will use the most "elegant" version of the ones presented, which is to pass the tables as a list of parameters in the `Python.Execute()` function. Let's see in detail how to accomplish this:

1. Click on **Enter Data** in the **Home** menu to enter new table data manually:

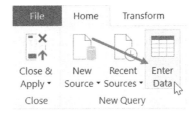

Figure 14.13: Enter a new table manually

2. Leave the table empty for now and name the new table `Result`, then press **OK**:

Figure 14.14: Create the empty Result table

3. Click on **Run Python script** in the **Transform** menu, keeping the **Result** query selected.
4. Leave just the default comment in the Python editor without entering any new code and press **OK**.
5. Go back to the **Home** menu and click **Advanced Editor**, keeping the **Result** query selected.
6. Just remove the code from `Source` to `text}})`, (including the comma) and make sure your code is the following:

```
let
    #"Run Python script" = Python.Execute("# 'dataset' holds the input
data for this script#(lf)",[dataset=#"Changed Type"])
in
    #"Run Python script"
```

7. Basically, you have the execution of an empty Python script in the M script. For now, do not press **Done**.

8. Replace the default [dataset=#"Changed Type"] parameters list with the following: [warehouse_supply_df=WarehouseSupply, country_demands_df=CountryDemand, shipping_cost_df=ShippingCost]. Then click **Done**.

9. You may get the following error: Formula.Firewall: Query 'Merge1' (step 'Run Python script') references other queries or steps, so it may not directly access a data source. Please rebuild this data combination.

10. If privacy levels are not already ignored, go to the Power Query editor **Options and settings**, then **Options**, and click on **Privacy** under the **Current File** section. Then, select the **Ignore the Privacy Levels and potentially improve the performance** option and press **OK**:

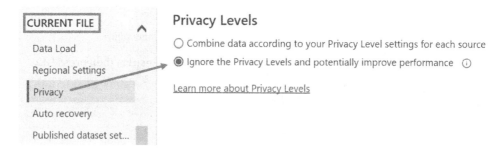

Figure 14.15: Ignore the Privacy Levels for the current file

11. Go to the **Home** tab and click on **Refresh Preview**.

12. Sometimes, it is necessary to give Power BI permission to run Python code. If so, click **Permission required** in the yellow warning ribbon and press **Run** in the next window.

13. At this point, you can finally enter the Python code to calculate the lowest possible cost while satisfying all imposed constraints. To do this, select the **Result** query and click on the gearwheel next to the **Run Python script** step in the **Applied Steps** panel.

14. Enter the script you can find in the Python\02-linear-optimization-in-power-bi-with-python.py file in the Chapter 14 folder, and press **OK**.

15. Click on **Table** for the result_df DataFrame:

Figure 14.16: Selecting the result_df table

16. You will see the contents of the following table, which shows the values of shipped quantities provided by the solution to the linear optimization problem for each combination of warehouse and country, and the corresponding costs:

	$^{AB}_C$ warehouse_name	$^{AB}_C$ country_name	$^{12}_3$ shipped_qty	$^{12}_3$ cost
1	Warehouse ITA	Italy	40000	320000
2	Warehouse ITA	France	0	0
3	Warehouse ITA	Germany	10000	140000
4	Warehouse ITA	Japan	0	0
5	Warehouse ITA	China	0	0
6	Warehouse ITA	USA	0	0
7	Warehouse DEU	Italy	0	0

Figure 14.17: Calculated optimal results

17. Click on **Close & Apply**.

Note that if you followed step 13, then the source privacy level control will be disabled. You should turn it back on at the end of this project to combine data according to the privacy level settings of each file, and to be warned of possible data leaks due to query folding mechanisms.

 Remember that if you want to publish your report to the Power BI service, the privacy level of all data sources must be set to **Public**.

Did you know that everything you've seen about LP problems can also be implemented in R too? Let's see how to do it.

Solving the LP problem in R

If the Python community is very active, the R community is certainly not standing still! In fact, the **Optimization Modeling Package (OMPR)** is available (https://dirkschumacher.github.io/ompr/), which is a domain-specific language designed for modeling and solving LP problems in R.

In general, all other packages developed in R that serve the same purpose are mostly matrix-oriented, forcing you to transform all objects into matrices and vectors before passing them to the solver. This task may seem simple enough at first glance, but when the problems to be solved become more complex, it can become difficult to turn everything into matrices and vectors in R to solve them.

The ompr package, on the other hand, provides enough expressiveness to allow you to model your LP problems incrementally, thanks also to the use of the %>% pipe. As a result, you will feel like you are writing code as if you were using dplyr functions, forgetting about matrices and vectors.

In addition, the ompr package relies on another package called ompr.roi to be able to select the preferred engine for solving LP problems. This package uses, behind the scenes, a sophisticated framework for handling linear and non-linear optimization problems in R called the **R Optimization Infrastructure (ROI)**, which is provided by another package called ROI (http://roi.r-forge.r-project.org/).

In our examples, we'll use the **GLPK** solver added as a plugin by ROI.

So, let's see how to set up the LP problem we described in the previous sections in R using the ompr package.

First, you need to install the packages necessary for ompr to work correctly. To do so, follow these steps:

1. Open RStudio and make sure it is referencing your latest CRAN R version (version 4.2.2 in our case).
2. Click on the **Console** window and enter this command: `install.packages('ompr')`. Then, press *Enter*.
3. Enter this command: `install.packages('ompr.roi')`. Then, press **Enter**.
4. Enter this command: `install.packages('ROI.plugin.glpk')`. Then, press **Enter**.

You will find all of the code shown below in the `R\01-linear-optimization-in-r.R` file in the Chapter 14 folder.

First, you will need to import the necessary packages and the data from the `RetailData.xlsx` Excel file, which you will find in the Chapter 14 folder:

```
library(dplyr)
library(tidyr)
library(readxl)
library(ompr)
library(ompr.roi)
library(ROI.plugin.glpk)
warehouse_supply_tbl = read_xlsx(r'{ D:\<your-path>\Ch14 - Calculating Columns
Using Complex Algorithms, Optimization Problems\RetailData.xlsx}', sheet =
'Warehouse Supply')
country_demands_tbl = read_xlsx(r'{ D:\<your-path>\Ch14 - Calculating Columns
Using Complex Algorithms, Optimization Problems\RetailData.xlsx}', sheet =
'Country Demand')
cost_matrix_tbl = read_xlsx(r'{ D:\<your-path>\Ch14 - Calculating Columns Using
Complex Algorithms, Optimization Problems\RetailData.xlsx}', sheet = 'Shipping
Cost')
```

Then you can compute the arrays and the cost matrix from the tibbles, which are needed to build the model with ompr:

```
n_warehouses <- cost_matrix_tbl %>%
    distinct(warehouse_name) %>%
    count() %>%
    pull(n)

n_countries <- cost_matrix_tbl %>%
    distinct(country_name) %>%
```

```
        count() %>%
        pull(n)
warehouse_supply <- warehouse_supply_tbl %>%
        pull(product_qty)

country_demands <- country_demands_tbl %>%
        pull(product_qty)

# Get the cost matrix from the tibble
# using the pivot_wider function
cost_matrix <- data.matrix(
        cost_matrix_tbl %>%
            pivot_wider( names_from = country_name,
                            values_from = shipping_cost ) %>%
            select( -warehouse_name )
)
rownames(cost_matrix) <- warehouse_supply_tbl %>% pull(warehouse_name)
```

To switch from the vertical form of the cost data in the `cost_matrix_tbl` tibble to the horizontal form, we used the very handy `pivot_wider()` function provided by the `tidyr` package.

At this point, defining the model using the functions exposed by `ompr` is almost straightforward if we follow the mathematical model shown in the *Formulating the LP problem* section:

```
model <- MIPModel() %>%
    # define the x integer variables
    add_variable( x[i, j], i = 1:n_warehouses, j = 1:n_countries,
                    type = "integer", lb = 0 ) %>%

    # define the objective function
    set_objective( sum_expr(cost_matrix[i, j] * x[i, j],
                    i = 1:n_warehouses, j = 1:n_countries),
                    sense = 'min' ) %>%

    # add warehouse supply constraints
    add_constraint( sum_expr(x[i, j], j = 1:n_countries) <= warehouse_
supply[i], i = 1:n_warehouses ) %>%

    # add customer demand constraints
    add_constraint( sum_expr(x[i, j], i = 1:n_warehouses) >= country_
demands[j], j = 1:n_countries )
```

The sum_expr() function may seem confusing at first glance. Let's take this piece of code as an example:

```
sum_expr(x[i, j], j = 1:n_countries)
```

It can be read in full as follows: take the decision variables x[i,j] obtained by substituting values ranging from 1 to n_countries (i.e., 6) for j, and then sum the resulting variables. In summary, you are asking to calculate:

```
x[i,1] + x[i,2] + x[i,3] + x[i,4] + x[i,5] + x[i,6]
```

At this point, once the model is defined, you can solve it using the glpk solver with this code:

```
result <- model %>%
solve_model(with_ROI(solver = 'glpk'))
```

The results obtained coincide (obviously, since the solution is optimal) with those already seen using Python's PuLP module:

```
decision_var_results <- matrix(result$solution, nrow = n_warehouses, ncol = n_
countries, )
rownames(decision_var_results) <- warehouse_supply_tbl %>% pull(warehouse_name)
colnames(decision_var_results) <- country_demands_tbl %>% pull(country_name)
decision_var_results
```

Here's the solution:

```
               Italy France Germany Japan China   USA
Warehouse ITA 40000      0   15000     0     0     0
Warehouse DEU     0      0    5000     0     0     0
Warehouse JPN 10000      0       0     0     0 25000
Warehouse USA     0  10000       0 40000  5000 25000
```

But wait, even if the value of the objective function for this solution is 2,270,000, which is the same value found with Python, the values of the variables are different. This means that the minimum achievable value of the objective function is unique (global minimum), but there is more than one way to achieve it.

Did you see that you can also solve an LP problem in R? Nothing too complex, right? Very well done! Now let's apply what you have seen to Power BI.

Solving the LP problem in Power BI with R

The implementation complexities of solving our LP problem in Power BI have already been exposed in the *Solving the LP problem in Power BI with Python* section.

Therefore, we will walk through the steps using R here without going into the details:

1. Open Power BI Desktop, go to **Options and settings**, then **Options,** and click on **Privacy** under the **Current File** section, then select the **Ignore the Privacy Levels and potentially improve the performance** option and press **OK.**

2. Click **Excel workbook** on the ribbon (or **Import data from Excel** in the main canvas), select the `RetailData.xlsx` file in the `Chapter 14` folder, and click **Open.**

3. Select the **CountryDemand, ShippingCost,** and **WarehouseSupply** tables (the ones with a blue header) and then click **Transform Data.**

4. Click on **Enter Data** in the **Home** menu to enter a new table data manually.

5. Leave the table data empty and name the new table `Result`, then press **OK.**

6. Click on **Run R script** in the **Transform** menu, keeping the **Result** query selected.

7. Leave just the default comment in the R editor without entering any new code and press **OK.**

8. Go back to the **Home** menu and click **Advanced Editor,** keeping the **Result** query selected.

9. Just remove the code from `Source` to `text}})`, (including the comma) and make sure your code is the following:

```
let
    #"Run R script" = R.Execute("# 'dataset' holds the input data for
this script",[dataset=#"Changed Type"])
in
    #"Run R script"
```

10. Basically, you have the execution of an empty R script in the M script. For now, do not press **Done.**

11. Replace the default `[dataset=#"Changed Type"]` parameters list with the following: `[warehouse_supply_df=WarehouseSupply, country_demands_df=CountryDemand, shipping_cost_df=ShippingCost]`. Then press **Done.**

12. If privacy levels are not already ignored, go to the Power Query editor **Options and settings,** then **Options,** and click on **Privacy** under the **Current File** section, then select the **Ignore the Privacy Levels and potentially improve the performance** option and press **OK.**

13. Sometimes, it is necessary to give Power BI permission to run R code. If so, click **Permission required** in the yellow warning ribbon and press **Run** in the next window.

14. At this point, you can finally enter the R code to calculate the lowest possible cost while satisfying all imposed constraints. To do this, select the **Result** query, and click on the gearwheel next to the **Run R script** step in the **Applied Steps** panel.

15. Enter the script, which you can find in the `R\02-linear-optimization-in-power-bi-with-r.R` file in the `Chapter 14` folder, and press **OK.**

16. You may be asked to click on **Table** for the `result_df` DataFrame.

17. You will see the contents of the following table, which shows the values of shipped quantities provided by the solution of the linear optimization problem for each combination of warehouse and country, and the corresponding cost:

	ABC warehouse_name	ABC country_name	1.2 shipped_qty	1.2 cost
1	Warehouse ITA	Italy	40000	320000
2	Warehouse ITA	France	0	0
3	Warehouse ITA	Germany	10000	140000
4	Warehouse ITA	Japan	0	0
5	Warehouse ITA	China	0	0
6	Warehouse ITA	USA	0	0
7	Warehouse DEU	Italy	0	0
8	Warehouse DEU	France	10000	100000
9	Warehouse DEU	Germany	15000	120000

Figure 14.18: Contents of the Result table

18. Click on **Close & Apply**.

Note that if you followed step 11, the source privacy level control is disabled. You should turn it back on at the end of this project to combine data according to the privacy level settings of each file, and to be warned of possible data leaks due to query folding mechanisms.

Summary

In this chapter, you learned how to solve the simplest optimization problems by first turning them into mathematical models and then solving them using specialized Python and R packages. You applied what you learned to a real-world demand optimization case in Power BI.

In the next chapter, you'll see how statistics can add a little spice to your business analysis.

References

- *George B. Dantzig and Systems Optimization* (https://web.stanford.edu/group/SOL/GBD/GBDandSOL.pdf)
- *Lecture Notes in Linear Programming modeling* (https://www.hds.utc.fr/~dnace/dokuwiki/_media/fr/lp-modelling_upt_p2021.pdf)

Test your knowledge

1. What is linear programming and how is it applied in data analysis?
2. How can linear optimization problems be formulated mathematically?
3. How can linear optimization problems be solved using Python and R?
4. How can multiple solutions provide the same optimal value in linear optimization problems?

Learn more on Discord

To join the Discord community for this book – where you can share feedback, ask questions to the author, and learn about new releases – follow the QR code below:

https://discord.gg/MKww5g45EB

15

Adding Statistical Insights: Associations

In the previous chapter, we discussed the process of enriching your data, which involves improving the quality and depth of information through the use of complex algorithms. However, there are additional methods that can be used to extract valuable insights from data. One effective approach is to apply statistical techniques. Statistics plays a critical role in data analysis by providing a framework for examining the relationships between variables in your dataset. By using statistical methods, you can gain meaningful insights into the relationships between different variables.

In this chapter, we will cover the basic concepts of some statistical procedures. By understanding these statistical techniques, you will be able to gain a deeper understanding of your data and make informed decisions based on the insights gained from the analysis. You will learn about the following topics:

- Exploring associations between variables
- Correlation between numeric variables
- Correlation between non-numeric variables
- Correlation between non-numeric and numeric variables

Technical requirements

This chapter requires you to have a working internet connection and **Power BI Desktop** already installed on your machine (version 2.118.828.0, 64-bit, June 2023). You must have properly configured the R and Python engines and IDEs as outlined in *Chapter 2, Configuring R with Power BI*, and *Chapter 3, Configuring Python with Power BI*.

Exploring associations between variables

At first glance, you may wonder what the point of finding relationships between variables is. The ability to understand the behavior of a pair of variables and to identify a pattern in their behavior helps business owners identify key factors that can skew certain indicators of business health in their favor.

Knowing the pattern that binds the trend of two variables gives you the power to predict one of them with some certainty by knowing the other. So, knowing the tools to uncover these patterns gives you a kind of analytical superpower that is always attractive to business owners.

In general, two variables are *associated* if the values of one are somehow related to the values of the other. If you can somehow measure the extent of the association between two variables, it is called a correlation. The concept of **correlation** is directly applicable in a case where the two variables are numerical. Let's see how.

Correlation between numeric variables

The first thing we generally do to understand whether there is an association between two numeric variables is to plot them on the two Cartesian axes to obtain a **scatterplot**:

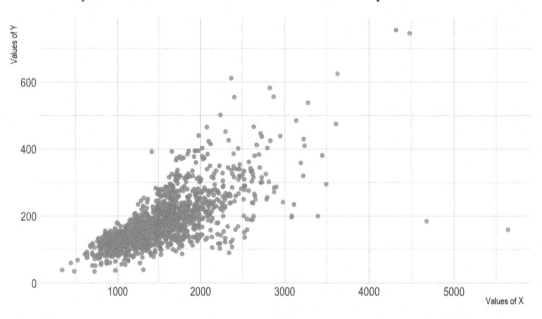

Figure 15.1: A simple scatterplot

Using a scatterplot, it is possible to identify three important characteristics of a possible association:

- **Direction:** This can be *positive* (increasing), *negative* (decreasing), or *not defined* (no association found – or both increasing and decreasing at the same time). If the increment of one variable is in accordance with the increment of the other, the direction is positive; if the increment of one variable is in accordance with the decrement of the other, it is negative; otherwise, it is not defined:

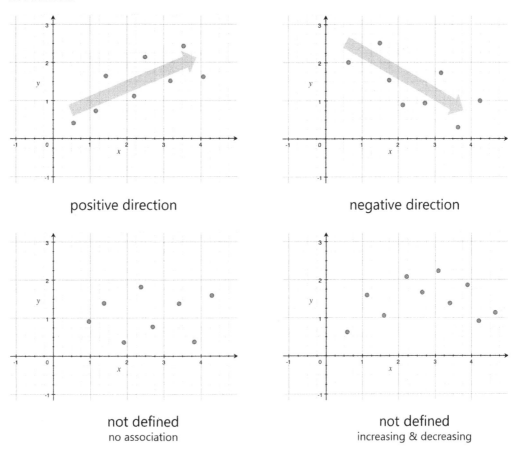

Figure 15.2: Direction types of the association

- **Form:** This describes the general form that the association takes in its simplest sense. Obviously, there are many possible forms, but there are some that are more common, such as *linear* and *curvilinear* (nonlinear) forms:

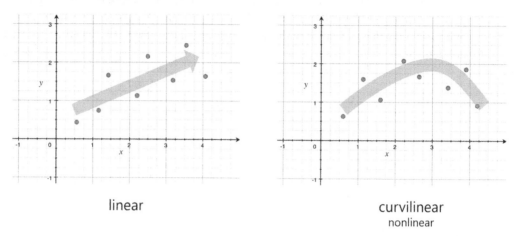

linear

curvilinear
nonlinear

Figure 15.3: Shapes of the association

- **Strength:** The strength of an association is determined by how closely the points in the scatterplot follow the line that draws the general shape of the association.

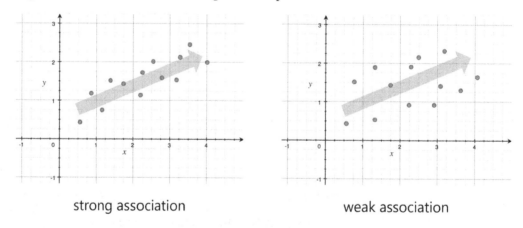

strong association

weak association

Figure 15.4: Strength of the association

As these visual patterns become measurable through the application of mathematical concepts, we can define different types of correlations between numeric variables.

Pearson's correlation coefficient

Pearson's correlation coefficient (r) measures the degree of linearity of the association between the variables being analyzed. That is, if $r = 1$ or $r = -1$, the two variables have a *perfect linear relationship*. The sign of the coefficient determines the direction of the association. If instead r is close to 0, on either the negative or positive side, it means that the association between the variables is *very weak*. The coefficient cannot take values outside the range [-1, 1].

The square of Pearson's coefficient ($R2$) is called the **coefficient of determination** and measures the percentage of **variance** (which measures the dispersion of observations from their mean value) in one variable that is due to the variance of the other variable, assuming the association is linear. For example, if the correlation coefficient r between a person's weight and height variables is 0.45, it can be said that about 20% (0.45 x 0.45) of the change (variance) in a person's weight is due to the change in their height.

The calculation of the correlation coefficient r is rarely done by hand, since every data management platform provides a function that easily calculates it. If you are curious, given a dataset of n entities, identify the variables x and y for which you want to calculate the correlation coefficient – this is the formula that allows you to calculate it:

$$r_{xy} = \frac{\sum_{i=1}^{n}(x_i - \bar{x})(y_i - \bar{y})}{\sqrt{\sum_{i=1}^{n}(x_i - \bar{x})^2}\sqrt{\sum_{i=1}^{n}(y_i - \bar{y})^2}}$$

Figure 15.5: Formula for the Pearson correlation coefficient

The $\bar{x}$ and $\bar{y}$ values correspond to the means of the variables x and y, respectively, in the dataset. Note that Pearson's correlation function is **symmetric**, which means that the order of the columns for which it is computed does not matter.

Examples of the correlation coefficient r calculated for some specific associations (**Boigelot distributions**) are shown in the following figure:

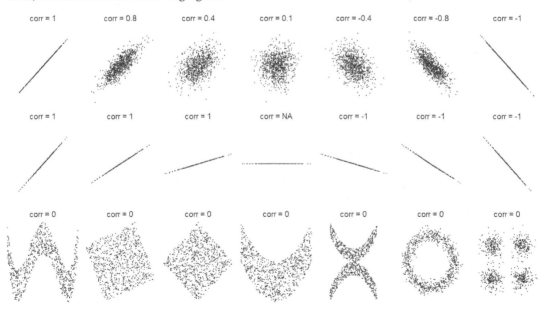

Figure 15.6: Pearson's correlation calculated over Boigelot distributions

The first row of scatterplots in *Figure 15.6* gives an idea of how the magnitude of the correlation measures the strength of the association, which tends to be linear.

The second row shows that whatever the angle of the linear relationship, the correlation coefficient r is always equal to 1 in absolute value, i.e., it always correctly identifies the linear relationship and its direction. The only exception is the case of the horizontal linear relationship at the center, for which the coefficient r is undefined since, for all values of x, there is a single value of y.

The third row shows one of the most important limitations of the correlation coefficient as detailed in the following note.

IMPORTANT NOTE

Pearson's correlation coefficient is not able to detect a pattern in the association between two variables when the relationship is nonlinear.

These are the other limitations:

- With a very small dataset size (e.g., 3–6 observations), the perception of an association might be misleading, suggesting a relationship where no relationship actually exists.
- The correlation coefficient is very sensitive to outliers (observations that are far away from most others). It can also happen that outliers give a false idea of the existence of an association, as shown in the following figure:

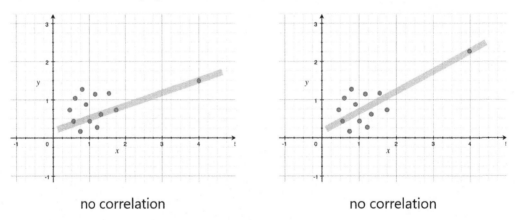

no correlation   no correlation

Figure 15.7: No correlation due to outliers

We will discuss outliers in more detail in *Chapter 16, Adding Statistical Insights: Outliers and Missing Values*.

- If the observations in the dataset are divided into different clusters, this can also create a false sense of association:

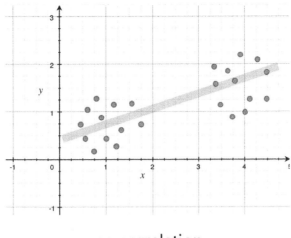

no correlation
due to clusters

Figure 15.8: No correlation due to clusters

- The variables used to calculate the correlation coefficient must be defined on a continuous scale. For variables based on a discrete scale, such as a 1–10 rating of a service, you must use Spearman's rank correlation, which we will look at in the next section.

- When there is a variable in an association that has unequal variability with a range of values of a second variable, we have a case of **heteroscedasticity**. The scatterplot takes on the typical shape of a cone, as in *Figure 15.1*. In this case, the correlation coefficient could identify a false linear relationship (more than one linear relationship would satisfy the conic shape of the scatterplot):

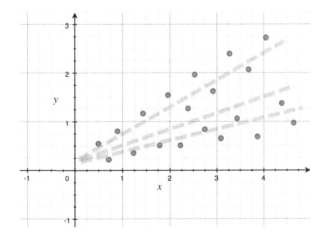

wrong correlation
due to heteroscedasticity

Figure 15.9: Wrong correlation value due to heteroscedasticity

- The variables used to calculate the Pearson correlation coefficient should not be highly **skewed**; that is, the distribution of the variables should not be skewed or asymmetrical with respect to a symmetrical bell curve (normal distribution, where the mean, median, and mode are equal); otherwise, the true magnitude of the correlation may be reduced:

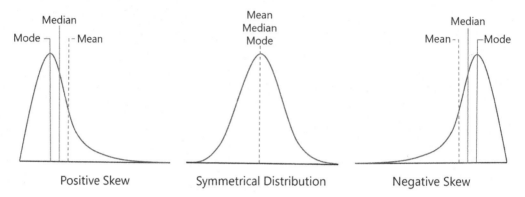

Figure 15.10: Types of distribution skewness

Having clarified these limitations, the first question that comes up is: how can I compute the correlation between two numeric variables when the association is nonlinear, when the variables are based on an ordinal scale, or when they have a skewed distribution? One of the possible solutions to this problem was provided by Charles Spearman.

Charles Spearman's correlation coefficient

Charles Spearman introduced a nonparametric alternative to Pearson's correlation. A **nonparametric statistical method** refers to the fact that it does not assume that the data on which it is calculated follows specific models described by a handful of parameters. This method is summarized in a new correlation coefficient called **Spearman's rank-order correlation coefficient** (denoted by ρ, *rho*). Spearman's coefficient measures the strength and direction of the association between two variables after their observations have been ranked according to their value. The formula used to calculate it is:

$$\rho = 1 - \frac{6 \sum d_i^2}{n(n^2 - 1)}$$

Figure 15.11: Spearman's rank-order correlation coefficient formula

The value d^i is the difference between the two ranks of each observation. For more details on the calculation, see the references at the end of the chapter. Note that Spearman's correlation function is also symmetric.

Spearman's correlation coefficient ranges from -1 to +1. The sign of the coefficient is an indication of whether it is a positive or negative monotonic association.

IMPORTANT FEATURES OF SPEARMAN'S CORRELATION

Because Spearman's correlation applies to ranks, it provides a measure of a **monotonic association** between two continuous random variables and is the best-fitting correlation coefficient for ordinal variables. Because of the way it is calculated, Spearman's correlation, unlike Pearson's, is robust to outliers.

Note that an association is said to be **monotonic** if it is increasing over its entire domain or decreasing over its entire domain (not a combination of the two):

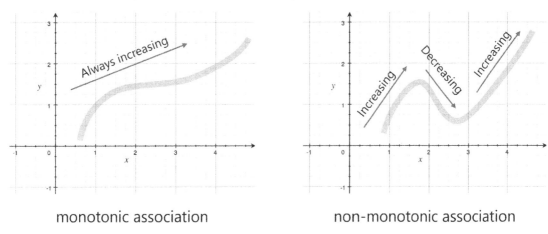

Figure 15.12: Monotonic and non-monotonic associations

IMPORTANT NOTE

It is important to check the monotonicity of the association since, in general, the correlation coefficients are generally unable to accurately describe non-monotonic relationships.

If you compute Spearman's correlation coefficient for the Boigelot distributions, you get this:

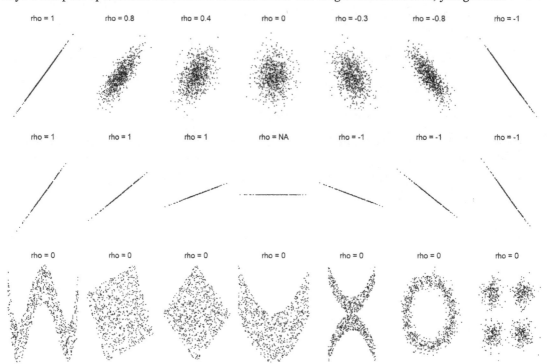

Figure 15.13: Spearman's correlation calculated on Boigelot distributions

Even Spearman's correlation does not capture the nonlinear patterns you observe in the third row of distributions in *Figure 15.13*. This is not due to the nonlinearity of these associations, but to their non-monotonicity. On the other hand, for monotonic nonlinear associations, Spearman's correlation is better suited than Pearson's:

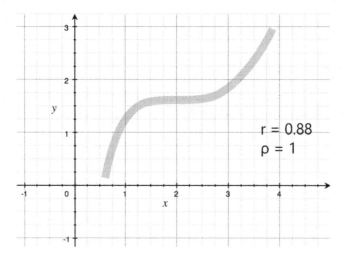

Figure 15.14: Pearson's and Spearman's correlation on a nonlinear monotonic association

Spearman's correlation is not the only one that uses data ranking in its calculation. Kendall's also uses this strategy. Let's take a look at its characteristics.

Maurice Kendall's correlation coefficient

Kendall's rank correlation coefficient (τ, tau) is also a nonparametric method for detecting associations between two variables. Its calculation is based on the concept of **concordant pairs** and **discordant pairs** (see the *References* section for more details). The formula for calculating Kendall's correlation coefficient is as follows:

$$\tau_C = \frac{2(n_c - n_d)}{n^2 \frac{(m-1)}{m}}$$

Figure 15.15: Kendall's correlation coefficient formula

The n_c value represents the number of concordant pairs, the n_d value represents the number of discordant pairs, and n represents the number of all the pairs. The m value is the minimum between the number of rows and columns of the **contingency table**, which compares the elements of the variables to be related. Like the other correlation functions, Kendall's is symmetric. See the *References* section for more details on contingency tables.

All of the assumptions made for Spearman's correlation also apply to Kendall's. Here is a comparison of the two correlations:

- Both correlations handle ordinal data and nonlinear continuous monotone data very well.
- Both correlations are robust against outliers.
- Kendall's correlation is preferred to Spearman's correlation when the sample size is small and when there are many tied ranks.
- Kendall's coefficient is usually smaller than Spearman's.
- Kendall's correlation is more computationally intensive than Spearman's.

That said, let's use all three correlation coefficients in a real-world scenario.

Description of a real case

Your boss has asked you to perform an analysis of the world population as requested by a client. Specifically, you need to understand if there is a relationship between life expectancy and **gross domestic product (GDP)** per capita over the years, and if so, how strong the relationship is.

As you search the web for useful data for this purpose, you realize that there is a portal that can help your case called **Gapminder** (https://www.gapminder.org/). It fights devastating misconceptions and promotes a fact-based worldview that everyone can understand by combining data from multiple sources into unique coherent time series that can't be found anywhere else. The portal accurately presents data on life expectancy (http://bit.ly/life-expectancy-data) and GDP per capita (http://bit.ly/gdp-per-capita-data). In addition, someone has transformed the data to collect it in a more suitable form for our purposes and has shared their work with the community in a CSV file (http://bit.ly/gdp-life-expect-data).

Awesome! You have everything you need to start your analysis. Let's see how to do it with Python first.

Implementing correlation coefficients in Python

To run the code in this section, you need to install the Seaborn module in your pbi_powerquery_env environment. As you've probably learned by now, you need to do the following:

1. Open Anaconda prompt.
2. Enter the command conda activate pbi_powerquery_env.
3. Enter the command pip install seaborn==0.12.2.

The code you'll find in this section is available in the file Python\01-gdp-life-expectancy-analysis-in-python.py in the Chapter 15 folder.

At this point, let's take a quick look at the data in the preceding CSV file, while also importing the forms needed for the rest of the operations:

```python
import pandas as pd
import matplotlib.pyplot as plt
import seaborn as sb
dataset_url = 'http://bit.ly/gdp-life-expect-data'
df = pd.read_csv(dataset_url)
df.head()
# If you're not using VS Code run this instead
# print(df.head())
```

You'll see something like this:

	country	year	pop	continent	lifeExp	gdpPercap
0	Afghanistan	1952	8425333.0	Asia	28.801	779.445314
1	Afghanistan	1957	9240934.0	Asia	30.332	820.853030
2	Afghanistan	1962	10267083.0	Asia	31.997	853.100710
3	Afghanistan	1967	11537966.0	Asia	34.020	836.197138
4	Afghanistan	1972	13079460.0	Asia	36.088	739.981106

Figure 15.16: A sample of the GDP and life expectancy dataset

The variables we are interested in are lifeExp and gdpPercap. Before you draw a scatterplot of them, we want to look at the distribution of each of them. So, let's define the functions we will use for the plots and draw the distributions:

```python
def distPlot(data, var, title, xlab, ylab, bins=100):
    hplot = sb.distplot(data[var], kde=False, bins=bins)
    plt.title(title, fontsize=18)
```

```
        plt.xlabel(xlab, fontsize=16)
        plt.ylabel(ylab, fontsize=16)

        return hplot
def scatterPlot(data, varx, vary, title, xlab, ylab):
        hplot = sb.scatterplot(varx, vary, data=data)
        plt.title(title, fontsize=18)
        plt.xlabel(xlab, fontsize=16)
        plt.ylabel(ylab, fontsize=16)

        return hplot
distPlot(data=df, var='lifeExp', title='Life Expectancy', xlab='Life Expectancy
years', ylab='Frequency')
# In case you're not using a Jupyter notebook run also the following:
# plt.show()
distPlot(data=df, var='gdpPercap', title='GDP / capita', xlab='GDP / capita
($)', ylab='Frequency')
# In case you're not using a Jupyter notebook run also the following:
# plt.show()
```

The plots created are as follows:

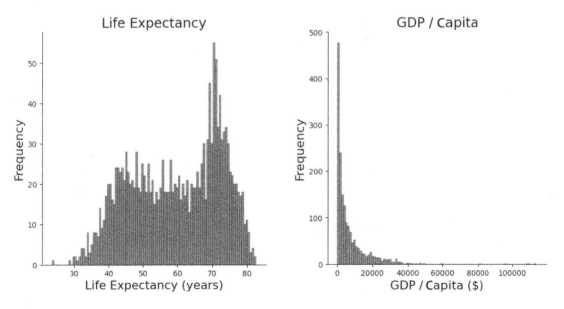

Figure 15.17: Distributions of life expectancy and GDP variables

As you can see, while the life expectancy distribution more or less approximates the normal distribution, the GDP distribution is completely positive-skewed. If there is a significant association between the two variables, you should then expect a likely nonlinear scatterplot. Let's check it out:

```
scatterPlot(data=df, varx='lifeExp', vary='gdpPercap', title='Life Expectancy
vs GDP/Capita', xlab='lifeExp', ylab='gdpPercap')
# In case you're not using a Jupyter notebook run also the following:
# plt.show()
```

This gives you the following plot (for better viewing, a color image is also available for download):

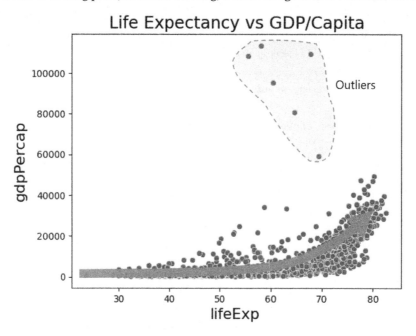

Figure 15.18: Scatterplot of life expectancy versus GDP per capita

Figure 15.18 shows that the association between the two variables is obvious and, as expected, is nonlinear (shown by the arrow in the background). In addition, there are outliers, which are highlighted at the top. You are therefore faced with two assumptions that invalidate Pearson's correlation. Fortunately, the association is monotonically increasing, so the Spearman and Kendall correlations should capture the pattern more accurately.

The Python implementation of the three correlation coefficients is already provided by pandas. Correlation analysis is therefore straightforward:

```
df[['lifeExp','gdpPercap']].corr(method='pearson')
df[['lifeExp','gdpPercap']].corr(method='spearman')
df[['lifeExp','gdpPercap']].corr(method='kendall')
```

The corr() function of a pandas DataFrame returns the correlation calculation for each pair of its numeric columns. Since the correlation functions are symmetric (i.e., the order of the columns for which they are computed does not matter), the three calls return three DataFrames, each with all the numeric features as rows and columns, and the correlations between the features as values:

Pearson

	lifeExp	gdpPercap
lifeExp	1.000000	0.583706
gdpPercap	0.583706	1.000000

Spearman

	lifeExp	gdpPercap
lifeExp	1.000000	0.826471
gdpPercap	0.826471	1.000000

Kendall

	lifeExp	gdpPercap
lifeExp	1.000000	0.636911
gdpPercap	0.636911	1.000000

Figure 15.19: Correlation coefficients between life expectancy and GDP per capita

As you can see, all three correlations show a positive association between the two variables. As expected, the strength detected by Pearson's correlation is the weakest ($r = 0.58$). In contrast, the Spearman and Kendall correlations have a higher magnitude, $\rho = 0.83$ and $\tau = 0.64$, respectively. The Spearman's correlation in particular indicates that the two variables are strongly correlated.

It often happens that in a data science project, when you have a large number of columns, you need to select the variables that are most predictive of a target variable to be predicted. The technique of correlation can certainly help us do this: assuming that the target variable is GDP per capita, we could decide to keep as predictors all those variables that have a correlation with the target variable greater than 0.7. You understand that, in this case, it is important to consider the correct correlation method; otherwise, you would risk rejecting a variable that is highly correlated with the target.

Great! Let's see how we can replicate this analysis in R as well.

Implementing correlation coefficients in R

One of the packages we recommend for computing correlation coefficients in R is **corrr** (https://github.com/tidymodels/corrr). It allows you to easily explore and rearrange the tibbles returned by the correlate() function according to the practices suggested by Tidyverse. Therefore, you need to install the corrr package in the latest version of CRAN R you have:

1. Open RStudio and make sure it is referencing your latest CRAN R (version 4.2.2 in our case).
2. Click on the **Console** window and enter this command: install.packages('corrr'). Then press *Enter*.

The code you'll find in this section is available in the file R\01-gdp-life-expectancy-analysis-in-r.R in the Chapter 15 folder.

So, let's proceed to import the necessary libraries, load the data from the CSV file on the web into a tibble, and display the first few lines:

```
library(readr)
library(dplyr)
library(corrr)
library(ggplot2)
```

```
dataset_url <- 'http://bit.ly/gdp-life-expect-data'
tbl <- read_csv(dataset_url)
tbl
```

You will see this in the console:

```
# A tibble: 1,704 × 6
   country      year       pop continent lifeExp gdpPercap
   <chr>       <dbl>     <dbl> <chr>       <dbl>     <dbl>
 1 Afghanistan  1952   8425333 Asia         28.8      779.
 2 Afghanistan  1957   9240934 Asia         30.3      821.
 3 Afghanistan  1962  10267083 Asia         32.0      853.
 4 Afghanistan  1967  11537966 Asia         34.0      836.
 5 Afghanistan  1972  13079460 Asia         36.1      740.
 6 Afghanistan  1977  14880372 Asia         38.4      786.
 7 Afghanistan  1982  12881816 Asia         39.9      978.
 8 Afghanistan  1987  13867957 Asia         40.8      852.
 9 Afghanistan  1992  16317921 Asia         41.7      649.
10 Afghanistan  1997  22227415 Asia         41.8      635.
# … with 1,694 more rows
# i Use `print(n = ...)` to see more rows
> |
```

Figure 15.20: First rows of the population tibble

Also, in this case, we define the functions necessary to draw a distribution plot and a scatterplot and use them to generate the plots of the distributions of the variables lifeExp and gdpPercap:

```
distPlot <- function(data, var, title, xlab, ylab, bins=100) {

    p <- ggplot( data=data, aes( x=.data[[var]]) ) +
        geom_histogram( bins=bins, fill="royalblue3", color="steelblue1",
alpha=0.9) +
        ggtitle(title) +
        xlab(xlab) +
        ylab(ylab) +
        theme(
          plot.title = element_text(size=22),
          axis.title = element_text(size=16),
          axis.text = element_text(size=14) )


    return(p)

}



scatterPlot <- function(data, varx, vary, title, xlab, ylab) {
    p <- ggplot( data=data, aes_string( x=.data[[varx]], y=.data[[vary]])) +
        geom_point(
```

```
                color='steelblue1', fill='royalblue3',
                shape=21, alpha=0.8, size=3
            ) +
            ggtitle(title) +
            xlab(xlab) +
            ylab(ylab) +
            theme(
                plot.title = element_text(size=22),
                axis.title = element_text(size=16),
                axis.text = element_text(size=14) )

    return(p)
}
p1 <- distPlot(data = tbl, var = 'lifeExp', title = 'Life Expectancy',
          xlab = 'Life Expectancy (years)', ylab = 'Frequency')
p1


p2 <- distPlot(data = tbl, var = 'gdpPercap', title = 'GDP / capita',
          xlab = 'GDP / capita ($)', ylab = 'Frequency')
p2
```

These are the plots we get:

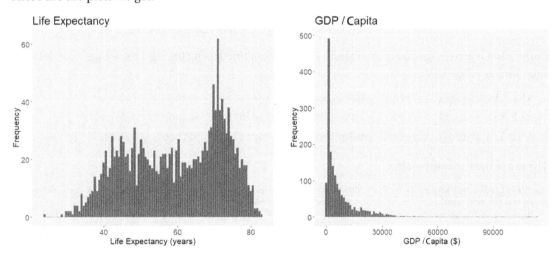

Figure 15.21: Distribution plots of life expectancy and GDP per capita

You can get the scatterplot between the two variables as follows:

```
p3 <- scatterPlot(data = tbl, varx = 'lifeExp', vary = 'gdpPercap', title =
'Life Expectancy vs GDP/Capita', xlab = 'lifeExp', ylab = 'gdpPercap')
p3
```

This is the graph you get:

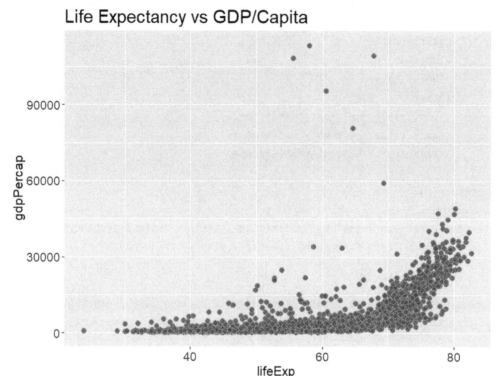

Figure 15.22: Scatterplot between life expectancy and GDP per capita

Correlation matrices (persisted in tibbles) are easily obtained using the corrr package's correlate() function, as follows:

```
tbl %>% select( lifeExp, gdpPercap ) %>% correlate( method = 'pearson' )
tbl %>% select( lifeExp, gdpPercap ) %>% correlate( method = 'spearman' )
tbl %>% select( lifeExp, gdpPercap ) %>% correlate( method = 'kendall' )
```

These are the console results:

```
Correlation computed with        Correlation computed with        Correlation computed with
• Method: 'pearson'              • Method: 'spearman'             • Method: 'kendall'
• Missing treated using: 'pair   • Missing treated using: 'pair  • Missing treated using: 'pair
wise.complete.obs'               wise.complete.obs'              wise.complete.obs'
# A tibble: 2 × 3               # A tibble: 2 × 3               # A tibble: 2 × 3
  term    lifeExp gdpPercap       term    lifeExp gdpPercap       term    lifeExp gdpPercap
  <chr>     <dbl>    <dbl>         <chr>     <dbl>    <dbl>         <chr>     <dbl>    <dbl>
1 lifeExp    NA      0.584       1 lifeExp    NA      0.826       1 lifeExp    NA      0.637
2 gdpPercap 0.584    NA          2 gdpPercap 0.826    NA          2 gdpPercap 0.637    NA
```

Figure 15.23: Correlation coefficients in tibbles

Pretty simple, right? Now that you know how to get correlation coefficients in both Python and R, let's apply what you've learned to Power BI.

Implementing correlation coefficients in Power BI with Python and R

Power BI has the ability to introduce a minimum level of statistical analysis for the data that has been loaded into the data model thanks to DAX. For a list of the statistical functions you can use, see this link: `http://bit.ly/dax-stats-func`. As for the simple Pearson correlation, you can use it for columns in an already loaded table thanks to the predefined quick measures that add some sometimes non-trivial DAX code for you behind the scenes. For more details, you can use this link: `http://bit.ly/power-bi-corr-coef`. However, there is no easy way to implement the Spearman and Kendall correlation coefficients.

There is no direct way to calculate the Pearson, Spearman, and Kendall correlation coefficients in Power Query (not even using DAX). The only way to proceed is to use Python or R. Let's see how to do that.

In this case, due to the simplicity of the code, we will implement the correlation coefficients in both Python and R in one project. Here are the steps:

1. Open Power BI Desktop through the shortcut that activates the `pbi_powerquery_env` environment.
2. Make sure Power BI Desktop is referencing the `pbi_powerquery_env` environment in the Python scripting tab.
3. Click on **Get data** and then select **Web**:

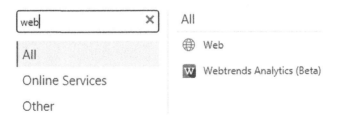

Figure 15.24: Get data from the web

4. Enter the `http://bit.ly/gdp-life-expect-data` string into the **URL** textbox and click **OK**.
5. You'll see a preview of the data. Then click **Transform Data**.
6. Click **Transform** on the ribbon and then **Run Python script**.
7. Enter the following Python script and then click **OK**:

```
import pandas as pd
corr_df = dataset.corr(method='pearson')
# You need to convert row names into a column
# in order to make it visible in Power BI
corr_df.index.name = 'rowname'
corr_df.reset_index(inplace=True)
```

You can find this code in the file Python\02-gdp-life-expectancy-analysis-in-power-bi-with-python.py in the Chapter 15 folder.

8. If you get the Firewall privacy level mismatch error, select a **Public privacy** level for the web URL data source and press **OK**. You are prompted to expand a DataFrame calculated in the Python script.

9. We are only interested in the data in corr_df. So, click on its **Table** value.

10. You'll see the preview of the Pearson correlation coefficients between all the numeric columns of the dataset.

11. Click **Home** on the ribbon and then click **Close & Apply**.

12. Repeat *steps 3* to *5*.

13. Click **Transform** on the ribbon and then **Run R script**.

14. Enter the following R script and then click **OK**:

```
library(dplyr)
library(corrr)
# You need to select only numeric columns
# in order to make correlate() work
corr_tbl <- dataset %>%
    select( where(is.numeric) ) %>%
    correlate( method = 'spearman' )
```

You can find this code in the file R\02-gdp-life-expectancy-analysis-in-power-bi-with-r.R in the Chapter 15 folder.

15. You'll see the preview of the Spearman correlation coefficients between all the numeric columns of the dataset.

16. Click **Home** on the ribbon and then click **Close & Apply**.

Note that the corr() function in Python calculates the correlation between two identical variables as 1, while the correlation() function of the corrr package in R returns NA in the same case. This is simply a convention.

Awesome! You have just calculated the Pearson and Spearman correlation coefficients for the numeric columns of a source dataset in Power BI with Python and R. Easy, right?

You're probably wondering, *Okay, all clear on the numeric variables. What if I have categorical (non-numeric) variables? How do I calculate the correlation between them?* Let's take a look at how to approach this type of analysis.

Correlation between non-numeric variables

We have shown that, in the case of two numeric variables, you can get a sense of the association between them by looking at their scatterplot. Obviously, this strategy cannot be used when one or both variables are non-numeric. Note that a variable is **categorical** (or qualitative or nominal) when it takes on values that are names or labels, such as smartphone operating systems (iOS, Android, Linux, and so on). Let's see how to analyze the case of two categorical variables.

The first question that comes to mind is the following: is there a graphical representation that helps us to understand whether there is a significant association between two categorical variables? The answer is yes, and it is called a **mosaic plot**. In short, the goal of the mosaic plot is to show, at a glance, the strength of the association between the individual elements of each variable by the color of the tiles representing the pairs of elements in question.

In this section, we will use the Titanic disaster dataset as a reference dataset. To get an idea of what a mosaic plot looks like, let's consider the variables Survived (which takes the values 1 and 0) and Pclass (*passenger class*, which takes the values 1, 2, and 3). Since we want to study the association between these two variables, we'll look at the following mosaic plot generated by them:

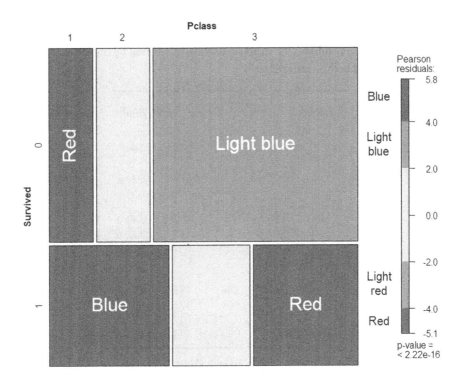

Figure 15.25: Mosaic plot of the Survived and Pclass variables

IMPORTANT NOTE

Basically, the more the color of the tile tends toward dark blue, the more there are observations represented by that tile compared to the expected amount in the case of variables independent of each other.

On the other hand, the more the color of the tile tends toward dark red, the fewer observations are represented by that tile compared to the expected amount in the case of variables independent of each other.

Looking at the top row of tiles in *Figure 15.25* associated with *Survived = 0*, we can say that, among the non-survivors, more than 50% of the people belong to the third class and the number is larger than expected if there was no association between survivors and classes. So, in general, we can say that there is a *positive association* of medium strength between the non-survivors and the third-class people. In other words, it is quite likely to find third-class people among the non-survivors. In contrast, the number of first-class people among the non-survivors is much lower than would be expected if there were no association between survivors and classes. So, there is a strong negative association between the non-survivors and the first-class people. Thus, it is very likely that there are no first-class people, or perhaps only a small number, among the non-survivors.

If we focus instead on the bottom row of tiles in *Figure 15.25*, we have confirmation of what we have already said: it is very likely that we will find first-class people among the survivors, and very unlikely that we will find third-class people.

The numbers behind the plot in *Figure 15.25* are based on conditional probabilities and can be found by calculating the **contingency table** (also called **crosstab**) generated by the various elements of each of the categorical variables being analyzed:

Survived	*Pclass*			*Total*
	1	2	3	
0	80	97	372	549
	133	113	303	549
	14.6 %	17.7 %	67.8 %	100 %
	37 %	52.7 %	75.8 %	61.6 %
1	136	87	119	342
	83	71	188	342
	39.8 %	25.4 %	34.8 %	100 %
	63 %	47.3 %	24.2 %	38.4 %
Total	216	184	491	891
	216	184	491	891
	24.2 %	20.7 %	55.1 %	100 %
	100 %	100 %	100 %	100 %

$\chi^2 = 102.889 \cdot df = 2 \cdot$ *Cramér's* $V = 0.340 \cdot p = 0.000$

observed values
expected values
% within Survived
% within Pclass

Figure 15.26: Contingency table of the variables Survived and Pclass

See the *References* section for more details on contingency tables and mosaic plots.

But in a nutshell, how do we numerically determine the global strength of the association between two categorical variables? The answer lies in the coefficient shown in *Figure 15.26*, namely *Cramér's V*. Let's see what it is all about.

Harald Cramér's correlation coefficient

Cramér's correlation coefficient (V) measures the strength of the association between two categorical variables and it ranges from 0 to +1 (it doesn't allow negative values, unlike the coefficients seen so far). This coefficient is based on **Pearson's chi-square statistic (χ2)**, which is used to test whether two categorical variables are independent. Cramér's V formula is as follows:

$$V = \sqrt{\frac{\varphi^2}{\min(k-1, r-1)}} = \sqrt{\frac{\chi^2/n}{\min(k-1, r-1)}}$$

Figure 15.27: Cramér's V formula

In the formula in *Figure 15.27*, $\varphi^2 = \chi^2/n$, the value n is the sample size, k is the number of columns in the contingency table, and r is the number of rows in the table.

Cramér's V is biased because it relies on the chi-square statistic, which can be influenced by the sample size and number of categories in the contingency table. This can result in an overestimation of the association between two categorical variables, particularly in cases with many categories or small sample sizes. The bias creates the illusion of a stronger relationship between the variables than actually exists.

Bergsma and Wicher proposed a correction method to address this bias. The method adjusts the calculation of Cramér's V to account for the effect of table size and structure. Their solution involves a more refined statistical approach that normalizes the chi-square value by a factor that is more sensitive to the dimensions of the contingency table and the distribution of the data within it.

Cramér's V coefficient is a symmetric function, and the guidelines of *Figure 15.28* can be used to determine the magnitude of its effect size:

Magnitude of Effect Size	Cramér's V Ranges
Small	[0 - 0.3)
Medium	[0.3 - 0.5)
Large	[0.5 - 1]

Figure 15.28: Cramér's V effect size ranges

The fact that *V* is a symmetric function leads to an important loss of information. Let's see why.

Henri Theil's uncertainty coefficient

To understand this concept clearly, imagine that you have a dataset in which there are some fraudulent bank transactions. In addition to the variable that determines whether the user is a fraudster or not, there is also a variable that identifies the user's hobbies. So, suppose you have the two categorical variables IsFraudster and Hobby, with distinct values as shown in the following dataset:

IsFraudster	Hobby
Non-fraudster	Basket
Non-fraudster	Piano
Non-fraudster	Basket
Fraudster	Chess
Fraudster	Chess
Fraudster	Bodybuilding

Figure 15.29: Sample dataset of categorical variables

Any value of the Hobby variable can be associated with a unique value of the IsFraudster variable (for example, *Chess → Fraudster*). However, the reverse is not true (for example, *Fraudster → [Chess, Bodybuilding]*). Therefore, the strength of the association *Hobby → Fraudster* (I know Hobby and need to determine IsFraudster) is of higher magnitude than the association *Fraudster → Hobby* (I know IsFraudster and need to determine Hobby). Unfortunately, using Cramér's coefficient *V* loses this distinction because it is a symmetric function. To maintain the asymmetric nature of the relationship, we need to introduce Theil's uncertainty coefficient.

Theil's uncertainty coefficient, also called the **entropy coefficient,** between two variables, *X* and *Y*, has a range of [0, 1] and is defined as follows:

$$U(X|Y) = \frac{H(X) - H(X|Y)}{H(X)}$$

Figure 15.30: Theil's uncertainty coefficient formula

It is based on the concept of **entropy**, which provides information about the variation or diversity (and therefore uncertainty) of the information contained in one variable, given by $H(X)$. Then it's also based on the **conditional entropy** (or **joint entropy**) $H(X|Y)$, which measures the diversity of data associated with the two variables X and Y.

For example, again considering the Titanic disaster dataset, the coefficient *U(Survived|Pclass)* is 0.06; conversely, *U(Pclass|Survived)* is 0.09. As you can see, Theil's *U* gives you the strength of the association, including the direction of the association.

Let's see which coefficient to consider when dealing with associations where one variable is numeric and the other is categorical.

Correlation between non-numeric and numeric variables

If you want to graphically represent an association between a numeric variable and a categorical (non-numeric) variable, the boxplot or violin plot will be the graphical representation for you. If you have already come across the problem of having to represent the distribution of a variable by highlighting key statistics, then you should be familiar with a **boxplot**:

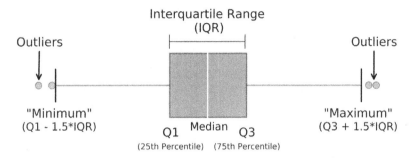

Figure 15.31: Graphical explanation of a boxplot

A **violin plot** is nothing more than a combination of a histogram/distribution plot and a boxplot for the same variable:

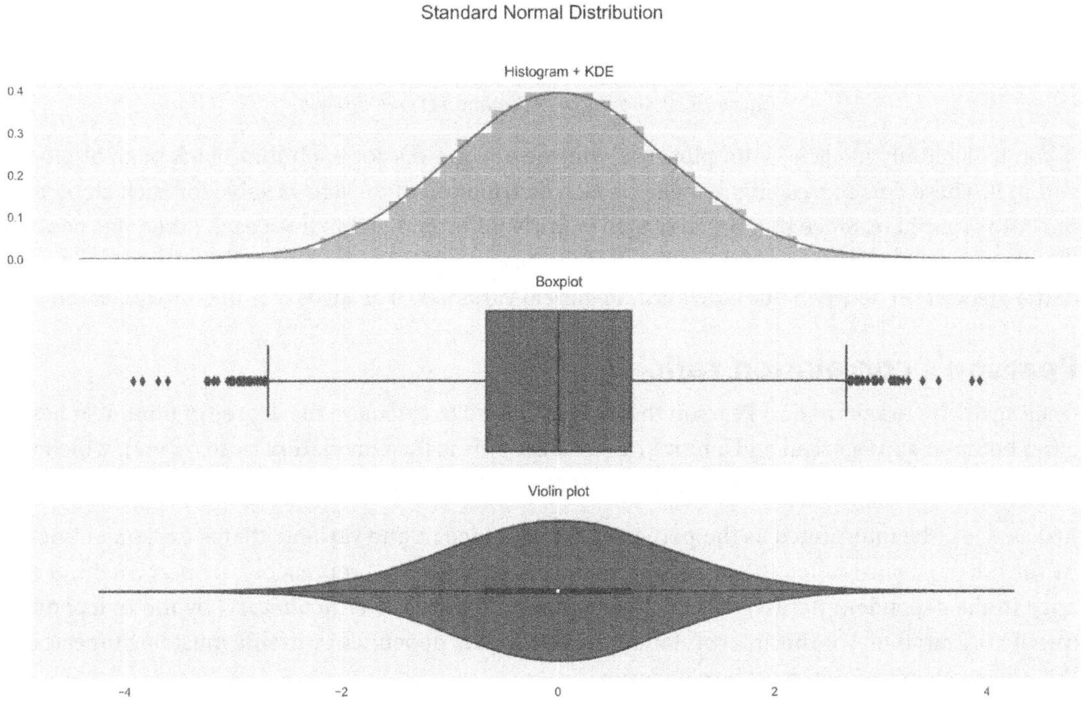

Figure 15.32: Graphical explanation of a violin plot

See the *References* section for more details about boxplots and violin plots.

If you need to relate a numeric variable to a categorical variable, you can create a violin plot for each element of the categorical variable. Returning to the example of the Titanic disaster dataset, given the Pclass (categorical) and Age (numeric) variables, you get this multiple-violin plot:

Figure 15.33: Graphical explanation of a violin plot

If you look closely at each violin plot, you will see a white dot for each thin black boxplot plotted within it. These dots represent the mean of each distribution of the Age variable for each element of the Pclass variable. Since they are arranged at fairly different heights from each other, it is possible that the Pclass variable is a good predictor of the Age variable. But how do we measure the strength of the association between numeric and categorical variables? The answer is the *correlation ratio*.

Pearson's correlation ratio

Once again, it's thanks to Karl Pearson that we have a tool to calculate the degree of nonlinear association between a categorical and a numeric variable. This is the **correlation ratio** (η, eta), which was introduced during the study of **analysis of variance** (**ANOVA**), and it ranges from 0 to +1.

Just as $r2$ can be interpreted as the percentage of variance in one variable that is explained linearly by the other, $\eta2$ (also called the **intraclass correlation coefficient**) represents the percentage of variance in the dependent (target) variable that is explained *linearly or nonlinearly* by the independent (predictor) variable. For this interpretation to be valid, the dependent variable must be numeric and the independent variable must be categorical.

The correlation ratio is an asymmetric function only if the categorical variable is an ordinal one (i.e., days of the week can be converted to integers); otherwise, it makes sense only in one way. The formula for the interclass correlation coefficient (from which we immediately derive the correlation ratio by applying the square root) is as follows:

$$\eta^2 = \frac{\sum_x n_x (\bar{y}_x - \bar{y})^2}{\sum_{x,i} (y_{xi} - \bar{y})^2} = \frac{\sigma_{\bar{y}}^2}{\sigma_y^2}$$

Figure 15.34: Correlation ratio's formula

The value $\bar{y}_x$ is the mean of y broken down by category x and $\bar{y}$ is the mean of the total y (cross-category). Since σ represents the *variance* of a variable, we can read $\eta 2$ as the ratio of the dispersion of the variable y weighted for each category of x to the total dispersion of y.

IMPORTANT NOTE

The more $\eta 2$ tends to 1, the less the observations disperse around their mean for each individual category. Therefore, the total dispersion of the numeric variable is all due to the division into categories, and not to the individual dispersions for each category. Therefore, in this case, we can say that there is a strong association between the numeric variable and the categorical variable.

To better understand the concept presented above, consider the analysis of grades in three subjects. If the grades for each subject are spread out, you have a certain eta. On the other hand, if the grades for each subject are uniform, then eta is equal to 1. This statement is illustrated in *Figure 15.35*, where each observation is plotted as a point in the violin plots:

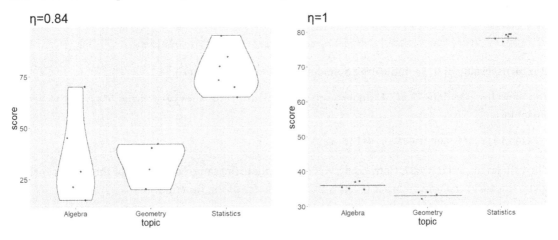

Figure 15.35: Differences in η after changing grade distributions per topic

So, let's now implement the correlation coefficients described in this section in Python.

Implementing correlation coefficients in Python

The Python community is very lucky because Shaked Zychlinski has developed a library with many data analysis tools, including a function that takes into account the data type of the columns in a pandas DataFrame and generates a DataFrame with the appropriate correlations.

This library is called **Dython** (http://shakedzy.xyz/dython/) and can be installed using pip. If you want to create mosaic plots, you will also need to install **statsmodels** (https://www.statsmodels.org/) in your pbi_powerquery_env environment. Proceed as follows:

1. Open Anaconda prompt.
2. Enter the command conda activate pbi_powerquery_env.
3. Enter the command pip install dython==0.7.4.
4. Enter the command pip install statsmodels==0.14.0.

The code you'll find in this section is available in the Python\03-titanic-disaster-analysis-in-python.py file in the Chapter 15 folder.

Of all the utilities in Dython, we need those in the nominal module. After loading the main libraries, we also create a helper function to draw a violin plot.

At this point, you can load the Titanic disaster data from a CSV file published on the web and convert the numeric columns Survived and Pclass (passenger class) to strings, since they are categorical variables:

```
dataset_url = 'http://bit.ly/titanic-dataset-csv'
df = pd.read_csv(dataset_url)
categ_cols = ['survived', 'Pclass']
df[categ_cols] = df[categ_cols].astype(str)
```

It is then possible to calculate *Cramér's V* coefficient between the two categorical variables:

```
cramers_v(df['survived'], df['Pclass'], bias_correction=False)
```

It returns a value of 0.34, indicating a moderate association strength.

You can also calculate *Theil's U* uncertainty coefficient of the Survived variable given the Pclass variable:

```
theils_u(df['survived'], df['Pclass'])
```

The value returned is 0.087. Conversely, you can calculate the same coefficient for the Pclass variable given the Survived one, in order to show the asymmetry of the function:

```
theils_u(df['Pclass'], df['survived'])
```

This one returns 0.058. So, it's clear that the association *Pclass → Survived* is stronger than the opposite one.

How about calculating the *correlation ratio η* between the variables Age (passenger age) and Pclass? Let's do that:

```
correlation_ratio(categories=df['Pclass'], measurements=df['Age'])
```

The result is 0.366. Now, what if you want to get a correlation value for each pair of columns regardless of their data type? In this case, the associations() function is our friend. You just have to specify whether you want to use Theil's U coefficient (nom_nom_assoc = 'theil') or Cramér's V one (nom_nom_assoc = 'cramer') for categorical variables, and that's it:

```
ass = associations(df, nom_nom_assoc = 'theil',
                   num_num_assoc = 'pearson',
                   figsize=(10,10), clustering=True)
```

The result is a beautiful heatmap that helps you understand at a glance which columns have the strongest correlation (for better viewing, a color image is also available for download):

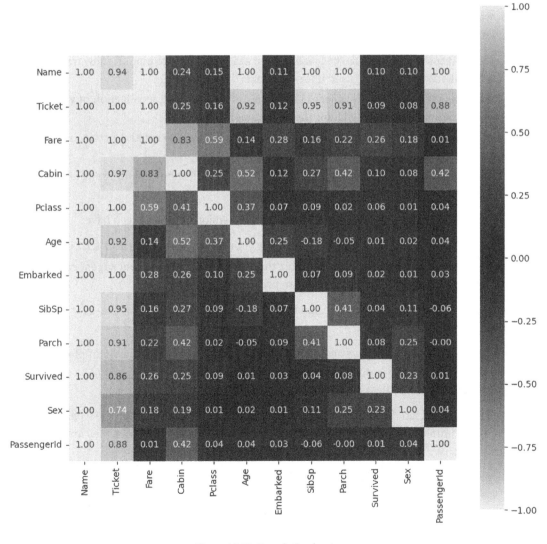

Figure 15.36: Correlation heatmap

As you may have noticed, you can also select the type of correlation to be used between numeric variables (Pearson, Spearman, and Kendall) using the `num_num_assoc` parameter. In addition, you can access the coefficient DataFrame using the code `ass['corr']`.

Now let's see how to implement the same things in R.

Implementing correlation coefficients in R

There is no R package on CRAN similar to Dython that allows you to calculate correlations between columns in a tibble regardless of their data type. There is also no package that implements the correlation ratio as defined above. Therefore, based on the source code of the Dython package, we created it from scratch.

Instead, we used some CRAN packages that expose some of the correlation functions introduced in the previous sections. In particular, these packages are:

- **rstatix** (`https://github.com/kassambara/rstatix`), an intuitive pipe-friendly framework for basic statistical testing. We used it for the `cramer_v()` function.
- **DescTools** (`https://andrisignorell.github.io/DescTools/`), a collection of various basic statistical functions. We used it for the `UncertCoef()` function.
- **vcd** (`https://cran.r-project.org/web/packages/vcd/index.html`), a collection of visualization techniques and tools for categorical data.
- **sjPlot** (`https://strengejacke.github.io/sjPlot/`), a collection of plotting and tabular output functions for data visualization.

So, you need to install these packages in the most recent version of CRAN R you have:

1. Open RStudio and make sure it is referencing your latest CRAN R (version 4.2.2 in our case).
2. Click on the **Console** window and enter this command: `install.packages(c('rstatix', 'DescTools', 'vcd', 'sjPlot'))`. Then press *Enter*.

The code you'll find in this section is available in the file `R\03-titanic-survive-class-analysis-in-r.R` in the `Chapter 15` folder.

After loading the main libraries, we again created a helper function to plot a violin plot. After that, we defined the `correlation_ratio()` function to compute the eta and `calc_corr()` to compute the correlation of a tibble regardless of the data type of the given columns.

At this point, you can load the Titanic disaster data from a CSV file published on the web and convert the numeric columns `Survived` and `Pclass` (passenger class) into factors, since they are categorical variables:

```
dataset_url <- 'http://bit.ly/titanic-dataset-csv'
tbl <- read_csv(dataset_url)
tbl <- tbl %>%
    mutate( across(c('survived', 'Pclass'), as.factor) )
```

It is then possible to calculate *Cramér's V* coefficient between the two categorical variables:

```
rstatix::cramer_v(x=tbl$Survived, y=tbl$Pclass)
```

It returns a value of 0.34, indicating a medium association strength.

You can also calculate *Theil's U* uncertainty coefficient of the Survived variable given the Pclass variable:

```
DescTools::UncertCoef(tbl$Survived, tbl$Pclass, direction = 'row')
```

The returned value is 0.087. Also, in this case, we can calculate the *correlation ratio* η between the numeric variable Age and the categorical Pclass one:

```
correlation_ratio( categories = tbl$Pclass, measurements = tbl$Age, numeric_
replace_value = 0)
```

The result is 0.366. This allows you to get the correlation value for any pair of columns, regardless of their data type, using the calc_corr() function we've developed. All you have to do is specify whether you want to use *Theil's U* coefficient (set theil_uncert=True) or *Cramér's V* (set theil_uncert=False) for categorical variables:

```
# Create two data frames having the only column containing the tibble column
names as values
row <- data.frame(row=names(tbl))
col <- data.frame(col=names(tbl))
# Create the cross join data frame from the previous two ones
ass <- tidyr::crossing(row, col)
# Add the corr column containing correlation values
corr_tbl <- ass %>%
    mutate( corr = map2_dbl(row, col, ~ calc_corr(data = tbl, row_name = .x,
col_name = .y, theil_uncert = T)) )
corr_tbl
```

You'll see something like this as a result:

```
# A tibble: 144 × 3
      row    col              corr
      <chr>  <chr>            <dbl>
 1 Age     Age              1
 2 Age     Cabin            0.524
 3 Age     Embarked         0.249
 4 Age     Fare             0.136
 5 Age     Name             1
 6 Age     Parch           -0.0488
 7 Age     PassengerId      0.0381
 8 Age     Pclass           0.366
 9 Age     Sex              0.0250
10 Age     SibSp           -0.185
# ... with 134 more rows
```

Figure 15.37: Correlation tibble you get from the Titanic one

You can also plot a heatmap of the correlation tibble just created using the following code:

```
corr_tbl %>%
    ggplot( aes(x=row, y=col, fill=corr) ) +
    geom_tile() +
    geom_text(aes(row, col, label = round(corr, 2)), color = "white", size = 4)
```

Here is the result:

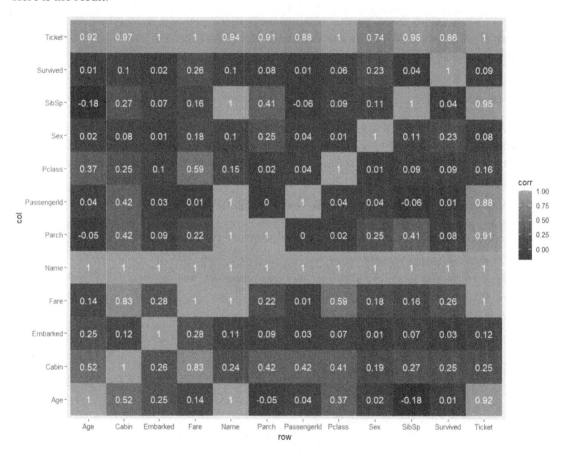

Figure 15.38: Heatmap of the correlation tibble

Awesome! You have just implemented all of the correlation coefficients studied in this chapter in R as well. Let's now see how to implement them in Power BI, both with Python and with R.

Implementing correlation coefficients in Power BI with Python and R

Obviously, Power BI was not born as an advanced statistical analysis tool, so you will not find, for example, all you need to implement all the correlation coefficients seen in the previous sections. In this case, the support given by Python and R is of fundamental importance for this purpose.

Also, in this case, due to the simplicity of the code, we will implement the correlation coefficients in both Python and R in one project.

First, make sure that Power BI Desktop references the correct versions of Python and R in **Options**. Then follow these steps:

1. Click on **Get data**, then select **Web**.

2. Enter the `http://bit.ly/titanic-dataset-csv` URL into the **URL** textbox and click **OK**.

3. You'll see a preview of the data. Then click **Transform Data**.

4. Click **Transform** on the ribbon and then **Run Python script**.

5. Enter the script you can find in the file `Python\04-correlation-analysis-in-power-bi-with-python.py` in the `Chapter15` folder.

6. We are only interested in the data in `result_df`. So, click its **Table** value.

7. You'll see the preview of all correlation coefficients between all the columns of the dataset.

8. Click **Home** on the ribbon and then click **Close & Apply**.

9. Repeat *steps 1* to *3*.

10. Click **Transform** on the ribbon and then **Run R script**.

11. Enter the script you can find in the file `R\04-correlation-analysis-in-power-bi-with-r.R` in the `Chapter15` folder.

12. We are only interested in the data in `corr_tbl`. So, click its **Table** value.

13. You'll see the preview of all correlation coefficients between all the columns of the dataset.

14. Click **Home** on the ribbon and then click **Close & Apply**.

Amazing! You have just calculated the correlation coefficients for all the numeric columns of a source dataset in Power BI with both Python and R!

Summary

In this chapter, you discovered several methods for calculating the correlation coefficient for different types of variables in your data analysis. First, you learned how to calculate the correlation coefficient using the Pearson, Spearman, and Kendall methods for two numeric variables. These methods help you understand the strength and direction of the relationship between two numeric variables. You also explored how to calculate the correlation coefficient for two categorical variables using Cramér's V and Theil's coefficient of uncertainty. Finally, you learned how to calculate the correlation coefficient between a numeric variable and a categorical variable using the correlation ratio.

In the next chapter, you will see how statistics are really important for identifying outliers and imputing missing values in your dataset.

References

For additional reading, check out the following books and articles:

- *Spearman's Rank-Order Correlation* (`https://statistics.laerd.com/statistical-guides/spearmans-rank-order-correlation-statistical-guide.php`)

- *Concordant Pairs and Discordant Pairs* (`https://www.statisticshowto.com/concordant-pairs-discordant-pairs/`)

- *Mosaic Plot and Chi-Square Test* (`https://towardsdatascience.com/mosaic-plot-and-chi-square-test-c41b1a527ce4`)

- *An intuitive introduction to Boxplots* (`https://medium.com/dataseries/an-intuitive-introduction-to-boxplots-e5babae2f04f`)

- *Violin plots explained* (`https://towardsdatascience.com/violin-plots-explained-fb1d115e023d`)

- *The Search for Categorical Correlation* (`https://towardsdatascience.com/the-search-for-categorical-correlation-a1cf7f1888c9`)

Test your knowledge

1. Why is it important to explore associations between variables in data analysis?

2. What are the different types of associations between variables?

3. How can we measure the strength and direction of an association between numeric variables?

4. What are Cramér's V coefficient, Theil's U uncertainty coefficient, and Pearson's correlation ratio, and how are they used in analyzing associations between categorical and numeric variables?

5. How can we use correlation coefficients to identify key predictors in a dataset?

6. How can we visualize associations between variables?

Learn more on Discord

To join the Discord community for this book – where you can share feedback, ask questions to the author, and learn about new releases – follow the QR code below:

`https://discord.gg/MKww5g45EB`

16

Adding Statistical Insights: Outliers and Missing Values

In the previous chapter, we explored a range of statistical functions in Power BI, including calculating correlations between variables. Now, we will continue to extend the data enrichment possibilities in Power BI through statistical functions by focusing on methodologies to detect univariate and multivariate outliers in your dataset. Additionally, we will explore advanced techniques to impute possible missing values in datasets and time series.

In this chapter, we will delve into what outliers are, highlight their impact on analysis accuracy, and provide strategies for dealing with them in Power BI. Furthermore, missing values can cause significant issues during data analysis and reporting. Unfortunately, Power BI lacks native tools, but luckily we can turn to Python or R to fill this gap. Therefore, understanding how to diagnose missing values accurately and implement effective imputation algorithms becomes crucial for reliable analysis results.

By the end of this chapter, readers will be equipped with the necessary knowledge and skills to identify outliers accurately and handle missing values effectively using advanced statistical techniques within the Power BI environment. The topics covered in this chapter are:

- What outliers are and how to deal with them
- Identifying outliers
- Implementing outlier detection algorithms
- What missing values are and how to deal with them
- Diagnosing missing values
- Implementing missing value imputation algorithms

Technical requirements

This chapter requires you to have a working internet connection and **Power BI Desktop** installed on your machine (version: 2.118.828.0 64-bit, June 2023). You must have properly configured the R and Python engines and IDEs as outlined in *Chapter 2*, *Configuring R With Power BI*, and *Chapter 3*, *Configuring Python with Power BI*.

What outliers are

Generally, outliers are defined as observations that are at an unusual distance from other observations in a data sample. In other words, they are uncommon values in a dataset. The abnormal distance we're talking about doesn't have a fixed measure, of course, but is strictly dependent on the dataset you're analyzing. Simply put, it will be the analyst who decides the distance beyond which others will be considered abnormal distances, based on their experience and functional knowledge of the business reality represented by the dataset.

> **IMPORTANT NOTE**
>
> It makes sense to talk about outliers for numeric variables, or for numeric variables grouped by elements of categorical variables. It does not make sense to talk about outliers only for categorical variables.

But why is there so much focus on outlier management? The answer is that they very often have undesirable macroscopic effects on some statistical operations. The most striking example is that of a linear correlation in the presence of an outlier in an "uncomfortable" position and the same thing calculated by eliminating the outlier:

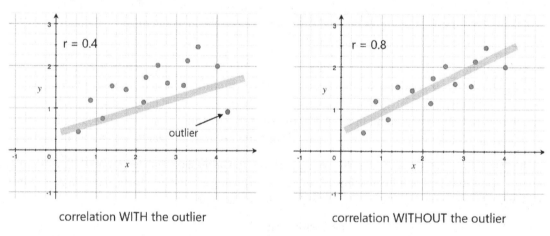

Figure 16.1: A simple scatterplot

As shown in *Figure 16.1*, and as you learned in *Chapter 15, Adding Statistical Insights: Associations*, Pearson's correlation r suffers greatly from outliers.

But then, is it always enough to remove outliers *a priori* to solve any problems you might find downstream in your analysis? As you can imagine, the answer is "no," because it all depends on the type of outlier you are dealing with.

The causes of outliers

Before considering any action to be taken on the outliers of a variable, it is necessary to consider what may have caused them. Once the cause is identified, it may be possible to correct the outliers immediately. Here is a possible categorization of the causes of outliers:

- **Data entry errors:** There may be an analyst collecting the data who made a mistake in compiling the data. For example, if the analyst is collecting the birth dates of a group of people, the analyst may write 177 instead of 1977. If the dates collected are in the 1900-2100 range, it is easy to correct the outlier created by the data entry error. Other times, it is not possible to recover the correct value.

- **Intentional outliers:** Very often, the introduction of "errors" is intentional on the part of the individuals to whom the measurements apply. For example, adolescents typically do not accurately report the amount of alcohol they consume.

- **Data processing errors:** Data transformation processes commonly applied to analytic solutions can introduce unintentional errors, which in turn can lead to possible outliers.

- **Sampling errors:** Sometimes, the data on which you perform your analysis must be sampled from a much larger dataset. In this case, the analyst may not select a subset of data that represents the entire population of data. For example, you need to measure the height of athletes, and you accidentally include some basketball players in your dataset.

- **Natural outliers:** So-called "natural" outliers exist because they are part of the nature of the business and are not the result of any kind of error. For example, it's pretty much a given that shopping malls sell more products during the holiday season.

Now that you know the most common causes of outliers, you need to figure out how to identify them.

Identifying outliers

There are different methods for detecting outliers, depending on whether you are analyzing one variable at a time (**univariate analysis**) or several variables at once (**multivariate analysis**). In the univariate case, the analysis is fairly straightforward. The multivariate case, however, is more complex. Let's examine it in detail.

Univariate outliers

One of the most direct and common ways to identify outliers for a single variable is to make use of boxplots, which you learned about in *Chapter 15, Adding Statistical Insights: Associations*. Some of the key points of a boxplot are the **interquartile range (IQR)**, defined as the distance from the **first quartile (Q1)** to the **third quartile (Q3)**, the **lower whisker** (Q1 - 1.5 x IQR), and the **upper whisker** (Q3 + 1.5 x IQR):

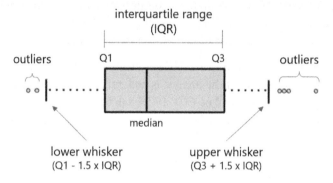

Figure 16.2: Boxplot's main characteristics

Specifically, all observations that are before the lower whisker and after the upper whisker are identified as outliers. This one is also known as **Tukey's method**.

Identification becomes more complicated when dealing with more than one variable.

Multivariate outliers

Identifying outliers when dealing with more than one variable (**multivariate outliers**) is not always straightforward. It depends on the number of variables involved and their data type.

Numeric variables and categorical variables

As long as you need to analyze how a numeric variable is distributed among the different elements of a categorical variable, you can still do it with the tools we have seen so far. In fact, you simply plot a boxplot for the values of the numeric variable grouped by each element of the categorical variable:

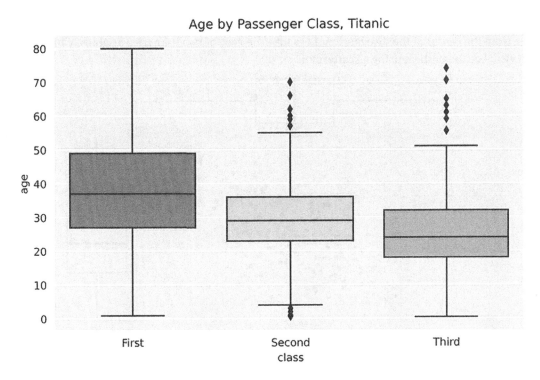

Figure 16.3: Numeric versus categorical variables

Although a numeric variable may not exhibit outliers within its range, when segmented by the levels of a categorical variable, outliers may emerge that are specific to these subsets. These outliers are identifiable only within the context of their respective categories and would otherwise remain undetected in an analysis of the combined dataset. Examining the data within each categorical segment is important to capture a more nuanced understanding of the variable's behavior across different groups.

All numeric variables

In general, the inexperienced analyst tends to simplify the determination of outliers in multidimensional cases when there are only numeric variables.

IMPORTANT NOTE

One might assume that an observation that is extreme in any variable is also a multivariate outlier, and this is often true. However, the opposite is not true: if variables are correlated, you can have a multivariate outlier that is not a univariate outlier in any variable.

When dealing only with numeric variables, it is still possible to use algorithms that measure the distance from the center of the distribution. Let's take the case of two numeric variables, which allows us to visualize the outliers using a scatterplot:

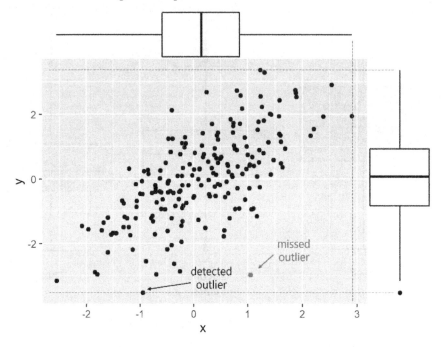

Figure 16.4: Scatterplot of two numeric variables

As you can see in *Figure 16.4*, we have also added in the margins the two boxplots for each individual variable under analysis to verify that for each of them, there are no outliers, except for the one detected at the bottom. You can also see that there is one outlier that is clearly different from all the other observations but is not detected as an outlier by the two boxplots.

Imagine fixing a hypothetical center of the distribution and defining a distance from the center (Euclidean distance) above which the observations are to be considered outliers:

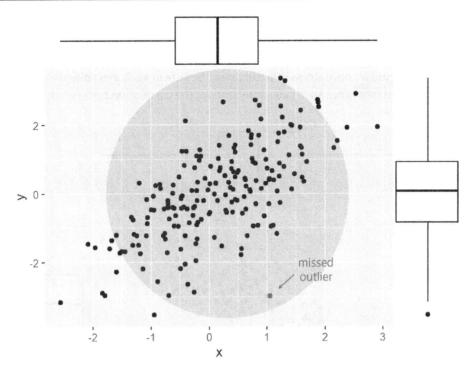

Figure 16.5: Euclidean distance from the center of the distribution

The above rule defines a circle centered on the center of the distribution. If you look at a circle with the radius you see in *Figure 16.5*, you will identify several outliers (perhaps false positives?) that were not identified by looking at the boxplots alone, but the outlier that you did not identify before remains unidentified in this case as well. As you can well understand, the problem is that the distribution has an ellipsoidal shape, which is distributed along the main diagonal of the Cartesian plane. A circle is, as you would imagine, only appropriate for analyzing a circular distribution.

What if there was a distance that also took into account the shape of the distribution? This is exactly what the **Mahalanobis distance** does. This new distance differs from the others because it considers the **covariance** between the two variables. Covariance and Pearson's correlation are two quantities associated with very similar concepts, so in some cases, they are interchangeable (see the references). The fact that the Mahalanobis distance takes into account the correlation between the two variables is evident in *Figure 16.6*:

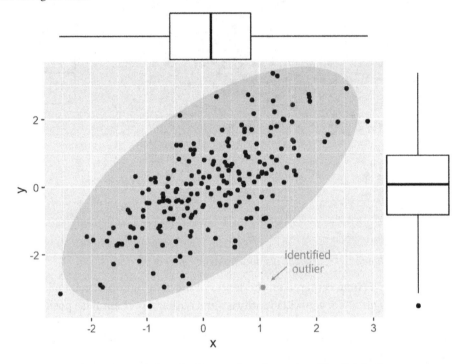

Figure 16.6: Mahalanobis distance from the center of the distribution

For the curious, this is the formula to calculate it:

$$d_M(\vec{x}, Q) = \sqrt{(\vec{x} - \vec{\mu})^{\mathsf{T}} S^{-1} (\vec{x} - \vec{\mu})}$$

Figure 16.7 – Mahalanobis distance formula

$\vec{x}$ is a multivariate observation, $\vec{\mu}$ is the multivariate mean of all observations, and S is the covariance matrix. The fact that the Mahalanobis distance depends on the mean of all observations (a very unstable measure, very sensitive to outliers) and on the covariance matrix shows that the same limitations apply as for Pearson's coefficient, which are:

- Possible outliers in inconvenient locations can greatly affect the multivariate center, which is defined by the mean of all observations. If the center is not calculated well, it is very likely that the Mahalanobis distance application will identify spurious outliers, as seen in *Figure 16.6*. This is easily solved by computing the center using a median-based formula, which is much more robust to the presence of extreme observations.

- In the presence of extreme outliers, the covariance matrix may also be negatively affected. This problem is also addressed by adopting a robust version of the covariance matrix using the **Minimum Covariance Determinant (MCD)**. This method not only provides a robust covariance matrix but also provides a robust estimate of the center of the observations.

- It is very likely that using the Mahalanobis distance will return false outliers in the case of *skewed, nonlinear,* or *heteroscedastic* distributions. In these cases, it is necessary to resort to transformations of the variables involved, as far as possible, before applying distance calculations. The goal of the transformations is to obtain distributions that are as normal as possible and to make the associations between different variables as linear as possible. In these cases, **Box-Cox transformations** or **Yeo-Johnson transformations** are used.

Identifying outliers becomes much more complicated when dealing with mixed variables (numeric and categorical) in numbers greater than two. It is necessary to use different data science techniques (feature engineering techniques for categorical variables, handling of unbalanced datasets, etc.) and to apply specific machine learning anomaly detection algorithms. For this reason, such cases are out of the scope of this book (see *References* for more details).

Once the outliers (both univariate and multivariate) are identified, it is up to the analysts to decide which method to use to try to fix them, if possible. How do they go about it? There are several common ways to correct outliers that can be considered.

Dealing with outliers

The most widely used approaches to deal with outliers are as follows:

- **Dropping them:** The analyst concludes that eliminating the outliers altogether will guarantee better results in the final analysis.

- **Capping them:** It is common to use the strategy of assigning a fixed extreme value (cap or **winsorize**) to all those observations that exceed it (in absolute value) when it is certain that all extreme observations behave in the same way as those with the cap value.

- **Assigning a new value:** In this case, outliers are eliminated by replacing them with null values, and these null values are imputed using one of the simplest techniques: the replacement of null values with a fixed value that could be, for example, the mean or median of the variable in question. You'll see more complex imputation strategies in the next sections.

- **Transforming the data:** When the analyst is dealing with natural outliers, very often the histogram of the variable's distribution takes on a skewed shape. Right-skewed distributions are very common, and if they were used as they appeared, many statistical tests that assume a normal distribution would give incorrect results. In this case, it is common to transform the variable by applying a monotonic function, which in some way "straightens out" the imbalance (this is the case of the log() function, for example). Once transformed, the new variable satisfies the requirements of the tests and can therefore be analyzed without errors. Once the results have been obtained from the transformed variable, they must be transformed again by the inverse function of the one used at the beginning (if log() was used, then the inverse is exp()) in order to have values that are consistent with the business variable under analysis.

Now let's see how to implement outlier detection algorithms based on what you learned in the previous sections.

Implementing outlier detection algorithms

The first thing you'll do is implement what you've just learned in Python.

Implementing outlier detection in Python

In this section, we will use the *Wine Quality* dataset created by Paulo Cortez et al. (`https://archive. ics.uci.edu/ml/datasets/wine+quality`) to show how to detect outliers in Python. The dataset contains as many observations as there are different types of red wine, each described by the organoleptic properties measured by the variables, except for the `quality` variable, which provides a measure of the quality of the product using a discrete grade scale from 1 to 10.

You'll find the code used in this section in the `Python\01-detect-outliers-in-python.py` file in the `Chapter 16` folder.

Once you have loaded the data from the `winequality-red.csv` file directly from the web into the `df` variable, let's start by examining the `sulphates` variable. Let's check if it contains any outliers by displaying its boxplot, which was obtained through a wrapper function that we have defined in the code:

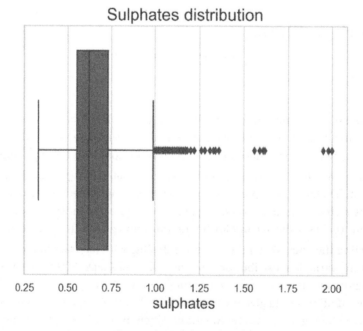

Figure 16.8: Sulphates boxplot

It appears that there are many values after 1.0. To be able to find them in the dataset, we created a function that takes a dataframe as input and the name of the numeric column to consider and returns the dataframe as output with the addition of a column of Boolean values, containing `True` if the value of the column is an outlier, and `False` otherwise:

```python
def add_is_outlier_IQR(data, col_name):
    col_values = data[col_name]

    Q1=col_values.quantile(0.25)
    Q3=col_values.quantile(0.75)
    IQR=Q3-Q1

    outliers_col_name = f'is_{col_name.replace(" ", "_")}_outlier'
    data[outliers_col_name] = ((col_values < (Q1 - 1.5 * IQR)) | (col_values >
(Q3 + 1.5 * IQR)))

    return data
add_is_outlier_IQR(df, 'sulphates')
```

Once we have identified the outliers from the initial distribution of the sulphates variable, we can plot its boxplot by removing the outliers to see what changes:

```python
df_no_outliers = df.loc[~df['is_sulphates_outlier']]
```

The resulting boxplot is as follows:

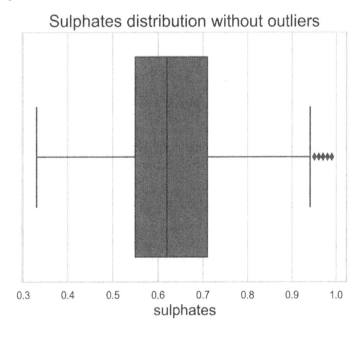

Figure 16.9: Sulphates boxplot once outliers were removed

As you can see, some outliers are still visible. This is because removing the outliers from the original distribution changed the distribution (changed its statistical properties). So, what you see in *Figure 16.9* are the outliers of the new distribution that was created.

As explained earlier, it is up to the analyst to determine whether the identified outliers should be corrected in some way, eliminated, or left where they are. In this case, assume the outliers in the second distribution are natural outliers. Let's try to break the new distribution down to the individual values of the quality variable and draw a boxplot for each of them:

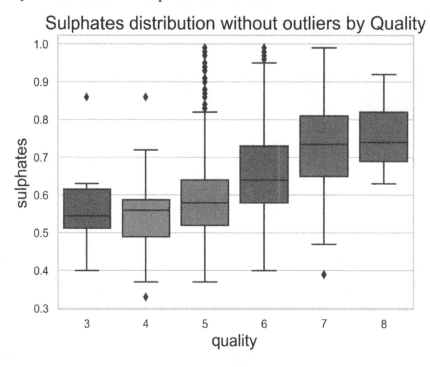

Figure 16.10: Sulphates boxplots for each quality value

As shown in *Figure 16.10*, the distribution of sulphates for wines that received a score of 5 has several outliers. This could lead the analyst to try to understand how much the presence of sulphates affects the final rating given to the wine by users, paying particular attention to the case of a wine considered to be of average quality.

On the other hand, if we wanted to identify multivariate outliers for all numeric variables in the dataset, except for the quality variable, we would have to change our approach and try to apply the Mahalanobis distance, as you learned in the previous section. We assume that the elimination of outliers has been validated for each individual variable. So, let's try to find out if there are multivariate outliers for the numeric variables in the df_no_outliers dataframe. First, however, it is necessary to check whether the distributions of the variables under analysis are skewed. Therefore, we try to draw a histogram for each of the variables:

```
df_no_outliers.drop('quality', axis=1).hist(figsize=(10,10))
plt.tight_layout()
plt.show()
```

The resulting plots are as follows:

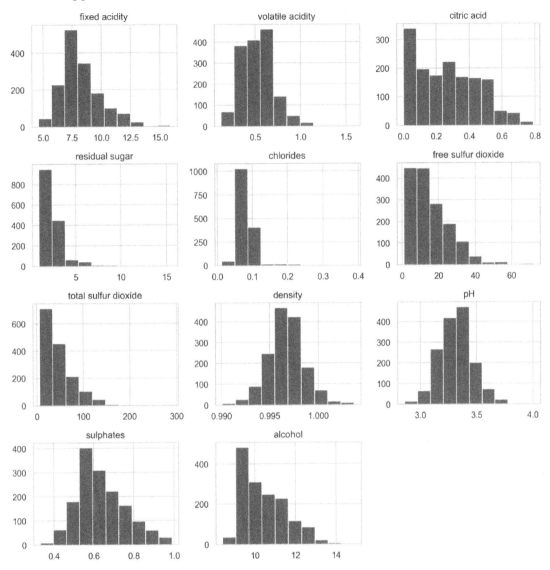

Figure 16.11: Histograms of all the wine quality variables without outliers

It is obvious that some of them are extremely right-skewed (*residual sugar*, *chlorides*, *total sulfur dioxide*, etc.), therefore it is necessary to try to apply transformations that try to "normalize" the individual distributions. In general, *Box-Cox transformations* are used. If they are applied to zero or negative values, the result may be undefined or negative, which is outside the intended use of the transformation. This situation can occur if the data has not been properly prepared, or if it has been assumed that all values are positive when in fact some are not. Since, in this case, some values of the distributions are not positive, it is not possible to apply them. Therefore, it is necessary to use another transformation that has the same objective but accommodates zero and negative values, called *Yeo-Johnson*. More details about these transformations can be found in the references.

For convenience, we have created a wrapper function that transforms a pandas DataFrame of numeric variables only by applying Yeo-Johnson transformations and also returns the corresponding lambda values:

```python
from sklearn.preprocessing import PowerTransformer
def yeo_johnson_transf(data):
    pt = PowerTransformer(method='yeo-johnson', standardize=True)
    pt.fit(data)
    lambdas = pt.lambdas_
    df_yeojohnson = pd.DataFrame( pt.transform(data), columns=data.columns.
values )
    return df_yeojohnson, lambdas
```

Then, once you've transformed the dataframe accordingly, try plotting histograms of the distributions of the transformed variables to see if the skewness has been smoothed out:

```python
df_transf, lambda_arr = yeo_johnson_transf(df_no_outliers[numeric_col_names])
df_transf.hist(figsize=(10,10))
plt.tight_layout()
plt.show()
```

This is the plot you get:

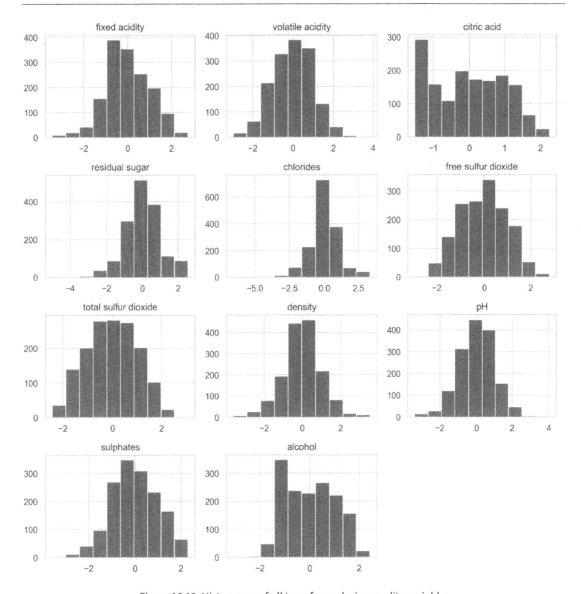

Figure 16.12: Histograms of all transformed wine quality variables

It is quite obvious that the distributions now look more like the "bells" of normal distributions. You can now compute Mahalanobis distances with the confidence that outliers will be detected with fewer errors.

Outliers are identified using a robust estimator of the covariance, the *MCD*. Since the squared Mahalanobis distance behaves like a Chi-Squared distribution (see the references), we can calculate the threshold value above which an observation is considered an outlier thanks to this distribution, passing the desired cutoff value to its *percent point function* (ppf()):

```
from sklearn.covariance import MinCovDet
robust_cov = MinCovDet(support_fraction=0.7).fit(df_transf)
center = robust_cov.location_
D = robust_cov.mahalanobis(df_transf - center)
cutoff = 0.98
degrees_of_freedom = df_transf.shape[1]
cut = chi2.ppf(cutoff, degrees_of_freedom)
```

Once you have determined the threshold value, you can add two columns to the dataframe: a column that indicates whether the observation (the row) is an outlier according to Mahalanobis, and a column that reports the probability that an observation is not an outlier by chance:

```
is_outlier_arr = (D > cut)
outliers_stat_proba = np.zeros(len(is_outlier_arr))
for i in range(len(is_outlier_arr)):
    outliers_stat_proba[i] = chi2.cdf(D[i], degrees_of_freedom)
df_no_outliers['is_mahalanobis_outlier'] = is_outlier_arr
df_no_outliers['mahalanobis_outlier_stat_sign'] = outliers_stat_proba
df_no_outliers[df_no_outliers['is_mahalanobis_outlier']]
```

You will see a dataframe chunk like this:

	fixed acidity		is_mahalanobis_outlier	mahalanobis_outlier_proba
14	8.9		True	0.998026
15	8.9		True	0.998662
33	6.9		True	0.983783
34	5.2		True	0.999955
38	5.7		True	0.999998
...	...		...	...
1570	6.4		True	0.999999
1571	6.4		True	0.980983
1574	5.6		True	1.000000
1589	6.6		True	0.989673
1598	6.0		True	0.989881

Figure 16.13: Outliers information shown in the dataframe

Wow! With a minimum of statistical knowledge, you were able to identify multivariate outliers of numeric variables in Python.

It is possible to get the same results in R. Let's see how.

Implementing outlier detection in R

You'll find the code used in this section in the `R\01-detect-outliers-in-r.R` file in the `Chapter 16` folder. To run it properly, you need to install new packages:

1. Open RStudio and make sure it is referencing your latest CRAN R (version 4.2.2 in our case).
2. Click on the **Console** window and enter this command: `install.packages('robust')`. Then press *Enter*.
3. Enter this command: `install.packages('recipes')`. Then press *Enter*.

Once you have loaded the data from the `winequality-red.csv` file directly from the web into the `df` variable, you'll plot the boxplot of the `sulphates` variable using the `boxPlot()` wrapper function:

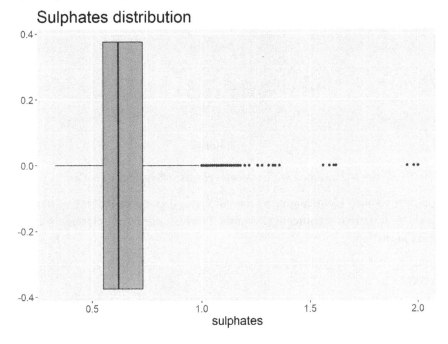

Figure 16.14: Boxplot of the sulphates variable

Since there are many outliers visible in *Figure 16.14*, they are identified using the add_is_outlier_ IQR() function, which adds an identifier column to the dataframe. As the name implies, the function identifies the outliers based on the interquartile range. At this point, the boxplot of the same variable is drawn again, this time eliminating the previously identified outliers:

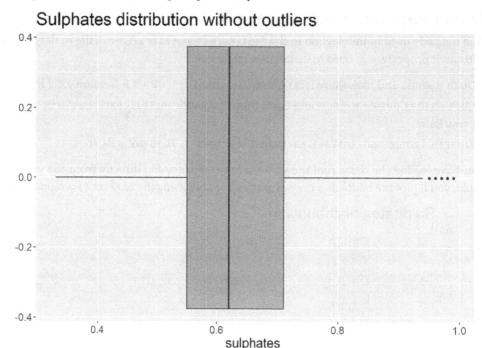

Figure 16.15: Boxplot of the sulphates variable after removing outliers

Assuming you now want to identify multivariate outliers, it is worth looking at the histograms of each variable to see if there is significant skewness. The histograms are plotted using the following dataframeHist() function:

```
dataframeHist <- function(data, bins = 10) {
    data %>%
        tidyr::pivot_longer( cols = everything() ) %>%
        ggplot( aes(value) ) +
        geom_histogram( fill='orange', na.rm = TRUE, bins = bins )+
        theme( ... ) +
        facet_wrap(~ name, scales = "free")
}
```

A special feature of this function is that it uses the pivot_longer() function from the tidyr package to transform the dataset from a wide format to a long format. It does this by consolidating all column names into a single name column, while transposing the original data values corresponding to those column names into a new value column:

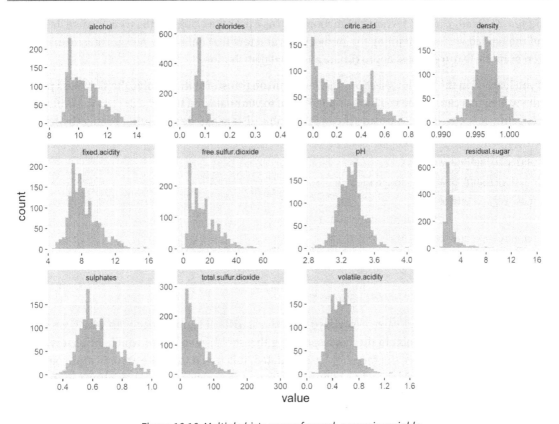

Figure 16.16: Multiple histograms for each numeric variable

Since the skewness is obvious, you can apply Yeo-Johnson transformations thanks to the yeo_johnson_transf() wrapper function we created for you:

```
yeo_johnson_transf <- function(data, target_name) {
  rec <- recipe(data, as.formula(paste0(target_name, ' ~ .')))
  rec <- rec %>%
    step_center( all_numeric(), - all_outcomes() ) %>%
    step_scale( all_numeric(), - all_outcomes() ) %>%
    step_YeoJohnson( all_numeric(), -all_outcomes() )
  prep_rec <- prep( rec, training = data )
  res_list <- list( df_yeojohnson = bake( prep_rec, data ),
                    lambdas = prep_rec$steps[[3]][["lambdas"]] )
}
```

The peculiarity of this function is that it uses a ready-made step in the recipes package, which simplifies the entire preprocessing phase, including centering, scaling, and applying the Yeo-Johnson transformation to all numeric columns, except the target column. The target column name is passed as a parameter because the function assumes that you are preparing the data for a machine learning model, where the target variable (the outcome you want to predict) should not be transformed in the same way as the predictor variables. To learn more about using recipes, see the references.

The yeo_johnson_transf() wrapper function returns a list of two objects: the transformed dataframe and the named vector containing the numeric parameters that define the power transformation for each numeric feature to best approximate a normal distribution.

As you learned in the previous section, the Yeo-Johnson transformations solve the skewness problem quite well in this case. Once you have applied them to your data and have the df_transf transformed dataframe, it is possible to try using the Mahalanobis distance to detect outliers using the following code:

```
data <- df_transf %>%
    select( numeric_col_names )
cov_obj <- data %>%
    covRob( estim="mcd", alpha=0.7 )
center <- cov_obj$center
cov <- cov_obj$cov
distances <- data %>%
    mahalanobis( center=center, cov=cov )
```

At this point, given a cutoff value associated with the statistical significance with which we want to identify outliers, we can obtain the corresponding threshold value above which an observation is considered an outlier. Once the threshold is calculated, it is trivial to create an indicator column for the outliers. It is also possible to add a column indicating the probability that an observation is not a random outlier, thanks to the pchisq() function:

```
cutoff <- 0.98
degrees_of_freedom <- ncol(data)
outliers_value_cutoff <- qchisq(cutoff, degrees_of_freedom)
df_no_outliers <- df_no_outliers %>%
    mutate(
        is_mahalanobis_outlier    = distances > outliers_value_cutoff,
        mahalanobis_outlier_proba = pchisq(distances, ncol(data)) )
df_no_outliers %>% filter( is_mahalanobis_outlier == TRUE ) %>% select( fixed.
acidity, is_mahalanobis_outlier, mahalanobis_outlier_proba)
```

The following is a partial representation of the output:

```
# A tibble: 180 × 3
   fixed.acidity is_mahalanobis_outlier mahalanobis_outlier_proba
           <dbl> <lgl>                                       <dbl>
 1           8.9 TRUE                                        0.997
 2           8.9 TRUE                                        0.998
 3           6.9 TRUE                                        0.982
 4           5.2 TRUE                                        1.00
 5           5.7 TRUE                                        1.00
 6           7.5 TRUE                                        1.00
 7           4.6 TRUE                                        1.00
 8           7.7 TRUE                                        0.998
 9           5.6 TRUE                                        1.00
10           7.7 TRUE                                        0.981
# … with 170 more rows
```

Figure 16.17: Final tibble containing the multivariate outlier information

Well done! You were also able to identify multivariate outliers in R.

At this point, it is trivial to apply the Python and R code you have seen so far to Power BI.

Implementing outlier detection in Power BI

Power BI has tools that allow you to view outliers graphically and then analyze them by hovering over them. One of them was introduced in the November 2020 release and is the **Anomaly Detection** feature. The other one is the **Outliers Detection** custom visual. Let's see what the main differences are:

- **Anomaly Detection** is available directly in Power BI. It is *only supported for line chart visuals* with *time series data* in the axis field.

- **Outliers Detection** is an open-source R custom visual that must be installed separately (https://github.com/microsoft/PowerBI-visuals-outliers-det). It is a bit outdated, but it can be built using the methodology you will learn in *Chapter 22, Interactive Custom Visuals in R*.

As you may have noticed, both of these tools are Power BI visuals.

IMPORTANT NOTE

Any transformations performed within Python or R visuals may modify the dataframe (# dataset) that will later be the object of the visualization, but the changes cannot be persisted in the data model in any way.

For this reason, we have decided to illustrate some outlier detection methods that can be applied in Power Query using Python or R. This way, you can identify observations that are outliers by simply filtering your data model tables accordingly. For the simplicity of the code, we will also implement the correlation coefficients in both Python and R in one project.

First, make sure that Power BI Desktop is referencing the correct versions of Python and R in **Options**. Then follow these steps:

1. Open Power BI Desktop through the shortcut that activates the `pbi_powerquery_env` environment.

2. Make sure Power BI Desktop is referencing the `pbi_powerquery_env` environment in the Python scripting tab, and the latest available engine (in our case 4.2.2) in the R scripting tab in **Options**.

3. Click on **Get data**, then **Web**.

4. Enter `https://archive.ics.uci.edu/ml/machine-learning-databases/wine-quality/winequality-red.csv` into the URL textbox and click **OK**.

5. If the **Authentication** dialog box appears, select **Anonymous** and click **Connect**.

6. You'll see a preview of the data. Then click **Transform Data**.

7. Click **Transform** on the ribbon and then **Run Python script**.

8. Enter the script you can find in the `Python\02-detect-outliers-in-power-bi-with-python.py` file in the `Chapter 16` folder.

9. If you get the Firewall privacy level mismatch error, select a **Public** privacy level for the web URL data source and click **OK**. You are prompted to expand a dataframe calculated in the Python script.

10. We are only interested in the data in `df_no_outliers`. So, click on its **Table** value.

11. You'll see a preview of the dataset that also has the new columns to identify outliers.

12. Click **Home** on the ribbon and then click **Close & Apply**.

13. Repeat *steps 3 to 6*.

14. Click **Transform** on the ribbon and then **Run R script**.

15. Enter the script you can find in the `R\02-detect-outliers-in-power-bi-with-r.R` file in the `Chapter 16` folder.

16. We are only interested in the `df_no_outliers` tibble. So, click on its **Table** value.

17. You'll see the preview of the dataset that also has the new columns to identify outliers.

18. Click **Home** on the ribbon and then click **Close & Apply**.

Amazing! You have just identified outliers of a numeric dataset in Power BI using both Python and R!

What missing values are and how to deal with them

Data describing real-world phenomena often has a lot of missing data. A lack of data is a fact that cannot be overlooked, especially if the analyst wants to do an advanced study of the dataset to understand how much the variables in it are correlated.

The consequences of mishandling missing values can be many:

*   The *statistical power* of variables with missing values is reduced, especially if a significant number of values are missing for a single variable.

*   The *representativeness of the dataset* subject to missing values may also be diminished, and thus the dataset in question may not correctly represent the substantive characteristics of the set of all observations of a phenomenon.

- Any statistical estimates may not converge to the values of the entire population, thus *introducing bias*.
- The results of the analysis performed may not be correct.

But, first, let's look at the possible causes of missing values in a dataset.

The causes of missing values

There can be many causes of a lack of values, determined by intentional or unintentional behaviors. Here is a non-exhaustive list:

- Corruption of data due to write, read, or transfer errors
- Replacing outliers that excessively skew the dataset with null values
- Refusal to answer a survey question
- Lack of knowledge about the subject matter of a survey question

However, all of these causes can be grouped into *four types of cases*:

- **Missing Completely at Random (MCAR):** The causes that generate the null values are completely independent of both the hypothetical values they would have if they were valued (Y) and of the values of the other variables in the dataset (X). They depend only on external variables (Z). From a statistical point of view, the advantage of data that are MCAR is that the dataset consisting of only complete values for both variables X and Y is an *unbiased sample* of the entire population. Unfortunately, MCAR cases are rare in real-world data.
- **Missing At Random (MAR):** The missing data of a partially incomplete variable (Y) is related to some other variables in the dataset that do not have null values (X), but not to the values of the incomplete variable (Y) itself. The dataset consisting of only complete values for both variables X and Y in the case of MAR is a *biased sample* of the entire population because it will surely miss all those values of X on which the null values of Y depend, resulting in a dataset that is not representative of the entire phenomenon. MAR is a more realistic assumption than MCAR.
- **Missing Not at Random due to external variables Z (MNAR Z):** The missing data of a partially incomplete variable (Y) depends on variables not included in the dataset (external variables). For example, consider a dataset that is missing a variable for "income level." There may be observations missing data for "luxury goods ownership." It's plausible that individuals with higher incomes, who are the primary purchasers of luxury goods, may choose not to disclose their ownership details due to privacy concerns. Therefore, eliminating observations that have a zero value for the "age" variable would produce a *biased dataset*.
- **Missing Not at Random due to missing values Y (MNAR Y):** The missing data of a partially incomplete variable (Y) depends on the hypothetical values it would have if it was imputed. For example, it is well known that adolescents tend never to disclose the fact that they consume alcohol. Therefore, if we remove from the dataset those observations for which the value for alcohol consumption is null, we implicitly risk removing from the dataset most of the observations related to adolescents, thus obtaining a *biased dataset*.

There are also statistical tests that allow you to understand whether the distribution of missing data is MCAR (see the references). However, as mentioned above, cases of MCAR are so rare that it is better to assume that the distribution of missing values of a given dataset is either MAR or MNAR.

Depending on the type of missing data distribution, specific strategies can be used to sanitize the missing values.

Handling missing values

The first thing to do, when possible, is to understand together with the referent of the data the reason for the missing values in the dataset, and whether it is possible to recover them. Unfortunately, in most cases, it is not possible to recover missing data from the source, and different strategies have to be adopted, depending on the case.

Discarding data

The first solution to the missing values that comes to the analyst's mind is surely to eliminate the problem at its source, i.e., to eliminate the missing values. There are several ways to eliminate them:

- **Listwise** or **Complete-Case Analysis (CCA) deletion:** This method involves *deleting any observation (row) that contains at least one missing data element in any variable*. It is often used when the number of missing values is small, and the number of observations is large enough. As you've seen in the classification of the four types of missing data, the only case where applying this solution does not result in a biased dataset is MCAR, a very rare case among datasets describing real-world phenomena. Therefore, listwise deletion is not a good strategy if you do not face a case of MCAR with a sufficiently high number of observations in the dataset.

- **Pairwise** or **Available-Case Analysis (ACA) deletion:** Depending on the variables being considered in a statistical analysis, this method *eliminates only those observations (rows) that have null values for the only variables involved*. Null values in variables not included in the analysis are not a reason to eliminate observations. Again, using this method does not produce a biased dataset only if the case being analyzed is MCAR. The most obvious disadvantage of this method is that if you need to compare different analyses, you cannot use it because the number of observations in the sample varies as the variables involved in the different analyses vary.

- **Variable deletion:** This method considers *removing the entire variable from the analysis* under consideration (and not from the dataset a priori!) when the proportion of missing value ranges is 60% and above. It makes sense to drop a variable if, after careful consideration, it is determined that it does not contain important information for the analysis at hand. Otherwise, it is always preferable to try an imputation method. In general, the elimination of a variable is always a last resort and should only be considered if the final analysis will benefit from it.

If the analyst is still left with a missing value problem after trying these elimination techniques, they must resort to imputation techniques. Let's look at the most commonly used methods.

Mean, median, and mode imputation

There is an intuitively attractive method, also known as **single imputation**, where you fill in missing values with predefined values. Unfortunately, the simplicity is offset by some not-insignificant problems.

Perhaps the most common replacement for null values is the **mean** of the distribution of the variable resulting from ignoring missing values. The motivation behind this choice is that *the mean is a reasonable estimate of an observation drawn at random from a normal distribution*. However, if the distribution in question is skewed, the analyst runs the risk of making highly biased estimates, even if the missing value distribution of the dataset is MCAR.

The skewness problem can be solved by using the **median** of the variable. However, the fact remains that the common problem with single imputation is that it replaces a missing value with a single value and then treats it as if it were the true value. As a result, single imputation ignores uncertainty and almost always underestimates variance (remember that variance is synonymous with information; a variable with 0 variance is a constant value variable that usually does not enrich statistical analyses).

Mode (the most repeated value) imputation is often used with categorical data represented as numbers. Even this method, when used without having strong theoretical justification, introduces bias, so much so that analysts sometimes prefer to create a new category specifically for missing values.

Multiple imputation is often preferable to single imputation because it overcomes the problems of underestimating variance by accounting for both within-imputation and between-imputation variance. Let's see what this is all about.

Easy imputation by hand

There may be cases of variables that are *obvious to impute by hand*. For example, in the correspondence of the "blue" value of the variable "color," you will notice that the variable "weight" always takes the value of 2.4, except in a few cases where it is null. In these cases, it is easy to impute the missing values of the variable "weight" in relation to the color "blue" with the value 2.4.

Multiple imputation

It is thanks to Donald B. Rubin that in 1987 a methodology for dealing with the problem of underestimation of variance in the case of single imputation was published. This methodology is called **multiple imputation** and consists of the following steps:

1. **Imputation:** This step is very similar to the single imputation step, except that this time, values are extracted m times from a distribution for each missing value. The result of this operation is a set of m imputed datasets, for which all observed values are always the same, with different imputed values depending on the uncertainty of the respective distributions.

2. **Analysis:** You use all m imputed datasets for the statistical analysis you want to perform. The result of this step is a set of m results (or analyses) obtained by applying the analysis in question to each of the m imputed datasets.

3. **Pooling:** The m results are combined in order to obtain unbiased estimates with the correct statistical properties. The m estimates of each missing value are pooled to obtain an estimated variance that combines the usual sampling variance (**within-imputation variance**) and the additional variance caused by missing data (**between-imputation variance**).

The whole process can be summarized in *Figure 16.18*:

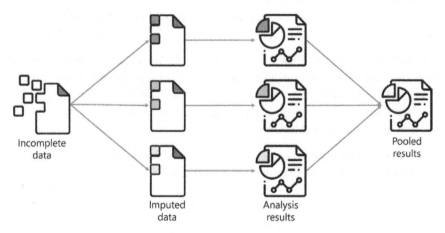

Figure 16.18: Multiple imputation process

Multiple imputation can be used when the data are MCAR, MAR, and even when the data are MNAR if there are enough auxiliary variables.

The most common implementations of multiple imputation are as follows:

- **Multivariate Imputation by Chained Equations (MICE):** This imputes missing values by focusing on one variable at a time. Once the focus is on one variable, MICE uses all other variables in the dataset (or an appropriately chosen subset of those variables) to predict missing values in that variable. Missing value prediction is based on linear regression models for numeric variables and logistic regression models for categorical variables.

- **Amelia II:** Named after Amelia Mary Earhart, an American aviation pioneer who disappeared over the central Pacific Ocean in 1937 while attempting to become the first woman to fly around the world. Amelia II combines a bootstrapping-based algorithm with an **Expectation–Maximization (EM)** algorithm, making it fast and reliable. It also works very well for time series data.

Recently, multiple imputation also has been implemented using deep learning algorithms. In particular, the **Multiple Imputation with Denoising Autoencoders (MIDAS)** algorithm offers significant advantages in terms of accuracy and efficiency over other multiple imputation strategies, especially when applied to large datasets with complex features.

Now let's add a layer of complexity that requires special considerations for accurately interpolating missing values while respecting the inherent temporal structure of the data.

Univariate time-series imputation

The problem of missing data affects not only multivariate tabular datasets but also time series datasets. For example, sensors that continuously collect data on a phenomenon may stop working at any time, creating holes in the series. Often, the analyst is faced with a time series that has missing values and they must somehow impute these values because the processes to which the series is to be submitted do not handle null values.

The constraint on the sequencing of events imposed by the time dimension forces the analyst to use specific imputation methods for time series. Let's look at the most common methods:

- **Last Observation Carried Forward (LOCF) and Next Observation Carried Backward (NOCB):** In the LOCF method, the last observed (that is, non-null) measure of the variable in question is used for all subsequent missing values. The only condition in which LOCF is unbiased is when the missing data is completely random, and the data used as the basis for LOCF imputation has exactly the same distribution as the unknown missing data. Since it can never be proven that these distributions are exactly the same, all analyses that make use of LOCF are suspect and will almost certainly generate biased results.

  The NOCB method is a similar approach to LOCF, but works in the opposite direction, taking the first (non-null) observation after the missing value and replacing it with the missing value. It obviously has the same limitations as LOCF.

- **Exponentially Weighted Moving Average (EMWA):** In general, the moving average is commonly used in time series to smooth out fluctuations due to short-term effects and to highlight long-term trends or cycles. EWMA is designed such that older observations are given lower weights. The weights decrease exponentially as the observation gets older (hence the name "exponentially weighted"). Missing values are imputed using the values of the resulting "smoothed" time series.

- **Interpolation:** The interpolation technique is one of the most widely used techniques to impute missing data from a time series. The basic idea is to use a simple function (such as a linear function, a polynomial function, or a spline function) that fits with the non-zero points near the missing value, and then interpolate the value for the missing observation.

- **Seasonally Decomposed Imputation:** If the time series under analysis has seasonality, this method could give very good results. The procedure adopted is to remove the seasonal component from the time series, perform the imputation on the seasonally adjusted series, and then add the seasonal component back.

There are also algorithms for imputing missing values for multivariate time series.

Multivariate time series imputation

This topic is beyond the scope of this chapter, but we simply wanted to point out that the *Amelia II* algorithm we discussed earlier is also used to impute missing values in a multivariate time series, whereas it is not suitable for imputation in univariate time series. See the *References* section for further reading about this topic.

To figure out whether to impute missing values, we must first identify them in the dataset. Let's see how to do that.

Diagnosing missing values in R and Python

Before thinking about imputing missing values in a dataset, we first need to know the extent to which the missing values affect each individual variable.

The code used in this section can be found in the R\03-diagnose-missing-values-in-r.R and Python\03-diagnose-missing-values-in-python.py files in Chapter 16. To properly run this code and the code in the following sections, you must install the required R and Python packages as follows:

1. Open Anaconda Prompt.
2. Enter the `conda activate pbi_powerquery_env` command.
3. Enter the `pip install missingno==0.5.2` command.
4. Enter the `pip install upsetplot==0.8.0` command.
5. Then, open RStudio and make sure it is referencing your latest CRAN R (version 4.4.2 in our case).
6. Click on the **Console** window and enter `install.packages(c("naniar", "imputeTS", "forecast", "ggpubr", "missForest", "mice", "miceadds"))`. Then press *Enter*.

At this point, let's see what features will come in handy when you are faced with analyzing missing values in a dataset.

The R package `naniar` provides the `vis_miss()` function, which displays the missing values of the entire dataframe in a single image:

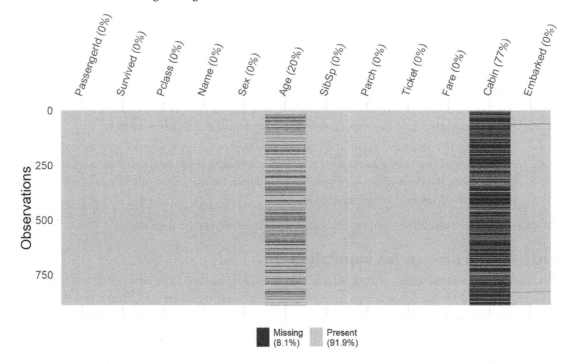

Figure 16.19: Plot of missing values in the entire dataset

You can draw similar graphs in Python thanks to the `missingno` library (https://github.com/ResidentMario/missingno).

Knowing only the percentage value of the number of missing values compared to the total number of values of the variable under consideration can be limiting. Therefore, it's often useful to also know the details for each column as well, using the `miss_var_summary()` function:

```
> miss_var_summary(tbl)
# A tibble: 12 × 3
   variable      n_miss  pct_miss
   <chr>          <int>     <dbl>
 1 Cabin            687      77.1
 2 Age              177      19.9
 3 Embarked           2     0.224
 4 PassengerId        0         0
 5 Survived           0         0
 6 Pclass             0         0
 7 Name               0         0
 8 Sex                0         0
 9 SibSp              0         0
10 Parch              0         0
11 Ticket             0         0
12 Fare               0         0
```

Figure 16.20: Missing values summary

We have developed a similar function from scratch in Python in the code you can find in the repository.

It would be interesting to be able to visualize combinations of missing values and missing intersections between variables. The R package `naniar` (https://github.com/njtierney/naniar) allows you to do exactly this kind of analysis thanks to the `gg_miss_upset()` function:

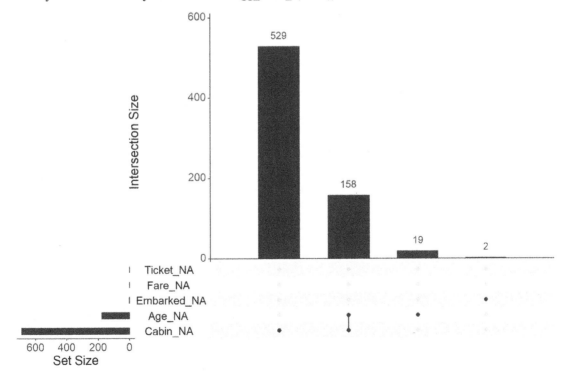

Figure 16.21: UpSet plot of dataset's missing values

To get the same plot in Python, the process is a bit more complicated. You must first use the upsetplot module (https://github.com/jnothman/UpSetPlot). The problem is to provide the UpSet() function exposed by this package with an input dataframe in the required format. For this reason, we have created the helper function upsetplot_miss(), which you will find in the code, to easily create the upset plot of missing values in Python as well.

In case you need to get an idea of the missing values in a time series, the imputeTS R package provides the ggplot_na_distribution() function, which shows the holes in the time series very clearly:

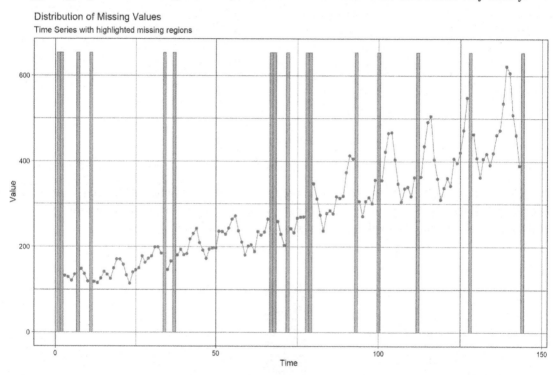

Figure 16.22: Detecting missing values in a time series

On the other hand, if you need to get more complete details about the statistics of missing values in a time series, the statsNA() function is for you:

```
> statsNA(air_missing_df$value)
[1] "Length of time series:"
[1] 144
[1] "------------------------"
[1] "Number of Missing Values:"
[1] 16
[1] "------------------------"
[1] "Percentage of Missing Values:"
[1] "11.1%"
[1] "------------------------"
[1] "Number of Gaps:"
[1] 13
[1] "------------------------"
[1] "Average Gap Size:"
[1] 1.230769
[1] "------------------------"
[1] "Stats for Bins"
[1] "  Bin 1 (36 values from 1 to 36) :       5 NAs (13.9%)"
[1] "  Bin 2 (36 values from 37 to 72) :      4 NAs (11.1%)"
[1] "  Bin 3 (36 values from 73 to 108) :     4 NAs (11.1%)"
[1] "  Bin 4 (36 values from 109 to 144) :    3 NAs (8.33%)"
[1] "------------------------"
[1] "Longest NA gap (series of consecutive NAs)"
[1] "2 in a row"
[1] "------------------------"
[1] "Most frequent gap size (series of consecutive NA series)"
[1] "1 NA in a row (occurring 10 times)"
[1] "------------------------"
[1] "Gap size accounting for most NAs"
[1] "1 NA in a row (occurring 10 times, making up for overall 10 NAs)"
[1] "------------------------"
[1] "Overview NA series"
[1] "  1 NA in a row: 10 times"
[1] "  2 NA in a row: 3 times"
```

Figure 16.23: Statistics of missing values in a time series

Once you have carefully studied the distributions of each variable's missing values and their intersections, you can decide which variables to keep in the dataset and which to subject to the various imputation strategies. Let's see how to do imputation in R and Python.

Implementing missing value imputation algorithms

So far, we have often used Python and R indiscriminately to implement solutions to the problems addressed in this book. But when it comes to missing value analysis, we will focus on R over Python. There's a compelling reason for this choice. R has traditionally been used by statisticians and data miners for statistical software development and data analysis, and it has an extensive collection of packages designed specifically for statistical analysis. Some of these packages, designed specifically for missing value analysis, are truly unrivaled when compared to Python's ecosystem. In other words, R comes bundled with powerful, statistically specialized tools that are not only more sophisticated than their Python counterparts but also very easy to use.

So, suppose you need to compute the Pearson correlation coefficient between the two numeric variables Age and Fare of the Titanic disaster dataset. Let's first consider the case where missing values are dropped.

Removing missing values

The effect of applying listwise and pairwise deletion techniques is evident in the calculation of Pearson's correlation between numeric variables in the Titanic dataset. Let's load the data and select only numeric characteristics:

```r
library(dplyr)
dataset_url <- ' http://bit.ly/titanic-dataset-csv'
tbl <- readr::read_csv(dataset_url)
tbl_num <- tbl %>%
  select( where(is.numeric) )
```

If you now compute the correlation matrix for the two techniques separately, you will notice the differences:

```r
# Listwise deletion
cor( tbl_num, method = 'pearson', use = 'complete.obs' )
# Pairwise deletion
cor( tbl_num, method = 'pearson', use = 'pairwise.complete.obs' )
```

You will see the following result:

```
> # Listwise deletion
> cor( tbl_num, method = 'pearson', use = 'complete.obs' )
              PassengerId      Survived      Pclass          Age        SibSp       Parch         Fare
PassengerId   1.00000000    0.02934016  -0.03534911   0.03684720  -0.08239772  -0.01161741   0.00959178
Survived      0.02934016    1.00000000  -0.35965268  -0.07722109  -0.01735836   0.09331701   0.26818862
Pclass       -0.03534911   -0.35965268   1.00000000  -0.36922602   0.06724737   0.02568307  -0.55418247
Age           0.03684720   -0.07722109  -0.36922602   1.00000000  -0.30824676  -0.18911926   0.09606669
SibSp        -0.08239772   -0.01735836   0.06724737  -0.30824676   1.00000000   0.38381986   0.13832879
Parch        -0.01161741    0.09331701   0.02568307  -0.18911926   0.38381986   1.00000000   0.20511888
Fare          0.00959178    0.26818862  -0.55418247   0.09606669   0.13832879   0.20511888   1.00000000
> # Pairwise deletion
> cor( tbl_num, method = 'pearson', use = 'pairwise.complete.obs' )
              PassengerId      Survived      Pclass          Age        SibSp        Parch         Fare
PassengerId   1.000000000  -0.005006661  -0.03514399   0.03684720  -0.05752683  -0.001652012   0.01265822
Survived     -0.005006661   1.000000000  -0.33848104  -0.07722109  -0.03532250   0.081629407   0.25730652
Pclass       -0.035143994  -0.338481036   1.00000000  -0.36922602   0.08308136   0.018442671  -0.54949962
Age           0.036847198  -0.077221095  -0.36922602   1.00000000  -0.30824676  -0.189119263   0.09606669
SibSp        -0.057526834  -0.035322499   0.08308136  -0.30824676   1.00000000   0.414837699   0.15965104
Parch        -0.001652012   0.081629407   0.01844267  -0.18911926   0.41483770   1.000000000   0.21622494
Fare          0.012658219   0.257306522  -0.54949962   0.09606669   0.15965104   0.216224945   1.00000000
```

Figure 16.24: Correlation matrix calculated using listwise and pairwise deletion

The code used in this section can be found in the R\04-remove-tabular-missing-values-in-r.R file in Chapter 16.

Let's see how to impute missing values in the case of a tabular dataset.

Imputing tabular data

Again, starting with the Titanic disaster dataset, the first thing you need to do is remove the Name and Ticket columns because they have a high number of different values.

> **IMPORTANT NOTE**
>
> It is important to eliminate categorical variables that have a high number of distinct values because otherwise, the MICE algorithm would fail due to excessive memory requirements. In general, high cardinality variables are not useful for imputing null values of other variables. There are cases where the information contained in these variables could be fundamental for the imputation (for example, zip codes). In this case, it is necessary to use transformations that reduce the cardinality without losing the information contained in the variables. For more information, see the references.

Since the missing values in the Cabin column represent more than 70% of all values, we decided to remove them as well. The categorical variables Survived, Sex, and Embarked are then transformed as factors:

```
tbl_cleaned <- tbl %>%
  select( -Cabin, -Name, -Ticket ) %>%
  mutate(
    Survived = as.factor(Survived),
    Sex = as.factor(Sex),
    Embarked = as.factor(Embarked)
  )
```

At this point, it is possible to compute the Pearson correlation for each pair of numeric variables by applying the pooling technique provided by Rubin in multiple imputations. The miceadds package exposes wrapper functions that simplify this operation for the most common statistical analysis given the result of the mice() function as a parameter. In our case, the function of interest is micombine. cor(), and we use it in our corr_impute_missing_values() function:

```
corr_impute_missing_values <- function(df, m = 5, variables, method =
c('pearson', 'spearman')) {
  method <- method[1]
  df_imp_lst <- mice(df, m = m, printFlag = FALSE)
  corr_tbl <- miceadds::micombine.cor(df_imp_lst, variables = variables, method
= method) %>%
    as_tibble() %>%
    arrange( variable1, variable2 )
  return( corr_tbl )
}
```

It is therefore easy to obtain the above correlations:

```
# Get the indexes of numeric columns
numeric_col_idxs <- which(sapply(tbl_cleaned, is.numeric))
corr_tbl <- corr_impute_missing_values(tbl_cleaned, variables = numeric_col_
idxs, method = 'pearson')
corr_tbl
```

Here is the result:

```
# A tibble: 30 × 11
   variable1 variable2           r    rse fisher_r fisher_rse   fmi      t         p lower95 upper95
   <chr>     <chr>           <db1>  <db1>    <db1>      <db1> <db1>  <db1>     <db1>   <db1>   <db1>
 1 Age       Fare          0.0902 0.0357   0.0905     0.0360 0.139   2.51 1.20e- 2  0.0199   0.160
 2 Age       Parch        -0.193  0.0332  -0.195      0.0345 0.0538 -5.66 1.49e- 8 -0.257   -0.127
 3 Age       PassengerId   0.0417 0.0391   0.0417     0.0391 0.290   1.07 2.86e- 1 -0.0350   0.118
 4 Age       Pclass       -0.378  0.0353  -0.398      0.0412 0.370  -9.67 4.23e-22 -0.445   -0.307
 5 Age       SibSp        -0.308  0.0411  -0.318      0.0454 0.503  -7.00 2.60e-12 -0.386   -0.225
 6 Fare      Age           0.0902 0.0357   0.0905     0.0360 0.139   2.51 1.20e- 2  0.0199   0.160
 7 Fare      Parch         0.216  0.0320   0.220      0.0336 0       6.55 5.88e-11  0.153    0.278
 8 Fare      PassengerId   0.0127 0.0336   0.0127     0.0336 0       0.377 7.06e- 1 -0.0531   0.0783
 9 Fare      Pclass       -0.549  0.0234  -0.618      0.0336 0     -18.4  1.18e-75 -0.594   -0.502
10 Fare      SibSp         0.160  0.0327   0.161      0.0336 0       4.80 1.60e- 6  0.0950   0.223
# ... with 20 more rows
```

Figure 16.25: Statistical inference for correlations for multiple imputed datasets

Note that due to the stochastic nature of the MICE algorithm, you may get slightly different results than those shown in *Figure 16.25*.

Without going into too much detail about the other fields, the correlation coefficient between the variables is given by the r column. Since the *r* coefficient is the result of an inferential process, the lower95 and upper95 columns define the upper and lower 95% confidence interval limits.

IMPORTANT NOTE

If you get an error like **Error in matchindex(yhatobs, yhatmis, donors) : function 'Rcpp_precious_remove' not provided by package 'Rcpp'**, you are probably running a recent version of a package that was compiled with an earlier version of Rcpp. Updating Rcpp with the install.packages('Rcpp') command should fix this.

Sometimes, the goal of your analysis is not to get results from statistical functions but to simply fill in the holes left by missing values because the dataset in question must then be used to train a machine learning algorithm that does not allow null values. The latest versions of scikit-learn (currently in the experimental phase) expose the impute module with its SimpleImputer, KNNImputer, and IterativeImputer methods. In this way, it is possible to impute the missing values of a dataset using machine learning algorithms (k-nearest neighbors; linear regression), among other more naïve methods (fixed value replacements: mean, median, or mode), and also to get an average score of how the algorithm performs in general (cross-validated mean squared error). You'll see an example of one of these methods in *Chapter 17, Using Machine Learning without Premium or Embedded Capacity*.

The code used in this section can be found in the R\05-impute-tabular-missing-values-in-r.R file in Chapter 16.

On the other hand, if you need to impute missing values from a univariate time series, how would you do it? Let's see.

Imputing time series data

Consider a time series of the average number of airline passengers per month. Let's duplicate it and randomly eliminate 10% of the values from it, as well as eliminating a few duplicated values by hand. Then, we'll merge the two time series into a single tibble:

```
air_df <- read.csv('https://bit.ly/airpassengers')
# Create 10% of missing values in the vector
set.seed(57934)
value_missing <- missForest::prodNA(air_df['value'], noNA = 0.1)
# Force a larger gap in the vector
value_missing[67:68,] <- NA
# Add the vector with missing values to the dataframe
air_missing_df <- air_df %>%
    mutate( date = ymd(date) ) %>%
    rename( complete = value ) %>%
    bind_cols( value = value_missing )
```

You will then get a dataframe that contains a column with the dates the measurements were taken, a full column with all the values of the measurements, and a value column with the values of the measurements that are sometimes missing, as shown in *Figure 16.26*:

```
> air_missing_df
             date complete value
1      1949-01-01      112    NA
2      1949-02-01      118    NA
3      1949-03-01      132   132
4      1949-04-01      129   129
5      1949-05-01      121   121
6      1949-06-01      135   135
7      1949-07-01      148    NA
8      1949-08-01      148   148
9      1949-09-01      136   136
10     1949-10-01      119   119
11     1949-11-01      104    NA
12     1949-12-01      118   118
```

Figure 16.26: Complete time series with artificially created missing values

The imputeTS package provides convenient functions that implement the missing value imputation described in the *Univariate time series imputation* section. If you need a quick graphical representation of missing values in a time series, the ggplot_na_distribution() function is for you. In fact, you can simply use the ggplot_na_distribution(air_missing_df$value) script to highlight regions containing missing values, as shown in *Figure 16.22*.

To get numerical statistics on missing values instead, the `statsNA()` function can be used. Once the values have been imputed using the various algorithms and parameters provided by `imputeTS`, it is possible to calculate the accuracy, since the complete time series is also known. We use the `accuracy()` function exposed by the `forecast` package to calculate the final accuracy using various metrics, such as *mean absolute error* and *root mean squared error*:

```
# A tibble: 10 × 6
     strategy    ME   RMSE    MAE      MPE   MAPE
     <chr>     <dbl>  <dbl>  <dbl>    <dbl>  <dbl>
 1 locf       1.11   11.8    3.10   0.133   1.22
 2 nocb       1.20   11.6    2.92   0.0728  1.05
 3 ewma_1     1.17    8.66   2.20   0.135   0.849
 4 ewma_2     1.27    9.87   2.48   0.134   0.944
 5 ewma_3     1.30   11.3    2.75   0.129   1.03
 6 ewma_6     1.33   12.5    3.10   0.131   1.14
 7 ewma_9     1.34   12.6    3.13   0.130   1.15
 8 linear     1.16    8.58   2.21   0.107   0.845
 9 spline     0.261   5.71   1.58  -0.0913  0.714
10 seadec     0.900   5.47   1.36   0.365   0.547
```

Figure 16.27: Error metrics for imputed values in a time series

The **Seasonally Decomposed Imputation** (**seadec**) strategy seems to be the best one. Here's the plot of missing values according to this strategy:

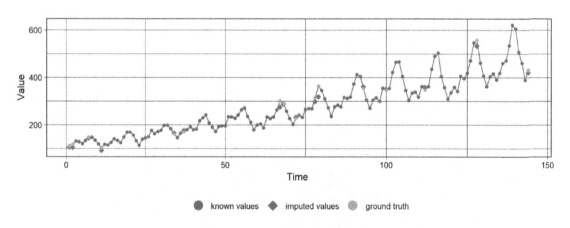

Figure 16.28: Representation of imputed values in the time series

In green (circles) are the original values of the measurements before they were removed to simulate missing values. The code used in this section can be found in the `R\06-impute-time-series-missing-values-in-r.R` file in Chapter 16.

Now let's see how you can use what you've learned so far about missing values in Power BI.

Imputing missing values in Power BI

We have delved into the theory and techniques of imputing missing values, whether you are dealing with a tabular dataset or a time series, precisely because in Power BI there is no way to impute them using native tools, except for the naïve solution of replacing them with a default value (such as a fixed value, mean, or median). In fact, when business analysts need to fill in gaps in data, they often seek the help of a data scientist or someone with the statistical skills to solve the problem. Now that you've studied this chapter, you're ready to tackle it on your own!

Let's apply what we did in the previous sections to tabular and time series data in Power BI:

1. Open Power BI Desktop and make sure it is referencing the latest available engine (in our case 4.2.2) in the R scripting tab in **Options**.
2. Click **Get data**, then **Web**.
3. Enter the following URL and click **OK**: `http://bit.ly/titanic-dataset-csv`.
4. On the next import screen, click **Transform Data**.
5. Go to the **Transform** tab, click on **Run R script**, copy the script in the `R\07-impute-tabular-missing-values-in-power-bi-with-r.R` file in the `Chapter 16` folder, paste it into the editor, and then click **OK**.
6. If you get the Firewall privacy level mismatch error, select a **Public** privacy level for the web URL data source and press **OK**. You are prompted to expand a dataframe calculated in the R script.
7. We are only interested in the data in `corr_tbl`. So, click on its **Table** value.
8. As a result, you'll see the table containing the correlation coefficients calculated using MICE and the pooling method provided by the multivariate imputation technique:

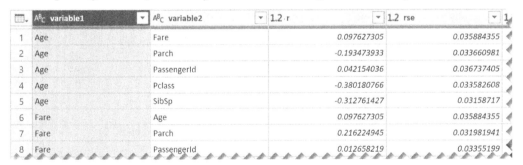

	$^{A^B}_C$ variable1	$^{A^B}_C$ variable2	1.2 r	1.2 rse	1
1	Age	Fare	0.097627305	0.035884355	
2	Age	Parch	-0.193473933	0.033660981	
3	Age	PassengerId	0.042154036	0.036737405	
4	Age	Pclass	-0.380180766	0.033582608	
5	Age	SibSp	-0.312761427	0.03158717	
6	Fare	Age	0.097627305	0.035884355	
7	Fare	Parch	0.216224945	0.031981941	
8	Fare	PassengerId	0.012658219	0.03355199	

Figure 16.29: Correlation table calculated with the multivariate imputation technique

9. Go to the **Home** tab and click **Close & Apply**.
10. Click **Get data** and then click on the **Text/CSV** connector.
11. Select the `air.csv` file you can find in the `Chapter 16` folder and click **Open**.
12. On the next import screen, click **Transform Data**.

13. Power BI automatically interprets the date text field as a date field, and therefore applies a **Changed Type** operation from Text to Date. As you learned in *Chapter 4, Solving Common Issues When Using Python and R in Power BI*, dates must be in Text format to be processed correctly in an R script that uses the lubridate package. Therefore, you must delete the **Changed Type** step by clicking on the red cross before inserting the R script:

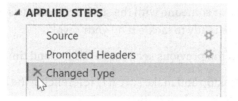

Figure 16.30: Delete the Changed Type step

14. Go to the **Transform** tab, click on **Run R script**, copy the script in the R\08-impute-time-series-missing-values-in-power-bi-with-r.R file in the Chapter 16 folder, paste it into the editor, and then click **OK**.

15. If you get the Firewall privacy level mismatch error, select a **Public** privacy level for the CSV file. Once done, click on **Refresh Preview** in the **Home** tab. You are prompted to expand a dataframe calculated in the R script.

16. As a result, you'll see the table containing the original time series (the value column) and other time series obtained through different imputation algorithms (each in a different column):

	date	1²₃ value	1.2 locf	1.2 nocb	1.2 ewma_1	1.
1	1/1/1949	null	132	132	131	
2	2/1/1949	null	132	132	131	
3	3/1/1949	132	132	132	132	
4	4/1/1949	129	129	129	129	
5	5/1/1949	121	121	121	121	
6	6/1/1949	135	135	135	135	
7	7/1/1949	null	135	148	141.5	
8	8/1/1949	148	148	148	148	
9	9/1/1949	136	136	136	136	

Figure 16.31: Table with imputed time series

17. Go to the **Home** tab and click **Close & Apply**.

Impressive! You have applied the most complex missing value imputation algorithms to a tabular dataset and a time series in Power BI with minimal effort. Congratulations!

Summary

In this chapter, you learned about outliers, their definition, common causes, and how to deal with them. You were also introduced to methods for identifying outliers using Python and R, taking into account the number of variables and their types.

Another focus of this chapter was on filling in missing values in tabular and time series datasets. You also learned how to diagnose missing values and implement imputation techniques using R. Next, you applied these imputation algorithms in Power BI.

In the next chapter, we will explore how you can use machine learning algorithms in Power BI without Premium or Embedded capabilities.

References

For additional reading, check out the following books and articles:

- *Add Marginal Plot to ggplot2 Scatterplot Using ggExtra Package in R* (`https://statisticsglobe.com/ggplot2-graphic-with-marginal-plot-in-r`)
- *5 Things You Should Know About Covariance* (`https://towardsdatascience.com/5-things-you-should-know-about-covariance-26b12a0516f1`)
- *Mahalanobis Distance and its Limitations* (`https://rpubs.com/jjsuarestra99/mahalanobis`)
- *The Box-Cox transformation for a dependent variable in a regression* (`https://blogs.sas.com/content/iml/2022/08/17/box-cox-regression.html`)
- *How to Use Power Transforms for Machine Learning* (`https://machinelearningmastery.com/power-transforms-with-scikit-learn/`)
- *The Relationship between the Mahalanobis Distance and the Chi-Squared Distribution* (`https://markusthill.github.io/mahalanbis-chi-squared/`)
- *Unsupervised anomaly detection algorithms on real-world data: how many do we need?* (`https://arxiv.org/abs/2305.00735`)
- *Using the recipes package for easy pre-processing* (`http://www.rebeccabarter.com/blog/2019-06-06_pre_processing/`)
- *Anomaly detection* (`https://docs.microsoft.com/en-us/power-bi/visuals/power-bi-visualization-anomaly-detection`)
- *Missing data: mechanisms, methods, and messages* (`http://www.i-deel.org/uploads/5/2/4/1/52416001/chapter_4.pdf`)
- *Multiple imputation by chained equations: what is it and how does it work?* (`https://www.ncbi.nlm.nih.gov/pmc/articles/PMC3074241/`)
- *Amelia II: A Program for Missing Data* (`https://www.jstatsoft.org/article/view/v045i07`)
- *Deep Learning for Multivariate Time Series Imputation: A Survey* (`https://arxiv.org/abs/2402.04059`)
- *All about Categorical Variable Encoding* (`https://towardsdatascience.com/all-about-categorical-variable-encoding-305f3361fd02`)

Test your knowledge

1. What are outliers and why are they important to consider in data analysis?
2. What are the causes of outliers and how can they be categorized?
3. What are the different approaches to deal with outliers?

4. What are missing values and why do they pose challenges in data analysis?

5. How can missing values be diagnosed and visualized in a dataset?

6. What is the concept of multiple imputation and how does it overcome the limitations of single imputation?

7. How can missing values be imputed in a time series dataset?

8. Why is R often considered more suitable than Python for conducting missing value imputation?

Learn more on Discord

To join the Discord community for this book – where you can share feedback, ask questions to the author, and learn about new releases – follow the QR code below:

`https://discord.gg/MKww5g45EB`

17

Using Machine Learning without Premium or Embedded Capacity

Advances in computing power have made data analysis much more powerful and efficient. In particular, with the advent of **machine learning** (**ML**) models, you can now gain valuable insights and enrich your analysis effortlessly. Fortunately, Power BI includes several AI capabilities that seamlessly integrate with ML models, allowing you to act on these insights immediately. Within the Power BI ecosystem, there are integrated tools designed to enhance your analysis with ML. These tools are tightly integrated with Power BI Desktop and Power BI dataflows, allowing you to leverage ML models created by your data scientists on Azure Machine Learning. In addition, Power BI allows you to harness the power of models trained and deployed through Azure AutoML. Furthermore, you can easily access services exposed by Cognitive Services directly through an easy-to-use graphical interface.

It is important to note that these tools (known as **advanced AI**) are only available if you have an **Embedded Capacity**, **Premium Capacity**, or **Premium Per User** (**PPU**) license. This may lead to the misconception that users with a Pro license, who primarily use Power BI Desktop or the Power BI service, cannot benefit from the ML capabilities. However, this is not the case, as users can access and utilize ML algorithms and models in their Power BI workflows by leveraging the extensive capabilities of the Python and R programming languages.

In this chapter, you will cover the following topics:

- Interacting with ML in Power BI with dataflows
- Using AutoML solutions
- Embedding training code in Power Query
- Using trained models in Power Query
- Using trained models in script visuals
- Calling web services in Power Query

Technical requirements

This chapter requires you to have a working internet connection and **Power BI Desktop** already installed on your machine (version: 2.119.986.0 64-bit, July 2023). You must have properly configured the R and Python engines and IDEs as outlined in *Chapter 2, Configuring R with Power BI,* and *Chapter 3, Configuring Python with Power BI.*

Interacting with ML in Power BI with dataflows

You can access **advanced AI features** directly through Power BI Desktop or you can access **advanced AI features for dataflows** through Power BI dataflows, which are easy-to-use self-service tools for transforming big data into insights to be shown in dashboards. But, as mentioned in the introduction, both modes require specific licenses.

These features are accessible from Power BI Desktop, in the **Power Query Home** ribbon (click **Transform data** to access Power Query):

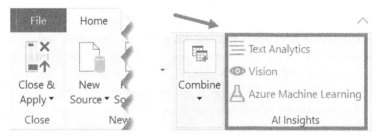

Figure 17.1: AI insights in Power BI Desktop

By default, these icons are disabled in Power BI Desktop if you are not logged in with your user in a tenant with one of the following Premium capacity SKUs: *EM2, A2,* or *P1* and above. You can still use these features if you have a PPU license, but not through Power BI Desktop (unless you have set up Azure AI Services for text analytics), only by creating a dataflow directly in the Power BI portal:

Figure 17.2: AI insights in Power BI dataflows

Going back to Power BI Desktop, the first two options (**Text Analytics** and **Vision**) that you can see in *Figure 17.1* use **Azure AI Services** behind the scenes, specifically the **Azure AI Language** and **Azure AI Vision** services. Basically, with these Power BI features, you can use four functions to enrich your data with the power of ML:

- **TagImages**: Analyzes images to generate tags based on what they contain
- **ExtractKeyPhrases**: Evaluates unstructured text and returns a list of key phrases for each text column
- **DetectLanguage**: Evaluates text input and returns the language name and ISO identifier for each column
- **ScoreSentiment**: Evaluates text input and returns a sentiment score for each document, ranging from 0 (negative) to 1 (positive)

Another option with AI Insights is the ability to use models hosted in Azure Machine Learning as scoring functions in Power Query. The following screenshot shows an example of this:

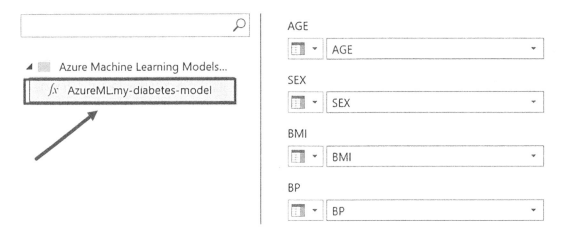

Figure 17.3: Azure Machine Learning functions in Power BI

Advanced AI features also include the ability to build ML models on the fly through a GUI, thanks to **AutoML for dataflows**. AutoML solutions are very convenient, especially for the analyst who doesn't have much experience with ML.

This is quite an in-depth topic, but for now, all you need to know is that you can create two types of models in Power BI: **classifications** (binary or general, that is, multi-label) and **regressions**:

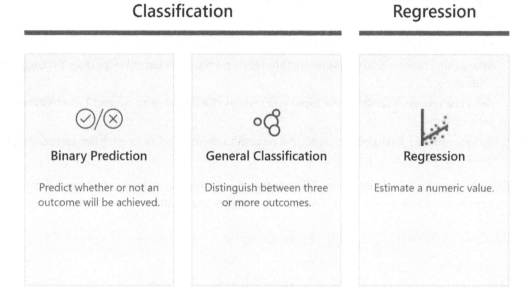

Figure 17.4: AutoML for dataflows in Power BI

Behind the scenes, there's the Azure AutoML service, which allows you to train models, but by leveraging dataflows, you don't need to instantiate a ML workspace to run AutoML experiments.

A user with only a Power BI Pro license cannot access these amazing features directly from the Power BI GUI. However, thanks to the introduction of Python and R in Power BI, it is now possible to use ML algorithms or external services that make it easy to implement them with just a few lines of code.

You may wonder if it is really possible to train a ML model with just a few lines of code. Where is the trick? Let's explore the secret.

Using AutoML solutions

Writing code from scratch to perform ML requires specific knowledge that a general analyst using Power BI often doesn't have. That's why we recommend using AutoML processes from here on out for analysts who don't have a data science background. Does this mean that anyone can build an accurate ML model without knowing the theory behind the science, just by using AutoML algorithms? Absolutely not! It's important to keep the following in mind:

IMPORTANT NOTE

An AutoML tool relieves the analyst of all the repetitive tasks typical of a ML process (hyperparameter tuning, model selection, etc.). Often, the tasks that require specific theoretical knowledge on the part of the analyst (e.g., missing value imputation, dataset balancing strategies, feature selection, and feature engineering) are left out of the automated steps. As a result, if the appropriate transformations known only to an expert are not applied to the dataset before starting an AutoML process, a baseline model will be generated. While this model may be sufficiently accurate, it may not ensure production performance.

You might think that AutoML tools are hated by data scientists. This is also a myth. Many of them use them as a quick-and-dirty prototyping tool and as an executor of repetitive steps while they focus on more critical tasks.

In this chapter, we will be satisfied with obtaining discrete performance models (sometimes very good ones, if we are lucky enough to have a properly transformed training dataset), so the outputs provided by AutoML solutions are more than adequate.

Furthermore, we will only use AutoML solutions in Python, as it is the most widely used language in most third-party ML platforms. The R language is slightly less widely used than Python, but that doesn't mean that the results you get in R are any less valid. On the contrary, as you may have noticed in previous chapters, some specialized packages of statistical functions that allow high flexibility in data manipulation exist only for R and not for Python.

Simply put, working with ML in Python allows models to be easily shared between popular platforms. Therefore, we recommend it for Power BI analysts who may prefer to delegate model building to more specialized platforms and then import them into Power BI.

Let's look at the AutoML tools we'll be using in the code for this chapter.

PyCaret

PyCaret (https://pycaret.org/) is an open-source, low-code ML library in Python that automates the cycle of ML experiments, democratizing access to these advanced techniques to business analysts and domain experts, and also helping data scientists to become more efficient and productive.

The types of problems that PyCaret can solve include:

- **Classification** (predicting a categorical target variable)
- **Regression** (predicting a numeric target variable)
- **Clustering** (grouping observations into specific sets, each with its own characteristics)
- **Anomaly detection** (the process of finding outliers in a dataset that are far fewer in number than the usual observations)

- **Natural Language Processing** (**NLP**) (transforming text into useful features for classification and regression)
- **Association rules** (a rule-based technique that uses probability theory to find important relationships between features)

For more experienced users, PyCaret also provides convenient functions for model ensembling and model explanation.

FLAML

FLAML (**Fast and Lightweight AutoML**) is a Microsoft lightweight Python library for efficiently automating ML and AI operations, including the selection of models, hyperparameters (parameters that are set for a ML algorithm before the learning process begins and are used to control the learning process), and other tunable choices of an application. It is an open-source Python package (`https://github.com/microsoft/FLAML`) that can tell you the ML model that would be the best fit for low computational cost. Thus, it removes the burden of the manual process of choosing the best model and the best parameters.

In addition, FLAML is used in Synapse Data Science in Microsoft Fabric to facilitate hyperparameter tuning and to provide a simple interface for performing AutoML.

Azure AutoML

Azure AutoML is a cloud-based service that can be used to automate the construction of ML pipelines for classification, regression, and forecasting tasks. Such pipelines include a preprocessing phase of the dataset to better match the training algorithms used in the next phase. After tuning and training multiple models, Azure AutoML selects the most accurate model among them, while also considering two other models resulting from the ensembling of the previously trained models.

The available tasks are as follows:

- Classification
- Regression
- Time series forecasting

For more detailed coverage of this platform, please see the references.

AutoQuant for R

For the sake of completeness, we also recommend one of the AutoML solutions for R, **AutoQuant** (`https://github.com/AdrianAntico/AutoQuant`). It is a set of functions that facilitate the use of many of the AutoML packages available for R (CatBoost, LightGBM, XGBoost, and H2O). In addition to giving the novice analyst the ability to create ML models with a few lines of code thanks to AutoML, this library also contains very advanced features (e.g., time series forecasting), often used by more experienced analysts.

Now let's look at the different ways you can use ML models in Power BI.

Embedding training code in Power Query

One of the easiest ways to train a ML model is to write the necessary code directly in Power Query, right after you import a dataset on which you want to build the model.

Training a model on a fairly large dataset typically takes a significant amount of time. Because you embed the code in Power Query, it runs every time the data is refreshed, and this can result in a non-negligible delay in getting the data online. Therefore, the following applies:

IMPORTANT NOTE

This solution is recommended if you are confident that the time required to complete the model training is acceptable.

Now let's look at an example of how to write some training code with PyCaret.

Training and using ML models with PyCaret

Let's take the Titanic disaster dataset to train a ML model. Specifically, we want to build a model that predicts whether a passenger survives (the Survived column) based on their attributes described by the other features in the dataset. Obviously, this is a *binary classification* (do they survive? Yes or no) that we can easily implement with PyCaret.

As PyCaret is constantly evolving, and so are all the other dependent libraries, you must also install the **Visual C++ Build Tools** to build the necessary wheels and avoid errors like *Failed building wheel for <package>*. Here are all the steps needed to install PyCaret correctly for Windows:

1. If you did not install the Visual C++ Build Tools mentioned in the *Deduplicating emails with Python* section of *Chapter 12, Calculating Columns Using Complex Algorithms: Distances*, you must do so in order to properly install PyCaret. Therefore, follow the steps described in that section.

2. Let's create a new environment specifically for the installation of PyCaret and all its dependencies. Run Anaconda Prompt and enter the following command to create the new **pycaret_env** environment with Python 3.9 and the IPython kernel for Jupyter (used by VS Code):

   ```
   conda create --name pycaret_env python=3.9 ipykernel
   ```

   Type y when prompted to download dependencies.

3. Enter the following command to switch to the new environment:

   ```
   conda activate pycaret_env
   ```

4. Enter the following command to install the full version of PyCaret:

   ```
   pip install pycaret==3.0.4
   ```

Once this is done, you can move on to viewing the model's training code. The only minor hiccup is the handling of missing values in the dataset (you had a chance to analyze them in *Chapter 16, Adding Statistical Insights: Outliers, and Missing Values*).

Unfortunately, PyCaret currently supports only the simplest methods of handling missing values, namely imputing the mean or median for numeric values, and imputing using the mode or a fixed string for categorical values. Since we want to show you how to impute missing values using the **K-Nearest Neighbors (KNN)** algorithm, as mentioned in *Chapter 16*, you will need to write a few more lines of code than usual.

The code used to impute the missing values using the KNN algorithm is used in the first transformation step in Power BI, after the data is imported from the Titanic dataset. You can find the code in the `Python/01-impute-dataset-with-knn.py` file in the `Chapter 17` folder (remember to follow the instructions in the comments to run the code outside of Power BI). First, it performs a simple feature selection to eliminate those fields that might cause noise during model training. After that, since the previous imputation algorithm exposed by scikit-learn via the **KNNImputer** module does not handle categorical variables in the dataset, the code also takes care of doing the encoding of the categorical variables using the **ordinal encoding** technique (using a mapping of categories to integers) thanks to the `OrdinalEncoder` module of scikit-learn.

At this point, the code imputes the missing values using the default distance measure, which is a Euclidean distance measure that does not include NaN values when calculating the distance between members of the training dataset.

Once the imputed dataset is available, you can train the model, which you will then use to score a test dataset. You can find the code in the `Python/02-train-model-with-pycaret.py` file in the `Chapter 17` folder. For convenience, you will use 95% of the imputed dataset to train the model, while the remaining 5% will be used as a test dataset. All of this is done in a transformation step that follows the previous one used to impute missing values in Power BI.

You'll split the dataset into training and test sets thanks to scikit-learn's `train_test_split()` method. After that, the model training is done very easily by calling PyCaret's `setup()` and `compare_models()` functions. In the `setup()` function, you will define which DataFrame to use for training, the target variable (`Survived`), and which are the categorical and which are the ordinal variables. The `compare_models()` function trains and evaluates the performance of all models provided by PyCaret for classification using cross-validation. In addition to returning the best-performing model, this function also returns the performance values of each model returned by cross-validation:

	Model	Accuracy	AUC	Recall	Prec.	F1	Kappa	MCC	TT (Sec)
gbc	Gradient Boosting Classifier	0.8322	0.8728	0.7304	0.8072	0.7648	0.6352	0.6388	0.4710
lightgbm	Light Gradient Boosting Machine	0.8271	0.8835	0.7215	0.8068	0.7568	0.6241	0.6305	0.2670
rf	Random Forest Classifier	0.8220	0.8722	0.7170	0.7952	0.7521	0.6141	0.6179	0.6310
lr	Logistic Regression	0.8186	0.8655	0.7126	0.7882	0.7460	0.6059	0.6100	0.2420
et	Extra Trees Classifier	0.8136	0.8530	0.7219	0.7723	0.7442	0.5982	0.6009	0.5990
ada	Ada Boost Classifier	0.8119	0.8423	0.7441	0.7630	0.7478	0.5987	0.6041	0.3640
nb	Naive Bayes	0.8102	0.8343	0.7532	0.7507	0.7486	0.5965	0.5999	0.1880
lda	Linear Discriminant Analysis	0.8051	0.8648	0.6992	0.7670	0.7284	0.5773	0.5813	0.1950
ridge	Ridge Classifier	0.8034	0.0000	0.6947	0.7662	0.7256	0.5734	0.5776	0.1420
dt	Decision Tree Classifier	0.7932	0.7735	0.6943	0.7440	0.7139	0.5531	0.5576	0.1890
svm	SVM - Linear Kernel	0.7136	0.0000	0.6105	0.5991	0.5630	0.3769	0.4059	0.1480
qda	Quadratic Discriminant Analysis	0.7085	0.8096	0.7575	0.6324	0.6684	0.4249	0.4537	0.1960
knn	K Neighbors Classifier	0.6966	0.7543	0.5549	0.6126	0.5782	0.3427	0.3466	0.1950
dummy	Dummy Classifier	0.6220	0.5000	0.0000	0.0000	0.0000	0.0000	0.0000	0.1970

Figure 17.5: Performance of all models

Figure 17.5 shows several typical classification metrics for each model. In yellow, you can see which models correspond to the highest values for each classification metric. One of the most commonly used is the **Area Under the ROC Curve** (**AUC** or **AUC-ROC**) when the dataset is almost balanced (in other words, when there is a slight disproportion between the number of observations associated with one class of the target variable and the other class). For imbalanced datasets, one of **Precision**, **Recall**, **F1-score**, or **Area Under the Precision-Recall Curve** (**AUC-PR**) is a better metric. The following note applies:

IMPORTANT NOTE

Unlike previous versions of PyCaret, the latest version we are using (specifically 3.0.4) implements a parallelism system that can also be used by Power BI. Therefore, if you don't set n_jobs to a specific value in the `compare_models()` function, PyCaret defaults it to -1 (maximum parallelism), allowing the model to be trained faster using multi-threading, even in Power BI.

With an AUC of about 0.88 (it can vary as the process is stochastic), the **Light Gradient Boosting Machine (LightGBM) classifier** appears to be the best model obtained by training 95% of the imputed dataset. It is also saved as a PKL file for future use. Then you will use the newly trained model (best_model) to obtain predictions on the remaining 5% of the dataset using PyCaret's predict_model() function. You will get a result similar to this one:

	Pclass	Sex	Age	SibSp	Parch	Fare	Embarked	Survived	prediction_label	prediction_score
0	3	1.0	25.000000	0.0	0.0	7.0500	2.0	0	0	0.8663
1	3	1.0	25.000000	0.0	0.0	7.2500	2.0	0	0	0.8373
2	3	1.0	33.000000	0.0	0.0	7.8958	2.0	0	0	0.9491
3	3	1.0	47.799999	1.0	0.0	7.7500	1.0	0	0	0.9584
4	3	1.0	24.400000	2.0	0.0	23.2500	1.0	1	0	0.7690
...	...	...	...	...	...	...	...	...	...	...
839	3	1.0	16.000000	1.0	3.0	34.3750	2.0	0	0	0.8558
840	3	0.0	26.000000	1.0	0.0	16.1000	2.0	0	0	0.6101
841	3	1.0	19.000000	0.0	0.0	0.0000	2.0	0	0	0.9233
842	3	0.0	13.000000	0.0	0.0	7.2292	0.0	1	1	0.8942
843	3	1.0	28.400000	0.0	0.0	7.8958	0.0	0	0	0.9518

Figure 17.6: Predictions of the test dataset

As you can see, the result vgenerated by scoring the dataset consists of two new columns for classification: the Score column represents an estimate of a measure, such as the probability that the predicted classes are those reported in the Label column. If you are interested in having a true probability estimate, you need to **calibrate** the model (see the references for more details). By default, the predicted class is 1 if the predicted probability is greater than or equal to 0.5.

Let's take a look at how you can implement what we've covered here in Power BI.

Using PyCaret in Power BI

First, make sure to create the run_power_bi_in_pycaret_env.bat file and its shortcut to run Power BI by enabling the pycaret_env environment. To do this, follow the steps in the *A practical solution to the problem* section in *Chapter 4, Solving Common Issues When Using Python and R in Power BI*. Then follow these steps:

1. Open Power BI Desktop from the shortcut you've just created that activates the **pycaret_env** environment.
2. Make sure Power BI Desktop is referencing the **pycaret_env** environment in the Python scripting tab of the **Options** menu.
3. Click on **Get data**, then **Web**.
4. Enter the http://bit.ly/titanic-dataset-csv URL into the URL textbox and click **OK**.
5. You'll see a preview of the data. Then, click **Transform Data**.
6. Click **Transform** on the ribbon and then **Run Python script**.

7. Enter the script you can find in the `Python\01-impute-dataset-with-knn.py` file in the **Chapter 17** folder.

8. We are only interested in the data in the **df_imputed** DataFrame. So, click on its **Table** value.

9. You'll see a preview of the dataset with all the missing values imputed.

10. Click **Transform** on the ribbon and then **Run Python script** again.

11. Enter the script you can find in the `Python\02-train-model-with-pycaret.py` file in the Chapter 17 folder.

12. We are only interested in the data in the **predictions** DataFrame. So, after the few minutes needed to train the model, click on its **Table** value.

13. You'll see a preview of the dataset with the predictions generated by the model and the input dataset.

14. Click **Home** on the ribbon and then click **Close & Apply**.

Amazing! You have just trained a ML model and then scored a test dataset with a few lines of Python code thanks to PyCaret!

You can also use another open-source package to train a model using AutoML. Let's see what it is.

Training and using ML models with FLAML

As with PyCaret, we will try to train a ML model with FLAML that can predict whether a passenger on the Titanic survived or not. We need to create a new `flaml_env` environment, which will be used to install the FLAML package:

1. Let's create a new environment specifically for the installation of FLAML and all its dependencies. Run Anaconda Prompt and enter the following command to create the new **flaml_env** environment with Python 3.9 and the IPython kernel for Jupyter (used by VS Code):

   ```
   conda create --name flaml_env python=3.9 ipykernel
   ```

   Type y when prompted to download dependencies.

2. Run Anaconda Prompt and enter the following command to switch to the new environment:

   ```
   conda activate flaml_env
   ```

3. Enter the following command to install FLAML with the extension of AutoML:

   ```
   pip install flaml[automl]==2.0.0
   ```

4. Because Power BI uses a wrapper that loads the matplotlib package to run the Python code, you must also install matplotlib. Enter the following command to install it:

   ```
   pip install matplotlib
   ```

It was not necessary to explicitly install matplotlib in the `pycaret_env` environment, because this package was a requirement of PyCaret, so it was installed behind the scenes.

Now you can train the model with the AutoML feature of FLAML using the code in the `Python/04-train-model-with-flaml.py` file in the `Chapter 17` folder. Remember to edit the `main_path` variable at the beginning of the script.

This script closely follows the previous script used for PyCaret training, so you will be able to follow it well on your own. In particular, using FLAML's AutoML is really easy. The AutoML execution configurations are declared in the dictionary `settings`. In our case, we declare the maximum execution time (10 minutes), the metric to be used for selecting the best-performing algorithm (in our case ROC AUC), the type of task (a classification), the name of the log file in which FLAML will log all the information from the training phases, and a seed that allows reproducibility of the results despite the use of stochastic functions.

After waiting 10 minutes from the execution of the `automl.fit()` function, it is possible to get the name and performance information of the best estimator identified by the AutoML procedure. In our case, the best estimator is the same one also selected by PyCaret, the **LightGBM** classifier, which obtained a ROC AUC of 0.8887. Again, the model is saved in Pickle format for future use.

At this point, the newly trained model can be used to obtain predictions using the test dataset and the `predict()` and `predict_proba()` methods.

IMPORTANT NOTE

The models generated by FLAML's AutoML feature are fully compatible with scikit-learn models (they are scikit-learn-style estimators). Therefore, the best estimator obtained from FLAML implements the same `predict()` and `predict_proba()` methods as a scikit-learn model to obtain the predicted class and class probabilities, respectively. This ensures that a model trained using FLAML can be used in any Python script by simply making sure that scikit-learn and any other dependent packages (e.g., LightGBM or xgboost) are installed and unpickling the model, without having to import the AutoML class from the flaml package, unlike PyCaret. In this case, all you need to do is extract the scikit-learn estimator from the trained FLAML AutoML object.

For compatibility with the dataset obtained from predictions made with PyCaret, the prediction_score column shows the probability scores of the class types predicted in the `prediction_label` column, not just everything related to class 1. To be clear, if the predicted class is 0 and the probability of it being 1 is 0.2, you will find the value *1 - 0.2 = 0.8* as the probability of class 0. Instead, data scientists generally work by always referring to the probability that the predicted class is positive because if you want to set a threshold other than 0.5 to determine the positive predicted class, you can calculate it yourself from the predicted probabilities of class 1 like this: *if predict_proba_class_1 >= selected_threshold then 1, otherwise 0*.

Let's take a look at how we train models with FLAML in Power BI.

Using FLAML in Power BI

Similar to what we did when using PyCaret in Power BI, we will train our model with FLAML using a version of the Titanic dataset for which missing values have already been imputed. To simplify things, instead of using the Python script for the imputation step, we will directly import the imputed dataset via the `titanic-imputed.csv` file. First, make sure to create the `run_power_bi_in_flaml_env.bat` file and its shortcut to run Power BI by enabling the `flaml_env` environment. To do this, follow the steps in the *A practical solution to the problem* section in *Chapter 4, Solving Common Issues When Using Python and R in Power BI*.

Here are the steps to do this:

1. Open Power BI Desktop from the shortcut you've just created that activates the `flaml_env` environment.
2. Make sure Power BI Desktop is referencing the **flaml_env** environment in the Python scripting tab of the **Options** menu.
3. Click on **Get data**, then select **Text/CSV**.
4. Select the `titanic-imputed.csv` file in the Chapter 17 folder and click **Open**.
5. You'll see a preview of the imputed Titanic dataset. Then, click **Transform Data**.
6. Click **Transform** on the ribbon, followed by **Run Python script**.
7. Enter the script you can find in the `Python\04-train-model-with-flaml.py` file in the **Chapter 17** folder. In case of a bug caused by xgboost, make sure that you are using xgboost version 1 (in our case 1.7.6), and not version 2.
8. We are only interested in the data in the **predictions** Dataframe. So, after the few minutes needed to train the model, click on its **Table** value.
9. You'll see a preview of the dataset with the predictions generated by the model and the input dataset.
10. Click **Home** on the ribbon and then click **Close & Apply**.

Can you believe it? You just trained a ML model in Power BI using FLAML with just a few lines of code.

So far, you have seen how to train a model directly in Power BI and reuse it for scoring. Now let's see what you do if you train a model on a platform other than Power BI and want to use that model in Power BI to predict values.

Using trained models in Power Query

As you already saw in *Chapter 5, Importing Unhandled Data Objects*, you used to pass objects that were the result of complex, time-consuming processing (including a ML model) in a serialized format specific to the language you were using. At that point, it was very easy to deserialize the file and get the model ready to use in Power Query to predict the target variable from new observations. However, it is important to know the dependencies needed by the scoring function (which takes the new observations as input and returns the predictions) because they are closely related to how the model was trained.

For this reason, we recommend the following:

> **IMPORTANT NOTE**
>
> If you need to use a serialized ML model provided by a third party, make sure that whoever developed it also provides you with a working scoring function in order to avoid unnecessary headaches when predicting target values for unknown observations.

If you think about it, the ability to serialize and deserialize a ML model could somehow solve the delay problem raised in the previous section in the case of training the model directly in Power Query. Suppose you run the embedded training code for the first time. Immediately after that, you serialize the model and save it to disk. The next time you refresh, instead of running the training code again, you can check to see if the serialized model file exists in the expected path. If yes, you load the file, deserialize it, and use that model for the next steps; otherwise, you rerun the training code.

Obviously, the above process requires the intervention of an expert who decides to eliminate the serialized file if the model starts to perform poorly, perhaps because the business data has changed significantly in the meantime so that the previous model is no longer as accurate as it was after the training with the past data (a process known as **model drift**; see the references for more details).

We will not go into the implementation details of this solution, because you will be implementing similar solutions in the following sections.

Let's now implement the scoring of a dataset of unseen observations in Power BI using an already-trained PyCaret model.

Scoring observations in Power Query using a trained PyCaret model

If you recall, in the previous section, you saved the model you trained in Power BI to a PKL file on disk. You also exported the test dataset computed in the same code to CSV. In this section, you will use the serialized model directly, loading it with the `load_model()` function, and the CSV test dataset to score in Power BI. Since the model was trained using PyCaret, the scoring function to use is simply given by the `predict_model()` function. Note that the scoring function may be more complex if you are not using a framework like PyCaret that simplifies things.

These are the steps to follow in Power BI:

1. Open Power BI Desktop from the shortcut you've just created that activates the **pycaret_env** environment.
2. Make sure Power BI Desktop is referencing the **pycaret_env** environment in the Python scripting tab of the **Options** menu.
3. Click on **Get data**, then **Text/CSV**.
4. Select the `titanic-test.csv` file in the Chapter 17 folder and click **Open**.
5. You'll see a preview of the test data. Then, click **Transform Data**.

6. Click **Transform** on the ribbon and then **Run Python script**.

7. Enter the script you can find in the Python\03-score-dataset-using-pycaret-model.py file in the Chapter 17 folder.

8. If you get the Firewall privacy level mismatch error, select a **Public** privacy level for the CSV data source and press **OK**. Then click on **Refresh Preview**. You are prompted to expand a DataFrame calculated in the Python script.

9. We are only interested in the **predictions** DataFrame. So, click on its **Table** value.

10. You'll see a preview of the test dataset with two additional columns – **prediction_label** and **prediction_score**.

11. Click **Home** on the ribbon and then click **Close & Apply**.

As you can see, this is the most immediate and common way to use a custom ML model for scoring in Power BI. In fact, we recommend the following:

IMPORTANT NOTE

It is convenient to perform training and generally manage a ML model in platforms outside of Power BI to decouple any development/tuning of the model from the rest of the report.

You can do the same with a pre-trained FLAML model. Let's see how to score a dataset in Power BI using this type of ML model.

Scoring observations in Power Query using a trained FLAML model

Just as you did for PyCaret, you will also use the previously created serialized FLAML model and load it with the usual open() and pickle.load() functions. Since the FLAML model is a custom scikit-learn estimator, you can simply use the model's predict() and predict_proba() methods. In this case, there is no need for a complex scoring function.

These are the steps to follow in Power BI:

1. Open Power BI Desktop from the shortcut you've just created that activates the **flaml_env** environment.

2. Make sure Power BI Desktop is referencing the **flaml_env** environment in the Python scripting tab of the **Options** menu.

3. Click on **Get data**, then **Text/CSV**.

4. Select the titanic-test.csv file in the Chapter 17 folder and click **Open**.

5. You'll see a preview of the test data. Then, click **Transform Data**.

6. Click **Transform** on the ribbon and then **Run Python script**.

7. Enter the script you can find in the Python\05-score-dataset-using-flaml-model.py file in the Chapter 17 folder. Remember to edit the main_path variable.

8. If you get the Firewall privacy level mismatch error, select a **Public** privacy level for the CSV data source and press **OK**. Then click on **Refresh Preview**. You are prompted to expand a DataFrame calculated in the Python script.

9. We are only interested in the **predictions** DataFrame. So, click on its **Table** value.

10. You'll see a preview of the test dataset with two additional columns – **prediction_label** and **prediction_score**.

11. Click **Home** on the ribbon and then click **Close & Apply**.

Even with FLAML, scoring a dataset using a pre-trained ML model is very easy.

Let's try something a little more tricky: using serialized ML models directly in **Script Visuals**.

Using trained models in script visuals

As you learned in *Chapter 5, Importing Unhandled Data Objects*, thanks to object serialization and its string representation, you can import any object into a Python or R visual as a DataFrame of strings. Once this DataFrame is available in the script visual, you can convert it back to the original object using inverse deserialization transformations. Of course, since you can do what we've described with any object, you can also do it with ML models that have already been trained outside of Power BI.

When the appropriately deserialized model is available in the *script visual* session, new observations can be immediately predicted using the scoring function described in the previous section.

The first thing you might ask is what's the point of being able to score a dataset within a script visual if the data always has to be available first in the Power BI data model to be used in the visual? In fact, if the data of the observations to be used as input to the model is already found in the Power BI data model, it might be better to apply batch scoring directly in Power Query and so use the predictions as a new column of the dataset. This is all absolutely true. However, there are some cases where it is convenient to use a script visual, such as is highlighted in the following note:

> **IMPORTANT NOTE**
>
> It is convenient to use a ML model in a script visual when you need to realize some simulation reports that allow you to explore the outputs of the model and vary the variables in play dynamically without having to refresh the entire report.

In this case, we recommend using **what-if parameters** (https://bit.ly/power-bi-what-if) in Power BI for numeric features, which are dynamic and give the user a very usable report. For categorical variables, you can manually enter their contents in Power BI using the **Enter Data** feature, which creates a disconnected table. What-if parameters create unrelated tables by default in the data model.

To properly understand this section, make sure you understand the content of *Chapter 5, Importing Unhandled Data Objects*. Suppose you need to provide observations to a ML model that expects two variables as input – one numeric and one categorical.

When you pass the information to the DataFrame of the script visual, in addition to the fields of the serialized model's DataFrame (model_id, chunk_id, and model_str) that come from Power Query, you must also assign the corresponding values to the two parameter slicers associated with the two input variables. Since only one value is selected at a time for each parameter during slicing, the set of all the parameters forms a tuple, which in our case is (numeric_value, category_id). This tuple is replicated as many times as there are rows in the string chunk DataFrame (consisting of the model_id, chunk_id, and model_str columns), and concatenated to it in order to provide the final DataFrame that will be available in the variable named dataset in the script visual session. A picture is worth a thousand words:

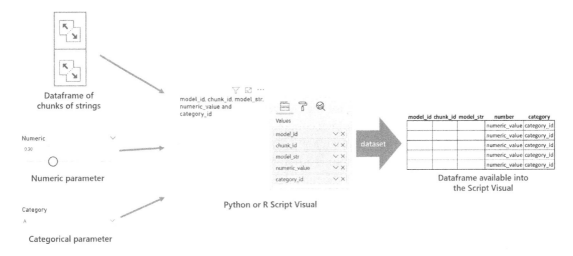

Figure 17.7: Deserializing an external file content into a script visual

Once you have the DataFrame of the dataset available in the script visual, you can apply the deserialization transformations only to the columns (model_id, chunk_id, and model_str) and obtain the ML model ready for use. If instead you select only the columns (number and category) and apply the distinct function to all the rows of the resulting DataFrame, you get back the tuple of parameters to provide as input to the deserialized model. Thus, you can compute the predicted value from the model by giving it the tuple of parameters as input. You can then use the prediction in the graph to be displayed in the script visual.

Let's see in practice how to dynamically predict values from a ML model in a Python script visual.

Scoring observations in a script visual using a trained model

The first thing you will do is properly serialize the ML models (in our case, only one) contained in a dictionary in Power Query. In this way, a DataFrame is obtained that contains the representation in strings of each serialized model of the aforementioned dictionary. Thus, it is possible to select the model of interest using a slicer in the report. In this way, the corresponding part of a DataFrame is used in a Python script visual, within which it is possible to deserialize the contents of the DataFrame and thus obtain the model to be used for scoring.

Both the PyCaret model and the FLAML model can be used to score the data used in this report. In fact, you will find two versions of Python scripts 06 and 07, each based on one of the above models. In our case, we will refer to the files that use the model trained with FLAML. If you want to use the model trained with PyCaret, you can decide to use the other pair of files, 06 and 07.

So, let's move on to develop our report in Power BI. Here are the steps to follow:

1. Open Power BI Desktop from the shortcut that activates the **flaml_env** environment.

2. Make sure Power BI Desktop is referencing the **flaml_env** environment in the Python scripting tab of the **Options** menu.

3. Click on **Get data** and then **More...**. Start typing **script** into the search textbox and double-click on **Python script**. The Python script editor will pop up.

4. Copy the contents of the Python\06-serialize-flaml-ml-models-in-power-query.py file in the Chapter 17 folder. Then, paste it into the Python script editor, changing the absolute path to the PKL file accordingly, and then click **OK**.

5. The Navigator window opens, allowing you to select which DataFrame to import. Select both the **model_ids_df** DataFrame (which contains the model IDs) and the **models_df** DataFrame (which contains the string representation of the serialized models), and then click **Load**. Behind the scenes, a 1:* relationship is automatically created between the model IDs and the serialized model DataFrame via the **model_id** fields. Check it by clicking on the **Model view** on the left of the canvas:

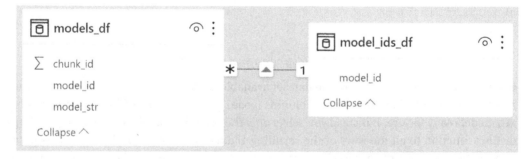

Figure 17.8: Automatically created relationship between modeled tables

This relationship allows you to filter the set of rows in the **models_df** table to be used in the Python visual, corresponding to the ID of the model you select via the slicer you'll create in the next step.

6. Go back to the **Report view** and click on the **Slicer** visual icon.

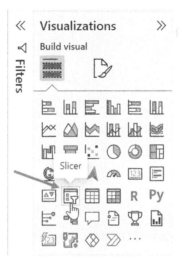

Figure 17.9: Selecting the Slicer visual

Then, click on the **model_id** measure of the **model_ids_df** table.

Figure 17.10: Click on the model_id measure to display it in the Slicer

7. Click on the Slicer **Format** options, expand **Slicer settings**, and select the **Dropdown** style option:

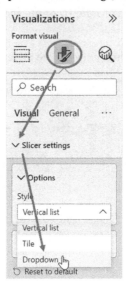

Figure 17.11: Selecting the Dropdown slicer style option

8. Then, switch on the **Single select** selection option, and then add the title **Model IDs** for the **Slicer header:**

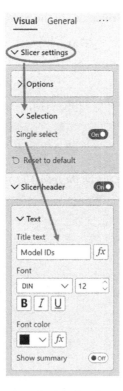

Figure 17.12: Setting the slicer options

Then, resize the bottom edge of the slicer and move it to the top center of the report.

9. You will now add a set of what-if parameters with their slicers associated with each variable to be passed as input to the model. Click on the **Modeling** tab on the ribbon, and then click on **New parameter's Numeric range** option:

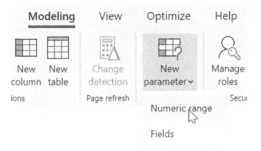

Figure 17.13: Numeric range parameter option

10. In the next dialog box, leave **Numeric range** selected, type `Pclass param` in the **Name** field, leave `Data type` as **Whole number**, type 1 in the **Minimum** field, type 3 in the **Maximum** field, leave **Increment** as 1, and type 2 in the **Default** field.

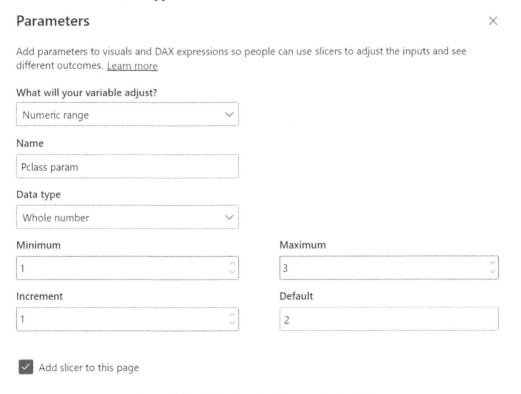

Figure 17.14: Adding the what-if parameter for Pclass

Keep **Add slicer to this page** selected and then click **Create**.

11. Resize the bottom edge of the Pclass slicer. Then, add the title **Passenger class** for the **Slicer header.** Then move it to the top left of your report.

12. Be sure to rename the **Pclass** value of **Pclass param** to the same name as the variable that represents it in the model, namely, **Pclass.**

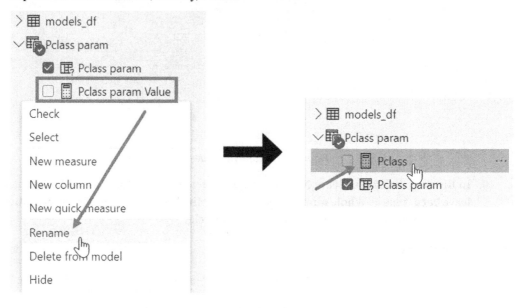

Figure 17.15: Renaming the Pclass parameter value

13. Because the Sex variable is categorical (F or M), you'll manually create a separate table for it. To do this, click the **Home** tab on the ribbon and click **Enter data**.

14. Create the first column, **Sex**, of the table and add the values 0 and 1 to it. Then, create the new column, **SexLabel**, and enter **Female** where **Sex** is 0 and **Male** where **Sex** is 1.

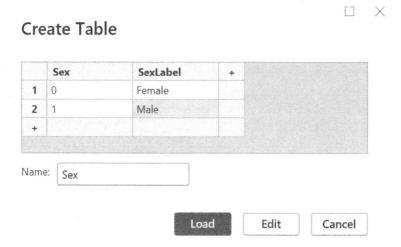

Figure 17.16: Manually enter data for Sex

Enter Sex as the table name and then click **Load**.

15. Let's add a slicer for the **Sex** variable. Click on an empty spot in the report canvas first and click the slicer visual to add a slicer to the report. Then, click on the **SexLabel** field and then on the **Sex** field (the order is important). Then, click on the Slicer **Format options**, expand **Slicer settings**, and select the **Dropdown** style option. Then, expand the **Selection** option group, and set **Single select** to on. Then, expand the **Slicer header** option group, and enter **Sex** as the **Title text**. Resize its bottom edge and move it under the **Passenger class** slicer:

Figure 17.17: A new drop-down slicer for Sex

16. Let's create a new what-if parameter for the **Age** variable. Click on the **Modeling** tab on the ribbon, and then click on **New parameter's Numeric range** option. On the next dialog, enter **Age param** in the **Name** field, leave the data type as **Whole number**, enter **1** in the **Minimum** field and 80 in the **Maximum** field, leave **Increment** as 1, and enter 30 in the **Default** field. Keep **Add slicer to this page** selected and then click **Create**.

17. Resize the bottom edge of the Age slicer and enter the title Age as the **Title text**. Then, move it to the top left of your report in the Sex slicer.

18. Be sure to rename the **Age** value of **Age param** to the same name as the variable that represents it in the model, namely, **Age**.

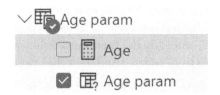

Figure 17.18: Renaming the Age parameter value

19. Let's create a new what-if parameter for the **SibSp** variable. Click on the **Modeling** tab on the ribbon and then on **New parameter, Numeric range**. On the next dialog, enter **SibSp param** in the **Name** field, leave the data type as **Whole number**, enter 0 in the **Minimum** field and 8 in the **Maximum** field, leave **Increment** as 1, and enter 0 in the **Default** field. Keep **Add slicer to this page** selected and then click **OK**.

20. Resize the bottom edge of the SibSp slicer and enter the title **Siblings/spouse aboard** for the **Slicer header**. Then move it to the top left of your report.

21. Be sure to rename the **SibSp param Value** to the same name as the variable that represents it in the model, namely, **SibSp**:

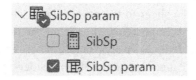

Figure 17.19: Renaming the SibSp parameter value

22. Let's create a new what-if parameter for the **Parch** variable. Click on the **Modeling** tab on the ribbon and then on **New parameter, Numeric range**. On the next dialog, enter **Parch param** in the **Name** field, leave **Whole number** as the data type, enter **0** in the **Minimum** field and **6** in the **Maximum** field, leave **Increment** as **1**, and enter **0** in the **Default** field. Keep **Add slicer to this page** selected and then click **Create**.

23. Resize the bottom edge of the Parch slicer and enter the title **Parents/children aboard** for the **Slice header**. Then, move it to the top left of your report under the SibSp slicer.

24. Be sure to rename the **Parch param Value** to the same name as the variable that represents it in the model, namely **Parch**:

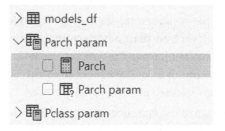

Figure 17.20: Renaming the Parch parameter value

25. Let's create a new what-if parameter for the **Fare** variable. Click on the **Modeling** tab on the ribbon and then on **New parameter, Numeric range**. On the next dialog, enter **Fare param** in the **Name** field, select **Decimal number** as the data type, enter **0** in the **Minimum** field and **515** in the **Maximum** field, enter **1** in the **Increment** field, and then enter **250** in the **Default** field. Keep **Add slicer to this page** selected and then click **Create**.

26. Resize the bottom edge of the Fare slicer and enter the title **Fare** as the title text. Then, move it to the top left of your report under the Parch slicer.

27. Be sure to rename the **Fare param Value** to the same name as the variable that represents it in the model, namely, **Fare**.

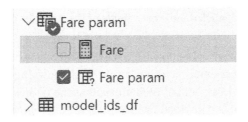

Figure 17.21: Renaming the Fare parameter value

28. Let's add a slicer for the **Embarked** variable. Because the **Embarked** variable is categorical (0, 1, or 2), you'll manually create a separate table for it. To do this, click the **Home** tab on the ribbon and click **Enter Data**.

29. Create the first column, **Embarked** (this name must correspond to that of the model's variable), of the table and then add the values 0, 1, and 2 to it. Then, create a new column, **Embarked-Label**, and enter **Cherbourg**, **Queenstown**, and **Southampton**, corresponding to 0, 1, and 2, respectively.

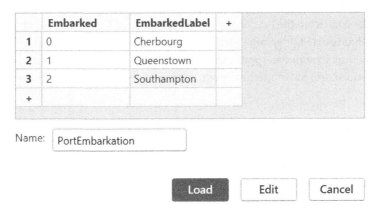

Figure 17.22: Entering data manually for Embarked

Enter PortEmbarkation as the table name and then click **Load**.

30. Let's now add a slicer for the **Embarked** variable. Click on an empty spot in the report canvas first. Then, click on the slicer visual in order to add a slicer to the report. Click first on the **EmbarkedLabel** field and then on the **Embarked** one (the order is important). Then, click on the Slicer **Format options**, expand **Slicer settings**, and select the **Dropdown** style option. Then, expand the **Selection** option group, and set **Single select** to on. Then, expand the **Slicer header** option group, and enter **Port of embarkation** as the **Title text**. Resize its bottom edge and move it to the Passenger class slicer.

31. Now, click on an empty spot in the report canvas, then on **Python Visual** in the **Visualizations** field, and enable it when you're prompted to do so. After that, move it to the center of your report.

32. Keeping it selected, click on all three fields of the **models_df** table (**chunk_id, model_id**, and **model_str**).

33. Still with the Python visual selected, also click on all the measures (those with a calculator icon) of all the parameters entered, as well as on the identifying fields of the categorical variables (the **Embarked** and **Sex** fields). Remember that the names of the measures must match the names of the variables provided by the model for the report to work. Keep the **model_id** field of the **model_ids_df** table *out of the selection*. At the end, you should see all the names of the measures plus those of the fields of the **models_df** table inside the Python visual.

Figure 17.23: Selected measure names visible in the Python visual

34. Now, click on the Python visual's **Format** options, expand the **Title** area, change the text to **Prediction**, and increase the font size to 28 point.

35. Copy the code from the `Python\07-deserialize-flaml-ml-models-in-python-visual.py` file in the `Chapter 17` folder and paste it into the Python visual script editor. Then, click on the **Run script** arrow icon in the upper-right corner of the Python script editor. You'll get a prediction (label and score) of whether a person described by the parameters you selected will survive.

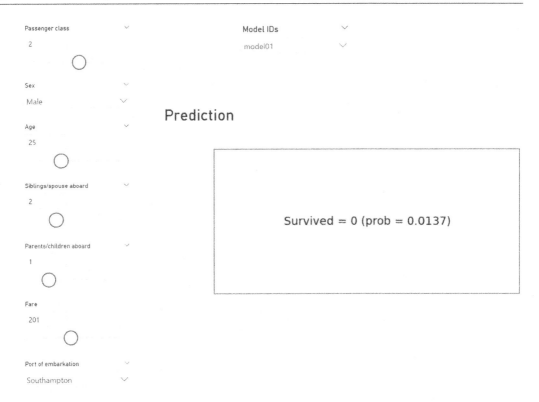

Figure 17.24: Full prediction simulation report for the Titanic model

Note that the same report can be generated using models trained in R with the same methodology used here. In fact, for completeness, in Chapter 17 we added to the repository the R folder containing the scripts corresponding to those used in this section, which are useful for obtaining the same results as those obtained here. In these scripts, we trained the model using a predefined algorithm (**Random Forest**) and used the recently introduced **tidymodels** framework, which makes use of the Tidyverse principles. See the references for more details.

IMPORTANT NOTE

Currently, the report you've just created cannot be published on the Power BI service even if you use scikit-learn's best estimator (in our case LightGBM), because the libraries needed to score the datasets (e.g., LightGBM, xgboost, and PyCaret) are missing. Should Microsoft decide to add these packages to the engines on the service, the report could be functional once published.

Wow! You've created a dynamic predictive report in Power BI!

Now let's see how you can invoke the AI and ML services provided by Microsoft in Power BI, even if you don't have a Premium, Embedded, or PPU license.

Calling web services in Power Query

Another way to interact with ML models in Power Query is to call web services. As you may already know, a ML model can be used to score many observations in batch mode against a trained model (the process described earlier). Another way to interact with a ML model is to expose it as a web service so that it can be called via REST APIs. You learned how to work with external APIs in *Chapter 11, Calling External APIs to Enrich Your Data*.

IMPORTANT NOTE

Keep in mind that you can't consume external services via REST API calls from a Python or R visual because internet access is blocked for security reasons. Therefore, you can only consume these services in Power Query.

As an example, in this section, you'll see how to invoke predictions from a released endpoint via **Azure Machine Learning,** and how to use the services exposed by the **Azure Text Analytics** feature of Cognitive Services. You could use some M code in Power Query to access these services, although it's not exactly straightforward. Fortunately, there are SDKs that make it much easier to access the exposed services. These SDKs are developed for Python, so our examples will be in Python only.

First, let's look at how to interact with a model trained with Azure AutoML.

Using Azure AutoML models in Power Query

In this section, you'll first see how to train a ML model using the Azure AutoML GUI. Then, you will use the model published to an Azure container instance as a web service in Power BI.

Training a model using the Azure AutoML UI

To use Azure AutoML, you must first have access to an Azure subscription (remember you can create a free account by following this link: `https://bit.ly/azure-free-account`). After that, you need to create an **Azure Machine Learning workspace** to train models using the different technologies that Azure provides. You can do this by simply following the steps on the page at this link: `https://bit.ly/create-azureml-workspace`. Once the workspace is assigned, you'll be able to sign in to **Azure Machine Learning Studio**, an environment that organizes all the ML resources you'll be working with. Follow these steps to log in to Azure ML Studio and start an AutoML experiment:

1. Go to `https://ml.azure.com/`. You can select your workspace from the recent ones if you've already signed in to it, or you can select it by clicking on Workspaces on the left and then clicking on your workspace in the list on the next page:

Figure 17.25: Azure ML Studio portal

2. First, you need to import the dataset you want to use to train the model. You will use the same dataset that you used to impute missing values in the previous sections. Click on **Data** on the left menu, and then click **Create**:

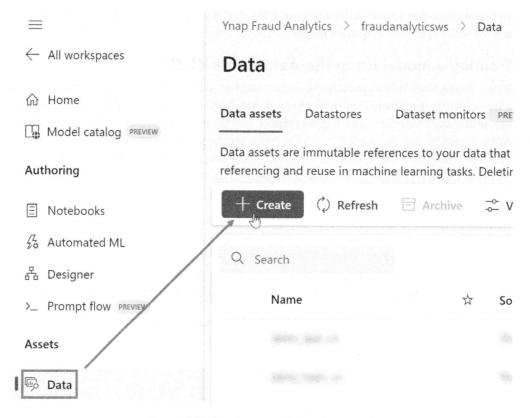

Figure 17.26: Creating a new dataset in Azure ML

3. You'll be prompted for the data asset name and type. Enter **titanic-imputed** as the name and leave **Tabular** as the type.

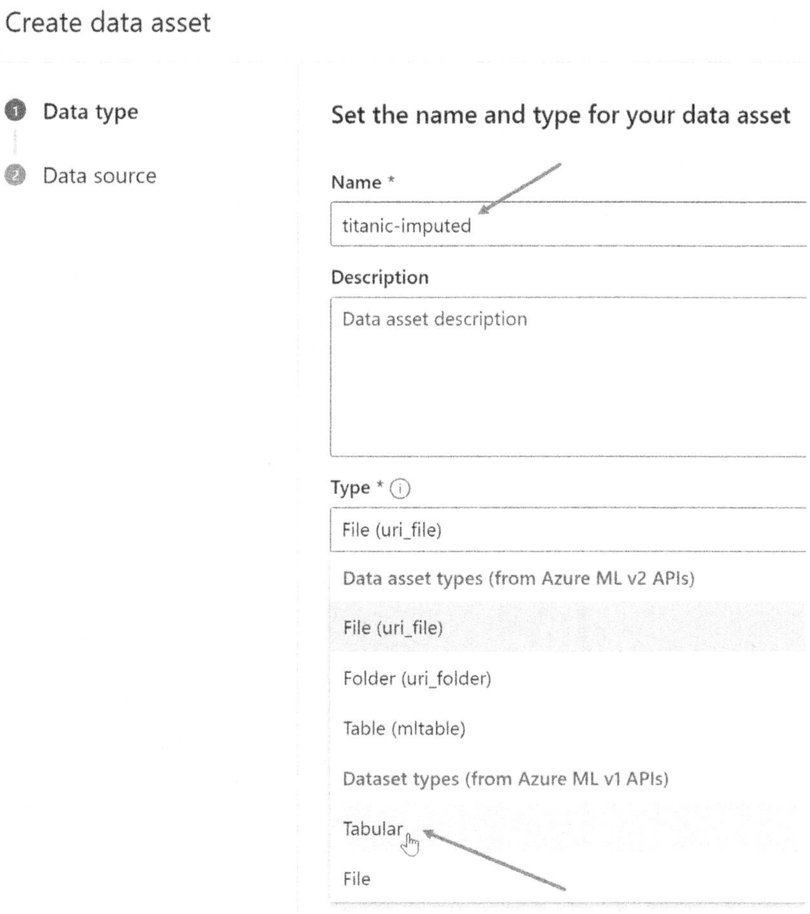

Create data asset

Figure 17.27: Selecting your data asset name and type

Then, click **Next**.

4. You have to upload the CSV file containing the Titanic disaster imputed data. So, select **From local files**, and then click **Next**.

5. Next, you need to select a datastore in the cloud where Azure ML will store the data you select from your machine. Keep **Azure Blob Storage** as **Datastore type** and select the **workspaceblobstore** datastore that Azure ML creates by default when the workspace is created. Click Next.

6. Next click on **Upload** and then on **Upload files**, and finally select the `titanic-imputed.csv` file in the `Chapter 17` folder via the **Open file** dialog. Click **Next**.

7. On the next page, you'll see a preview of the record you're importing. The engine automatically chooses the best import options for you. However, if you'd like to change anything, you can do so on this page. If everything is OK, click **Next**.

8. On the next page, you can change the imputed schema of the data you're reading. In this case, leave the derived type for each field because the exported CSV file has numeric values with integers and decimals. Then click **Next**.

9. A summary page will be displayed. Just click **Create** and your dataset will be added to Azure ML.

10. Now you need to create a compute cluster to use for model training. Click on the **Compute** tab on the left menu, then click on **Compute clusters,** and finally click on **New**.

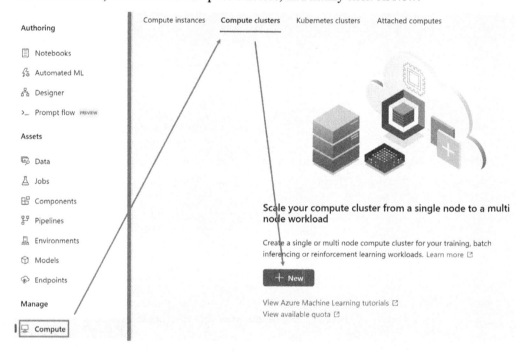

Figure 17.28: Creating a new compute cluster

11. Then you can select your preferred location for the cluster and the virtual machine type and size to use for each cluster node. You can leave the default selection and click **Next**.

12. Choose a name for your cluster (in our case **cluster**), the minimum number of nodes (leave it at 0 so it will automatically shut down when not in use), and the maximum number of nodes (set it to 2). Set the **Idle seconds before scaling down** value to 300. Then click **Create** to provision your compute cluster.

13. Now, click on the **Automated ML** tab on the left menu and then on **New Automated ML job**.

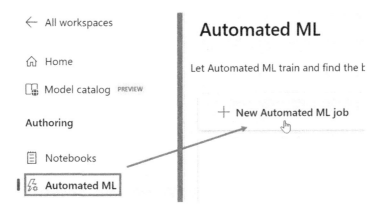

Figure 17.29: Creating a new AutoML job

14. On the next page, select the **titanic-imputed** dataset and click **Next**.

15. Now you can configure the job by specifying the name of the new experiment (a virtual folder) that will contain all the AutoML jobs (we used **titanic** for the name), the ML target column (**Survived**, the one to be predicted), the compute type (**Compute cluster**), and the compute cluster to use to run the AutoML jobs (the **cluster** you created earlier):

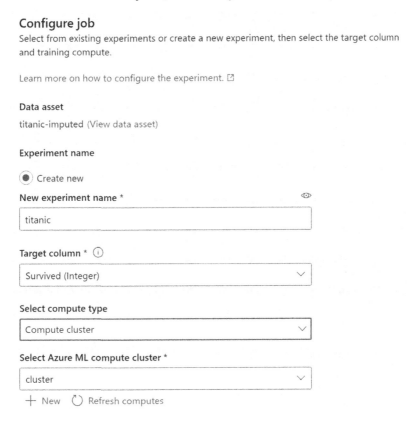

Figure 17.30: Configuring your AutoML job

Then click **Next**.

16. You can then declare the type of ML experiment you want to run. In our case, this is a classification:

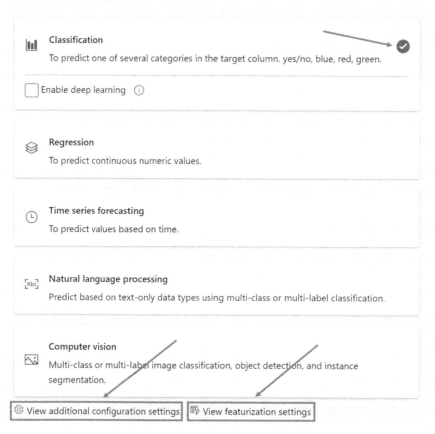

Select task and settings

Select the machine learning task type for the experiment. To fine tune the experiment, choose additional configuration or featurization settings.

Classification
To predict one of several categories in the target column. yes/no, blue, red, green.

☐ Enable deep learning ⓘ

Regression
To predict continuous numeric values.

Time series forecasting
To predict values based on time.

Natural language processing
Predict based on text-only data types using multi-class or multi-label classification.

Computer vision
Multi-class or multi-label image classification, object detection, and instance segmentation.

⚙ View additional configuration settings   🖽 View featurization settings

Figure 17.31: Setting up the AutoML task type

17. Click **View additional configuration settings** to select the primary metric to be used in your experiment. Leave **AUC-weighted** selected, expand **Additional classification settings**, and declare the positive class of the target variable of the training dataset by typing **1**:

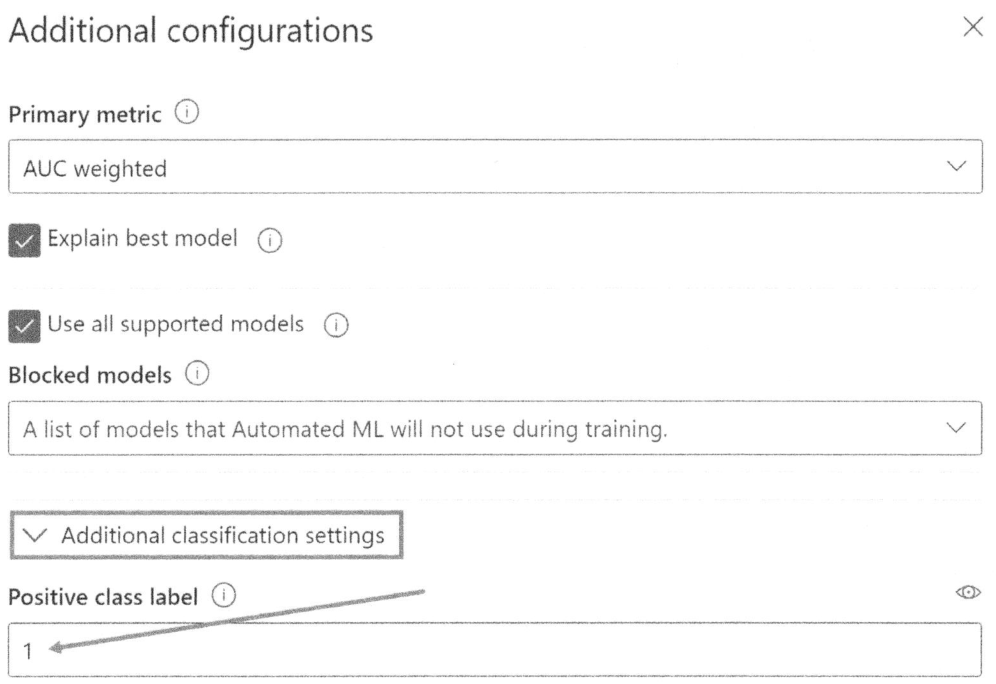

Figure 17.32: Setting the Positive class label

It is very important to declare the positive class label; otherwise, the feature algorithm might discard all variables and the job would fail. Then click **Save**.

18. By clicking **View featurization settings**, you can enable the auto-feature option provided by AutoML. It's enabled by default. You can also select the feature type for each column and the missing value imputation strategy for each of them (the strategies are the naive ones). Leave everything set to **Auto**, and then click **Save**. Click **Next**.

19. You can then select the validation type and an optional test data asset to evaluate with the model to be trained. Leave **Auto** for the **Validation type** and **No test data asset required** for the **Test data asset**.

20. You can now click **Finish** to start your AutoML job. You'll be redirected to the just started job page, and after a while, you'll see it running:

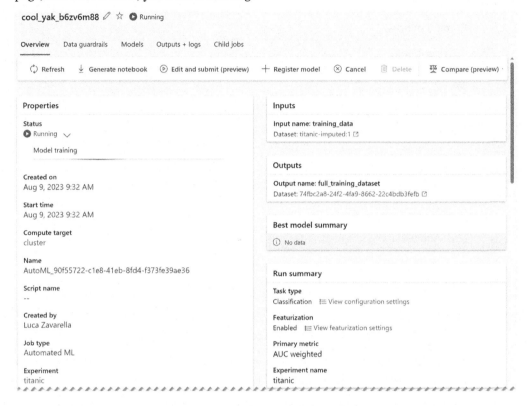

Figure 17.33: Your AutoML experiment running

The job will be given a random name. You can rename it if you need to recognize it when you run multiple jobs.

21. After about 30 minutes (depending on Azure workloads), the job should be complete. Click on the **Models** tab on the **AutoML Run** page and you will see the training pipelines sorted by the best-performing ones (you can also see them while the AutoML job is running):

Figure 17.34: Best-performing pipelines found by AutoML

22. For the best-performing model (**VotingEnsemble**), the **Explainability Dashboard** is also automatically generated and can be accessed by clicking **View Explanation**. See the references for more details. Now click on the **VotingEnsemble** link to go to the specific run that trained the model using this pipeline. Click **Deploy** and then **Real-time endpoint**:

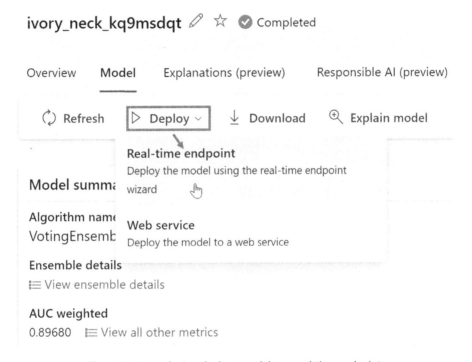

Figure 17.35: Deploying the best model to a real-time endpoint

In this way, you are releasing the model to the real-time endpoints that are fully managed by Azure ML. If you had chosen **Web service** deployment instead, you could have released your model on an **Azure Container Instance** or **Azure Kubernetes Service** (**AKS**) with the ability to set custom deployment configurations.

Anyway, once you've clicked on **Real-time endpoint**, a new panel will appear on the right asking for information about the virtual machine type and instances you want to use for your deployment according to the workload you expect, and endpoint settings. Select the cheaper VM for this example (in our case, Standard_DS1_v2), as the model you'll deploy is small. A single VM instance is enough. Give the model endpoint the name titanic (you may need to change this name to make the endpoint URL unique), and type titanic-model-01 for **Deployment name** (you may have multiple deployments behind a single endpoint). Then, click on **Deploy** and wait for the model to be deployed.

23. Click **Deploy**. After that, a model summary page will show the deployment status of your model. Click on **Refresh** every time to know the current status of your deployment:

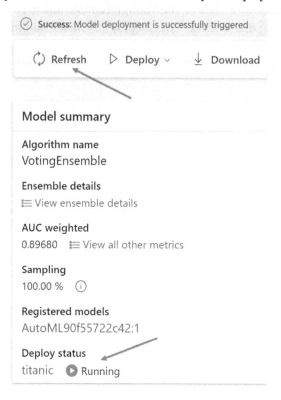

Figure 17.36: Checking the deployment status

24. When the **Deployment status** field in **Model summary** changes to **Succeeded** after about 10 minutes (it depends on the Azure workload), click the **titanic** (or whatever name you chose) endpoint link.

25. The endpoint **Details** page contains all the information about the service. You can click on the **Test** tab to test your endpoint by providing it with test input data. The tab we are most interested in is the **Consume** tab, which provides the REST endpoint URL and authentication key for calling the REST API from an external system. You can also directly copy the Python code snippet in the **Consumption option** section, which allows you to consume the service:

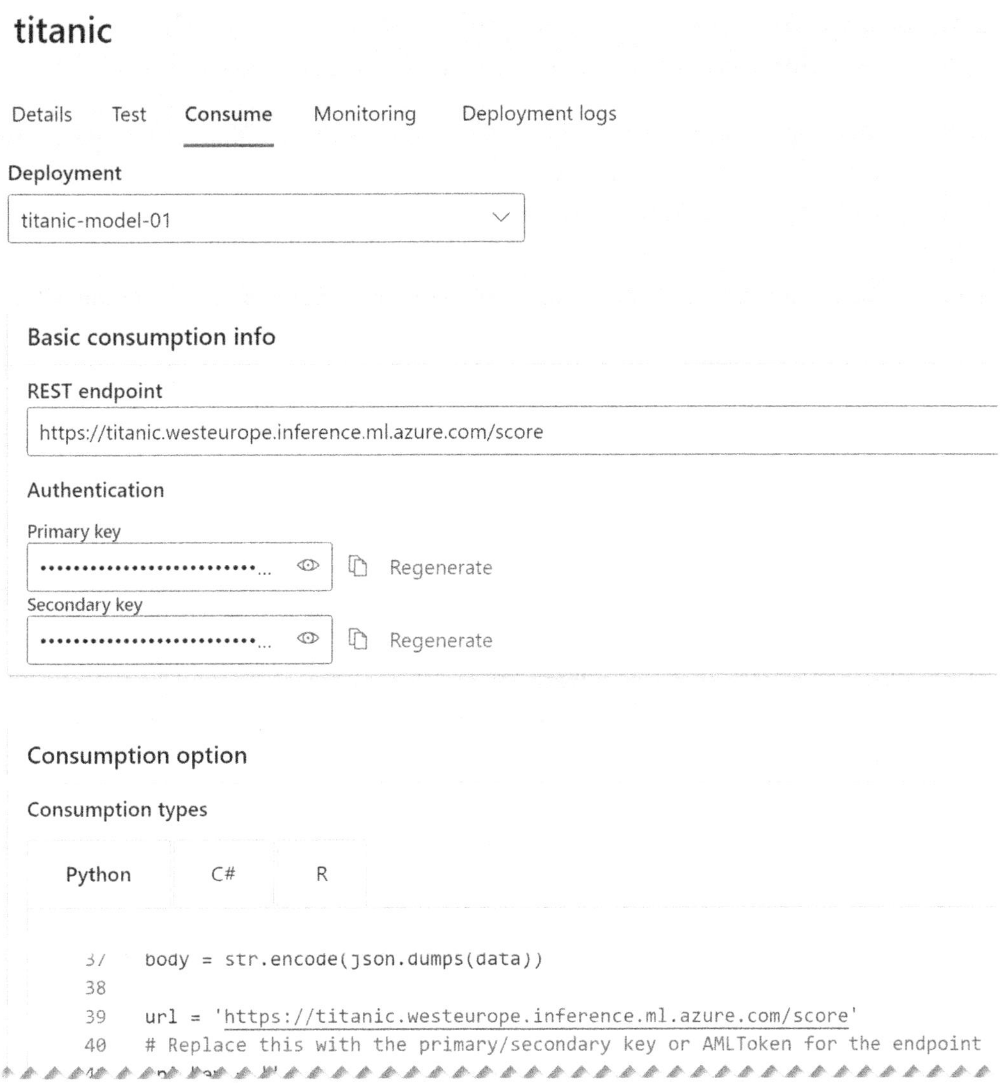

titanic

Details   Test   **Consume**   Monitoring   Deployment logs

Deployment

titanic-model-01	⌄

Basic consumption info

REST endpoint

https://titanic.westeurope.inference.ml.azure.com/score

Authentication

Primary key

•••••••••••••••••••••••...	👁	📋 Regenerate

Secondary key

•••••••••••••••••••••••...	👁	📋 Regenerate

Consumption option

Consumption types

Python	C#	R

```
37    body = str.encode(json.dumps(data))
38
39    url = 'https://titanic.westeurope.inference.ml.azure.com/score'
40    # Replace this with the primary/secondary key or AMLToken for the endpoint
```

Figure 17.37: Consumption details of your real-time endpoint

We will use a variation of this code to score test observations in Power Query.

26. Remember to make a note of the REST endpoint URL and one of the endpoint authentication keys to use in your Python code.

At this point, the model is ready on a web service to be consumed via REST APIs. Now let's use it in Power Query.

Consuming an Azure ML-deployed model in Power BI

Using a variation of the Python code suggested by the **Endpoint Consume** tab in Azure ML Studio, we created a function that takes as parameters the endpoint URL, the API key, and a DataFrame containing the observations to score. In the output, we get a DataFrame containing only the `predicted_proba` column with the probability score of each observation and the `predicted_label` column with the label of each observation (1 or 0). We compare the probabilities with the passed threshold (default is 0.5): if the probability is greater than or equal to the threshold, then the score is 1; otherwise, the score is 0.

Before implementing the code in Power BI, you must assign the endpoint URL and authentication key to the `ENDPOINT_URL` and `ENDPOINT_API_KEY` environment variables, respectively, as you learned in *Chapter 11, Calling External APIs to Enrich Your Data*. You can follow this guide to permanently set up the environment variables on your system: `https://phoenixnap.com/kb/windows-set-environment-variable`. To retrieve the predictions of a test dataset from a model trained with Azure AutoML and deployed as a real-time endpoint in Power BI, follow these steps:

1. Open Power BI Desktop through the shortcut that activates the **pbi_powerquery_env** environment.
2. Make sure Power BI Desktop is referencing the **pbi_powerquery_env** environment in the **Python scripting** tab.
3. Click on **Get data**, then select **Text/CSV**.
4. Select the `titanic-test.csv` file in the `Chapter 17` folder and then click **Open**.
5. You'll see a preview of the test data. Click **Transform Data**.
6. Click **Transform** on the ribbon and then **Run Python script**.
7. Enter the script you can find in the `Python\08-use-azure-ml-web-service-in-power-bi.py` file in the `Chapter 17` folder.
8. We are only interested in the **scored_df** DataFrame. So, click on its **Table** value.
9. You'll see a preview of the test dataset with the additional **predicted_proba** and **predicted_label** columns.
10. Click **Home** on the ribbon and then click **Close & Apply**.

Amazing! You were able to consume a model trained on Azure ML and deploy it to a real-time endpoint without having either a PPU license or a Premium capacity.

Using Azure AI Language in Power Query

Azure AI Language is a cloud-based service that provides NLP capabilities for understanding and analyzing text. You can use this service to build intelligent applications using the web-based Language Studio, REST APIs, and client libraries. The Language service unifies the following previously available Azure AI services: Text Analytics, QnA Maker, and LUIS. It also provides several new features that are either *preconfigured* or *customizable*. Preconfigured features are those whose AI models are not customizable: you simply submit your data and use the feature's output in your applications. Customizable features require you to train an AI model using the Azure AI Language tools to specifically fit your data.

Some of the features provided by Azure AI Language include **named entity recognition (NER)**, detection of **personally identifiable information (PII)** and **personal health information (PHI)**, language detection, sentiment analysis and opinion mining, and summarization.

We will show you how to perform sentiment analysis on some text using Python and the preconfigured templates provided by Azure AI Language. First, however, you need to deploy a new **Language service** through the Azure portal.

Configuring a new Language service

You must have an Azure subscription to use these services. Then you need to create a Language service by following these steps:

1. Go to the Azure portal (`https://portal.azure.com/`) and click on the search resources textbox at the top of the page. Start typing the **language** string in the search textbox and the **Language** option will appear under **Services**. Click on it. After the Language service page is displayed, click on the **Create language** button in the middle of the page.

2. Leave all **Custom features** unselected, and click **Continue to create your resource**.

3. On the **Create Language** page, create a new resource group by clicking on **Create new** and naming it **rg-language-services**. Then select your preferred region and give the service a name (in our case, `textanalytics555`; you can use a unique name of your choice). Then, select the **Free F0** pricing tier, check the **Responsible AI Notice** option, and click on **Review + create**. On the next summary page, click **Create**.

4. When the resource deployment is complete, click on **Go to resource group** and then click on the service name on the next page. Then, click on the **Keys and Endpoint** menu on the left to get access to the service keys. Note the details of one of the two keys of your choice (you can click on the **Copy to clipboard** icon on its right) and the endpoint URL. You'll use this information in your Python code.

Your resource is now ready to be used via the dedicated Python SDK.

Configuring your Python environment and Windows

To consume text analytics, you must first install the **Azure Text Analytics client library for Python** by following these steps:

1. Open Anaconda Prompt.

2. Switch to your PyCaret environment by entering this command: `conda activate pycaret_env`.

3. Install the client library by entering this command: `pip install azure-ai-textanalytics==5.3.0`.

After that, to prevent the *ssl module in Python is not available* error on Windows machines, you need to add the `pycaret_env\Library\bin` path to the Windows environment `PATH` variable. In addition, you need to add the two `LANGUAGE_URL` and `LANGUAGE_API_KEY` system variables to be used in your Python code. These are the steps to do it:

1. Click on the Windows **Start** icon in the lower-left corner of your screen and start typing the **variable** string. Then, click on **Edit the system environment variables**.

2. Click on the Environment Variables... button, then double-click on the **Path** variable under **System variables**. In the **Edit environment variable** dialog that appears, click on the **New** button and add the path `C:\ProgramData\Miniconda3\envs\pycaret_env\Library\bin`. Then, click **OK**.

3. Click the **New...** button to add a new environment variable. Type `LANGUAGE_URL` as the variable name and `https://<your-service-name>.cognitiveservices.azure.com/` as the variable value, replacing `<your-service-name>` with the name you've chosen for your Language service. Then click **OK**.

4. Click the **New...** button to add another environment variable. Type `LANGUAGE_API_KEY` as the variable name and type your service key as the variable value. Then click **OK**.

5. Click **OK** in the **Environment Variables** dialog box, and click **OK** on the **System Properties** dialog box.

6. You must restart your system for the change to take effect.

You are now ready to consume the service from Power Query.

Consuming the Text Analytics API in Power BI

In this section, we will show you how to perform sentiment analysis using a Language service on the fictional company *Fabrikam Fiber*. The company provides cable television and related services in the United States and allows users to leave comments on its website. Your goal is to define the degree of positivity, neutrality, and negativity for each comment.

Basically, once a client is authenticated with a URL and a key, you can easily perform sentiment analysis thanks to the `analyze_sentiment()` method without knowing anything about NLP. Keep in mind that the free tier of Text Analytics is limited to processing only 10 documents (in our case, comments) at a time. For this reason, the code we built consists of grouping the comments into groups of 10 and calling the API for each group.

Let's see how to do that:

1. Open Power BI Desktop from the shortcut you've just created that activates the **pycaret_env** environment.

2. Make sure Power BI Desktop is referencing the **pycaret_env** environment in the Python scripting tab of the **Options** menu.

3. Click on **Get data**, then **Text/CSV**.

4. Select the `FabrikamComments.csv` file in the `Chapter 17` folder and click **Open**.

5. You'll see a preview of the Fabrikam dataset. Then, click **Transform Data**.

6. Click **Transform** on the ribbon, followed by **Run Python script**.

7. Enter the script you can find in the `Python\09-use-text-analytics-in-power-bi.py` file in the `Chapter 17` folder.

8. If you get the Firewall privacy level mismatch error, select a **Public** privacy level for the CSV data source and press **OK**. Then click on **Refresh Preview**. You are prompted to expand a DataFrame calculated in the Python script.

9. We are only interested in the **sentiment_enriched_df** DataFrame. So, click on its **Table** value.
10. You'll see a preview of the Fabrikam dataset enriched with the following additional columns: **comment_sentiment**, **overall_positive_score**, **overall_neutral_score**, and **overall_negative_score**:

comment	comment_sentiment	overall_positive_score	overall_neutral_score	overall_negative_score
I ordered three widgets last week and just received them. I am VERY d...	mixed	0.12	0.11	0.77
Can't believe you fools shipped me the wrong items AGAIN. If you wer...	negative	0.01	0.19	0.8
Wow! I had NO IDEA that reciprocating garombles of such high quality...	mixed	0.49	0.12	0.39
Jake, I've had similar problems tracking down another source of thinga...	mixed	0.29	0.22	0.49
That hand model needs a manicure, stat!	neutral	0.07	0.83	0.1
I put my wedding ring in a Bag of Holding I purchased from you guys (f...	positive	0.54	0.44	0.03
David, sorry, it's whatchamacallits I'm looking for. I should have been ...	negative	0.03	0.18	0.79
Hi folks. According to your encabulator brochure, the hydrocoptic mar...	negative	0.01	0.14	0.85
Jake, it's probably none of my business, but you will probably get a bet...	positive	0.38	0.36	0.26

Figure 17.38: Additional sentiment analysis columns

11. Click **Home** on the ribbon and then click **Close & Apply**.

That's amazing! Thanks to the `azure-ai-textanalytics` Python library, you were able to perform sentiment analysis in just a few lines of code. With the same ease, you can also use the other services that Azure AI Language provides through other Python SDKs in Power BI.

Summary

In this chapter, you learned how Power BI interacts with Microsoft AI services by default through the Power BI Desktop and dataflow features. You also learned that by using AutoML platforms, you can get around the licensing issue (PPU license or Premium capacity) that Power BI presents for interfacing with Microsoft AI services. You used both an on-premises AutoML solution (PyCaret) and Azure AutoML on the cloud to solve a binary classification problem. You also used Azure AI Language to perform some sentiment analysis directly using a Python SDK.

You've learned that AI enrichment is mostly done in Power Query (which provides access to the web using the data gateway), although you've seen a case where it can be convenient to use a ML model directly in a Python visual.

In the next chapter, you will see how to implement data exploration of your dataset in Power BI.

References

For additional reading, check out the following books and articles:

- *Use AI Insights in Power BI Desktop* (`https://learn.microsoft.com/en-us/power-bi/transform-model/desktop-ai-insights`)
- *AI with dataflows* (`https://docs.microsoft.com/en-us/power-bi/transform-model/dataflows/dataflows-machine-learning-integration`)
- *PyCaret repository* (`https://github.com/pycaret/pycaret`)
- *FLAML repository* (`https://github.com/microsoft/FLAML`)
- *A Review of Azure Automated Machine Learning (AutoML)* (`https://medium.com/microsoftazure/a-review-of-azure-automated-machine-learning-automl-5d2f98512406`)

- *Automated Machine Learning with Microsoft Azure, by Dennis Michael Sawyers, Packt Publishing* (`https://www.amazon.com/Automated-Machine-Learning-Microsoft-Azure/dp/1800565313/`)
- *A Gentle Introduction to Concept Drift in Machine Learning* (`https://machinelearningmastery.com/gentle-introduction-concept-drift-machine-learning/`)
- *Machine Learning Basics with the K-Nearest Neighbors Algorithm* (`https://towardsdatascience.com/machine-learning-basics-with-the-k-nearest-neighbors-algorithm-6a6e71d01761`)
- *Python's "predict_proba" Doesn't Actually Predict Probabilities (and How to Fix It)* (`https://towardsdatascience.com/pythons-predict-proba-doesn-t-actually-predict-probabilities-and-how-to-fix-it-f582c21d63fc`)
- *Use the Interpretability Package to Explain ML Models and Predictions in Python* (`https://docs.microsoft.com/en-us/azure/machine-learning/how-to-machine-learning-interpretability-aml`)
- *Get Started with Tidymodels* (`https://www.tidymodels.org/start/`)

Test your knowledge

1. What AutoML solution language is recommended for Power BI analysts to use?
2. What precautions should you take when incorporating training code into Power Query?
3. What is the benefit of FLAML's AutoML feature in terms of model compatibility?
4. What is the importance of having a working scoring function in Power Query when using a serialized ML model?
5. How can you solve the delay problem caused by training the model directly in Power Query?
6. Why is it recommended to train and manage ML models outside of Power BI?
7. What is the purpose of being able to score a dataset within Script Visual?
8. How can I interact with third-party ML models in Power Query if I do not have the serialized model?
9. Why can't you consume external services via REST API calls from a Python or R visual in Power BI?
10. What is Azure AI Language and what services does it provide?

Learn more on Discord

To join the Discord community for this book – where you can share feedback, ask questions to the author, and learn about new releases – follow the QR code below:

`https://discord.gg/MKww5g45EB`

18

Using SQL Server External Languages for Advanced Analytics and ML Integration in Power BI

As we dive into this chapter, you may find the topic a bit tangential at first. The primary focus of this book is on using the Python and R analytics engines within Power BI to add valuable insights to our reports. However, in this chapter, we will explore a different avenue by examining how we can use the Python and R analytic engines configured within SQL Server (or Azure SQL Managed Instance). Why explore this alternative approach? Well, when you're dealing with Microsoft's **relational database management system** (**RDBMS**) as one of your report data sources, it's worth considering because integrating these analytics directly into the database layer can significantly streamline your data processing workflows, enhance the performance of your data analytics, and provide a more seamless and efficient way to generate insights directly from your data source, reducing the need for data movement and enabling more real-time analytics.

It's interesting to note that the technology used by SQL Server allows not only Python and R, but also Java and C# to be integrated into the database engine itself. While the prospect of maintaining an instance with all of these components may not appeal to all database administrators, it's important to understand that these languages are primarily used within an external platform that is integrated as a data source in a Power BI report. Therefore, if we use Java or C# in a SQL Server stored procedure and we import the output result set into Power BI, we cannot say that Power BI directly enables the use of Java and C#.

Now, you may be wondering why we devoted an entire chapter to using Python and R in an external platform rather than focusing solely on Power BI. The reason for this decision is twofold. First, SQL Server is one of the most widely used components within data architectures built on the Microsoft stack.

Therefore, understanding its capabilities for working with Python and R in conjunction with Power BI is highly beneficial. Second, there are situations where certain limitations prevent the use of Python and R within Power BI. However, by using Python and R within SQL Server and then importing the pre-processed dataset into Power BI, we can work around these limitations.

This chapter does not attempt to cover every conceivable use case involving SQL Server, as that would take up a large portion of this book. Instead, we will focus on the basic principles that enable SQL Server to run external code. We will cover configuring the engine to run Python and R code, and we will highlight scenarios where integrating Python or R code directly into SQL Server may prove more advantageous than implementing the same use case in Power BI alone. That being said, the following topics will be covered:

- Introducing SQL Server Machine Learning Services
- Installing Python and R custom runtimes for SQL Server
- The need for external languages with Power BI
- Using external languages with Power BI

Technical requirements

This chapter requires you to have a working internet connection and Power BI Desktop already installed on your machine (version: 2.121.644.0 64-bit, September 2023). You must have properly configured the R and Python engines and IDEs as outlined in *Chapter 2*, *Configuring R with Power BI*, and *Chapter 3*, *Configuring Python with Power BI*. In addition, you must have properly configured SQL Server Express as outlined in *Chapter 8*, *Logging Data from Power BI to External Sources*.

Introducing SQL Server Machine Learning Services

SQL Server Machine Learning Services is an in-database technology that enables advanced analytics and machine learning directly in Microsoft SQL Server. By integrating advanced algorithms and machine learning models into SQL Server, users can process and analyze large volumes of data without having to move it to a separate analytics platform.

Prior to the introduction of Machine Learning Services, the only way to integrate external data processing via Python or R into a transformation pipeline was to run external code that would read the data from the SQL Server instance via **open database connectivity** (**ODBC**) and then write the output to a staging table in case the processed data was needed for further processing in SQL Server. An example of a framework that arose to integrate processing done with R and SQL Server before the advent of Machine Learning Services is the one developed by Tomaz Kastrun, which is available at this link: https://bit.ly/manual-r-integration-sql. It is evident how complicated it was to configure it to allow this integration. Machine Learning Services mitigated the obvious problems that arose with the aforementioned "manual" integration, namely:

- *Data security* is enhanced because the execution of external language scripts takes place within SQL Server itself. This eliminates the need to move sensitive data to external platforms, minimizing the risk of data breaches or unauthorized access. By keeping analysis close to the data source, organizations can ensure the confidentiality and integrity of their data.

- *Speed* is another major benefit provided by SQL Server Machine Learning Services. The inherent optimization of databases for set-based operations allows for efficient processing of large volumes of data. By harnessing the power of SQL Server's built-in capabilities, users can perform complex analytical tasks without sacrificing performance.

- Ease of *deployment and integration* is a key benefit of using SQL Server Machine Learning Services. SQL Server serves as a central hub for various data management tasks and applications within an organization. Leveraging the data residing in the database ensures compatibility and consistency between the language extension and the data being analyzed.

The tool that allows Machine Learning Services to execute Python or R code using external engines is the SQL Server *Extensibility Framework*.

 Machine Learning Services is only available in SQL Server (on-premises) and in **Azure SQL Managed Instance**, a **platform-as-a-service (PaaS)** offering with near-perfect compatibility with the latest SQL Server database engine in Enterprise Edition.

Let's take a closer look at what this is all about.

The Extensibility Framework to run Python and R scripts

The **Extensibility Framework** of SQL Server Machine Learning Services gives you the powerful ability to execute code in an external language runtime environment directly from within SQL Server. This framework allows you to run scripts in languages such as R or Python outside of the core database engine. You can easily invoke the external runtime environment through a stored procedure called `sp_execute_external_script`. This stored procedure acts as a bridge, facilitating communication between SQL Server and the external runtime.

Without going into too much architectural detail, let's say that from version 2016 through version 2019, Microsoft used proprietary components that allowed the SQL Server service responsible for communicating with external engines (the **Launchpad process**) to run Python and R scripts. In fact, when you install Machine Learning Services from SQL Server Setup and also select the Python and R options as languages, you are actually installing the proprietary components that were mentioned previously:

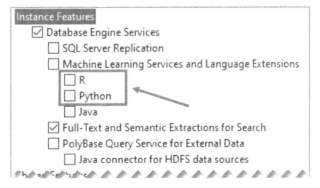

Figure 18.1: Proprietary components for communicating with Python and R engines

These components provide Python version 3.7.1 and R version 3.5.2 in SQL Server 2019. In addition, starting with version 2019, Microsoft was able to introduce Java as an additional language in SQL Server by using an additional component in the basic Extensibility Framework architecture: the **External Host process**. Basically, thanks to the External Host, it was possible to add any external compiled language such as Java using the Extensibility Framework API. Such languages are commonly called **external languages**. Within a short time, Microsoft open sourced the Java Extension API, along with the Language Extensions, including files. Soon after, the open source Language Extensions for Python and R were also released (`https://github.com/microsoft/sql-server-language-extensions`), allowing newer versions of the engines to be linked to SQL Server.

So here it is, starting with SQL Server 2019 with **Cumulative Update** 3 (CU3) (a rollup of several hotfixes tested as a group), it is possible to manually install newer versions of the Python and R engines thanks to the Extensibility Framework and the open source Language Extensions.

 Beware of installing the Python and R languages directly from SQL Server Setup, because, until version 2019, there will always be the aforementioned proprietary components for Python and R with outdated versions.

Starting with SQL Server 2022, you will no longer be able to install the proprietary components for Python and R from the setup wizard; you will need to manually install the engines and manually connect them to SQL Server. Therefore, the process of installing external languages in SQL Server 2022 has some additional installation tasks compared to SQL Server 2019 (see *References* for details).

So, let's see how we install our custom Python and R runtimes on SQL Server.

Installing Python and R custom runtimes for SQL Server

In *Chapter 8, Logging Data from Power BI to External Sources*, you installed an instance of SQL Server 2019 to test its ability to use Python and R to log information from Power BI. Our goal now is to install the latest Python and R engines on SQL Server 2019. As mentioned in the previous section, we need to have at least SQL Server 2019 with at least CU3 installed. We assume that you have system administrator privileges on your machine. So, let's take a look at how to do it.

Updating SQL Server

Referring to the SQL Server 2019 builds table (available at `https://bit.ly/sqlserver2019-build-numbers`), you can see that the minimum allowed version corresponding to CU3 is `15.0.4023.6`:

SQL Server 2019 Cumulative Update (CU) builds

CU Name	SQL Server build version	SQL Server (sqlservr.exe) file version	Analysis Services build version	Analysis Services (msmdsrv.exe) file version	Knowledge Base number	Release date
CU22 (Latest)	15.0.4322.2	2019.150.4322.2	15.0.35.41	2018.150.35.41	KB5027702	August 14, 2023
CU3	15.0.4023.6	2019.15.0.4023.6	15.0.34.9	2018.150.34.9	KB4538853	March 12, 2020
CU2	15.0.4013.40	2019.15.0.4013.40	15.0.34.1	2018.150.34.1	KB4536075	February 13, 2020
CU1	15.0.4003.23	2019.150.4003.23	15.0.32.52	2018.150.32.52	KB4527376	January 07, 2020
RTM	15.0.2000.5	2019.150.2000.5	15.0.32.50	2018.150.32.50	SQL Server 2019 release notes	November 04, 2019

Figure 18.2: Minimum SQL Server build version number to install

Therefore, the first step is to check which SQL Server build version you have installed. To do this, follow these steps:

1. Open the **SQL Server Management Studio (SSMS)** app.

2. You are prompted to connect to an instance of SQL Server. You have already installed the default instance (MSSQLSERVER) on your machine by following the instructions in *Chapter 8*. So, make sure you connect to the **.** SQL Server instance (the default one) using Windows Authentication:

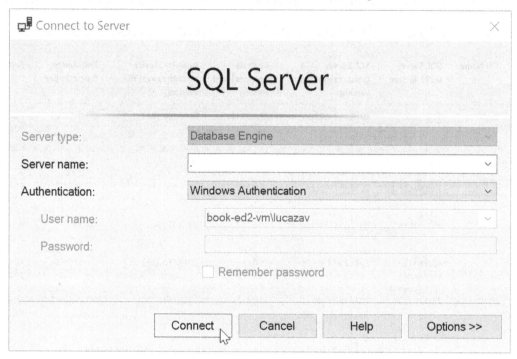

Figure 18.3: Connect to your local SQL Server instance

3. Once it is connected, in **Object Explorer** on the left, you can see the SQL Server build version in three parts:

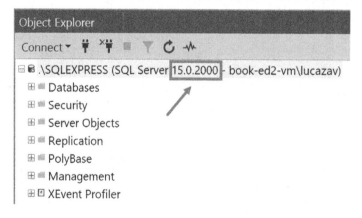

Figure 18.4: SQL Server build version in three parts

4. If you also want to see the fourth part of the build version, you must click **New Query** to write a new query, write the SELECT @@version script, and click **Execute**:

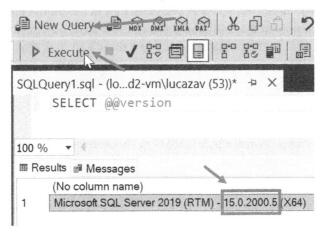

Figure 18.5: SQL Server build version in four parts

In our case, the installed build of SQL Server 2019 is the **release To manufacturing** (RTM) version (15.0.2000.5), which is the initial version of SQL Server 2019 without any hotfixes or cumulative updates (CUs). Therefore, you must install any CU greater than or equal to 3 to have the ability to link a custom Python or R runtime to SQL Server 2019. Let's see how you install the latest CU:

1. Go to the latest SQL Server updates page at this link: https://bit.ly/sqlserver-updates.

2. Click the most recent CU for SQL Server 2019 (in our case, CU22):

Figure 18.6: Download the latest CU for SQL Server 2019

3. On the page that opens, click **How to obtain or download the latest cumulative update package for Windows (recommended)** to expand the section, and then click the **Download the latest cumulative update package for SQL Server 2019 now** link.

4. The official download page for the latest CU for SQL Server 2019 (version 15.0.4322.2) opens. Click **Download** to download the installation package and save it on your machine.

5. Run the CU22 installation package. You will be asked to accept the license agreement. Check the box and click **Next**.

6. On the next screen, the installer identifies the current installation and automatically selects the checkbox for the identified instance to be updated. Click **Next**.

7. The installer checks the SQL Server service files in use on the machine to determine which can be restarted automatically and which can be restarted manually to avoid a machine reboot. We are going to do the restart anyway, so go ahead and click **Next**.

8. The next screen displays a summary of the items that will be updated. Click **Update** to proceed with the upgrade.

9. When the update is complete, a message will appear to remind you to restart your computer. Close all applications and restart the operating system.

10. After your computer restarts, use SSMS to check the SQL Server version again to verify that the upgrade was successful.

Great! You've just updated your SQL Server 2019 instance to the latest available build. Let's take a look at how you can add the Machine Learning Services component to SQL Server 2019.

Installing Machine Learning Services and Language Extensions

If you followed the instructions we gave you in *Chapter 8* about which features to install in addition to the database engine, the *Machine Learning Services and Language Extensions* option was unchecked, as shown in *Figure 18.7*. So, you need to install this feature, which will then allow you to integrate Python and R custom runtimes with SQL Server. These are the steps to do so:

1. On the machine where you installed the SQL Server 2019 instance, open the **Start** menu, locate the **Microsoft SQL Server 2019** program group, and click **SQL Server 2019 Installation Center (64-bit)**:

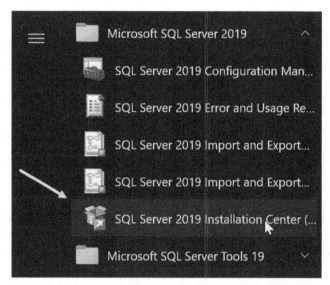

Figure 18.7: Open SQL Server 2019 Installation Center

2. Click on the **Installation** tab on the left and then select **New SQL Server stand-alone installation or add features to an existing installation:**

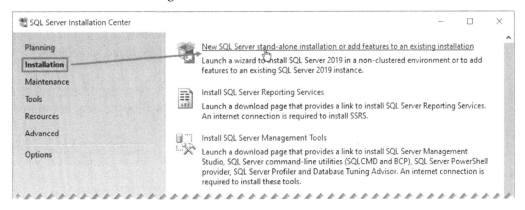

Figure 18.8: Add new features to the SQL Server 2019 instance

3. You are prompted to select the folder where the SQL Server Setup file is located. During the instance installation, the process created a supporting setup folder in the C:\ root. In our case, the folder that contains the SETUP.EXE file is C:\SQL2019\ExpressAdv_ENU:

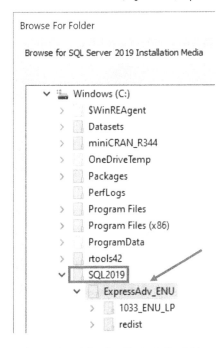

Figure 18.9: Selecting the installer folder

Select the **ExpressAdv_ENU** folder and click **OK.**

4. On the next screen, select the option to use Microsoft Update to check for updates, and then click **Next.**

5. The process checks the setup files and then attempts to identify any potential problems. Only a warning about Windows Firewall will be displayed to inform you that remote access to your SQL Server instance might not be possible. This is not a problem in our case, so you can click **Next**.

6. You need to add a new feature to the SQL Server instance installed on your computer, so select **Add features to an existing instance of SQL Server 2019**, make sure the default instance (**MSSQLSERVER**) is selected, and click **Next**.

7. On the next screen, select only the **Machine Learning Services and Language Extensions** option. *Do not* select either **R** or **Python** as you will be installing the custom runtimes later:

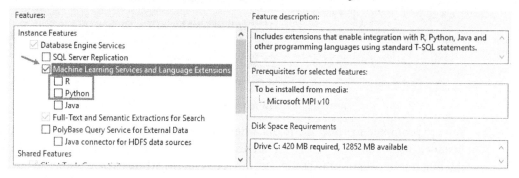

Figure 18.10: Adding the Machine Learning Services and Language Extensions feature

8. A recommendation about service accounts is shown on the next screen. Click **Next**.

9. You'll receive a successful status message when the installation finishes successfully. Click **Close**.

Great! You have just installed the components to connect the latest Python and R custom runtimes to SQL Server.

 Until recently, there was a bug in Machine Learning Services that did not allow scripts to run in the intended languages if the SQL Server instance was a named instance. It appears that the bug has been fixed, at least in SQL Server 2022. See the references for more details.

Now, let's install the Python runtime compatible with SQL Server.

Installing the Python runtime

The first thing you might wonder is why it is necessary to install a new Python runtime when we have been working with the various Miniconda environments so far. The problem is the same one you encountered when setting up Power BI and Python in *Chapter 4, Solving Common Issues When Using Python and R in Power BI*: the need to activate a Conda environment before you can use it. This is why even the Microsoft documentation on installing a custom Python runtime (see the **References**) suggests installing the standard Python distribution (www.python.org). We could have used a batch file to first enable the correct Conda environment and then run the SQL Server service, just as we did with Python, but in this case, it is better to follow a standard so as not to violate any corporate policies a SQL Server **database administrator** (**DBA**) may have to follow.

To decide which version of Python you need to install, you need to see which version is supported by the latest Python language extension released. In our case, the latest version is 1.2.0, which supports up to Python 3.10 (`https://bit.ly/python-language-extension-120`). We then install the latest compatible version.

At the time of writing, the latest version of Python 3.10 is 3.10.13. Unfortunately, this version, which contains only security fixes, does not provide an installer for Windows. The latest version that does have an installer is 3.10.11. If you find a version of Python 3.10.x that has a Windows installer for an *x* (called a patch in a three-part version number) greater than 11, you can safely install it. Anything we say about version 3.10.11 will be valid for a newer version as well. So, let's continue with the installation of this version:

1. Go to the Python 3.10.11 release page at `https://www.python.org/downloads/release/python-31011/`.

2. Scroll to the bottom of the page and click the **Windows installer (64-bit)** download link:

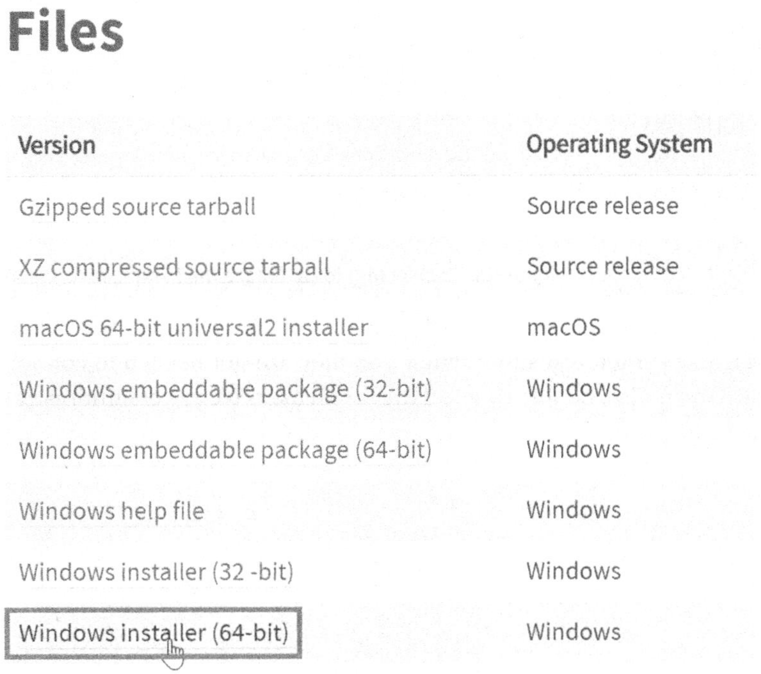

Files

Version	Operating System
Gzipped source tarball	Source release
XZ compressed source tarball	Source release
macOS 64-bit universal2 installer	macOS
Windows embeddable package (32-bit)	Windows
Windows embeddable package (64-bit)	Windows
Windows help file	Windows
Windows installer (32 -bit)	Windows
Windows installer (64-bit)	Windows

Figure 18.11: Downloading the Python 3.10.11 installer for Windows

3. Once the file is downloaded, run it. The first screen will ask if you want to continue with a basic or custom installation. Be sure to select **Add python.exe to PATH** first, and then click **Customize installation:**

Figure 18.12: Selecting to customize the Python installation

4. The next screen allows you to select some optional features. You can uncheck the **tcl/tk and IDLE** and **Python test suite** options, as they are not needed to connect a Python engine to SQL Server. Also, be sure to select the **for all users (requires administrator privileges)** option. Then click **Next**.

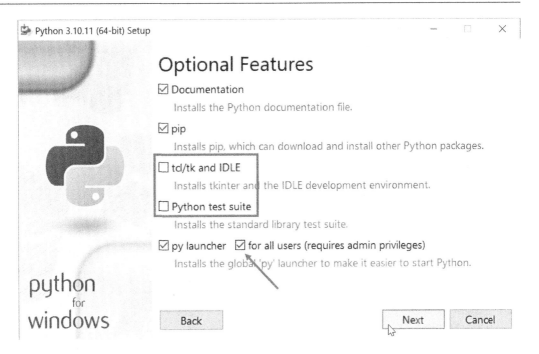

Figure 18.13: Selecting the optional features

5. You can then select the advanced options. Make sure that **Install Python 3.10 for all users** and **Add Python to environment variables** are checked. You can uncheck the two options regarding debugging tools. Also, take note of the path where the binaries will be installed:

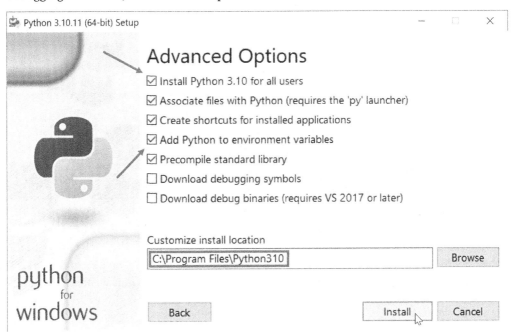

Figure 18.14: Selecting the advanced options

6. On the last screen, if the installation was successful, you have the option to disable the annoying limitation in Windows that prohibits paths longer than 260 characters. Select it and click **Close**:

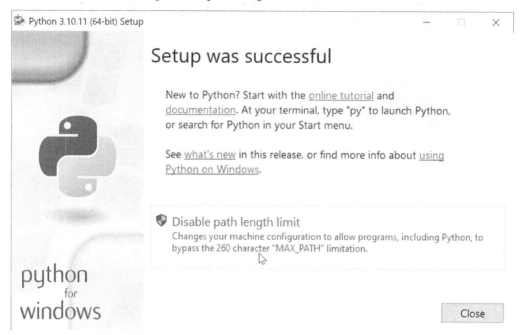

Figure 18.15: Disabling the path length limit

Great! You have installed the latest version of Python that is compatible with SQL Server 2019.

If you now open a command prompt with administrator privileges and run `pip -V` from any path to see the version of pip, you can verify that pip is installed with Python 3.10:

```
Administrator: Command Prompt
Microsoft Windows [Version 10.0.20348.1249]
(c) Microsoft Corporation. All rights reserved.

C:\Users\lucazav>pip -V
pip 23.0.1 from C:\Program Files\Python310\lib\site-packages\pip (python 3.10)

C:\Users\lucazav>
```

Figure 18.16: Checking the pip version

pip from Python 3.10 is automatically used because the path to it is in the PATH environment variable. Then, to install a package in the base installation of Python 3.10, simply type `pip install <package-name>` from the simple command prompt. Give it a try by installing pandas with `pip install pandas`!

Now, let's install the R runtime to connect to SQL Server.

Installing the R runtime

The latest R language extension available at the time of writing is 1.2.0 (`https://github.com/microsoft/sql-server-language-extensions/releases/tag/R-v1.2.0`), which supports R from version 3.3 to the latest one. Since the suggested distribution for SQL Server is CRAN R, you can use the latest version you have been using (4.2.2 in our case) for R scripts at this point.

While the Python installer takes care of adding the path to the engine folder to the PATH environment variable, the R installer does not. Therefore, you must manually add the R engine path to the PATH variable. You should be familiar with adding and editing environment variables by now. For completeness, here are the necessary steps:

1. Click on the **Start** menu, type `environment`, and click on **Edit the system environment variables.**
2. Click on the **Environment Variables...** button an the bottom-right of the System Properties window.
3. Select the **PATH** variable in the **System variables** list and click **Edit.**
4. Click the **New** button and add the path to the \bin\x64 folder of your R installation path. In our case, the path is `C:\Program Files\R\R-4.2.2\bin\x64`. Click **OK.**
5. Click **OK** in the **Environment Variables** window, and then click **OK** in the **System Properties** window.

For proper integration between SQL Server and R, the **Rcpp** package must be installed in the engine, allowing you to seamlessly integrate C++ code into your R projects for efficiency and performance. Even if the engine you have been using already has this package installed, here are the steps to follow if you are installing a new engine:

1. Run the RGui you just installed (in our case, the **R x64 4.2.2** application, which you can find in the recently added applications or the R application group).
2. Enter the following command and press **Enter:** `install.packages("Rcpp")`.
3. You may be asked to select which CRAN mirror to use to download the package if it's the first package you're installing. Leave CRAN mirror **0-Cloud [https]** selected and click **OK.**
4. At the end of the installation, close the RGui without saving the workspace image when prompted.

So, we have the SQL Server engine and the Python and R engines working. We just need to configure them so that they can talk to each other. Let's see how to do that.

Configuring the SQL Server Language Extensions

In the previous sections, we anticipated that the main actor in the communication between SQL Server and external languages is the Launchpad service, which in turn calls the `ExtHost.exe` service, delegated to run code on an external language.

Therefore, the configurations that must be made for Python and R code to run from SQL Server are twofold:

1. Make the Launchpad service and anything it runs in **AppContainers** for isolation issues (see *References* for details) have read and execute permissions on the Python 3.10 and R 4.2.2 installation folders and their subfolders.

2. Install the latest version of SQL Server Language Extensions required to run Python and R from SQL Server, reference them using T-SQL commands, and test a sample script.

Let's look at what needs to be done in detail.

Granting access to Launchpad

The **Integrity Control Access Control List** (**icacls**) command in Windows allows you to change the permissions of a directory by granting specific permissions.

Open an elevated command prompt and run the following commands to give the Launchpad service access to the Python 3.10 and R 4.2.2 installation folders:

```
icacls "C:\Program Files\Python310" /grant "NT Service\MSSQLLAUNCHPAD":(OI)(CI)
RX /T
```

```
icacls "C:\Program Files\R\R-4.2.2" /grant "NT Service\MSSQLLAUNCHPAD":(OI)(CI)
RX /T
```

The *object inherit* (OI) and *container inherit* (CI) parameters ensure that permissions are granted to all files and subfolders. The permission types granted are *read* (R) and *execute* (X). The /T flag is used to perform the operation on all specified files in the current directory and its subdirectories.

Now, you need to do the same thing for AppContainers. There is the **ALL APPLICATION PACKAGES** group that is part of the security context for Windows Store applications running in these containers. Since the **security identifier** (**SID**) that identifies the **ALL APPLICATION PACKAGES** security group is S-1-15-2-1, the same grants that were given to the Launchpad service must also be given to this SID with the following commands:

```
icacls "C:\Program Files\Python310" /grant *S-1-15-2-1:(OI)(CI)RX /T
```

```
icacls "C:\Program Files\R\R-4.2.2" /grant *S-1-15-2-1:(OI)(CI)RX /T
```

You could also have assigned access to this folder to the same NT Service\MSSQLLAUNCHPAD and ALL APPLICATION PACKAGES users via the GUI using the folder properties. For example, you can check the Security properties of the Python310 folder after running the preceding commands:

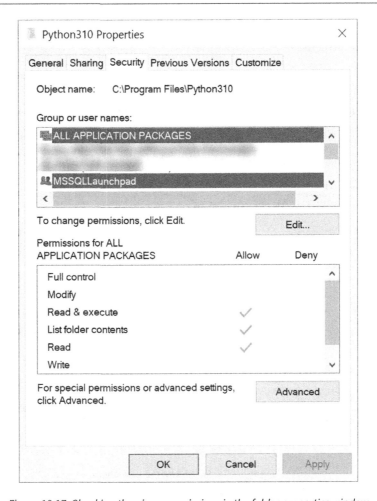

Figure 18.17: Checking the given permissions in the folder properties window

These may not be the only grant activities you need to perform:

If the external language script needs to access a specific folder in the file system for business-related purposes, you must also give the preceding permissions (for both the NT Service\MSSQLLAUNCHPAD and ALL APPLICATION PACKAGES users) to the folder that the engine needs to access. Consider adding write permission (**W**) to the folder as well, if necessary.

For the new permissions assigned to Launchpad to take effect, you must restart the service. Here are the steps to do this correctly:

1. Open the **SQL Server Configuration Manager** application in the **Microsoft SQL Server 2019** application group.

2. Click the **SQL Server Services** option on the left, right-click on **SQL Server Launchpad (MS-SQLSERVER)**, and then click **Restart**.

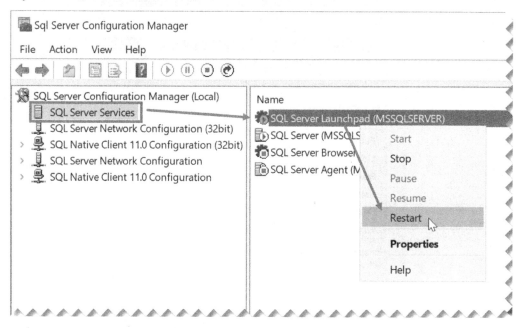

Figure 18.18: Restarting the Launchpad service

Once we've ensured that the services can access the analytics engine folders and any other folders for business needs, we'll install and configure the Language Extensions for Python and R.

Configuring the Language Extensions

To download and register the Python and R Language Extensions, follow these steps:

1. Download the latest version of SQL Server Language Extensions for Python and R from this link: `https://github.com/microsoft/sql-server-language-extensions/releases`. The files you need to download are `python-lang-extension-windows-release.zip` and `R-lang-extension-windows-release.zip`. You can find them in the **Assets** section of each language. These ZIP files contain the DLL used to let external engines communicate with SQL Server, `pythonextension.dll` and `libRExtension.dll` respectively.

2. Make sure you save these files in a folder that SQL Server has access to; in our case, we created a new folder: `C:\LanguageExtensions`.

Now, it's time to register the external Language Extensions in the database from the specified file paths. Each new external language has a specific name that identifies it in SQL Server.

The names "R" and "Python" are reserved and cannot be used to create your external languages with these exact identifiers. It's also important to note that names are case sensitive in this context.

In our case, we use py310 and r422 as external language names. Let's configure them using T-SQL:

1. Open **SQL Server Management Studio** and login to the default instance you created in *Chapter 8* using a . (dot) as the server name. Then, click **New Query** in the top command bar.

2. The first command you will use is CREATE EXTERNAL LANGUAGE, which allows you to register external Language Extensions in the database. The parameters accepted by the command specify the ZIP file to associate with the external language, the DLL file to reference in the ZIP archive, and any environment variables. These are set before the external process is started. This makes it possible to dynamically assign, for example, the Python or R HOME variables used by the external language. Here is the command to create the Python external language:

```
CREATE EXTERNAL LANGUAGE [py310]
FROM (CONTENT = N'C:\LanguageExtensions\python-lang-extension-windows-
release.zip',
    FILE_NAME = 'pythonextension.dll',
    ENVIRONMENT_VARIABLES = N'{"PYTHONHOME": "C:\\Program Files\\
Python310"}');
GO
```

Note that environment variables are passed as a dictionary in a string.

3. The corresponding command to create the external language associated with the R runtime is as follows:

```
CREATE EXTERNAL LANGUAGE [r422]
FROM (CONTENT = N'C:\LanguageExtensions\R-lang-extension-windows-release.
zip',
    FILE_NAME = 'libRExtension.dll',
    ENVIRONMENT_VARIABLES = N'{"R_HOME": "C:\\Program Files\\
R\\R-4.2.2"}');
GO
```

4. You need to enable external scripts in your instance with this script:

```
sp_configure 'external scripts enabled', 1;
RECONFIGURE WITH OVERRIDE;
```

5. The sys.external_languages catalog view allows you to verify that external languages have been created correctly:

```
SELECT * FROM sys.external_languages;
```

The output will be as follows:

	external_language_id	language	create_date	principal_id
1	1	R	2023-09-16 12:48:44.800	4
2	2	Python	2023-09-16 12:48:44.803	4
3	65537	py310	2023-09-16 13:24:34.830	1
4	65539	r422	2023-09-17 13:08:32.377	1

Figure 18.19: The newly created external languages

Great! Now, you're ready to run some sample Python and R scripts from SQL Server.

The tool in T-SQL that allows you to execute a script written in a supported language is the system-stored procedure sp_execute_external_script. The essential input parameters for a quick test of the success of the configuration are the external language identifier and the string containing the script to execute. To test the correct Python configuration, run this script:

```
EXEC sp_execute_external_script
@language =N'py310',
@script=N'
import sys
print(sys.path)
print(sys.version)
print(sys.executable)';
```

The output should look like this:

```
Messages
    STDOUT message(s) from external script:
    ['', 'C:/Program Files/Microsoft SQL Server/MSSQL15.MSSQLSERVER/MSSQL/ExternalLibraries/1/65537/1',
    3.10.11 (tags/v3.10.11:7d4cc5a, Apr  5 2023, 00:38:17) [MSC v.1929 64 bit (AMD64)]
    C:\Program Files\Microsoft SQL Server\MSSQL15.MSSQLSERVER\MSSQL\Binn\exthost.exe


    Completion time: 2023-09-18T13:42:10.4837366+00:00
```

Figure 18.20: Output of the Python script

Wow! This means that Python is configured correctly. Now, let's do the same test with R:

```
EXEC sp_execute_external_script
    @language =N'r422',
    @script=N'
print(R.home());
print(file.path(R.home("bin"), "R"));
print(R.version);
print("Hello RExtension!");'
```

Here is the output:

```
Messages
   STDOUT message(s) from external script:
   [1] "��C:/Program Files/R/R-4.2.2��"
   [1] "��C:/Program Files/R/R-4.2.2/bin/x64/R��"
                   ��_��
   ��platform��        ��x86_64-w64-mingw32��
   ��arch��           ��x86_64��
   ��os��             ��mingw32��
   ��crt��            ��ucrt��
   ��system��         ��x86_64, mingw32��
   ��status��         ����
   ��major��          ��4��
   ��minor��          ��2.2��
   ��year��           ��2022��
   ��month��          ��10��
   ��day��            ��31��
   ��svn rev��        ��83211��
   ��language��       ��R��
   ��version.string�� ��R version 4.2.2 (2022-10-31 ucrt)��
   ��nicknam
   STDOUT message(s) from external script:
   e��          ��Innocent and Trusting��
   [1] "��Hello RExtension!��"

   Completion time: 2023-09-18T13:46:03.4143176+00:00
```

Figure 18.21: Output of the R script

As you can see, there is a display problem due to string encoding, because R produces output in UTF-8, but SMSS expects *stdout* (console) output to be in UTF-16. However, this is a known problem of the R language extension 1.2.0 that does not affect the operation of the engine. Again, we can say that R was configured correctly!

The T-SQL scripts used in this section are all collected in the 01-configure-ml-services-python-R.sql file in the Chapter 18 folder.

One thing to keep in mind that often gets lost is the following:

The **CREATE EXTERNAL LANGUAGE** statement creates an external language specifically in the database on which the query is executed. In particular, since no database has been created in the instance yet, by default a query is executed on the master database. This means that the external languages we create exist only in the master database. If you need the ability to run Python and R scripts on a different database, you must run **CREATE EXTERNAL LANGUAGE** queries on that database too.

You have noticed that to execute a script via external languages, you need to call the system-stored procedure `sp_execute_external_script`. Let's take a closer look at this.

A closer look at sp_execute_external_script

The `sp_execute_external_script` system-stored procedure is the tool needed to execute a script provided as an input argument to the procedure itself via Machine Learning Services and Language Extensions. For the sake of simplicity, our examples will be in Python, but everything said applies to R as well. So, let's take a closer look at the parameters the stored procedure provides to handle input and output data.

Understanding input and output parameters

The runtimes used must first be defined using the CREATE EXTERNAL LANGUAGE statement, then they can be referenced by the stored procedure by passing the name of the external language as the `@language` parameter. This way, the stored procedure will execute the script using the supported external language.

In general, a Python or R script applies more or less complex transformations to an input dataframe. The `sp_execute_external_script` accepts two parameters, `@input_data_1` and `@input_data_1_name`, which allow you to specify the input dataframe and the name of the variable to which it is referenced within the script, respectively.

For example, suppose you want to count the rows in the `sys.configurations` system view of your SQL Server instance in Python. You could do this:

```
EXEC sp_execute_external_script
@language = N'py310',
@script = N'
import pandas as pd
print(configs_df.shape[0])',
@input_data_1 = N'SELECT configuration_id, name FROM sys.configurations',
@input_data_1_name = N'configs_df';
```

If you print the result to the standard Python output stream, you will see the output in the **Messages** tab of SSMS:

```
Messages
    STDOUT message(s) from external script:
    83

    Completion time: 2023-09-23T11:38:44.0267066+00:00
```

Figure 18.22: Output of the row count calculation in Messages

Great! There are 83 configurations in our instance. This value may not match what you get on your instance. In that case, this is not a problem; you simply have a different number of configurations.

Based on how we formatted the string representing the Python code in the previous SQL script, the following applies:

 Since a Python script is sensitive to indentation, it always pays to insert the code in the `@script` parameter, aligning everything left in the SSMS editor to avoid execution errors.

This way you can see the output as a message in SSMS, but what if you want to reuse this data in a later data stream instead? This can be done by passing the result of a script variable to a SQL Server variable thanks to the `@params` argument and the `OUTPUT` parameters of the `sp_execute_external_script` stored procedure. Once you have defined the `@row_count` variable in SQL Server, you can use the `row_count` variable in your script and then declare it first in `@params` and then as an `OUTPUT` parameter. Let's see how to do this:

```
DECLARE @row_count INT;

EXEC sp_execute_external_script
@language = N'py310',
@script = N'
import pandas as pd
row_count = configs_df.shape[0]
print(row_count)',
@input_data_1 = N'SELECT configuration_id, name FROM sys.configurations',
@input_data_1_name = N'configs_df',
@params = N'@row_count INT OUTPUT',
@row_count = @row_count OUTPUT;

SELECT NumRows = @row_count;
```

Besides as a message, you can now see the output in **Results** because of the use of the variable in the last `SELECT`:

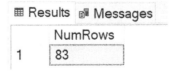

Figure 18.23: Output of the row count calculation in Results

However, it is often necessary to apply transformations to the input dataframe and output the transformed result set. The stored procedure `sp_execute_external_script` has the ability to generate output also in the result set format (i.e., a Python or R-side dataframe). By default, you simply associate the transformed dataframe with the `OutputDataSet` variable in your script to get a result set as output from the stored procedure.

For example, suppose you want to add the id_name column to the output result set that is given by the concatenation of configuration_id and name. Here is how to do that:

```
EXEC sp_execute_external_script
@language = N'py310',
@script = N'
import pandas as pd
configs_df["id_name"] = configs_df["configuration_id"].astype(str) + configs_
df["name"]
OutputDataSet = configs_df',
@input_data_1 = N'SELECT configuration_id, name FROM sys.configurations',
@input_data_1_name = N'configs_df';
```

The output is as follows:

▦ Results ▦ Messages

	(No column name)	(No column name)	(No column name)
1	101	recovery interval (min)	101recovery interval (min)
2	102	allow updates	102allow updates
3	103	user connections	103user connections
4	106	locks	106locks
5	107	open objects	107open objects
6	109	fill factor (%)	109fill factor (%)
7	114	disallow results from triggers	114disallow results from triggers

Figure 18.24: Output of the transformed result set without column names

You can definitely see that the new column was added at the end of the others, but the output result set does not have the column names. By default, sp_execute_external_script doesn't return column names. You need to use the WITH RESULT SETS clause to specify an output schema for your result set. You can also set the @output_data_1_name parameter to change the default output variable name to use in your script. Let's see an example of this:

```
EXEC sp_execute_external_script
@language = N'py310',
@script = N'
import pandas as pd
configs_df["id_name"] = configs_df["configuration_id"].astype(str) + configs_
df["name"]
transformed_df = configs_df',
@input_data_1 = N'SELECT configuration_id, name FROM sys.configurations',
@input_data_1_name = N'configs_df',
@output_data_1_name = N'transformed_df'
```

```
WITH RESULT SETS(
    (
        configuration_id INT NOT NULL,
        name VARCHAR(150) NOT NULL,
        id_name VARCHAR(200) NOT NULL
    )
);
```

This is the output:

	configuration_id	name	id_name
1	101	recovery interval (min)	101recovery interval (min)
2	102	allow updates	102allow updates
3	103	user connections	103user connections
4	106	locks	106locks
5	107	open objects	107open objects
6	109	fill factor (%)	109fill factor (%)
7	114	disallow results from triggers	114disallow results from triggers
8	115	nested triggers	115nested triggers

Figure 18.25: Output of the transformed result set with column names

Wonderful! We like the output result set now! One comment is worth making:

> In order to map a correct pattern to the output result set, it is necessary to know the data type of each column of the dataframe generated in the script and, in the case of strings, their maximum length. Unfortunately, it is not possible to do this mapping automatically in SQL Server.

On the other hand, if there is a need to persist the output result set to a table, the T-SQL script gets a bit complicated because it is necessary to first create the table (if it does not already exist) and then do an INSERT of the output of the sp_execute_external_script stored procedure into the target table. In this case, however, we do not need the WITH RESULT SET clause because we want to persist the output to a table whose schema has already been defined. Assuming you need to persist the output to a temporary table (see *References* for details on temporary tables), this is an example:

```
DROP TABLE IF EXISTS #InstanceConfigurations;

CREATE TABLE #InstanceConfigurations (
    configuration_id INT NOT NULL,
    name VARCHAR(150) NOT NULL,
    id_name VARCHAR(200) NOT NULL
```

```
);

INSERT INTO #InstanceConfigurations
EXEC sp_execute_external_script
@language = N'py310',
@script = N'
import pandas as pd
configs_df["id_name"] = configs_df["configuration_id"].astype(str) + configs_
df["name"]
transformed_df = configs_df',
@input_data_1 = N'SELECT configuration_id, name FROM sys.configurations',
@input_data_1_name = N'configs_df',
@output_data_1_name = N'transformed_df';


SELECT * FROM #InstanceConfigurations;
```

There is a restriction on the @input_data_1 parameter that accepts the input data query:

 The query passed to the @input_data_1 parameter can be as complex as you like, but it must be in the form of SELECT ... FROM .... This means that you cannot pass an EXEC query that executes a stored procedure, for example.

It can sometimes happen in the script that more than one result set needs to be used as input to get the desired output result set. Let's see what to do in such cases.

Managing loopback requests

The sp_execute_external_script syntax includes a parameter called @input_data_1, which allows you to pass input data to the external script using a T-SQL query. You might think that since the parameter is named input_data_N, you can pass multiple parameters like @input_data_2 to the stored procedure. However, this is not the case. Although Microsoft named the parameter to suggest the possibility of multiple input records in the future, it is not currently supported.

In SQL Server, it is usually better to use the database engine to transform data whenever possible. However, there are situations where you may need to use multiple data streams in an external script, especially for unique transformations that are only available in the external language. In such cases, you can connect back to SQL Server from the external script using an ODBC connection. This process is often referred to as a **loopback request**. In *Chapter 8, Logging Data from Power BI to External Sources*, you saw how to read from and write to SQL Server using Python and R. We will use some of the code you saw in that chapter.

First, install the pyodbc package in the Python environment installed for SQL Server:

1. Open an elevated command prompt.
2. Enter the pip install pyodbc command.

The RODBC library should already be installed at this point in the latest version you use for R scripts (4.2.2 in our case). If not, be sure to read *Chapter 8* to install the necessary packages.

For the sole purpose of demonstrating the possibility of loopback, let's read the data from the same system view as before directly into Python via pyodbc:

```
EXEC sp_execute_external_script
@language = N'py310',
@script = N'
import pandas as pd
import pyodbc

conn = pyodbc.connect(
    "Driver={ODBC Driver 17 for SQL Server};"
    "Server=.;"
    "Database=Master;"
    "Trusted_Connection=yes;")

configs_df = pd.read_sql("SELECT configuration_id, name FROM sys.
configurations", conn)
configs_df["id_name"] = configs_df["configuration_id"].astype(str) + configs_
df["name"]
transformed_df = configs_df',
@output_data_1_name = N'transformed_df'
WITH RESULT SETS(
    (
        configuration_id INT NOT NULL,
        name VARCHAR(150) NOT NULL,
        id_name VARCHAR(200) NOT NULL
    )
);
```

When you run this command, you may get an error like this:

```
A 'py310' script error occurred during execution of 'sp_execute_external_
script' with HRESULT 0x80004004.
STDOUT message(s) from external script:
```

```
2023-09-23 15:42:18.32    Error: Python error: <class 'pyodbc.
OperationalError'>: ('08001', '[08001] [Microsoft][ODBC Driver 17 for SQL
Server]Named Pipes Provider: Could not open a connection to SQL Server [5].
(5) (SQLDriverConnect); [08001] [Microsoft][ODBC Driver 17 for SQL Server]
Login timeout expired (0); [08001] [Microsoft][ODBC Driver 17 for SQL Server]
A network-related or instance-specific error has occurred while establishing
a connection to SQL Server. Server is not found or not accessible. Check if
instance name is correct and if SQL Server is configured to allow remote
connections. For more information see SQL Server Books Online. (5)'):   File
"<string>", line 5, in <module>
```

You are prompted to verify that SQL Server is configured to accept remote connections. Follow these steps:

1. Open **SQL Server Configuration Manager** from the **Microsoft SQL Server 2019** application group.

2. Expand the **Protocols for MSSQLSERVER** option. The managed protocols appear on the right.

3. Ensure that **TCP/IP** is enabled:

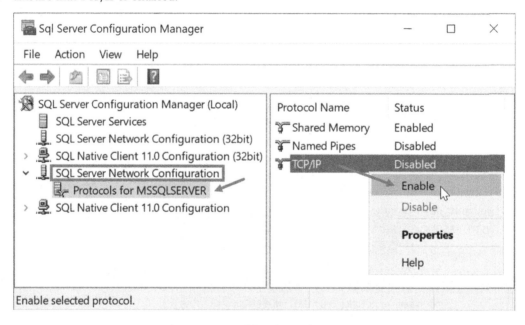

Figure 18.26: Enabling the TCP/IP protocol

4. You will be prompted to restart the service. Click **OK** to close the warning message. To do this, click **SQL Server Services** in the upper-left corner, right-click **SQL Server (MSSQLSERVER)**, and select **Restart**.

When you try to run the previous script again, you get the following:

	configuration_id	name	id_name
1	101	recovery interval (min)	101recovery interval (min)
2	102	allow updates	102allow updates
3	103	user connections	103user connections
4	106	locks	106locks
5	107	open objects	107open objects
6	109	fill factor (%)	109fill factor (%)
7	114	disallow results from triggers	114disallow results from triggers
8	115	nested triggers	115nested triggers

Figure 18.27: Output using a loopback call to the database from the script

For simplicity, we have shown an example where the reading of database data is done in the script, but as we mentioned earlier, this functionality is needed when another data stream comes from the @input_data_1 parameter query. In this case, it is important to note the following:

> ODBC performance (using RODBC in R or pyodbc in Python) uses the TCP/IP protocol, which is generally slower than other protocols used by SQL Server. Therefore, embedded calls to ODBC are typically used to retrieve "secondary" datasets, such as lookup tables, needed for analysis. The main, larger dataset is always passed through the @input_data_1 parameter of the sp_execute_external_script stored procedure, which uses *Shared Memory* protocol for faster data transport between SQL Server and the external process (e.g., the Launchpad) on the same machine.

Great! You now have all the tools you need to fully exploit the potential of external languages in SQL Server.

Let's see if it's possible to manage multiple installations of Python and R with external languages as well.

Managing different Python environments or R installations

Installing external languages like Python and R on SQL Server is a bit tricky because it's tied to environment variables. This means that you can only set up one Python environment and one R environment. If you want to manage multiple Python or R environments, you have to manually tweak configuration files and change environment variables, which isn't easy. What's more, there's no easy way to automate these changes. You could use the xp_cmdshell stored procedure to do this, but that's not recommended because it's insecure and goes against best practices.

Given the preceding limitations and the complexity of managing multiple Python and R environments in SQL Server, we recommend that you stick to a single environment for Python and a single environment for R when using external languages. This approach simplifies setup and avoids the need for complicated manual adjustments to configuration files and environment variables.

At this point, you might be wondering how, when, and why you use this indirect way of integrating the Python and R languages into Power BI. Let's take a look at it together.

The need for external languages with Power BI

If we have introduced the possibility of using SQL Server external languages to apply advanced analytics techniques to data, it is because sometimes it may be necessary to do so instead of using the standard Python and R integration feature in Power BI. The first case is related to the policies of the company that needs to use this feature. Let's see what that is.

Architectural and security policy constraints

So far, we have taken for granted a basic requirement for using Python and R in Power BI that turns out to be a bit of a stretch in the context of enterprise architecture: we are talking about using the Power BI *on-premises data gateway in personal mode*. As you may already know, Power BI limits each user to running only one data gateway in personal mode. This means that if a user installs another data gateway in personal mode, even on a different computer, the latest installation will replace any previous installation. You can understand that if the ability to use analytical languages in Power BI is strictly for a component designed for single-user use, it means that this feature is not yet designed for an enterprise architecture. In fact, the unofficial architectures suggested in *Chapter 2, Configuring R with Power BI*, and *Chapter 3, Configuring Python with Power BI*, are essentially a stretch for the purpose of using the data gateway in personal mode in an enterprise-level architecture.

The other major limitation of using Python and R in Power BI is the fact that the privacy level of the datasets used as a data source by an analytics engine *must necessarily be public*. In Power BI, when the public data source privacy level is used, it allows data from one data source to be folded into another. This means that multiple data sources can be combined and integrated seamlessly, without worrying about potential data leakage issues due to exposed sensitive data.

Given these significant limitations, some organizations may not want to use the default Python and R integration features in Power BI. In this case, if the organization is already using SQL Server (or Azure SQL Managed Instance) as the main repository of its business data, it is possible to inject advanced logic directly into the database using external languages and then read the already transformed or enriched data into Power BI.

Another situation where you might need to use SQL Server external languages is when the analytical script needs to take a fairly large dataset stored in SQL Server as input.

Running analytical scripts on data stored in SQL Server

You saw how to process large amounts of data in Power BI in *Chapter 9, Loading large datasets beyond the available RAM in Power BI*. Most of the time, the data you were processing was in CSV or parquet format. There are times when there is a fairly large amount of data persisted in a SQL Server instance (or Azure Managed Instance) that needs to be processed using Python or R. The engines referenced by the external languages are the standard Python and R engines, so they process the data by loading it all into memory. Often, database servers have quite a large amount of RAM and can therefore handle processing a fairly large amount of data via Python or R. Among other things, it is possible to decide how much RAM to allocate to the database engine and how much to the external languages using SQL Server's *Resource Governor* (see the References for details). Therefore, in these cases, some organizations prefer to inject processing via analytical languages into SQL Server to keep the entire data stream safely in one place.

Then there is another, more technical type of limitation that might cause the analyst to use external languages. It is the need to publish a report to the Power BI service that contains script visuals whose code uses libraries that do not exist in the engines provided by the service.

Missing libraries in the Power BI service

You already know that, especially for Python, the number of packages available on the Power BI service is by no means exhaustive. As a result, you may often develop a script for a visual script that runs in Power BI Desktop (since you can install any Python or R packages you need on your machine). However, when you go to publish the report to the Power BI service, you discover that one of the packages needed to run the script is missing.

A possible solution to this problem would be to follow the logic shown in *Chapter 5, Importing Unhandled Data Objects*, generate all the images given by the possible combinations of filters that can be set by the report, and persist them to the file system in serialized format. After that, only the image corresponding to the filters selected in the report can be deserialized in the visual script. However, sometimes the number of filter combinations is so large that this solution is no longer applicable for obvious performance reasons.

Or imagine the situation illustrated in *Chapter 17, Using Machine Learning without Premium or Embedded Capacity*, when you use an externally trained machine learning model in a visual script. If the model used is an *xgboost* or *lightgbm* (widely used models because they perform well), you don't have the ability to publish the report to the Power BI service.

At this point, you can turn to SQL Server external languages and the ability to make Direct Query calls to SQL Server in Power BI. We will not give specific examples of image generation with external languages here, as it would make the chapter extremely long. Instead, we will solve the machine learning case in *Chapter 17* to publish the working report on the Power BI service.

Let's look at an example of how to put this technique into practice.

Using external languages with Power BI

In this section, we will try to solve the problem of publishing to the Power BI service the report that shows the value predicted by the Titanic Survival machine learning model based on the parameters selected in the report itself, which you saw in *Chapter 17, Using Machine Learning without Premium or Embedded Capacity*.

In this particular case, any change to the parameters in the report will update the value predicted by the model without having to update the Power BI dataset. If we think about how this translates to the use of external languages, it means that each time the parameters are changed, a query to SQL Server must be launched that runs the model scoring script, passing the various parameters selected in the report. In other words, we need the **DirectQuery** mode to have real-time data. Power BI doesn't store any data. Instead, every time you create a visualization or run a query, Power BI sends a request directly to the data source. Let's try to understand what this means from a more practical point of view.

You have seen in the previous sections that to execute an analytical script in SQL Server, you need to call the `sp_execute_external_script` stored procedure with the appropriate parameters. If the output of the previous stored procedure needs to be further enriched with other data that is persisted in the database, it is convenient to wrap both the execution of the script and the data enrichment operations in another stored procedure to simplify querying this data. In general, it is also common to wrap the simple execution of `sp_execute_external_script` to avoid having to write the entire script string as a parameter. In short, to run an analytical script in SQL Server, you must always run a stored procedure. Going back to the integration with Power BI, you then need to be able to run a stored procedure in DirectQuery.

Here is the first problem you will encounter with this implementation:

> When you try to use a query of type `EXEC <my-stored-procedure> …` in a DirectQuery dataset, everything works fine in Power Query, but when you click **Close & Apply**, you get the mysterious *Incorrect syntax near the keyword 'EXEC'* error. Instead, everything runs smoothly when you use Import mode.

The mystery is solved by analyzing the queries that Power BI sends to SQL Server as it checks the result set metadata of the query entered. The query is as follows, which is syntactically incorrect:

```
select * from (
    EXEC <my-stored-procedure> … WITH RESULT SETS ((…))
) SourceQuery where 1 = 2
```

In practice, Power BI assumes that the query you enter can be considered a subquery of a generic `SELECT * FROM` query in which the `WHERE` clause has a false condition by definition (1 = 2). This is a little trick to return an empty result set super fast but with well-defined metadata. The downside is that to be a valid subquery, the query you enter must also be in the form of `SELECT * FROM`. So how do you get rid of the problem? Let's see how.

Converting an EXEC to SELECT ... FROM

In SQL Server, you can retrieve data from external sources using OLE DB providers in one-shot mode by providing a connection string and the query you want to inject into the external source using the **OPENROWSET** function. The typical way to use this feature is as follows:

```
SELECT *
FROM OPENROWSET('<provider>', '<connection-string', <query>')
```

The SQLNCLI, which is the OLE DB provider for connecting to a SQL Server database, comes pre-installed as part of the SQL Server Setup.

In SQL Server, the **OPENQUERY** function is another way to access external data, but it works in conjunction with **linked servers** rather than the ad hoc connection approach of OPENROWSET. Linked servers in SQL Server are configurations that provide remote database access, allowing SQL Server to execute commands against OLE DB data sources outside the local server environment. They facilitate queries against different database systems or SQL Server instances, allowing you to join tables across servers, execute commands, or retrieve data from a remote source. OPENQUERY executes a pass-through query on the specified linked server, which SQL Server treats as an object representing a server outside the local server environment. The command sends the query to the linked server and returns the result set as if it were a table.

These two commands seem very similar. OPENROWSET is typically used for ad hoc, one-time queries. In this case, there is the overhead of establishing a connection each time an OPENROWSET query is executed. This can also contribute to performance overhead, especially if many such queries are run repeatedly over time. On the other hand, OPENQUERY uses predefined linked servers, which can be more efficient for repeated queries to the same external server because the connection details are configured once and reused, potentially providing better performance through optimized connections.

In the following examples, we will use OPENROWSET because we assume that the execution is a one-time operation. So, you can use it to retrieve data from any database, including the same database where the OPENROWSET query originates. For example, the following query should work:

```
SELECT *
FROM OPENROWSET('SQLNCLI', 'server=.;Trusted_Connection=yes;',
        'SELECT configuration_id, name FROM sys.configurations')
```

The first time you run the above query, you receive the following error:

```
Msg 15281, Level 16, State 1
SQL Server blocked access to STATEMENT 'OpenRowset/OpenDatasource' of component
'Ad Hoc Distributed Queries' because this component is turned off as part
of the security configuration for this server. A system administrator can
enable the use of 'Ad Hoc Distributed Queries' by using sp_configure. For more
information about enabling 'Ad Hoc Distributed Queries', search for 'Ad Hoc
Distributed Queries' in SQL Server Books Online.
```

The *Ad Hoc Distributed Queries* feature is disabled by default on your SQL Server instance. It must be enabled to use the OPENROWSET function for ad hoc queries. To enable it, you'll need to run the following commands as a system administrator:

```
-- To show advanced options
EXEC sp_configure 'show advanced options', 1;
RECONFIGURE;


-- To enable Ad Hoc Distributed Queries
EXEC sp_configure 'Ad Hoc Distributed Queries', 1;
RECONFIGURE;
```

It's important to note that enabling *Ad Hoc Distributed Queries* can be a security risk if not managed carefully. It can potentially allow SQL injection attacks or unauthorized data access if misused. That's why it is disabled by default.

If you now try to run the previous OPENROWSET query again, you will get the following result:

	configuration_id	name
1	101	recovery interval (min)
2	102	allow updates
3	103	user connections
4	106	locks
5	107	open objects
6	109	fill factor (%)

Figure 18.28: Output of the OPENROWSET query showing the configurations

Great, it works! But wait a minute. What if we try to run an EXEC query through the OPENROWSET function? Let's try that with the system-stored procedure used to show the databases in the instance:

```
SELECT *
FROM OPENROWSET('SQLNCLI', 'server=.;Trusted_Connection=yes;',
                'EXEC [sys].[sp_databases]')
```

Here's the result:

	DATABASE_NAME	DATABASE_SIZE	REMARKS
1	master	15936	NULL
2	model	16384	NULL
3	msdb	38784	NULL
4	tempdb	16384	NULL

Figure 18.29: Output of the OPENROWSET query using an EXEC

Amazing! You managed to execute a stored procedure using the SELECT * FROM form with a little trick. Now you are confident that you can call a stored procedure from a DirectQuery datasource in Power BI without any errors.

At this point, let us prepare everything necessary in SQL Server to perform the scoring of the machine learning model used in *Chapter 17*.

Implementing the predictive stored procedure

If you recall, the Python\04-train-model-with-flaml.py script in *Chapter 17* trains a machine learning model using the FLAML AutoML feature. At the end of the script, both the final AutoML object, which contains all the properties captured during the training of the different models, and the best estimator in scikit-learn format identified by the training are persisted in pickle format. We will use the latter model to score the parameters passed from the report to Power BI.

This section assumes a minimum level of familiarity with T-SQL. If you need to learn the basics of programming in T-SQL in detail, see *References*.

In short, what you need to do is:

- Set up the model in pickle format in a folder accessible by SQL Server.
- Create a new supporting database on SQL Server in which to create the Python external language.
- Persist the model in binary format in a table in the aforementioned database.
- Create a stored procedure that generates the predicted label and prediction probability given the model references to be used and the values of an input instance as parameters.

Here are the steps to put them into practice (you can find the T-SQL scripts in the 03-configure-mlmodels-database.sql file in the Chapter 18 folder):

1. Create the folder C:\MLModels.
2. Copy the Python\titanic-best-model-flaml.pkl model file from the Chapter 17 folder created with FLAML and paste it into the C:\MLModels folder.
3. Open the **Command Prompt** with administrator privileges.
4. Enter the following command: icacls "C:\MLModels" /grant "NT Service\ MSSQLLAUNCHPAD":(OI)(CI)RX /T.
5. Enter the following command: icacls "C:\MLModels" /grant *S-1-15-2-1:(OI)(CI)RX /T.
6. Open **SQL Server Management Studio**, connect to your instance, click the **New Query** button, and create a new database by running the following script: CREATE DATABASE [MLModels].
7. Create a new table which will contain the binary version of your models by running the following script:

```
USE [MLModels];
GO


CREATE TABLE models (
```

```
        model_name         VARCHAR(100)      NOT NULL,
        model_version      INT NOT NULL DEFAULT 1,
        model              VARBINARY(MAX) NOT NULL
);
```

8. Also, create the `py310` external language for the `MLModels` database by running this script:

```
CREATE EXTERNAL LANGUAGE [py310]
FROM (CONTENT = N'C:\LanguageExtensions\python-lang-extension-windows-
release.zip',
    FILE_NAME = 'pythonextension.dll',
    ENVIRONMENT_VARIABLES = N'{"PYTHONHOME": "C:\\Program Files\\
Python310"}');
```

9. Create the stored procedure that will load a model given its name from the default models folder, and will output the binary version of the model:

```
CREATE PROCEDURE dbo.stp_generate_binary_model
    @model_file_name NVARCHAR(200) = N'titanic-best-model-flaml.pkl',
    @model_bin VARBINARY(MAX) OUTPUT
AS
BEGIN

    DECLARE @python_script AS NVARCHAR(MAX) = N'
import pickle
import os

main_path = r''C:\MLModels''

with open(os.path.join(main_path, r''' + @model_file_name + '''), ''rb'')
as f:
    model = pickle.load(f)

model_bin = pickle.dumps(model)
'

    EXECUTE sp_execute_external_script @language = N'py310'
, @script = @python_script
    , @params = N'@model_bin varbinary(max) OUTPUT'
    , @model_bin = @model_bin OUTPUT;

END
```

10. Populate the models table with the FLAML model file you've just copied by running this script:

```
DECLARE @model varbinary(max);

DELETE FROM dbo.models
WHERE
    model_name = 'titanic_flaml'
    AND model_version = 1;

EXECUTE stp_generate_binary_model @model_bin = @model OUTPUT;

INSERT INTO dbo.models (model_name, model_version, model)
VALUES ('titanic_flaml', 1, @model);
```

11. Finally, create the stored procedure used to predict if someone will survive on the Titanic:

```
CREATE PROCEDURE stp_predict_titanic_survivors
        @ModelName          AS VARCHAR(100)
    , @ModelVersion     AS INT
    , @Age              AS INT
    , @Embarked         AS FLOAT
    , @Fare         AS FLOAT
    , @Parch        AS FLOAT
    , @Pclass       AS INT
    , @Sex          AS INT
    , @SibSp        AS FLOAT
AS
BEGIN
    SET NOCOUNT ON;

    DECLARE
        @binary_model VARBINARY(MAX),
        @input_query NVARCHAR(MAX);

    SET @input_query = CONCAT(N'
        SELECT
          Age       = ', @Age, N'
        , Embarked    = CAST(', @Embarked, N' AS FLOAT)
        , Fare        = CAST(', @Fare, N' AS FLOAT)
        , Parch     = CAST(', @Parch, N' AS FLOAT)
        , Pclass    = ', @Pclass, N'
        , Sex       = ', @Sex, N'
```

```
        , SibSp = CAST(', @SibSp, N' AS FLOAT)')

    SELECT TOP 1
        @binary_model = model
    FROM dbo.models
    WHERE
        model_name = @ModelName
        AND model_version = @ModelVersion;

    EXECUTE sp_execute_external_script
        @language = N'py310'
            , @script = N'
import pandas as pd
import pickle

model = pickle.loads(binary_model)

prediction_label = model.predict(input_tuple_df)[0]
prediction_score = model.predict_proba(input_tuple_df)[:,1][0]

print(f''Prediction label: {prediction_label}'')
print(f''Prediction score: {prediction_score}'')

output_data = {
    ''prediction_label'': [prediction_label],
    ''prediction_score'': [prediction_score]
}

output_df = pd.DataFrame(output_data)'

        , @input_data_1 = @input_query
        , @input_data_1_name = N'input_tuple_df'
        , @output_data_1_name = N'output_df'
        , @params = N'@binary_model VARBINARY(MAX)'
        , @binary_model = @binary_model
    WITH RESULT SETS ((
        prediction_label INT
        , prediction_score DECIMAL(5,4)
    ));

END
```

12. The input query forces a cast of some decimal values to float because there is no match between SQL Server's `DECIMAL` data type and Python's `float64` for decimal numbers (see `https://bit.ly/sqlserver-python-data-types`).

Great! The predictive stored procedure is ready to use. Let's check if it works fine by running this script:

```
EXEC stp_predict_titanic_survivors
      @ModelName           = 'titanic_flaml'
    , @ModelVersion     = 1
    , @Age                = 74
    , @Embarked          = 2.0
    , @Fare          = 7.775
    , @Parch        = 0.0
    , @Pclass        = 1
    , @Sex          = 1
    , @SibSp        = 0.0
```

Here is the output:

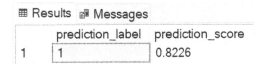

Figure 18.30: Prediction data returned by the predictive stored procedure

Awesome! The output returns the predicted label and its probability. You have the primary tool used to provide the values predicted by the model for your report in Power BI. Let's see how to integrate them into the report.

Calling a stored procedure in DirectQuery

The report you will use will be virtually identical to the one you created in the *Scoring Observations in a Script Visual Using a Trained Model* section of *Chapter 17, Using Machine Learning without Premium or Embedded Capacity*. In fact, we ask that you follow the steps outlined in *Using trained models in script visuals* in *Chapter 17* to create the report skeleton. First, you can open Power BI Desktop without using any shortcuts that activate a specific environment.

 There is no need to worry about the local Python environment that needs to be referenced because all Python code is executed on the SQL Server side, not through the built-in engine in Power BI.

Therefore, you can skip *steps 1* through *8*. Then, just follow *steps 9* through *30*, and you should have all the slicers associated with the model parameters ready to go:

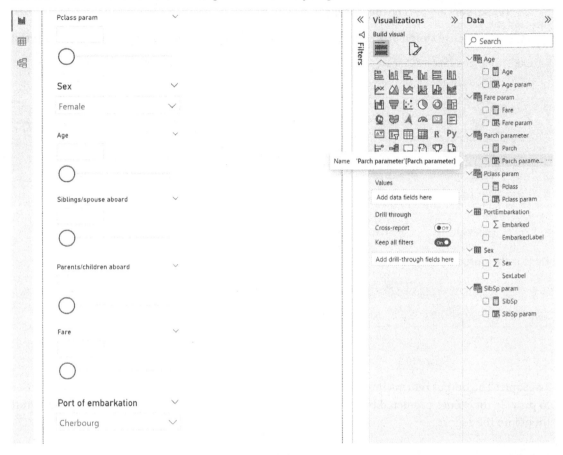

Figure 18.31: Ready-to-use report skeleton

Let's now add the parameters in Power Query that will be associated with the various sliders, which will then be used in the query that calls the stored procedure:

1. On the **Home** ribbon, click **Transform data** to go to the Power Query Editor.

2. On the Power Query Editor **Home** ribbon, click **Manage Parameters**, and then click the **New** link at the top of the new window that appears:

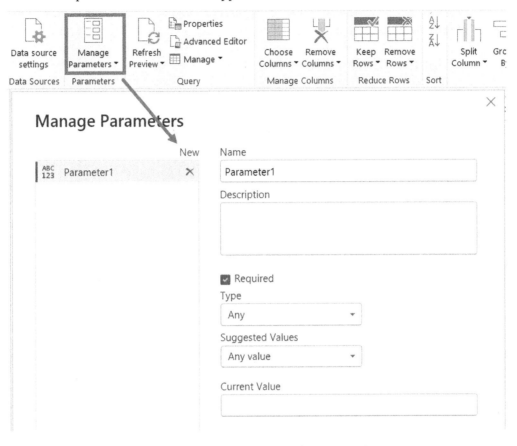

Figure 18.32: Create a new Power Query parameter

3. Change the parameter **Name** in _Pclass (the underscore is used to prevent naming conflicts), leave the **Required** option selected, set the **Type** as **Decimal Number**, and enter any default value, such as **1**.

4. Repeat the steps in order to enter as parameters as the needed model input values (_Sex, _Age, _Parch, _SibSp, _Fare, and _Embarked, other than the just added _Pclass), and fill in the parameter settings in the same way you've just done for the _Pclass one. In the end, you'll have the following situation:

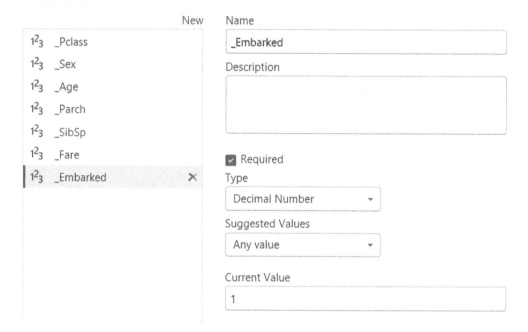

Figure 18.33: Create Power Query parameters

Then, click **OK**.

5. Now right-click on the empty area of the **Queries** pane on the left, hover over **New Query**, and select **SQL Server**:

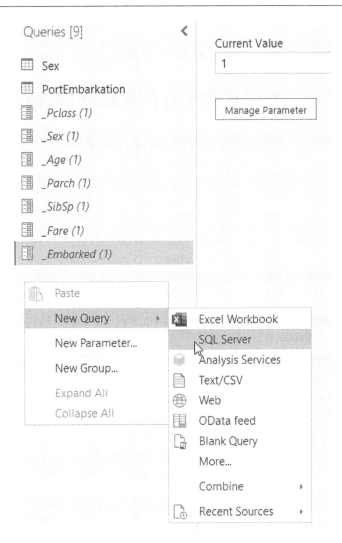

Figure 18.34: Create a SQL Server query

6. Specify the **.** (dot) as the **Server**, MLModels as the **Database**, select **DirectQuery** as the **Data Connectivity mode**, expand the **Advanced options**, and enter the following **SQL statement** that we used in the previous section to test the stored procedure:

```
EXEC stp_predict_titanic_survivors  @ModelName = 'titanic_flaml', @
ModelVersion = 1, @Age = 74, @Embarked = 2.0, @Fare = 7.775, @Parch =
0.0, @Pclass = 1, @Sex = 1, @SibSp = 0.0
```

Then press **OK**.

7. You'll get the same results as in the previous section, but this time in Power Query:

Local SQL database: MLModels

prediction_label	prediction_score
1	0.8226

Figure 18.35: Output of the executed stored procedure in Power Query

Then press **OK**. But wait a minute: you chose the DirectQuery option, so will running stored procedures not work fine with DirectQuery as well? Unfortunately not! It works fine in Power Query, but if you leave the query as is, you'll get an error when you click **Close & Apply**. So, you need to modify the definition of the query you just added using the OPENROWSET trick.

8. Rename the query you just created from `Query1` to `Predictions` by right-clicking on it and selecting **Rename**.

9. On the **Home** ribbon, click **Advanced Editor** with the **Predictions** query selected.

10. You can see the M query that runs the stored procedure. It is quite easy to replace the EXEC query ... in the corresponding OPENROWSET query in this way:

```
SELECT * FROM OPENROWSET('SQLNCLI','server=.;Trusted_
Connection=yes;','EXEC MLModels.dbo.stp_predict_titanic_survivors  @
ModelName = ''titanic_flaml'', @ModelVersion = 1, @Age = 74, @Embarked =
2.0, @Fare = 7.775, @Parch = 0.0, @Pclass = 1, @Sex = 1, @SibSp = 0.0'
```

First, notice the two single quotes around the `titanic_flaml` string. They are double because the entire EXEC query becomes a string used in the OPENROWSET, and so the quotes used in the EXEC must be escaped. In addition, you must reference the stored procedure to be called using its three-part name when OPENROWSET is used. Therefore, the complete M expression becomes as following:

```
let
    Source = Sql.Database(".", "MLModels", [Query="SELECT * FROM
OPENROWSET('SQLNCLI','server=.;Trusted_Connection=yes;'
    ,'EXEC MLModels.dbo.stp_predict_titanic_survivors  @ModelName =
''titanic_flaml'', @ModelVersion = 1, @Age = 74, @Embarked = 2.0, @Fare =
7.775, @Parch = 0.0, @Pclass = 1, @Sex = 1, @SibSp = 0.0')"])
in
    Source
```

In addition, to display the result of the titanic model prediction based on the user's selection, the parameters just created in Power Query must be inserted into the above expression. You can do this with the M Text.From(…) function, which returns the text representation of a value passed as a parameter. Specifically, you need to replace the fixed values in the previous M expression with the text representation of the parameters. Therefore, the expression becomes:

```
let
    Source = Sql.Database(".", "MLModels", [Query="SELECT * FROM
OPENROWSET('SQLNCLI','server=.;Trusted_Connection=yes;'
    ,'EXEC MLModels.dbo.stp_predict_titanic_survivors  @ModelName =
''titanic_flaml'', @ModelVersion = 1, @Age = " & Text.From(_Age) & ", @
Embarked = " & Text.From(_Embarked) & ", @Fare = " & Text.From(_Fare) &
", @Parch = " & Text.From(_Parch) & ", @Pclass = " & Text.From(_Pclass)
& ", @Sex = " & Text.From(_Sex) & ", @SibSp = " & Text.From(_SibSp) &
"')"])
in
    Source
```

Then press **OK** in the Advanced Editor.

11. Your permission is required to execute the query on the database. To do this, click the **Edit Permission** button on the yellow ribbon at the top of the canvas, and then click **Run** in the **Native Database Query** window. If you type the M expression correctly, you will see predictions as a result in Power Query, this time by using parameters. Wonderful! The stored procedure is executed correctly using the parameters, but those parameters are just default values for now because you still have to somehow connect them to the slicers so that they change based on user selections.

12. Click **Close & Apply**, and in the case of a potential security risk warning, click **OK**. If you don't get any errors, it means that you managed to execute a SQL Server store procedure in DirectQuery, which seemed impossible at first!

13. To bind Power Query parameters to slicers, click the **Model view** button on the left. Select the **Pclass param** field of the **Pclass** table, expand its **Advanced** properties, and set the _Pclass parameter in the **Bind to parameter** combo box:

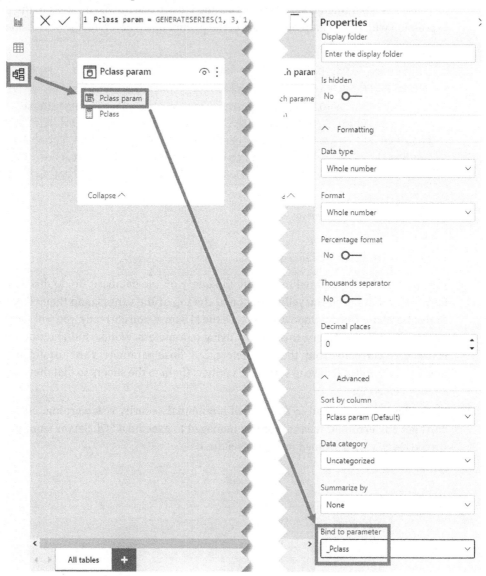

Figure 18.36: Linking Power Query parameters to slicer values

If a potential security risk warning pops up, click **Continue**.

14. Repeat *step 13* for all the other tables. In the case of tables created from the **Enter data** activity, you have to bind parameters to their numeric fields. For example, you have to select the Sex field for the Sex table, set None for the Summarize by combo box, and set the _Sex parameter in the **Bind to parameter** combo box:

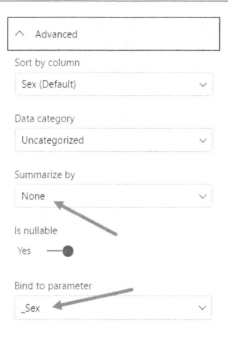

Figure 18.37: Linking parameters for Enter data tables

Set also **Summarize by** to **None** for the **Predictions** table fields. From this point on, any changes the user makes to the slicers are reflected in an `EXEC` query to the predictive stored procedure with appropriate parameter passing. All that is left to do is to display the result that is returned by the stored procedure.

15. Go back to the visuals by clicking the **Report view** button on the left. Click on an empty space of the canvas and click on the **Card** (new) visual:

Figure 18.38: Adding the Card visual

16. To display a formatted string in the Card, click on the **Predictions** table ellipsis (more options) in the **Data** panel on the right, and select **New Measure**. Then type the following DAX formula for the new measure:

```
prediction_text = "Survived = " & MAX('Predictions'[prediction_label]) &
" (prob: " & MAX('Predictions'[prediction_score]) & ")"
```

17. Select the Card visual, then select the **prediction_text** measure you just created. If prompted, click **Run** in the **Native Database Query** window that appears. You will then see the result of the prediction in the Card:

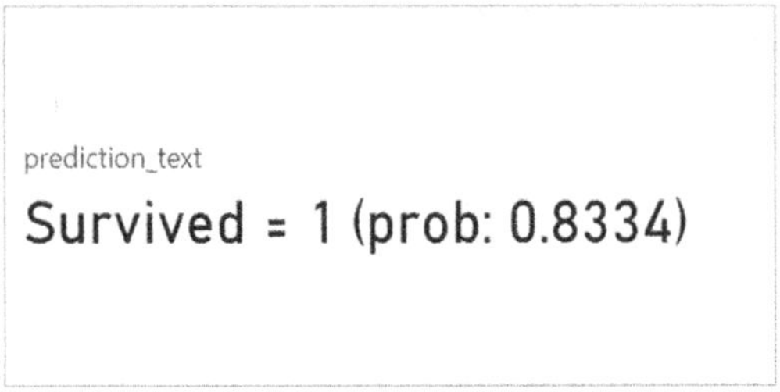

prediction_text

Survived = 1 (prob: 0.8334)

Figure 18.39: SQL Server predictions displayed in a Card

Awesome! You can get the predictions of a machine learning model through DirectQuery execution of a stored procedure on SQL Server!

Unfortunately, as of today (October 2023) there are some bugs when working with Power Query parameters in Power BI:

- The moment you bind a parameter to a field in a table using the **Bind to parameter** option, the slicer formatting associated with that field is lost. For example, you can no longer display slicers in **Single Value** style, only **Vertical List**, **Tile**, or **Dropdown**:

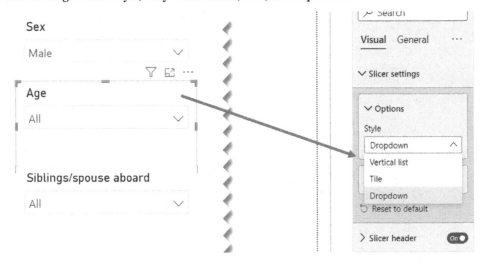

Figure 18.40: Slider style lost

- Although the binding of parameters with values that result from **Enter data** activities (specifically for **Sex** and **Embarkment**) has been performed correctly, changes to the associated slicers are not reflected in the parameters by Power BI.

Once the Power BI product team fixes these bugs, the report will be fully functional.

In the specific case of using machine learning models for scoring in SQL Server, the following applies:

It is true that the use of external languages is only allowed on on-premises SQL Server and Azure Managed Instance. However, if a machine learning model has been created using one of the algorithms supported by the *RevoScaleR* or *revoscalepy* packages and has been persisted in binary format in a table, the native **PREDICT** function can also be used to generate the values predicted by the model in Azure SQL Server. See *References* for more details.

Now, let's see whether publishing the report to the Power BI service will continue to make the predictions work.

Publishing the report to the Power BI service

For the report to work after it is published, you need the Power BI service to be able to communicate with the on-premises SQL Server instance that you installed as described in this chapter. Therefore, it is necessary to install a data gateway on a machine that is located on the same network as the database server and is not restricted from accessing it. In this case, you can use the default data gateway instead of the one in personal mode. If you want to do so, follow the steps in the following link to install it on your machine: `https://bit.ly/install-default-data-gateway`. In your case, since you already have a data gateway installed in personal mode, you can use that to connect to the database if you want. For demonstration purposes, we will use the newly installed default data gateway. You must then publish your report by following these steps:

1. Click **Publish** on the **Home** ribbon of Power BI Desktop. You may be prompted to save the report in its current state. Click **Save**.

2. Select your preferred workspace to publish the report to. Once the report is published, you'll be notified that the report dataset is disconnected and it needs to be configured on the service. Click **Open dataset settings**.

3. When the dataset settings page opens, expand the **Gateway and cloud connections**, turn on the **Use on-premises or VNet data gateway** switch, click the gear icon to the right of your default data gateway name (**book-ed2-vm** in our case), and click the **Add to gateway** link to fix the data source connection:

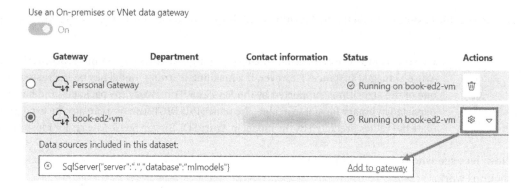

Figure 18.41: On-premises gateway configurations

4. Enter the connection name (`MLModels` in our case), set **Windows** as the **Authentication method**, enter your local Windows credentials and add the domain name to the username, then press **Create**:

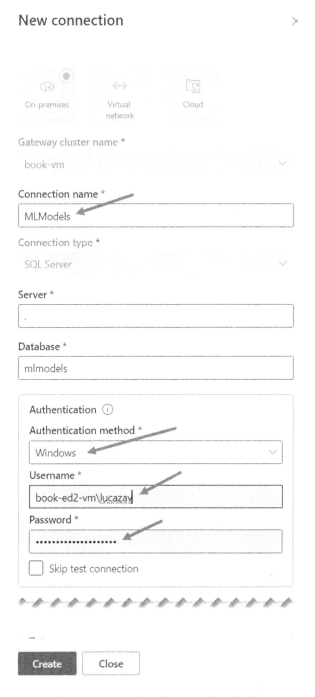

Figure 18.42: Entering the connection details

For simplicity, we entered the credentials of the machine administrator who installed the SQL Server instance. Therefore, we are sure that this user has read access to the database. Normally, the best practice is to use a service user, create a login on SQL Server for that user, and make sure that the user has read access to the MLModels database and the permissions to execute stored procedures on that database at all times.

5. Now, you can set the **Maps to** combo box to the newly created connection (**MLModels**):

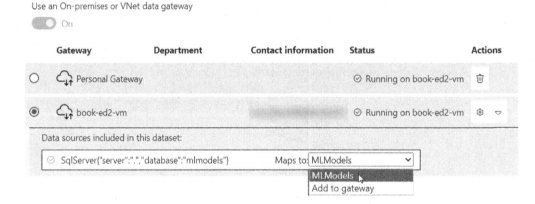

Figure 18.43: Mapping the connection to the SQL Server data source

Click **Apply**.

6. Go back to the workspace in which you published the report and open the report.

7. Select different values for the slicers to see the predictions change accordingly:

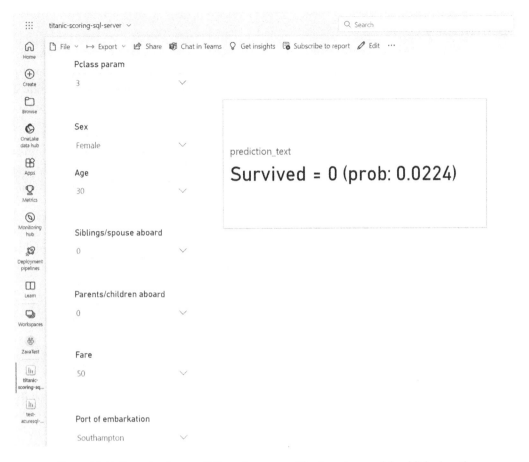

Figure 18.44: Report using predictions from a machine learning model published on the service

Great! Your report updates in real time on the Power BI service, generating predictions from a machine learning model queried in Python on SQL Server. This would not be possible if you were using the Python language provided by Power BI.

Summary

In this chapter, you learned about using external languages in Power BI to integrate advanced analytics and machine learning capabilities directly into SQL Server. External languages allow you to execute Python or R scripts within SQL Server, eliminating the need to transfer data to separate analytics platforms. This provides benefits such as improved data security, faster processing, and easier deployment and integration.

You also learned about the SQL Server Extensibility Framework, which enables the execution of Python or R code using external engines. The framework allows for the execution of scripts in an external runtime environment, facilitating communication between SQL Server and the external languages.

Additionally, you learned about the challenges of managing multiple Python or R environments in SQL Server and the benefits of using external languages in scenarios where Power BI's default integration may not be suitable due to architectural and security policy constraints, the need for real-time data processing, or the lack of required libraries in the Power BI service.

In the next chapter, we'll finally start working with R and Python scripts in Power BI, doing some data ingestion and data transformation.

References

For additional reading, check out the following books and articles:

- *Bring Your Own R & Python Runtimes to SQL Server Extensibility Framework* (https://nielsberglund.com/post/2020-12-29-bring-your-own-r--python-runtimes-to-sql-server-extensibility-framework/)

- *Install a Python custom runtime for SQL Server* (https://learn.microsoft.com/en-us/sql/machine-learning/install/custom-runtime-python)

- *Install SQL Server 2022 Machine Learning Services (Python and R) on Windows* (https://learn.microsoft.com/en-us/sql/machine-learning/install/sql-machine-learning-services-windows-install-sql-2022)

- *Fix: Getting R and Python to actually work on SQL Server 2022* (https://blog.greglow.com/2024/03/04/fix-getting-r-and-python-to-actually-work-on-sql-server-2022/)

- *SQL Server on Windows: Isolation changes for Machine Learning Services* (https://learn.microsoft.com/en-us/sql/machine-learning/install/sql-server-machine-learning-services-2019)

- *Overview and Performance Tips of Temp Tables in SQL Server* (https://www.sqlshack.com/overview-and-performance-tips-of-temp-tables-in-sql-server/)

- *Manage Python and R workloads with Resource Governor in SQL Server Machine Learning Services* (https://learn.microsoft.com/en-us/sql/machine-learning/administration/resource-governor)

- *Native scoring using the PREDICT T-SQL function with SQL machine learning* (https://learn.microsoft.com/en-us/sql/machine-learning/predictions/native-scoring-predict-transact-sql)

Acknowledgements

I would like to thank my technical editor, Art Tennick, for his timely feedback on the topics covered in this chapter, of which he is an unabashed advocate!

Test your knowledge

1. What is SQL Server Machine Learning Services?
2. What were the challenges before the introduction of Machine Learning Services?
3. What is the role of the SQL Server Extensibility Framework in executing Python or R code with Machine Learning Services?
4. Which products have Machine Learning Services available?
5. What is the purpose of the Launchpad service in SQL Server Machine Learning Services?
6. How do you give SQL Server's Launchpad service access to folders where you have downloaded external language DLLs or folders that need to be accessed by scripts?
7. Why would you need external languages with Power BI?
8. How do you call a stored procedure in DirectQuery mode in Power BI?
9. How is the SQL Server machine learning model table used in the examples shown in this chapter?
10. Why do you need to use OPENROWSET to execute a stored procedure? Wouldn't it be enough to use EXEC?
11. What are the benefits of running a stored procedure in DirectQuery in Power BI?
12. In the predictive reporting example given in the book, what is the big advantage of using the external language instead of using the built-in Python in Power BI?

Learn more on Discord

To join the Discord community for this book – where you can share feedback, ask questions to the author, and learn about new releases – follow the QR code below:

`https://discord.gg/MKww5g45EB`

19

Exploratory Data Analysis

In *Chapter 17*, we discussed the challenges of using machine learning without premium or embedded capacity. One of the key pitfalls we highlighted was blindly applying **automated machine learning (AutoML)** solutions to a dataset, which often results in inaccurate models. To overcome this limitation, a critical step is to gain a deep understanding of the inherent characteristics of the dataset.

To accomplish this, this chapter introduces the concept of **exploratory data analysis (EDA)**. This approach to analysis, pioneered by John Tukey, encourages statisticians to thoroughly explore the data and formulate hypotheses. By doing so, we can extract valuable information that ultimately enhances our understanding of the dataset and leads to the discovery of meaningful patterns among the variables.

By using EDA techniques, you can make informed decisions when selecting the most appropriate machine learning models and feature engineering methods. This chapter explores the basic techniques and tools needed to perform effective EDA, enabling you to extract meaningful insights from your dataset and ultimately build more accurate models.

In this chapter, you will learn about the following topics:

- What is the goal of EDA?
- EDA with Python and R
- EDA in Power BI

Technical requirements

This chapter requires you to have a working internet connection and Power BI Desktop already installed on your machine (version: 2.121.644.0 64-bit, September 2023). You must have properly configured the R and Python engines and IDEs as outlined in *Chapter 2, Configuring R with Power BI*.

What is the goal of EDA?

The primary goal of EDA is to ensure that the dataset used for complex processes is clean and reliable. This involves addressing two critical aspects: eliminating missing values and outliers that have the potential to skew subsequent analyses, and selecting relevant variables that contribute substantive information while discarding those that are primarily noise.

By thoroughly cleaning the dataset, we eliminate potential sources of inaccuracy in the conclusions derived from subsequent processes. Missing values and outliers can disrupt the integrity of statistical analyses and lead to inaccurate results. Therefore, one of the first focuses of EDA is to identify and handle missing values appropriately, either by imputing appropriate estimates or by removing them altogether. Similarly, outliers, extreme observations that deviate significantly from the overall pattern, are identified and treated to avoid undue influence on subsequent analyses.

In addition to ensuring data cleanliness, EDA involves a comprehensive exploration of the relationships between variables within the dataset. This exploration helps uncover insights that can justify and guide any subsequent complex processing. Identifying relationships, dependencies, and patterns between variables allows us to understand the underlying relationships and draw meaningful conclusions. Such insights gained during the EDA phase can justify the use of specific data preprocessing techniques or guide the selection of appropriate machine learning algorithms for later stages.

Ultimately, by conducting thorough EDA, we enhance the quality and reliability of the dataset, mitigate potential sources of error or bias, and lay the foundation for more accurate and effective analyses to be performed in subsequent stages. The main phases of EDA are as follows:

1. Understanding your data
2. Cleaning your data
3. Discovering associations between variables

Let's take a closer look at each of these types of analysis.

Understanding your data

In this first phase, it is important to understand the meaning of each variable in the context of the problem that the dataset represents. Once the measurable business entities with which the variables are associated are clear, it is easier to infer how they interact with each other.

Having an idea of **the size of the dataset,** understood as the number of variables and the number of observations (rows), will help you get a first idea of the size of the data you will be dealing with. Next, it is crucial to identify and immediately define the **type of variables** involved (which can be numerical or categorical) in order to visualize them in the most appropriate way.

Then, knowing the **descriptive statistics** of the **numerical variables** in the dataset helps to gain greater sensitivity to their values. In addition, when you're looking at them and trying to figure out how they're distributed, there are a few different types of graphs that can help you get a clearer picture:

- **Histogram**: Imagine you have test scores for a class and you want to know how many students got scores within a certain range. A histogram takes all those scores and puts them into bins or ranges. For example, you can see how many students scored between 60-70, 70-80, and so on. The height of each bar tells you how many students are in each range.

- **Density plot**: This is like a smooth version of a histogram. Instead of bars, you get a curve that shows you where the scores are most concentrated. It's good for understanding the shape of your data. For example, you can see if most of the test scores are clustered at the high end or the low end.

- **Raincloud plot**: This is like a combo meal of graphs. It usually includes a box plot (which you learned about in *Chapter 16*, *Adding Statistical Insights: Outliers and Missing Values*), a density plot (as mentioned above), and sometimes individual data points (often represented as dots or small markers, sometimes literally hanging like "rain") all in one graph. It's super useful for understanding how your numbers are distributed, how they vary, and where most of the data points are.

Each of these charts gives you a unique way to understand how your numerical data is distributed, which can help you make better decisions or gain insights from it.

When dealing with **categorical variables**, such as favorite fruits or car brands, a bar chart is often the first choice for visualization. In a bar chart, which can be either vertical or horizontal, each category is represented by its own bar. The length or height of that bar correlates to how often that particular category appears in your dataset. So if you're conducting a survey about favorite fruits, a longer or taller bar for "apple" indicates that it's a popular choice among respondents.

But what if you have a lot of categories, like 50 different book genres? Showing them all on a single graph can make it messy and hard to interpret. In situations like this, it's a good idea to limit the number of categories you actually show – maybe just the top 10 most common genres. What happens to all the other categories? Typically, you combine them into a catch-all category called "Other." This keeps the chart clean and focused on the most common or important categories, while still giving you a sense that there are other possibilities in the data. This combination is usually done in a later phase of machine learning projects (called **feature engineering**) to avoid, for example, having a model that is not generic enough for all the cases to which it needs to be applied (the phenomenon of **overfitting**) and thus determining poor performance.

Giving the analyst the ability to visually explore how two variables relate to each other is critical to understanding more complex relationships in a dataset (this is called **multivariate analysis**). As you may recall from *Chapter 15*, *Adding Statistical Insights: Associations*, the choice of visualization technique depends on the type of data you're working with. If both variables are numerical, such as height and weight, a scatterplot is the chart of choice. It shows individual data points plotted in a two-dimensional space and helps you see if, for example, taller people tend to be heavier.

If you're working with two categorical variables, such as favorite fruit and age group, a mosaic chart is a solid choice. This plot uses rectangular tiles to represent the frequency of each combination of categories, making it easier to spot patterns or trends. You will see an example of this type of chart later in this chapter.

But what if you're mixing a numerical variable with a categorical one? For example, if you're looking at test scores (numerical) in different subjects (categorical)? In this case, you can use multiple boxplots (or even raincloud plots) for each category. These plots give you a snapshot of how the numerical data behaves within each categorical group, showing things like the average test score in math versus history. An example of these plots is shown later in this chapter.

At this point, we can move on to describe the data cleaning phase.

Cleaning your data

As you learned in *Chapter 16, Adding Statistical Insights: Outliers and Missing Values*, these are the two most important activities for obtaining a statistically robust dataset that is as close as possible to the real case it represents:

- Identifying and managing **outliers**
- Imputation of **missing values**

During the EDA process, it is important to use all visual and non-visual tools to easily detect outliers and missing values. This will allow any anomalies found to be corrected at a later stage.

As you learned earlier, for **univariate outlier analysis**, it is very useful to be able to display individual distributions using box plots for numerical variables. It would also be very useful to be able to see which outliers remain or are added after transforming the variable using Yeo-Johnson transformations. This way, you can see if it might be worth trying to normalize the distribution to have as few outliers as possible.

It is also convenient to be able to perform a **bivariate analysis of the outliers** considering a numerical variable and a categorical variable so that you can study the anomalies of the distribution of the numerical variable broken down by each label of the categorical variable.

After careful study and identification of possible outliers, it is also important to have a convenient visualization of the combinations and intersections of **missing values** between variables. Therefore, the goal is not only to know the number and relative percentage of missing values of each variable, but also to have a convenient visualization of how these missing values interact with each other, thanks to an upset plot.

Finally, let's turn to the analysis of associations between variables.

Discovering associations between variables

As you learned in *Chapter 15, Adding Statistical Insights: Associations*, knowing the **degree of association between variables** in the dataset will certainly help you understand which ones carry the most information and which ones are mostly just noise. Selecting the most informative variables and using them to train a machine learning model will certainly help you to get more stable and performant results.

Having visual tools to interpret the associations between pairs of numerical-numerical, numerical-categorical, and categorical-categorical variables certainly helps with the difficult task of feature selection.

There are tools that allow you to automatically generate EDA reports. Let's see what they are.

EDA with Python and R

If you need to do data exploration using only Python or R, there are tools that automatically generate a number of visualizations to make your life easier. We have two lists below, one for Python tools and the other for R tools, in case you need them. It is easier to find tools for interactive data analysis in Python than in R. Packages available in R often provide wrappers that greatly simplify EDA via coding.

The Python libraries for EDA are as follows:

- **Sweetviz** (https://pypi.org/project/sweetviz/): An open-source Python library that generates beautiful, high-density visualizations to kickstart EDA with just two lines of code
- **Lux** (https://lux-api.readthedocs.io/): A Python library that facilitates fast and easy data exploration by automating the visualization and data analysis process
- **pandas Profiling** (https://pandas-profiling.github.io/pandas-profiling/): Generates profile reports from a pandas DataFrame for data analysis
- **pandasGUI** (https://github.com/adamerose/pandasgui): A GUI for viewing, plotting, and analyzing pandas DataFrames
- **D-Tale** (https://github.com/man-group/dtale): The combination of a Flask backend and a React frontend to bring you an easy way to view and analyze pandas data structures

The R packages for EDA are the following:

- **ExPanDaR** (https://github.com/joachim-gassen/ExPanDaR): ExPanDaR is a Shiny-based app supporting interactive exploratory data analysis. The repository is a bit outdated, but it's still a valid application.
- **Explore** (https://github.com/rolkra/explore): An R package that simplifies exploratory data analysis. It allows users to interactively explore data using a few easy-to-remember functions. It also enables users to generate automated reports with one line of code.
- **ggquickeda** (https://github.com/smouksassi/ggquickeda): An R Shiny app/package that enables you to quickly explore your data and to detect trends on the fly thanks to scatterplots, dot plots, boxplots, bar plots, and so on.
- **summarytools** (https://github.com/dcomtois/summarytools): An R package for data cleaning, exploring, and simple reporting. It integrates well with commonly used software and tools for reporting in R (such as RStudio).
- **DataExplorer** (https://boxuancui.github.io/DataExplorer/): Aims to automate most data handling and visualization so that users can focus on studying the data and extracting insights.

Check out the references for more details on the above tools.

Unfortunately, if you want to take advantage of Power BI as a visualization tool, you cannot use many of the visualizations that are automatically generated by the Python tools mentioned previously. Therefore, we will use R packages to generate what we need for basic EDA via code, because R allows you to get very high-quality graphics of any complexity quite easily. Let's see how.

EDA in Power BI

In this section, we will make extensive use of the ggplot2 package, an advanced R library designed for creating plots based on the **Grammar of Graphics.** It is not our intention to go into detail about every feature exposed by the package, even though it is used quite extensively in the code that accompanies the chapter. Our goal, as always, is to provide code that can be easily adapted for use in other projects and, above all, to provide a starting point for a more detailed look at the functions used. For more details, see the *References* section in this chapter.

In addition to the tools provided by Tidyverse in R (including ggplot2), we will also use the summarytools and DataExplorer packages to create EDA reports in Power BI. It is therefore necessary to install them:

1. Open RStudio and make sure it is pointing to your latest CRAN R (version 4.2.2 in our case).
2. Check that the Rcpp package is installed in the **Packages** tab on the bottom-right side of RStudio. If it is not installed, click on the **Console** window and type this command: install. packages('Rcpp'). It's a summarytools dependency. Then, press *Enter*.
3. Type this command: install.packages('summarytools'). Then, press *Enter*.
4. Type this command: install.packages('DataExplorer'). Then, press *Enter*.

After the installation of DataExplorer, it could happen that the dependent library igraph conflicted with other libraries. To check this, run library(igraph) in the console. If you get an error like *Unable to load shared object 'C:/Program Files/R/R-4.2.2/library/igraph/libs/x64/igraph.dll'*, then try to uninstall the library with the command remove.packages("igraph"), restart RStudio, and then reinstall the library with the command install.packages("igraph"). This should solve the problem.

At this point, we can start implementing our EDA reports. First, however, it is important to emphasize that the data type of variables must be defined in each R script that you will use in your report.

IMPORTANT NOTE

For the purpose of EDA, it is important to define the data type of the variables in the dataset to be analyzed. Depending on the data types of the features, different analysis strategies are applied. The data types of columns in a Power BI table in the data model do not map one to one to the data types handled by R. Therefore, it is necessary to define the data types of the columns directly in an R script to prevent Power BI from overwriting them.

In addition, the R\00-init-dataset.R script that you will find in the Chapter 19 folder will be used as the *official CSV connector* of your EDA report in Power BI, since in this case it is more convenient to load data directly into R for each script in which it is used. After loading your data into it, you need to define the columns to drop, both categorical and integer. Columns specified as integers are considered to be either numerical or categorical variables, allowing the analyst to select them according to the function that best describes the phenomenon being analyzed. All other columns should be numerical:

```
library(readr)
library(dplyr)
```

```
dataset_url <- 'http://bit.ly/titanic-dataset-csv'
src_tbl <- read_csv(dataset_url)
vars_to_drop <- c('PassengerId')
categorical_vars <- c('Sex', 'Ticket', 'Cabin', 'Embarked')
integer_vars <- c('Survived', 'Pclass', 'SibSp', 'Parch')
```

If you need to import an Excel file instead of a CSV file, you already know how to make changes to the code from what you learned in *Chapter 8, Logging Data from Power BI to External Sources*.

The script then defines the tbl tibble by applying the appropriate transformations:

```
tbl <- src_tbl %>%
  mutate(
    across(categorical_vars, as.factor),
    across(integer_vars, as.integer)
  ) %>%
  select( -all_of(vars_to_drop) )
```

This script will be preloaded into any other R script you develop for the EDA report, so you can be sure to have the dataset with the exact data types specified in memory.

So, let's start developing the report from the basic statistics of the dataset.

Dataset summary page

The first page of the EDA report is responsible for providing the analyst with an overview of the data contained in the dataset. Some **basic information** is exposed that enriches the output of the **DataExplorer** package's introduce() function. This information is as follows:

- Number of rows and columns
- Number of discrete (categorical) and continuous (numerical) columns
- Number of columns having all missing values
- Total number of missing values in the dataset
- Number of complete rows, that is, not having missing values
- Total number of observations in the dataset, given by the number of rows multiplied by the number of columns
- Memory used in KB
- Number of duplicated rows

Then, a **summary statistics table** for the entire dataset is computed from the output of the dfSummary() function of the summarytools package. It contains the following information for each variable:

- Variable name and data type
- Basic statistics according to the data type
- Number of unique valid values (not null)

- Frequencies of valid values
- Number of valid values and their percentage
- Number of missing values and their percentage

Finally, more extensive **descriptive statistics** are available for numerical variables thanks to the descr() function of the summarytools package. In addition to the most common ones, the following statistics are added:

- **Median absolute deviation** (*mad*): Unlike variance and standard deviation, this is a robust measure of how widely distributed outliers are in a dataset. It is typically used for non-normal distributions.

- **Interquartile range** (*IQR*): As you saw with the box plots, this is a measure of where the bulk of the distribution values lie.

- **Coefficient of variation** (*cv*): This is a measure of relative variability as it is the ratio of the standard deviation to the mean.

- **Coefficient of skewness** (*skewness*): A measure of the lack of symmetry in a distribution.

- **Kurtosis:** It is a measure of whether the data is heavy-tailed or light-tailed relative to a normal distribution.

With this information, the analyst can get a complete picture of the shape of the data contained in the dataset.

Let's see how to implement them in Power BI. First, make sure that Power BI Desktop is pointing to the correct versions of R in **Options**. Then, follow these steps:

1. Click on **Get data, More …**, search for script, select **R script**, and click on **Connect**.

2. Enter the script found in the file R\01-basic-info.R in the Chapter 19 folder. Make sure that the init_path variable points to the correct absolute path of the 00-init-dataset.R file located in the same folder.

3. In the **Navigator** dialog box, select the basic_info_tbl, the numeric_vars_descr_stats_tbl, the summary_tbl, and the sample_tbl tables. Then click on **Load**.

4. After the four tables are loaded in the **Data** panel on the right in Power BI Desktop, you can add them to your report canvas by simply checking their column names. For example, expand the basic_info_tbl content and check the attribute (string field) and value (numerical field) fields in this order to get a table chart (if you click on the numerical field first, you'll get a column chart). A table appears on your canvas:

attribute	Sum of value
all_missing_columns	0.00
columns	11.00
complete_rows	183.00
continuous_columns	6.00
discrete_columns	5.00
duplicated_rows	0.00
memory_usage	184,456.00
rows	891.00
total_missing_values	866.00
total_observations	9,801.00
Total	**196,219.00**

Figure 19.1: Basic info table in its first state

In this case, the **Total** row makes no sense. This is because Power BI considers a numerical column to be summed by default.

5. Make sure that the table visual is selected, then click on the **Build visual** options (the form icon) in the **Visualizations** panel on the right. Expand the options of the **Sum of value** field in the **Columns** section and select **Don't summarize**:

Figure 19.2: Select to not summarize the value field

You will notice that the **Totals** row disappears. Then expand the **Specific column** section in the **Format** pane and type 0 in the **Value decimal places** text box – in later versions of Power BI Desktop, click the **Data** pane, choose **Value**, and enter 0 in the ribbon. Finally, select the **General** options (the **Format** pane in later versions), switch on the **Title** option, and expand its options. Then enter the label Basic Dataset Info in the text box.

6. Now click on an empty area of the canvas, expand the summary_tbl fields in the **Data** pane, and check them in the following order: **Variable**, **Stats Values**, **Unique Valid**, **Freq of Valid**, **Valid**, and **Missing**. Then expand the right edge of the visual in order to see all the columns. Feel free to resize individual columns to have the header in a single row. Make sure that all numerical fields have **Don't summarize** selected and use this string as the title label: Dataset Summary. You will get something like the following:

Dataset Summary

Variable	Stats Values	Unique Valid	Freq of Valid	Valid	Missing
Age [numeric]	Mean (sd) : 29.7 (14.5) min < med < max: 0.4 < 28 < 80 IQR (CV) : 17.9 (0.5)	88 distinct values	88 distinct values	714 (80.1%)	177 (19.9%)
Cabin [factor]	1. A10 2. A14 3. A16 4. A19 5. A20 6. A23 7. A24 8. A26	147 distinct values	1 (0.5%) 1 (0.5%) 1 (0.5%) 1 (0.5%) 1 (0.5%) 1 (0.5%) 1 (0.5%) 1 (0.5%)	204 (22.9%)	687 (77.1%)

Figure 19.3: The Dataset Summary table visual

7. Now click on an empty area of the canvas, expand the numeric_vars_descr_stats_tbl fields in the **Data** panel, and check them in the following order: **variable**, **mean**, **sd**, **min**, **q1**, **med**, **q3**, **max**, **mad**, **iqr**, **cv**, **skewness**, and **kurtosis**. Then expand the right side of the visual in order to see all the columns. Also, in this case, make sure that all numeric fields have **Don't summarize** selected and use this string as the title label: Descriptive Statistics for Numeric Variables. You'll get something like this:

Descriptive Statistics for Numeric Variables

variable	mean	sd	min	q1	med	q3	max	mad	iqr	cv	skewness	kurtosis
Age	29.70	14.53	0.42	20.00	28.00	38.00	80.00	13.34	17.88	0.49	0.39	0.16
Fare	32.20	49.69	0.00	7.90	14.45	31.00	512.33	10.24	23.09	1.54	4.77	33.12
Parch	0.38	0.81	0.00	0.00	0.00	0.00	6.00	0.00	0.00	2.11	2.74	9.69
Pclass	2.31	0.84	1.00	2.00	3.00	3.00	3.00	0.00	1.00	0.36	-0.63	-1.28
SibSp	0.52	1.10	0.00	0.00	0.00	1.00	8.00	0.00	1.00	2.11	3.68	17.73
Survived	0.38	0.49	0.00	0.00	0.00	1.00	1.00	0.00	1.00	1.27	0.48	-1.77

Figure 19.4: The Descriptive Statistics table visual

8. Now click on an empty area of the canvas, expand the `sample_tbl` fields, and check them all in the order you want after checking **Name** first (if you check a non-numerical field first, the visual selected by default will be the table). Make sure that all numerical fields have **Don't summarize** selected and use this string as the title label: `Dataset Sample`. You'll get something like this:

Dataset Sample

Name	Age	Sex	Pclass	SibSp	Parch	Ticket	Fare	Cabin	Embarked	Survived
Ahlin, Mrs. Johan (Johanna Persdotter Larsson)	40.00	female	3	1	0	7546	9.48		S	0
Allen, Mr. William Henry	35.00	male	3	0	0	373450	8.05		S	0
Andersson, Miss. Erna Alexandra	17.00	female	3	4	2	3101281	7.93		S	1
Andersson, Mr. Anders Johan	39.00	male	3	1	5	347082	31.28		S	0
Andreasson, Mr. Paul Edvin	20.00	male	3	0	0	347466	7.85		S	0
Arnold-Franchi, Mrs. Josef (Josefine Franchi)	18.00	female	3	1	0	349237	17.80		S	0
Asplund, Mrs. Carl Oscar (Selma Augusta Emilia Johansson)	38.00	female	3	1	5	347077	31.39		S	1
Backstrom, Mrs. Karl Alfred (Maria Mathilda Gustafsson)	33.00	female	3	3	0	3101278	15.85		S	1
Beesley, Mr. Lawrence	34.00	male	2	0	0	248698	13.00	D56	S	1

Figure 19.5: The Data Sample table visual

9. After repositioning the visuals on the canvas, you'll get your first EDA report page, like the one below:

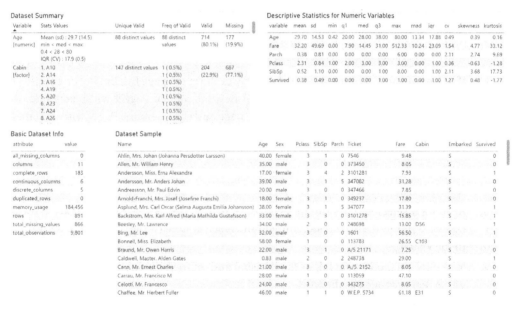

Figure 19.6: Summary page of the EDA report

10. Simply rename the page (right-click on the bottom page tab and click **Rename Page**) using the `Summary` label.

IMPORTANT NOTE

To view the sample details of the dataset, you must properly select its fields and use them as columns in the Power BI table visual. This means that if you want to change the source dataset, you must manually edit the visual sample details.

Nice work! You have just developed the first page of your EDA report. Now let's try to develop a page dedicated to the missing values analysis.

Missing values exploration

Although some information about the missing values is available in text format on the newly developed **Summary** page, providing a page with visuals dedicated to the missing values is definitely an advantage for the analyst.

In addition to displaying a simple **lollipop plot** showing the percentage values of missing values for each variable, you will also use an **upset plot** to allow the analyst to see which combinations of variables are found to be missing altogether, just as you learned in *Chapter 16, Adding Statistical Insights: Outliers and Missing Values*.

So, let's start developing the **Missing Values Analysis** page:

1. If it does not already exist, create a new Power BI report page by clicking on the plus icon next to the tabs at the bottom of the canvas. A new tab named **Page 1** will be created. Rename it (right-click on the tab at the bottom of the page and click **Rename Page**) with the label Missing Values Analysis.

2. Next, click an empty space on the report canvas first. Then click on the **R Visual** icon in the **Visualizations** pane (or in **Insert** on the **Home** ribbon) and enable it when you're prompted to do so. Next, move it to the left side of the page and resize it in order to fill half of the page.

3. Keeping it selected, click on the attribute field of the basic_info_tbl table. You won't use this field in the R Visual code, but you must select at least one column to activate the script in the visual.

4. Now click on the **Format** tab of the R Visual and, in the **Title** section, enter the string Missing Value Percentages as the title.

5. Copy the code from the R\02-missing-values-plot-1.R file into the Chapter 19 folder and paste it into the R Visual script editor. Remember to change the init_path variable accordingly. Then click on the **Run script** arrow icon in the upper-right corner of the R script editor (enable the R Visual each time you're prompted to do so). You'll see the lollipop plot in it, like this one:

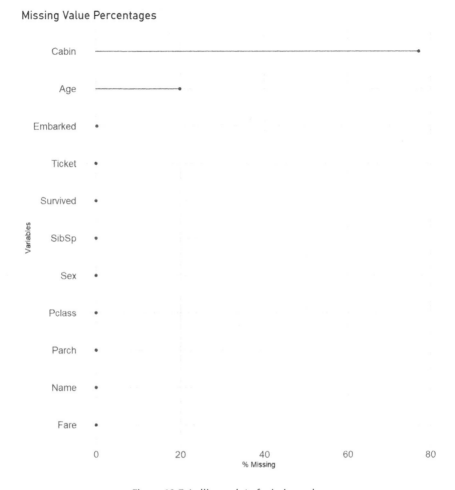

Figure 19.7: Lollipop plot of missing values

6. Click again on an empty area of the report canvas first. Then click on the **R Visual** icon in the **Visualizations** pane and enable it when you're prompted to do so. Next, move it to the right side of the page and resize it in order to fill half the page.

7. Keeping it selected, click on the `attribute` field of the `basic_info_tbl` table. You won't use this field in the R Visual code, but you must select at least one measure to enable the script in the visual.

8. Now click on the R Visual's **Format** tab, and in the **Title** section, enter the string `Variables Missing Together` as the title.

9. Copy the code from the R\03-missing-values-plot-2.R file into the Chapter 19 folder and paste it into the R Visual script editor. Then click on the **Run script** arrow icon in the top-right-corner of the R script editor (enable the R visual each time you're prompted to do so). You'll see the upset plot in it, like the following one:

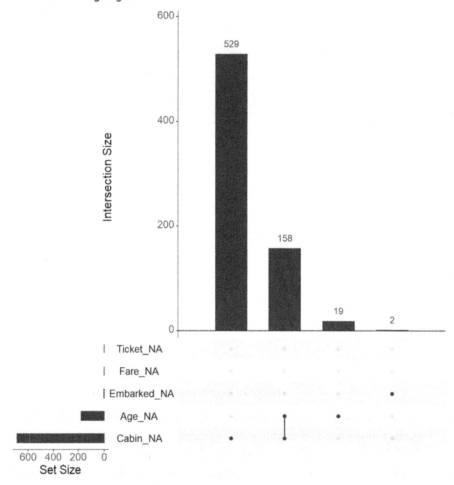

Figure 19.8: Upset plot of missing values

Nice work! It is now much easier for the analyst to understand the impact of missing values on the dataset. The whole page will look like this:

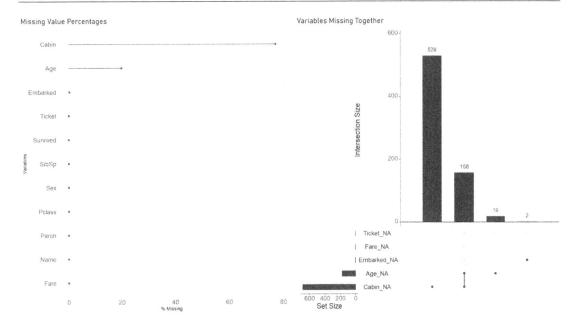

Figure 19.9: Missing values analysis page of the EDA report

Let's now turn to the development of a page dedicated to the univariate analysis of the dataset.

Univariate exploration

The one-dimensional analysis of a dataset consists of analyzing the distributions of the variables that make up the dataset. Depending on the data type of the variables, different visual tools are used to facilitate this analysis. The selection of variables to display in Power BI is done through drop-down slicers. If a variable is of the integer type, it will appear in both the numerical and categorical variable drop-down menus, allowing the analyst to visualize it in the way they deem appropriate.

Because the preceding graphs must be displayed using R visuals, if you want to publish the EDA report to the Power BI service, you must make sure that the R packages you are using are compatible with the version of the R engine found on the Power BI service (version 3.4.4 as of today). Also remember that Power BI Desktop can only reference one R engine at a time, which is the one used for both Power Query and R visuals on your machine. Therefore, if you plan to use the latest R engine for Power Query after you publish the report, you should also install the packages needed to render the report on that engine on your machine. This will ensure that the report renders correctly on Power BI Desktop during your testing.

However, in this particular case, the report uses some packages that unfortunately were not available when the R engine version 3.4.4 was released (e.g., `ggdist`). Therefore, the report we develop will only be usable on Power BI Desktop. In these cases, what do you do if you need to publish the report to the Power BI service?

TIP

If you have an on-premises SQL Server instance or Azure SQL Managed Instance to use as a repository, you can use the techniques described in *Chapter 18, Using the SQL Server Extensibility Framework's R and Python Engines with Power BI*. Basically, instead of saving lists of `Ggplot` objects to disk (as you will see below), you can save lists of PNG images generated in R directly to SQL Server tables or as in-memory pandas DataFrames (then there is no overhead of saving to files or into tables) and then embed them in binary text format and view them directly in Power BI using the technique shown at this link (you can also use Fabric lakehouse/warehouse to store pandas DataFrames graphics columns or SVG or PNG binary files): `https://bit.ly/embed-images-powerbi`.

You just have to be careful in cases where images are large and their binary text representation exceeds 32,766 characters (the limit on the length of a text value that can be loaded into Power BI). The solution involves both the splitting technique you learned in *Chapter 5, Importing Unhandled Data Objects*, and a bit of DAX to reassemble the whole string, as Chris Webb nicely points out in his post at this link: `https://bit.ly/embed-large-images-powerbi`. This technique results in the image being a measure – not all image visuals support measures, therefore the next step would be to convert the measure into a calculated column which conveniently is no longer subject to the 32,766 limit.

With that said, let's install the packages that we need to develop this report on Power BI Desktop:

1. Open RStudio and make sure it is referencing your CRAN R dedicated to Power Query (version 4.2.2 in our case).

2. Click on the **Console** window and enter this command: `install.packages('cowplot')`. It's like an extension of ggplot2, providing themes and functions to align, arrange, and annotate plots. Then, press *Enter*.

3. Enter this command: `install.packages('ggpubr')`. It provides some easy-to-use functions for creating and customizing ggplot2 based publication-ready plots. Then, press *Enter*.

4. Enter this command: `install.packages('ggExtra')`. It is a collection of functions and layers to enhance ggplot2, mostly used for its ggMarginal function, which adds marginal histograms/boxplots/density plots to scatterplots. Then, press *Enter*.

5. Enter this command: `install.packages('RColorBrewer')`. It is an essential tool to manage colors and palettes with R. Then, press *Enter*.

6. Enter this command: `install.packages('ggmosaic')`. It is designed to create visualizations of categorical data, in particular, mosaic plots. Then, press *Enter*.

7. Enter this command: `install.packages('ggdist')`. It is designed to visualize statistical distributions, illustrate uncertainty, and enhance ggplot2 graphics. Then, press *Enter*.

Now you can start developing the new page of your report dedicated to the univariate analysis of the dataset:

1. If it does not already exist, create a new Power BI report page by clicking on the plus sign next to the tabs at the bottom of the canvas. A new tab named **Page 1** will be created.

2. Click on **Get data, More ...**, search for script, select **R script**, and click on **Connect**.

3. Enter the script you can find in the file R\04-serialize-univariate-plots.R in the Chapter 19 folder. Make sure that the folder variable points to the correct absolute path of the Chapter 19 folder. This script serializes to disk the lists of plots associated with each variable according to its type. Once you click **OK**, you will find the following files on disk: histodensity_lst.rds, histodensity_transf_lst.rds (numerical variables transformed according to Yeo-Johnson), and barchart_lst.rds. Pre-computing lists of graphs and serializing them to disk is a good strategy when the possible combinations of the variables involved are small.

4. In the **navigator** dialog, select the categorical_df and numeric_df tables. As you can see, the numeric_df table contains the names of the numeric variables in the numeric_col_name column, repeated twice, once for each type of transformation in the transf_type column to be applied to them (standard and yeo-johnson):

numeric_df

numeric_col_name	transf_type
Age	standard
Age	yeo-johnson
Fare	standard
Fare	yeo-johnson
Parch	standard
Parch	yeo-johnson
Pclass	standard
Pclass	yeo-johnson
SibSp	standard
SibSp	yeo-johnson
Survived	standard
Survived	yeo-johnson

Figure 19.10: numeric_df table contents

Then click **Load**.

5. Click on the slicer visual icon. Then expand the numeric_df table under the **Fields** panel (or in the **Data** pane) and check the numeric_col_name measure.

6. Click on the **Format** options icon on the right, expand **Slicer settings**, and select the **Dropdown** slicer type. Expand the **Selection** options and enable the **Single select** option. Expand the **Slicer header** options and edit **Title text** to Numeric Variables.

7. First, click on an empty space on the report canvas. Then click the slicer visual icon. Then expand the numeric_df table under the **Fields** panel (or in the **Data** pane) and check the transf_type measure.

8. Click on the **Format** options icon on the right, expand **Slicer settings,** and select the **Dropdown** slicer type. Expand the **Selection** options and enable the **Single select** option. Expand the **Slicer header** options and edit **Title text** to Transformations.

9. Now, click on an empty space on the report canvas. Then click on the **R Visual** icon in the **Visualizations** pane and enable it if you're prompted to do so. Next, move it under the two slicers you've just created.

10. Keeping it selected, click on both fields of the **numeric_df** table (**numeric_col_name** and **transf_type**).

11. Now click on the **Format** pane of R Visual and uncheck the **Title** option.

12. Copy the code from the R\05-plot-numeric-variables.R file in the Chapter 19 folder and paste it into the R Visual script editor. Remember to edit the folder variable. Then click on the **Run script** arrow icon in the upper-right corner of the R script editor (enable R Visual each time you're prompted to do so). You'll get the univariate analysis of the untransformed Age variable:

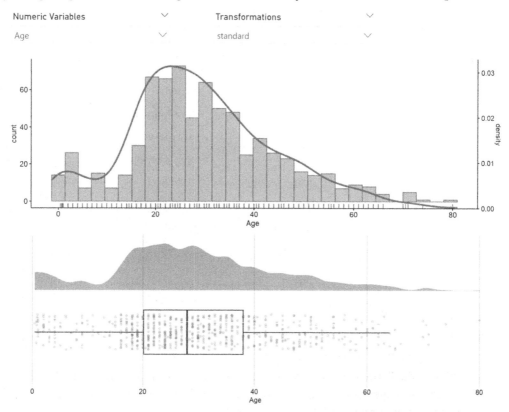

Figure 19.11: Univariate analysis of the Age variable

13. If you select the yeo-johnson transformation from the **Transformations** drop - down list, the plots will update accordingly:

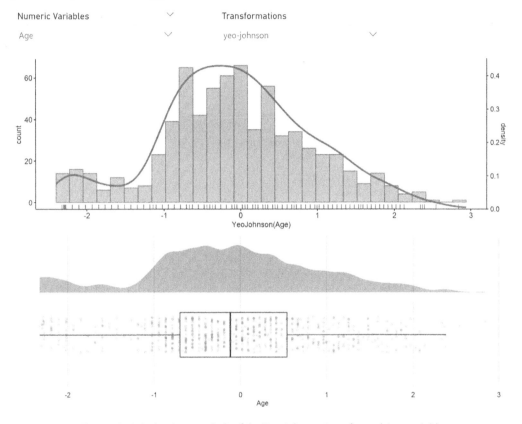

Figure 19.12: Univariate analysis of the Yeo-Johnson transformed Age variable

14. Now let's create the categorical variable slicer. Click on an empty spot in the report canvas first. Then click on the **Slicer** visual icon. Then expand the categorical_df table in the **Fields** panel (or in the **Data** pane) and select the categorical_col_name measure.

15. Click on the **Format visual** options icon on the right (or in the **Format** pane), expand **Slicer settings**, and select the **Dropdown** slicer type. Expand the **Selection** options and enable the **Single select** option. Expand the **Slicer header** options and edit **Title text** to Categorical Variables.

16. Now, first click on an empty space on the report canvas. Then click on the **R Visual** icon in the **Visualizations** (or **Insert** on the **Home** ribbon) pane and enable it if you're prompted to do so. Next move it under the slicer you've just created.

17. Keeping it selected, click on the field of the **categorical_df** table (**categorical_col_name**).

18. Now click on the **Format** tab of R Visual and uncheck the **Title** option.

19. Copy the code from the R\06-plot-categorical-variables.R file in the Chapter 19 folder and paste it into the R Visual script editor. Remember to edit the folder variable. Then click on the **Run script** arrow icon in the upper-right corner of the R script editor (enable R Visual each time you're prompted to do so). You'll get the univariate analysis of the Cabin variable:

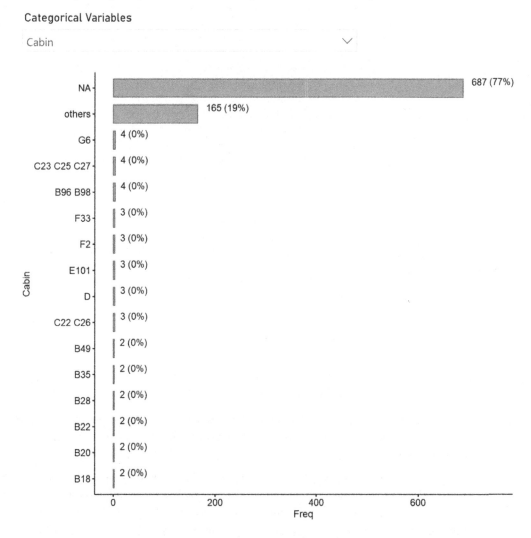

Figure 19.13: Univariate analysis of the Cabin variable

20. Simply rename the current page (right-click on the tab at the bottom of the page and click **Rename Page**) with the label Univariate Analysis.

Well done! You have just developed a great EDA report page dedicated to univariate dataset analysis. If you play with the slicers, the whole page will look like this:

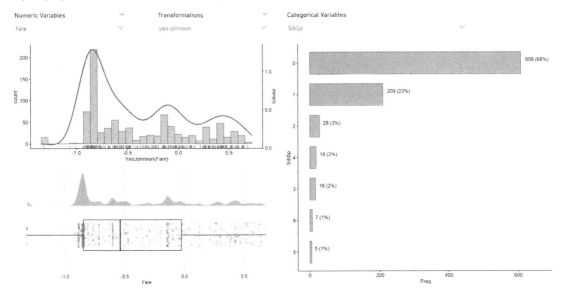

Figure 19.14: The Univariate Analysis EDA report page

Now it is time to develop a report page dedicated to multivariate dataset analysis.

Multivariate exploration

In general, analyzing variables individually is never enough to give the analyst a complete view of the dataset. Being able to use visualizations that allow the interaction of multiple variables depending on their data type is definitely a step towards a more accurate analysis of the dataset.

The most common visualization used to analyze the interaction of two numerical variables is the **scatterplot**. In our case, we will use an enriched version of this plot, adding the **marginal distributions** of the variables at the edges. It's also possible to color the points according to another categorical variable.

In this way, the analyst can examine the interaction of three variables. *Figure 19.15* shows an example of this plot for the Age and Fare variables grouped by the Sex variable:

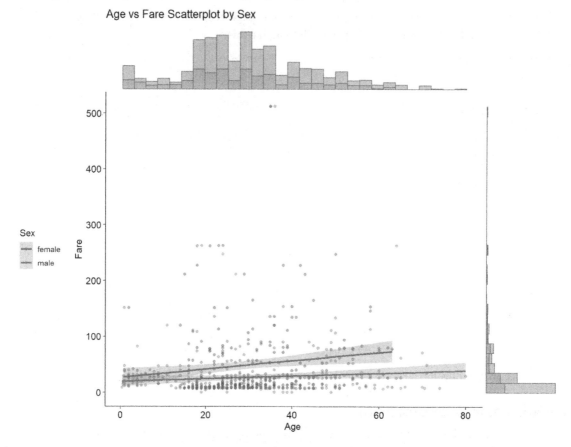

Figure 19.15: Scatterplot with marginal histograms for Age and Fare by Sex

As you can see, there are as many regression lines as there are categories of the grouping variable. In the case of a missing grouping variable, the regression line is unique, and the plot also shows the values of Pearson's R coefficient, Spearman's **rho**, and Kendall's **tau**, with the p-value derived from the respective tests. In short, the **p-value** in this case represents the probability that the correlation between x and y in the sample data occurred by chance (take a look at the references to learn more about p-values):

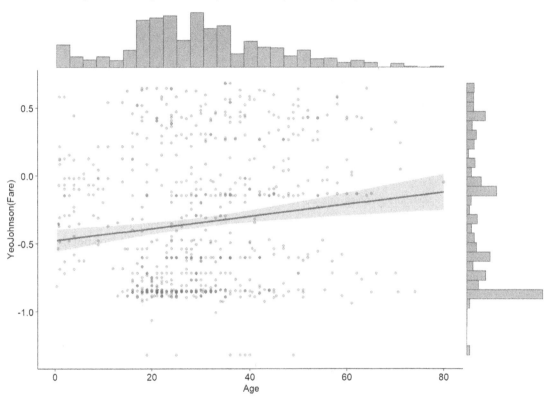

Figure 19.16: Scatterplot for Age and Fare (transformed) without grouping

When the variables you want to study the interaction of are categorical, the **mosaic plot** comes in handy. In *Figure 19.17*, you can see the mosaic plot of the SibSp and Pclass variables grouped by Sex (for better viewing, a color image is also available for download):

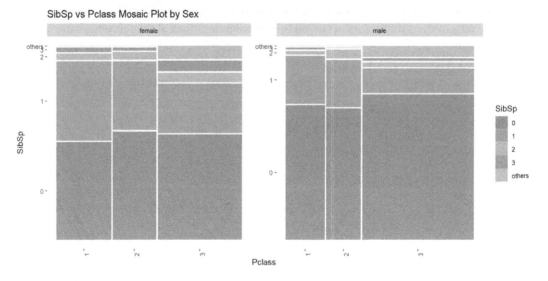

Figure 19.17: Mosaic plot for Pclass and SibSp grouped by Sex

Finally, it is possible to study the interaction of a numerical variable with a categorical variable by visualizing **raincloud plots for each category**. In addition, it is always possible to split the plot by a third categorical variable, as in the previous cases. *Figure 19.18* shows an example of this plot for the Fare (transformed by Yeo-Johnson for better visualization) and Pclass variables by the Sex variable:

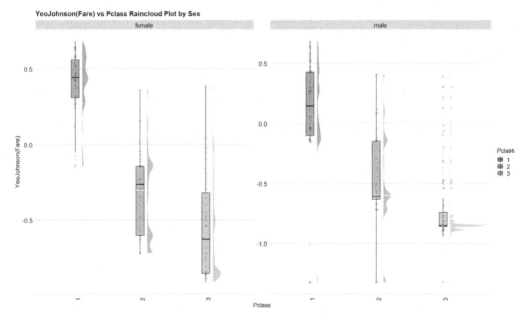

Figure 19.18: Raincloud plots for the Fare and Pclass variables grouped by Sex

The new page of your report dedicated to the multivariate analysis of your dataset is now ready to be developed:

1. If it does not already exist, create a new Power BI report page by clicking the plus sign next to the tabs at the bottom of the canvas. A new tab named **Page 1** is created.

2. Click on **Get data.More …**, search for `script`, select **R script**, and click on **Connect**.

3. Paste the script found in the R\07-create-multivariate-objects.R file into the Chapter 19 folder. Make sure that the folder variable points to the correct absolute path of the Chapter 19 folder.

4. In the **Navigator** dialog, select the multivariate_df table, and click **Load**. In this case, the code to generate the plots will be written directly in R Visual, without the need to serialize them first and recall them at the time of visualization. This strategy is opposite to the one used for the univariate analysis page, because in this case the number of combinations between the variables in the game is much higher, and generating the same number of plots in a list and serializing everything is not very efficient. The multivariate_df table is a DataFrame that is the result of a cross-join of all the variables involved in the multivariate analysis (two numerical variables, a variable associated with the type of transformation for each of them, two categorical variables, and another categorical variable for the grouping: seven variables in total) for more than 100,000 lines:

	x	x_transf_type	y	y_transf_type	cat1	cat2	grp
1	Age	standard	Age	standard	Cabin	Cabin	<none>
2	Age	standard	Age	standard	Cabin	Cabin	Cabin
3	Age	standard	Age	standard	Cabin	Cabin	Embarked
4	Age	standard	Age	standard	Cabin	Cabin	Name
5	Age	standard	Age	standard	Cabin	Cabin	Parch
6	Age	standard	Age	standard	Cabin	Cabin	Pclass
7	Age	standard	Age	standard	Cabin	Cabin	Sex
8	Age	standard	Age	standard	Cabin	Cabin	SibSp
9	Age	standard	Age	standard	Cabin	Cabin	Survived
10	Age	standard	Age	standard	Cabin	Cabin	Ticket
11	Age	standard	Age	standard	Cabin	Embarked	<none>

Figure 19.19: multivariate_df table's content

5. Click on the **Slicer** visual icon. Then expand the multivariate_df table under the **Data** pane and check the x column.

6. Click on the **Format visual** options icon on the right, expand **Slicer settings**, and select the **Dropdown** slicer type. Expand the **Selection** options and enable the **Single select** option. Expand the **Slicer header** options and edit **Title text** to x numeric. Click **General**, enable **Title**, expand its section, and enter Analysis Variables as the title text.

7. First, click on an empty spot in the report canvas, and then on the **Slicer** visual icon. Expand the multivariate_df table on the **Data** pane and check the x_transf_type column.

8. Click on the **Format visual** options icon on the right, expand **Slicer settings**, and select the **Dropdown** slicer type. Expand the **Selection** options and enable the **Single select** option. Expand the **Slicer header** options and edit **Title text** to x transformation.

9. Repeat steps 5 to 8 in order to create the **y numeric** and **y transformation** slicers, making sure to select the y and y_transf_type columns respectively. Keep the **Title** section switched off for them also.

10. Click on an empty space on the report canvas, and then click on the **Slicer** visual icon. Expand the `multivariate_df` table on the **Data** pane, and check the `cat1` column.

11. Click on the **Format visual** options icon on the right, expand **Slicer settings,** and select the **Dropdown** slicer type. Expand the **Selection** options and enable the **Single select** option. Expand the **Slicer header** options and edit **Title text** to `cat1 categorical`.

12. Repeat steps 10 through 12 to create the **cat2 categorical** slice. Be sure to select the **cat2** column for it.

13. Click on an empty spot in the report canvas first and then on the **Slicer** visual icon. Expand the `multivariate_df` table on the **Data** pane and check the `grp` column.

14. Click on the **Format visual** options icon on the right, expand **Slicer settings,** and select the **Dropdown** slicer type. Expand the **Selection** options and enable the **Single select** option. Expand the **Slicer header** options and edit **Title text** to `grp categorical`.

15. Try to align all these sliders on a single row at the top of your page, like the following, after aligning and resizing them a bit:

Figure 19.20: Multivariate page's slicers at the top of the page

16. First, click on an empty area of the report canvas. Then click the **R Visual** icon in the **Visualizations** pane and enable it if you're prompted. Next, move it under the row of slicers you've just created and resize it to fill the page.

17. Keeping it selected, click on all the fields of the `multivariate_df` table.

18. Now click on the **Format** tab of R Visual and uncheck the **Title** option.

19. Copy the code from the `R\08-plot-multivariate-plots.R` file in the `Chapter 19` folder and paste it into the R Visual script editor. Then click on the **Run script** arrow icon in the upper-right corner of the R script editor (you'll need to activate R Visual each time you're prompted to do so). You'll see all the multivariate analysis plots.

20. Simply rename the current page (right-click on the tab at the bottom of the page and click **Rename Page**) using the label `Multivariate Analysis`.

Amazing! This EDA report page dedicated to multivariate analysis is very enlightening for an analyst. If you play with the slicers, the whole page will look like this:

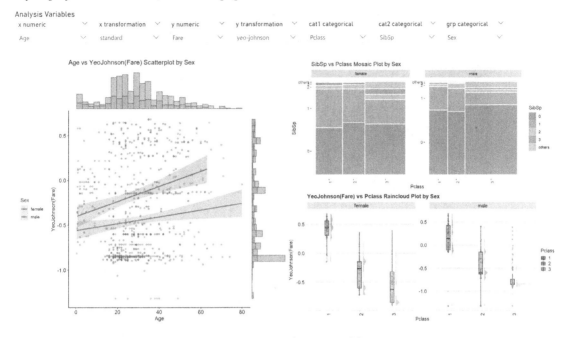

Figure 19.21: Multivariate analysis page of the EDA report

Note that the numerical **y** variable is used as the y-axis for both the scatterplot and the raincloud plot. The categorical variable **cat1** is used as the x-axis for both the raincloud plot and the mosaic plot. The categorical **grp** variable is used to group all three plots by their labels.

You've just seen how powerful and flexible R is for professional graphics development. Now let's see how to develop a variable association page.

Variable associations

As you learned in *Chapter 15, Adding Statistical Insights: Associations*, knowing the correlation coefficient that links two variables gives you the ability to estimate the predictive power of one variable over the other. In that chapter, you also learned how to calculate the correlation coefficient based on combinations of the different types of variables involved.

In this section, we will use what you have learned to develop a page for the EDA report that contains a **heatmap plot** colored according to the intensity of the correlation coefficient. Here is an example:

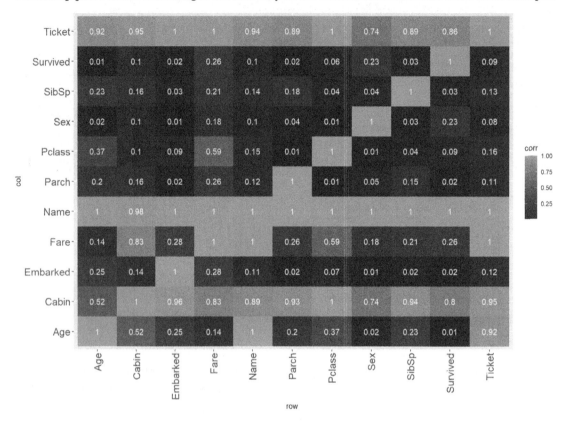

Figure 19.22: Correlation heatmap of the dataset

The correlation coefficient is calculated according to the choice that the analyst can make thanks to two slicers: one that allows you to choose the method to use for the correlation between numerical variables and another that allows you to choose the method to use for the correlation between categorical variables.

So, let's start developing the **Associations** page:

1. If it does not already exist, create a new Power BI report page by clicking on the plus sign next to the tabs at the bottom of the canvas. A new tab named **Page 1** is created.

2. Click on **Get data, More ...**, search for `script`, select **R script**, and click on **Connect**.

3. Enter the script you can find in the file `R\09-create-association-objects.R` in the `Chapter 19` folder. Make sure that the `folder` variable points to the correct absolute path of the `Chapter 19` folder.

4. In the **Navigator** dialog, select the `corr_tbl` table. This table is the result of several transformations. First, for each combination of correlation methods (for numerical and categorical variables), a column containing the corresponding correlation coefficient was computed.

This was accelerated by using parallel computing for R introduced in *Chapter 11, Calling External APIs To Enrich Your Data*. A pivot operation was then performed that combined all of these columns into the single column corr and created the new column, corr_type, which contains the string identifying the combination of methods used. Finally, the corr_type column was split into two separate columns, one for use in the correlation method slicer for numerical variables and the other for use in the correlation method slicer for categorical variables. Here is an example of the resulting table:

corr_tbl

row	col	numeric_corr_type	categorical_corr_type	corr
Age	Age	pearson	theil	1
Age	Age	pearson	cramer	1
Age	Age	spearman	theil	1
Age	Age	spearman	cramer	1
Age	Age	kendall	theil	1
Age	Age	kendall	cramer	1
Age	Cabin	pearson	theil	0.524193719
Age	Cabin	pearson	cramer	0.524193719
Age	Cabin	spearman	theil	0.524193719

Figure 19.23: corr_tbl table contents

Then click on **Load**.

5. Click on the slicer visual icon. Then expand the corr_tbl table on the **Data** pane and check the numeric_corr_type column.

6. Click on the **Format visual** options icon on the right, expand **Slicer settings**, and select the **Dropdown** slicer type. Expand the **selection** options and enable the **Single select** option. Expand the **Slicer header** options and edit **Title text** to Numeric correlation type. Click **General**, enable **Title**, expand its section, and enter Analysis Variables as the title text.

7. Click on an empty spot in the report canvas, and click then on the slicer visual icon. Expand the corr_tbl table on the **Fields** panel, and check the categorical_corr_type column.

8. Click on the **Format visual** options icon on the right, expand **Slicer settings**, and select the **Dropdown** slicer type. Expand the **Selection** options and enable the **Single select** option. Expand the **Slicer header** options and edit **Title text** to Categorical correlation type.

9. Try to align all these sliders on a single row at the top of your page like the following:

Figure 19.24: Association page's slicers at the top of the page

10. First, click on an empty area of the report canvas. Then click the **R Visual** icon in the **Visualizations** pane and enable it if you're prompted. Next, move it under the row of slicers you've just created and resize it to fill the page.

11. Keeping it selected, click on the col, corr, and row fields of the corr_tbl table.

12. Click on R Visual's **Format** tab and, in the **Title** section, enter the string Categorical Heatmap as the title.

13. Copy the code of the R\10-plot-association-plots.R file in the Chapter 19 folder and paste it into the R Visual script editor. Then click on the **Run script** arrow icon in the upper-right corner of the R script editor (enable R Visual each time you're prompted to do so). You'll get all the multivariate analysis plots in it.

14. Simply rename the current page (right-click on the tab at the bottom of the page and click **Rename Page**) using the label Association Analysis.

It's impressive how easy it was to create a correlation heatmap with R and ggplot!

Playing with the slicers, the whole page will look like the following:

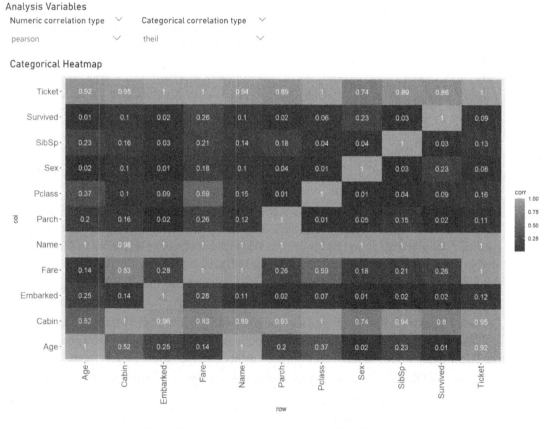

Figure 19.25: Association analysis page of the EDA report

Wow! You have completed your first EDA report. You have to admit that the result is already amazing!

Summary

In this chapter, you learned what **EDA** is used for and what goals it helps achieve. You also learned which tools are most commonly used to perform automated EDA using Python and R. Finally, you developed a complete and dynamic EDA report to analyze a dataset using R and its most popular graphing packages.

In the next chapter, you'll see how to develop advanced visualizations.

References

For additional reading, check out the following books and articles:

- *Powerful EDA (Exploratory Data Analysis) in just two lines of code using Sweetviz* (`https://towardsdatascience.com/powerful-eda-exploratory-data-analysis-in-just-two-lines-of-code-using-sweetviz-6c943d32f34`)
- *Lux: A Python API for Intelligent Visual Data Discovery* (`https://www.youtube.com/watch?v=YANIids_Nkk`)
- *pandas Profiling of the Titanic Dataset* (`https://docs.profiling.ydata.ai/latest/`)
- *pandasGUI Demo* (`https://www.youtube.com/watch?v=NKXdolMxW2Y`)
- *A Comprehensive Guide to the Grammar of Graphics for Effective Visualization of Multi-dimensional Data* (`https://towardsdatascience.com/a-comprehensive-guide-to-the-grammar-of-graphics-for-effective-visualization-of-multi-dimensional-1f92b4ed4149`)
- *The Complete ggplot2 Tutorial* (`http://r-statistics.co/Complete-Ggplot2-Tutorial-Part1-With-R-Code.html`)
- *Everything you need to know about interpreting correlations* (`https://towardsdatascience.com/eveything-you-need-to-know-about-interpreting-correlations-2c485841c0b8`)

Test your knowledge

1. What is the primary goal of **Exploratory Data Analysis** (**EDA**)?
2. What are the essential phases in the EDA process?
3. What does the EDA process entail when it comes to understanding or getting to know your data?
4. How can you visualize categorical variables in EDA?
5. In EDA, what types of graphs can be used to understand the relationship between two different variables?
6. What is the process of cleaning or tidying up your data in EDA?
7. What is the primary objective when identifying connections between variables during EDA?
8. Why is the definition of data types important in EDA and how does it relate to Power BI and R?
9. How can I ensure the graphs utilizing R packages are displayed correctly in the Power BI service?

10. What should I do if the report we developed can only be used on Power BI Desktop because some packages are not available on the R engine that is on the Power BI service?

11. Given the large number of variables involved in multivariate analysis, how does this affect the code-writing strategy for generating plots?

Learn more on Discord

To join the Discord community for this book – where you can share feedback, ask questions to the author, and learn about new releases – follow the QR code below:

```
https://discord.gg/MKww5g45EB
```

20

Using the Grammar of Graphics in Python with plotnine

Coined from the *Grammar of Graphics* as implemented in R, ggplot2 has become the tool of choice for many data visualization professionals. Its popularity stems from its consistent underlying graphics grammar, making the syntax reasonable to learn and master. Once you understand the basics, it's possible to create different visualizations using the same syntax structure.

One feature of ggplot2 that makes life easier for developers is its layering approach. This feature allows the user to add or remove elements at will. Users can plot simple graphs as well as create complex custom visualizations thanks to the higher level of control provided by this approach.

This is not to say that it is impossible to create graphs as complex as those created with ggplot2 in Python. Simply, the tools provided by Matplotlib in Python are a bit more complicated to use and have a more intricate syntax to achieve the same things in ggplot2. A notable simplification has been introduced by the *Seaborn* package for Python developers. Of course, the immediacy of ggplot2 could not be achieved with Seaborn.

This was true until the release of the *plotnine* package, which implements the Grammar of Graphics for Python. That said, the following topics will be covered in this chapter:

- What is plotnine?
- Analyzing Titanic data with plotnine
- Using plotnine in Power BI

Technical requirements

This chapter requires you to have a working internet connection and Power BI Desktop already installed on your machine (version: 2.123.742.0, 64-bit, November 2023). You must have properly configured the R and Python engines and IDEs as outlined in *Chapter 2, Configuring R with Power BI*, and *Chapter 3, Configuring Python with Power BI*. Knowledge of the topics covered in *Chapter 5, Importing Unhandled Data Objects*, is recommended.

What is plotnine?

In the dynamic field of data visualization in Python, *plotnine* is emerging as a compelling library in the Python ecosystem. It is based on Leland Wilkinson's Grammar of Graphics, a comprehensive framework for creating complex and meaningful graphics from data. The Grammar of Graphics empowers users to visually describe what they want to present, rather than the procedural details of plotting, which plotnine skillfully translates into beautiful visual representations. The library mirrors the functionality of R's ggplot2, providing a Pythonic approach to sophisticated data visualization.

plotnine features an intuitive and powerful syntax, making it a favorite for exploratory data analysis where speed and efficiency in data visualization are critical. The library provides a consistent and flexible framework for constructing plots, a benefit of the Grammar of Graphics approach, which eases the learning curve and broadens its application to diverse data visualization needs. In addition, its seamless integration with pandas, Python's leading data manipulation library, streamlines the data visualization process.

As expected, plotnine is designed to closely mimic ggplot2, offering an almost identical style and approach to creating visualizations. The main differences between the two may be nuanced and related to the depth of integration with R's broader ecosystem, rather than significant differences in the visualization capabilities themselves. For example, ggplot2's integration with R's data structures and types may provide greater fluidity in managing and visualizing data directly from R's various data analysis packages. In addition, R's rich statistical and data manipulation libraries can provide a more streamlined workflow for certain types of complex data analysis and visualization tasks when using ggplot2.

Let us take a closer look at the main concepts of plotnine.

plotnine core concepts

In plotnine, the basic concepts are borrowed from the Grammar of Graphics and form the basis for creating and customizing visualizations:

- **Aesthetics**, often abbreviated to *aes*, refers to the visual aspects of plot objects. This includes attributes such as color, shape, size, and position, which are crucial for distinguishing and highlighting different parts of the data.

- **Geometries**, known as *geom*, are central to determining the type of visualization. Each geometry corresponds to a different type of plot. For example, `geom_point` creates scatter plots, `geom_line` is used for line plots, and `geom_bar` is used for bar plots. This categorization allows for a wide range of visual representations, depending on the nature and requirements of the data.

- **Facets** are a feature that allows the creation of multiple related plots within a single figure. This is particularly useful for comparing different subsets of data. By dividing the data based on a categorical variable, facets allow side-by-side comparisons, making it easier to see patterns and differences between categories.

- **Scales** play a critical role in how data is mapped to visual properties. They are the mechanisms by which data values are translated into visual elements such as color, size, or position. Scales can be manipulated to change aspects such as the color palette of a graph or the range and limits of axes, providing control over how data is visually represented.

- **Coordinate systems** define the spatial layout of a graph. The most common system is the Cartesian coordinate system, but plotnine also supports others, such as polar coordinates. This choice affects the overall layout and appearance of the plot, offering different perspectives and ways of presenting the data.

- **Themes** affect the overall aesthetics and appearance of the plot. They control elements such as the background, gridlines, and fonts. Themes allow for extensive customization, allowing users to fine-tune their visualizations for both aesthetic appeal and clarity. This includes changing everything from color schemes to text styles to ensure that the final visualization meets specific presentation needs or preferences.

Let us see how these concepts can be used in practice in an exploratory data analysis.

Analyzing Titanic data with plotnine

We will now demonstrate the simplicity of using plotnine for recurring tasks such as exploratory analysis.

First, you need to install the plotnine package. Here are the steps to do that:

1. Open Anaconda Prompt.
2. Switch to your pbi_powerqery_env environment by entering this command: conda activate pbi_powerqery_env.
3. There are two ways to install plotnine: either install the package with the default options with a simple pip install plotnine==0.12.4 or install some extra features with pip install plotnine[all]==0.12.4 (the extra packages installed are scikit-learn and scikit-misc for loess and Gaussian smoothing). The default installation is sufficient for the code you will find in this chapter.

Then, you can import the necessary libraries and functions and load the Titanic data into the df variable with the following code:

```
import pandas as pd
from plotnine import (
    options, theme_tufte, ggplot, aes, geom_bar,
    geom_text, after_stat, geom_histogram, facet_grid, labs
)

dataset_url = 'http://bit.ly/titanic-dataset-csv'
df = pd.read_csv(dataset_url)
```

Now, suppose that you want to count the number of passengers on the Titanic by class. First, assuming that the Titanic dataset is contained in the df DataFrame, you need to initialize the graph by setting df as the data source with ggplot(df). Using the aes() function, you can map the x-axis to the Pclass column of the Titanic dataset (i.e., the different passenger classes are plotted along the x-axis). The geom_bar() function adds bar geometry to the graph.

By default, it creates a histogram, which, in this case, counts the number of occurrences (frequency) of each unique value in the Pclass column, effectively providing the number of passengers in each class. Finally, the labs() function adds labels to the graph to improve readability. title sets the title of the graph. The x and y parameters are used to label the x and y axes, respectively. In this case, the x-axis is labeled Class and the y-axis is labeled Count. The contribution of each function is added to the plot by the plus sign (+) operator. The above translates to the following code:

```
p = (
        ggplot(df)
        + aes(x='Pclass')
        + geom_bar()
        + labs(title='Passenger Count by Class', x='Class', y='Count')
)
p
```

Here are the results:

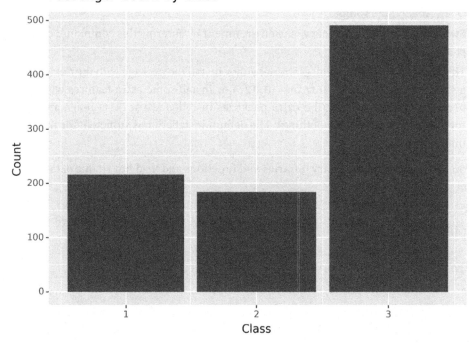

Figure 20.1: Bar chart of passengers by class

The monochromatic scheme of this chart may be visually unappealing, and the grid may distract the viewer. To improve its aesthetic appeal, consider assigning different colors to the bars for each class and removing the grid by applying a minimalist theme such as the Tufte theme. This theme, inspired by Edward Tufte's principles in *Chapter 6, Data-Ink Maximization and Graphical Design*, of *The Visual Display of Quantitative Information*, focuses on data-ink maximization and clean design.

You can add the color fill option using the plus operator and the `fill` parameter of the `aes()` function, which is set to the string `factor(Pclass)`. Note how, in this case, plotnine borrows the `factor` function for categorical variables directly from R. The title of the legend can be customized using the `fill` parameter of the `labs()` function. Again, using the plus operator, you can easily "add" the Tufte theme to the plot. Here is the resulting code from these additions alone:

```
p = (
    p
    + aes(fill="factor(Pclass)")
    + labs(fill='Class')
    + theme_tufte()
)
p
```

Here is the resulting plot (remember that you can access the color images online, as mentioned in the *Preface*):

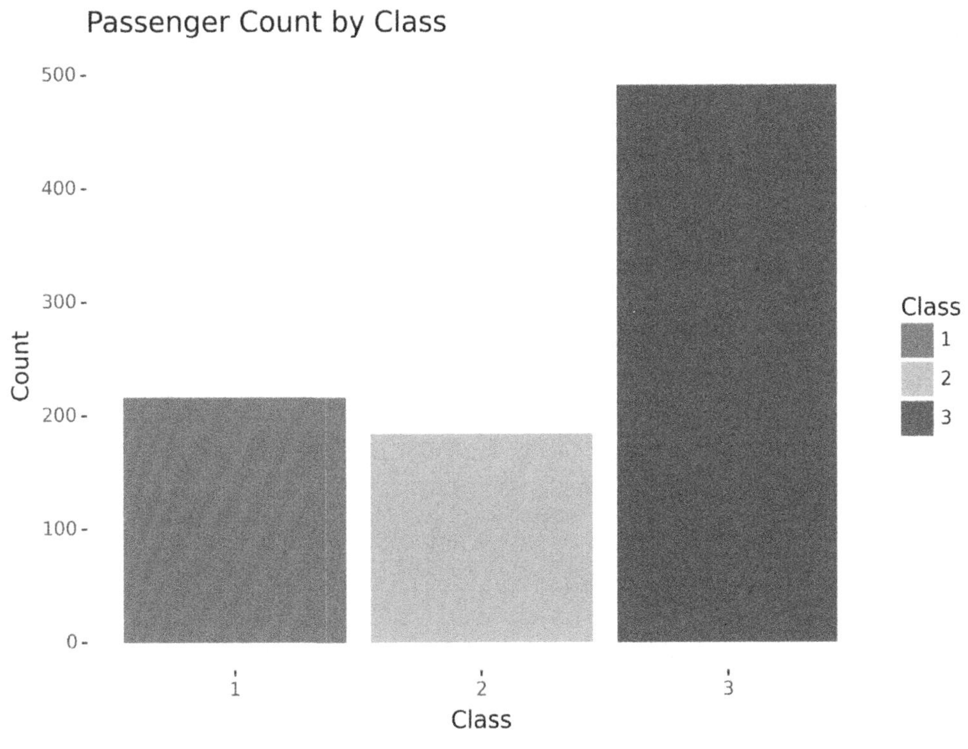

Figure 20.2: Colored bar chart of passengers by class

Figure 20.2 is very similar to *Figure 19.1* in *Chapter 19, Exploratory Data Analysis*. It is missing only the number of passengers in each class and the percentage of the total that number represents at the top of each bar. If you also want to add these numerical values for each bar of the graph, think of adding two text labels, one for the number of passengers and one for the percentage of the total.

The numerical values of the labels are calculated thanks to the `after_stat()` function, whose main purpose is to access the results of statistical transformations applied to the data during the plotting process. These values can then be formatted thanks to the `format_string` parameter, and their placement on the graph can be adjusted thanks to the `nudge_x`, `nudge_y`, and `va` (vertical alignment) parameters.

For the sake of clarity, we report all the code together:

```python
p = (
        ggplot(df)
        + aes(x='Pclass', fill="factor(Pclass)")
        + geom_bar()
        + geom_text(
            aes(label = after_stat('count')),
            stat = 'count',
            nudge_x = -0.14,
            nudge_y = 0.125,
            va = 'bottom',
            size = 8
        )
        + geom_text(
            aes(label = after_stat('prop*100'), group=1),
            stat = 'count',
            nudge_x = 0.14,
            nudge_y = 0.125,
            va = 'bottom',
            format_string = '({:.1f}%)',
            size = 8
        )
        + labs(title='Passenger Count by Class',
                x='Class', y='Count', fill='Class')
        + theme_tufte()
)
p
```

The resulting plot is as follows:

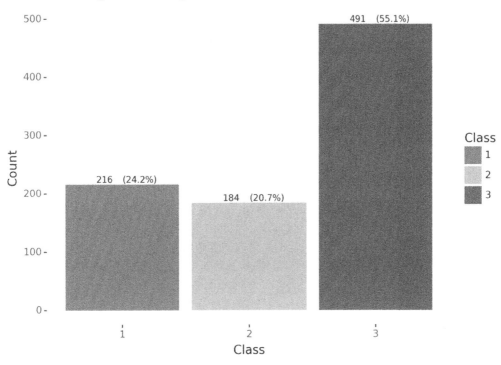

Figure 20.3: Colored bar chart of passengers by class complete with statistics

Impressive for how simple it is, isn't it? Also, you can easily plot the histogram of passenger ages with this code:

```
(
    ggplot(df)
    + aes(x='Age')
    + geom_histogram(binwidth = 10, color = 'brown', fill = 'orange')
    + labs(title = 'Age Distribution of Passengers',
            x='Age', y='Count')
    + theme_tufte()
)
```

Here is the resulting plot:

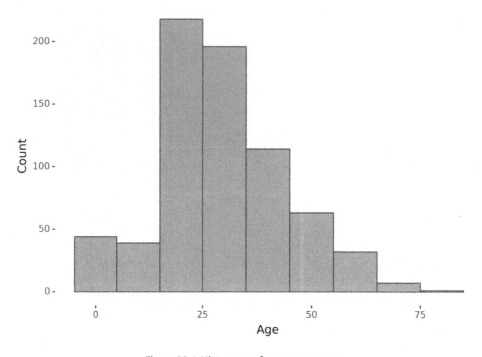

Figure 20.4: Histogram of passenger ages

If you want to analyze the frequency of passenger ages by gender, you simply divide the previous plot by the values taken by the Sex variable, thanks to the facet_grid() function. At the code level, it is a matter of adding a simple line to the previous code:

```
(
    ggplot(df)
    + aes(x='Age')
    + geom_histogram(binwidth = 10, color = 'brown', fill = 'orange')
    + facet_grid('. ~ Sex')
    + labs(title = 'Age Distribution of Passengers by Sex',
           x='Age', y='Count')
    + theme_tufte()
)
```

The resulting plot is as follows:

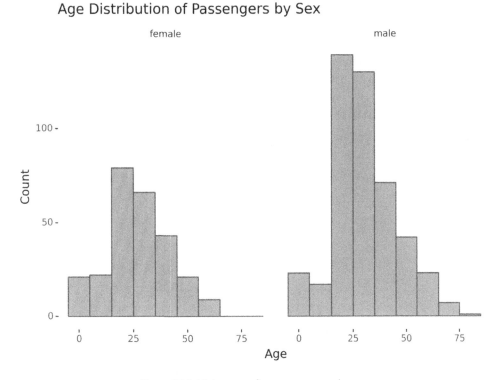

Figure 20.5: Histogram of passenger ages by sex

You can find all the scripts in the `01-titanic-analysis-plotnine.py` file in the `Chapter 20` folder.

Thanks to plotnine, those who have experience in analysis with ggplot2 in R will also feel at home with Python. The ease of use of a package that implements the `Grammar of Graphics` cannot fail to impress even the most ardent Pythonist.

With a little patience, you can then replicate the EDA report created in R in *Chapter 19*, *Exploratory Data Analysis*, with Python, but this time, using plotnine!

Now let's take a look at how we can use the plots we get from plotnine in Power BI.

Using plotnine in Power BI

The plots returned by plotnine have a data type specific to the package used. Assuming you have assigned a plotnine plot to the variable p, this is what you get:

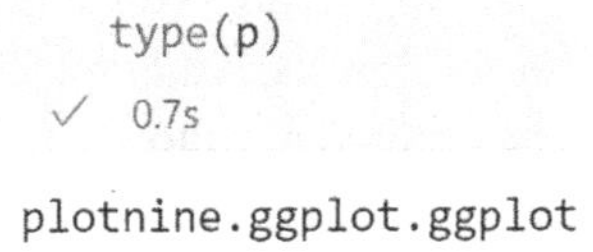

```
type(p)
```
✓ 0.7s

```
plotnine.ggplot.ggplot
```

Figure 20.6: Data type of a plotnine plot

As you probably remember, by default, the graphs handled in Python script are of the Matplotlib plot type. Also, If you consult Microsoft's documentation on the Python packages installed in the Python engine of the Power BI service as of the time of writing (`https://bit.ly/powerbi-python-limits`), the plotnine package is not among them. So, how can you take advantage of the full potential of plotnine if the package does not seem to be installed on the service? You have three options. Let's see what they are.

Working with plotnine and getting an image

One of the most immediate options is to use the string of the binary representation of the plot image generated by plotnine, as briefly mentioned in the *Univariate exploration* section of *Chapter 19, Exploratory Data Analysis*.

Basically, a ggplot object is transformed into a Matplotlib figure thanks to the `draw()` function:

```
type(p.draw())
✓  0.4s
```

```
matplotlib.figure.Figure
```

Figure 20.7: Data type of a Matplotlib figure

At this point, the Matplotlib figure stored in the p variable, as seen in *Figure 20.3*, can be saved as a PNG image and then converted to a byte stream that can be represented as a string. To do so, you need to import the io and base64 modules as follows:

```
import io
import base64
mplt = p.draw()

with io.BytesIO() as buffer:
    mplt.savefig(buffer, format='png')
    buffer.seek(0)
    image = buffer.getvalue()
    image_to_string = base64.b64encode(image).decode('latin1')
```

Note that if you want to save your plot, the ggplot object exposes the `save()` method, which supports these extensions: `.eps`, `.jpeg`, `.jpg`, `.pdf`, `.pgf`, `.png`, `.ps`, `.raw`, `.rgba`, `.svg`, `.svgz`, `.tif`, `.tiff`, and `.webp`.

Back to our code, since the `image_to_string` string representing our plot is more than 32,766 characters long, we need to break it into several parts. An empirical function useful for calculating the maximum length of a text chunk can be defined as follows:

- The chunk size must be a multiple of 10,000 that is less than or equal to the length of image_to_string.
- It must not exceed 30,000.

You can find the code that implements the preceding logic in the following find_largest_chunk_length() function:

```python
def toCut(obj, width):
    return re.findall('.{1,%s}' % width, obj, flags=re.S)


def find_largest_chunk_length(n):
    # Calculate k so that k*10000 <= n and k*10000 <= 30000
    # to respect the limit of 32,766 characters for the
    # length of a string in a dataset cell in Power Query
    k = min(n // 10000, 3)

    # Return the larger value of k * 10000 that fits in n
    # so that k * 10000 <= 30000
    return k * 10000


str_len = len(image_to_string)
max_len = find_largest_chunk_length(str_len)


image_to_string_splitted = toCut(image_to_string, max_len)


num_chops = ceil(len(image_to_string) / max_len)


tmp_data = {
        'plot_name': ['plot01'] * num_chops,
        'chunk_id': list(range(1, num_chops+1)),
        'plot_str': image_to_string_splitted
    }


img_to_str_splitted_df = pd.DataFrame(tmp_data, columns = ['country_
name','chunk_id','plot_str'])
```

We named the plot plot01 because it is possible to handle multiple plots in the data structure we thought of.

In order for the string to be interpretable as an image, it must first be reassembled from its chunks and then prefixed with the data URI for a Base64-encoded PNG image (data:image/png;base64,). This can be accomplished with a simple DAX expression using the CONCATENATEX function, which combines values from a table into a single text string in an order determined by sorting the chunk_id column in ascending order:

```
Display Image =
IF(
    HASONEVALUE('img_to_str_splitted_df'[plot_name]),
```

```
    "data:image/png;base64, " &
    CONCATENATEX(img_to_str_splitted_df, img_to_str_splitted_df[plot_str], ,
img_to_str_splitted_df[chunk_id], ASC)
)
```

But once you have the string of the byte representation of the image, how do you display it? The most direct way to do this is to use CloudScope's own custom visual *Image Pro* (https://bit.ly/image-pro-powerbi), which takes such a string as input and displays it. This visual was free until the end of 2023. Given the considerable effort required to keep it up to date with Power BI version changes, the vendor decided to make it available as a trial version for testing purposes. Since we generally prefer free solutions, we can use Vincent Faigt's *Simple Image* visual (https://bit.ly/simple-image-powerbi) as an alternative.

The main difference between Image Pro and Simple Image is that, with Image Pro, you can use both a table column or a *measure* defined by a DAX expression to generate the string that represents the image, whereas with Simple Image, you are forced to use a *column* (whether created in Power Query or as a calculated column defined by a DAX expression). Because a DAX measure is dynamic by definition, Image Pro is able to display a picture based on the user's interaction with the report. Because a new column via a DAX expression is a static calculation performed for each row, it cannot change its content based on user interaction with the report. Therefore, if you need to display multiple images based on user interaction with the report, you should consider the purchase of the Image Pro visual.

Let's see how it all comes together in Power BI using Simple Image:

1. Open Power BI Desktop from the shortcut that activates the pbi_powerquery_env environment.

2. Make sure Power BI Desktop is referencing the pbi_powerquery_env environment in the Python scripting tab of the **Options** menu.

3. Then, click on **Get data** and then **More ....** Start typing script into the search textbox and double-click on **Python script**. The Python script editor will pop up.

4. Open the 02-ggplot-as-picture.py file in Visual Studio Code or Notepad and copy its content. Then, paste it into the Python script editor and click **OK**.

5. The **Navigator** window will open, giving you the option to select which DataFrame to import. Select the **img_to_str_splitted_df** one:

Navigator

Figure 20.8: Import byte representation DataFrame of the image in Power BI

Then click **Load**.

6. Click the **Slicer** visual to add a slicer in the canvas that allows you to select the image to show. Expand the **img_to_str_splitted_df** table under the Data panel and select the **plot_name** field.

7. Click the **Format visual** tab for the slicer, expand **Slicer settings**, expand the **Selection** section, and then enable the **Single select** option. Then, resize the Slicer visual in the upper-left corner of the canvas.

8. In order to have the string that represents the image, you have to create a new measure. So, click on the **Modeling** menu, click **New column**, and enter the following DAX code:

```
Display Image =
IF(
    HASONEVALUE('img_to_str_splitted_df'[plot_name]),
    "data:image/png;base64, " &
    CONCATENATEX(img_to_str_splitted_df, img_to_str_splitted_df[plot_
str], , img_to_str_splitted_df[chunk_id], ASC)
)
```

Then, click the **Commit** icon (the tick on the left):

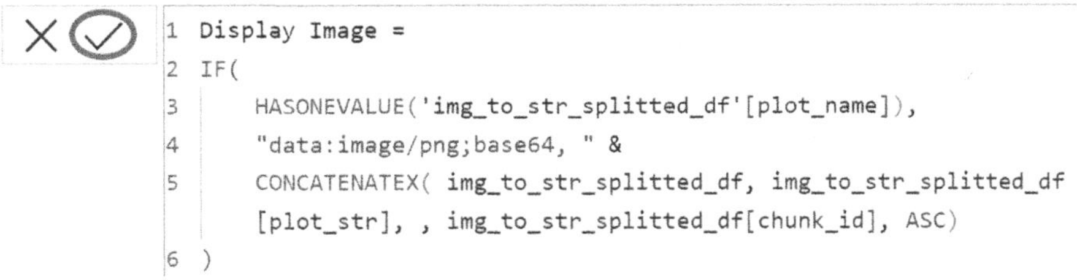

```
1  Display Image =
2  IF(
3      HASONEVALUE('img_to_str_splitted_df'[plot_name]),
4      "data:image/png;base64, " &
5      CONCATENATEX( img_to_str_splitted_df, img_to_str_splitted_df
       [plot_str], , img_to_str_splitted_df[chunk_id], ASC)
6  )
```

Figure 20.9: Entering the DAX formula to generate the image string

Note the following:

 If you needed dynamic images using Image Pro, you should have put the DAX expression in a **New Measure**, not a **New Column**.

9. In the **Data** panel, under the **img_to_str_splitted_df** table, you will find the new **Display Image** field with the symbol of a calculated measurement:

Figure 20.10: The newly added Display Image measure

10. Now you need to add the Simple Image custom visual to Power BI. Then, click on the **Get more visuals** ellipsis:

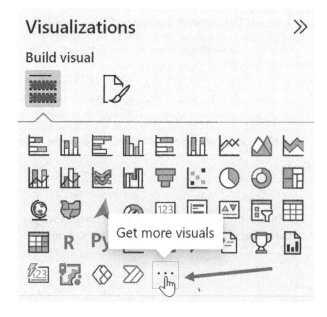

Figure 20.11: Getting more visuals in Power BI

11. Search for `simple` in the next window and click the **Simple Image** visual:

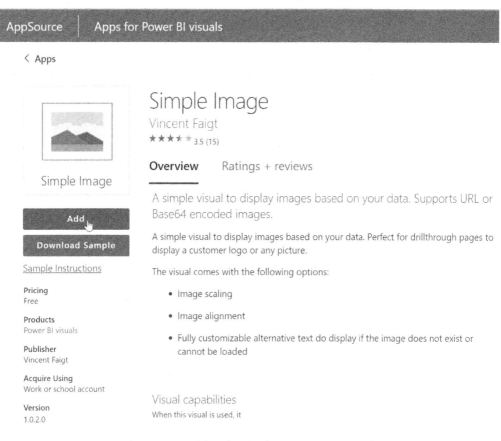

Figure 20.12: Adding the Simple Image custom visual

Click **Add** and a dialog box appears informing you that you've successfully imported the visual. Then click **OK**.

12. Now, click on the newly added **Simple Image** visual:

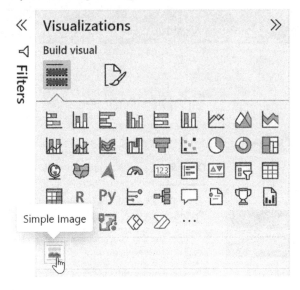

Figure 20.13: Adding the Simple Image visual to the canvas

13. Once the visual appears on the canvas, expand it and place it next to the plot name slider. Then, with the visual still selected, click on the newly added **Display Image** column. You will see the following:

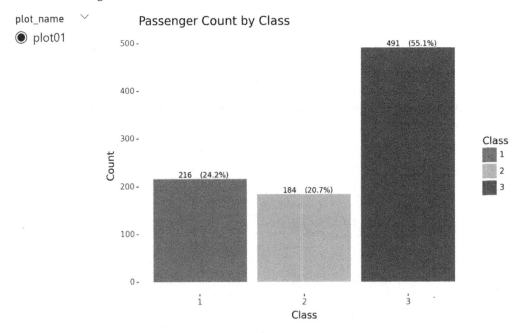

Figure 20.14: Image is shown using its byte representation

In this way, you were able to visualize a plot generated with plotnine by the byte representation of its PNG image. This ensures that the plot will definitely be displayed when the report is published to the Power BI service.

 If the Simple Image visual is used, the **img_to_str_splitted_df** table must contain only one image to be displayed correctly (limitation due to the use of a calculated column). The slicer is therefore useless in this case. However, we decided to include it in the report in case you need to display more images using the Image Pro visual.

Some of you might think that the *new card visual* could be used instead of the previously mentioned visuals. But images in cards can only point to files or URLs for images, not to measures or columns containing Base64 images.

Now let's see how to use the Matplotlib plot directly in a Python script visual.

Working with plotnine and getting a Matplotlib figure

Sometimes, it is not enough to simply display an image of a plot. It may be necessary to dynamically change the Matplotlib object representing it in real time, based on certain selections made with slicers. In this case, it is best to use the Matplotlib figure directly, perhaps after making changes to that object through the Python script's visual code.

You saw in the previous section that a ggplot plotnine object can be converted to a Matplotlib figure using the draw() method. If you then encode the Matplotlib figure to get a string representation of it, as seen in *Chapter 5, Importing Unhandled Data Objects*, you can use the string DataFrame in a Python script visual, decode it into the Matplotlib object, and display it as such.

Unfortunately, this Matplotlib figure seems to hide something sufficiently complex in its definition to cause an error when serializing with Pickle using plotnine 0.12.4. The error you get is:

```
NotImplementedError: Sorry, pickling not yet supported.
```

I submitted a bug report on GitHub, and the author successfully resolved it. So, to install the latest update of the plotnine GitHub repository using pip, we ran this command in the Anaconda Prompt after enabling the pbi_powerquery_env environment:

```
pip install "plotnine @ https://github.com/has2k1/plotnine/archive/master.zip"
```

To ensure reproducibility, we have specified version 0.12.4 for the installation of plotnine at the beginning of this chapter. Note that if a version later than 0.12.4 is available at the time of your plotnine installation, you can install it and avoid installing the development version. In this case, just use the standard pip install plotnine command.

We followed the trace of the deserialization code found in the 06-deserialize-plots-object-from-pkl-in-power-bi.py script in *Chapter 5* to convert the Matplotlib image into a DataFrame of multi-byte strings. The difference is that instead of loading the image object from a Pickle file on disk, we used an in-memory bytes buffer. The new code can be found in 03-ggplot-as-matplotlib-encoding.py in *Chapter 20*.

You can use it to import the string byte DataFrame `plot_df` of the barplot using the Python source connector.

In the last section of the preceding code, we have included the (commented) deserialization code from the Python script visual, originally from the `07-deserialize-plots-df-into-python-visual.py` file in *Chapter 5*. By uncommenting and running this code within VS Code, the barplot is successfully generated. Oddly enough, when the exact code from the `07-deserialize-plots-df-into-python-visual.py` file of *Chapter 5* is used in the Python script visual, it results in an empty plot. However, we've included the encoding code as a reference in case the issue is due to a Power BI bug that may be fixed in the future.

What if we wanted to use plotnine's ggplot object directly in the Python script visual instead?

Working with plotnine in the Python script visual

One of the methods we indicated in *Chapter 3, Configuring Python with Power BI*, for selecting packages to install in the environment that replicates the contents of the environment currently on the Power BI service is to rely on what is stated in the Microsoft documentation. Specifically, the page in question can be found at `https://bit.ly/powerbi-python-limits`, and to date, the `plotnine` package is not listed on the list provided by that page.

Some time ago, we had an email exchange with the product team working on analytics in Power BI, suggesting that the presence of plotnine on the service would certainly be welcomed by analysts. The product team replied that it was indeed a very good idea and that they would look into it.

Out of curiosity, we tried to think of a way to verify this information through a Power BI report published on the service and came up with an interesting solution. Here are the steps to reproduce it:

1. Open Power BI Desktop from the shortcut that activates the `pbi_powerquery_env` environment.
2. Make sure Power BI Desktop is referencing the `pbi_powerquery_env` environment in the Python scripting tab of the **Options** menu.
3. Click **Enter data** on the **Home** ribbon, name the column `num_packages`, enter the values **10**, **20**, and **30**, and rename the table `NumPackages`:

Create Table

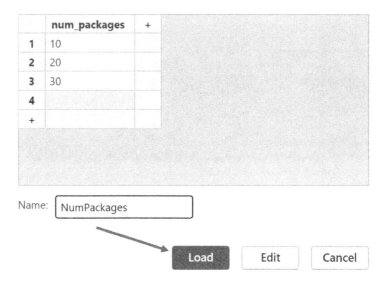

Figure 20.15: Creating the NumPackages table

Then click **Load**.

4. On the **Home** ribbon, click **Transform data** to get to Power Query, right-click on an empty area of the **Queries** panel on the left, then select **New Query** and then **Blank query**. The Query1 query appears in the panel. Right-click on it and rename it NumPages. Keep it selected and click **Advanced Editor** on the **Home** ribbon. Replace all of the code with the following to create a table with a num_pages column having values from 1 to 20:

```
let
    Source = Table.FromList(List.Numbers(1, 20), Splitter.
SplitByNothing(), {"num_pages"})
in
    Source
```

Then click **Done**. Your **NumPages** table will look like the following:

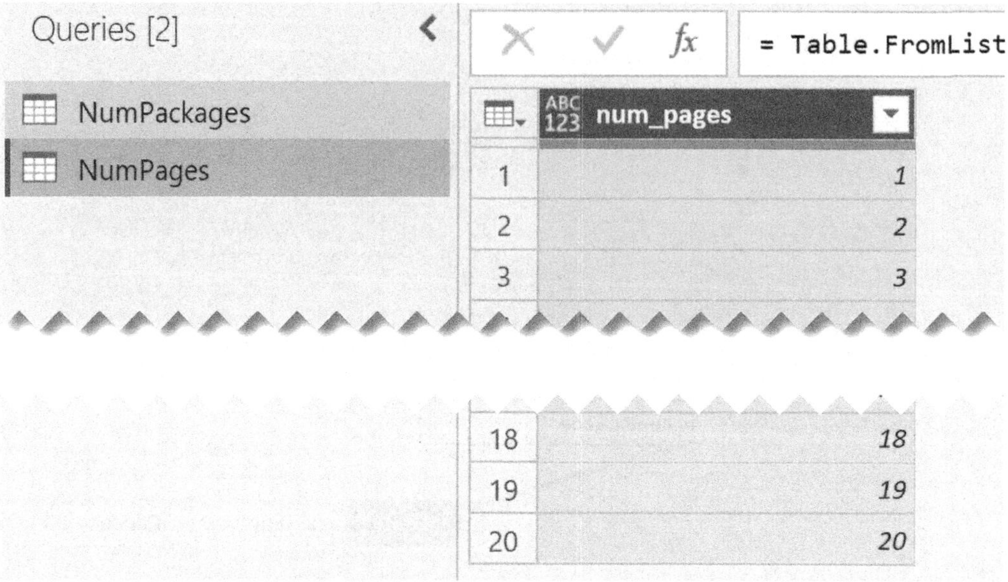

Figure 20.16: The NumPages query

5. Now we need to create a cross-join query between **NumPackages** and **NumPages** to use as the data source for the Python visual. We add a custom constant numeric column for each table on the fly that acts as the key for the join, ensuring that every row in the first table joins every row in the second table. To do this, right-click on **NumPackages** and select **Reference**. The new **NumPackages** query (2) will appear. Right-click it and rename it PackagesPages. Keep it selected and click **Advanced Editor** on the **Home** ribbon. Replace all of the code with the following to create a cross-join table:

```
let
    Source = NumPackages,
    // Add a constant column to NumPackages
    NumPackagesWithKey = Table.AddColumn(Source, "Key", each 1, Int64.
Type),
    // Add a constant column to NumPages
    NumPagesWithKey = Table.AddColumn(NumPages, "Key", each 1, Int64.
Type),
    // Perform a cross join on the constant column
    CrossJoin = Table.NestedJoin(NumPagesWithKey, {"Key"},
NumPackagesWithKey, {"Key"}, "NumPackages", JoinKind.Inner),
    // Expand the NumPackages table to show num_packages column
    ExpandedCrossJoin = Table.ExpandTableColumn(CrossJoin, "NumPackages",
{"num_packages"}),
```

```
    // Remove the constant column as it's no longer needed
    FinalTable = Table.RemoveColumns(ExpandedCrossJoin, "Key"),
    // Sort values
    SortedTable = Table.Sort(FinalTable,{{"num_pages", Order.Ascending},
{"num_packages", Order.Ascending}})
in
    SortedTable
```

Then click **Done**. Your **PackagesPages** table will look like the following:

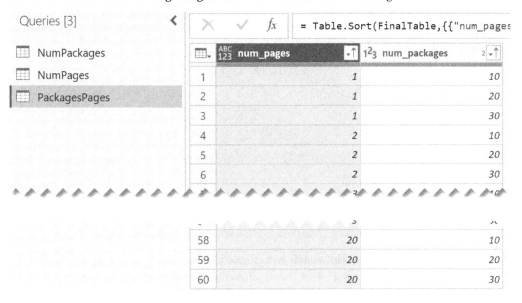

Figure 20.17: The PackagesPages query

Then click **Close & Apply**.

6. Notice that two relationships have been created behind the scenes, linking the two tables **NumPackages** and **NumPages** to the cross-join table, **PackagesPages**. You can verify this by clicking on **Model view** on the left:

Figure 20.18: Relationships between tables

7. Now click on the **Slicer** visual, expand the **NumPackages** table under the **Data** panel on the right, and click on the **num_packages** field.

8. Then, click on the **Format visual** tab of the slicer, expand the **Slicer** settings, and select the **Vertical list** option. Then, expand the **Selection** section and enable the **Single select** option. At the end, resize the visual area and keep it in the upper-left corner of the canvas.

9. Repeat steps 5 and 6, but this time, in order to create a slicer for the **num_pages** field. You will end up with something like this:

Figure 20.19: Slicers ready for number of packages and number of pages

10. Now select a **Python script visual** and enable it. Select the **num_packages** field under Data in order to enable the script editor, even if this field is not used in the code.

11. Open the 04-show-python-version-powerbi.py file from the Chapter 20 folder and copy its content. Then, paste it into the Python script editor. Click the run icon to check if it works.

12. Click on the **Format visual** tab of the Python visual, expand the **Title** section, and edit the text with Python Version.

13. Click on an empty area of the canvas and then click on **Python script visual** again. Select the **num_packages** and **num_pages** fields under **Data** in order to enable the script editor.

14. Open the 05-show-installed-packages-powerbi.py file from the Chapter 20 folder and copy its content. Then, paste it into the Python script editor. Click the run icon to check if it works.

15. Click on the **Format visual** tab of the Python visual, expand the **Title** section, and edit the text with Installed Packages.

16. At the end, you have a report that, after you select the number of packages to display for each page, allows you to display all the packages on the selected page in alphabetical order. You will see something like this:

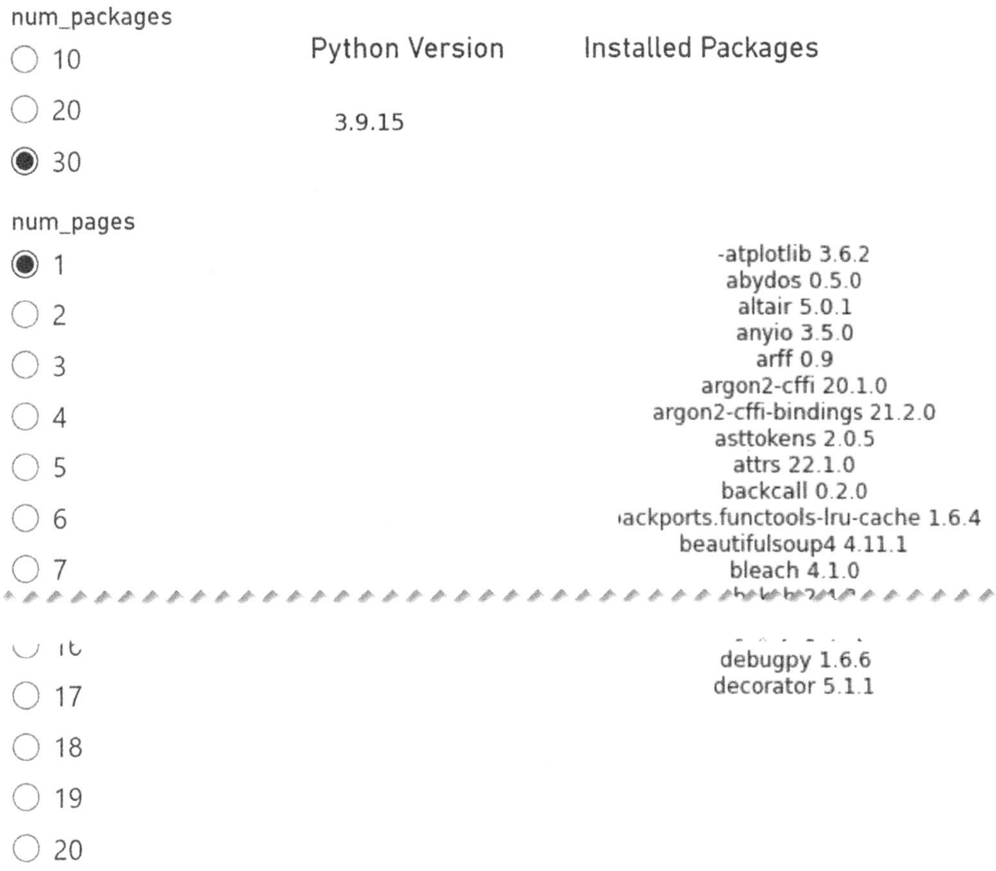

num_packages

○ 10

○ 20

◉ 30

Python Version

3.9.15

Installed Packages

num_pages

◉ 1

○ 2

○ 3

○ 4

○ 5

○ 6

○ 7

-atplotlib 3.6.2
abydos 0.5.0
altair 5.0.1
anyio 3.5.0
arff 0.9
argon2-cffi 20.1.0
argon2-cffi-bindings 21.2.0
asttokens 2.0.5
attrs 22.1.0
backcall 0.2.0
ackports.functools-lru-cache 1.6.4
beautifulsoup4 4.11.1
bleach 4.1.0

○ 16

○ 17

○ 18

○ 19

○ 20

debugpy 1.6.6
decorator 5.1.1

Figure 20.20: Report to check the Python version and the installed packages

As you can see, you can now check the packages installed in your environment on your machine with just a few clicks. Simply publish this report to the service to see what packages are installed on the Power BI service. To do this, follow these steps:

1. Click on **Publish** on the **Home** ribbon. You are prompted to save your report. Do so.

2. Click **My workspace** in the **Publish to Power BI** window, and then click **Select**.

3. When you are finished publishing, go to the Power BI service using this link: app.powerbi.com. Select **My Workspace** and click on the report with the name you chose for the report you just saved. Click **30** for the number of packages per page, and you will see the following:

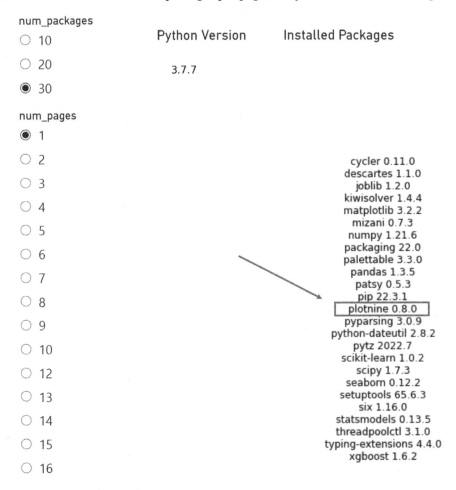

Figure 20.21: Python packages actually installed on the Power BI service

Wow! The version of Python is the same as in the Microsoft docs. But contrary to what the Microsoft docs say, the plotnine package is available in version 0.8.0 on the service! Okay, so it's not the latest version of plotnine, but it's there! Note that there are also additional descartes, mizani, and palettable packages that are not listed in the Microsoft docs. These are some plotnine dependencies. Then, you can use Python code to generate a ggplot graph directly within a Python script visual, not only to display the plot on Power BI Desktop but also to display it on the service when the report is published. Let's give it a try:

1. Open Power BI Desktop from the shortcut that activates the pbi_powerquery_env environment.

2. Make sure Power BI Desktop is referencing the pbi_powerquery_env environment in the **Python scripting** tab of the **Options** menu.

3. Click **Get data**, then **Web**, type the URL `http://bit.ly/titanic-dataset-csv`, click **OK**, and then click **Load** in the next dialog box.

4. Now select a **Python script visual** and enable it. Select the **PassengerId** and **Pclass** fields under **Data** in order to enable the script editor. Note that the **PassengerId** field is necessary to prevent the dataset's `drop_duplicates()` method from dropping all **Pclass** duplicates.

5. Open the `06-ggplot-plotnine-powerbi.py` file from the `Chapter 20` folder and copy its content. Then, paste it into the Python script editor. Click the run icon to check if it works. You will see something like this:

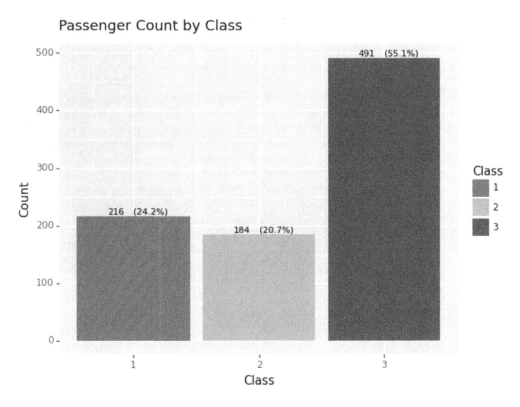

Figure 20.22: Plot created from a Python visual using plotnine

Note that, in this case, we did not import and use the `theme_tufte` library because the 0.8.0 version of the service does not provide it. Also, the usual code for injecting a Matplotlib figure into the standard Python device that you saw in *Chapter 5, Importing Unhandled Data Objects*, (using `plt.get_current_fig_manager()`) will not work with plotnine. In this case, we use a simple `print(p)` to display the ggplot object.

Good! Now everything works because you are using the plotnine package installed in your environment on your machine.

Now try to publish the report to the service by following the same steps as for the `Installed Packages` report. After publishing successfully, open the report on the service and you will see this:

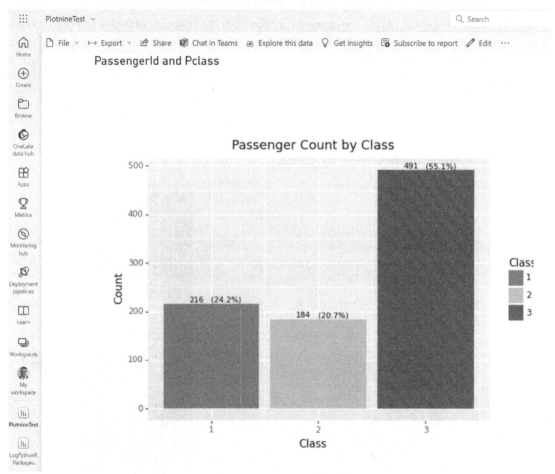

Figure 20.23: Report on the service using plotnine

Did you ever think that you could use plotnine in a Python script visual, even though Microsoft docs doesn't list it among the packages installed on the service? In this chapter, we have shown you that it is possible!

Summary

This chapter provided an in-depth exploration of data visualization techniques using the plotnine package in Python. It began with an introduction to ggplot2, a popular data visualization tool in R, and its Python equivalent, plotnine, which is based on the Grammar of Graphics concept.

The core concepts of plotnine were discussed in detail, providing a basic understanding necessary for creating and customizing visualizations.

In addition, the chapter illustrated the practical application of plotnine through an in-depth analysis of the Titanic dataset. This included comprehensive instructions on installing plotnine, importing the necessary libraries, and creating different types of visualizations such as bar charts and histograms. In addition, the chapter delved into the integration of plotnine visualizations with Power BI, providing step-by-step instructions on how to convert plotnine graphics for use in Power BI, facilitating a seamless integration process. In the next chapter, we'll finally start working with R and Python scripts in Power BI, doing data ingestion and data transformation.

References

For additional reading, check out the following books and articles:

- *The Grammar of Graphics* (http://ndl.ethernet.edu.et/handle/123456789/59587)
- *A Grammar of Graphics for Python* (https://plotnine.readthedocs.io/)

Acknowledgment

I would like to thank my technical reviewer, Art Tennick, for his timely feedback that Image Pro had been removed from Microsoft AppSource, and a hint about possible alternatives.

Test your knowledge

1. What is the difference between ggplot2 and plotnine and how are they related?
2. How can plotnine be used in Power BI?

Learn more on Discord

To join the Discord community for this book – where you can share feedback, ask questions to the author, and learn about new releases – follow the QR code below:

https://discord.gg/MKww5g45EB

21

Advanced Visualizations

As you saw in *Chapter 19, Exploratory Data Analysis*, you can create very professional-looking graphs using the ggplot2 package and its extensions. In this chapter, you'll learn how to create advanced and attractive custom graphs, with a special focus on **circular barplots**. Circular barplots are particularly useful for showing relationships in data that are periodic or cyclical in nature, providing a visually appealing and space-efficient way to display such patterns. They are ideal for comparing categories that are parts of a whole, such as hours in a day or months in a year, where the circular layout emphasizes the cyclical nature.

The visualization of such plots will be done exclusively using R programming, as it offers robust support for creating these intricate graphics. This is because, despite Python's extensive capabilities with libraries like matplotlib, it is quite challenging to build circular plots with it. In addition, plotnine, the popular Python library for creating graphics using the Grammar of Graphics approach that you learned about in *Chapter 20, Using the Grammar of Graphics in Python with plotnine*, does not yet support creating circular plots, making R the preferred choice for this specific type of visualization.

You will learn about:

- Choosing a circular barplot
- Implementing a circular barplot in R
- Implementing a circular barplot in Power BI

Technical requirements

This chapter requires you to have a working internet connection and **Power BI Desktop** already installed on your machine (version: 2.121.644.0 64-bit, September 2023). You must have properly configured the R engine and IDEs as outlined in *Chapter 2, Configuring R with Power BI*.

Choosing a circular barplot

Very often, we need to display the measures associated with different categorical entities using a **bar chart** (or **barplot**). However, when the number of entities to be represented exceeds 15 or 20, the graph begins to become unreadable, even if it is arranged vertically:

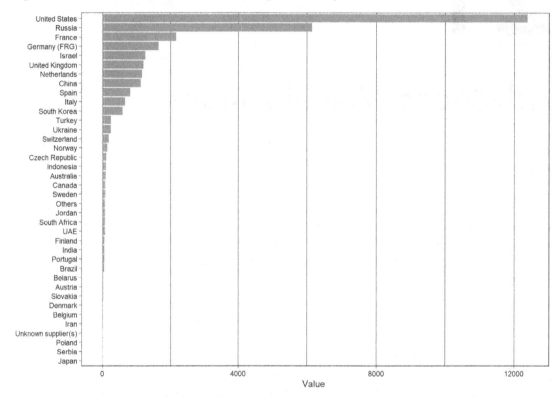

Figure 21.1: A barplot of worldwide weapons sellers

In this case, as you saw in *Chapter 19*, *Exploratory Data Analysis*, it is often a good idea to plot a maximum number of entities and then group the subsequent entities into a single category (in our case, the *Others* category). This preserves the readability of the graph, but loses some of the information you want to represent.

If it is absolutely necessary to display all entities with all their dimensions, we often resort to a more eye-catching organization of the space occupied by the barplot, wrapping it in a circular shape, thus obtaining a **circular barplot**:

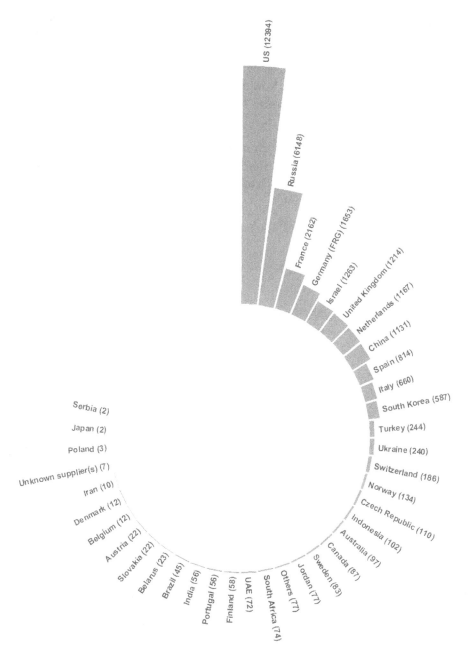

Who sells more weapons?

Figure 21.2: Circular barplot of worldwide weapons sellers

The code needed to create the plot in *Figure 21.2* can be found in the `barplot-worldwide-weapons-sellers.R` file in the *Chapter 21* folder. You will understand it better once you have finished studying the chapter.

In the world of data analysis, creating a clear, cohesive visualization is key to understanding a complex set of data. When you're dealing with multiple entities and characteristics, such as a list of 24 speakers rated on four different attributes, a grouped bar chart can be a valuable tool. In our example, we have 24 speakers at an event, each of whom was rated by the audience on a scale of 1 to 5 for *Expectation*, *Interesting*, *Useful*, and *Oral Presentation* skills. Now we want to display this feedback for all speakers but also categorize it by each trait. This translates to 24 (speakers) x 4 (skills), or a whopping 96 entities to plot.

Enhancing the graph with additional layers by grouping the entities by traits makes the data more accessible and straightforward to understand. Here, using a grouped bar graph, where we have a cluster of bars for each speaker representing each of the four skills, would simplify the display. Here is an example of a circular grouped bar graph:

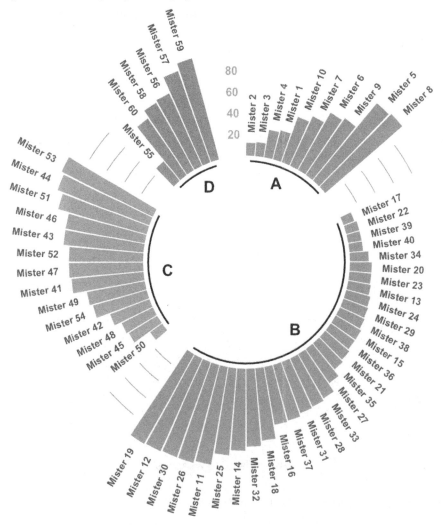

Figure 21.3: Example of a circular grouped bar graph

In the next section, you'll use the R programming language and the `ggplot2` package to construct the outlined circular barplot.

Implementing a circular barplot in R

In this section, you'll find R code inspired by the code available to the entire R community at the **R Graph Gallery** website (`https://www.r-graph-gallery.com/index.html`). Along with some minor additions, we've refactored and generalized this code into a function called `circular_grouped_barplot()`. This was done using the **tidy evaluation** framework (see the included references for more information). The main benefit of this change is that our function can now handle any dataset.

You may recall from previous chapters that when dealing with R functions, column names were passed to functions as strings. However, with the advent of **tidy evaluation**, these column names can now be passed using **tidyverse grammar** instead. Essentially, this allows column names to be passed directly through a pipeline. Consider the example below for a better understanding:

```
circular_grouped_barplot(data = speakers_tbl,
                         grp_col_name = 'Characteristics',
                         label_col_name = 'SpeakerName',
                         value_col_name = 'Value')
```

Instead of this call for the previous function, you will have the following one:

```
speakers_tbl %>%
  circular_grouped_barplot(grp_col_name = Characteristics,
                           label_col_name = SpeakerName,
                           value_col_name = Value)
```

Notice how the quotes identifying the strings have disappeared in the last script. You are now referencing the `speakers_tbl` columns directly.

Let's take a step-by-step look at what this function does. The code you will find here is taken from the file `01-circular-grouped-barplot.R`, which you can find in the Chapter 21 folder. Let's proceed as follows:

1. First, make sure the `scales` package is already installed in your CRAN R engine dedicated to R visuals (in our case, version 3.4.4). Just check whether its name is in the list you can find in the bottom-right **Packages** tab in RStudio. If not, install it as usual with the command `install.packages('scales')`.

2. The dataset you will use comes from the `Scores.csv` file in the Chapter 21 folder. As mentioned in the previous section, it contains the average feedback that 24 speakers received from attendees at a conference on some of the characteristics they displayed during the speech.

The tibble looks like this:

```
> dataset
# A tibble: 96 x 3
   SpeakerName      Characteristic Votes
   <chr>            <chr>          <dbl>
 1 Sloan Combs      Expectation     3.93
 2 Tobias Hobbes    Expectation     4
 3 Paislee Jež      Expectation     4.07
 4 Kristine Harland Expectation     4.2
 5 Evander Corvi    Expectation     4.23
 6 Rhianna Clarke   Expectation     4.41
 7 Purdie Badcock   Expectation     4.5
 8 Sonny Rodríguez  Expectation     4.5
 9 Delta Shelby     Expectation     4.6
10 Elsabeth Fabbro  Expectation     4.71
# ... with 86 more rows
>
```

Figure 21.4: The speakers tibble

3. Looking at the code for the `circular_grouped_barplot()` function, you can see the internal `rescale100()` function, which is used to rescale the values of the entire dataset (in our case, the votes) to a scale of 0 to 100.

4. The execution of the arguments passed to the function via `enquo()` will then be delayed (see the references for more details):

```
grp_var <- enquo(grp_col_name)
label_var <- enquo(label_col_name)
value_var <- enquo(value_col_name)
```

5. The categorical variables of the input dataset are transformed into factors, and the values are scaled thanks to the previously defined function, all using tidy evaluation:

```
data <- data %>%
  mutate(
    !!quo_name(grp_var) := as.factor(!!grp_var),
    !!quo_name(label_var) := as.factor(!!label_var),
    !!quo_name(value_var) := rescale100(!!value_var) )
```

6. To separate each group of bars, a few empty bars are added at the end of each group. First, define an empty bars DataFrame:

```
empty_bars <- 3
# Create the empty dataframe to add to the source dataframe
data_to_add <- data.frame(matrix(NA, empty_bars * nlevels(data[[quo_
name(grp_var)]]), ncol(data)) )
colnames(data_to_add) <- colnames(data)
```

```
data_to_add[[quo_name(grp_var)]] <- rep(levels(data[[quo_name(grp_
var)]]), each = empty_bars)
```

It looks like the following:

```
        SpeakerName   Characteristic Votes
     1           NA      Expectation    NA
     2           NA      Expectation    NA
     3           NA      Expectation    NA
     4           NA      Interesting    NA
     5           NA      Interesting    NA
     6           NA      Interesting    NA
     7           NA OralPresentation    NA
     8           NA OralPresentation    NA
     9           NA OralPresentation    NA
    10           NA           Useful    NA
    11           NA           Useful    NA
    12           NA           Useful    NA
```

Figure 21.5: The empty bars DataFrame

7. Then, the empty DataFrame is added to the source DataFrame (the data one). When the resulting DataFrame is reordered for the grouping variable and values, the rows of the empty bar DataFrame are automatically distributed at the end of each group:

```
data <- rbind(data, data_to_add)
# Reorder data by groups and values
data <- data %>% arrange(!!grp_var, !!value_var)
```

8. A bar identifier is added:

```
data$id <- seq(1, nrow(data))
```

It is used to calculate the angle at which each label must be displayed:

```
# Get the total number of bars
number_of_bars <- nrow(data)
# Subtract 0.5 from id because the label must have the angle of the
center of the bars,
# Not extreme right(1) or extreme left (0)
angles_of_bars <- 90 - 360 * (data$id - 0.5) / number_of_bars
```

9. We define the DataFrame of the labels, starting from the data one, taking into account the correct alignment of the labels with the bars and the correct angle they must have to be readable:

```
label_data <- data
label_data$hjust <- ifelse( angles_of_bars < -90, 1, 0)
label_data$angle <- ifelse( angles_of_bars < -90, angles_of_bars + 180,
angles_of_bars)
```

10. A base line DataFrame for groups is defined. It contains the start and end IDs (bars) of each group, the average ID of each group (used as a base point for group text labels), and the angle at which each text label should be rotated:

```
base_data <- data %>%
  group_by(!!grp_var) %>%
  summarize(start = min(id),
            end = max(id) - empty_bars) %>%
  rowwise() %>%
  mutate(title = floor(mean(c(start, end)))) %>%
  inner_join( label_data %>% select(id, angle),
              by = c('title' = 'id')) %>%
  mutate( angle = ifelse( (angle > 0 & angle <= 90) |
                          (angle > 180 & angle <= 270),
                          angle-90, angle+90 ) )
```

11. An `if` clause determines whether to initially define a barplot with only one group or with multiple groups, depending on the content of the source dataset. In our case, since there are four groups, the code is as follows:

```
p <- data %>%
  ggplot(aes_string(x = 'id', y = quo_name(value_var), fill = quo_
name(grp_var))) +
  # Add a barplot
  geom_bar(stat = 'identity', alpha=0.5) +
  # Add 100/75/50/25 indicators
  geom_segment(data = grid_data,
      aes(x = end, y = 100, xend = start, yend = 100),
      colour = 'grey', alpha=1, size=0.3 ,
      inherit.aes = FALSE ) +
  geom_segment(data = grid_data,
      aes(x = end, y = 80, xend = start, yend = 80),
      colour = 'grey', alpha=1, size=0.3 ,
      inherit.aes = FALSE ) +
  geom_segment(data = grid_data,
      aes(x = end, y = 60, xend = start, yend = 60),
      colour = 'grey', alpha=1, size=0.3 ,
      inherit.aes = FALSE ) +
  geom_segment(data = grid_data,
      aes(x = end, y = 40, xend = start, yend = 40),
      colour = 'grey', alpha=1, size=0.3 ,
      inherit.aes = FALSE ) +
  geom_segment(data = grid_data,
```

```
        aes(x = end, y = 20, xend = start, yend = 20),
        colour = 'grey', alpha=1, size=0.3 ,
        inherit.aes = FALSE ) +
    # Add text showing the value of each 100/75/50/25 lines
    annotate('text', x = rep(max(data$id), 5),
            y = c(20, 40, 60, 80, 100),
            label = c('20', '40', '60', '80', 100) ,
            color='grey', size=3,
            angle=0, fontface='bold', hjust=1)
```

The barplot looks like this:

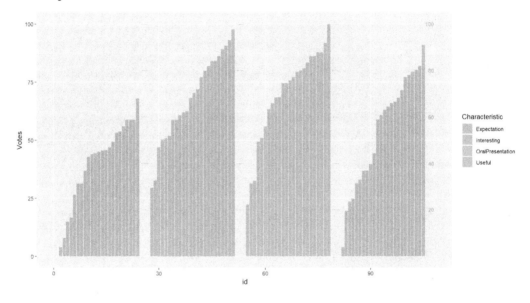

Figure 21.6: The representation of the first draft of the barplot

12. After defining a text justification vector, the previous plot is stripped of unnecessary graphical frills, and it is magically wrapped into a circular shape simply by using the coord_polar() function:

```
p <- p +
    # The space between the x-axis and the lower edge of the figure will
    implicitly define the width of the empty circle inside the plot
    ylim(-120,120) +
    theme_minimal() +
    theme(
        legend.position = 'none',
        axis.text = element_blank(),
        axis.title = element_blank(),
        panel.grid = element_blank(),
```

```
    plot.margin = unit(rep(-1,4), 'cm')
) +
# Wrap all in a circle!
coord_polar()
```

What you will get is the following first draft of the plot:

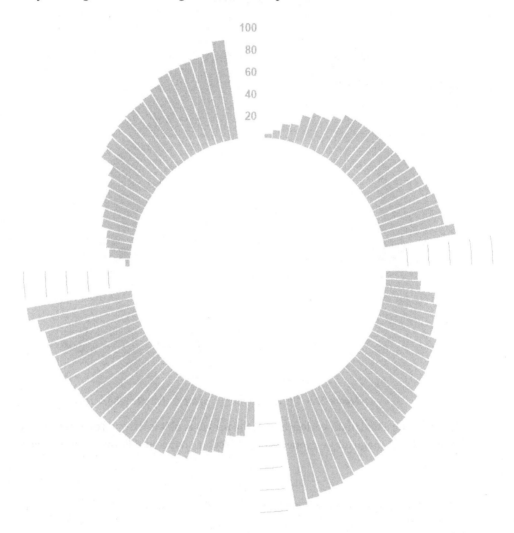

Figure 21.7: The first draft of the circular barplot

Unfortunately, the `coord_polar()` function does not rotate or curve the labels. So, if you need them rotated, you'll have to do it manually.

13. Finally, let's add appropriately rotated bar labels, group base lines, and group text labels:

```
p <- p +
  # Add labels
  geom_text(data = label_data %>% mutate( y_pos = !!value_var + 10),
      aes_string(x = 'id', y = 'y_pos',
                    label = quo_name(label_var),
                    hjust = 'hjust'),
      color = 'black', fontface = 'bold',
      alpha = 0.6, size = 3,
      angle = label_data$angle,
      inherit.aes = FALSE) +

  # Add base lines of groups
  geom_segment(data = base_data,
      aes(x = start, y = -5, xend = end, yend = -5),
      colour = 'black', alpha=0.8,
      size=0.6 , inherit.aes = FALSE ) +

  # Add groups text
  geom_text(data = base_data %>% mutate(y = -14),
      aes_string(x = 'title', y = 'y',
                    label=quo_name(grp_var),
                    angle = 'angle'),
      hjust = text_horiz_justification,
      colour = 'black', alpha=0.8, size=4,
      fontface='bold', inherit.aes = FALSE)
```

The result is as follows:

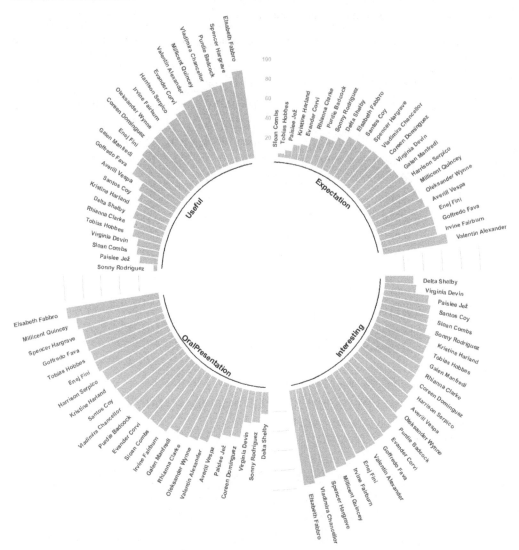

Figure 21.8: The final circular barplot

This is just a demonstration of how effective it is to create complex graphs with `ggplot2` by taking advantage of the *Grammar of Graphics*. As you have seen, this framework allows you to approach the creation of a complex graph by adding modular pieces of logic one at a time and testing the result intuitively.

IMPORTANT NOTE

The code used in this section uses an old version of tidy evaluation, which is tied to older versions of rlang, dplyr, and ggplot2. This choice is forced by the fact that the Power BI service uses an older version of the R engine (3.4.4) with older versions of the preceding packages.

Starting with versions 4.0 of rlang, 3.0.0 of ggplot2, and 1.0.0 of dplyr, the syntax used for tidy evaluation has been simplified and standardized. For an example of the same function that draws a circular barplot translated for the new versions of the previous packages, see the 02-circular-grouped-barplot-new-tidy-eval.R file.

Now let's see how to implement the circular barplot in Power BI.

Implementing a circular barplot in Power BI

As you have already seen in the previous chapters, Power BI is able to render graphs developed with ggplot2 using R visuals. So, no matter how complex the graph you created with ggplot2 is, you can be sure that Power BI will handle it well.

To create a circular barplot in Power BI, follow these steps:

1. Make sure that Power BI Desktop is pointing to the version of CRAN R that is dedicated to R visuals in **Options**.

2. Click on **Get data**, and then click **Text/CSV**.

3. Select the Scores.csv file located in the Chapter 21 folder and click **Open**.

4. You will see a preview of the CSV file. Be sure to select 65001: Unicode (UTF-8) for **File Origin**. This will ensure that special characters in speaker names are displayed correctly. Then, click on **Load**.

5. Click on the **R Visual** icon in the **Visualizations** panel, enable it, and then resize the visual to fit the entire available canvas.

6. With the R visual selected, expand the Scores table under the **Fields** panel and check all its fields (Characteristic, SpeakerName, and Votes).

7. Click on the **Format** tab of the R visual and disable **Title**.

8. Copy the code from the 01-circular-grouped-barplot.R file into the Chapter 21 folder and paste it into the R visual script editor. Then, click on the **Run script** arrow icon in the upper-right corner of the R script editor. You'll see the circular barplot.

9. First, click on an empty spot in the report canvas, then click on the slicer visual icon. Then, expand the Scores table under the **Fields** panel and select the Characteristic column.

10. Click the slicer's **Format** options, expand **Slicer settings**, expand **Options**, and select the **Dropdown** slicer type. Then expand the **Selection** section and enable the **Show "Select All"** option.

11. Resize the bottom and right edges of the slicer and move it to the center of the circular barplot.

You can now filter multiple characteristics (using the *Ctrl* key) and the circular barplot will update accordingly:

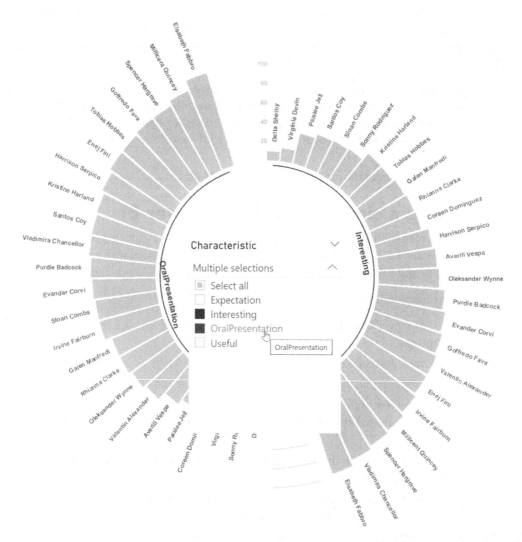

Figure 21.9: The circular barplot filtered by a slicer in Power BI

Pretty impressive, huh? With a little practice with `ggplot2` and R, you can get as many impressive graphs as you want to enrich your analysis.

Summary

In this chapter, you learned how to create sophisticated and visually appealing custom graphs, with a particular focus on circular barplots. First, the merits of circular barplots were discussed, especially when dealing with large numbers of entities or categories. From there, you learned the ins and outs of creating these barplots in R, using the ggplot2 package and the tidy evaluation framework.

In addition, this chapter explored how to integrate R scripts into Power BI to render complex ggplot2 graphs. It provided a step-by-step walk-through for importing data into Power BI, creating an R visual, and then customizing the circular barplot within that environment.

In the next chapter, you'll learn how to develop interactive custom visuals in R and Power BI.

References

For additional reading, check out the following articles:

- *Who Sells More Weapons?* (`https://www.data-to-viz.com/story/OneNumOneCat.html`)
- *Circular barplot with groups* (`https://www.r-graph-gallery.com/297-circular-barplot-with-groups.html`)
- *Down the rabbit hole with tidy eval — Part 1 (the old tidy eval way)* (`https://colinfay.me/tidyeval-1/)https://colinfay.me/tidyeval-1/`)
- *Tidy eval helpers* (`https://ggplot2.tidyverse.org/reference/tidyeval.html`)

Test your knowledge

1. Why are circular barplots particularly useful?
2. What is the recommended approach for utilizing column names in R functions, emphasizing the direct use of column names instead of passing them as strings?
3. What is the meaning of the `coord_polar()` function in ggplot2?

Learn more on Discord

To join the Discord community for this book – where you can share feedback, ask questions to the author, and learn about new releases – follow the QR code below:

`https://discord.gg/MKww5g45EB`

22

Interactive R Custom Visuals

In our journey through the fascinating world of data visualization, we most recently arrived at *Chapter 21, Advanced Visualizations*, and discovered the amazing potential to construct intricate and visually compelling graphs, such as circular bar plots, thanks to the exceptional flexibility offered by ggplot. However, as we navigated these waters of complex graphing, an underlying question may have arisen – are we exploiting the full potential of the data by simply presenting it in these imaginative graphs? Or are we somehow limited by the lack of user interaction?

The feeling is not unfounded. One could argue that an inherent limitation of static charts is their lack of responsiveness to user input, in the form of tooltips and other interactive features. This missing element has the potential to limit the way we understand and interpret data from these visualizations.

To further deepen your understanding and ability to create engaging and interactive visualizations, this chapter will take a leap from where we left off in ggplot. You'll be introduced to a new dimension of creating custom graphs with R. We'll explore how to build interactivity into these graphs directly using *HTML widgets*.

In addition, it is important to note that in this chapter, as in the previous one, we are using R exclusively for the creation of interactive custom visualizations. This is primarily because the pbiviz tools we are using do not support any technology that uses Python behind the scenes. To ensure compatibility and to take full advantage of the pbiviz tools in creating our interactive visualizations, our focus will remain strictly on R.

Here are the topics we will cover:

- Why interactive R custom visuals?
- Adding a dash of interactivity with Plotly
- Exploiting the interactivity provided by HTML widgets
- Packaging everything into a Power BI custom visual
- Importing the custom visual package in Power BI

Technical requirements

This chapter requires you to have a working internet connection and **Power BI Desktop** installed on your machine (version: 2.123.742.0 64-bit, November 2023). You must have properly configured the R engine and IDEs as outlined in *Chapter 2, Configuring R with Power BI*.

Why interactive R custom visuals?

Let's start with a graph you've already implemented in R. For example, consider the raincloud plot of `Fare` versus `Pclass` variables introduced in *Chapter 19, Exploratory Data Analysis* (this time not grouped by `Sex`):

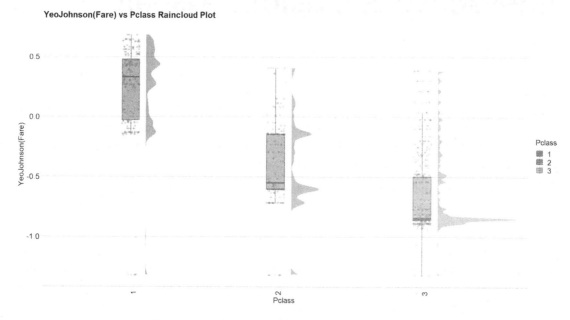

Figure 22.1: Raincloud plot for Fare (transformed) and Pclass variables

Focus for a moment just on the boxplots you see in *Figure 22.1*. Although the Fare variable is already transformed according to Yeo-Johnson to try to reduce skewness, there are still some extreme outliers for each of the passenger classes described by the categorical variable Pclass. For example, if you wanted to know the values of the transformed variable Fare that correspond to the whiskers (fences) of the boxplot on the left so that you could then identify the outliers that are beyond these whiskers, it would be convenient to have these values appear when you hover the mouse near this boxplot. It would be even more interesting to know the actual value of a particular isolated outlier when you hover the mouse over the point that represents it.

There is no doubt that these interactive features would be welcomed by the analyst reading the graphs if they were introduced. So, let's see how to add these interactive features to an existing graph developed with ggplot.

Adding a dash of interactivity with Plotly

There is an open source JavaScript library for data visualization, which is declarative, high-level, and allows you to create dozens of types of interactive graphs called **Plotly.js**. This library is the core of other Plotly client libraries, developed for Python, Scala, R, and ggplot. In particular, the library developed for R, called **Plotly.R** (https://github.com/ropensci/plotly), provides the ggplotly() function, which does all the magic for us: it detects all the basic attributes contained in an existing graph developed with ggplot and transforms it into an interactive web visualization. Let's see an example.

First, you need to install the Plotly.R library (https://github.com/ropensci/plotly) on your latest CRAN R engine using the install.packages('plotly') script.

IMPORTANT NOTE

For simplicity, we'll make sure to run the custom visual on the latest version of the CRAN R engine, since all the necessary libraries have already been installed in the previous chapters. If the goal is to publish a report with the custom visual on Power BI, you need to make sure that the custom visual renders correctly on the same R engine that is present on the Power BI service (in our case, CRAN R 3.4.4).

Then run the script found in the 01-interactive-boxplots.R file in the Chapter 22 folder. The contents of the script are extrapolated from the various scripts used in *Chapter 19, Exploratory Data Analysis*, so you won't see anything new. The only part of the script you haven't seen before is the following:

```
plotly::ggplotly(rc, tooltip = c('x', 'y'))
```

It's the piece of code that turns a static graph into a dynamic HTML-based one, and as you can see, it's a simple call to the ggplotly() function. The result looks like this:

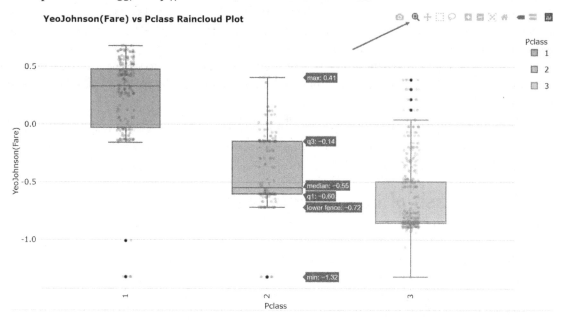

Figure 22.2: Result of applying the ggplotly() function to the raincloud plot

As you can see, in RStudio the result is no longer displayed in the **Plots** tab, but in the **Viewer** tab, which is dedicated to HTML output. You will also notice the presence of the **modebar** in the top-right corner, which allows you to set some operations on the chart, such as zoom and hover options.

But the most striking thing is that you no longer see a series of raincloud plots, as you expected, but simple boxplots! If you look at the RStudio console, you will notice that there are three identical warning messages, one for each raincloud plot that should have been displayed:

```
In geom2trace.default(dots[[1L]][[3L]], dots[[2L]][[1L]], dots[[3L]][[1L]]) :
geom_GeomSlabinterval() has yet to be implemented in plotly.
If you'd like to see this geom implemented,
Please open an issue with your example code at
https://github.com/ropensci/plotly/issues
```

You may have noticed that only the density plots have disappeared. This means that the current version of Plotly (4.10.1) does not yet manage the objects created by the ggdist library. Also, ggplotly() renders fill and color aesthetics differently than ggplot's static graphs. Certainly, this functionality needs to be improved and, most likely, these bugs will be fixed in future releases. In any case, the graph is still usable and shows how easy it is to add interactivity to a ggplot graph.

At this point, you might think that any chart created in HTML and JavaScript could then be used in Power BI. This is not the case.

IMPORTANT NOTE

Any interactive graph that can be used in Power BI must be an HTML widget.

In fact, Plotly.R exposes charts via HTML widgets. Let's see what that's all about.

Exploiting the interactivity provided by HTML widgets

HTML widgets are R packages that allow you to create interactive web pages. These packages are generated by a framework that creates a binding between R and JavaScript libraries. This framework is provided by the `htmlwidgets` package developed by RStudio. HTML widgets are always hosted inside an R package, including the source code and dependencies, to ensure that the widgets are fully reproducible even without access to the Internet. For more details on how to develop an HTML widget from scratch, see the references.

In addition to being able to embed HTML widgets in **RMarkdown** files (dynamic documents with R) or **Shiny** applications (interactive web applications built directly from R), the `htmlwidgets` package allows you to save them also in standalone web page files thanks to the `saveWidget()` function.

However, there are hundreds of R packages that expose their functionality in HTML widgets. You can browse the **htmlwidgets gallery** (`http://gallery.htmlwidgets.org/`) to search for interactive graphics that may be of interest to you.

Okay, it is possible to visualize these HTML widgets, both those in the gallery and those created through Plotly, in Power BI. That sounds great. But how do you embed a dynamic chart created in HTML and JavaScript in Power BI? You need to compile an R-powered visual using the *pbiviz tools*.

Let's see how it's done.

Packaging it all into a Power BI custom visual

Power BI Visual Tools (pbiviz) are the easiest way to create custom visuals in Power BI. They are written in **JavaScript** (using **Node.js**) and are used to compile the source code of **.pbiviz packages**. A `.pbiviz` package is a zipped version of the **Power BI visual project**, which in turn is a set of folders, scripts, and assets needed to create the custom visualization you want to implement. In general, a standard Power BI visual project is created from a template using the `pbiviz` command-line tools. The contents of the template depend on the method you want to use to create the custom visual (**TypeScript**, **R visual**, or **R HTML**).

IMPORTANT NOTE

The pbiviz tools do not support any technology that uses Python behind the scenes, such as the ipywidget widgets.

With this in mind, it is worth learning a little more about R and ggplot to be able to develop interesting custom visuals using the R visual and R HTML modes. In addition to this, as mentioned at the end of *Chapter 2*, *Configuring R with Power BI*, take the following note into account:

IMPORTANT NOTE

The Publish to Web option in Power BI does not allow you to publish reports that contain standard R visuals. You can work around this limitation by creating R custom visuals that are allowed to be published with this option.

Now let's see how to install the pbiviz tools.

Installing the pbiviz package

The pbiviz command-line tools provide everything you need to develop visuals and test them in reports and dashboards on the Power BI service. For the last reason mentioned, you also need to install an SSL certificate so that your laptop can interact securely with the Power BI service.

Let's see how to do everything step by step:

1. Go to https://nodejs.org/en/ and install the version of Node.js recommended for all users, following the default options set by the installer.

2. Reboot your machine, as this is mandatory for the command in *step 4* to work.

3. Click on the Windows **Start** button, type power, and click the **Windows PowerShell** application.

4. In the PowerShell console, type the following command: npm i -g powerbi-visuals-tools@4.0.5. We install a specific version of the Power BI Visual Tools to use the Power BI Visuals API 3.8.0. Power BI Visual Tools version 4.0.5 is the latest to use API 3.8.0. More recent versions of Power BI Visual Tools use newer versions of the Power BI API (5.3.0), but they are still poorly documented with few working examples. Since it is still possible to use API 3.8.0 in the latest versions of Power BI Desktop, we have preferred to continue using these APIs. If you see any deprecation warnings, don't worry and wait for the installation to complete.

5. In the PowerShell console, type the following command: pbiviz install-cert. It opens a **Certificate** pop-up window telling you that the certificate is not trusted and that you should install it in the Trusted Root Certification Authorities store to trust it.

6. Click **Install Certificate...** on the window, leave **Current User** as Store Location, and click **Next**.

7. Select **Place all certificates in the following store**, click **Browse...**, select the **Trusted Root Certification Authorities** folder, and click **OK**. Click **Next** in the pop-up window, and then click **Finish**.

8. You'll get a **Security Warning** window asking if you want to install the certificate. Click **Yes** and a **The import was successful** dialog box will appear. Click **OK**. Then click **OK** on the pop-up window.

9. In order to verify that everything went well, go back to the PowerShell console, type the pbiviz command and press **Enter**. You should see the following output:

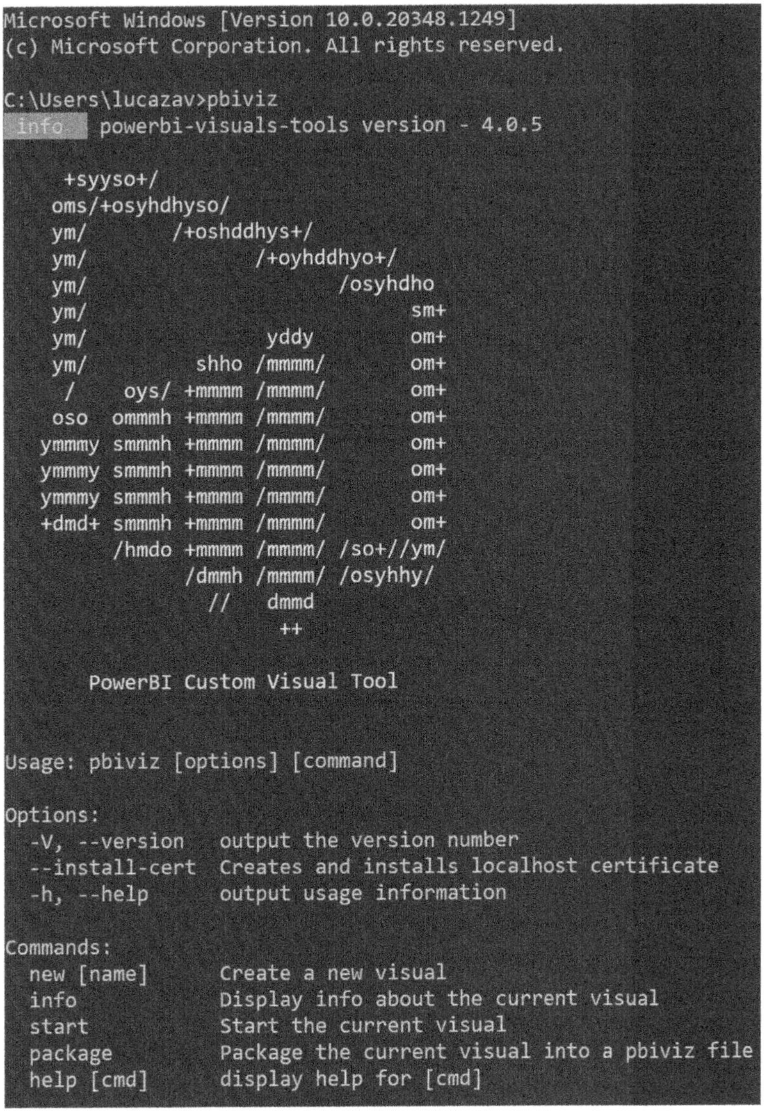

```
Microsoft Windows [Version 10.0.20348.1249]
(c) Microsoft Corporation. All rights reserved.

C:\Users\lucazav>pbiviz
 info    powerbi-visuals-tools version - 4.0.5

    +syyso+/
   oms/+osyhdhyso/
   ym/        /+oshddhys+/
   ym/             /+oyhddhyo+/
   ym/                   /osyhdho
   ym/                         sm+
   ym/            yddy          om+
   ym/        shho /mmmm/       om+
   /    oys/ +mmmm /mmmm/       om+
  oso  ommmh +mmmm /mmmm/       om+
 ymmmy smmmh +mmmm /mmmm/       om+
 ymmmy smmmh +mmmm /mmmm/       om+
 ymmmy smmmh +mmmm /mmmm/       om+
 +dmd+ smmmh +mmmm /mmmm/       om+
       /hmdo +mmmm /mmmm/ /so+//ym/
             /dmmh /mmmm/ /osyhhy/
               //   dmmd
                     ++


      PowerBI Custom Visual Tool


Usage: pbiviz [options] [command]

Options:
  -V, --version   output the version number
  --install-cert  Creates and installs localhost certificate
  -h, --help      output usage information

Commands:
  new [name]      Create a new visual
  info            Display info about the current visual
  start           Start the current visual
  package         Package the current visual into a pbiviz file
  help [cmd]      display help for [cmd]
```

Figure 22.3: pbiviz is installed correctly

Great! Now you have your pbiviz tools properly configured and ready to compile a custom visual.

Let's put them to the test right now with an R HTML custom visual.

Developing your first R HTML custom visual

To create a custom R HTML visual, you must first create a standard Power BI visual project of type *R HTML* from the template provided by pbiviz tools. Then, you just need to modify the scripts provided by the project in order to create the visual you want to develop.

In this section, you will package the dynamic boxplots graph that you met in a previous section.

Here are the steps to get the `.pbiviz` package:

1. Open the **Windows PowerShell** console from the **Start** menu if you have closed it since you last used it. By default, the folder where the console starts is `C:\Usersers\<your-username>`.

2. Create a folder for custom visuals named `Power-BI-Custom-Visuals` by using the `md` `Power-BI-Custom-Visuals` command.

3. Go to the folder you just created with the `cd` `Power-BI-Custom-Visuals` command.

4. Generate a standard R HTML Power BI visual project from the template by using the `pbiviz new interactiveboxplotsviz -t rhtml` command.

5. In VS Code, open the template folder you just created. After trusting this folder, you should see something like this in **Explorer**:

Figure 22.4: Contents of the interactiveboxplots folder in VS Code

You can find a complete buildable project in the PBI-Visual-Project\interactiveboxplotsviz folder in the Chapter 22 repository. You can use it as a reference for the next steps.

6. Open the pbiviz.json file of the template you just created to enter the basic information about the custom visual you want to create. Format it properly (right-click in the document canvas and click **Format Document**). *Figure 22.5* and the following figures show a portion of the template code on the left and how it should be modified on the right:

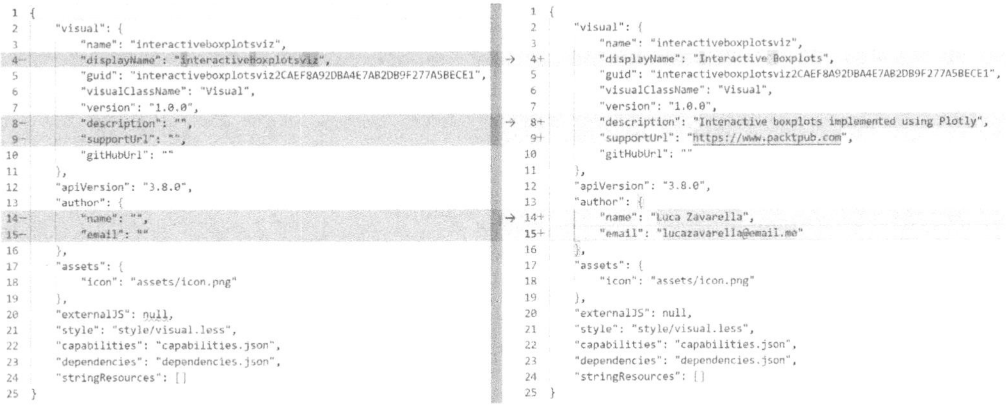

Figure 22.5: Editing the contents of the pbiviz.json file in VS Code

Here are the details of the attributes to edit for the "visual" node:

- "displayName": "Interactive Boxplots"
- "description": "Interactive boxplots implemented using Plotly"
- "supportUrl": "https://www.packt.com"

Here are the details of the attributes to edit for the "author" node:

- "name": "<full-name-of-the-author>"
- "email": "<email-of-the-author>"

7. Now open the capabilities.json file. It is used to declare what data types the visualization accepts, what customizable attributes to put in the properties panel, and other information needed to build the visualization. It contains several root objects. The first one whose contents you need to edit is dataRoles (https://bit.ly/pbiviz-dataroles). In this section, you can define the data fields that your visual expects. The default template has only the unique Values field by default, like the standard R visual.

In our case, the multivariate boxplot visual needs three fields:

```
1  {                                    1  {
2     "dataRoles": [                    2     "dataRoles": [
3        {                              3        {
4-          "displayName": "Values",  → 4+          "displayName": "X Split Variable",
                                        5+          "description": "Integer or categorical variable used on x axis
                                         +          to split boxplots",
5          "kind": "GroupingOrMeasure", 6          "kind": "GroupingOrMeasure",
6-         "name": "Values"          → 7+          "name": "x"
                                        8+       },
                                        9+       {
                                        10+         "displayName": "Y Quantitative Variable",
                                        11+         "description": "Numeric variable (integer or double) used on y
                                         +          axis, whose distribution is displayed in boxplots",
                                        12+         "kind": "GroupingOrMeasure",
                                        13+         "name": "y"
                                        14+      },
                                        15+      {
                                        16+         "displayName": "Grouping Variable",
                                        17+         "description": "Integer or categorical variable used to group
                                         +          data into facets",
                                        18+         "kind": "GroupingOrMeasure",
                                        19+         "name": "grp"
7        }                              20      }
8     ],                               21     ],
```

Figure 22.6: Editing the dataRoles section of the capabilities.json file

8. Based on the elements added in `dataRoles`, you must modify the contents of the `dataViewMappings`
    root object in the `capabilities.json` file (`https://bit.ly/pbiviz-dataviewmappings`). They
    describe how data roles relate to each other and allow you to specify conditional requirements
    for data visualization. In our case, we need to declare the three fields created in `dataRoles` as
    components of the script's input dataset:

```
 9    "dataViewMappings": [              22    "dataViewMappings": [
10      {                                23      {
11        "scriptResult": {              24        "scriptResult": {
12          "dataInput": {               25          "dataInput": {
13            "table": {                  26            "table": {
14              "rows": {                 27              "rows": {
15                "select": [             28                "select": [
16                  {                     29                  {
17                    "for": {            30                    "for": {
18~                     "in": "Values"  →31+                     "in": "x"
                                         32+                    }
                                         33+                  },
                                         34+                  {
                                         35+                    "for": {
                                         36+                      "in": "y"
                                         37+                    }
                                         38+                  },
                                         39+                  {
                                         40+                    "for": {
                                         41+                      "in": "grp"
19                    }                  42                    }
20                  }                    43                  }
21                ],                     44                ],
22                "dataReductionAlgorithm": {  45                "dataReductionAlgorithm": {
23                  "top": {}            46                  "top": {}
24                }                      47                }
25              }                        48              }
26            }                          49            }
27          },                           50          },
28          "script": {                  51          "script": {
29            "scriptProviderDefault": "R",  52            "scriptProviderDefault": "R",
30            "scriptOutputType": "html",    53            "scriptOutputType": "html",
31            "source": {                54            "source": {
32              "objectName": "rcv_script",  55              "objectName": "rcv_script",
33              "propertyName": "source"     56              "propertyName": "source"
34            },                         57            },
35            "provider": {              58            "provider": {
36              "objectName": "rcv_script",  59              "objectName": "rcv_script",
37              "propertyName": "provider"   60              "propertyName": "provider"
38            }                          61            }
39          }                            62          }
40        }                              63        }
41      }                                64      }
42    ],                                 65    ],
```

Figure 22.7: Editing the dataViewMappings section of the capabilities.json file

As you can see, the `"script"` subsection of the template refers to the `rcv_script` object. We will see that this is defined in the next section.

9. The `objects` section of the `capabilities.json` file describes the customizable properties that are associated with the visual and that appear in the **Format** pane (`https://bit.ly/pbiviz-objects`). In our case, we want to parameterize the type of transformation we can apply to the variable y. Therefore, we will make sure that the user can select the transformation type from the **Y Transformation Type** combobox, which is located in the **Variables Settings** section just below the **General** section. The necessary changes to the script are as follows:

```
66   "objects": {                          66   "objects": {
67     "rcv_script": {                      67     "rcv_script": {
68       "properties": {                    68       "properties": {
69         "provider": {                     69         "provider": {
70           "type": {                        70           "type": {
71             "text": true                    71             "text": true
72           }                                72           }
73         },                                73         },
74         "source": {                       74         "source": {
75           "type": {                        75           "type": {
76             "scripting": {                  76             "scripting": {
77               "source": true                 77               "source": true
78             }                                78             }
79           }                                79           }
80         }                                 80         }
81       }                                   81       }
                                            82+    },
                                            83+    "settings_variable_params": {
                                            84+      "displayName": "Variables Settings",
                                            85+      "description": "Settings to control the transformations applied to the
                                               +      variables",
                                            86+      "properties": {
                                            87+        "y_transf_name": {
                                            88+          "displayName": "Y Transformation Type",
                                            89+          "description": "Type of transformation to be applied to the variable
                                               +          Y. The type 'Standard' indicates that no transformation is applied",
                                            90+          "type": {
                                            91+            "enumeration": [
                                            92+              {
                                            93+                "displayName": "Standard",
                                            94+                "value": "standard"
                                            95+              },
                                            96+              {
                                            97+                "displayName": "Yeo-Johnson",
                                            98+                "value": "yeo-johnson"
                                            99+              }
                                            100+            ]
                                            101+          }
                                            102+        }
                                            103+      }
82     }                                    104    }
83   },                                     105    },
84   "suppressDefaultTitle": true           106   "suppressDefaultTitle": true
85 }                                        107 }
```

Figure 22.8: Editing the objects section of the capabilities.json file

The `suppressDefaultTitle` parameter at the end of the `capabilities.json` file allows you to suppress the title that typically appears at the top left of each R visual. As you can see in *Figure 22.8*, this section defines the `rcv_script` object referenced in the `dataViewMappings` section. Unlike the one you just added (`settings_variable_params`), the `rcv_script` object is not intended to appear in the **Format** pane but is used only to describe the attributes of the `source` and `provider` objects that define the R script. To actually declare which parameters to display in the **Format** pane, you need to make a small change to the `settings.ts` file. Let's see how.

10. Open the settings.ts file located in the src folder of your Power BI visual project. It contains the settings in TypeScript for the items you want to be displayed in your visual. Instead of displaying the rcv_script object, we can display the settings_variables_params object, which contains our parameter associated with the type of transformation to apply to the y variable:

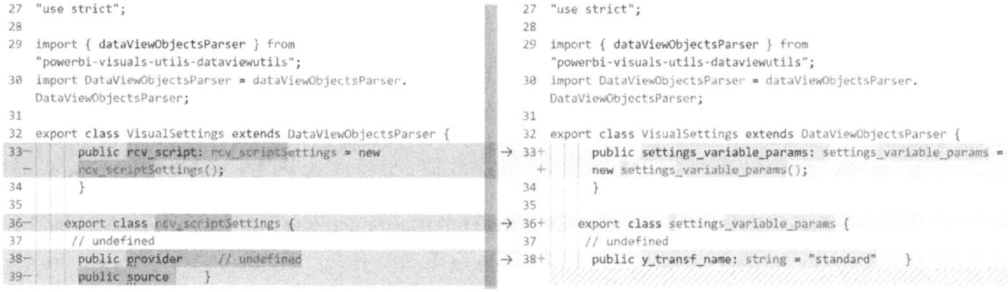

```
27  "use strict";                                          27  "use strict";
28                                                         28
29  import { dataViewObjectsParser } from                  29  import { dataViewObjectsParser } from
    "powerbi-visuals-utils-dataviewutils";                    "powerbi-visuals-utils-dataviewutils";
30  import DataViewObjectsParser = dataViewObjectsParser.  30  import DataViewObjectsParser = dataViewObjectsParser.
    DataViewObjectsParser;                                    DataViewObjectsParser;
31                                                         31
32  export class VisualSettings extends DataViewObjectsParser {  32  export class VisualSettings extends DataViewObjectsParser {
33-     public rcv_script: rcv_scriptSettings = new      → 33+     public settings_variable_params: settings_variable_params =
 -      rcv_scriptSettings();                                +      new settings_variable_params();
34      }                                                  34      }
35                                                         35
36-     export class rcv_scriptSettings {               → 36+     export class settings_variable_params {
37         // undefined                                    37         // undefined
38-        public provider    // undefined             → 38+        public y_transf_name: string = "standard"    }
39-        public source    }
```

Figure 22.9: Editing the settings.ts file

For more details about the classes used in this script, see the references.

11. Open the dependencies.json file. It contains a reference to each library used in the R code that generates the visual. In addition to the ones already present (ggplot2, plotly, htmlwidgets, and xml2), you will need to add the following: RColorBrewer, cowplot, dplyr, purrr, forcats, and recipes. Just follow the syntax already used for the existing libraries and change the URLs, keeping in mind that you can put any string in displayName.

12. Finally, you can enter the R code that generates the visual in the script.r file. You can replace all of its contents with the contents of the file of the same name, which you can find in the Power BI visual project shared in the GitHub repository for *Chapter 22*.

At the beginning of the script are some commented lines that can be used to debug any problems in RStudio. Then there is a source() command that loads the utility functions from the provided flatten_HTML.r file in the r_files folder. These help to convert Plotly or widget objects into self-contained HTML. The following code is very similar to what you've already seen in the previous sections. There are built-in pieces of code to handle the presence of the fields passed to the visual as input data and the parameter that handles the type of transformation of the variable y. Here's an example:

```
y_transf_name <- 'standard'
if(exists("settings_variable_params_y_transf_name")){
  y_transf_name <- as.character(settings_variable_params_y_transf_name)
}
```

The name of the variable settings_variable_params_y_transf_name is given by the union of the name of the section containing the parameter and the name of the parameter itself.

Finally, there are two pieces of code at the end of the script. One is used to remove some of the icons from the Plotly Modebar:

```
disabledButtonsList <- list(
    'toImage', 'sendDataToCloud', 'zoom2d', 'pan',
    'pan2d', 'select2d', 'lasso2d',
    'hoverClosestCartesian', 'hoverCompareCartesian')
p$x$config$modeBarButtonsToRemove = disabledButtonsList
p <- config(p, staticPlot = FALSE, editable = FALSE, sendData = FALSE,
showLink = FALSE, displaylogo = FALSE,  collaborate = FALSE, cloud=FALSE)
```

The other is a workaround for a Plotly bug that displays the outliers of a boxplot despite passing the outlier.shape = NA parameter to geom_boxplot():

```
hideOutliers <- function(x) {
  if (x$hoverinfo == 'y') {
    x$marker = list(opacity = 0)
    x$hoverinfo = NA
  }
  return(x)
}
p[["x"]][["data"]] <- purrr::map(p[["x"]][["data"]], ~ hideOutliers(.))
```

Finally, the internalSaveWidget(p, 'out.html') command uses one of the utility functions loaded at the beginning of the script to generate the flattened visual in a self-contained HTML with the default name out.html, which is properly managed by Power BI.

The last command calls the ReadFullFileReplaceString() function. It allows you to replace strings in the out.html file generated by the code in order to modify the default configurations generated by Plotly. Specifically, the command used here corrects a padding setting of the generated HTML widget.

13. Now go back to the Windows PowerShell console and make sure that you are in the Power-BI-Custom-Visuals\interactiveboxplotsviz folder. If you were in the Power-BI-Custom-Visuals folder, simply use the cd interactiveboxplotsviz command. Then, type the pbiviz package command to compile the .pbiviz package that contains your custom visual. At the end of compiling your pbiviz package, you will see something like this:

```
(base) PS C:\Users\lucazav\Power-BI-Custom-Visuals\interactiveboxplotsviz> pbiviz package
info    powerbi-visuals-tools version - 4.0.5
info    Building visual...
info    Certificate is valid.
info    Start preparing plugin template
info    Finish preparing plugin template
info    Start packaging...
(node:2624) [DEP_WEBPACK_COMPILATION_ASSETS] DeprecationWarning: Compilation.assets will be frozen in future, all modifi
cations are deprecated.
BREAKING CHANGE: No more changes should happen to Compilation.assets after sealing the Compilation.
        Do changes to assets earlier, e. g. in Compilation.hooks.processAssets.
        Make sure to select an appropriate stage from Compilation.PROCESS_ASSETS_STAGE_*.
(Use `node --trace-deprecation ...` to show where the warning was created)
info    Package compression enabled
info    Package created!
info    Finish packaging
Webpack Bundle Analyzer saved report to C:\Users\lucazav\Power-BI-Custom-Visuals\interactiveboxplotsviz\webpack.statisti
cs.prod.html

warn    Please, make sure that the visual source code matches to requirements of certification:

info    Visual must use API v3.2.0 and above
info    The project repository must:
info    Include package.json and package-lock.json;
info    Not include node_modules folder
info    Run npm install expect no errors
info    Run pbiviz package expect no errors
info    The compiled package of the Custom Visual should match submitted package.
info    npm audit command must not return any alerts with high or moderate level.
info    The project must include Tslint from Microsoft with no overridden configuration, and this command shouldn't retu
rn any tslint errors.
info    https://www.npmjs.com/package/tslint-microsoft-contrib
info    Ensure no arbitrary/dynamic code is run (bad: eval(), unsafe use of settimeout(), requestAnimationFrame(), setin
terval(some function with user input).. running user input/data etc.)
info    Ensure DOM is manipulated safely (bad: innerHTML, D3.html(<some user/data input>), unsanitized user input/data d
irectly added to DOM, etc.)
info    Ensure no js errors/exceptions in browser console for any input data. As test dataset please use this sample rep
ort

info    Full description of certification requirements you can find in documentation:
info    https://docs.microsoft.com/en-us/power-bi/power-bi-custom-visuals-certified#certification-requirements
(base) PS C:\Users\lucazav\Power-BI-Custom-Visuals\interactiveboxplotsviz>
```

Figure 22.10: Compile custom visual successfully

Very nice job! You have compiled your very first R HTML custom visual using the pbiviz tools. Okay, but where is the compiled package? Don't worry, look inside the newly created dist folder of your Power BI visual project:

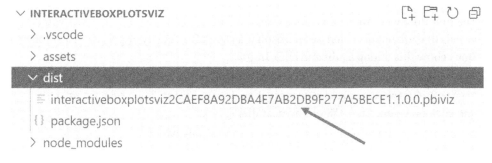

Figure 22.11: Your .pbiviz package just compiled

There it is! Now let's import it into Power BI.

Importing the custom visual package into Power BI

Now that the bulk of the work is done, importing your custom visual into Power BI is a breeze. First of all, you need to install the xml2 package in your R engine, as it is used by the provided utility functions:

1. Open RStudio and make sure it is pointing to your latest CRAN R (version 4.2.2 in our case).
2. Click on the **Console** window and type this command: `install.packages('xml2')`. If you remember, this library is listed in the dependency file you saw in the previous section. Then, press **Enter**.

Now let's import the custom visual into Power BI:

1. Make sure that Power BI Desktop is pointing to the correct R engine (the latest one) in **Options**.
2. Click on **Get data**, search for web, select **Web**, and click on **Connect**.
3. Type the following URL as the source: `http://bit.ly/titanic-dataset-csv`. Then click **OK**.
4. Make sure that the **File Origin** is **65001: Unicode (UTF-8)** and click **Load**.
5. Click the ellipses below the **Visuals** pane, and then click on **Import a visual from a file**:

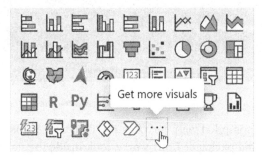

Figure 22.12: Import a custom visual from a file

6. The first time you import a custom visual, a dialog box appears that warns you that custom visuals that are not provided by Microsoft may contain security or privacy risks. You can select **Don't show this dialog again** and click **Import**.
7. In the window that opens next, browse to the following folder: `C:\Users\<your-username>\Power-BI-Custom-Visuals\interactiveboxplotsviz\dist`. Then select your `.pbiviz` package and click on **Open**. Click **OK** on the next dialog box.
8. As you can see, a new icon has appeared in the **Visuals** pane:

Figure 22.13: Import a custom visual from file

If you want to use a custom icon for your visual, simply replace the icon.png file in your Power BI visual project's assets folder before compiling.

Click on it to add your custom visual to your report canvas. Then click **Enable** in the next dialog box.

9. Enlarge your custom visual area, then expand the **titanic-dataset-csv** table on the **Fields** pane and check first the **Pclass** field, then the **Fare** field:

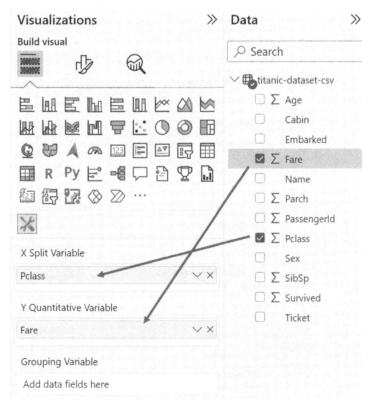

Figure 22.14: Select the Pclass and Fare fields as X and Y variables

Make sure that the **Don't summarize** option is selected for each of the **Pclass** and **Fare** variables added as variables of the custom visual.

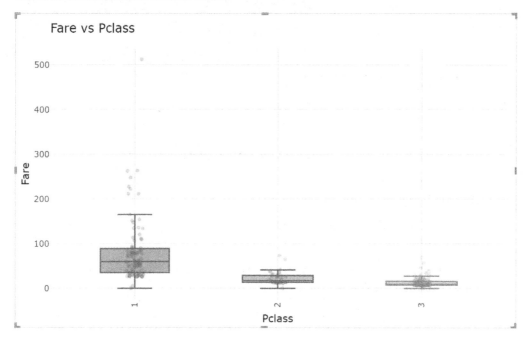

Figure 22.15: Your custom visual showing boxplots for Fare vs. Pclass

10. Now click on the **Format** icon of the visual, expand the **Variables Settings** section, and select Yeo-Johnson for **Y Transformation Type**:

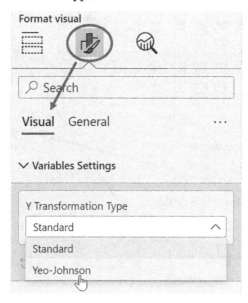

Figure 22.16: Select Yeo-Johnson for Y Transformation Type

Now look at your custom visual again. You will see something like this:

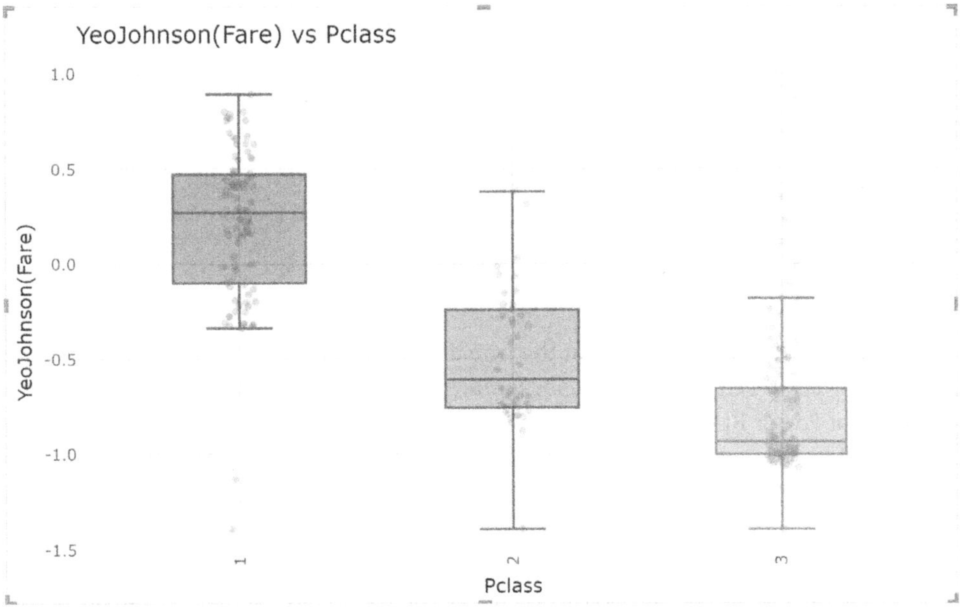

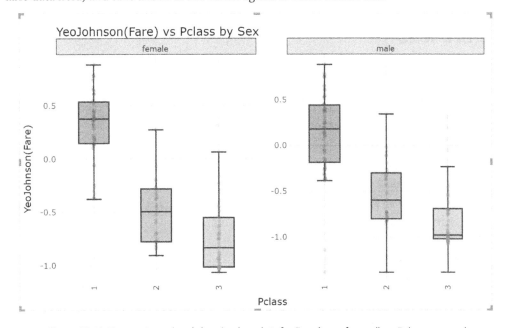

Figure 22.17: Your custom visual showing boxplots for Fare (transformed) vs. Pclass

11. Now click the build visual icon to see the data required by the custom visual, then go to the **titanic-dataset-csv** table in the **Fields** pane, drag the **Sex** field into the visual's **Grouping Variable** data field, and take a look at the visual again. It will look like this:

Figure 22.18: Your custom visual showing boxplots for Fare (transformed) vs. Pclass grouped by Sex

Really impressive! Your custom interactive visual is awesome and works great!

Summary

In this chapter, you learned about the advantages of using an interactive visual over a static visual in some cases. You learned how to add some basic interactivity to charts developed with ggplot using Plotly.

You learned that the key to creating interactive visuals in Power BI is that they are based on HTML widgets. So you were guided step by step through the creation of a custom visual, compiled using the pbiviz tools.

Finally, you imported the compiled package into Power BI to test its functionality.

As we close this edition, we reflect on the transformative journey we've been on together. In addition to adding advanced analytics to your toolbox, you've mastered the art of combining the robust capabilities of Power BI with the analytical power of Python and R. With these skills, you'll be able to go beyond traditional data analysis limitations and turn complex data into powerful stories and predictive insights. This book has been designed to guide you through the complex landscape of data analysis, ensuring that you are equipped to tackle real-world challenges with confidence and creativity. The journey through these pages has been about more than learning; it has been about broadening your perspective, enhancing your skills, and empowering you to use data in transformative ways. As you move forward, remember that every dataset tells a story, every analysis reveals a truth, and your expertise now allows you to uncover and tell them with unprecedented clarity and impact. Take the knowledge, practices, and curiosity you've developed here and let them lead you to new horizons in your analytical endeavors. Thank you for joining us on this enlightening journey, and may your future analyses be insightful, impactful, and inspiring.

References

For additional reading, check out the following books and articles:

- *Plotly R Open Source Graphing Library* (https://plotly.com/r/)
- *[Course] R: Interactive Visualizations with htmlwidgets* (https://www.linkedin.com/learning/r-interactive-visualizations-with-htmlwidgets/welcome)
- *Creating a widget* (http://www.htmlwidgets.org/develop_intro.html)
- *Power BI visual project Structure* (https://docs.microsoft.com/en-us/power-bi/developer/visuals/visual-project-structure)
- *Power BI Custom Visual Part 5 – Formatting* (https://shetland.azurewebsites.net/2021/02/18/power-bi-custom-visual-part-5-formatting/)

Test your knowledge

1. Why choose interactive visuals over static charts?
2. How does the chapter suggest adding interactivity to ggplot graphs?
3. How can a user create an interactive Power BI custom visual with R?

4. Is it possible to publish standard R visuals to the web using the Publish to Web feature?

5. Is it possible to use Python with pbiviz to create interactive custom visuals?

Learn more on Discord

To join the Discord community for this book – where you can share feedback, ask questions to the author, and learn about new releases – follow the QR code below:

```
https://discord.gg/MKww5g45EB
```

Answers

Chapter 1

1. The stages are data loading, data transforming, and data viewing.
2. You can't use a Python dictionary as a data source. Only pandas DataFrames are recognized by Power BI as allowed data sources.
3. You can't use an R list as a data source. Only R data frames are recognized by Power BI as allowed data sources.
4. In the case of both the Python script and R script, the name of the variable that contains the transformation data obtained up to the previous step is **dataset**.
5. You must drag the fields you want to use in your script to the **Values** area.
6. You must refresh the data in order to re-run a Python or R script added as a Power Query step (either in the loading phase or in the transforming phase) – or set a **Page Refresh** property for DirectQuery imports of data frames.
7. Python and R script visuals are updated whenever you interact with other visuals in the report (cross-filtering).
8. The internet cannot be accessed from a Python or R script visual published on the Power BI service due to security issues. The same script visual can access resources on the internet on Power BI Desktop without problems.
9. Python and R script visuals can be used in Power BI Desktop, the Power BI service, and Power BI embedded.

Chapter 2

1. The available R engines are CRAN R, Microsoft R Open, and Microsoft R Client. Of these, Microsoft's engines are being discontinued.
2. The most obvious advantage of Microsoft's R distributions is that they include out-of-the-box use of the Intel MKL multi-threading libraries.
3. Yes, it is possible to introduce BLAS and LAPACK multi-threading libraries also for CRAN R. It is not possible to do this from the installer, but a manual configuration using the libraries exposed by Intel oneMKL is required.
4. In order to publish a report that contains transformations done via R scripts, you must install an instance of the on-premises data gateway in personal mode on a machine that you manage, on which you must install the same version of the R engine that you have installed on your development machine.

5. You will not encounter any errors on Power BI Desktop, because the R code present in both Power Query and the R script visual is injected into the R engine installed on your machine. When you publish the report, the R code used in Power Query will be injected into the R engine on the machine where the data gateway in personal mode is installed, and therefore you will not receive any errors. Instead, the R code used in the R script visual will be injected into specific virtual machines allocated for the service, which have a specific version of the R engine and specific packages installed. Therefore, it may be the case that the R script visual code that you tested with a newer version of R and with newer packages on your machine will give an error when published to the service.

6. Yes, you can do the refresh without installing the data gateway in personal mode only in the special case where the report datasets are only fed by online services.

7. You can interact with the R IDE from Power BI only if you want to debug the code of an R script visual.

8. R script visual input data is exported to a temporary folder in CSV format.

9. Although your report works properly on Power BI Desktop, it will generate an error when it is published and must access the internet because, for security reasons, access to the World Wide Web is precluded for an R script visual on the Power BI service.

10. It is not possible to publish a report that contains an R script visual via "**Publish to web**". You can, however, bypass this limitation by implementing a custom R visual, as shown in *Chapter 22*.

Chapter 3

1. The Python distributions most widely used by data scientists are Anaconda and Miniconda.

2. The most widely used tools for installing packages in Python are the pip and conda package managers. The pip package manager has the **Python Package Index** (**PyPI**) as the source repository for packages. The conda one has several conda channels as source repositories. The most important are the default one, maintained by Anaconda Inc., and the conda-forge one, maintained by the Python community.

3. To ensure the reproducibility of Python script results in Power Query and Python script visuals, it is enough to install a single instance of the Python engine, taking care to create two virtual environments to handle the two separate cases.

4. Your colleague did not follow the best practices you learned in this chapter. When Python script visuals are published to Power BI Desktop, they run the scripts on a Python engine already prepared and maintained by the service, so your colleague should have created a virtual environment containing the same version of the Python engine provided by the service, with the same versions of the packages as those installed on the service.

5. Since the data source is on the web, the dataset will refresh without requiring any special configuration. If your data source was on-prem (files in shared folders, databases, etc.), you would have had to install the Power BI data gateway in personal mode, configure it with the appropriate user (your own or service), and associate it with the dataset in question.

6. Since dot products are linear algebra operations, we know that their execution times can be optimized through the BLAS and LAPACK libraries. NumPy uses precisely these libraries behind the scenes, so it is worth using the numpy.dot() function if you want better performance. Also, if you install NumPy via conda from its default channel, the Intel MKL implementation of the above libraries is used behind the scenes, which performs better than all others on Intel processors.

7. When you use # %% within a Python script, VS Code interprets it as the beginning of a Jupyter notebook cell, which ends at the next similar code. VS Code then gives you the ability to execute the cell code.

8. To get the data obtained from the Power Query transformations, simply add a Python script visual to the report canvas, provide it with the necessary fields as input obtained from multiple transformation steps in Power Query, and click on the *Launch Python IDE* button, found on the right side of the Python script editor title bar. VS Code will create a CSV file containing the above data in a temporary folder.

9. Unfortunately, Power BI does not allow the development of custom Python visuals. If you need to publish a report on the web containing a plot that can only be realized by scripts, you must necessarily use a custom R visual.

10. Both reports reference a single data gateway representing the service user. This means that the data gateway in question is referencing only one of the two environments A and B, as indicated in the PythonSettings.xml file. Therefore, the dataset using the environment not referenced by the configuration file will give an error when it is refreshed, because it will not find the packages it needs for processing. If the published reports refer to more than one environment, it is necessary to instantiate as many separate machines as there are environments, installing a data gateway in personal mode on each one and using a separate login for each environment. This is why it is usually preferred to use only one environment and to install as few packages as possible in it.

Chapter 4

1. The ADO.NET error referring to the inability to import the NumPy library is raised seemingly for no reason when you use a conda environment that is not previously enabled.

2. The Firewall is responsible for ensuring that possible data leakage does not occur during the query folding process.

3. The two possible errors raised by the Firewall are that of incompatible privacy levels between queries, and that of indirect access to a data source. The first error (incompatible privacy levels) is raised when Python or R scripts (depending on the language you are using) have a privacy level that does not allow possible sharing of information with the referenced data source (with incompatible privacy level). The second error (indirect access to a data source) is raised when the script step references a query that directly accesses a data source, and thus the check for possible shared information is no longer enforceable by the Firewall.

4. When you publish a report to Power BI service, its datasets do not maintain the same privacy levels set in Power BI Desktop. These must be set again at the service level.

5. In this case, the Firewall first raises the error of incompatible privacy levels. You must therefore first align the privacy level of the data source with that of the Python scripts (set to Public, a choice forced by the fact that otherwise, to date, you cannot publish the report on the service). After that, the Firewall will also raise the indirect access error to the data source.

6. The method of combining transformations involves replicating the steps required to obtain a table before applying a script step to it. This means that, should the table itself be used in the report and the transformation logic generating it change, the replicated steps in the new query with the script step would also need to be aligned. In contrast, using encapsulation by function grants the new query the same benefits as a referenced query. That is, any changes to the referenced query will automatically be reflected in the new query to which a script step is added, without any manual intervention.

7. The method for applying a full join between two queries to be passed into a Python or R script does not necessarily require that at least one of their fields serve as a key for the join. This method works even for completely different tables.

8. The list of tables passed as a parameter to the `Python.Execute` or `R.Execute` function may not necessarily contain the "dataset" table that references the result of all transformations applied up to that point to the query in which the script step is added. For example, this is necessary when you want to generate a new table as a direct result of applying a Python or R function to two tables in the data model.

9. It is necessary to transform Date, Date/Time, or Time type fields into the text format before adding a Python or R script step because otherwise the field values would not be interpreted correctly by Python or R even as simple strings, showing the string `Microsoft.OleDb.<data-type>` for all of them.

10. If you need to use the Time data type within the logic of a script step and do not have the ability to have specific packages installed that could implement it in the most appropriate way, it is definitely worth using Python. This is because Python also installs by default the Datetime module, which allows you to deal appropriately with the Time data type. In order to work properly with it in R, you need to install third-party packages.

Chapter 5

1. It may happen that a team of data scientists makes use of a lot of computational resources for a long time in order to generate an object using Python or R. For the purpose of being able to reuse the result obtained without having to spend time and resources again, the team can serialize the object to a file. This file can also be reused in Power BI.

2. There is no specific format for serializing an R object to be deserialized in Power BI. In fact, in Power BI, you can deserialize an object of any format, either in an R step in Power Query or in an R script visual by loading the serialized file from the file system.

3. The alternative method is a necessary workaround to make the use of the report more interactive, without necessarily having to deserialize the object from the file system at each interaction with the report itself.

4. The alternative method for injecting a serialized object from Power Query into a script visual involves these steps in Power Query:

    1. Deserialize the list of objects from the file system.
    2. From the list, create a dataframe containing only the names associated with the objects, and serialize each object in the list into its byte string representation.
    3. Split each string representation of the object in multiple chunks due to a limitation of Power BI.
    4. The named list of string chunks can be easily transformed into a dataframe whose fields can be passed to a script visual.

    Then, in a script visual:

    5. Merge chunks to reconstruct the byte string representation of objects.
    6. Transform each string of bytes back into an object.
    7. Use the object in the script visual code.

5. The relationship between the two tables allows only the byte string representation of the object associated with the single name selected in the Slicer to be passed to the script visual. This way, the deserialization activity within the script visual involves only one object and is faster, allowing for faster interaction with the report.

Chapter 6

1. The main purposes of using regexes are:

    a. Text validation: Regexes can be used to check if a piece of text matches a certain pattern. This is useful for tasks such as verifying email addresses, dates, or other types of structured data.
    b. Text searching and filtering: Regexes can be used to search for patterns in large amounts of text, such as finding all instances of a particular word or phrase in a document. This can also be used to filter out unwanted data, such as removing all instances of a certain word or phrase from a document.
    c. Text manipulation and formatting: Regexes can be used to manipulate text in various ways, such as finding and replacing certain words or phrases, formatting text, or converting text from one format to another.
    d. Web scraping and data extraction: Regexes can be used to extract specific data from web pages or other structured documents, such as extracting all email addresses from a website or extracting data from a log file.
    e. Programming and scripting: Regexes are widely used in programming and scripting languages to perform text manipulation and processing tasks. Many programming languages, including Python and JavaScript, have built-in support for regexes.

2. Python provides built-in support for regular expressions through the re module. It provides basic regular expression operations such as searching, matching, and substitution. Sometimes the regex package, a more advanced regular expression engine, is needed. It has additional features such as lookarounds, named capture groups, and better Unicode support.

3. R provides several built-in functions for working with regular expressions, which are part of the base package (e.g. grep, grepl, sub, gsub, etc.). To adhere to the Tidyverse framework, functions from the stringr package were used, which consistently expose the same functionality as the core functions. However, if you need to use named capture groups with a simpler syntax, the nameCapture or nc packages are recommended.

4. To extract useful information from free text in tabular form, one must first identify the values of the entities of interest with regex patterns for each of them. After that, since these entities may appear in a different order depending on who enters the text, one must provide a main pattern for each of the ways they might appear, using the individual patterns of each entity to be matched.

Chapter 7

1. The most obvious disadvantage of anonymization is that it removes significant value from the data involved. This is because once the anonymization process is complete, it becomes impossible to trace the identities that generated the data. This means that any information or insights that could be gained from analyzing the data in its original form may be lost after anonymization.

2. Pseudonymization and anonymization are both de-identifying processes that are used to protect sensitive information. The main difference between the two methods is that pseudonymization replaces direct or indirect identifiers with pseudonyms, while retaining the possibility of re-identifying the data. In contrast, anonymization removes all identifiable information from the data so that it cannot be linked to specific individuals or entities, and it cannot be re-identified.

3. The pseudonymization architecture described in this chapter ensures compliance with the GDPR's deletion requirements by making it impossible to identify the subject once the personal data is deleted, and by preserving the analytical correlations between the remaining data. Specifically, when a request is made for the deletion of personal data by an individual, the corresponding association between the individual and their personal data is removed from the lookup table.

4. It is necessary to use NLP techniques, such as Named Entity Recognition (NER), to identify personally identifiable information (PII) in free text because PII is often represented in a wide variety of formats, and regular expressions are not able to capture the complexity and variety of these formats.

5. One of the best Python packages for de-identifying personally identifiable information (PII) is Presidio, which is an open-source package released by Microsoft. Presidio provides identification and anonymization for entities found in free text and images, such as credit card numbers, names, locations, social security numbers, email addresses, and financial information. Presidio uses NLP engines to recognize the entities, and it supports both spaCy (the default one) and Stanza.

6. spacyr was used to identify PII in text and it is an R package that can use spaCy's NLP engine in Python for tasks like Named Entity Recognition (NER) by using the reticulate package.

7. Pseudonyms are fictitious names or identifiers used in place of a person's real name or other personally identifiable information (PII) in order to protect their privacy or identity.

8. The packages used to generate pseudonyms were Faker for Python and Charlatan for R.

Chapter 8

1. The to_csv() function of the pandas module has been used in Python. It uses the default character \r\n as the end-of-line character. The write_csv() function from the readr package was used in R. Unlike the one used in Python, this one requires you to specify the newline character if you want to use \r\n, otherwise, the default is \n.

2. You can use pandas' to_excel() function in Python, but remember that you must first install the openpyxl module. In R, on the other hand, you can use the write.xlsx() function from the openxlsx package.

3. The ODBC driver for SQL Server was used to connect to an (Azure) SQL database.

4. This chapter used the pyodbc module for Python and the DBI and odbc packages for R to connect to an Azure SQL Database.

5. One of the easiest ways to prevent exposing credentials in the connection string is to use environment variables.

Chapter 9

1. The primary limitation on reading files in Power BI Desktop is the amount of RAM available on the machine on which it is installed. This limitation directly affects the size of files that can be read, because files that are larger than the available RAM cannot be imported directly.

2. For datasets larger than available memory, it is possible to use special packages that implement distributed computing systems in both Python and R without having to rely on sophisticated big data platforms such as Apache Spark-based backends.

3. Dask uses lazy evaluation, where data read operations are queued but not executed until explicitly requested, allowing efficient management of large datasets without immediate memory consumption.

4. Apache Arrow provides a language-independent columnar storage format for efficient data exchange and operations on large datasets. It reduces overhead and improves processing time by loading only relevant columns into memory.

Chapter 10

1. Parquet is an open-source columnar storage format designed to optimize file efficiency. It stores data in a way that allows for the efficient compression and encoding of data, resulting in faster query execution times and reduced storage requirements. Parquet can handle complex data structures and uses binary encoding to enhance data security. It is compatible with interactive and serverless technologies like Azure Synapse Analytics, and Azure Databricks and Fabric and can be used in Power BI with Python and R. Basically, Parquet is a high-performance storage format that is well suited for storing and processing large, complex datasets.

2. The native Parquet connector in Power BI allows users to select only the necessary columns for analysis and can be advantageous in cases where GROUP BY transformations are needed. However, the connector does not support parallel processing, predicate pushdown, or partition pruning, which can significantly improve query execution times. Manual intervention or the use of Python or R may be necessary to optimize queries and take advantage of these performance-enhancing features.

3. *Predicate pushdown* refers to the technique of pushing down filters (i.e., predicates) to the data source, so that only the necessary data is read into memory. When a query is executed, filters are typically applied after the data has been read into memory. However, by applying filters earlier in the query execution, you can significantly improve performance by getting rid of non-matching records earlier, saving unnecessary processing time and resources later.

    Partition pruning, on the other hand, involves dividing a dataset into smaller, more manageable partitions based on specific criteria or attributes, such as date or region. By doing this, the framework can efficiently process only the relevant partitions, instead of scanning the entire dataset. However, this is only possible if the Parquet files representing the dataset have been partitioned for the selected key fields used as a filter.

4. Dask generally provides better performance for large datasets that cannot fit into memory, while PyArrow may be faster for smaller datasets that can fit into memory. PyArrow is optimized for working with Arrow-based data structures and can provide faster performance for operations like reading and writing Parquet files. Dask's parallel and distributed computing capabilities can introduce additional overhead, which may not be significant for larger datasets but could be noticeable for smaller datasets or when compared against more optimized libraries like PyArrow.

5. To transform referenced data from an Arrow dataset into R, no special API is required. It is sufficient to use the constructs of dplyr applied directly to the dataset.

Chapter 11

1. The design model that is becoming the de facto standard for public web services is REST. This model uses the JSON data format to exchange information.

2. The most convenient method is to apply() from a pandas DataFrame. It allows you to send each row to a function by setting the parameter axis=1.

3. To parallelize the web service calls for each row, simply use a Dask DataFrame, which also exposes the `apply()` method like pandas.

4. You can use the `map()` family of functions from the purrr library.

5. It is possible to make web service calls in parallel in R thanks to the `furrr` package, which exposes methods equivalent to the various purr `map()` methods. This makes it very easy to parallelize code that already uses `map()`.

6. The advantage of using an SDK to call a web service is that it saves you from having to navigate through the JSON response to extract the information you need by exposing a simple and clear interface.

7. To parallelize calls to a web service in Power BI, you can only use Python through the Dask package. The latest versions of Power BI Desktop do not properly resolve R `futures`, so R is not currently usable for parallelization in Power BI.

Chapter 12

1. The concept of distance is particularly valuable in data analysis and pattern recognition because it provides a common metric for comparing and evaluating different types of data. Regardless of whether the data consists of numerical attributes, categorical variables, or complex structures like images or text, distances can be defined and calculated to quantify the dissimilarity between instances.

2. The introduction of the Haversine function made it possible to reformulate the law of Cosines distance in a much simpler way, allowing navigators of yesteryear to easily calculate distances thanks to pre-calculated Haversine tables.

3. The assumption that has provided greater accuracy to Vincenty's formula is that Earth is considered to be an ellipsoid, not a sphere.

4. The packages used are PyGeodesy in Python and geosphere in R.

5. Although the computational complexity of Hamming distance is linear, the fact that it can only be applied to strings of equal length and is based on simple character substitution does not allow it to be applied to typical string comparison problems.

6. It is recommended to use the Damerau-Levenshtein distance in all cases where character transpositions are common. For example, it can be used to suggest corrections for misspelled words by finding the closest matches in a dictionary or to detect and correct errors in an **optical character recognition (OCR)** system.

7. The Jaro-Winkler distance is particularly useful when it is necessary to identify duplicate or similar records that almost always have the same prefix and small variations in the string subsequence. This is because it gives more weight to the corresponding characters at the beginning of the strings.

8. The Jaccard distance is preferable in use cases where the focus is on comparing sets and the order or frequency of elements is not considered. It is particularly useful when dealing with categorical or binary data and provides a simple and intuitive measure of dissimilarity or similarity between sets.

9. The packages used are TextDistance in Python and stringdist in R.

Chapter 13

1. Fuzzy matching is a data analysis technique that allows items from separate data sources to be compared and merged based on their similarity. It identifies and merges similar items by applying algorithms that measure the similarity between instances. Fuzzy matching is particularly useful when dealing with datasets that may contain errors, inconsistencies, or variations in data values.

2. The benefits of fuzzy matching in data analysis include the ability to merge and compare data from different sources, identify similar records even with variations or errors, and improve data quality and accuracy. Use cases for fuzzy matching include data integration, record linkage, deduplication, data cleansing, user matching, and clustering analysis. It is especially valuable in scenarios where exact matching is not possible or practical.

3. The default fuzzy matching algorithm in Power BI is very efficient in most cases, even with very large datasets. Its only limitation is that it does not provide the flexibility for users to customize or select different similarity measures, so it may not provide optimal results in certain scenarios where more advanced or specific matching techniques are required.

4. Common data cleaning steps performed before applying fuzzy matching algorithms include converting strings to lowercase for case insensitivity; removing leading and trailing spaces to avoid mismatches due to extraneous spaces; standardizing date/time formats to ensure consistent comparison; handling abbreviations by replacing them with full words for standardization; removing stopwords (commonly used words like "a" and "the") that don't impact matching accuracy; applying stemming or lemmatization to reduce words to their base or root form for matching similar meanings; preserving numerical values if they are essential for matching; and handling special characters by removing or replacing them consistently for consistent matches.

5. The algorithm implemented in Power BI overcomes the computational complexity of comparing large datasets by using a filtering-verification architecture. Instead of evaluating the similarity function on each pair of records, which is not feasible for large datasets, the algorithm uses **Locality Sensitive Hashing (LSH)** to generate signatures for each string in the input tables. These signatures serve as compact representations of the strings and help filter out pairs of records that are unlikely to have a similarity above a specified threshold.

6. Probabilistic record linkage works by assigning probabilities to determine the likelihood that two records belong to the same entity. It does this by comparing attributes or characteristics of records and calculating similarity measures between them. These similarity measures are used to estimate match and non-match probabilities. Probabilistic models, such as the Fellegi-Sunter model, use these probabilities along with predefined rules to make record linkage decisions. The goal is to identify matches and non-matches with higher accuracy, even when dealing with variation, errors, or inconsistencies in the data.

7. This chapter uses the following libraries to apply probabilistic record linkage algorithms: Splink in Python and reclin2 in R.

8. One of the most direct and simple ways to measure the accuracy and performance of probabilistic record linkage algorithms is to use the confusion matrix. This matrix provides a comprehensive summary of the model's predictions (matches and non-matches) and their corresponding actual values (truth). It includes true positives, false positives, true negatives, and false negatives.

Chapter 14

1. Linear programming is a mathematical optimization technique used to find the best possible solution to a problem with linear constraints and a linear objective function. In data analysis, linear programming is used to optimize resource allocation, decision making, and planning problems. It can help determine the most efficient allocation of resources, maximize or minimize a specific objective, and make informed decisions based on quantitative models and constraints.

2. Linear optimization problems can be formulated mathematically by defining decision variables, an objective function, and a set of constraints. Decision variables represent the unknown quantities to be determined. The objective function defines the goal, whether it is to maximize or minimize a certain quantity. Constraints represent limitations and requirements that must be met. All variables, objectives, and constraints are expressed in the form of linear equations or linear inequalities. The goal is to find the values of the decision variables that optimize the objective function while satisfying all constraints.

3. Linear optimization problems can be solved using Python and R with the help of libraries and packages specifically designed for mathematical optimization. In Python, the PuLP library can be used to formulate and solve linear programming problems. It provides a simple and intuitive syntax for defining variables, constraints, and the objective function. In R, the ompr package, along with the ompr.roi and ROI.plugin.glpk packages, can be used to formulate and solve linear programming problems.

4. In linear optimization problems, multiple solutions can provide the same optimal value if there is more than one feasible solution that achieves the same optimal objective function value. This means that different combinations of decision variable values can lead to the same optimal objective function value while satisfying all constraints. This occurs when the feasible region contains multiple points that all yield the optimal solution. In these cases, the decision maker may have the flexibility to choose from multiple optimal solutions based on other considerations or preferences.

Chapter 15

1. Exploring associations between variables is important in data analysis because it helps you understand the relationships and patterns between different variables. With this knowledge, you can identify key factors that may influence certain indicators of business health or outcomes. By uncovering these associations, you gain insights that can be used for decision-making, forecasting, and optimization. You can understand and predict the behavior of one variable based on the behavior of another, leading to more effective strategies and informed decisions.

2. The different types of associations between variables include positive association (an increase in one variable corresponds to an increase in the other), negative association (an increase in one variable corresponds to a decrease in the other), and no association (no relationship can be found between the variables). These associations can be linear or nonlinear.

3. Assessing the magnitude and orientation of the relationship between numerical variables is essential for interpreting how these variables interact within statistical and data analytical contexts. Techniques such as Pearson's correlation coefficient, Spearman's rank correlation coefficient, and Kendall's tau can be used to determine the magnitude and orientation of this relationship.

4. Cramér's V coefficient, Theil's U uncertainty coefficient, and Pearson's correlation coefficient are statistical measures used to analyze associations between categorical and numeric variables. Cramér's V coefficient quantifies the strength of the association between two categorical variables. It ranges from 0 to 1, with higher values indicating stronger associations. Theil's U uncertainty coefficient, also known as the entropy coefficient, measures the amount of information shared between two variables. It ranges from 0 to 1 and captures both linear and nonlinear associations. Pearson's correlation ratio assesses the strength of the association between a numeric variable and a categorical variable. It provides the proportion of variance in the numeric variable that is explained by membership in the category of the categorical variable.

5. Correlation coefficients can be used to identify key predictors in a dataset by measuring the strength and direction of relationships between variables. Higher correlation coefficients indicate stronger associations, suggesting that these variables may have a greater influence on the target variable or outcome of interest. Positive correlations suggest that as one variable increases, the other tends to increase as well, while negative correlations suggest an inverse relationship. However, it's important to consider other factors such as context, domain knowledge, and statistical significance when determining the key predictors in a dataset.

6. Associations between variables can be visualized using a variety of techniques. Scatterplots are effective at showing relationships between two numeric variables, allowing us to identify trends, direction, and strength of associations. Line plots or bar graphs can show associations over time or across categories. For categorical variables, mosaic plots provide a visual representation of the strength of the association by color-coding tiles. Violin plots combine histogram-like distributions and boxplots to compare numeric variables across categories. Heatmaps provide a comprehensive view of associations in tabular datasets by using colors to represent the magnitude of correlation coefficients. These visualization techniques help analysts better understand the relationships and patterns between variables in their data.

Chapter 16

1. Outliers are observations in a data sample that are significantly different from the rest of the data. These observations are typically characterized by being extremely high or low compared to the majority of data points. Outliers can have a significant impact on data analysis because they can greatly distort statistical operations and lead to inaccurate results. Outliers can also affect the accuracy of predictive models. Algorithms such as linear regression are sensitive to outliers, and the presence of outliers can result in models with poor fit and prediction.

2. Outliers in a dataset can have several causes, which can be categorized based on their origin and characteristics. One cause of outliers is data entry errors, which occur when mistakes are made during the data collection or entry process. For example, a typographical error or misplaced decimal point can result in an extreme value that is significantly different from the other data points. Intentional outliers are another type, where individuals deliberately introduce inaccurate or exaggerated values. This can occur in surveys or self-reported data, where respondents may provide false information for a variety of reasons. Data processing errors can also lead to outliers. These errors can occur during data transformation or manipulation processes, such as data cleaning or the application of outlier detection algorithms. Sampling errors are another source of outliers. When data is sampled from a larger population and the sampling process is not representative, outliers can occur. For example, if certain subgroups of the population are excluded from the sample, the outliers in those subgroups may not be represented in the dataset. Finally, natural outliers are outliers that occur due to inherent characteristics of the data generation process. These outliers are not the result of errors but are a normal part of the data distribution. Identifying the specific cause of outliers makes it easier to decide on the appropriate course of action, whether it is to remove the outliers, correct the data, or consider them part of the natural variation in the dataset.

3. There are several methods for dealing with outliers in data analysis. Each method has its own advantages and disadvantages, and the choice of method depends on the specific context and objectives of the analysis. One approach is to completely remove outliers from the dataset, known as dropping outliers. This method ensures that the extreme values do not affect the final analysis. Another approach is capping, or winsorizing, which replaces extreme outlier values with a threshold. This helps to limit the impact of outliers on the analysis. Another method is to assign a new value to the outliers. This can be done by replacing them with a fixed value, such as the mean or median of the variable. Another approach is to transform the data by applying mathematical transformations, such as logarithmic or exponential functions, to the variable containing the outliers. Finally, contextual analysis plays an important role. It involves considering the specific context and domain knowledge to determine the validity and appropriate handling of outliers. It's important to note that there is no one-size-fits-all approach to outlier handling. The choice of method depends on the specific dataset, the objectives of the analysis, and the domain expertise.

4. Missing values refer to the absence of data for certain variables or observations within a dataset. They can pose challenges in data analysis due to the loss of valuable information, potential bias in analysis results, incomplete analysis, reduced statistical power, difficulty in data imputation, and challenges in interpretation. Missing values represent a loss of valuable information, and not handling them properly can lead to biased results.

5. There are several techniques for diagnosing and visualizing missing values in a dataset. One common approach is to calculate the percentage of missing values for each variable in the dataset. This provides an overview of the extent of missing values in the data. In addition, it is helpful to visualize missing values using graphs or plots. One method of visualization is to use heat maps or color-coded matrices. In this approach, missing values are represented by a distinct color, making it easy to identify patterns and clusters of missingness. Another technique is to use the `missingno` library in Python or the `naniar` package in R.

These tools provide functions such as `miss_var_summary()` and `gg_miss_upset()` that generate dataframes or visualizations to display missing values in the dataset in a proper way.

6. Multiple imputation is an approach that estimates missing values based on observed data to create multiple imputed records. It incorporates imputation uncertainty and provides unbiased estimates by accounting for both within-imputation and between-imputation variances. Machine learning techniques can also be used to predict missing values based on other variables in the dataset. These include techniques such as k-nearest neighbours, regression models, or deep learning algorithms. The choice of method depends on the specific dataset and analysis requirements, as each technique has its own advantages and limitations.

7. Missing values in a time series dataset can be imputed using several techniques. One approach is to use interpolation, where a function is used to estimate the missing values based on the values before and after them in the series. This can be done using linear interpolation, polynomial interpolation, or spline interpolation. Another method is to use an **Exponential Weighted Moving Average (EWMA)**, where older observations are given less weight than more recent observations. This method smooths the time series and imputes missing values based on the smoothed values. Seasonal decomposition of time series can also be used for imputation, where the seasonal component is removed, the missing values are imputed on the seasonally adjusted series, and then the seasonal component is added back. In addition, machine learning algorithms can be used to impute missing values in time series datasets, such as k-nearest neighbors or linear regression. These algorithms predict the missing values based on the values of other variables and the pattern of the time series. By applying these imputation techniques, the missing values in a time series dataset can be filled in, allowing for more complete analysis and interpretation of the data.

8. R is often considered better than Python for missing value imputation in Power BI because it has a stronger focus on statistical analysis and a large collection of specialized packages. R packages such as *MICE*, *miceadds*, *imputeTS*, and *Amelia II* offer comprehensive and well-documented functions specifically designed for missing value imputation. In addition, R's programming syntax and ecosystem make it easy to work with dataframes and effectively manipulate missing values. The *tidyverse* collection of packages, which includes *dplyr* and *tidyr*, provides powerful data cleaning and manipulation tools that are well suited to the principles of missing value analysis.

Chapter 17

1. For Power BI analysts who prefer to delegate model building to more specialized platforms and then import them into Power BI, working with AutoML solutions in Python is recommended. Python is widely used and allows for the easy sharing of models between popular platforms.

2. You can consider embedding the training code in Power Query if you are confident that the time required to train the model is acceptable.

3. The advantage of FLAML's AutoML feature is that the generated models are fully compatible with scikit-learn models. This means that the best estimator obtained from FLAML can be used in any Python script by simply unpickling the model, making sure that scikit-learn and dependent packages like LightGBM are installed, without having to import the AutoML class from the flaml package.

4. It is important to have a working scoring function in Power Query when using a serialized ML model because the scoring function is closely related to how the model was trained. If the scoring function is not provided, it can cause unnecessary headaches when predicting target values for unknown observations.

5. The ability to serialize and deserialize a ML model can solve the delay problem by saving the serialized model to disk after the initial training run. In subsequent refreshes, instead of running the training code again, the serialized model can be loaded, deserialized, and used for further steps. This saves time and avoids the delay caused by re-running the training code.

6. It is recommended that you train and manage ML models outside of Power BI to decouple the development and tuning of the model from the rest of the report. This allows for more flexibility and agility in model development and keeps model training and management separate from the reporting process in Power BI.

7. The purpose is to be able to explore the outputs of a ML model and dynamically vary the variables in play without having to refresh the entire report. It enables simulation reports and provides a convenient way to visualize the model's predictions.

8. One way to interact with ML models in Power Query is to call web services. ML models can be exposed as web services, so they can be invoked through REST APIs.

9. You can't consume external services via REST API calls from a Python or R visual in Power BI because internet access is blocked for security reasons. You can only consume external services in Power Query.

10. Azure AI Language is a cloud-based service that provides natural language processing capabilities. It unifies services such as Text Analytics, QnA Maker, and LUIS, and provides capabilities such as named entity recognition, language detection, sentiment analysis, and summarization.

Chapter 18

1. SQL Server Machine Learning Services is an in-database technology that allows advanced analytics and machine learning to be performed directly in Microsoft SQL Server. It integrates advanced algorithms and models into SQL Server, allowing users to process and analyze large volumes of data without needing to move it to a separate analytics platform.

2. Before Machine Learning Services, the only way to integrate external data processing via Python or R into a transformation pipeline was to run external code that would read the data from the SQL Server instance via ODBC and then write the output to a staging table for further processing in SQL Server.

3. The SQL Server Extensibility Framework is the tool that allows Machine Learning Services to execute Python or R code using external engines. It acts as a bridge between SQL Server and the external runtime environment, facilitating communication and enabling the execution of code in an external language runtime environment directly from within SQL Server.

4. Machine Learning Services are available in SQL Server (on-premises) and in Azure SQL Managed Instance, which is a PaaS offering. Azure SQL Managed Instance provides near-perfect compatibility with the latest SQL Server database engine in the Enterprise Edition.

5. The Launchpad service in SQL Server Machine Learning Services is responsible for communicating with external engines and running Python and R scripts. It acts as a mediator between SQL Server and the external runtime environment, facilitating the execution of scripts and coordination of data processing.

6. To grant access to the Launchpad service, you need to use the `icacls` command in Windows to change the permissions of the necessary folders. You need to grant read and execute permissions to the Launchpad service and the `ALL APPLICATION PACKAGES` group for the mentioned folders. These permissions ensure that the Launchpad service can access the necessary files and execute external scripts.

7. External languages are needed with Power BI when the standard Python and R integration is not sufficient. This can be due to organizational policies, architectural and security constraints, the need to process large datasets stored in SQL Server, or the unavailability of certain libraries in the Power BI service.

8. To call a stored procedure in DirectQuery mode in Power BI, you can use the OPENROWSET function in the Power Query Editor. You create a new query and specify the OPENROWSET function with the appropriate parameters to execute the stored procedure. This allows you to retrieve the results of the stored procedure and include them in your Power BI report.

9. In the examples, the `models` table in the MLModels database stores the binary versions of machine learning models. It allows you to persist models in binary format and retrieve them when needed for prediction or analysis. This table serves as a central repository for the machine learning models used in your SQL Server environment.

10. By wrapping the `EXEC` statement within the OPENROWSET function, the result set is treated as if it were a subquery of a `SELECT` statement, allowing the Power Query engine to recognize and process the metadata correctly. This ensures that the result set can be seamlessly integrated into Power BI datasets and used for further analysis, visualization, and reporting.

11. Running a stored procedure in DirectQuery in Power BI provides flexibility and real-time data analysis capabilities. It allows you to leverage the power of stored procedures in SQL Server to perform complex calculations, data transformations, and predictive analytics. By incorporating the results directly into your report, you can deliver timely insights to your users.

12. The great advantage of using external languages for this predictive report is that you can publish the fully functional report to the Power BI service using any library needed in Python. If you used standard Python in Power BI, you would have received an error when scoring using the model on the published report in the Power BI service.

Chapter 19

1. The primary goal of Exploratory Data Analysis (EDA) is to ensure that the dataset used for more complex processes is clean and reliable. It involves eliminating missing values and outliers, selecting relevant variables that provide meaningful information, and discarding those that are primarily noise.

2. The key stages of the EDA process include getting to know your data, cleaning your data, and identifying relationships among variables.

3. During this phase, you understand the context of each variable in the dataset, including its size (in terms of variables and observations), the type of variable (numerical or categorical), and its descriptive statistics. Depending on the type of variable, different types of graphs such as histograms, density plots, and rain cloud plots are used for better visualization.

4. Categorical variables, such as favorite fruits or car brands, are often visualized using a bar chart. Each category is represented by its own bar, and the length or height of that bar correlates to how often that particular category appears in your dataset.

5. The choice of visualization technique depends on the type of data. For two numerical variables, a scatterplot is used; for two categorical variables, a mosaic chart is used; and for a numerical variable with one categorical variable, we can use multiple box plots or even raincloud plots for each category to see how the numerical data behaves within each categorical group.

6. The data cleaning phase involves identifying and managing outliers and imputing missing values. Visualization tools such as box plots are used for outlier analysis, while an upset plot is used to visualize the combination and intersection of missing values between variables.

7. This phase helps to understand the degree of association between variables in the dataset. Knowing which variables carry the most information and which are mostly noise can significantly impact feature selection for a machine learning model, leading to more stable and powerful results.

8. Defining the data types of variables in EDA is critical because it determines the applicable analysis strategies. However, Power BI does not map one to one to the data types handled by R (or Python) in data modeling. Therefore, it is essential to define the data types of columns directly in an R script to prevent Power BI from overwriting them and to ensure accurate and effective EDA.

9. To ensure proper rendering, verify that the R packages you're using are compatible with the version of the R engine on the Power BI service. Remember that Power BI Desktop only references one R engine at a time, so if you plan to use the latest R engine after publishing, you will need to install the necessary packages for that engine on your machine to successfully render reports.

10. If your report is only usable in Power BI Desktop due to package limitations, you can use an on-premises SQL Server instance or Azure SQL Managed Instance as a repository. You can store lists of PNG (or base64) images generated in R directly in SQL Server tables on in-memory pandas DataFrames, then embed them in binary text format and view them directly in Power BI. However, if the images are large and their binary text representation exceeds 32,766 characters, you will need to use a splitting rows technique and a bit of DAX to reassemble the entire string to display it correctly in Power BI.

11. For large numbers of variables, the strategy shifts to writing the plot generation code directly in R Visual. This is specifically chosen because, given the large number of variable combinations, generating and serializing a large number of plots becomes truly inefficient.

Chapter 20

1. ggplot2 is a very popular data visualization tool in R, known for its effectiveness and ease of use. plotnine is a Python package that emulates the principles of ggplot2 – in particular, the concept of Grammar of Graphics. plotnine is an attempt to bring the powerful visualization capabilities of ggplot2 to Python users, allowing them to create complex and aesthetically pleasing visualizations using a similar syntax and approach.

2. This chapter covered two different methods for using plotnine in Power BI. The first approach involves generating a binary encoded string of an image, such as PNG, within Power Query. The encoded string is then displayed using a custom visualization tool, specifically Image Pro (or Simple Image).

   The second method takes a more direct strategy by using plotnine code within a Python visual in Power BI. Unexpectedly, the plotnine package is available on the Power BI service, despite Microsoft's documentation suggesting the contrary. This capability allows for the creation and on-the-fly manipulation of visualizations within the Python script visual.

   Both methods ensure that your report can be published to the Power BI service. Just make sure your code is compatible with plotnine 0.8.0.

Chapter 21

1. Circular barplots are adept at showing relationships in data with periodic or cyclical patterns, providing an aesthetically pleasing and compact way to visualize such data. In addition, they are particularly effective for managing datasets with large numbers of points, ensuring clarity and readability even in complex datasets.

2. You can handle column names in R functions by directly using the column names, rather than passing them as strings, following the tidyverse grammar.

3. The coord_polar() function in ggplot2 is used to create polar coordinate plots. Essentially, it transforms a plot from the standard Cartesian coordinate system (with x and y axes) to a polar coordinate system. In our case, it is used to wrap a barplot into a circular shape, transforming a linear barplot into a circular one.

Chapter 22

1. Interactive visuals are preferable because they offer responsiveness to user input, such as tooltips and other interactive features that enhance the understanding and interpretation of data beyond what static charts can provide.

2. The chapter suggests using Plotly.R, an open source data visualization library, and its `ggplotly()` function to transform existing ggplot graphs into interactive web visualizations.

3. The user can create an interactive Power BI custom visual by using Power BI Visual Tools (pbiviz) to create, compile, and package custom visuals, focusing specifically on R HTML custom visuals.

4. Standard R visuals cannot be published using the Publish to Web option in Power BI, but this limitation can be circumvented by creating custom R visuals.

5. pbiviz tools do not support technologies that use Python behind the scenes.

Glossary

A

Ad Hoc Distributed Queries in SQL Server: A feature in SQL Server that allows execution of ad hoc queries using OPENROWSET and OPENDATASOURCE, providing flexibility in data retrieval from various sources.

ADO.NET: A framework in the .NET ecosystem for data access.

AdventureWorksLT: A sample database provided by Microsoft for learning and demonstration purposes.

Aesthetics (aes): In plotnine, refers to the visual aspects of plot objects like color, shape, size, and position, crucial for distinguishing different parts of the data.

Agglomerative Hierarchical Clustering (AHC): A method of cluster analysis which seeks to build a hierarchy of clusters, used in fuzzy clustering.

Anchors: Symbols in regex (like '^' and '$') that specify the position in the string where a match must occur.

Anomaly Detection: Two entries define it as identifying data points that significantly deviate from the majority or are rare, raising suspicions due to their significant difference from the majority.

Anonymization: The process of removing or altering personal data so it cannot be associated with a specific individual, making it impossible to reverse-engineer the identity of the subjects.

ANOVA (Analysis of Variance): A statistical method used to test differences between two or more means.

Apache Arrow: A cross-language development platform for in-memory data, enhancing the performance and efficiency of data processing.

Arrow for R: An R package providing an interface to the Apache Arrow data processing framework, including support for Parquet files.

Association Analysis: A set of techniques used in machine learning to discover patterns or relationships in large datasets.

Association Rules: Used in machine learning to find interesting relationships (associations and correlations) between variables in large databases.

Azure AutoML: A cloud-based service on Microsoft Azure for automating the process of applying machine learning algorithms to data. It simplifies model building, tuning, and deployment.

Azure Cognitive Services: A suite of cloud-based services from Microsoft that provide AI capabilities, like text analytics and computer vision, to applications without requiring expertise in AI.

Azure Machine Learning: A cloud-based service for creating and managing machine learning solutions. It provides tools to train, test, deploy, manage, and track machine learning models.

Azure SQL Server: A cloud-based relational database service provided by Microsoft Azure.

B

Backreference (regex): A reference in regex to a previously matched group, typically denoted as \1, \2, etc.

Bar Chart: A graphical representation used for displaying categorical data, where each category is represented by a bar, and the length or height of the bar represents its value.

Batch Processing: Processing large volumes of data in a batch or group, often involving efficient handling of numerous records.

Binary Classification: A type of classification task in machine learning where the model is trained to categorize data into one of two different categories (e.g., yes/no, true/false).

Box Plot: A standardized way of displaying the data distribution based on a five-number summary: minimum, first quartile, median, third quartile, and maximum.

C

Character Class: A set of characters that may match at a point in the string, specified within square brackets (e.g., [A-Z]).

Chunk Files: Parts of a dataset stored separately, typically used in processes where data is too large to fit into memory.

Circular Barplot: A graphical representation where bar plots are arranged in a circular manner, often used to display relationships in periodic or cyclical data. It provides an aesthetically pleasing and space-efficient way to display patterns, ideal for comparing categories that are parts of a whole.

Clustering: A machine learning technique that involves grouping sets of objects in such a way that objects in the same group (cluster) are more similar to each other than to those in other groups.

Conda: A package management system and environment management system for installing multiple versions of software packages and their dependencies and switching easily between them.

Confusion Matrix: A tool for summarizing the performance of a classification algorithm, showing the correct and incorrect predictions.

Constraints: Limitations or requirements in an LP problem that the solution must satisfy.

Contingency Table: A type of table in a matrix format that displays the frequency distribution of the variables.

Coord_polar(): A function in ggplot2 used to transform a plot from the Cartesian coordinate system to a polar coordinate system. This function is particularly useful for creating circular plots or graphs.

Coordinate Systems: Define the spatial layout of a graph in plotnine. Common systems include Cartesian and polar coordinates.

Correlation Coefficient: A measure that describes the extent of the statistical relationship between two continuous variables.

Correlation Heatmap: A graphical representation of correlation data in which matrix values are represented as colors, used to visualize the correlation between multiple variables.

Correlation Ratio (η): Assesses the strength of the relationship between a categorical independent variable and a continuous dependent variable.

Cramér's V: A measure of association between two nominal variables, giving a value between 0 and +1.

CRAN R: The Comprehensive R Archive Network, a network of servers containing the R source code and documentation.

CSV (Comma-Separated Values): Three entries describe CSV as a simple file format used for storing tabular data in plain text.

Custom Visual Package: A package in Power BI that contains a custom visual. It is created using pbiviz tools and can be imported into Power BI for use in reports and dashboards.

D

Dask DataFrame: A parallel DataFrame used in Python for handling large datasets by breaking them into smaller chunks.

Dask: A flexible parallel computing library for analytic computing in Python, enabling the manipulation of large datasets.

Data Aggregation: The process of combining data from multiple sources and summarizing it into a simpler form for analysis or reporting.

Data Append: The process of adding new data to an existing dataset, often used for incremental data loads.

Data Cleaning: The process of detecting and correcting (or removing) corrupt or inaccurate records from a dataset, ensuring the quality of data in analytics.

Data Deduplication: The process of removing duplicate records from a dataset, often used in database management and data storage.

Data Enrichment: The process of enhancing, refining, and improving raw data, particularly from external sources such as web APIs.

Data Gateway (Enterprise): A Power BI feature that allows you to connect to data sources on-premises or in the cloud.

Data Gateway in Personal Mode for Power BI: A configuration in Power BI that enables individual users to connect to various data sources for importing data or for DirectQuery purposes.

Data Imputation: Two entries describe it as the process of replacing missing data with substituted values.

Data Logging: The process of recording events, transactions, or observations over time for further analysis.

Data Masking: Technique for hiding sensitive information by replacing it with obfuscated data or other characters.

Data Partitioning: The process of dividing a dataset into smaller segments, often based on certain criteria, to improve data management and query performance.

Data Perturbation: Adding noise or synthetic data to original data to prevent identification.

Data Preprocessing: The process of transforming raw data into an understandable format for analysis.

Data Privacy Firewall: A feature in Power BI designed to prevent sensitive data from being inadvertently transferred between data sources, especially during query folding.

Data Privacy Levels in Power BI: Settings in Power BI that determine how data from different sources can be combined and integrated, with implications for data security and confidentiality.

Data Refresh: Two entries describe it as the process of updating data in Power BI reports or dashboards to reflect more recent data.

Data Swapping: Technique where values in a dataset are shuffled to mask the identity of individuals.

Data Table Structure (data.table): A data structure in R used for optimized in-memory data manipulation, employed in reclin2 for performance enhancement.

Data Type Transformation: The process of converting data types in Power Query before using them in Python or R scripts, particularly important for date/time fields.

Data Visualization: The graphic representation of data. It involves producing images that communicate relationships among the represented data to viewers.

Data Wrangling: The process of cleaning, structuring, and enriching raw data into a desired format for better decision-making in less time.

Dataflows: In Power BI, dataflows are used to ingest, transform, integrate, and enrich big data from various sources into insights which can be visualized in reports and dashboards.

DataFrame: A two-dimensional, size-mutable, and potentially heterogeneous tabular data structure with labeled axes (rows and columns).

Data-Ink Maximization: A principle focusing on maximizing the data information in a plot while minimizing non-data ink, used for creating clear and concise graphics.

DAX (Data Analysis Expressions): A collection of functions, operators, and constants that can be used in a formula or expression to calculate and return one or more values.

DBI and odbc Packages in R: R packages used for connecting to and interacting with databases via ODBC drivers.

Decision Variables: Variables that represent the choices to be made in an LP problem.

De-identification Techniques: Methods used to remove or alter personal data to prevent identification of individuals.

Density Plot: A smoothed version of a histogram, often used to visualize the distribution of a data variable. It shows the probability density function of the variable.

Deserialization: The process of converting a serialized object back into its original format.

DirectQuery in Power BI: A feature in Power BI that allows real-time data querying, without importing or storing the data in Power BI.

Disk.frame: An R package for manipulating larger-than-RAM datasets using a disk-based approach.

Distance: In data analysis and pattern recognition, a quantitative measure that captures the dissimilarity or similarity between objects or points in a given space.

DuckDB Backend: An in-memory analytical database used for executing SQL statements in data linking operations with Splink.

Duplicate Query: A method in Power Query where a query is duplicated and modified to avoid indirect access errors.

E

Ellipsoid: A mathematical representation of the Earth's shape, more accurate than a simple spherical model.

Encryption: The process of encoding data to prevent unauthorized access, with the ability to decrypt it back into its original form.

Enterprise Gateway: A more robust version of the On-premises Data Gateway designed for larger-scale deployments.

Excel Files: Files created by Microsoft Excel, used for storing and manipulating data in a tabular form.

Expectation Maximization Algorithm: A statistical technique for maximum likelihood estimation in data with missing or incomplete information.

Exploratory Data Analysis (EDA): A process in statistics and data analysis where the characteristics of the data are examined and summarized before the application of more formal analysis. EDA aims to identify patterns, spot anomalies, test hypotheses, and check assumptions through the use of summary statistics and graphical representations.

External Language Runtime Environment: A feature within SQL Server Machine Learning Services that allows execution of scripts in languages like R or Python, functioning outside the core database engine but integrated into SQL Server's processes.

F

Facets: A feature in plotnine for creating multiple related plots within a single figure, useful for comparing different subsets of data.

Faker and Mimesis: Python libraries used for generating fake data for pseudonymization.

Feasible Region: The set of all possible points that satisfy all the constraints in an LP problem.

Fellegi-Sunter Model: A widely used probabilistic method for record linkage, based on estimating the probability of matches and non-matches between records.

FLAML (Fast and Lightweight AutoML): A Microsoft lightweight Python library for efficiently automating machine learning operations, including model and hyperparameter selection.

Formula.Firewall Error: An error in Power BI that occurs due to the Data Privacy Firewall blocking data flow between different data sources.

FST Format: A format for fast serialization of data frames, used in R for efficient storage and access.

Function Encapsulation in Power Query: A technique to create functions from queries, retaining the benefits of referenced queries without causing Firewall blocks.

Functional Programming: A programming paradigm where programs are constructed by applying and composing functions.

Fuzzy Matching: A process that identifies non-exact matches of dataset entries. Used when merging data from separate sources to find similar items.

G

General Data Protection Regulation (GDPR): European Union regulations for data protection and privacy.

Generalization: Replacing specific data with broader categories to maintain privacy.

Geocoding: The process of converting addresses into geographic coordinates (latitude and longitude).

Geographic Distance: The measurement of distance between two points on the Earth's surface, often calculated using spherical or ellipsoidal models.

Geometries (geom): Central to determining the type of visualization in plotnine. Each geometry corresponds to a different type of plot (e.g., scatter, line, bar plots).

ggplot2: A data visualization package for the statistical programming language R, based on the Grammar of Graphics, which provides a powerful and flexible way to create graphs.

ggplotly() Function: A function in Plotly.R that converts existing ggplot graphs into interactive web visualizations, adding dynamic HTML-based interactivity to the visuals.

Global Search Flag (g): A regex modifier that matches all occurrences within the given string.

GLPK (GNU Linear Programming Kit): An open-source software package for solving large-scale linear programming (LP) problems.

Grammar of Graphics in R: A concept in R programming that provides a systematic approach to building graphs by combining elements like data, geoms, and aesthetics.

Grammar of Graphics: A framework for creating complex and meaningful graphics from data, focusing on visually describing what to present rather than procedural plotting details.

Great Circle Distance: The shortest distance between two points on the surface of a sphere, measured along the surface.

Greedy and Lazy Matches: Greedy quantifiers match as much text as possible, while lazy quantifiers (appended with '?') match as little as possible.

H

Hamming Distance: A measure of the difference between two strings of equal length, calculated by counting the number of positions at which the corresponding characters are different.

Hashing: Transforming data into a fixed-size string of characters, which is typically a one-way operation.

Haversine Formula: A formula to calculate the great-circle distance between two points on a sphere given their longitudes and latitudes.

Histogram: A graphical representation used to estimate the probability distribution of a continuous variable, typically displaying the number of data points that fall within a range of values, divided into bins or intervals.

HTML Widgets: R packages that enable the creation of interactive web pages and graphics. These widgets can be embedded in RMarkdown files, Shiny applications, or exported as standalone web pages.

HTTP Methods: Specific actions or operations used in HTTP requests, such as GET, POST, PUT, and DELETE.

Hyperparameter Tuning: The process of optimizing the parameters that govern the overall behavior of machine learning algorithms. Hyperparameters are set before the learning process begins and are crucial for controlling the learning process.

I

IDE (Integrated Development Environment): A software application that provides comprehensive facilities to computer programmers for software development.

IDE (Integrated Development Environment): An application providing comprehensive facilities to programmers for software development. Examples for Python include RStudio and Visual Studio Code.

Ignore Case Flag (i): A regex flag that enables case-insensitive search.

Image Pro Visual in Power BI: A custom visual for displaying images in Power BI reports, capable of showing dynamic content based on user interactions.

Import Mode: A data connection mode in Power BI where data is imported into Power BI's data model.

Imputation Using Deep Learning: A more advanced method of imputation using deep learning algorithms, particularly useful for large datasets with complex features.

Imputation: The process of replacing missing data with substituted values, often used in statistical analyses to maintain data integrity.

Incremental Load: A data loading technique where only new or changed data is added to an existing dataset, improving efficiency.

Indirect Access Error: An error related to the Data Privacy Firewall, occurring when a data source is indirectly accessed through another query, complicating data privacy checks.

Information Removal: The process of deleting specific data elements from a dataset to prevent identification.

Intel Math Kernel Library (MKL): A library of math processing routines to increase application performance and reduce development time.

Interactive Boxplots: A specific type of interactive visual in R, implemented using Plotly, that allows for dynamic interaction with boxplot elements in Power BI reports.

Interactive R Custom Visuals: Custom visuals in Power BI developed using R, which offer interactivity such as tooltips, zoom, and hover options, enhancing the user's data analysis experience.

IPython Kernel: An interactive computing environment that provides a combination of execution, rich text, mathematics, plots, and rich media.

J

Jaccard Distance: A statistic used for comparing the similarity and diversity of sample sets, defined as the size of the intersection divided by the size of the union of the sets.

Jaccard Similarity: A statistical measure used for gauging the similarity and diversity of sample sets, often employed in fuzzy matching algorithms.

Jaro-Winkler Distance: A measure of similarity between two strings, rewarding characters that match from the start of the strings and adjusting for transpositions.

JSON (JavaScript Object Notation): A lightweight data-interchange format that is easy for humans to read and write and for machines to parse and generate.

Jupyter Notebooks: An open-source web application that allows users to create and share documents containing live code, equations, visualizations, and narrative text.

K

Karney's Method: A method for calculating distances on an ellipsoid, providing accurate results even for nearly antipodal points.

Kendall's Tau Coefficient (τ): A measure of the strength and direction of association between two variables, based on the ranks of the data.

K-Nearest Neighbors (KNN): A simple algorithm that stores all available cases and classifies new cases based on similarity measures.

Koalas: A project that brings the pandas API to Apache Spark, allowing pandas code to execute on Spark clusters.

L

Lazy Evaluation: A programming strategy where the evaluation of an expression is delayed until its value is needed.

Levenshtein Distance: A string metric for measuring the difference between two sequences, quantifying the minimum number of single-character edits required to change one word into the other.

Linear Programming (LP): A mathematical method for determining a way to achieve the best outcome in a given mathematical model. Its functions are linear.

Listwise Deletion: A method for handling missing data by removing any rows in the dataset that contain a missing value.

Listwise Deletion: Removing entire rows from a dataset where at least one value is missing.

Literal Characters: Characters in a regex pattern that match exactly themselves.

Locality Sensitive Hashing (LSH): A method for dimensionality reduction, which is used in Power BI to efficiently compare large datasets.

Loopback Requests in SQL Server: A method where an external script, such as one written in Python or R, connects back to SQL Server using an ODBC connection for data retrieval or manipulation.

M

M Code: A code language used in Power BI's Power Query to perform data transformation and manipulation tasks.

M Language: A functional language used in Power Query to manipulate data.

Machine Learning (ML): A branch of artificial intelligence (AI) focused on building systems that learn from data to identify patterns and make decisions with minimal human intervention.

Machine Learning Services in SQL Server: A feature in SQL Server that integrates advanced analytics into the database engine, enabling the use of R and Python for data analysis and machine learning tasks directly within SQL Server.

Magrittr Pipe (%>%): An operator in R, borrowed from the magrittr package, used for chaining commands in a more readable format.

Mahalanobis Distance for Multivariate Outliers: A distance measure used to identify outliers in a multivariate context.

Mahalanobis Distance: A measure of distance between a point and a distribution, considering correlations.

Math Kernel Library (MKL): A library of optimized math routines for science, engineering, and financial applications.

Matplotlib Figure in Power BI: The use of Matplotlib, a Python plotting library, within Power BI for creating and displaying complex visualizations.

Merge Transformation in Power Query: A technique used to combine data from multiple datasets before applying Python or R scripts.

MICE (Multivariate Imputation by Chained Equations): An imputation method that deals with missing data by creating multiple imputations.

Microsoft R Open: Microsoft's enhanced distribution of R, offering improved performance and additional capabilities.

Miniconda: A minimal installer for Conda. It is a smaller alternative to Anaconda that includes only Conda, Python, the packages they depend on, and a small number of other useful packages.

Missing at Random (MAR): In MAR, the missingness is related to the observed data but not to the unobserved data. This suggests that the propensity for a data point to be missing is systematically related to observed data but not to the missing data itself.

Missing Completely at Random (MCAR): A scenario in which the missingness of data is independent of both observed and unobserved data. MCAR implies that the reasons for missing data are unrelated to the data itself, making it a completely random occurrence.

Missing Not at Random (MNAR): In MNAR, the missingness is related to the unobserved data, meaning the missing values themselves have a relationship with the reasons they are missing.

Missing Values: Data points that are not recorded or are absent in a dataset.

Mixed-Integer Linear Programming (MILP): A form of linear programming where some decision variables are required to have integer values.

Model Ensembling: In machine learning, it refers to the method of combining predictions from multiple models to improve the overall performance.

Model Explanation: Techniques used to explain the predictions made by machine learning models, helping to understand their behavior.

Monotonic Relationship: A relationship that is either entirely non-increasing or non-decreasing.

Mosaic Chart: A graphical method for visualizing data from two or more qualitative variables. It is a form of a bar chart that provides a visual representation of the data in terms of proportions.

Mosaic Plot: A graphical visualization of a contingency table showing the strength of the association between variables.

Multiline Flag (m): A regex flag that enables the start and end anchors to match the start and end of a line, respectively, instead of the whole string.

Multiple Imputation: A statistical technique for replacing missing values with multiple substituted values.

Multiple Imputation: A statistical technique where missing values are filled in multiple times to create several complete datasets. The results from these datasets are then pooled to get final estimations.

Multivariate Analysis: Analysis involving multiple variables to understand relationships and patterns.

N

Named Capturing Groups: Groups in regex that can be referred to by a specified name.

Natural Language Processing (NLP): A branch of artificial intelligence that helps computers understand, interpret, and manipulate human language.

Negated Character Class: A character class that matches any character not specified within it (e.g., [^0-9] matches any non-digit).

Non-Capturing Group: A group that matches a part of the string but is not captured for backreferencing, denoted as (?:...).

Nonparametric Statistics: Statistical methods not based on parameterized families of probability distributions.

NumPy: A Python library used for working with arrays, also supporting a large collection of high-level mathematical functions.

O

OAuth Authentication: An open standard for access delegation, commonly used as a way for internet users to grant websites or applications access to their information without giving them the passwords.

Objective Function: The function in an LP problem that needs to be maximized or minimized.

ODBC (Open Database Connectivity): A standard API for accessing database management systems, allowing SQL Server to communicate with external data sources, including for the execution of scripts in external languages.

ODBC Driver for SQL Server: A driver that enables connectivity to SQL Server from various programming environments including Python and R.

ompr (R package): An R package used for modeling and solving linear and mixed-integer linear optimization problems.

On-premises Data Gateway: A bridge that provides quick and secure data transfer between on-premises data (data that is not in the cloud) and several Microsoft cloud services.

OpenBLAS: An open-source implementation of the BLAS (Basic Linear Algebra Subprograms) and LAPACK (Linear Algebra Package) libraries with many optimizations for specific processor types.

OPENROWSET Function in SQL Server: A function that enables data retrieval from external sources using OLE DB providers, often used for executing stored procedures or ad hoc queries in SQL Server.

Optimization Modeling: The process of defining and solving mathematical models for decision-making problems.

Outlier Detection: The identification of rare items, events, or observations which raise suspicions by differing significantly from the majority of the data.

Outliers: Observations in a data set that lie far outside the range of values typical for the data set. They can be univariate (in one variable) or multivariate (across multiple variables). Outliers can significantly skew the results of statistical analyses.

P

Pairwise Deletion: A method for handling missing data where analysis is conducted with all cases in which the variables of interest are present, regardless of missing values in other variables.

pandas DataFrame: A two-dimensional, size-mutable, and heterogeneous tabular data structure in Python with labeled axes.

pandas: A Python library used for data manipulation and analysis, offering data structures and operations for manipulating numerical tables and time series.

Parallel Computing for R: A method of computation where many calculations or processes are carried out simultaneously, often used to accelerate complex data analyses in R.

Parallel Processing in R: The use of R packages like furrr to execute tasks in parallel, improving performance for large data sets.

Parallel Processing: A computing technique where multiple processes or threads work simultaneously on different parts of a problem.

Parquet File Format: An open-source columnar storage format optimized for large-scale data processing and storage systems.

Parquet File: A columnar storage file format optimized for large-scale data processing and storage systems.

Partition Pruning: A technique for improving query performance by dividing a dataset into partitions based on specific criteria, and only processing relevant partitions.

pbiviz Package: A command-line tool used to develop and test custom visuals for Power BI, part of the Power BI Visual Tools. It also facilitates the interaction with the Power BI service for secure communication.

Pearson's Correlation Coefficient (r): Measures the linear relationship between two variables, ranging from -1 (perfect negative correlation) to +1 (perfect positive correlation).

Personal Gateway: A type of On-premises Data Gateway used for personal or small-scale data refresh scenarios.

Personally Identifiable Information (PII): Information that can be used to identify a specific individual.

PIP: A package manager for Python packages, or modules from the Python Package Index.

PKL File: A file format used by Python for storing serialized objects, typically created using the pickle library.

Plotly in R (Plotly.R): An open-source data visualization library in R that allows the transformation of static ggplot graphs into interactive web visualizations.

Plotnine: A Python library for data visualization, based on the Grammar of Graphics. It offers a Pythonic approach to sophisticated data visualization, similar to ggplot2 in R.

Power BI Desktop: A data visualization software by Microsoft that integrates with R and Python for advanced analytics and visualizations. It allows for the creation, manipulation, and sharing of interactive data visualizations and reports.

Power BI Embedded: A Microsoft Azure service that allows developers to embed interactive Power BI reports or dashboards into an application.

Power BI service Python Runtime: The version of the Python engine and its packages pre-installed in the Power BI service cloud, which users must adapt to.

Power BI service: A cloud-based service that enables users to share, collaborate, and publish their Power BI reports and dashboards.

Power BI Visual Tools (pbiviz): Tools used to create custom visuals in Power BI. Written in JavaScript (using Node.js), they compile the source code of .pbiviz packages, which are zipped versions of Power BI Visual Projects.

Power BI: A business analytics service by Microsoft. It provides interactive visualizations and business intelligence capabilities with an interface simple enough for end users to create their reports and dashboards.

Power Query: A data connection technology that enables you to discover, connect, combine, and refine data across a wide variety of sources. It's integrated into Power BI and other Microsoft products.

Predicate Pushdown: An optimization technique that involves applying filters directly on the data source, reducing data loading and processing time.

Presidio: A Microsoft open-source package for rapid identification and anonymization of entities in free text and images.

Privacy Levels in Power BI: Settings that determine how data is shared between different data sources, impacting how the Firewall manages data flow.

Probabilistic Record Linkage: A method used in data matching that utilizes probability and statistics to determine the likelihood of records referring to the same entity.

Pseudonymization: Replacing private identifiers with fake identifiers or pseudonyms, while maintaining a mapping to allow re-identification under controlled conditions.

PuLP (Python): A Python library used for linear programming.

PyArrow Dataset: A data structure in PyArrow representing a two-dimensional columnar dataset.

PyArrow: A Python library for managing and processing data in the Apache Arrow format, including Parquet files.

PyCaret: An open-source, low-code machine learning library in Python that automates the cycle of machine learning experiments. It simplifies the deployment of ML models and democratizes access to advanced techniques.

pyodbc: A Python library that facilitates connecting to ODBC databases, including SQL Server.

PyPI (Python Package Index): A repository of software for the Python programming language.

Python Engine: Software that interprets and executes Python code. Examples include the standard Python installation, ActivePython, and Anaconda.

Python Script Visual: A feature in Power BI that allows running Python scripts directly, enabling dynamic and complex data visualizations within reports.

Python SDK: A set of tools, libraries, and documentation that allows developers to build Python applications.

Python.Execute Function: An M function in Power Query used to run Python scripts, allowing parameters to be passed as dataframes.

Python/R Programming Languages: High-level programming languages used extensively in data analysis, machine learning, and scientific computing. They offer extensive libraries and frameworks for data manipulation and machine learning tasks.

Q

Quantifiers: Symbols in regex (like '+', '*', '?') that specify how many times the preceding element must occur.

Query Folding: A process in Power Query where steps are translated into a query language suitable for the data source, potentially leading to data privacy concerns.

R

R Client: A software application that allows users to interact with R, typically through a command-line interface or GUI.

R Graph Gallery: An online resource providing a comprehensive collection of R graphics and visualizations, showcasing various methods and techniques for creating advanced plots in R.

R HTML Custom Visuals: A type of custom visual in Power BI, developed using R and HTML, that allows for the inclusion of dynamic, interactive content in Power BI reports.

R Packages: Collections of R functions, data, and compiled code in a well-defined format.

R Script Visuals: Visualizations in Power BI that are created using the R programming language.

R visualR script visuals: A type of visual in Power BI that uses the R scripting language for data visualization.

R Visuals in Power BI: The feature in Power BI that enables the use of R programming language for creating custom visuals and advanced data visualizations directly within Power BI reports.

R.Execute Function: Similar to Python.Execute, this function in Power Query is used to run R scripts with the capability to pass parameters as dataframes.

Raincloud Plot: A combination of a box plot, a density plot, and a scatter plot, providing a more detailed view of the data distribution, including variability and density.

RDS File: A file format specific to R, used for storing serialized R objects.

read_csv (pandas): A function in pandas for reading CSV files into a DataFrame.

read_excel (pandas): A function in pandas for reading Excel files into a DataFrame.

Reclin2: An R package for probabilistic record linkage and data deduplication, implementing the Fellegi-Sunter model.

Regex Engine: The implementation of regex functionality in a programming language or tool.

Regression: A machine learning task where the goal is to predict continuous values (e.g., predicting house prices, temperatures).

Regular Expression (Regex): A sequence of characters defining a search pattern, commonly used for string-matching within texts.

Resource Governor in SQL Server: A feature in SQL Server used to manage the distribution of resources like CPU and RAM between the database engine and external services like Machine Learning Services.

RESTful Services: Web services that adhere to the REST (Representational State Transfer) architectural style, using HTTP requests to access and use data.

ROI (R Optimization Infrastructure): A sophisticated framework in R for handling linear and non-linear optimization problems.

RTools: A collection of tools to facilitate the development of R packages.

S

Scales: Mechanisms in plotnine by which data values are translated into visual elements, such as color or size, allowing control over data representation.

Scatterplot: A type of plot or mathematical diagram using Cartesian coordinates to display values for typically two variables for a set of data.

SciPy: An open-source Python library used for scientific and technical computing.

Script Visuals: In Power BI, script visuals are used to run R and Python scripts to create visuals that cannot be created with the standard visuals in Power BI.

Sentiment Analysis: A machine learning technique that detects polarity (such as positive, negative, neutral) within the text.

Serialized Object: In both R and Python, an object converted into a format that can be saved to a file or transferred over a network.

Shorthand Character Classes: Convenient symbols in regex representing common character types (e.g., \d for digits, \w for word characters).

Simple Image Visual in Power BI: A custom visual in Power BI that displays images, including those generated from Python scripts, as part of a report.

Single Imputation: Replacing missing values with a single value, like the mean or median of the dataset. It is a simpler form of imputation but can underestimate variability.

Snow Package in R: A package for parallel processing, enabling the distribution of data across multiple machines for efficient data handling.

sp_execute_external_script: A stored procedure in SQL Server used to execute scripts in external languages (like R and Python) within the context of the SQL Server environment.

sp_execute_external_script: A stored procedure in SQL Server used to execute scripts in external languages like Python and R. It's a crucial tool for integrating advanced analytics into SQL Server's data processing workflows.

Sparklyr: An R package that provides an interface to Apache Spark, enabling the use of dplyr-like syntax for data manipulation.

SparkR: An R package that provides a light-weight frontend to use Apache Spark from R.

Spearman's Rank Correlation Coefficient (ρ): A nonparametric measure of rank correlation, assessing how well the relationship between two variables can be described using a monotonic function.

Special Characters (Metacharacters): Characters in regex with a special meaning, like '.', '*', '+', etc.

Spherical Trigonometry: The study of spherical triangles, used for calculations on the sphere, such as in navigation and astronomy.

Splink: An open-source Python library designed for probabilistic record linkage, facilitating the implementation of such algorithms.

SQL Authentication: A method of connecting to SQL Server using a username and password.

SQL Server Express Edition: A free, lightweight edition of SQL Server ideal for small server applications and local data stores.

SQL Server Extensibility Framework: A framework in SQL Server that enables the execution of R and Python code within the SQL Server environment, allowing advanced analytics and machine learning directly in the database.

SQL Server Language Extensions: Extensions in SQL Server that enable the integration and execution of external languages such as Python, R, and Java within the SQL Server environment.

SQL Server Management Studio (SSMS): A software application for configuring, managing, and administering Microsoft SQL Server instances and databases.

SQL Server's Launchpad Process: A component in SQL Server responsible for communicating with external engines to run Python and R scripts.

Statistical Association: The relationship or dependency between two or more variables in a dataset.

Stored Procedures in SQL Server: Predefined functions in SQL Server that can perform operations in the database and return the results, often used for complex data processing tasks.

String Distance: A metric used to measure how dissimilar two strings (sequences of characters) are to one another.

Stringology: A subfield of computer science and mathematics focused on the study of strings, including their analysis, manipulation, and comparison.

Supply Chain Optimization: The use of mathematical models to optimize production, inventory, distribution, and other facets of supply chains.

T

Theil's U Uncertainty Coefficient: Measures the strength of association in one direction between two categorical variables.

Themes: In plotnine, themes control the overall aesthetics and appearance of the plot, including elements like background, gridlines, and fonts.

Tibble: A modern reimagining of data frames in R, part of the Tidyverse collection.

Tibble: A modern reimagining of the data frame in R, part of the Tidyverse collection.

Tidy Evaluation: A programming framework in R that simplifies how variables are used and manipulated in functions. It allows for more intuitive and flexible coding, particularly in data manipulation and visualization tasks.

Tidyverse: A collection of R packages designed for data science tasks, including data manipulation, exploration, and visualization.

Time Series Data: A series of data points indexed in time order, often used in statistics, signal processing, pattern recognition, econometrics, mathematical finance, weather forecasting, and earthquake prediction.

Time Series Imputation: Techniques for handling missing values in time series data, considering time dependencies.

Time Series Imputation: Techniques specifically designed for filling in missing values in time series data, considering the temporal sequence and structure.

to_csv (pandas): A function in pandas for writing DataFrame contents to a CSV file.

to_excel (pandas): A function in pandas for writing DataFrame contents to an Excel file.

Tokenization: Replacing sensitive data with unique identification symbols (tokens) that retain essential information without compromising its security.

Transportation Problem: A type of network flow problem in optimization that focuses on determining the most cost-effective way of distributing goods.

Trusted Connection: A method of connecting to SQL Server using Windows Authentication.

T-SQL (Transact-SQL): A proprietary extension to the SQL language used by Microsoft SQL Server and Azure SQL Database.

Tukey's Method: A statistical technique for identifying outliers based on interquartile range (IQR).

U

Univariate Analysis: Analysis of a single variable.

Upset Plot: A visualization tool used to analyze the intersections of sets, similar to Venn diagrams but more scalable for displaying complex relationships between multiple sets.

V

Vincenty's Formula: An iterative method to calculate the distance between two points on the ellipsoid earth, providing high accuracy.

Violin Plot: A method of plotting numeric data and its probability density.

Virtual Environment: An isolated environment that allows Python users and developers to manage different project dependencies separately.

W

Warehouse Optimization: A type of optimization problem focusing on the efficient allocation and distribution of resources in a warehouse setting.

Web Service: A software module hosted on a server, accessible over the internet to provide data in response to specific requests from a client.

packt.com

Subscribe to our online digital library for full access to over 7,000 books and videos, as well as in-dustry leading tools to help you plan your personal development and advance your career. For more information, please visit our website.

Why subscribe?

- Spend less time learning and more time coding with practical eBooks and Videos from over 4,000 industry professionals
- Improve your learning with Skill Plans built especially for you
- Get a free eBook or video every month
- Fully searchable for easy access to vital information
- Copy and paste, print, and bookmark content

At www.packt.com, you can also read a collection of free technical articles, sign up for a range of free newsletters, and receive exclusive discounts and offers on Packt books and eBooks.

Other Books You May Enjoy

If you enjoyed this book, you may be interested in these other books by Packt:

Mastering Microsoft Power BI - Second Edition

Greg Deckler

Brett Powell

ISBN: 9781801811484

- Build efficient data retrieval and transformation processes with the Power Query M language and dataflows
- Design scalable, user-friendly DirectQuery, Import, and Composite Data Models
- Create basic and advanced DAX measures

- Add ArcGIS Maps to create interesting data stories
- Build pixel-perfect paginated reports
- Discover the capabilities of Power BI mobile applications
- Manage and monitor a Power BI environment as a Power BI administrator
- Scale up a Power BI solution for an enterprise via Power BI Premium capacity

Expert Data Modeling with Power BI - Second Edition

Soheil Bakhshi

ISBN: 9781803246246

- Implement virtual tables and time intelligence functionalities in DAX to build a powerful model
- Identify Dimension and Fact tables and implement them in Power Query Editor
- Deal with advanced data preparation scenarios while building Star Schema
- Discover different hierarchies and their common pitfalls
- Understand complex data models and how to decrease the level of model complexity with different approaches
- Learn advanced data modeling techniques such as calculation groups, aggregations, incremental refresh, RLS/OLS, and more
- Get well-versed with datamarts and dataflows in PowerBI

Packt is searching for authors like you

If you're interested in becoming an author for Packt, please visit authors.packtpub.com and apply today. We have worked with thousands of developers and tech professionals, just like you, to help them share their insight with the global tech community. You can make a general application, apply for a specific hot topic that we are recruiting an author for, or submit your own idea.

Share your thoughts

Now you've finished *Extending Power BI with Python and R, Second Edition*, we'd love to hear your thoughts! Scan the QR code below to go straight to the Amazon review page for this book and share your feedback or leave a review on the site that you purchased it from.

https://packt.link/r/1837639531

Your review is important to us and the tech community and will help us make sure we're delivering excellent quality content.

Index

Download a free PDF copy of this book

Thanks for purchasing this book!

Do you like to read on the go but are unable to carry your print books everywhere?

Is your eBook purchase not compatible with the device of your choice?

Don't worry, now with every Packt book you get a DRM-free PDF version of that book at no cost.

Read anywhere, any place, on any device. Search, copy, and paste code from your favorite technical books directly into your application.

The perks don't stop there, you can get exclusive access to discounts, newsletters, and great free content in your inbox daily

Follow these simple steps to get the benefits:

1. Scan the QR code or visit the link below

https://packt.link/free-ebook/9781837639533

2. Submit your proof of purchase
3. That's it! We'll send your free PDF and other benefits to your email directly

Made in the USA
Coppell, TX
08 December 2024

41961887R00446